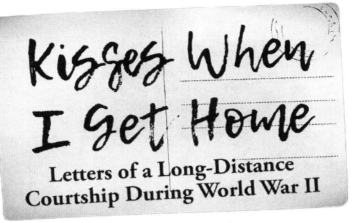

Kisses When I Get Home

Letters of a Long-Distance Courtship During World War II

Walter and Rita Klein

Richard E. Klein, Editor

DUMB
DICKIE
PRESS.

Table of Contents

Editor's Introduction

Love stories are timeless and universally endearing. Love stories set in turbulent times and upheavals in society are especially commanding. Hemingway's *A Farewell to Arms* was set in Northern Italy during the Great War, now commonly known as World War I. Hemingway's *For Whom the Bell Tolls* was set in the Spanish Civil War of the late 1930s. The movie *Titanic* harkened back to the ill-fated maiden voyage of the Titanic, which struck an iceberg on the night of April 14, 1912 and sunk to the cold depths of the North Atlantic Ocean by 2:20 a.m. on April 15. To my knowledge, these and many other love stories were fictional accounts, although based—in some cases—on a composite of real persons.

In stark contrast, the love story of Walter and Rita Klein is their actual account: a real-life story, a story lived by them. The Walter and Rita letters are set in the era of World War II. Unlike many popular love stories, *Kisses When I Get Home* is a true story, written by my Uncle Walter J. Klein and his betrothed, Rita Marie Lavery Klein.

Having been born February 11, 1939, I am old enough to have early childhood memories of the later years of WWII. I can remember Walter in his sharp Army uniform visiting back home. I remember backyard summer picnics with family gathered, including Walter and Rita. I distinctly remember how my grandfather, John F. Klein, shared letters, postcards, and photographs sent home.

Upon my discovery of the cache of Walter and Rita's WWII courtship letters, uncovered fifty years following the war's close, I was immediately drawn to them. As I paged through, the times described seemed to burst forth with life. I am both humbled and honored to have been the instrument to see that these letters—their love story—are now available for lovers of all ages. I sincerely hope you will find their story as compelling and spellbinding as I did.

As the war approached, Rita Marie Lavery was a young secretary. Walter was employed as a gravel truck driver. It seems that Rita, being sentimental, started keeping a scrapbook that recorded their first date and the ensuing days and years. I am hopeful that Rita's scrapbook survived and can be accessed. For now, the big prize is their trove of letters, their wartime courtship exchanges delivered by the mailman. Rita was sentimental to the point that most letters were secured in bundles with ribbons. Walter was more practical, using shoelaces to tie Rita's letters into small parcels.

World War II was fought by the Greatest Generation, generally described as those Americans born between 1905 and 1925. My Uncle Walter John Klein was born December 31, 1915. His betrothed, who became my Aunt Rita, was born December 5, 1918. Obviously, WWII deeply impacted their lives, although Walter remained stateside for the duration of the war. Walter was the fifth of six surviving Klein children, raised in Stratford, Connecticut. Rita was also the fifth child in the Lavery family. She was raised in nearby Bridgeport, Connecticut. Stratford and Bridgeport are situated adjacent to each other along the Connecticut shore of Long Island Sound. Bridgeport was then a factory town with numerous large industries. Stratford was a bedroom community to Bridgeport. Prominent industries in and near Bridgeport included Remington Arms, Bridgeport Brass, Singer Sewing Machine, General Electric, Chance Vought Aircraft, Sikorsky Helicopter, and Bullard Machine Tool Company. Walter's father, John F. Klein (1883-1968), worked as a machinist at Bullard Machine Tool Company. My father, Albert Klein (1910-1993), was also employed at Bullard's.

As a young child, Walter was severely burned in an accidental and tragic fire. Being a playful child, he was under the rear porch steps at 163 Jackson Avenue, the family's home in Stratford, Connecticut. Walter was with his younger sibling, my Aunt Martha Elizabeth Klein Mahlo, born January 1, 1917. Walter and Martha had been playing with matches in the tight confines under the porch steps. A fire trapped the two young and obviously unsupervised children. As told to me by my father, a passerby—a dentist—responded and was able to pull Walter and Martha to safety, thus saving their lives. The date of the fire was not recorded or has been lost, but the period of 1918-1919 seems likely. Other events imply that the fire occurred prior to July 1920. Martha's birth date, January 1, 1917, also provides another defined time marker.

Because of his extensive burns, young Walter was not expected to live. He was hospitalized for about a year following the fire. The medical costs for Walter's care constituted a devastating burden for the Klein family of eight. To compound the family's situation, Walter's mother—my grandmother Eva (Yvetta) Sablofski Klein (1886-1929)—was institutionalized in July of 1920. She was aged 34 at the time of her commitment. Eva was adjudicated in a Fairfield County court as insane. The family, being unable to provide for her financially, petitioned the court to declare Eva as a pauper. For the balance of her life, she was a ward of the state of Connecticut. On July 17, 1920, following a judicial hearing, she was admitted to the Connecticut Valley Hospital for the Insane in Middletown, Connecticut. Three medical doctors concurred in court records that she was insane, diagnosed with disorganized schizophrenia. The hospital was primarily focused on confinement of patients. The idea of treating patients with mental illnesses was distant at best. During her confinement, Grandmother Eva contracted and was subsequently diagnosed with pulmonary tuberculosis in July of 1928. She passed on May 10, 1929 at age 42, several weeks before her upcoming 43rd birthday.

Walter and his five siblings were raised in a working-class home largely devoid of a mother figure. My Aunt Helene was the oldest of the Klein children, born in 1907. Aunt Helene took on much of the burden of raising her younger siblings. Aunt Helene was just short of age 13 at the time of her mother's commitment.

Many years later, both Uncle Walter and his sister Aunt Martha remarked to me in personal interviews that they each had no memory of their mother, except that they as children each remembered seeing her body on display in her coffin. For the nine years that Eva was institutionalized, the six Klein children were never allowed by their father to visit or see their mother. I recount these facts and other details in my book *We're All Set: Selected Klein Family Memories*, published in 2018 and available through amazon.com.

Like many children of working class families of that era, Walter did not complete high school. Having an eighth-grade or ninth-grade education was considered as being educated. Of the six surviving Klein children, my father was the only one to complete high school.

As Walter became a young man in the 1930s, he enjoyed motorcycles, notably the Indian brand. Walter also liked smart clothing. He tended to dress well and look sharp. My mother, Ellen Klein (1914-2002), married to Walter's older brother Albert, once commented to me that she felt Walter was unwise in how he spent his money back then. My mother thought Walter was foolish to spend his money excessively on clothing and other things that she considered frivolous and non-essential.

The letters describe the Walter and Rita engagement as a two-step process. First, they mutually agreed to marry. The second step—which made it official—took place on Christmas Eve, December 24, 1942, when Rita received her diamond engagement ring. For her, the second step of getting the ring carried the greater significance.

The collection of letters is immense; something close to 800 in total. Rita's letters to Walter were typically four pages in length. Each letter commonly represented a daily description and accounting of life's happenings, joys, and struggles. Walter's letters were typically shorter, usually one page. The collection of letters presents a truly unique and detailed insight into the lives and emotions of these two engaged lovers.

Walter and Rita were profuse letter writers, especially Rita. In those days, the postman delivered mail twice daily—both mornings and afternoons. Rita, as a working secretary, developed the habit of writing daily, and at times twice daily.

For the 500 or so days of their correspondence, I have been able to find and transcribe approximately 800 letters. It is fair to say that Walter and Rita wrote each other most days. Rita, as evidenced in her writings, asked that Walter keep her letters. She didn't need to be told to keep his. All letters were put for safekeeping into a small cardboard box where she lived in a rental house at 1440 Stratford Avenue, Bridgeport. In an early letter written by Rita, dated February 1, 1943, she comments to Walter on the need to preserve the collection of letters. Rita told Walter of her desire that they may be able to read these letters some future day and look back upon their courtship.

Another fact is clear. Wartime letters were highly valued and shared—

shared with family, co-workers, and neighbors. Rita commonly wrote about calling a relative on the phone to read a Walter letter, or at least part of it. The letters as written were intended to be read and shared. In rare cases, Rita wrote instructing Walter to destroy a particular page after being read. As editor and the person who rescued these letters from destruction and oblivion, I feel comfortable knowing that the words written some 75 years ago are not lost.

My goal with these letters was to retype and preserve the voice of the original writers. Walter and Rita had strikingly different writing styles. Rita was a trained professional secretary. As such, her letters were virtually flawless in usage, spelling, and punctuation. As editor, in order to improve readability and clarity, the only changes were the insertion of an occasional comma, and at times the insertion of a missing period. These minor editing changes have not been marked. Rita commonly used a shorthand notation, such as the plus symbol (+) in lieu of "and." The letters are transcribed preserving Rita's obvious shorthand markings.

In contrast to Rita's letters, Walter's writing was filled with spelling and grammatical errors. Walter would sometimes let words run on but without using period marks and capitalization to denote sentence breaks. This is not to say Walter couldn't write correctly, but rather when writing at Army camp the urgency of writing took precedence over striving for today's standard of correctness. From my perspective as editor, the task of revising Walter's writing would destroy his voice. As such, Walter's letters are transcribed as close to his writing as possible. No effort was made to correct spelling, grammar, punctuation, or English usage.

Because the reader, especially younger readers, may not understand the culture and even language of the WWII era, my editorial policy was to add brief clarifying commentary as appropriate. These editorial insertions follow the respective letters. Such editorial additions are clearly noted.

This edition contains approximately 500 selected letters, representative of the thoughts and happenenings described by Walter and Rita. Some letters were omitted or shortened due to space considerations. Others were not included as they were damaged or contained personal material inappropriate for general audiences.

Peace and blessings to you,

Richard E. (Dickie) Klein, son of Albert Klein and nephew of Walter J. Klein

PART I: The First Days as War Sweethearts

Adjusting to Long-Distance Romance

In 1940, the approach of World War II brought Selective Service by an act of Congress, and thus the draft. Initially, all males between the ages of 21 and 36 were required to register with Selective Service. Uncle Walter, then age 24, registered in the fall of 1940. All registered males then had to report for medical examinations. Walter was originally classified as 4-F because of his burns suffered as a child. He was extensively scarred, especially on his upper body and arms, and also experienced nerve damage. Men were rejected from service for one or more of three disqualifications: physical, mental, or moral. In Walter's case the grounds for being unfit for the draft were due to physical defects.

As the war progressed, doctors became less picky, so Walter was reclassified as I-B. He then was subject to the draft but was restricted from any combat positions. He had been deemed fit for limited service.

The Walter and Rita wartime courtship letters began on January 13, 1943, as Walter entered the military. He reported to and went through an accelerated basic training at Fort Devens, Massachusetts. Walter's non-combat status is now an established historical fact, but during his conscription he was periodically reexamined by Army doctors. As medical standards relaxed, some men were reclassified and deemed fit for combat duty, some even sent overseas and into combat. The written letters suggest that Walter experienced other medical issues, including dizziness and headaches.

For the duration of his service time, up until July 1944, Walter was stationed at Army camps in Massachusetts. Until then, he was close enough to his hometown of Stratford, Connecticut, to get home some weekends. Travel was most commonly by train. At times, Walter served as a motor-pool driver for officers. One officer was from Stratford as well, so Walter was his assigned driver. That explains why Walter was able to arrive at my boyhood home in Stratford driving an army jeep. Weekend visits back to Stratford were frequent, roughly each month or so.

Walter and Rita depended heavily on each other as the war and their relationship progressed. This relationship was abundantly evident in their letters.

Rita shared a rental house at 1440 Stratford Avenue, Bridgeport, with her older sister Cele, her sister's husband Charlie, and her ne'er-do-well brother Thomas. Another sister of Rita's, Eleanor, lived there at times. Both of Rita's parents had passed prior to America's entry into the war. Her father died in 1936. Rita's mother died in 1941. Rita, being sentimental, noted in her wartime letters that a parent had passed "five years ago today." Given that Rita meticulously dated her letters, we can infer the dates of her parents' passings. Rita's living arrangements during the war and up to July of 1944 were tied to her much older sister Cele; Cele was 17 years older than Rita.

Rita kept Walter informed of the doings of her social circle, including members of her girls club (Dot Blake, Alice Blake, Dot Grant, and Dot Smith) and her office friends (Ann Preston, Ruth Landry, Betty Hughes). She also sent occasional news of her relatives, including her cousin Elwood, and Walter's family, including his sister-in-law Ellen and sisters Lillian, Helen, and Martha.

During WWII, Uncle Walter served in the Army. Because of burns he suffered as a child, he was restricted to stateside duty. He served in a number of positions, such as in Military Police, in the Quartermasters Corps, and as a driver assigned to a motor pool.

Letters: January 13, 1943 – March 31, 1943

Wednesday 1/13/43

Dearest,

This is my first day as a "war sweetheart".

I imagine this day for you was one of a lot of confusion and uncertainty.

I was very glad that I went to the station to "see you off" as otherwise you would have been alone. I went back to work about nine o'clock and everyone in the office was very much concerned over you, so you see you really rate high in everyone's opinion.

Ann Preston, in an endeavor to keep me from being too lonely, invited me to her home for dinner tomorrow (Thursday) night but, as I mentioned to you before, club was postponed this week until Thursday so I declined her invitation for the time being.

I am writing this letter after doing a few tasks around the house and I know you are sound asleep by this time, dearest, after your strenuous day. (It is now 9:30).

Try not to be discouraged darling, if everything seems very strange. It probably will for a while but I know you will adjust yourself to the best of your ability just as I will try too, dear.

Well, dearest, this is my first letter (I know it is very short) but there will be a lot more to follow.

Love always,
XX Rita XX

Darling I arrived safely, they just were showing me how to make a bed properly the food is good, I had diner + supper here already.

Love Walter

POST CARD

Darling do not write until I get stationed permanently, because I will only be here for a short while 4 or 5 days Everything is under control. I hope you + all are well at home.

Love
Pvt. W. Klein

Friday – Jan. 15, 1943 9:00 P.M.

Dearest Walter,

I can't tell you how happy I was when I received your two cards tonight when I came home from work, especially to hear that "everything is under control" as you said on one of them.

I miss you more each day dearest, but I'm trying my best to keep occupied as I know you want me to.

I imagine everything is happening to you so fast that you must feel as though you are in a different world. I know you will do your best to cooperate in every way no matter how difficult everything is. You always take everything in its stride.

I told the girls in the office what you said on one of the cards about learning how to make beds properly. They said you will make a very good husband learning those things. Ruth Landry said you would be "thoroughly housebroken" by the time you come home. Incidentally Ruth got word from her boyfriend that he just arrived in Seattle, Washington (3200 miles from here).

Darling, I took my watch to the jewelers last night and it won't be ready for five weeks. It has to be thoroughly cleaned and have a new stem, also the band shortened. It will cost $4.50. I left it there.

I went to club last night. It was at Dot and Alice Blake's house. Dot says Joe is stationed in Norfolk, Virginia for the time being.

Cele and Charlie send their regards and said if you ever want to make a phone call – and are short of money, don't hesitate to call and reverse the charges, also if you ever want to send a telegram you can send it "collect" if you don't happen to have much money at the time. If you need any of your laundry I can send it very easily if you let me know.

Well, dearest, I'll close now wishing for everything of the best for you,
Yours Always,
Rita [circled with X's]
P.S. "Your best foot forward." Remember, dearest, I love you.

1/16/43

Regards to all the family. Well Rita it is now Sat. noon, time sure does go by fast. The army is pretty good until you have to go on guard duty for 24 hrs. two hrs on and 4 hrs off, one has to sleep and eat in the same clothing for the full guard duty, If one lives through guard duty and K.P. they will become a good soldier. Well I am still living Love Walter.

Sunday 1/17/43 4:00 P.M.

Walter, dearest,

I am writing this a few hours after your phone call. It made me so happy to hear your voice – more than I can tell you. I realize, darling, that you have been kept busy every minute and you have to work very hard. You seemed in very good spirits over the phone in spite of it all and I know you are doing your very best. Anyway, dearest, you are not alone working so hard and I'll bet all the other fellows think you are "an all around good fellow". (You are).

Cel called Elwood's mother after you called and told her you said that he had already left Devens. She didn't tell her that you thought he had gone west because she might bank on it too much and then be disappointed if he didn't. I think that was the right thing for her to do.

Well, dearest, it seems so strange for me this weekend not being with you – I know it did for you too. The girls in the office (Ann and Ruth) had it all planned that the three of us would go to the show (last night, Saturday) but it so happened that Ann's boyfriend came home from Virginia on Friday to stay at her house for the weekend. Besides that, her brother left for Devens Saturday morning and she was quite upset. Ruth went to Trumbull to her boyfriend's house for the weekend (he wasn't home but his sister invited her. So that left me alone. Dot Smith had to work today and didn't feel like going to the show last night. Cel + Jeanie met me after work downtown and we went to eat in "Ye Old Tavern" and then went to the Merritt to see "Once Upon a Honeymoon" with Ginger Rogers and Cary Grant. It was very good – a comedy.

This morning I went to 10 o'clock Mass and have tried to keep busy all day. I washed my hair and did quite a bit around the house. This evening I'll probably read and listen to the radio. Anyway, darling, I will have a lot of time to catch up on my reading from now on.

I am writing with your pen. It writes very good doesn't it? It makes me feel a little closer to you being able to use something belonging to you.

Tomorrow after work I am going to have my picture taken in Larings. I'll send it to you, dear, as soon as it is ready. It will be a small miniature I think, colored. I hope you'll like it.

I called your sister-in-law, Ellen, up and told her you called me from Devens. She was glad to hear that everything was alright with you. She asked me who went to the station the day you left and I told her J. Bridges stopped for a few minutes but that was all besides Cel, Charlie and I. She was very much surprised and said she would have been there but she thought the train would leave very early. She said when you get stationed to send her your address and she'll write.

Here is a poem, dearest that seems to have been written especially for you and

I. The name of it is: "A Letter to My Soldier Boy" by Alice E. Meaney.

I promised I'd write often, dear
At least once every day,
You can't know how I've missed you
Ever since you went away.

I take our favorite walks alone
And as I count each star,
I pray that God will keep you safe
No matter where you are.

And there's a new thrill in my heart
For when the flag flies high,
I lift my head up proudly
For a soldier's girl am I."

Do you like it, Walter? I thought I would send you a little poem once in a while but if you would rather not have me I won't darling. Just let me know.

Well, darling, I must close now but before I do I just want to say I love you with all my heart.

Forever Yours,
Rita [circled with X's]

P.S. Keep your chin up.

Sun 1:30 P.M. Dec. 17. 1943 [Actually Jan 17. 1943]
Pvt. W. Klein
R.R.C. CO.F. BARRACK. 6
Fort. DEVENs MASS.

Dear darling you are my girl, yes you are darling, you are a good girl Rita dear. I have been keep busy every minute of the day and nite for the first four day's. boy they certainly do give you the once over here.

Your cousin Elwood Lavery was shipped out of here two day's after he was here, he sure is a smart boy he and I had guard duty together, while off for rest, he and I talked for quite a while, he was telling me a lot about school at Notra dame and Harvard, I heard that he was sent to some western camp. I hope everything is alright at your home and that they all feel well and happy how is my little girl Jenie making out. [The girl referred to as Jenie is Jeanie, Rita's niece Virginia.]

I droped Dot Smith a card yesterday, I hope you and her will get together quite often in the near future.

I was thinking of you last nite dear. I was thinking what you were doing on our usual Sat nite dance together, I didn't have much time to think about you before that dear. I just didn't have the time.

Dearest you are my little girl, you our a good girl.

Lots of Love
Walter.

1/19/43 Tuesday 8:30 P.M.

Dearest Walter,

Since you called me on the phone Sunday I have received two postals and one letter from you. It makes me so happy to hear from you although I do wish I could mail the letters I've written you but anyway I'm a little cheered by the fact I can send them as soon as I know where you will be stationed.

It certainly looks as though you are "taking it on the chin" as the saying goes from what you said on your cards and letter about all the guard duty and K.P. you've had, but I guess the routine will not be so strenous when you get located some place. I know, dearest, you are making the best of it as you do everything.

You mention in your letter that Elwood was sent to some western camp. Even so, he might be hundreds of miles away from his wife but I hope not.

Everyone is well and as for being happy, dear, speaking for myself, I'm trying my best as I told you in my other letters to adjust myself. I am very, very lonely but I know I will feel a little happier when I know where you are going to be and can write to you. Cele, Charlie and Jeanie miss you very much too.

Dot Smith read the card you sent her over the phone. It was nice of you to think of her, dear.

I have just finished eating my supper – that is about an hour ago. I had a 5:30 appointment with the dentist tonight so I went right from work. I only have one more filling to be done and then I'll be finished. Aren't you glad, dearest? I know you wouldn't want your girl to spend 3/4 of her life in the dentist's chair. I passed by your house on the way (I was in the bus). I didn't see your father's car but I saw a pair of his trousers on the line (ha ha).

Last night, after doing a few chores in the house, I read a good story in the February issue of "Redbook". The name of it was "The Time Between". It is the story of a young lieutenant (a pilot) in the Army. You would like it very much.

I am finally beginning to receive those books I ordered several months ago. You know, the ones I got from the drug store. I have 16 sets altogether so far. You and I will have quite a collection, won't we? Remember they are yours, too, dearest.

I saw a clipping in the "Want Ad" section of Sunday's paper put in by Pascone's for dump truck drivers. I hope they wouldn't offer you that kind of a job as I think your abilities are far beyond that.

Well, dearest, I'll close now and put this letter with the others until such time as I can mail them all.

Forever Yours,
Rita
XXXXXXXX

Thursday 7:30 P.M. 1/21/43

Dearest Walter,

As I haven't received any mail from you yesterday or today I imagine you are on your way to a new destination – although Jeanie did receive a postal from you postmarked Jan. 19th but you probably wrote that Sunday or Monday.

I am quite anxious to know what branch of the Army you will be in - - that is, Air Corps, Quartermasters', Signal Medical or maybe some other division but I know I will have to wait until I hear from you. I was also wondering how you made out on your tests at Devens. Were they hard and were they the type you thought they'd be?

I was supposed to go to Dr. McQueeny tonight and have the ganglion on my wrist removed but when I came home from work Cel said that his nurse called and said she would have to cancel the appointment as the doctor had to stay in the hospital tonight I have to call up tomorrow and make another one.

Dearest, last night I had my picture taken. The photographer was open until 9:00 o'clock so I went home from work and put on my velvet dress and the pearls you gave me. He took four poses of me but I don't know whether they will come out good or not as I found it very hard to smile. You know how it is when someone tells you to and you have to pose, you just can't smile naturally, it has to be forced. Well, anyway the proofs will be ready Saturday so I'll pick the best one out and send you the picture as soon as I get your address.

I went from Larings' to club. It was at Dot Grant's. All the girls were asking for you and I told them all about your calling from Devens and what you wrote me. Dot Smith says Ernie is wondering where you will be stationed. He said he would like to have you go to Camp Rucker so he could "pal around with you" but I suppose it's quite impossible.

Ann Preston's brother went to Devens Saturday (1/16) but expected to be moved any day now. He called up his girlfriend and his mother and said he likes Army life very much. His name is Joe.

Margaret Anton, another girl in the office, has a brother who left Bridgeport the day after you but her family had received only one letter up until today anyway. Of course everyone understands (including myself) that you are all kept busy practically every minute and do not have time to write. By the way, his name is Fred.

Well, dearest, I've been rambling on about my affairs for so long I hope you aren't bored. I would so much like to hear all about you – how you are getting along, where you are + "what you think of the whole set-up" as you would say but I know you will let me know how everything is as soon as you get settled.

You must get tired of having me tell you in all my letters not to get discouraged if everything seems difficult and the routine is very strenuous but you know, dearest, the only thing to do is try to make the best of everything. Of course I know you always do but I want you to be as happy as you can while you are away. I love you so much.

Well, darling, this is station R I T A signing off.

Love Always.

P.S. Joke of the week:

A girl went to the doctor for a physical exam as she was going to join the W.A.A.C.S. The doctor said she was in good physical condition but asked her why she dyed her hair. She said she didn't want to look old + felt white hair would make her look old. The doctor said: "What difference if there's snow on the roof as long as there's heat in the house." (Ha ha) Cel told me that one.

Rita

X X X X X X X X X

(This is your ninth day.)

POSTCARD

1/21/43 Thur.

Hello darling how are you dear. This morning dear I got shipping orders finally I got into a big truck and landed at the other side of the fort, and low and behow where should I land but in the Military Police

Love Walter

Jan. 21. 1943

Service Corp. 11.11

Military Police

Fort Devens Mass.

Dearest Rita

I hope you and all at home are feeling fine and that the weather is not to cold for you all I am now stationed at my permanent post, that is at the military police barracks about three miles from where I was. I am now begining by basic training, that will be for about three months, after that I may still be permanently stationed here, or eles be sent to any post in the united states or Europe, but I think I will be at deven's for a long time to come. All the rest of the boy's were shipped also. they were all spread all over the country for basic training. Well I think I am going to like it better than Medical duty, but what I was interested in was the quartermaster corp, there I could use my mechanical ability, well time will tell.

Darling I love you dearest you are my little girl, you are a nice little feminine girl Rita dear. You take good care of your self, for I will propably be home on furlough in the near furture, then we both can go out for a little fun together again Boy will I dance my head off, I will certainly appreciate some dervison by then, never mine then, I mean right now. Take good care dear, before you know it we will do the town again

Lots of Love

Walter.

Friday 7:00 P.M. 1/22/43

Dearest Walter,

I received your postal and letter today telling me you are in the Military Police. I was very much surprised to hear that you are to be stationed in Fort Devens at least for your basic training.

Although you probably don't realize it, according to your letter and what you thought about the M.P. before you went away, I think you are lucky dearest. Everyone I told about it, including Cel and Charlie thought so too. In spite of the fact that you cannot use your mechanical ability you will undoubtedly have just as much of a chance to advance.

I am very happy about the whole thing, darling, as you are near to home and as you said in your letter can come home on furlough possibly, once in a while. Then, too, you can call me up – remember you can always reverse the charges when you are short of change – so you see there are a lot of advantages.

Everyone here is well including myself except for the fact that I'm very lonesome. Now I will be much happier though, because I can write to you, that is, mail all the letters I've written you since you've gone. I just thought I would take a chance on sending this one now hoping you will receive it tomorrow. You will probably get all the other letters next week.

Well, dearest, I will make this one very short. Any time you get a chance, I would love to have you call up (reverse the charges). If you could call about the same time you did last Sunday this week, it would be nice. Anyway, I am home during the week every evening but Wednesday. If you don't call I'll know you haven't the time.

Love Always,
Rita
X X X X X X X X X X X

P.S. Chin up, remember I love you.

PVT. W. KLEIN
M.P. S.C.U. 11.11
Fort Devens MASS.
Friday 22. 1943

Dearest Rita,

Darling how I miss being with you, I never know how well off I was at home, their I could come and see you or call over the phone at nearly any time, darling I think of you and alway's have a picture in my mind of us together. I look at your picture's at least twelve times a day, I keep them in my pocketbook all the time, darling we did'ent know how lucky we were a few week's ago to be with each other at least four times a week. darling by being away for a week and half show's how we can miss each other so much that it seem's like two years darling by being separeted for so short a time and missing each other so much, that show's how much we love each other, now we love each other, twice as much, at least it seem's so darling, that test of being separeted to test our love show's how much we love each other, more than we though. Of course that test was not of our own making, but now we know how we really stand, now our love is not just one hundred percent but two hundred percent, darling dear.

darling you are one sweet girl, you are my little sweetheart, you are the sweetest girl in the world, today we had drill and studies all day, they keep me busy all the time, even after supper we have to study.

Love Walter

KISSES FOR YOU X X X X X

PVT. W. KLEIN
Military Police
Service Corp Unit
Fort Devens – Mass
Sat. Morning Jan. 23. 43

Dearest Rita,

We are still continueing to drill and study, we learn how to march and do the manual of arm's also we have to learn all of the articles of War and also all the general orders and also all special orders, we have to memorize all orders, it seem's just like back in school each morning we have to make our beds, and they have to be perfect, not half perfect, boy this army will either make or break a man, we get up at six oclock and go to bed at nine oclock at nite, we have to take a shower bath each day, we have inspection of barrack's each morning – In the morning fifthteen after 7 we get up, we all have to stand out side near the flat for reviellie and at nite for retreat, today we all have to get a army haircut.

Darling what I would'ent give to be with you tonite darling one never know's how much one's freedon is worth until then freedon is taking away from them, their is no better life than the civilian life, being with you and being at home with all the family is worth a million dollars. One get's a funny feeling after you are placed among a lot of strangers, It was'ent bad up at the Recruit reception center, there, we were among all our friend's, then I had Elwood Lavery and Bob Smiffen and another friend that live's near me at home.

Darling I love you, you are my little sweetheart.

Love. Walter

Rita dear you are my little sunshine, you are my life inspiration dear. You are the sweetest little girl in the world, you do not know how femenen you are dear Darling hope you and Dot Smith get together tonite and go out for a little fun Darling how is my little girl friend Jenie making out, is she still making eyes at the boy's at the meat market's and that gos for little Rosemary too, How is little Cel making out these day's also chick tell Tom I was asking for him, and also tell him how lucky he is to be able to get across the street for a short beer any time he feel like it, here in the army it is a different story, here one is getting orders all day long, boy it sure is hard to get used to it, tell him not to mind what other people think or how he feel's at times about feeling like being in the army because all the rest of the boy's are in, when one is in civilian life one is apt to take everything for granted, but regardles how he or vincent feel's at time's about going in the army, tell them how well off they are by being free to go and do as they please. Here we have to do guard duty also KP. also rubbish detail, besides taking care of our cloths, also washing all our cloths, making bed's drilling studying, marching, shine shoes sweep floors, mop floors and so many more details. Tell vincent regardles How hard he has to work or how long, or how much taxes one has to pay or that there is so many rationing's, in the end he is free to do as he pleases, his time is his own, and he does not have to take orders from some inferior dizzy greasy corpral, that is not have as intelligent as a new recruit, only the fact that he has been in the army for sometime, if one does not like ones look's, more K.P. to do, the army has it's good points to, but it has more bad prints than good one's, at least I think so If one gets placed right I think it would not be so bad, but they interview everybody, then insted of placing them for what they can do, they put them wherever they need men regardles of what they can do, me I should be in the quartermaster corp, to take care of machinery and to operate all mechanical thing, but once one get's into this outfit there is no transfer's to be had, as far as I know unless one is shipped to some other camp in the united states or Europe. I would rathy be shipped to some other camp close by home that has plenty opportunity, and not just do interior guard duty, but do town or train duty, to go places and do thing, and not be the same guard post every day In the post one has to be here Six months before he does town guard town duty.

Love, Walter

Well darling, I suppose we will get used to it eventually You are my <u>Love</u>. Rita dear.

Sunday 5:00 P.M. 1/24/43

Dearest Walter,

I thought perhaps you would call up this afternoon but of course I realize that you are kept very busy and probably did not have a chance.

I have been in the house since Friday night as I had a slight touch of the grippe. Several of the girls in the office were out with it so I had to have a few days vacation, too. I feel much better now and guess I'll go into work tomorrow.

How are you these days, dearest? I hope you are well – getting enough rest and good food even though you don't have any diversion as you said in your last letter. As you said also, you and I will certainly have to "do the town" when you come home. I will be there "with bells on" to greet you won't I dearest?

This week some time you will get a package. - - a sewing kit from Jeanie, writing paper from Cel and a carton of gum from me. I am telling you this so you will be on the lookout for it.

Friday night I called Martha up and gave her your address. She was very glad I called and said she would write soon. She was also glad to hear you are stationed so near. She said it is very hard for she and Adolph to go to your house on Saturday nights like they used to because of the gas shortage. She hasn't seen your father in a few weeks now, but thought he was alright as Helen called her up last Sunday and said he is working every day. Helen is still at Lilly's though.

All stores in Bridgeport, + I guess in all Connecticut, are going to be closed on Mondays from now on. Shows are going to be closed one day a week (not all on the same day though - - they will stagger it). Taverns are to be closed on Mondays too. All this is due to fuel shortage.

Elwood's mother called me up this morning and said she received a letter from Elwood yesterday – (the first one). He is in Alabama in a new camp and is in the Chemical Warfare Division. He will only be there for two weeks however and doesn't know where he will be stationed then. This division is something new. She didn't seem to think it was a good break for him. She thinks the M.P. is a good outfit to be in. She said when he sends her his permanent address she will send it to me and I can then send it to you. He told his mother he would like to write to you too.

Darling, there is something I would like to ask of you. Please do not feel you have to write to Cel, Charlie, Jeanie, Eleanor or Dot Smith. I can give them all the information about you when you write to me. The only ones you are obligated to write to are your father and I - - of course your sisters occasionally. Please do not think I am selfish in feeling this way. If you think this over I'm sure you will understand. I am the one who is the most concerned over you, darling, besides your father so don't you think if you have any time to write it should be to either one of us? Of course by that I don't mean that I expect mail everyday from you. For instance last week there were two days that I didn't get any mail at all from you (which was alright) but when I was talking to Dot Smith she had received a card from you – so had Eleanor and Jeanie. Everyone thought this was funny – that they should receive mail and not me. Do you see what I mean dearest?

Well, dearest, supper is ready so I must go – will write again Tuesday.

Forever Yours,

Rita [circled with X's]

P.S. Here is some philosophy as you would say:
"It's full of worth + goodness too,
With manly kindness blent
It's worth a million dollars
And it doesn't cost a cent."
(A smile)
I love you.

Monday 7:00 P.M. 1/25/43

My Darling,

Tonight when I came home from work I received two letters from you. One was dated 1/22 (a short one) and the other 1/23 (a six-page letter). You must have written this one when at your lowest ebb. I was very much surprised to know the way you feel because your letters and cards before have been very cheerful and I enjoyed your previous letters so much - - they sounded just like you.

I think I realize, dearest, just what you are going through but don't forget you won't be in the Army two weeks until the day after tomorrow – (1/27) and you must give yourself a lot more time than that to adjust. You are now going through an adjustment period which I know is very hard. As you said in your letter you are among strangers, are taking orders (all kinds) daily, and on the whole you have a strenuous routine. You also said in civilian life you feel free and your time is your own and do not have to take orders from anyone like you do now. I grant you, darling, that all this is true but no matter where you were stationed and what Division you were in you would still go through the same adjustment period. It is hard for any fellow at first but I always thought you could adjust yourself to almost anything because you have been through so much already.

I think you are wrong in feeling that you should be in the Quartermasters' Corps. I don't see how you think you would be any better off. As you say, it would give you a chance to use your mechanical ability but you will be able in the M.P. to show that you have leadership, can take discipline and will be able to cope with all types of people. Maybe after six months you will get a chance to do train or town guard duty. If you ever do get a pass for a week-end you can come home whereas if you were in the South or West you would probably get to the nearest town that's all.

I hope you don't feel that I am giving you a sermon telling you all this but darling, I wish you would please try to make the best of everything. When you have to take an order from an "inferior, dizzy, greasy corporal" as you say try to take it in good spirit even if it kills you. I know you resent this very much (I would myself) but I think "taking it on the chin" and trying to make the best of everything is the only thing to do. You know, dearest, this isn't going to last forever. When it's all over you and I have a lot to look forward to – just being together.

Although I didn't mention it in my last letter, Sunday (last) was a day of special significance for you and I – we were engaged for a month. Did you realize it? You gave me the ring on December 24th and Sunday was January 24th. It is such a beautiful ring as is a symbol of our love before you went away as well as the present and the future. I'm so glad I have it for this reason. I never get tired of looking at it and I'm very proud to show it to everyone. I know you feel the same too, darling.

I miss you just as much as you miss me, dear. This past week-end I was a shut-in with a cold as I told you in my last letter. Maybe this coming weekend I can get together with Dot Smith. Wouldn't it be wonderful if I got a 'phone call saying you were coming home. I suppose this is impossible. The things I have been trying to tell you in this letter are expressed in the following:

"Success is failure turned inside out –
The silver tint of the clouds of doubt –
And you never can tell how close you are,
It may be near when it seems afar;
So stick to the fight when you're hardest hit - -
It's when things seem worse that you mustn't quit."

Please, dearest, keep your courage, I know you can "take it".
Love Always,
Rita
X X X X X X X X X X X X X X

Military Police
11.11 Service Corp Unit
Fort Devens, Mass
Monday 25. 1943

Dearest Rita,

I tonite just recived Cel's and Jeanie letters and I am sure very happy to recive them, Cele is right, I think in the end this Fort won't be to bad after all, it could be better and it could be worse, one consolation is at least that I am not to far away, they sure do give us long undies they certainly keep us warm, I may be able to get my hands on a pair someday, that is if I can remove a pair from one of the boy's while he is sleeping, but I think that is to tough of a job.

Well I am so glad to hear that Elwood Lavery arrived safely at his destanation, he even though he was going West, but all the letter that he went to Alabama, It is nice and warm there,

I droped Eleanore and Vin a line to let them know a little about the army life, to bad I forgot to get Gertrude's address, but she will let me know. Give Tom my Regards Rita dear, Darling I am writeing more letters than I ever though I would, and I like to write very much, more than I though I would, it is a good way to express my self dear.

About the test's, one test was on ones mechanical ability, that test I did very good, another one was on the signal corp work, and the other was on your vocabulary and Math ability, On the whole test I did about average It was not to tough.

Darling I recived your first letter at Monday Noon, I was going to call you on the phone, but I was studying until about four Sun afternoon

Sunday Morning I went to one of the Chapel's on the grounds the churches are very beautiful inside considering they are army chapels.

Here they have a very large Co of Waac's, they do quite a few different

job's, mostly they work in the different offices at the Fort. They have about Six
Post exchange here, where one can buy almost anything, they also have about
six theatre here at the fort, I have gone to the show twice the show's are pretty
good,

Here at the Fort on the outskirts of the Fort they have a large Service Club
where all the boy's can go if they have the evening or any time off, we new
recruits do not get very much time off, he is keep busy almost all the time, we
will be keep busy like that for a few month's, Now I will get back to the service
club talk here they also have the most elaborate library that any person could
find, one can also buy a very good full course meal here, just in case he gets
tired of the food at the barrack's they also have a very nice ice cream parlor,
one can even get a strawberry Sunday there,

Each Sunday afternoon and Saturday night they hold dances at the Club,
quite a few waacs come, also the USO furnishs plenty of girl's from the USO
club, all the girls are chaperoned by the older women of the USO. the music is
furnished by the army band, and the mush is very good, I managed to go down
there Sunday at Six oclock for a short time with so of the boy's at the Post
Exchange there the boy's can buy that there too beer, it is not very strong, of
course this is all valable to the boy's that can get some time off, one that is not
very seldom.

There is now twenty five boy's in our patoon, Nine more just came in to
join us, they just come down from the reception center at the induction center.

Darling you are a good girl I droped Dot Smith a line the other morning,
while I had a few minutes Darling I sure do miss you, last nite how I wish I
could be near you dearest, I alway's carry your pictures with me.

Darling how are the girls at the office how is Betty doing and Bill Hughs
How is our bridge tender (Chick) doing you are my little sweet darling forever
dearest. I love you.

Love Walter
SIX Big Kisses X X X X X X

Tuesday 7:00 P.M. 1/26/43

Walter dearest,

Since your last letter was dated Saturday, 1/23, I was wondering how you
are. I hope you're well and as happy as you can possibly be under the
circumstances. I was also wondering if you have received any of my mail yet. If
you have, will you let me know, dearest?

The weather was very bad today - - it was raining and snowing. Tonight
the roads are very slippery. I have a few new magazines and am going to spend
a quiet evening reading.

Dot Smith said she received a letter from Ernie saying that his second
application for a furlough has been cancelled. One of the officers told him he
is needed in the camp very badly as they haven't enough fellows who do his
type of work. It looks as though he won't be home for a long time. Dot is

going to take her vacation in March and go down to Alabama to see him.

Anne Preston's brother, as I told you in a previous letter, went to Devens the Saturday after you. He is now stationed in Camp Edison, New Jersey in the Signal Corps. He says Army life is just the type of a life he likes - - cleanness, neatness and order. He is only 20 years old so I suppose adjusts himself easily.

Ruth Landry's boyfriend is on his way to Alaska. When he landed in Seattle he was told he would be there for about ten days and Ruth has not heard from him in about a week and a half now.

Darling, I think of you constantly and hope you are well. Try not to get too discouraged and although the Army's way of thinking is altogether different from your way (and mine), I think you will make it easier for yourself if you take everything in its stride the way you always do. I know you will make lots of friends (of course this might take time) although it shouldn't for you.

If you really think it would be better if you were in another division couldn't you ask for a transfer? If I were you I would give yourself more time.

Well, darling, I would like to mail this before 7:30 so I'll close now. Please let me know how you feel and if things in general are any easier than they were the first few days.

Forever Yours,

Rita

X X X X X X

P.S. This was you when you were writing your last letter (ha ha)

Try to smile like this, dearest. I love you.

Tuesday Evening Jan. 26, 7 oclock.

Dearest Rita,

After supper tonight I recived all your letters, boy I was sure glad to have recived them all, the boy's all keep saying that I certainly do alright, they keep kidding me all the time about how evertime they look over at me I am writing a letter, they keep saying boy she must be a sweet kid.

Darling you are a very sweet girl, you are a very intelligent girl, you have so many fine qualaties dear, I love you very much. Today will make fourteen day's in the army for me, I seem like a old timer already, it seem's as if I have been here for month's, we have learned very much here already we will learn everthing in one month that usually would take three month's Now that I am attached to the M.P. it is not to bad, we do not have to do all the extra detail work, that we did, up at the reception center Here we learn the more technical angle today the sargent showed us all how to dismandle a rifle, we also learned how to present the Manual Arm's, today we also attended a movie on first aid all so on poison gases, they really teach us all the trick's, each morning we have to fall in for revellie and in the evening we have retreat, it is a very colorful ceromony, they have five bugelers sounding tap's, next week the sargent is going to teach us how to fire our rifles; this camp is about fifty square miles, and there is about fourth thousand men stationed at the fort, as far as I can see, I can not see anything but army building, today we had a little more snow,

Here at camp they have about four thousand trucks of all kinds, ready to be shipped to all parts of the country Don't tell nobody about the trucks or anything, I should of not said anything about them. I didn't relize it until I wrote it down.

How is my little girl Jeanie doing, I suppose she is still making eyes at the boy in the butcher market. Tonight I will take a shower and also wash my clothes, also study for a hour You are my sweet girl dearest.

Big six kisses X X X X X X dear Love Walter

Wed. Morning 8 A.M. Jan 27

Dearest Rita,

The poem's you sent me are very appropriate for the occasion dear. Charlie Chonka did not have very much luck with his girl somehow, I expected something like that from Ann.

It is now snowing and quite colder than yesterday, one inch, of snow has already fallen, to add to the other five inches, that has previously fallen.

Give my regards to Ann and Ruth at the office, I did not tell Ann's brother, because I am about two miles from the recruit reception center otherwise I might have seen him.

I hope Jeanie is progressing just as well as she has alway's been doing at school and that she does not have to stay after school because she has been naughty.

Rita dear you are my little Bunny, arn't you dear, about five hundred come into the reception center here at the fort, they come from all over the eastern part of the country. We have ten minute's of exercise in the morning, they sure do get all the kinks out of the body. I write to my father each day or sometimes every other day, I also drop my brother and sisters a line every other day.

Adolph Mahlo give me five dollars before I left for camp. I droped Martha a line too. I do not need the extra cloths of mine that you have at your home as yet. but maybe later. Thanks for getting them for me. Try to get Joe's Pavlick's present address I would like to drop him a line the discipline here is very good for a fellow it teaches a fellow how to get along with your fellow men, it teaches a person tolerance, witch is very good for any one,

Dearest you are my love, you are my little fiancee you are my sweetheart, and my good companion, and guide How is your pretty diamond,

I am writeing this card at 12 oclock noon.

Dear Rita I just ran out of writing paper, I will get some more at the Post exchange this morning the lieutent and our sargent gave us all a talk on what we can write and talk about, so that leaves me at a pretty tough spot, as to what

I say or write, as to what goes on here at camp.

At eight oclock this morning the saregent had us all outside in our O.d. army shirts to do the calisthenics, boy it certainly was cold out there, at least until we started to exercise. Our lieutent Mr. Vilerage and our saregent, Deshoie are pretty swell egg's but they are very stricked Our saregent is a Frenchmen our lieutent is a former World War Veteran, he has had plenty of experence You are my Love Rita dear, also my fiancee, Love Walter You are my little doll, you are also my little bunny. You are a very intelligent girl, Darling take good care of yourself.

Love Walter
PVT.

Thursday 11:30 A.M. 1/28/43

Hello Sweetheart,

I am writing this letter in bed as I decided to take a one-day vacation from work to doctor-up a very persistent cold I've had for almost a week. Don't worry about me, though, darling. I'll be fit as a fiddle in a day or so.

I have your last two letters in front of me as I am writing, one is dated Tuesday and the other Wednesday. They made me very happy – they are so interesting and you sound much more encouraging than you did last Friday. I can see you are getting used to the routine now and are making the best of the whole situation as a person with a fine character as you have would.

You said in one letter that your sargeant and lieutenant talked to you and the rest of the boys regarding what you should talk about in your letters. Well, dearest, just write whatever you think best but you don't have to worry about my saying anything to people about things I shouldn't. I always like to know just how you feel and how you are making out – in other words anything you want to write is of great interest to me. Your letters sound just like the way you talk, I read all of them over several times, I enjoy them so much.

I am so glad you are making new friends and that you have had a little time to see a few movies and go to the Service Club for a while. On the whole, Fort Devens sounds like quite a place after reading about your description of the Chapels, Post Exchanges, Library, Service Club etc.

Dot Smith and I haven't been able to get together as yet but we expect to this coming week-end. We are going to have dinner downtown after work Saturday and then go to the show. I might invite her over to the house Sunday if she doesn't have to work. During the week I have no desire to go out. Sometimes I work until six o'clock and when I come home I always find chores to do to pass away the time. I read quite a bit now too.

Dot read your letter sent to her over the phone. It was quite long. I'm glad you thanked her mother for inviting us for supper, it was thoughtful of you. Dot said you wrote to Ernie too. I would like to tell you again – Please do not feel you have to write to anyone other than your father, sisters and I. It takes a lot of your time to be writing all the time and as long as you write to your family and I that's all that's necessary. As I said in one of my previous letters I will give all these other people you are writing to the information about you, (how you are, etc.) Think this over again, darling, I don't want to be selfish but if you have a little extra time in which to write, please write to your father or I. You know how much your letters mean to me.

Last night I brought the proofs of the pictures I had taken back to Larings'. The one I chose for you is a smiling pose. (a natural smile too). I hope you like it. It is going to be in a small leather folder that you can carry around with you. The leather is called "ostrich leather". The picture will be colored and then when you receive it you can carry it instead of those dilapidated snapshots you have.

You said in your letter that you were all out of writing paper. Darling, I mailed you a package on Monday – writing paper from Cel, a sewing kit from Jeanie and gum from me. I hope you have received it by today. I notice so far I receive your mail much faster than you receive mine. I guess that's because there are so many new recruits it is hard.

Did you ever get a chance to talk to Joe Callahan (the fellow Vin knows) at the reception center? Vin says he comes home every other week-end. Do you think it will be possible for you to come home some week-end before you finish your basic training? If not, maybe you might after you finish it.

Dearest, do you mind if I give you a suggestion about answering my letters (as a matter of fact, anyone's letters?) If you take my last letter and put it in front of you and follow through while you are writing, it will make it easier for you to find things to write about besides answer any questions that might be in the letter. Do you see?

Cel, Charlie Jeanie and Tom are all well and send their regards. They are looking forward to seeing you some time in the near future (I hope). I always give them all the news of your letters (except the parts where you say how nice I am and how much you love me) ha, ha.

Enclosed you will find a little clipping about me which was in the company's newspaper, "The Clipper." You'll also find some jokes which may not make you laugh but maybe smile a little anyway. They were in the "Clipper" too. I am enclosing a poem, too, that I hope you will enjoy. It was in last night's paper. It suits you to a "t" doesn't it?

Dearest, the saying "Absence makes the heart grow fonder" certainly is true isn't it with you and I? I think our love is growing more each day, if such a thing could be possible. We are living from day to day for each other until such time as we can be together always. Please keep this in mind, dearest. I am living from day to day and am trying to do all the things I know you would want me to – always with the thought in mind that the whole situation is only temporary and you and I have a bright future to look forward to. These are the thoughts that make the days a little easier now. I know you think so too.

Well, soldier boy, I'll close now so I can get this out in the afternoon mail.

Forever Yours,
Rita [circled with X's]

P.S. Wish I could give you the above kisses in person.

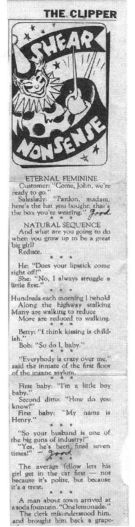

Thursday 28. 1943 Noontime

Dearest Rita,

I have just recived a letter from Gertrude in New York, she sure writes a nice letter, she congratulated us on our engagement. I also recived a letter from my brother and my nephew donald, donald now has the smallpox, he has been home from school for a week, my brother is fine, but work's quite long hours.

I also recived a letter from my sister Lillian, she is feeling quite well lately, Helen is still there, as far as I know, Joan and Carrol both have the smallpox Lillian says that Jack has the pox also and has not been at work for a week.

Yesterday I recived your letters and also A letter from Ellen, my brother's wife.

The boy's all say that I do alright as far as reciveing mail is concerned.

I still have to drop Pat Marino that is in Africa, also Charles Chonka up at Newfoundland

I am feeling fine and ajusting quite well, last nite I went out to the P.X to get this paper I am writeing on, it only cost me twenty cents, pretty cheap, the army gives us a break once in a while. This morning the lieutent was drilling us on the manual arms with our rifle, boy he can sure be strick, and hard and callous, but I gess he has to be, in order to drive everything home, we have to get everything in thirdty day's, which would ordinary would take three month's.

Our saregent, the frenchmen is very soft spoken, he is a good fellow.

This afternoon we all are going outside to learn the foundamental of marching it will be a four hour drill, this morning we drill with the rifle for three and ahalf hours, the gun weigh's about nine and ahalf pounds, and is a 1917 model, made in the Remington in Bridgeport Conn, during the last War. As yet we have not been on the fireing range, propably next week.

I droped Eleanore another nice card of the Service Club that I was telling her about in my last letter to her. I also droped my sister Helene a card. Darling you are my sweet little girl, I love you, I love you, very much.

Take good care of yourself dearest Keep busy, so that the time will go by very smooth and nice.

Give all, my regards

I will call you this coming Sunday if I dont have to be on any duty, but I dont think I will be on any details, I will call the same time as last.

X X X X X X six kisses

Love. Walter.

Friday 4:00 P.M. 1/29/43

Dearest Walter,

I just received your letter which you wrote Thursday noon. My one day vacation is turning out to be a three-day one. I have an attack of "the old-fashioned grippe." I am out of bed now though and feel much better - - I'll surely go to work Monday. You probably won't receive this letter until Monday (I am getting your mail much faster than you are receiving mine).

I am so glad to hear you are receiving so many letters - - from Gertrude, your sisters and brother. I know you appreciate it a lot.

It's too bad you had to buy writing paper. The package we mailed you last Monday has certainly been delayed in getting to you.

You seem to be learning everything very fast – fundamentals of marching, dismantling a rifle, and other things but as you said you are receiving three months' training in one month.

The snow fall we had yesterday amounted to 12 inches. Today the weather is nice, though, the sun is out and it looks nice outside shining on the snow.

I have been reading for a few hours this afternoon. I read quite a few interesting articles in the Reader's Digest. One was written by a woman who has lived in France for 40 years. She gives a detailed description on France (how the people live since it was taken over by the Germans) – another article is on the life of Stephen Foster (he wrote practically all the songs of the South – "Old Black Joe", "Swanee River" etc.)

In one of your recent letters you asked for Joe Pavlich's address. Dot Blake says he really isn't stationed in one place long enough to have an address. He was in Norfolk, Virginia for a while but now he is in New York dock again. She says he won't be long there either. As soon as I find out where he is stationed permanently I'll let you know.

Dot Smith is now planning her trip to Alabama. She is taking the last two weeks in March off and her mother is going with her. Ernie will be able to spend each evening with her as well as Saturday night and all day Sunday. I wouldn't be surprised if they were married while she is down there. She says not though.

We are all kidding Dot Grant because she's been buying so many things for her hope chest. She has already bought an electric iron and several blankets, sheets and pillowcases. She says the reason she's buying all these things is because there is going to be a shortage on them but we keep telling her she's going off any day now to get married. Jimmy expects to get another deferment in May.

Dearest, writing these few pages make me feel a little closer to you. It will make me so happy to hear your voice when you call Sunday, (if you can). I love you so much, dearest – you are so thoughtful and kind. I miss you more as time goes on but I'm trying to keep as busy as possible to make the time pass more quickly just as you told me to do.

With all my love

X X X X X Rita X X X X X

P.S. Your letters are my sunshine.

Friday Evening 7:00 1/29/43

Dear Rita,

Darling take care of yourself so that you will be in the Pink of condition.

Today we were out shoveling snow for about four hours, last night it snowed all through out the night, we had about a foot snowfall in all, the drift's were in some places about three feet high,

In the afternoon the lieutent and saregent showed us all how to dismandle a tommy gun, also a colt automatic pistol, and also a shotgun, yesterday he showed us how to handle the old infield rifle.

I recived your last letter that you wrote on Thursday at 11:30 a.m. at 5:30 P.M on friday, I am sure happy to recived your letters, I keep looking forward to each day when I can recive your letter, yesterday I was looking for your letter, but it did not arrive, boy now I know how a fellow feel's about letter's from home or there girl (Here I had a boy for a girl, some mistake. Hey Rita. friends, we alway's keep waiting for the mail, remember how I use to say about how two or three letters a week from a girl friend were enough, but now I think differently, after all, us boy's never grow up, it seem's, alway's looking for some consoleing. I am so glad that you enjoy my letters, I am now useing the method you seggested in writing a letter.

Yes Fort Deven's is a good a fort that any fellow would want to be at, a fort is alway's much better than a camp, because a fort is so much more permanently build. A camp is more or less just temporary,

I am so glad you and Dot are getting together this week end, I hope you both have a swell time together, now don't make eyes at the boy's you and Dot, Ha. Ha. You too are swell girls Darling I am so glad that you had your picture taken, I will be looking forward to reciving it very soon, dearest, I am sure it will be a very good picture of you, RIta dear.

When I was up at the Reception Center I did not see Joe Callahan, Vin's friend, when I was in the building that he work's in, I was moving so fast, that is reciving my cloth's that I did'ent even have time to look left or right, he propably was there at the time, when we started in at one end of his building we did not have any clothes on, but by the time we came to the other end we had a complete soldier's outfit of cloth's, two of everthing, even including a War helmet. It happened so fast we did'ent even know what happened. Boy they sure do have mass production here everything is at a mass production, no matter what it is.

The lieutent told us all the other day that we would not get any passes to go home for at least four weeks, not even to the town's nearly, just passes for about the fort. After our basic training we will get some liberty's, I hope.

I am so glad that you made the company newspaper. The jokes were very good also the poem was right to the T. you were right.

Saturday 12: oclock 1/30/43
Fort Deven's Mass.

Dear Rita,

At noon today I recived a letter that you wrote on Sunday afternoon at 5:00 P.M. 1/24/43 it must have gotten lost in all the mail, at the fot, here there is so much mail, it is bound to happen once in a while.

At noon I also recived your last letter that was writen at Friday at 4:00 P.M. 1/29/43 it sure did not take long for that letter to get here, it usually does not take over a day and a half for your letter's dear.

Yes darling I will write to you each day and to my father three times a week what I was trying to do was to write to everyone but I see I do not have the time to do that, if I tried I would have to neglect someone, so dearest I will only write to the one's that come first in my heart, than if I have any extra time I will continue to write to the other's of my friends.

Darling I did not mean to hurt you, by not writing to you for a day or two, but now I will never fail to write to you first each day, each day I only have time for two or three letters so you can count on hearing from me, that is if I can possibly make it, and that no special detail keep's me to busy all day, and part of the evening.

Darling take good care, take extra care dear, so, that you will feel one hundred percent.

Today we were all showed how to handle the automatic pistol, how to draw it from the holter, and also to bring it up for inspection when the officer's come around for inspection. It weights about two and ahalf pounds, and fire's accarate for about twenty five feet. I did'ent think it would snow as much as it did in Bridgeport, it snowed just as much in Bridgeport as it did here.

I am so glad you are doing a lot of reading after all to better yourself is the thing to do, you know I like you for one reason, that is because you are nice and also very intelligent.

I am so glad to hear that Dot Smith and her mother plan to go to see Ernest in the near future I hope they have a very fine trip.

It would'ent surpriss me if Dot Grant went off and got married, or married so quickly we would all be dumbfounded or something.

Tonight I just found out I am elected to be charge of quarter's for tonight, that detail's call's for me to be responsibly for everything that takes place in our barrack's, boy job is to put out lights in the building at nine P.M. to anser all questions from visitors, and to watch all proproty about my post. And I was counting on going to the service Club with the boy's Next time I will be more lucky, the boy's are all razzing me, there no all telling me how lucky I am, they are saying if there were a million soldiers, Kleiny would get the detail. Ha. Ha. Darling I love you. I will call you tomorrow if I can, I think I will make it.

Sunday 9:00 P.M. 1/31/43

Dearest,

I thought I would sit down and write a few lines as I am alone now. Dot Smith has just gone home and Cel is gone to a wake.

It made me so happy, dear, when you called this afternoon. I couldn't tell you over the phone because you know how it is - - time is so short and we both have so much to say — we both seemed to be talking at the same time. I was glad to hear that you were to have a little time to yourself after 5 o'clock this afternoon. I know you do have to have a little diversion once in a while. I hope you enjoyed the show. I think it is a pretty good idea to have the fellows take turns at taking charge of the barracks. I suppose it gives the officers a chance to see how some of the boys react when they are given authority that is, if they can give orders and have them carried out properly. It must be quite a hard job though. I hope you didn't have a big bill after you hung up.

Dot came over about an hour after you called. She had a hard time getting over (waiting for fuels). She is well and she was asking for you. She (and I too) are looking forward to seeing you in the near future. When she came I asked her if she would go down to church with me to make a visit as I was unable to go this morning. We did take a walk down and it was so nice to go outside – I hadn't been out since last Wednesday. We came back to the house and Dot stayed for supper. She talked a lot about her trip to Alabama – what she would wear etc. I was glad she came over. It was the first chance we had to get together since you left.

Last night (Saturday) Cel and Charlie were teaching me how to play Michigan Rummy. We played a few games and it was a lot of fun.

The girls from the office (Ruth, Ann, Agnes, + Betty) called me up yesterday to see how I was. It was nice of them wasn't it?

Ann Preston gave me a blue leather folder in which to put Bonds. It's very nice. It keeps them from getting soiled or lost.

Tom told me to tell you that there is a fellow who is in Devens whom he would like you to get in touch with. He left Bridgeport about the same time you did and is stationed in Devens working in the Post Office. He used to work with Tom in the Bpt. Post Office before being inducted. His name is Edward Hicks (Eddie). It seems that he noticed your mail going through Devens Post Office addressed to me and as he knows Tom he just took it for granted you were writing to Tom's sister. Of course he noticed your name on the envelope too. If you get a chance, dearest, it would be a good idea to get in touch with him. Just tell him your name, that you know Tom and that you are the fellow who is writing to me and he will know.

Darling, I was wondering if you are managing to keep the money you took with you or if you've had to spend a lot of it. It might be quite some time before you get paid so it would be a good idea to keep it as long as you can – you might have to use it (or some of it) if you come home after your basic training. I was very happy to know that you might be home after your training. This is something for the both of us to look forward to.

Ellen called me up late this afternoon just to say "hello" and to ask for you. She said she's very glad to see you are getting adjusted and to receive so much mail from you. I told her that I was surprised too at you - - that is I didn't think you liked to write as much as you do, but as you explained to me on the phone, it is a way to express yourself. The only reason I didn't think it was such a good idea, darling, was that if you spend all your spare time writing you wouldn't have any time for yourself to relax or go to the library in the Service Club or do anything else you might like to do. Do you understand, dearest? As long as you write to your father and sisters + brother occasionally and to me as much as possible that's all that's necessary.

Dearest, before I go I just want to tell you I love you. Please try to "keep smiling". I know you are doing your best every day and I'm very proud of you. You are such a good boy, I know you are a good soldier too. I'll send you something nice soon again, dearest.

Love Always,
X X X Rita X X X

Monday 4:30 P.M. 2/1/43

Walter dearest,

I just received the letter you wrote Sunday morning written on your new writing paper. I'm glad you like the paper. I thought your letter was so funny (humorous) that I thought I'd sit down and tell you how much I enjoyed it.

You certainly get good, wholesome food if the breakfast you mentioned is a sample of what you get every day. You couldn't have a better breakfast at home, could you?

It's too bad you missed Church yesterday, dear, but you can surely go next week (I hope).

It must be very hard to be on duty for 24 hours as you were this past week-end. It's a good thing you don't have this duty every week.

I'm so glad to hear you are feeling well, dearest, and that you have such a good appetite. As long as you eat the proper food (not too many sweets) plenty of milk, vegetables and some fruit you will feel well I know – and of course as much rest as you can possibly get. – You know all this darling, but I just feel like reminding you. Maybe you will gain a little weight now. I know you don't like a lot of weight but I think you could stand some.

I laughed and laughed at the part of your letter where you said the boys all kept kidding you and saying not to forget to wake them up and you asked them who would wake you up and that it would take bombs to wake some of them up after they've been to town on Saturday. Maybe if you were to tickle their feet or stick a pin in them, that might help to get them up (ha ha).

You say the Army is teaching you how to take orders and carry them out, and that when you come home and I give you an order you will do it without any questions. Well, darling, you don't ever have to worry about my giving you orders. I never did before and I don't think I ever could. You always call me your coach but this means that I might give you suggestions. I know you always like a good suggestion or idea once in a while. I know I do.

You don't have to worry either, dear, about ever getting caught with a bottle on you. That isn't one of your habits at any time I know. Now if Tom were in the Army that would apply to him. He is upstairs right now in his usual condition. Well, he is a good fellow when he's sober anyway.

Even though I don't know the boys in your company, say "hello" to them for me anyway. I bet they are nice fellows and have girls or wives at home the same as I am.

When Cele comes home from work I'll read the funny part of your letter to her. She'll like it.

I hope you are saving all the letters I write. I'm saving yours. If you find they take up too much room send them back to me (in one bunch) or bring them whenever you get home and I'll keep them for you. Some day it will be fun when you and I can sit down and read them all together.

You're the nicest sweetheart a girl could ever have and my thoughts are always with you, dearest.

Lots of love and kisses

xxx Rita xxx
P.S. Let's both keep our best foot forward.

Monday Evening 2/1/43
Fort Deven's Mass.

Dear Rita,

It made me so happy to be able to talk to you yesterday, darling, I hope you had a very enjoyable evening with Dorothy Smith last night dear, it made me feel so good to hear your voice, Darling take good care of yourself, yesterday your voice sounded a little weak, darling you must have had a very bad cold, I am so glad you are feeling better.

Darling I have everything under control here, and I am feeling very good, it seem's the earlier we get up the better we feel, I guess a very busy life is good for a person, there are about four irish fellow's in my barrack's, I pal around with two of them, Dennis H. Gainty and Paul N. Donnelly, Dennis comes from from New London, and Donnelly comes from Newton Mass. the other fellow is Martin J. Curran, he comes from Boston Mass, he was a policeman in Boston, Dennis worked building submarine's in New London, and Donnelly while in civilian life made a living as a tree surgeon, as I writing here they are all sitting down on a few beds singing all the irish song's, they are now singing (my wild Irish Rose) they were also singing about some (Patty Mckee.) they certainly are a happy go lucky three. Dennis is about 35 years old but looks about 30, he has a baby face, we all kidd him about when he was about twenty he must have had to beat the girls away from himself with a club, Because he was so good looking.

Here we have a boy that owned a resturant in Lawrance Mass, also a Jewish fellow from Cape Cod Mass. that operated a shoe store. We certainly do have some hot debates with him, he certainly is very sure of himself, he is a typical Jewish fellow, they are now beginning a hot debate if it keep's up much more, they will be a riot, All the boy's are saying that England is not doing there share, also they would loss to much, the Jewish Boy is saying that England is doing all right, he is also telling the boy's what a beating his people are, and have taking in Europe, the boy's are certainly hot tonight, I am just sitting tight, laying to write this letter, the boy's think that Germany, Italy, Japan all are no good, the Jewish boy thinks regardles weather Russia is a communistic country and that England is so bossy, they should be our friends just the same. Most of the boy's think that one is as bad as the other, the whole five country's put totegher, Boy if the lieutent should every walk in now we would all be in the guard house tomorrow, I am trying to be just spectator, but it is very hard, now they are debating about the negro's, one fellow in favor of the negro, against about six fellows darling maybe I should not be so uninterested writing this conversation.

Your Love Walter.

Gainty thinks you are nice.

It took me one hour to complete this letter, with the boy's debating. it is quite noisy. Darling you are my Love. I Love You.

Tuesday 2/2/43 – 9:30 P.M.

Dearest Walter,

I just came back from Dr. McQueeney's – I was supposed to have the ganglion on my wrist removed. Well, I still have the lump. The doctor said I would have to go to the hospital and take gas to have it taken off, as it is excess fluid under the skin forming a lump and is really a part of the wrist bone. It's nothing serious. He wants me to wait a while before I have it done, though. He gave me a very thorough examination while I was there and except for the fact that I'm underweight I'm O.K. He's a very nice doctor – he was kidding me all the time I was there. He asked me if I was in love and I told him about you being in the Army and guess what he said. "Did he have "hot lips?" I just laughed and laughed. Cel was with me and she thought he was so funny. He said "I can see love in your eyes." He didn't believe how old I was when I told him. Well, as I said before, he examined me thoroughly and thought I better take a few more days off from work and rest as I still have the cold in my system. I had a slight fever too. He gave me two prescriptions.

Well, dearest, I hope I don't bore you with all this talk of myself but I thought I'd tell you the result of my visit.

I didn't receive any mail from you today but I know I will tomorrow. I know you are busy, darling.

I went to work today and was glad to get back. Betty asked me for your address so you'll probably hear from her and Bill. All the other girls were asking for you too.

Well, dearest, I'll make this a short note for now. I'd like to give it to Tom to bring with him to the post office so it will go on the mail train tonight – just so you can receive it tomorrow.

I love you dearest, I guess the doctor is right when he says he sees love in my eyes (even if he is only kidding). I miss you more and more every day but I'm trying to make the best of everything just as I know you are. I might stay home again tomorrow from work. If I do I'll write a longer letter.

Love Always,
X X X Rita X X X

(P.S. Be a good boy, dear)

Fort Deven's
Massachusetts
Febuary 2. 1943 6:00 P.M.

Dear Rita,

So happy to recive your letters each day, they make me feel so close to you dearest, I look forward to reciving your mail darling. I am fine and all the boy's are well as could be expected, the boy's are <u>18</u> yrs to <u>35</u> yrs old, some are french, some are Greek, others are german, others Polish, one Jewish, there are no Italians in our group, we have one swedish boy from East Ave Bpt. his name is George Hanson, two other boy's are English, all in all they are some bunch. one little fellow that is English comes from Portland Maine, he and I go to the show and library quite often, he is now in the hospital being treated for a bad cold. his name is Richmond Eddy. This morning the lieutent had us out marching for three hours steady marching, boy he sure does give us a workout, if a fellow should get out of step or miss to many facing, boy I dont want to be that fellow, because the lieutent will make the fellow do some fast marching with the Sergeant for a few hours without stoping, than the boy's later will give the boy's a razzing this afternoon we all had drill with our gas mask on for a ¼ of a hour tomorrow we will drill for a ½ hours, than the next day for ¾ hours, so on, until we have them on for any lenght of time, without finding it to hard to breath or feeling to uncomfortable, of course it does feel funny with them on, some of the boy's kid one another how this or that one look's better with a gas mask on than with out one on, Boy it certainly is funny seeing the boy's get into them, they look like men from Mar's. We are certainly covering a lot of ground in a short time. Darling you are my little sweetheart you are my true love, you are a very sincere girl darling, Darling I love you. Darling I am saving all of your lovly letters. Of the twenty five boy's in our paltoon only four of them are married, they are in there early twenty's, Six of the boy's are engaged, <u>15</u> are not going steady at the present time, of the four married, none have children as yet, as far as they know? Dennis Gainty say's <u>he is quite a card</u>, the only smart people are the Irish. We are alway's kidding him.

Paul Donnelly was kidding me a bit, he said he would like to get your address so he could write to a sweet irish girl. I said I would not trust him with a load of banana's I said O. <u>yeah</u>.

Wednesday 6:30 P.M. 2/3/43

Walter darling,

Please excuse my crowding the writing on the paper like this – I am down to my last sheet of writing paper but I'll get some more tomorrow. I received your letters dated Monday and Tuesday and enjoyed both of them. I'm so glad to hear you're making so many friends – you are certainly with a nice group of fellows. I think one can learn a lot being in the company of so many different types of people. Tell your friends Dennis Gainty, Paul Donnelley and Martin Curran that it seems good to hear good, Irish names like theirs. They sound like happy-go-lucky fellows and I imagine are a lot of fun. Your friend Richmond Eddy sounds like a more serious type of a boy. It's too bad he's sick but with all you boys around to cheer him up he should be well in no time. The debate you said the boys were having when you wrote on Monday must have been good. I wish I were there to put my two cents worth into it. (ha ha).

Darling, your description of the fellows marching and drilling with your gas masks on sounds just like a story I read in the "Readers' Digest." The name of it is "See Here, Private Hargrove." Of course what I read was a brief summary of a book by that name that is now on the market. It's the funniest story. The fellow who wrote the book is now a Corporal in the Army but when he wrote it he was a private. It tells about all his experiences during his basic training and I laughed my head off when I read it. I was planning to buy the book – if I do – I'll send it to you. You'll enjoy it a lot.

Dearest, do you think there is any possibility of your coming home on a 24-hour pass? It would be grand if you could some Sunday. I know you mentioned getting a week-end off (maybe) after your training so that's something to look forward to anyway. Please let me know what you think about a 24-hour pass. Maybe it wouldn't be worthwhile as by the time you would get home (4 hours) and 4 hours to go back you wouldn't be here very long.

The club is coming here tonight – that is what there is of it – Dot Grant just called up and said she was sick she wouldn't be here. Dot Blake is working so that leaves only Alice, Dot Smith and I. Well, I'll enjoy having them over anyway. I think the real reason D. Grant isn't coming is it's her birthday today and she and Jimmy will probably celebrate. Well, happy birthday to her anyway.

I'm going to have Ann and Ruth come over some night next week. We can have some fun playing Michigan Rummy.

Dearest I've started the practice (about a week ago) of saying the "Memorare" (Prayer to the Blessed Virgin) for you every night. I'm going to Communion for you this week. I'm doing this for your continued good health. This seems to me about the best thing I could do for you. You are so deserving of the best of everything. You're certainly doing a wonderful job of adjusting yourself – making friends, learning something new every day – in other words – trying to do your job in the Army well – an all-around good fellow. I love you, dearest – you're the apple (I mean soldier) of my eye.

Love AlwaysRita

These aren't enough. → X X X X X X

Febuary 3. 1943 12:00 MOON

Dear Rita.

I hope you are in tip top shape today Rita dear, and that you feel like a million. Rita I have not as yet been able to get up to the post office to meet Tom's friend <u>Eddie</u>, there are about four post office's on this fort, if Tom knew what post or company he is attached to, it would be easy'er for me to find him unless he is working up at the main post office. On this fort there are about <u>40</u> thousand men. Tom propably has his address,

This morning the lieutent had us all out marching for two hours, we went outside at 8.A.M. to 10.AM, boy the weather sure was snappy, we only had one break in two hours, that is time of to warm our hands, and to wipe our noses.

At times our noses were red as beets, and if we march much longer, there would be ice icks hanging from our noses, if we dared to raise our hand to rub our ears and the luey or sergeant caugh us, we would get a bawling out.

This afternoon we are going to get more information on gun alinement, and how to fire our rifles, we do this up in icicles the attic, last night we had movies on correct marching, both pictures and sound, just like the movies in town. I went to show last night with Gainty and Donnelly, we saw Andy Hardy Pictures with Micky Roony, and Cecelia Parker it was quite humorous. I enjoyed it very much It is now very nice out, the sun has warmed up thing's very much.

Boy we all did sleep very sound last night, after that tough workout yesterday by our lieutent, the boy's call him by his pet name when he is not around, they call him Poker face, he even say's himself that he is a poker face once in a while, but that he has to be that way in order to drive home the points of the day, the boy's make sure he is not around when they mention, the name Poker face. The boy's are feeling fine, each noon they all congragate near where the fellow in charge gives out the mail, they look forward for mail very much, weather or not they are near or far from home. Rita you are my lifes inspiration, and you are my sweet little darling, Darling I think about you very often in fact each night as I go to sleep I picture in my mind, you and I together, maybe haveing a kiss or two, or a few long ones

Love Walter

Twelve KISSES, X X X X X X X X X X X X X

Thursday 6:00 P.M. 2/4/43

Dearest,

I stopped downtown tonight and bought this writing paper so now I'll have enough to last me for quite a while (maybe).

I enjoyed your last letter so much, dear. I had to laugh at the part where you said it was so cold when you were marching the other morning that there were icicles hanging from the boys' noses. You all would look funny marching like that. Anyway, one good point about your routine is that you are out in the air quite a bit. I know you must like that part of it. I can see where your lieutenant would have to be a "poker face" to drive home the points to all you boys. As long as you are on the alert at all times you have nothing to worry about. After all, dearest, you can't do anything more than your best. It's constant plugging along that most of the time brings one out on top.

I'm so glad you manage to get to the movies once in a while. Whenever there's any diversion to be had "Kleiny" will be right there if possible won't you darling? (I know you).

Tom says that the fellow I wrote you about is in the same company you are. This doesn't seem possible to me as he's in the post office and you, of course, are in the M.P. Tom said when he saw your return address on the mail going to me he noticed that you were both in the same company. If this is impossible, just don't bother as I know it's hard to locate anyone in such a large number of fellows.

Dot Smith says Ernie wrote and told her he had a nice surprise for her but he didn't tell her what it was – although he kept hinting a lot. She thinks he might be on his way home, as if he did get this furlough, it was supposed to start February 2nd, Tuesday. That means he would be home by late this afternoon. She said she'd let me know if he did but I haven't heard yet.

I haven't heard from Elwood's mother whether he arrived at his final destination or not. He was only supposed to be in Alabama for about ten days.

Eileen and the doctor will be married a year Sunday, Feb. 7th. I think I'll send them an anniversary card seeing I was bridesmaid at their wedding. Remember that day, dearest, when you and I danced so much? That's all a happy memory now.

Ann Preston and her family went to see her brother last Sunday. He's stationed at Camp Edison, New Jersey. (He left Bpt. for Devens the Saturday after you. He can have visitors on Sundays (the Sundays he's not on guard duty or other detail) from 10:30 A.M. to 5:30 P.M. Ann said she had a nice time. Joe, her brother, took the family around the camp and stayed with them all day. He expects to come home for a week-end this week. He's in the Signal Corps and likes the Army very much although he gets lonesome sometimes. Ann invited me to her home this coming Saturday for supper and then to the show. I might go if I feel better. I'm back to work now but the grippe certainly takes a lot out of anyone – but don't worry, dearest, I'll be in tip-top shape when you come home anyway.

Darling, sometimes I play the musical powder box you gave me. It sounds nice. I have so many things around me that you gave me – it makes me feel a little closer to you. I wear the bracelet every day, take turns with the pearls and locket, and of course I'm never without my diamond. You know how much I think of that. I'm using the "Evening in Paris" sch you gave me, too.

I was going to have your initials put on the watch I gave you but I noticed the place where the initials would go (on the back) is not gold like the rest of the watch. I didn't know this before. There is sort of a chrome finish and I don't think it would be a good idea to put the initials on that part. I guess it really isn't necessary to have initials on it anyway, but if you'd like them on I'll have them put on. Let me know, dearest.

Darling, I never get tired of having you tell me you love me – I always look for that little paragraph in your letters just for me. I know you do the same. It means so much to hear it every day - - that is, to see it written. When we're apart like this, it is the only way we can express our love – by telling each other over and over, but it makes me happy and I feel close to you even if we don't see each other. It doesn't seem possible that our love could be so deep and lasting does it? But you and I both know it is.

Love Always,
Rita

P.S. [I LOVE YOU spelled with X's] Aren't I artistic? (ha ha)

Fort Deven's January 4. 1943
Mass.Thursday 7:00 P.M.
[Actually February 4]

Dear Rita,

I just have recived a letter from Ernest Smith, he was very glad to hear from me, he also want's to congradulate us on our engagement, he thinks you are a swell girl, and that I am a lucky fellow. He writes in this letter how he has gotten a ten 10 day leave, he say's that he did everything under the sun to get it, he did not say when the leave started, only that he is leaving for Bridgeport, the letter was written Febuary 1. 1943, I prosume that his leave was going to start very soon, after he finished this letter, he said he hope that we could all get together, well if he starts his leave about the fifthteen of Feb. and has until the twenty fifth of Febuary we could all be together, because I think our weekend is going to come on the twenty,eth of Febuary, at least that is when our month basic training is over, that is when the lieutent promised us a pass, only half us may get a pass the first week, than the other half the next, maybe I will be lucky enough to get a pass the first week. Ernest say's he is fine and that he is thinking that soon he may get a rateing, he likes his work very much. today I also recived a letter from Al Hammer the boy that is in the navy he is stationed at the present in South Caroline, he is Elsie Hammer brother.

Today I also recived a letter from Michael Racky, he is stationed in Rhode Island in the Coast Artillery, he is Vinny's brother, he say's that I am very lucky to be stationed so close to home.

Yesterday I got a letter from my sister Martha, she was saying how you called last week, she say's you are a very nice girl.

My sister Emma also drop a line, they are all feeling fine, and she hopes I will get home soon, because they would all like to see how I look in my uniform, I should look very classy in my uniform, with my good look's, should bowl them over,. Ha. Ha.

About your ganglion on your wrist dear, I was thinking all the long, that when you have it treated, you would have to take an anaesthetic, I though that it would take more than just cut it, while you were watching, well darling it will come out all right, I am sure.

Darling you are my sunshine, you know that there is not much sunshine nowday's especially during the winter month's, even in the hot summer day's you are my sunshine and lifes inspiration. I love you very much.

Love. Walter.
Pvt. Walter Klein

Friday 6:00 P.M. 2/5/43

Dear Sweetheart,

I just received your card a little while ago when I came home from work. I think it's so cute. Wouldn't you and I look funny dressed like the picture of the little Indians on it? I got a big kick out of the way you changed the verse on it too. You're so thoughtful, darling.

You certainly are learning things fast in the Army – marching with your rifle and all the other things that go with your training. It just goes to show that the officers have to have "poker faces" and be strict – I guess that's the quickest way to have the fellows learn, being like that.

Last night Ruby Unsderfer's (Frenchy's sister) picture was in the paper announcing her engagement to a fellow by the name of Leahy from Dorchester, Mass. I thought you'd be interested to know.

Ruth Landry got a notice from the government that her boyfriend's mailing address would be Seattle, Washington from now on but that he was stationed somewhere else (it didn't say where). She knows that he's in Alaska by now – and she's very discouraged knowing he's so far away.

Darling, do you ever hear from Leo or any of the boys? I hope so. I wish I could give you some news about them once in awhile but of course it's impossible. I also hope you're writing to your father as often as possible as he must be very lonesome all by himself.

I was wondering what you thought of the card I sent you with the batch of letters sent all in one envelope. Did you like the little girl on it with a piece of glass for a tear? That's supposed to be me.

Cele and Charlie both told me to tell you they were asking for you.

Tomorrow night I'm supposed to go to Ann Preston's house for dinner and then to the show. I wish I could see you instead, dearest. I might go if I can.

I hope you find time to call me up Sunday, darling. I love to talk to you on the phone.

Well, darling, I'd like to mail this before 7:15 (that's the last pick-up of the mail around here.). I love you so much – you're such a good boy.

Love Always,
X X X Rita X X X

P.S. Joke: One farmer said to another: There was such a bad wind storm the other night that it blew my grandfather's nose for him. (ha ha)

Saturday 12:00 2/6/43

Dear Rita Marie,

Recived your 6:00 PM 2/5/43 letter at noon today, it did not take long to get here, you are very prompt with your mail dear.

Leo is soon to be inducted into the Army, what Harry Hammer has writen to me about the boy's, Leo should arrive at Fort Deven's about the 12th twelfth of Febuary, I have already droped him a card and a letter telling him how I would like to see him when he arrives at camp, I told him where I am stationed, and I told him the Layout of the recruit reception center I told him the army is not to bad once a fellow get's used to the scheme of the army, I write to Harry Hammer one of the boy's, he in turn tell's the boy's about the doing's at camp.

Yes darling the card that you sent with the letters all together in the envelope was very nice, you sure do have good taste, the little girl looked just like you darling. Darling you have a lot of good company in Bridgeport, now that all the boy's are being shipped to distant places, you have Ruth Landry and Ann Preston, also Dot Blake, and Dorothy Smith, I hope you all do go out quite often, because you all have the same interest, Boy Ann Preston boyfriend sure is quite a way's from home, it will be very hard for Ruth now, give my regards to all the girl's in the office, Ann, Ruth, Betty, Violite and the others.

This morning our lieutent, <u>Valenage</u>, is his name, our sergeant name is Sgt. Deschaie, they are both frenchmen, they are not to bad of fellows, the sergeant just resently had added to his family, a set of twins, he sure does all right for a frenchman, he lives in town with his wife each night, he commutes each day, now to get back to what I was going to say this morning we were out for a three hour hike, it was quite a workout the roads were very ice'y to complicate things, the boy's had planned a big time in the nearby town's but if you could see some of them now you would laugh, there are about twelve stretched out on there bunk now. To bad for the boy's, I am feeling pretty good right now.

Darling I Love you, you are my sweetheart, you are very sweet.

Love Walter.

Sunday 5:30 P.M. 2/7/43

Dearest,

Dorothy and Ernie just left a few minutes ago. They stayed for about an hour. Ernie looks very well, seems to weigh about the same though, but looks nice in his uniform. Charlie came home from work while they were here and served them a drink. We asked them to stay for supper but Mrs. Smith expected them back to the house. While we were sitting talking we all said it was too bad you couldn't be here too, dearest, but maybe sometime again he'll be home and you will have a chance to come home then. I was glad they came as it sort of broke the afternoon up for me – that is, it didn't seem so long.

It was wonderful to hear your voice this afternoon, darling, but I'm sorry you have a cold. If it gets any worse, please go to the doctor and have him give you something for it won't you? I don't want you to get sick, dearest. I'm glad you managed to get to church and Communion this morning – I know it makes you feel better.

I invited Ann, Ruth and Betty over to the house this coming Wednesday for the evening. I hope they come. It seems every time I plan anything lately it doesn't work out somehow (weather and other things).

Enclosed you will find a clipping that was in last night's paper. Your cousin Les's name is on the list and I thought you'd be interested to see it as there are probably a lot of fellows names you'll recognize. I'm surprised that Les went into the Navy. He must have preferred it and joined before he was drafted.

There is also a cartoon about Pfc. Peter Plink. Did you ever read it in the Post when you were home? I think it's funny. The other one "All in a Lifetime" I thought was funny too. Believe it or not, a lot of people are doing that right now – using all kinds of excuses so they can use their cars.

Dearest, I miss you so much but now I'm looking forward to seeing you in a few weeks. It seems as though you've been gone three years instead of three weeks. I know it seems long to you, too. Please take care of yourself, dear, remember I love you, you're such a good sweetheart. Try to get lots of sleep if you can – I want you to be as "fit as a fiddle" when you come home, dearest.

Love Always,

Rita [A heart made of X's]

This is a funny looking heart isn't it? ↑ (ha ha)

Monday 6:30 P.M. 2/8/43

Hello Sweetheart,

How're you today? I hope your cold is better.

I just came home from work and your letter you wrote Saturday was waiting for me. It's so nice to have your letters to look forward to every day.

I was glad to hear that Harry Hammer wrote you and gave you some news of the boys. I'll bet you were surprised to see Leo's name on the Navy list in the clipping I sent in my last letter.

Yes, dearest, as you said I have a lot of nice girl friends to keep me company and go out with while you're gone but as I mentioned before, up to the present time I haven't been out with any of them at all. It just so happens that one of us at least just couldn't make any plans at the time. Well, I'm hoping that Ann, Ruth + Betty come over Wednesday. We can have a nice evening together if they do.

As you've probably heard, men, women and children's shoes are being rationed starting today. Everyone will only be allowed to buy three pairs a year and are to use a certain coupon in the sugar ration book when we buy a new pair. I guess pretty soon they're going to ration all clothes. Well I guess it's just a matter of getting used to it. As Ernie said yesterday, he thinks sometimes that the fellows in the Services are better off than civilians — They have plenty of clothes, and good food. This seems true doesn't it?

Dearest, I mailed you a magazine this afternoon that I thought you might enjoy. There are some funny pictures and jokes in it – the ones I thought were good I marked – you'll see as you go through. Of course, this type of magazine is alright if you're in the mood for something funny but for some good reading I know you'd like to read "Life" or "Reader's Digest" or some of the other better magazines. I didn't know whether to send you any of these or not. I thought they would be available in the library you were telling me about. If they aren't, I'd be glad to send "Life" or whatever one you'd like once in awhile. I suppose you don't have much time to read though. Let me know about this.

Darling, if there are some days that you don't receive any mail from me you'll know I just couldn't make the last mail. It seems that the last pick-up around here is 7:15 P.M. That means I don't have much time between 6:30 + 7:15 (by the time I eat supper + everything) to mail a letter. Of course I write every night but I can't make the last mail every night. I know you understand.

Take good care of yourself, dearest, I don't want my sweetheart to be sick 'cause I love you so much. Well, good night, dear.

Love Always,
xxxxxx Rita xxxxxx

P.S. Keep <u>Smiling</u>

Tuesday 7:00 P.M. 2/9/43

Dear Rita,

You are my little sweetheart, Rita, dear, you are a very sincere girl darling,

I was very happy to learn that Leo my cusin was inducted into the navy, now that the new law is into effect, so many men that are inducted each month, some go into the army, some go into the navy, others go into the marine's, that is the way the men are being divided among all the branches so I think Leo was very lucky to get placed into the navy, he did not enlist into the navy, he was placed there by the goverment, I think he would of selected the navy if he had the choose between the army or navy, this is as far as I understand is the method that they use now.

We here at camp manage to get quite a few magazine's, also plenty of books, both from the library and Post Exchange plus what the boy's get from home, if you find some magazine that you think is very humorous or interesting you can send it to me, I will appreciate them very much, as now I have more books than time, but later I may have more time.

Darling do not strain yourself to much using so much effort to write each day, I know how time is so limided now day's, so if you do not find the time, or if you have to push your, self, darling wait until you do not have to rush so, you know after supper you have to relax some, after you have been working so hard at the office, so darling use your best Judgement, and do not tire yourself out, I will understand if I do not recive a letter for that day, although I look forward to each day so that I may recive a letter from you, to hear how you are, and the happening's at Bridgeport, boy I am a loulou, I am, but I can not help it, can I darling, you are my sunshine, and my inspiration Rita dear. I hope you like the heart shape box of candy that I sent also the valentine card. Darling you are my sweetheart. I hope you have a very happy Valentine day.

Love. Walter.
VALENTINE LOVE TO YOU
[heart with arrow through it]

Wednesday 11:15 P.M. 2/10/43

Dearest,

I thought I'd drop you a few lines before going to bed – as you can see on the top of this paper – it's quite late.

The girls have just left – that is, Ann and Ruth. Betty couldn't come as Bill hurt his eye at work so she had to be home to get his supper and help him doctor it up. It was too bad she couldn't come because we had a very nice evening. Ann brought over a lot of records and we played them and danced. We also played "parchesi" and it was such fun. Of course it would have been nicer if our boyfriends were here too but we consoled ourselves and said, "well, your days are coming."

Dearest, I received your valentine today and it was a lovely one – the verse was so nice. I'll put it with all my other nice cards I've received from you.

Last night there was a broadcast from Fort Devens' Reception Center. Were you there? I listened thinking maybe you'd say "hello" over the radio (ha ha). There were two bands and a few of the boys sang and some gave their impression of the Army. There were also a few W.A.A.C.S. It was very good.

Well, dearest, it's almost 12 o'clock so I must go to bed. I love you with all my heart.

Yours forever,
xxx Rita xxx

P.S. Chin up, dearest + your best foot forward.

Dear Rita.

Recived the magazine you send, It is just the type I like, it has some very good cartoons I say it also has plenty of class.

Love
Walter

Thursday 5:45 2/11/43

Dearest Walter,

I received your letter dated Tuesday and also the card. I had a good laugh over the pictures on the card. I'm glad you enjoyed the magazine – I'll send you another soon.

I didn't know all the fellows were placed in different branches of the service by the government. Well, I think Leo will like the Navy. He'll probably drop you a line when he gets established. Well, darling, there's Cele calling me for supper. I'll finish this when I come back.

I've eaten supper and while eating I had some very bad news. Dot Grant called me up and said Helen Banahan (Hainsworth) died yesterday (the girl in the club who was in Wallingford with tuberculosis). I'm so sorry to hear it and shocked. Dot Grant handles the money for our club so she's going to take some of the money and send flowers and a Mass Card from all of us. We are going to the wake (all the girls in the club) tomorrow night. She's going to be buried Saturday but I guess we won't be able to make the funeral. You remember, dearest, I wrote you a few weeks ago telling you she was very sick. I guess she just kept getting worse all the time. I certainly feel badly about it + feel sorry for Harry and her mother.

You mention in your letter that you sent me a box of candy. I haven't received it yet but I did receive your nice valentine as I told you before. It's so nice of you to remember me for Valentine's Day, dear, you're so kind and thoughtful. I know I will like the box when it does come. I'm sorry you won't have my picture by Saturday but I will send it as soon as I can get it.

How are you feeling now, is your cold all better? I hope so.

Dot Smith said Ernie is leaving Saturday noon. He has to be back in camp by Monday. She says she has something special to tell me when we're alone. I think she's going to tell me – either she's already married or will be very soon. I know Ernie wanted to get married while he was here but Dot didn't think she would. Well, I'll tell you when the whole thing is "official", dear, but for now don't mention it to anyone. Cele also thinks this is the way it is.

I guess I'll go to the store now + buy a few funny valentines for Ruth + Ann. We are going to exchange them Saturday between the three of us.

Well, dearest, that's all for tonight. Be a good boy (you are) 'cause I love you.

Love Always,
Rita
xxxxxx

(Ha Ha)

Sunday 3:45 P.M. 2/14/43
Valentine's Day

Hello Sweetheart,

I've just finished eating dinner (we had a late one today). You called just before we sat down to eat. It was nice of you to call, dear, as I know you only had an hour's free time. It's too bad you had to be on K.P. today – it must be very tiresome seeing so many dishes all day long as you said, and getting the food ready to be served. Well, as I told you on the 'phone, at least you have something nice to look forward to during this week – coming home next week-end.

I was surprised that you will be free from 1 o'clock on – I thought you wouldn't get a pass until late Saturday afternoon and then wouldn't get into Bpt. until late Saturday night. It certainly was wonderful news for me. You know how much I've been looking forward to seeing you even if only for a few hours. I know you'll want to spend some time with your father. If you go home as soon as you get off the train and spend a little time with him before you come to see me, it would be nice. I know he'll be glad. Then, of course, you can spend your usual Sunday morning as you did before – going to Church and then some more time home and then with me a little later. I seem to be planning your whole week-end, don't I dearest? It's just that I want you to have an enjoyable week-end without having to rush around here + there – just relax and "feel at home".

I opened the pink satin heart you sent me and we all had some candy. It's very good. The inside of the box was in topsy-turvey condition, that is, the candies were all jumbled up but of course this is to be expected – you know how packages are handled in the post office – just thrown around. Cel bought a new coffee table last week (it's near the divan) so I put the box on that. It looks nice there. I'll leave it there so you'll see it next week and have some candy (if there's any left).

Tom said the fellows in the post office received a card from Eddie Hicks. He was moved from Devens last week. He's now in Arkansas (still doing postal work). This is a good break for him, I think, doing the same type of work as he did before being inducted.

In my last letter I mentioned to you that Dot Smith said she had something she wanted to tell me when we were alone. Well, I was right assuming that it had something to do with she and Ernie getting married. She told me Friday that they plan to get married in August. They want Ernie's boyfriend Irving to be best man, Mary Ruane, a life-long friend of Dot's to be maid of honor. They also want you to be an usher + me a bridesmaid. This means of course, as you know, that you + I would be in the bridal party – you would be my partner. Isn't that good news? I wasn't surprised to hear this (that is that they would plan to get married as soon as possible). Of course, August is six months away and as they both said, anything could happen within that time. Dot said she thinks Ernie could get a furlough alright if he told them he is to be married but the hard thing about it is whether Irving, his boyfriend and you could get home at that time. She realized that you by that time might be in some camp in the South or West but on the other hand you might still be in Devens too. So it's hard to set any definite date yet but I guess they'll know by May the exact date – sometime in August. They've already bought the wedding ring. It would be nice if everything works out the way they plan. It would be a new experience for you, wouldn't it, and I would like to be a bridesmaid again. Ernie said he was going to write to you as soon as he gets back to camp so you'll probably hear more about it from him soon.

Last night, Ann, Ruth and I managed to get together (finally) and went to dinner and then to the show. We worked until 5 o'clock and went from work. We saw the picture at the Majestic "Journey for Margaret" with Robert Young + Lorraine Day and "Icecapades". Both pictures were very good. We ate dinner in the Barnum Coffee Shoppe and had some sherry wine first. It was a change for me to spend the evening like this. I enjoyed it a lot. Ann and Ruth are a lot of fun.

I brought the booklet you sent me into the office and showed the girls. They had a good laugh. I received the postal from you yesterday (the one with the picture on it of the soldier with the big feet). It was funny too. You said on this card that you were to go into a gas chamber Friday. How did you make out? Ernie was talking about that last Sunday. He had to go through one too. He said it was quite an experience, one he hoped he would never have to go through again.

Here's a poem that I think is nice. The name of it is "Buried Treasure" by C. Bonham.
"I shall keep the lovely dreams
That you and I have made
Way down within my secret heart,
Where they can never fade.

I'll label them "Do not disturb,"
And wrap in love for you,
So when you come to claim them, dear,
They'll be as good as new."

Here's a cute one:
"Let's nibble at love while we're young and ruthless
'Cause if we wait, We'll be old and toothless." (ha ha).

This is quite a long letter isn't it dear? I'll have to go now or I'll have "writer's cramp" (ha ha). Take good care of yourself, dear, so you'll feel tops for next week.

Love Always,
Rita

x x x x x x x x x x

Next week I'll give you this many in person. ↑ I love you, dearest
[This letter was missent to Chicopee Falls.]

Monday 7:30 P.M. 2/15/43

Dearest,

I just finished eating supper – I didn't get home until 6:30 as I had to work until 6. I know you probably won't get this letter until Wednesday or so because I missed the last mail (7:15). You understand though, I know you do, dear.

I received the card you wrote Saturday (the picture of a mailbox with little cards inside of it). It's such a cute card. I never saw one quite like it before – you have very good taste for picking out cards. I'm going to bring it into the office and show the girls just as I did your valentine and booklet. They enjoy looking at anything like that.

There is an epidemic of measles throughout the factory and a few people in the office have them too. I hope I don't get them. Maybe I wouldn't be so apt to as I've had them before. Bill Hughes went home today with them. By the way, he's going to have his local physical for the Army Friday. I guess he'll be in soon. I don't know what Betty will do then. I don't think she'd like to live all by herself.

We are in the midst of a cold spell now. This morning it was 10° below zero and it's almost that again tonight. I suppose it's just as cold in Devens too. I had quite a hard time getting to work this morning – you know how the buses are in the cold weather. I hope it will be warmer by Saturday, don't you, dear? – Maybe you and I won't know whether it's hot or cold anyway. We'll be oblivious to everything. (ha ha).

How are all the rest of the boys in your platoon? I suppose you are all managing to have a little fun along with your work. I hope so.

Maybe it won't take you as long as you think to get home Saturday (I guess you figure 5 hours). It might only take about 4 hours if you have good train connections. Let's keep our fingers crossed.

I'm going to do a few chores not in the house. I suppose at this time you are also washing or writing or talking with the boys. I always try to imagine what you're doing at different times. I wish I could be with you to tell you what a good boy you are (as I used to) and how much I love you. I wish, too, that I could be with you to hear all your problems (if any) and all the doings of each day. Well, anyway, dear, maybe I'll see you at the end of this week and that will be worth waiting for.

Love Always
Rita x x x x x x
I Love You.

Mon 7:P.M 2/15/43

Dear Rita,

Was very happy to hear your voice over the phone and be able to chat with you. Today the weather was about twelve below zero, this is very cold country up in these hills We drilled inside today and did some studies, also attended some military movies. I am looking forward to this Sat and Sunday Rita dear. Love Walter.

Tuesday 7:45 P.M. 2/16/43

Walter Dear,

I worked until 6 o'clock tonight again. I don't mind at all because it means that I'll be through work Saturday all the earlier.

I didn't receive any mail from you today but I know that you must have been very busy yesterday or maybe you felt as though you just didn't have any news or felt tired. It's alright, dear, I understand. It's funny though, isn't it, when you're used to getting a letter or card every day, you feel sort of "let down" if you don't happen to get one for just one day. I guess I'm just spoiled.

Betty is home with the measles. Bill also has them – as I told you in my last letter, there seems to be an epidemic in the factory and office. About ten of the girls in the office decided to send Betty a few dozen of red roses and a nice card with them. She'll probably be home for about eight to ten days.

Mrs. Ellicott (Mr. Lincoln's Secretary) – the woman who came out to the car the time you were waiting for me and talked to you) has left the office and gone back to New York. It seems she was compelled to move from where she lives (Greenfield Hill) as her land-lady wanted the rent. Well, she couldn't get a rent anywhere in Bridgeport, Black Rock or anywhere else so there was no other alternative but for she and her husband to go back to N.Y. She left the office tonight. Everyone hated to see her go as she's such a pleasant person. Some of us in the office are going to meet her Friday noon and treat her to lunch and give her a little gift.

Darling, it's still very cold here although a lot warmer than the zero weather we had. It would be a good idea for you to dress as warmly as possible when you come home (long coat + gloves if you have them). I know you realize this.

Enclosed you will find a clipping that was in Sunday's paper. The writer of this column interviewed Vin Saturday. It's just supposed to be the average bus driver's opinion on the bus stations in Bpt. at the present time. I don't know whether it's alright for me to send you the newspaper clipping or not. If it isn't, let me know, dear. You can destroy it when you read it anyway.

Tomorrow (Wednesday) you will be five weeks away. I'll bet it seems longer to you. It does to me. I think from what you've told me about your new life that there are a lot of advantages and you have certainly acquired a knowledge of a lot of things you didn't know before. (This applies to anyone). In your case, I think you are now beginning to realize your capacities and I'll bet they're above anything you ever thought you could do. This is something I think is very good in your case. Remember, dear, the time I said I hoped you would realize after you were in the Army awhile, just what you could and couldn't do. If you don't mind my saying, you were lacking confidence in yourself somewhat before you went away. Now I think you are gaining it in the right way. You're certainly doing your best in everything pertaining to the Army I know. I suppose you wonder where I get all these ideas. Well, just from reading your letters, I think you are taking a real interest in every thing you do. This is the best spirit, dear even though there might be a lot of things you don't like, too. (if any).

Well, dearest, I seem to be giving you a sermon, don't I? This is just a little "food for thought." If you just try to remember that our love is getting stronger each day in spite of your being away, I know you won't ever be discouraged. This is what I think anyway.

I'm counting the days now until I see you, dear. Take good care of yourself, sweetheart

Love Always,
Rita
X X X X X

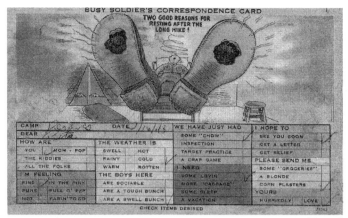

Tuesday 7: A.M.

Dear Rita,

It is about twenty below zero here this morning, boy we did not want to get up, but the good old buglar blew just the same. I feel pretty good this morning, got to bed a little early'er for a change we are kept very busy. Love, Walt

We get up a quarter to six every Morn.

Thursday 7:00 P.M. 2/18/43

Dearest Walter,

I received your postal dated Tuesday with the picture of the soldier resting with the big feet. (ha ha.) I also received the jig-saw puzzle and the card you wrote Wednesday. The puzzle is very cute. I took it all apart and put it into the little red bag that came with it. I'll put it together some day when I have time. Cele and Charlie said I should send it back to you and let you put it together (ha ha).

You said on the card that you expect to be in Bridgeport by 5 o'clock and to my house at 8. Darling, couldn't you come to see me a little earlier – about 7 or 7:30? I'll be so anxious to see you and the week-end will go by so fast, an extra hour or half-hour will mean a lot. Of course I know you'd like to spend some time home, too, but you'll be home Sunday morning.

You'll probably enjoy the train ride home Saturday seeing that you'll have lots of company, as you said all the other boys were going to Bridgeport too. You also said you and the boys would like some "smooching", well, I know you Kleiny, if they're like you, they must be anxious. (ha ha)

I only worked until 5 o'clock tonight. It seemed good to get home a little earlier. All the girls in the office envy me because you're coming home for the week-end. They all wish their boyfriends would too. Ruth received a letter from her boyfriend today from Alaska. This is the first mail she's had since before Christmas. It was an air mail letter and it took ten days to get here.

Ann's brother also has a 36-hour pass this week-end. He's in Camp Edison, N.J. This will be the second leave he's had.

Well, dearest, it won't be long now before we see each other. I know you can hardly wait, too. Cel, Charlie + Jeanie are all anxious to see you. Don't forget to dress as warmly as possible, dearest, because it's cold here also. Wear gloves if you have them. You and I will have to do a lot of "catching up" won't we after 5- 1/2 weeks?

Love Always,
x x x Rita x x x

P.S. I hope we have a little time alone as there's something I want to tell you. I didn't want to write it in my letters but don't worry, it's nothing to worry about. Good night, dearest - -

Monday 8:00 P.M. 2/22/43
Washington's Birthday

Dearest Walter,

I hope you had an enjoyable week-end and that you arrived back at the Fort safely.

The week-end turned out much differently than I expected. We didn't seem to be together enough. It really was no one's fault. Everyone wanted to see you and you wanted to see everyone too. People just didn't seem to realize that we would like to be together alone for a while. I guess it was because this was your first visit and the novelty of the whole thing (seeing you in uniform etc.) made everyone including yourself and I all excited.

It was nice of your brother to invite us out to dinner. Cel thought we'd come back here for supper as she said you told her Saturday night you intended to be here. It was sort of too bad because she spent practically her whole day cooking and then we weren't here anyway. Eleanor and Vin thought they were doing us a favor by taking you to the station. They meant well but I'd just as soon have taken the bus because then I could have been with you alone a little while anyway. Well, as I said before, it was your first visit home so I'm willing to overlook the whole thing.

In your excitement yesterday you made several cutting and unnecessary remarks which were probably unintentional but I couldn't help being hurt. You didn't have to tell everyone that you bought the pins in the 5 + 10¢ Store in Bridgeport. If you did, it's perfectly alright but not to tell everyone. Cel felt funny taking the extra one as she knew you didn't buy it for her in the first place. Well, she took it at my suggestion. Also when Irene and Charlie came in the restaurant and kiddingly asked us when we were going to be married you didn't have to say "All the girls are better off married because then they don't get sick so often etc. - - -) and then taking the attitude in front of everyone that you are playing "hard to get" making me feel as though I am over-anxious. I guess you mean all your remarks to be funny but they are anything but funny. You just put me in an embarassing position. This brings me to the subject I was going to talk to you about if we were alone.

I was going to suggest that you start sending money to me every month when you get paid. Maybe you intended to do this, I don't know, but I think it's a good idea no matter when we get married we'll need some money to get some kind of a home together. For my part, I'm going to start saving as soon as possible. I talked to Cel about this the other night and she thinks we ought to try to save as much as possible now. Your brother asked me if I was like "some of the Swedes" who go with a person for 10 years before they marry. Well, as you know, I'm not. You, I think, are inclined to think in these channels. While the war is on you'll probably say you don't believe in war marriages. After the war you'll say jobs are scarce and we'll have to have money. Now is the time to start saving. Cel said she thinks sometimes young couples like you and I are better to start with $400 or $500 than the way she and Charlie started with $5,000.<u>00</u> and now they have nothing as far as money goes but they have their health + a job. I would rather talk to you about these things when we're together but this is the next best thing (writing).

I guess you've forgotten common courtesy since you went away. I know it's hard for you to make introductions but at the station you made me wish I wasn't there at all.

There's also the question of my meeting your father at some time or other. I don't see why you don't tell him about me, at least if you only said yesterday you wanted to visit your girlfriend and had him drive you down here. It's about time he knew of our engagement from you and not from everyone else.

Well, Walter, don't think I'm just trying to pile up a lot of accusations against you. I just want you to sit down sometime within the next six weeks and take stock of yourself and try to get over your "smart-alec superior ways". The Walter I saw over the week-end was not the same boy who left six weeks ago. It was just someone I don't want to know too much of. You and I have a lot of facts to face, some we both might try to avoid, but I think it best that we bring everything out in the open. You have so many fine qualities too. I was happy to see you looking so well and that you are trying your best in everything pertaining to the Army. I imagine you were very tired today after so little sleep and the long ride back. Try to catch up on sleep this week.

I brought the roll of film in to be developed (in Lupe's). It will be ready Friday so I'll send you the pictures over the week-end.

I'm wearing the pin you gave me every day. I showed it to all the girls. I like it a lot.

In spite of this very depressing letter, dearest, my love is as strong as ever. Please don't think I'm mad. It's just that I want to have you face a few facts and wake up! You know I'd rather have a little kindness and courtesy than anything else in the world and of course your love.

I know the next time you come home I'll see more of you.

Love Always,
Rita
X X X X X X

Tuesday, 7:00 P.M. Feb. 23, 1943

Dearest Walter,

Vin borrowed my typewriter about a month ago and returned it yesterday so I thought I'd use it for a change.

I hope you managed to rest up a little since the week-end and are getting back into routine easily. I went to bed early last night myself - - I guess I'm just not used to "night life" any more. I'm an "early to bed, early to rise" girl now (ha ha).

Both Betty and Bill are back to work now after their measles. Ann Preston's mother called up the office this morning and said Ann had a headache and a fever and she thought possibly it was the measles just starting although she didn't have a rash. It looks as if the whole office will have them before long (maybe).

Enclosed you'll find an income tax form that I think you will have to file even if you don't pay it until after the war. I asked Mr. Sweeney, a cost accountant in the office, if you would and he said everyone in the United States whether the person is in the Army, Navy or any other branch of the service would have to at least fill out the form even if he does not intend to pay it until after he comes out of the service. Do you remember the amount of money you made last year? If you have the slip at home it would be a good idea to have someone send it to you and then fill this out. You could ask the other boys what they are going to do about theirs. I think you're familiar with this form as you used it last year. At the bottom (the signature space) I think you should sign your name as Private W. J. Klein. I have to pay $149.00 this year which means that paying it quarterly the first payment will be $37.25. I'm going to pay it this way because by July, if Congress decides on it, a certain amount will be deducted from everyone's pay each week for income tax. Then they'll just have to forget the last half of 1942 if they do this. That means that you and the rest of the boys, by letting it go until after the war, might only have to pay for the first half of 1942. This won't be so bad will it? Well that's enough on this dull subject.

I'm going to buy you something nice downtown this week and I'll send it over the week-end. I won't tell you what it is though so you'll be surprised.

If I don't see you for another six weeks it will seem such a long time. I'll try to keep as busy as possible so the time will go by fast. Maybe you'll be home before six weeks, do you think so darling?

I must go now and do my weekly wash, read a little and then to bed. I hope your cough is getting better. Take care of yourself, dear.

Love Always,

Rita

X X X X X X

P.S. Keep smiling!

Wednesday 8:30 2/24/43

Dear Rita,

I hope you are feeling fine and that you are happy after our weekend together, time went by so fast, on my next leave we will spend more time together, so many of my friends wanted to see me in my uniform, thats why I lost so much time from being with you more, I recived your letter that you wrote Monday evening, I also recived your letter of Tuesday evening, in the first letter you said, I said that I bought the pistol pins in a five and ten, I said as far as I remember that I bought them in the army and navy store down town, I said they are the same as the ones that they sell anywhere else, I would of bought them here at camp if they had them in stock, but we can hardly get them anywhere. I think you took me wrong. I did not mean it the way you took it. I am so sorry, I apologize for everything, I did not mean it in that light. I am still trying to think of when I did not introduce you and Cel to some of the boy's at the railroad station, I may be slow at introductions but I did not do anything on propose, I am so sorry for anything that I did wrong. darling when I read your letter I was so dumbfounded to hear of all the things I did wrong, it made me feel very bad to hear that I was very impolite and discouteous, I could hardly make it all out, I though a lot about what you wrote in the letter it was a shock to me to hear of all the things I did wrong, also to hear of all my infant ways, It never did hurt me so much to have you tell me in our conversation but to have it writen on paper, boy it sure does things to a fellow, propably just what I need, may be, I do not know. You know best Rita dear. I love you Rita dear, do not be mad at me, I will try my utmost to be polite and more couteous in the furture.

Was Cel mad at me for not coming back to eat, I did not think she was counting on us being there for supper so much. What does she think of the whole thing, does she think I was rude or not. About my brother saying that about the swedes, he did not say you were like the swedes in the way of going for a long time with a person before getting married, what he said was, after I said we have been going nearly for two ½ yrs, was that is the way the swedes seem to do it, he did not say you are like the swedes, he did not mean it the way you took it darling, I am sorry.

In the letter that you wrote Tuesday evening, you said how you were going to buy me something nice this coming Sat and have it sent this coming weekend, I am so glad to hear that darling, I love you dearest darling, you are a sweet girl Rita, I love you. I will love you no matter what you say to me in your letters, I know that you know best, darling I did not know I was so rude maybe this will teach me a lesson, next time I will know better, I will not be able to get a pass long enough to get home for about a month, as far as I know, but I am not sure of anything as yet darling.

Take good care of yourself darling I will write again soon

Darling I love you, I will love you no matter what you say, and I know you know best, and that you are right in most all cases darling

Love Walter

[picture of X's in the shape of a V with an arrow drawn through it, saying Walter on the left of the V and Rita on the right of the V]

Friday 6:45 P.M. 2/26/43

Hello Sweetheart,

Last Friday night at this time I was looking forward to your coming home Saturday. Tonight I'm still looking forward to seeing you again (in about a month).

I received the letter you wrote Wednesday tonight. As you explained in your letter, you didn't mean to say or do anything to hurt me intentionally, so let's forget the whole thing. Cel isn't mad about our not coming back for supper so don't worry. The whole point in my writing that letter is that I found it hard to take some of the things you said in front of everyone, that's all. I know you don't do these things purposely it's just that I don't like "out of the way" remarks in front of people. Do you understand now? I like to be treated with courtesy and kindness at all times but especially when anyone is with us. You know this. I understand you too well to know you don't do things and say things wrong intentionally.

I got the snapshots we took Sunday from the Drug Store tonight. They came out good I think. I'll send them to you Sunday. I'd like to bring them into the office first. Then you can send them back to me when you see them and I'll put them in our book. Is this O.K. with you?

Ruth and Ann want me to go to the show with them after work tomorrow but I went to the show Wednesday and I guess my finances won't allow me to go twice a week. (ha ha). It costs about $2.50 every time I go to the show with the girls (dinner etc.) I might go home and eat supper and then go I don't know yet.

I wish I could see you real soon again dearest. The next time you come home I'm going to plan a nice week-end if it's alright with you. We can go dancing someplace Saturday night and Sunday we can go for a nice walk along the seawall at Seaside and maybe take more pictures just like we used to.

Dot Smith is well again now. I guess she didn't have the grippe after all. She says Ernie is very discouraged because he can't get a rating. For some reason or other she's always saying it's too bad you're not in a different division. I told her you liked what you are in but I think Ernie must have told her about the letter you wrote him when you were discouraged. Of course you realize now you shouldn't write things like that to him. You know better now, don't you dearest?

I sent you the package I was telling you about today. You should get it Monday. It's not very much (not as much as I'd like to send) but I hope you enjoy them.

Love Always,
Rita

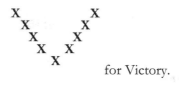

for Victory.

Sunday 3:45 P.M. 2/28/43

Dearest Walter,

I'm so glad you called today – as I told you on the phone I was wondering how everything was with you, how you were, etc. I know you didn't have much time to write during this past week and so after you called I was so glad to know everything was alright. I was happy to hear that you might get a pass in a few weeks. I won't count on it too much, though, as it's so indefinite as of yet.

Enclosed are the snapshots we took last week. I think they came out good. The one I like best of you is the one taken at the side of my house. The background isn't so good but you look nice in the picture. I'm going to keep this one in my wallet. I brought them into the office and all the girls thought you look nice in your uniform. I was going to have two sets of the pictures made and then you could keep one set, but I think after you see them you won't need to keep them, will you? When you send them back I'll put them in our album. The next time you come home we can take more.

I didn't go to the show with Ann and Ruth last night after all. Ann was sick in bed with a sore throat and Ruth said she'd rather wait until next week. I went with Dot Smith. It's the first time since you went away that Dot and I went out together. I had to work until 4:30 so Dot met me at 5 o'clock in Read's. Then we ate in the "Star" and went to the Majestic to see "Random Harvest" with Greer Garson and Ronald Colman. It was the best picture I've seen in a long time. If you haven't already seen it, don't miss it (if you ever find time). It was nice going out with Dot. She talked about Ernie and I talked about you. (ha ha). We just talked about the different things each of you like and dislike and Dot thinks you and Ernie are very much alike in your ways. I don't tho. She was also talking about her plans for the wedding (if everything works out). – that, is, what kind of gowns we would wear etc. I think it's too early to plan anything yet but I didn't say anything.

Dearest, try not to be too discouraged if you find it hard to get used to your new routine. It certainly must be hard to get up at 3 o'clock in the morning and then during the 8 hours that you're off to try to sleep when you can. Maybe you won't be on this schedule for too long a time. I hope not. Anyone is much better off if he sleeps a certain number of hours each night. Don't be too discouraged, dearest, I'll write to you as often as possible and send you different things from time to time. Then once in a while we can see each other. You and I have been lucky so far as you can call up occasionally and come home too. If the fellows who are far away get passes they can't come home, the only thing they can do is go to the nearest town. We love each other so much that no matter how far away you are we will be close. We just want each other to be as happy as possible while we are not together – Well, always, for that matter. When you're out on guard duty for four hours and you feel lonely, just remember that you and I are as close as we can possibly be and that I'm thinking of you all the time and praying this whole thing will be over soon. (you know what I mean).

Every Sunday, after Mass, the organist plays the National Anthem and everyone stands so quietly you can hear a pin drop. It's a nice feeling to know someone close to you is in the Service but at the same time I have the feeling of wanting us to be together too. Well, it's hard to explain – you understand.

The factory is trying to put a deferment through for Bill Hughes but it's uncertain yet whether he'll get it. Betty is worried. She said she's going to live at the Y.W.C.A if he goes.

Here's a joke.

First Private: "It must have been embarrassing when the M.P. poked his head in your parked car. Wasn't it?"
Second Private: "It sure was, for a minute, his wife and I were both speechless"
　　(ha ha)
　　Here's another:

First Rooky: "So you'd like to go to town tonight? What's coming off?"
Second Rooky: "The dress of the burlesque queen."

Do you like those? I got them from "Army Laughs" book. A girl in the office had it.

Well, dearest, I'd better go and look at the chicken in the oven.

Love Always,
Rita
X X X X X X
X X X X X X

P.S. Your best foot forward!

Monday 6:30 P.M. 3/1/42 [The year should be 43.]

Hello Sweetheart,

How are you today darling? I hope you are getting used to your new routine – also that you received the mixed nuts today and enjoyed them. I tried to get you a fruit and nut assortment of candy but I guess they're not making them any more as I didn't see any in the stores I tried.

I only had to work until five tonight. Ann Preston is still out sick also Irene Noonan is out with a touch of bronchial pneumonia (that's the lady I work for) whom you met outside of Carpenter's one day.

There's going to be a black-out at 8:15 tonight until 9:00 o'clock. We were notified in the papers. They're going to try some new signals out.

We had fried chicken, creamed onions, potatoes, cake + tea for supper. How does that sound to you? Good? We're practically living on chicken lately, it's so hard to get other meat.

This afternoon during rest period in the office there were about six of us girls having a debate on the pro's and con's of getting married while the war was continuing. It seems as though that question comes up in our office a lot. Ruth said if her boyfriend comes home in May from Alaska they'll be married war or no war. Betty was all for it, along with about four other girls. Violet was against it. I was "betwixt and between." They all gave different arguments for it. Well it was a lot of fun anyway.

Take care of yourself, dearest, so when you do come home you'll feel "tops". I'm feeling very well again now.

Lots of Love

Rita [circled with X's]
Keep Smiling!

Monday 29, 1943 12:30 P.M.
Fort Devens Mass.

Dear Rita,

How is my sweet little darling, you are my love Rita dear, I think of you each day, and each morning while I am on duty at my post at four a.m. to eight a.m. I think of you while you are snozing in your warm little bed, this shift is the hard one, the other that is from 4: P.M. to 8 p.m. is not to bad, darling I wish I had you with me on my posts at the motore Pole, than we could talk and maybe have a kiss or two. Ha. Ha. Today is pay day, I recived $41.85 after my reductions for insurance and bonds, I will send twenty dollars to you for our saving funds, it is not to safe to keep to much money here. I will send it the first change I get I do not have to much extra time but I may get to the post office this week.

Darling I would like to give you a few nice long kisses dear, you know me, I can really kiss nice when I put my mind to it, darling you are very sweet, I hope maybe in two weeks from now that I am able to get home to your house for 36 hours, than darling we can both canter about town to have some fun, we can go to a nice dance on sat night, than Sun I can go to church with you, than in the afternoon we can go for a nice walk in the park and maybe take some snapshots, just like old times darling, remember.

Boy darling as I continue to write this letter, I keep getting a stronger desire in wanting to embrace you, and kiss you tenderly, dearest, boy I am getting romantic dearest. darling I enjoy your letters so much I look forward to each mail call, darling it seems I cannot keep up to you with our correspondence, but darling you understand, first I do not have to much extra time, second I cannot spell off letters to easyly, I guess I am like all boy's, we seem to be good only in making love or smoozing.
Love Walter

Tuesday 6:45 P.M. 3/2/43

Dearest Walter,

I was so happy to receive your letter dated yesterday, it was such a nice letter – it sounded just like you.

I imagine it does seem as though the time goes by very slowly when you're on duty from 4:00 A.M. to 8:00 A.M. I wish I could be there at that time to keep you company so you wouldn't feel lonely.

I was so glad to hear that you're going to send some money home to me – I'll put it away for you, dearest, I know just where I'll keep it. Remember that tin box of candy you gave me about a year ago? Well, I'll put it in there – I still have the box. If you keep sending this amount each month, you'll have about $250.<u>00</u> at the end of the year. Then with what I save we should have a pretty good little sum. What do you think about it, dearest?

The kind of a week-end you have planned when you do come home is just the kind of a one I was thinking of. It will be so nice to go someplace and have a few dances, talk and a little snack like we used to. I can hardly wait to see you again, darling.

I am enclosing a money order blank all filled out. The reason I'm sending it is it might save you a little time when you go to the post office. All you'll have to do is give it to the clerk and you'll be all set then. Darling, please don't think I'm sending this just to make sure you'll send the money — it's just that I think it might help you a little. Cele laughed and laughed when I told her I was sending it. You understand tho, don't you?

Here's a little news that might interest you. Violet Santucci has been going out with Tommy Curnin (Celece's brother — the one who's lame). I think you met him once. I was surprised to hear this as she had been going with a fellow who's in the Navy but now for the past month she's been going out with Tom about three times a week. She's been to his house a couple of times and everything but I guess it won't develop into anything serious. You know Violet. She likes to have a flock of boy friends.

Tomorrow the club is at Dot Smith's I guess I'll go.

I went for a walk this noon during lunch hour with Betty. It was nice out.

I had to laugh at your letter when you said you'd like a few kisses when you're on duty and that all the boys are good only for smooching. You're funny, Kleiny. I wish I could be with you to give you a few kisses. We'll both be getting out of practice won't we? (ha ha).

Love Always,
Rita

X X X X X X X X X X X X

I love you very much dear

How do you like this shorthand? This is what it means ↑

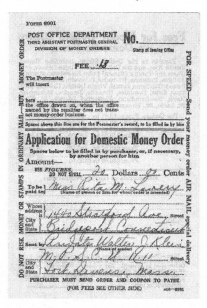

March 2 1943 Tues 4: p.m.

Dearest I just recived your nice box of assorted nuts Boy thanks a lot for remembering me dearest I like them very much. I also recive your latest letter dearest, I like your letters very much darling.

The last letter that I mailed 3/2/43 Tuesday morning I put down the date as Feb. 30 Boy I guess I got lost on the even added a day to tell time.

Tues 12: noon 2/30/43
Fort Devens Mass.
[Here is the 2/30 mentioned in postcard.]

Dear Rita,

How is my sweet little irish girl the boy's here think you are a sweet little girl dear. I showed the pictures to a few of the boys, and they say boy she is all right, they said I do allright by myself.

Darling you look very nice in all the pictures, they all came out very good I think dear.

Darling I love you very much. I could give you some very nice kisses darling right now, but I think that my disiness will not be satisfied until I see you soon.

Darling we will start the ball going with thirdty dollars to start with, darling we can add some each month, in that way we can accumalate a few hundred dollars to meet our expenses in the furtur dear. Darling I love you very much Darling here are ten big kisses for you, X X X X X – X X X X X They are very big ones dear. Darling you are very sweet, I am getting to love you more and more each day. It is good to know that I have such a fine girl waiting home for me, I hope to see you soon dearest.

Love Walter

P.S. Be a good girl Rita dear. I know you are always darling. How is my little Jeanie girl doing with her boy friends. I kept one film with me dear.

Wednesday 8:00 P.M. 3/3/43

Dearest Walter,

When I came home from work tonight I received your letter, money order and pictures. I was very much surprised (but glad) that you sent $30.00. I hope you didn't leave yourself short of money, dearest. I'll cash it tomorrow and put it away. As you said in your letter, it's something to start the ball rolling. I'll do my best from now on to add to it, every week, if possible and pretty soon we'll have a big ball (ha ha). In saving this way, each month for you and a little each week for me, we'll be both working together dearest, with the same purpose or aim in view. I think it's a nice feeling to know that we're both working together, not only in saving money but just doing things that we know will make the other happy.

You said it's good to know you have a fine girl waiting home for you. Well, dearest, I hope I can always be fine in your opinion as you are in mine. Our love certainly is strong, isn't it?

Dot Smith said she got a letter from Ernie and he received a rating. He's now a corporal. Isn't that good? She said he only expected a first class private's rating but he got two at the same time – I guess because he had a year's service before. I'm glad he finally got a rating as he deserved it especially on account of being in the service before.

Bill Hughes got his notice to go to Hartford next Thursday. I guess he'll go to Devens the following Friday after that. Betty feels very badly about it as now they'll have to break up their home and I guess she'll go back to her sister's house. She doesn't want to do this but I guess there's no other alternative. The factory couldn't get a deferment for him.

Cel, Charlie and Jeanie are all well and are asking for you. They hope you do come home the week after next, too.

I'm going to give this letter to Thomas on his way to work tonight. I hope you get it tomorrow. Well, dearest, I guess I'll have to go now and do some nightly chores. Take care of yourself, try not to get any colds or anything.

Love Always,
Rita
X X X X X X X X X X

P.S. Chin up, darling.

Friday 5. 1943
Fort Devens Mass.

Dear Rita

How is my sweet little irish <u>colleen</u> dear. you are my love Rita dear I could give you about a dozen big kisses right now dear I hope you are feeling fine and that you are happy as could be under the circumstances darling. I am getting along fine and manag to get along O.K. they keep us plenty bush. Uncle Sam belives in keeping us boys busy, so that we will not get into mischief.

Darling I love you very much dearest you do not know how much, darling I wish I could show you how much I do Love you You are very sweet. very sweet. I am looking forward in seeing you soon. I will let you know as soon as I can get more dope on the subject.

Lots of Love darling.
Walter
2 dozen large kisses Honey Bunch <u>Walter</u>
["LOVE TO YOU DEAREST" written in a V of 2 dozen X's]

Rita

Darling I could kiss you very passionatly dearest. Boy I am very hungry for some good loving dearest. I am a bad boy feeling like that. Am I not Rita. But I can not help it you understand don't you Rita. See us boys do are always looking for some nice smooching by our girls.

Love Rita Dear.

Love Walter.

Monday 7:45 P.M. 3/8/43

Dearest,

I hope you arrived at the Fort safely and managed to get a few hours sleep on the train. We had a wonderful day together yesterday, didn't we, dearest? I hope you enjoyed it as much as I did. The next time you come home we'll surely be together Saturday night too. Then you can plan on staying here all night.

All day today I was thinking of all the things we did yesterday – how nice it was of you to go to Church all by yourself even though you were a little late. I was certainly happy when I saw you in the back of the Church – it took a lot of courage I'll bet for you to go in alone. It was nice of your father to let you take his car – we had such a nice time riding and taking pictures – also visiting Lillian and Jack + to see Helene. Their children are all good looking aren't they? The baby will be a "killer diller" when he grows up I bet. I'm so glad I met your father and I know you are too. He was very pleasant and did his best to have everyone enjoy themselves. You are a "chip off the old block" – if you know what I mean. In the short time I was with him I could see so many of your characteristics in him.

I worked until 5:30 tonight. Ann Preston is back after her illness also Irene Noonan (the lady I work for). Ann must have been quite sick as she lost quite a bit of weight. She didn't lose her personality, though, that's something.

I called your sister-in-law Ellen about an hour ago. She said she just got the measles today. She noticed the rash on her this afternoon and tonight her throat was sore. She said she felt well enough to be up though. She expected the children to get them now although they all had them once before. I told her that you came home Saturday night late and that you really didn't expect a pass but found out about it late Saturday afternoon. She wanted to know what we did yesterday. I didn't tell her we visited Lillian + Jack. I just said that we had such little time that we decided not to do much visiting this time. Was that alright, dearest? I don't know whether Lil and Jack will say we were there or not. Anyway, she said not to do anything about the pictures until she gets over the measles and then she might stop here some day and look at them and pick out the ones she wants made up. She didn't think she'd want all of them. I'll wait until I hear from her I guess.

Dearest, I hope you aren't worrying about my crying Sunday before you left. It's hard to understand. I sometimes try to analyse myself for the reason but I don't understand myself. As you said, Cel and Charlie are as nice as they can possibly be to me and do their best towards making this my home. I do think of my mother very often and the whole thing runs through my mind, as though it just happened yesterday. I'm always wishing I had her here to talk to. I suppose the average person would think that after a year or so one gets over those things and forgets. I know you understand better than anyone. They say "time heals." Well, I suppose this is true but it will take a longer time for me to get over the feeling of aloneness than a person who doesn't feel things like me. You also said it's nice to come home but partings are hard on anyone. Last night I just had the feeling again of being so alone – your going back and thinking of my mother all the time – that's the only way I can explain it, dearest. Please don't worry about me. I'll get over my childish ways slowly but surely. It's funny, but just last week I was priding myself on getting over those ways as I hadn't felt depressed in a long time about my mother – Well, dearest, I don't want you to see me that way any more if I can help it. You certainly are the most understanding person in the world with me. That's just one of your fine qualities. I hope you aren't bored with all this explaining, dearest.

Here's a little humor Ruth gave me.
"The Wolf Song"
If he parks his little flivver
Down beside the moonlight river,
And you feel him all-a-quiver
Baby, he's a <u>wolf</u>.

If he says you're gorgeous lookin-
And that your dark eyes set him cookin,
And your eyes aren't where he's lookin
Baby, he's a <u>wolf</u>.

When he says you're an eyeful,
But his mind begins to trifle,
And his heart pumps like a rifle.
Baby, he's a <u>wolf</u>.

If by chance when you're a kissin
You can feel his heart a-missin,
And you talk but he won't listen
Baby, he's a <u>wolf</u>.

If his arms are strong like sinew
And he stirs the gypsy in you,
So that you want him close-a'gin you
Baby, he's a <u>wolf</u>.

What do you think of that, darling? That's Ruth's idea of humor. Her girlfriend in New York sends her things like this.

Well, dearest, I'll write again tomorrow. Take care of yourself – get as much rest as possible.

Love Always,
Rita
I love you, dearest – X X X X X X

YOU ARE MY LIFES INSPIRATION RITA DEAR.
Darling Be Brave.

Monday 8. 43

Dear Rita

You are my sweetheart Rita dear. I love you very much. You are my sweet little girl for always and always. I love you so much.

I arrived at the railroad 10:05 P.M. I had plenty of time, the train came in at 10:30 P.M. I arrived at Ayer Mass at 5:30 A.M. the train was 1 ½ late. I managed to get some sleep on the train. I resived your humours book. It is very good darling. You are so though full. I was looking at it after lunch. I got some good laughs from it. This morning we had to shovel snow, here they had snow instead of rain, about a foot of it. I got another shot in the arms also this morning, the last of them. I am glad. This morning the louie had us drilling with Pistols. This school learning is very good we get through at 4:30, and can go to bed at 9. oclock. boy that is the life. All the boys like the schooling also. we can sleep until 10 min to six in the morning when going to school.

Darling I love you so much. I had such a enjoyable time with you. You make me so happy. This morning I was reviewing the happenings of the weekend. boy they were pleasant happenings darling.

Darling I am feeling very good today. All I need is some sleep, I will get some tonight to catch up. Darling I think of you all the time. Dearest we love each other so much, Dont we bunny. Keep your Chin up Rita dear. everything will be all right. You and I will work everything out as time goes on.

Rita dear I found it so hard to leave you last night, you found it very hard too dear. We Love each other so much. thanks for being so nice to me over the weekend. Rita dear. I also want to thank Cele and Charlie for being so nice and accomadating. Love Walter

Tuesday 7:30 P.M. 3/9/43

Dearest Walter,

I received the letter you wrote yesterday – it was such a comforting letter – you're so kind and thoughtful. The time will go by fast until I see you again because I know you're so understanding.

I was glad to hear that you got to the station in plenty of time and managed to get a little sleep on the train. It certainly was late getting into Ayer, wasn't it? Well, as long as you could catch up on your sleep a little last night it isn't so bad. It would be a good idea to get as much sleep as possible so that next week when you're on duty, it won't seem so hard. I was also glad to hear you enjoyed the week-end so much just as I did. As I said before, next time we'll have to top the other two times and have a little fun Saturday night dancing + a little snack etc. I was also glad to hear you enjoyed the magazine. I'll send you more later.

I can see where you would like school better than being on duty – learning something every day is much more interesting than being on guard. Then, of course, your hours are better too. You can manage to have a little diversion once in a while too.

Tomorrow is Ash Wednesday and the first day of Lent. I'm going to church tomorrow night as the priest distributes ashes (he blesses the people's forehead with them). That's the procedure every year on Ash Wednesday. It's to remind one that we were made from the dirt of the earth – you know – "Ashes to ashes, dust to dust." I usually give something up every year like candy but this year I don't think I'll cut down on sweets as I can't afford to lose weight. I'll just make special efforts in making visits to the Church, praying more etc. I hope you aren't bored, dearest, with this explanation but I thought you might find it interesting information.

Betty brought the card you sent them into the office and showed it to me. It was cute the way you marked the pictures. Some of the girls saw it too and laughed. Betty is all upset about Bill's going away. Everyone can tell she's worried just to look at her. She's pale and doesn't say a word. Maybe she'd feel better if she could at least talk about it instead of keeping it all to herself. It's hard to know what to say to her. Well, that's just her way – she can't help it I guess. She's hoping he won't pass in New Haven but he probably will.

Dearest, I love you so much. I want to do everything to make you happy. You've helped me so much and you do now too, just by writing such nice letters and being so understanding. I'm very lucky to have you stationed in Mass. We can see each other once in a while and talk to each other on the phone. We're both very lucky.

Enclosed you'll find some more humor that Ruth gave me. It's pretty good I think. What do you think of it?

Well, dearest, I'll have to go now and do my washing. I'm going to give this letter to Tom to mail as I'm too late for the last mail around here. I hope you get it tomorrow.

Love Always,
Rita

[Heart made of X's with two arrows through it forming an X, one arrow labeled Rita and the other Walter]

This is supposed to be a heart (ha ha)

Ten Commandments of Love

1. Remember thy Sweetheart at all times.
2. Thou shalt not tease.
3. Thou shalt not make eyes at other girls.
4. Thou shalt not do anything in public, but in private.
5. Thou shalt not ask for a kiss, but take it.
6. Thou shalt not love but one. (me).
7. Thou shalt not kiss to love, but love to kiss.
8. Thou shalt not kiss other girls.
9. Thou shalt always kiss your sweetheart when she says no, because she hates to say yes.
10. Thou shalt not have any other love but me, or before me.

12:30 P.M. March 9. 1943
Fort Devens Mass.

Dearest Rita,

This morning we had a military movie on, <u>why</u> <u>we</u> <u>are</u> <u>fighting</u> <u>and</u> <u>what</u> <u>for</u>. it was held at the No. 1 Theatre. the modern theatre that I told you about. Later at ten oclock to 11:30 we were taught how to handle a Thompson

Submachine gun, also how to dismandle it. It fires faster than one can say <u>Jack rabbit</u>. Yesterday afternoon, the sergeant talk to us about the Law and arrests of the Military Police. It was very interesting, it lasted for three hours. Darling you are the sweetest girl in the world, you are the only one girl in the world for me. All I want in my companion you possess darling. You are very intelligent Rita dear. You are a very feminine. You are very <u>curvey</u> dear. Ha. Ha.

Darling I am a one girl man. I am so glad that I am. You are the one of my life.

Darling I love you so much I can not show you enough dear I am going to buy something nice the first chance I get. Rita I could kiss you very much now. It is now my lunch hour, we have from 11:30 to one oclock to ourselves during school hrs. Rita I think of you each day and each hour, at night when I go to bed I think of you and the fun and very good companionship we have with each other. I sometimes lie on m bunk for ten minutes, Rita dear you mean so much to me.

Keep brave and keep as happy as you can dear. We will spend many more enjoyable hours in the near future together. Darling I could kiss you so passionately right now. boy do I feel like smooching. ha. ha.

I love you. I love you. I love you. I can't seem to be able to right enough dear to let you know how much I love you.

Kisses lots of them for you Rita.

X X X X X X X X X X X X X X X X X X X X X X X X X X X X X X X X

X X X

35 of them.

Thursday 6:30 P.M. 3/11/43

Dearest Walter,

Tonight I came home from work and of course the first thing I did was look on the buffet (that's where your mail is) but there wasn't any there tonight. Charlie had hidden your letter on me just to be funny. He told me there wasn't any mail. Well, he finally gave me your letter – boy – was I glad!

I'm glad you enjoy my letters every day and that you liked the humor I sent. Map reading must be interesting after one learns how. It's nice that you can get to bed early and still have a little time to go to the show or some other places to relax for a little enjoyment.

I forgot to mention in my other letters that I brought the roll of film to Lupe's Monday night after work. The pictures won't be ready until this coming Monday. It takes a little longer to have pictures developed now.

Ruth and Ann have been kidding the life out of me. They said they're going to write to you and tell you what a bold, brazen hussy I am. They'll probably compose some kind of a funny poem about me. So be prepared, dearest. I told them you wouldn't be surprised no matter what they write because you know me too well. They're cooking up something but I don't think they'll let me see it before they send it to you.

We're going to get our tickets for the play "Claudia" Monday. Ruth wants to get $2.00 seats. The prices are $1.00, $1.50 + $2.00. Dot Smith is coming with us. It's playing March 25th 26th + 27th. We're going on the opening night, Mar. 25th, Thursday. The following Saturday you'll be home (I think).

Dearest, there's some more of Ruth's jokes enclosed. This is a "little on the shady side" if you know what I mean. She was going to send it to her boyfriend and she said if I sent it to you, I shouldn't tell you she gave it to me. I told her you're very broad-minded and wouldn't care who gave it to me. You'll probably get a big kick out of it.

Dearest, I enjoy your letters a lot and I'm so glad to hear from you each day. It's the nicest part of the day when I read your letters. I'd rather read them than have dessert for supper. (ha ha). I like those nice, big, kisses you put at the bottom of your letters – but of course I like them in person better (ha ha).

Lots + lots of Love,

Rita

(12) --> X X X X X X X X X X X X X

A solider returning to camp after a two-week furlough received this letter from his girl. She had written this song for him.

M is for the many times you made me.

O is for the other times you tried

T is for the tourist camps we stayed in

H is for the hell we raised inside

E is for the energy exerted

R is for the reck you made of me

Put them all together and they spell Mother, That's what I'm going to be.

The next day the soldier answered her letter and returned the compliment by dedicating this song to her:

F is for your funny little letter

A is for my answer to gain note

T is for your tearful accusation

H is for your hope that I'm the goat

E is for the ease with which I made you

R is for the rogue you thought I'd be.

Put them all together and they spell Father, But you're crazy if you think it's me!

Thursday 12:30 3/11/43

Fort Devens Mass.

Dear Rita,

Lots of love to you dearest. I Love you so much Rita dear. Yes dear our love could come up to Ann First description of real honest to goodness love any day.

Rita dear you are curvey, you are too I am not fooling. I like you just as you are darling. But of course later on you will become more curvey dear, <u>Ha</u>. <u>Ha</u>. when we are married. Yes Rita as far as I can understand the 27th of March is the date when I can get my next leave. I will know better at a future date. Thats good about my income tax. I sent in the form yesterday. to bad about Ruths letters not reaching her boy friend. Give Ann and the girls my regard, this morning we had 3 hrs of marching and all the facings and all the manual with over 30-30 rifles. I am getting along very good in this mans army.

Today from 12:00 A.M. too tomorrow at 12:00 A.M. I am on duty as Super Nuemerary. that is what they call us that are extra men, selected each day for 24 hrs, ready to relive any of the boy in case they may become sick. Sometime out of each 24 hrs one may have to work 4 or eight hrs. the army makes sure we are always busy.

Rita I could kiss you now, about three dozen big ones. Rita you and I get along so well, we have a very strong love dear. It is worth to me all the money in the world. Rita you are so sweet to me you are everything. Rita my heart says you are the one girl of my life. It makes me so happy to know that. Besides I say you are the one girl of my life. Rita boy my heart is doing <u>flipers</u> while I am writing this.

Be brave and keep yourself busy I know you are the best girl in the world and capable of handling all siduations.

Love Walter

Sat. 5:00 P.M. 3/13/43
Fort Devens Mass.
Military Police.

Dear Rita,

How do you like my new writing paper that I got at the USO in Ayer Center, it is given free of charge, It is quite a swell layout at the USO, they have pink ponk tables that us boys were using, also pool tables, they also furnish playing cards for us boys to play rummy or pinnacle, they have a nice place furnished for us boys.

Yes dear my heart does <u>flippers</u> for you very often, I am beginning my new post duty tonight, from 8 to 12:00 P.M. and then from 8 in the morning to 12:00 A.M. Noon. I am on the third relief. it is divided into three 4 hrs. reliefs. we keep going around the clock. If I was on the same post as last week I would of probably stand a chance to see Bill Hughes, because that post which is post 24<u>B</u> is the Motor Pool which is right next to the railroad when all the trains come in with the new recruits I am now on post 6<u>A</u> which is about one mile from the railroad and about one mile from the recruit reception center. this post is the post laundry and warehouses.

I hope I can manage to get some time to be able to get up to the reception center but I doubt it. If I was in school I would have the evenings off and be able to rumble about the fort.

I am in what they call the quadrangle barracks up on the hill about one mile from the Reception Center the Poem fits us both dear. I like them and all the other humorous Jokes you send.

You are my sweetheart Rita dear, I love you so much, darling you are a sweet Irish girl.

Love Walter.

Sunday 3:30 P.M. 3/14/43

Dearest,

Since you called at 12:45 I've eaten dinner and taken a bath, also read a little. I was so glad you called – it was nice to talk with you.

The schedule you're on now is better than the last once – you'll have a little more time to sleep now. Will you continue on that same schedule for the next two weeks or will you go back on the other one next week?

Friday night I called up your sister, Martha. She was glad I called. She said they had a batch of baby chicks Thursday – about 50 of them. They must be cute. She was telling me about a new bedroom set she bought for Richard. It must be very nice. There are three pieces – bed, dresser and chest of drawers. The chest of drawers opens out in the middle and can be used as a desk. The set is maple. Martha said she and Adolph stopped at your sister Lillian's last Tuesday and Lil told her you were home the week-end before. She said she realizes that you and I can't get up to Easton every time you come home but said to go up to see them when we have time.

I met Dot Smith about 5 o'clock + as I told you on the 'phone we went to the show. I enjoyed it. I think you can enjoy yourself a lot when you just go out one night a week. Dot said Ernie will probably have a sergeant's rating pretty soon. She said now with a corporal's rating he has quite a few privileges. He shares a room with another fellow and they have a radio in the room. They can keep the lights on until late at night if they want. She said now there's a possibility of his being moved nearer home. That would be nice wouldn't it? She was also talking about the wedding. It will be a nice one if everything is in their favor by that time. While we were downtown we saw a beautiful bridal gown in a window in the Arcade. We went in to price it. It was $39.00 which is reasonable. Dot thought it was too early, though, to buy her gown. She said when Ernie was home they bought the wedding ring. It matches her diamond – that is, it's the mate to it.

When I was in Read's yesterday I saw a box of goodies I thought you might like – as I told you I bought it and you'll probably receive it Tuesday or Wednesday. I won't tell you just what's in it but it's something to eat. Dot sent Ernie one too.

How did you like the humor I sent last week? Ruth said her girlfriend in New Jersey sent it to her and she passed it all around the office. I thought you'd have a few laughs over it. Did you?

Well, dearest, this letter is quite "newsy" isn't it? I guess I'm all talked out.

I could go on and on telling you how much I love you, but I'll save that until you come home. I'll only tell you once for now. I love you very, very much, dearest.

With all my heart,
Rita [circled with X's]

P.S. Wednesday is St. Patrick's day. You and the boys ought to sing a few Irish songs for me. "When Irish Eyes are Smiling" That's my favorite. (ha ha).

Monday 7:30 P.M. 3/15/43

Dearest,

Tonight when I came home from work your letter written Saturday and the folder of pictures written Friday were waiting for me. I enjoyed the pictures a lot, especially the way you wrote on different ones. I'd like to see Sweetheart Monument. The scenery around it must be very pretty if it's anything like the picture. I'd also like to see all the other places, the library, chapels, reveille and retreat. Maybe some Sunday I'll go up to see you and you can show me all the different places of interest. I'll bet you'd like that.

Tom said whenever post cards or folders of that type go through the post office and the clerks recognize the name to whom they're addressed, they open the folders and read what's inside or if it's a postal card they read everything himself included no doubt. I guess they've read quite a bit of your mail addressed to me. I don't like that at all do you? I guess there's just no privacy as far as you and I are concerned but we can't do anything about it can we?

Guess what? Ann Preston said her boyfriend asked her if she would accept a diamond for her birthday (April 13th). He visited her over the week-end and talked it over with her mother and father. Her mother + father thought it was alright as long as she doesn't get married for a while because she's so young. I guess she'll accept it. She just told Ruth + I about it and will keep it a secret until her birthday. That's nice don't you think so? Ann is going with Dot Smith, Ruth + I to the Klein too when we go. We called up and asked them to hold the tickets until this coming Thursday (pay day). They'll be very good seats. They're in the fifth row in the middle.

Here are the pictures, dearest. Do you think they came out good? You can tell it was a very windy day the way our coats are blown. The one of you with your overcoat on is nice also the one of you in Lordship. Darling, when you finish with them you can return them. Keep any of them you might like tho.

Dearest, I hope the time doesn't go by too slowly while you're on duty these days. It won't be long before you're home again and then you and I will have some fun together won't we?

Lots of Love,
Rita

x x x x x x x x x x

P.S. Keep smiling.

Marcy 16. 1943 5:00 P.M.
Fort Devens Mass.

Dear Rita Marie,

I recived your box of assortments dear, you are so nice dear, I like them very much, I recived them Mon Noon with your letter.

The pictures came out very good, you and I manage to get some good takes now and then, I am going to keep one of you, you look very sweet dearest in the picture.

I also recived some very nice writing stationery, who ever sent it did not put they name on it, I think It was from Ellen. I can always use stationery.

I will not send any more open post cards if I can help it, because everyone reads whatever is in side. I should know better dearest.

Best of wishes to Ann Preston, It was quite a surprise too me to here of the latest news.

It is nice of you girls to be able to get together and go to Klein's. I am now chasing prisoners, that is what they call it, when we guard the prisoners while at work or other details, that is for 4 hrs, while the other 4 hrs I spend on interior guard. Well I am now progressing right along, before long I may be able to get some of the gravey Jobs. Maybe. Ha Ha. You are such a nice girl. I love you dearest.

Rita you are the apple of my eye and the irish girl of my heart.

Lots of love and kisses.

Love
Walter.

Monday 7:00 P.M. 3/22/43

Dearest Walter,

I hope you managed to get a seat on the train and catch a little sleep on the way back to the fort, also that you met the fellows at the station you usually go back with. It's nice that you'll be going to school this week, you can get more rest.

Did you have an enjoyable week-end? I hope you can come home again April 3rd – of course we'll just have to wait and see.

I asked Violet if she and Tom went out Saturday night and she said she didn't call me up because they didn't feel like going any place special. They just stopped in a little place in Devon and had something to eat. She said she'd like to go out with us sometime in the future, though. Tom comes home almost every week-end.

I've been thinking about your sister Emma since yesterday. She surely will be over-burdened now. I think it would be nice if you dropped her a card or wrote a letter telling her you hope she feels alright and when you come home again you could stop in to see her. Remember, when you and I were talking to her at the pond and she said when you come home to stop and see her as she would like to see you in your uniform. She's such a nice person. It seems a shame not to be in contact with her at all. What do you think about this?

Betty came back to work today. She said Bill called her up Saturday and Sunday and expected to be moved from Devens today. He doesn't know what division he's in yet but probably will know when he arrives at his destination. Betty seems to be in much better spirits now but of course she's hoping he won't be moved too far away.

Ann Preston said her brother is going to apply for Officers' Training School soon. He probably will make out well if he can pass all the tests. He's the type of a fellow who likes strict, military discipline. He is very neat about everything and is very conscientous. He's only twenty years old.

It will be nice when you take your car from Easton and leave it either here or in your own yard. Cele thinks there will be enough room here if you want to leave it. It's up to you.

I just saw the mail truck go by so I know I'm too late for the mailman tonight. I guess I'll just have to take a chance on Thomas taking this letter. I hope you get it tomorrow.

Here are a few cute jokes:

Cop: "No parking, you can't loaf along this road."
Voice in car: "Who's loafing?"

One of the new W.A.A.C.'s stepped up to the sergeant and asked where did she eat,
"You mess with the soldiers," said the sarge.
"I know that," she said, "but where do I eat?"

Girl – "I'd like to buy a brassiere."
Salesman – "What bust?"
Girl – "Nothing, it just wore out."

Boy – I'll bet you never saw any dancing like this back in the Gay Nineties, heh, uncle?
Uncle – Yep, once + then the place was pinched.

Ha Ha! Do you like them?

Well, dearest, I guess this is all for now. I'll be looking forward to seeing you soon again.

Love Always,
Rita
x x x x x x

Mon. 12:30 P.M. 3/22/43

Dear Rita,

I managed to get a seat on one of the new coaches and had a good snooz for my self, I also got a few hours <u>sleep</u> in the barracks from 4 AM to 6 AM. Boy those new coaches sure are nice, they ride so nice and smooth and do not jar like those old cars. Rita you are a very sweet Irish girl, I love you, you are my sweetheart.

I kissed you so nice dearest over the weekend did'ent I dear. I love your kisses Rita I never get tired of your loving, I had a very nice week end.

On my next time home I will spend all our time together, we will be with each other for the full time that I am home, whatever you plan we will do dearest.

It will be your day dearest.

Lots of love Rita.

Be a good girl.

Take care of yourself and dont make eyes at the boys – <u>ha</u>. <u>ha</u>.

The next time I am home I will catch you, you were just to fast for me to catch you dearest, you are some kid.

I love you so much. Here are 1 one hundred kisses One Hundred big ones.

Love Walter

Tuesday 6:30 P.M. 3/23/43

Dearest Walter,

I just finished reading the letter you wrote yesterday. I was glad that you had a little sleep and rode in one of the new coaches.

You say the next time you come home we will be together all the time. Well, I've come to the conclusion it's just as well we do a lot of visiting when you come home. It really is better that way. I'd like to be with you alone every minute if I could but it's bad for both of us. As far as your "catching me" the next time, I hope I'm always too fast for you (until we're married).

I finished work at five o'clock tonight (unusual). This noon I mailed you a book I told you about quite a while ago – "See Here, Private Hargrove" is the title of it. It has been very much discussed and is supposed to be a favorite book of the Army. I liked it a lot. I know you probably won't have time to read very often but even if you only read part of it I think you'll enjoy it. Let me know what you think of it.

Don't be hurt, darling, if you don't get your mail on time after this. Thomas doesn't want to take the letters with him any more so now I'll just have to try to make the 7:15 mail. Sometimes I work late and this is impossible so if you don't receive them the day after I write them, you'll understand won't you?

Don't worry about my making eyes at the boys as you said. You're the only one for me. I miss you so much, dearest, the weeks I don't see you. Please take care of yourself until I see you again and get as much rest as possible. Then your cold will go away.

Love Always,
Rita [circled with X's]

P.S. Do your very best so you can get a rating in a few months.

Sat. 4:30 P.M. 3/27/43

Dear Rita,

I am so glad that you and the girls enjoyed the comedy at Klein's, it is so nice that you all get together once in awhile. Yes I am going to be on from 12:00 to 4:00 shift, you sure do have a good memory, I did not think you would know what relief I would be on from the short discription I gave you of the reliefs.

Give my regards to Betty, to bad Bill is so far away from her, he propably will be there only for a short time maybe.

Rita you are a swell girl.

I love you Rita dearest. I could kiss you for a bout a hour and ahalf, than I will get a little shuteye, then eat a little, later go on my post, way up in the hills, you are my lovely sweetheart, you are the sweetest girl in the <u>U.S.A.</u>

Be a good girl until I see you again soon.

Love <u>Walter</u>

Walter Love Rita   Lots of <u>Love</u>

P.S. Yes I like this USO stationary it is so nice and small. Ha. Ha.

Sunday 1:00 P.M. 3/28/43

Dearest Walter,

I'm eating a Milky Way candy bar while I'm writing this letter I'm so hungry and we aren't going to have dinner until later. I imagine while I'm writing this you are on duty or detail of some sort. I hope if you call up it's before 4 o'clock because Dot Smith asked me to go over to her house for supper and to spend the evening with her.

I received the letter you wrote Friday yesterday. It's nice that you had Thursday afternoon off and could get outside to play volley ball. That's a good game – I used to play it when I was in Normal School. It must have been a long day for you Friday doing "prisoner chasing" all day.

Yesterday I worked until 3 o'clock and at 6 o'clock I met Eleanor Keaterig, (the one who teaches in Groton, Conn.) and we went to see Bob Hope (at the Polis') in "They Got Me Covered". It was funny. The other picture was "On the Front". It was about the fighting in North Africa + was in technicolor. You might like to see it if you get a chance – it was interesting.

After the show Eleanor said she was hungry so we went into the "Star" and had a club sandwich. I asked Eleanor if she would like a cocktail but I might as well have asked her to cut off her right arm. I was trying to introduce her to a "Scarlett O'Hara" telling her what a nice taste they have and everything but no, she's just a regular school mar'm who doesn't drink. (Leave it to me to try to lure her into taking a drink, heh, darling?). (ha ha). I was home by 10 o'clock. I enjoyed going with her though, as I hadn't seen her in so long, we had a lot of things to talk about.

Friday after work I bought a nice pair of patent leather shoes (of course with No. 17 Coupon). If you come home, Palm Sunday or Easter, dearest, I'll be all dressed up.

I imagine you'll receive the packages I sent you tomorrow or Tuesday at the latest. I won't tell you what's in them but I do hope you like them. There are so many things I'd like to send you. I get a lot of pleasure out of buying nice things for you. I guess I even get more of a kick out of sending you things than you do receiving them. What do you think, darling?

Last night I was thinking how lucky you and I are to be able to see each other once in a while and that you can call frequently. There are so many couples who don't see one another for months and months and can never talk on the 'phone either. I surely do hope you can continue to be near me for the duration but of course one can't plan on that.

Dinner is almost ready, darling, so I'm going to set the table. I hope I haven't left for Dot's house when you call.

Love Always,

x x x Rita x x x

P.S. Can't you feel how strong our love is? – I can.

Monday 6:30 P.M. 3/29/43

Dearest,

As I didn't receive any mail from you today and you didn't call yesterday, I'm a little worried.

Yesterday I waited until 4:15 before going to Dot's house, thinking you would call. I know you probably just didn't have time or there is some other very good reason why you couldn't. I do hope you aren't sick or anything, dearest. Please let me know how everything is won't you?

As I said before, I went to Dot's for supper and stayed until about 9:30. I had a nice time – talking and listening to records. She was also discussing her wedding plans. As far as she knows now, the date will be August 21st, on a Saturday.

Dot said she was talking to Dot Blake yesterday and she said Joe just came back from Casa Blanca. He's stationed in Brooklyn at the present time but expects to go out on a boat soon again. He didn't say anything about the trip but just said he was glad to be home again.

I told Mrs. Smith and Dot the next time you come home we would stop over to see them and they said they'd like to see you.

It would be nice if you could come home this coming week-end but I suppose that's impossible if you are on detail or something this week. If you do happen to find out the last minute like the last time, you can call up here or the office.

I do hope everything is alright with you, dearest. I hope I get some mail from you tomorrow. I'll feel much better if I do.

Love Always

Rita

x x x x x x x x x x

P.S. I love you.

11:30 A.M. Monday. 29. 1943

Fort Devens Mass.

Dear Rita,

How is my little sweet heart today, I hope you are in the best of spirits dearest, you are a very sweet girl.

I recived a letter from Ernie today, as yet I have not had time to read it. I also recived your package, I have not opened it as yet, but I imagine it is the ties that you spoke about, you are a good girl Rita dearest.

I am now ready to go on post in the mess hall guarding five prisoners I will be on from 2:00 P.M. noon to 5:00 P.M. tonight. than I will go on again at 12:00 P.M. to right until 4:00 P.M. in the morning, I will be on post way up in the hills guarding the water supply.

Rita I did not have time to call yesterday. All I have time to do when I am on post is work, eat, sleep, and very little time for anything else.

Rita you are the sweetest girl in the world.

I love you dearest.

Love Walter.

Tuesday 7:00 P.M. 3/30/43

Dearest Walt,

I can't tell you how glad I was to receive your letters written Saturday and Monday — to know that you were not sick or anything. It was foolish of me to worry so much wasn't it? Tom says the mail is very heavy and therefore it's very slow in coming right now — there isn't enough help in the post office.

It's perfectly alright that you didn't call up Sunday — I know you didn't have any time.

You said in Monday's letter that you were guarding the prisoners in the mess hall from 2:00 to 5:00 P.M. and also going on your regular duty at 12 midnight 'till 4 in the morning. Does that mean that you are now having the detail you spoke about when you were home that you expected (your name was to come up soon)? If this is so, maybe you'll be home this coming week-end. We'll see. Dearest, the next time you come home let's make the most of every minute. We could go to the Ritz (if you want) or someplace nice. Are you going to bring your car home from Easton this next time or later? (I'm a nosey little thing, aren't I?) (ha ha).

We just found out yesterday that our house is for sale. The Agent asked

Charlie if he would like to buy it but Charlie said it would cost too much to fix and he wouldn't want to own such an old house. Cele thinks we'll have to move when it's bought as the people who buy it will want to move here themselves. I don't know where we'll find a rent as we really need six rooms. Cele is worried about it but I'm not. Everything will work out somehow.

Darling, you know that ◇①◇ that you wear on your arm signifying the area that you're in? Dot and Ernie are making a collection of insignias of the different areas. She showed me the ones they have so far and was wondering if you could get an extra one. You could bring it home the next time couldn't you? If you can't get one, it's alright.

You say you felt like kissing me Saturday. Maybe you'll have the chance this coming week (if you come home). I hope so.

Dearest, please try to get as much rest as possible when you're off duty. I love you so much, I don't want you to be tired or get sick.

Here's a funny poem.

To rest on Saturday sure seems well
But that long, old Sunday drags like H - - l,
Payday comes and the dollars clink
"I'm off for the week-end," So you think.
But Friday-night (and here's what's hard)
It's ten to one that you're on guard.
You drill all day, come in at nite,
And the shower house is a welcome sight.
The showers are swell, but if you're late
The water's cold as an old maid's date. (ha ha)
So by the time your term is done.
You're raring to quit and have some fun.
The day to leave shows up and then,
You go and sign right up again.

I got this poem from the book "Army Laughs."
Lots of Love,
Macushla (Rita)
[X's drawn around Macushla and Rita]
P.S. I was so glad to get your letters today, dearest.

Tuesday 4:30 P.M /3/30
Fort Devens Mass.

Dear Rita,

I recived your package of gum and your two letters this noon, I am so glad to recive your letters so regular dearest. I sent a letter Sat. Noon, you should of gotten it Monday but you know how it gets held up sometime.

I do not have very much time to myself when on for the weeks duty.

I am well and getting along O.K. everything is coming along alright dearest. I am so glad that you enjoyed your visit at Dot Smith house. you both seem to get along swell. Boy Joe sure has covered lot of territory in so short time that he has been in the navy. Best of luck to him. I would enjoy going with you to Dot Smith's home when I manage to get my next pass. God only know's when I will get my next pass, the way it looks now we may have to stay on duty for two weeks, than when the passes come due, I may catch special duty that all of us have to take turns at. That will mean that it will be some time until my chance comes around again. but it it hard to tell in this army. I never know from day to day what is going to happen the next day

Rita you are my sweetheart. I love you dearest. You are sweet.

Love Walter

Wednesday 12:10 P.M. March 31, 1943

Dearest Walter,

I thought I'd start a letter during my lunch hour and finish it when I go home tonight.

Last night, Cele, Charlie and I went out to Loretta and John Neary's in Fairfield (you met them). Irene was out there too. I haven't been to their house in a long time. We had a nice visit. They were asking for you and said it was nice you were stationed so near home. They have a beautiful home – it's been all re-papered and hard wood floors put in since I was there before.

Our hours in the office have been changed. Starting next week we're going to work from 8 to 12:30 (half-hour for lunch) and 1 to 5:30 and then 'till noon on Saturday. Every third Saturday some of us will have to work all day (in case any of the Army Ordnance men come in). I think I'll like this arrangement better than the present one as we'll have Saturday afternoon off. The Saturday that we work entitles us to a half-day off during the following week.

The Jewish girl (Mr. Lincoln's secretary) is getting married tomorrow (April Fool's Day) in New York City. She's all excited today and everyone is kidding her. She's marrying a fellow who is in his last year at Yale Medical School. Darling, you think I'm not domestically inclined. She doesn't know the first thing about cooking, making beds, washing, ironing or anything. In other words, she's a career girl (or something). I don't think I'll be that bad, do you? We all told her we feel sorry for her husband-to-be. (ha ha)

Tonight I'm going to Church (Lenten devotions). I'll say a prayer for you, dearest. I'll finish this letter when I go home tonight – that's all for now, sweetheart.

6:00 P.M. Here I am home from work. I didn't receive any mail from you today but I realize you must be very busy this week, dearest. I hope you are well and everything is hunky-dory with you.

I guess if you do happen to come home this coming week-end you'll need a rest after your busy week won't you darling?

I'll be so glad to see you when you do come home. Whichever week-end you do come, you can come here from the train and stay for supper or stop home to your house to let them know you're home, whatever you want do, darling, will be alright. If you call Friday or Saturday to let us know you're coming you can tell us then what you're going to do. o.k?

I'm enclosing a little cartoon I think is kind of funny.

Love Always,

Rita

X X X X X X X X X X X X

P.S. There are a dozen big kisses for you. I wish I could give them to you in person.

Wednesday Morn 9:00 A.M. 3/31/43

Fort Devens Mass.

Dear Rita,

I just got up from bed, I got in from post at 5:00 AM this Morning, I went on at 12:00 P.M. last night, <u>some</u> <u>fun</u>. Today is pay day, so we will line up down stairs for our money, ordinarily we are able to sleep until 11:00 AM. I will go on duty again at 12:00 Noon chasing prisoners about the Fort. We use forty five's, slung on our holsters at our sides Rita you are my sweetheart. I live for you Rita dear, I hope I can manage to get a pass soon so I can get to Bpt. to see you dearest. If and when I get information concerning the passes, and I am sure, I will get in contact with you on the phone.

How are you dear, I hope you are getting along O.K. and that the time is going by not to slow. How is my little Jeanie doing, is she still making eyes at the boys at the butcher market, to get on the right side of them to manage to get some precious butter or other food stuffs. Ha. Ha.

The line is forming out in the hallways for our money so I should get about $39.00 this month, now that they are going to decut $3.75 for War Bonds instead of $1.25 Rita you are my cute little irish collean, <u>Bunny</u> dear.

With Love

Walter

PART II: Life as We Know It

Everyday Life in the 1940s

In Rita's letters, she shares stories about her four older siblings. It seems that Thomas was a problem at times. He was described in various letters as lazy, and in general was a burden on his sisters. Thomas worked for the post office in Bridgeport but was not reliable. Yes, he tended to drink. Rita wrote in one letter that her brother was upstairs in his usual condition, obviously not sober.

As the letters reveal, lifestyle and economic issues were center-front in Walter and Rita's lives. Walter and Rita enjoyed the good life; things like a dinner out, taking in a show, stopping to have a Tom Collins, and even splurging on the purchase of sterling silver. On the other hand, they tried to save and economize. The two goals were often at odds. The situation that Walter and Rita confronted mirrored life, as we all necessarily make choices.

This WWII-era gas rationing coupon book was issued in my name. I assume that even children, being persons, qualified for rationing stamps. When making a fuel purchase, one paid in dollars and coins but also had to give gas rationing coupons to the attendant.

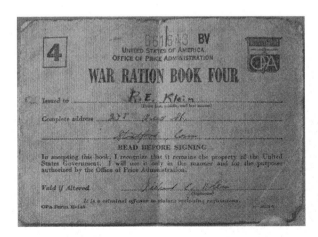

"Whichever day it was, the guy at the filling station was so overjoyed that he let us buy all the gas we wanted without giving him our gas rationing coupons.

It turned out his timing was off: gas rationing and coupons remained mandatory for some time following the war's end."

Letters: April 1, 1943 – July 18, 1943

Friday 11: AM 4/1/43

Dear Rita,

Recived your letter dated Wed. Morn 12:00 Noon.

This week I was on a 16 hour post, you see some post are 24 hrs and others are 16 hrs and some 12 hrs. So during the day where no guard is required on that perticular post I have to fill in doing prison chasing, so that acounts for my chasing prisoners during the day,

I have very little time now, I have to go on duty in the mess hall guarding fire birds in 15 minutes so I hope you will excuse my hasty writing dearest. Rita you are a good girl, I love you dearest. Be a good girl, I hope to see you as soon as possible dearest Lots of Love Rita Dear I could kiss you for a quick dozen times for I would have about 10 minutes before I have to go down stairs to fall in and be accounted for

Lots of Love
Walter

Sunday 12:30 P.M. 4/4/43

Walter dearest,

I'm writing this letter while dinner is in the making. How are you, sweetheart? I hope you didn't count too much on coming home this week-end as I know you'd be very disappointed if you did plan too much.

If your name comes up next week for detail as you said it might, you'll surely be home the following week (Palm Sunday) and that will be nice, dearest. I can wear my new spring clothes and we can go out together just like we did the past years on Easter. In other words, we can have our Easter a week ahead of time. (ha ha). No matter what week-end you come, it will be wonderful just to be together.

You said in Friday's letter that you had gone to the show Thursday. I was glad to hear that and that the picture was so good. Last night Ann Preston and I went to see Spencer Tracy and Katherine Hepburn in "Keeper of the Flame." It was a very good picture (of a serious vein). The other picture with it was a comedy, all about Army life + was a laugh riot – the name of it was "Fall In". It showed one part about the Military Police on duty in a town on a day the soldiers got paid. If it plays at the Fort, don't miss it, you'll have a lot of laughs. Ruth didn't go to the show with us last night because she was planning to go to New York for the day (today).

Yesterday Betty brought in some silk handkerchiefs Bill sent her. He's in the Air Corps in Miami and is stationed in one of the big hotels there. He says Miami is a beautiful place and he likes the Army very much so far. By the way, it's the Ground Crew of the Air Corps. He's been in swimming already. The weather is very warm there and he even has a tan.

Artie Sarnecky is still in Devens. He went in the Army in the early part of March. He expects to be stationed there for at least 13 weeks. He's in the Medical Corps of the Engineers' Division and is in limited service. Maybe you will see him some time. If you do happen to meet him some time it would be a good idea not to express any dislikes about the Army to him or about Devens. The reason I'm telling you this is because one night about three weeks ago Frank, his brother + Catherine were here visiting Cele and Charlie and he said he heard you were stationed in Devens and didn't like it much – that you'd rather be somewhere else. I told him I didn't know where he ever heard that because you were glad, as far as I knew, that you were there. He said he thought some of the fellows were telling Artie that they were talking to you. Well, anyway I told him they were all wrong thinking that. You know how Artie is so you won't say anything will you, dearest? You know how stories are apt to go around and people lie and exaggerate. I don't pay any attention that's all. The best thing to do, though, is not to say anything at all.

Friday night I listened to Frank Mund on the radio (9:30 P.M. – the Bayer Aspirin Program). He sang some nice songs. Have you heard "As Time Goes By"? That's a nice one. Some other good ones are "I've Heard That Song Before", "Don't Cry", "Saving Myself for Bill", + "Brazil". I'll bet you have to laugh at me liking all sentimental songs. Those are mostly what's played now with everyone away.

I don't know whether the boys in the Army realize how the food situation is here at home. Everything is in bad shape right now, especially the meat shortage. There are some days during the week that we don't have meat at all. We have to save the points so we can have a decent meal on Sunday. As you've probably heard, each person is allowed 16 points per week for meat. We have to use these points if we want butter or cheese (certain kinds) too. A lot of families are eating out one night a week now (we are) – of course the restaurants aren't affected too much yet, although when one does go to eat out, we just have to take whatever there happens to be. I don't understand what people with children are doing to get enough butter, meat, etc. The argument of the people in Bridgeport is that the defense workers will not be able to work such long hours without proper food. Even for cold meats (for sandwiches) it requires so many points. I guess the people wouldn't mind so much if our boys in the Army were getting it but some of the reports from the different camps aren't so good either. Do you manage to get enough meat and butter, etc. and is it good? When you come home the next time, dear, we might have to give you almost anything in the line of meat and vegetables, don't be surprised.

Some of the girls in the office (including myself) are going to get a raise soon. There were about six new girls hired in the last three months and started work with the same salary that we girls, who have been there quite a while, are getting. The older girls (Violet, Laura Lee, Agnes, Betty + I) resented this naturally, so each one of us talked to the office manager and said we didn't think it was fair. It was finally decided, after a lot of bickering back and forth that we will be given a substantial raise. It should come through in a few weeks. It probably will be about $4.<u>00</u> increase. You know how many times I talked about leaving. Well, the amount of money I get is really the only drawback to the job (or course the most important one). I like all the people in the office, the girls etc. and like stenographic work so that's why I hesitate to leave. When I talked to the office manager he told me they were thinking of giving me the job of Secretary to Mr. Lincoln, the Vice President + General Manager. That's the job the Jewish girl I told you about is now holding. He said he talked this over with Mr. Lincoln but he was satisfied with her even though I would "fill the bill" alright. I really don't know whether to believe it or not so I'm just taking it "with a grain of salt" (ha ha). You know me, dear.

I wish this whole mess was over (the war) so you and I could share our lives together before we're too old. I suppose that strikes you funny, darling, but that's the way I feel. We should have a little happiness from life while we can together, don't you think so? I was thinking about what you said the last time you were home about it being worse if we were separated after marriage than it is now. I don't think I could miss you any more after we are married than I do now or long to have you here any more than now. In your case, if a time came for you when we would be separated for a long, long, time, you would always let your head rule you + not your feelings. What do you think of your little girl expressing herself like this? I surprise even myself. Just as you said, dearest, we can tell at the end of the summer just about how everything will be for us.

You called a few minutes ago and as I told you, I was writing this long letter. I was tickled to death to talk to you, dear, it was so nice to know you are well and everything is going along pretty smoothly for you, now that you'll be going to school next week. I hope your bill wasn't too high. Cele said we were talking almost six minutes. It seemed like a minute to me. About the rosary beads, dearest, I'd like anything that you'd pick out but as I told you I do like blue. Don't spend too much money on them as I know you haven't much even though you did get paid. By the time you get the things you need – so much for amusements etc., and send me a money order you won't have hardly anything. Darling, don't forget to put some aside for your train fare the next time you come home.

We are having a lot of trouble with Thomas again – he's been home from work again on account of the usual thing – too much drinking. He's the cause of a lot of worry on everyone's part, Cele, Charlie + myself. I guess it will take a miracle to have him change. You understand how it is, dearest – I don't want to bore you with all the details. Maybe with a lot of prayers he might some day snap out of it.

Well, dearest, this is certainly a lengthy letter but as I told you on the phone I've written you rather short letters during the week – they are usually written hurriedly during lunch hour and then again sometimes I haven't much news or anything very interesting to write about. You understand, dearest, don't you?

There is a cartoon enclosed that I think is very funny, our friend Peter Plink is a big dope isn't he? I hope you enjoy it, dear.

I hope the next two weeks go by fast. I know the time seems long for you, dearest, but maybe after Palm Sunday you might come home every two weeks. Keep your chip up, honey-bunch.

Love Always,

X X X Rita X X X

(These are big ones) ↑

Wednesday 6:30 P.M. 4/7/43

Dearest Walter,

I didn't receive any letter from you today but I know that the mail is slow in coming through – I'll probably get two letters tomorrow (maybe).

How's everything, sweetheart? I'll bet you wish it were the end of next week so you could be getting ready to come home. (I do too).

Tonight I'm going to church – as usual to Lenten Devotions. Then I'll probably iron some clothes, maybe read a little and then go to bed. Tomorrow night Cele + I will go to my uncle's wake. He is laid out at the undertaker's (Cyril Mullins) not at his home because it's too small. We'll go to the funeral Friday morning too.

Here are a few jokes I took out of a book that came into the office:

"You certainly look cute in that gown."
"Oh, this? I wear it to teas."
"To tease whom?"

Wife – "I can't decide whether to go to a palmist or a mind reader."
Husband – "Go to a palmist, you have a palm."

Here's one that Betty gave me – Director Sam Wood and Lewis Stone were playing golf when Lana Turner walked by in a bathing suit. Wood turned to Stone + Stone turned to Wood, then they both turned to rubber.

Do you like that one, darling? I'll bet you like that one better than the first two. (ha ha).

I can hardly wait for the rest of this week and next week to go by – I'm looking forward to seeing you so much, dear. Imagine, it will be four weeks that we will not have seen each other. Oh me! Oh my!

Lots of Love and Kisses, Dear

Rita Marie

Thursday 12:30 P.M. 4/8/43

Fort Devens Mass.

Dear Rita

Recived your letters that you wrote Wednesday 6:30 PM was so glad to get recive it. so prompt.

Yes I can hardly wait for Palm Sunday to come along, so you and I can have a nice week end to gether. Right darling, dearest, The jokes were very good, especially the last one. Today we all had to fall out in our best dress for review, the diplomat and ambassador from Mexica paid us a visit at the Fort, boy we sure did have a big job on our hands, polishing all our brass, and leather and other equipment.

The review was very color full, about 5,000 soldiers turned out to pay their respects.

Last night I manage to get to Ayer Mass., and I bought you a nice string of rosary beads, they are sterling silver I hope you like them I send them insured, so you should get them all right.

Rita you are my sweet heart I love you dearest.

Be seeing you soon

Love Walter

Friday Morning 11:15 P.M. 4/9/43
[Probably meant A.M.]

Dearest Walter,

I came home from the funeral about a half-hour ago and am going into work at 12:30.

Dearest, I have so many things to thank you for – first of all, the beautiful rosaries you sent. How did you ever know that I would love Sterling silver ones? Then, as you said in Thursday's letter, you went into Ayer for them – that certainly was nice of you, dearest, - you have such good taste. I love them – they will always be one of my most cherished possessions. I went to my uncle John's wake last night and I asked Father Pat (he was there) to bless them for me. I told him you sent them to me and he thought they were very nice (he was surprised, darling). We always have religious articles such as rosaries, prayer books, medals, etc. blessed before using them.

It was very thoughtful of you to send the area insignia for Dot Smith. I know she'll appreciate it – also the pin of the officers' (M.P. insignia) for me to wear. It's a nice big one, isn't it, darling? Maybe I'll wear it on my new coat.

This morning I received Thursday's letter, also the money order which I will cash as soon as possible. That makes $50.00 we have now, dearest, isn't that good?

I hope you didn't leave yourself short of money, dearest, buying those nice things and then sending the M.O. Thanks again for everything, especially for the lovely rosaries.

The funeral this morning was very well attended (all the Laverys). Father Pat said the Mass. We went to the cemetery too. It was very cold, tho, in the Church and at the cemetery. I hope there won't be any more deaths in the family for a long while.

The menu you described in Tuesday's letter sounded very good. I'm glad you're getting such good food. The only thing that seems to be lacking a little is you don't seem to be getting much milk – in comparison to what you drank at home. I guess maybe you can make up for it in other foods, heh, darling?

That dress review must have been nice to see. I wish I could have seen it. I'll be thinking of you over the week-end and before we know it will be April 17th + you'll be home. (Oh boy!) Maybe I'll call your sister, Martha, up tonight and see how everyone is. Tomorrow night (Sat.) I might go to the show with Dot Smith – I'm not sure though.

Well, here I am at the office finishing this letter. I brought in the beads to show the girls and they all thought you had very good taste – they liked them a lot.

Tomorrow noon there are ten of us girls going out to lunch to celebrate Ruth's birthday, Ann's birthday (next Tuesday) Betty's Anniversary (Sunday) and last but not least my engagement. (Imagine after 3 – ½ months) The girls said that they never really celebrated our engagement yet so now they will. (ha ha). It's sort of a belated celebration isn't it? We'll all have a cocktail on you, dearest.

Well, dearest, I'm going to send this letter to the post office now with the office boy so I'll write again Sunday and give you all the details of everything. I wish it were next Friday at this time.

If you don't have time to call up Sunday, it will be alright, dearest.

Love Always,

Rita

P.S. You're such a good sweetheart, I love you so much – lots of love and kisses. X X X X X X

Sunday 1:15 P.M. 4/11/43

Dearest Walter,

It was nice to talk with you on the phone a little while ago – I'm glad everything is alright with you. As I said on the phone, being on duty from 8 to 12 isn't quite as bad as 12 to 4. The week will be over before you know it, dearest, and we'll be together for a nice week-end (I hope). The past three weeks, as we said, did seem very long but we won't mind waiting this week we'll both be looking forward to next week-end so much.

Yesterday noon ten of the girls from the office (me too) went to the Palms Restaurant in Black Rock for lunch. (I told you we were going in Friday's letter). We all had a nice time. We had two Manhattans – one of them to all the boys in the Army and the other one to Betty (her first anniversary is today) also to Ann Preston whose birthday is Tuesday. We went back to work about 1:15 (in good spirits) (ha ha).

I had to work until 4 o'clock yesterday afternoon to make up for being out Friday morning. Then I went to the post office downtown to cash your money order. The clerk who waited on me asked if I had anything with me to identify myself. I was surprised at this, I didn't know it was necessary. It so happened I didn't have a thing with me not even my pass. The clerk recognized the name and asked if Tom was any relation. Everything was O.K. when I told him he was my brother. I don't see why they want identification do you, dearest? I met Dot Smith at five o'clock yesterday and then we met Ruth + Ann and went to the Hitching Post for dinner and then to the Warner to see "Happy Go Lucky". I knew you saw it and liked it so I suggested it. It surely was good. We had a few laughs anyway.

Friday afternoon Thomas went to the local draft board for another physical. He doesn't know yet if they're going to send him to Hartford or New Haven for examination. He had to have X-Rays taken of his ear Friday and they showed that his ear drum is punctured slightly. The doctors told him if he was accepted of course he will be in a non-combat division. Maybe they would have him do postal work. He'll know sometime this week if he's going to New Haven. We all hope he is taken as it might straighten him out (somewhat anyway). Charlie thinks if he does go he'll be sick in the hospital within two weeks as his system will not be able to stand going without alcohol. He must be afraid of going or else the doctors must have told him he was definitely a 4-F on account of his dissipation because he's been drunk since Saturday morning. We had some horse meat in the Frigidaire for the cats and he ate it thinking it was roast beef, isn't that awful? The whole situation is really pathetic. I hope he is taken because maybe then we'll all have peace of mind at least. I hope you don't mind my telling you about him, dearest, but I know how you understand, don't you?

Vincent said he expects to be in by July at the latest. The C.R. + L. are working on a 90-day deferment now for him. Of course there will be nothing to keep him from going. Eleanor will have to live with her sister and put their furniture in storage I guess.

About the wedding tomorrow – Virginia's husband-to-be is not a Catholic so they will be married outside of the Altar (no Mass). He's been taking instructions to become a Catholic out in California where he's stationed but the priest in St. Charles didn't think he had enough instructions as yet to be baptized. He intends to continue his instructions when he goes back to his post though. Virginia teaches in St. John's School and is going out to California to live with him when school closes in June. He's a Staff Sergeant. If there is any picture or account of the wedding in the paper tomorrow I'll send it to you. You might like to see it. Cele doesn't think she can take any time off to go tomorrow because they're so busy, but she might. I think I'll work until 3 o'clock and then go to the reception for an hour or so with Eleanor and maybe Charlie. I'd rather go to the Church, tho, but it's very hard to get time off now.

I used my rosaries for the first time this morning in Church and I said them for you, dearest. Gosh, I surely do love them.

It would be a good idea, dear, if you dropped a card to Helen or your father saying you might be home next week-end just so they'll be on the lookout for you – that is – about leaving the lock off the door. Then maybe you wouldn't have to go home early in the evening. What do you think dearest?

I asked you in another letter if you were going to bring your car down to my yard from Easton the next time you come home or if you're going to leave it there a while longer. Maybe if Adolph knew you were going to bring it down here next week-end he could have it ready for you. You could drop him a card. It's up to you, dearest, I just thought I'd suggest it.

Well, dearest, I guess I'm all talked out this time. I'm going to wash my hair this afternoon and read a little. (and think of you).

Lots of love and kisses, dearest.

Rita Marie

big ones heh? ➔ X X X X X X X X X X X

Monday 10: AM.

Post No. 17.A

Powder Magazin Area

Fort Devens Mass.

Dear Rita,

I am now writing from my post way up in the hills, this post is the Fort Magazine dump. Her is where all the powder is stored, I am situated up in a thinlty foot towr, I can get quite a view of all the fort from here, during the day I am up in the towr but at night I am down near one of the gates, the sun is shining now and it is quite warm, No one ever comes around to where I am stationed so I always bring writing paper and a book to keep me busy when I am not observing about, I have a telephone up here, so I can call other posts that have phones (I also have to call the corpral of the guard ever 15 minutes after the hour.

I imagin this part of the country is beautiful in the summer or fall, but here we seem to have only two season's, winter and summer, they say summer comes about August. Ha. Ha.

They say we will be waring our over coats until the end of May, that what the boys that were here last year say. when they are kidding us.

Rita you are a good girl, I could give you a bout a hour of good loving dearest now, you know me.

Boy I am some <u>wolf</u>. Ha. Ha. Be <u>good</u> <u>dearest</u>

Love Walter.

Lots of <u>Love</u>.

Tuesday 12:30 P.M. 4/13/43

Dearest Walt,

How're you today, sweetheart? I hope you don't find the time this week going by too slowly. Tomorrow will be the middle of the week and before you know it you'll be rushing to catch the train home-bound (I hope). By the way, if you're on duty until 12 noon Saturday you will have to rush won't you? I hope you manage to get the early train in Springfield (the one that brings you in to Bpt. about 5:30). Then you can come to my house from the train and be here about 6 o'clock. I have it all figured out, haven't I, darling? Let's leave it this way. If I don't get any call from you, that will mean you're coming home but if by any chance you find out you're not getting a pass, you can call me, heh, dearest?

I certainly am looking forward to this coming week-end. I'm sure we'll have a wonderful one together.

Today is Ann Preston's birthday (she's 19) and she's invited Ruth and I to her house tonight for a while. Guess what Ruth + I gave her for her birthday! Sterling Silver Rosaries. We bought them before I received mine – it was a coincidence tho, wasn't it? They are smaller than mine. I like mine better. We paid $3.<u>98</u> for them in Howland's. She likes them a lot.

I guess I told you before that the club had broken up. Dot Grant was treasurer. We all had some money paid into it at the time it broke up so she sent all of us a money order so she wouldn't have the money on her hands any more. Mine amounted to $3.<u>75</u>. It certainly is a shame that we couldn't keep together especially while the boys are away but you know how girls are, don't you?

It's 6:15 now and I'm home but I haven't eaten supper yet. I just read the letter you wrote yesterday morning while you were on duty in the tower. I'd like to be up there with you, darling and be able to look down at the view of the Fort – it must be nice. It's good that you can read while you're up there and write a letter.

Betty said she received a Special Delivery Air Mail letter from Bill – pages + pages of how lonesome he is, how hard everything is, etc. It made her so worried that now she's says as soon as he is moved somewhere else (he expects to be any day) she's going to live with him. I don't see how she can do this because privates aren't allowed to live with their wives are they? Well I suppose she's thinking of the fact that whatever time he does have off he can spend it with her if she's near him.

Try to get as much rest as possible this week while off duty so you'll feel "in the pink" over the week-end.

Lots of love + kisses, dear

Rita

Tuesday Morning 9: AM. = 4/13/43

Post. 17A.

Dear Rita,

I recived your letter that you wrote Sunday afternoon, it sure was a nice letter. HOw is my sweet little irish darling this morning, I hope that you are in the best of spirits and that you are feeling just <u>hats</u>, <u>cats</u> <u>fine</u>.

The sun is shineing this morning and it is nice way up in the tower, the wind is blowing just a little. So glad that you and the girls had such a nice time together down town Saturday, Did you stay <u>sober</u>. <u>Ha</u>. <u>Ha</u>. That is the usual procedure that the post office use in asking for identification's when cashing money orders. I am quite surprised to hear that Tom and Vincent may be taken into the army, especially Thomas, because of the fact that they have not bothered him to much, and I though that they had forgot about him, but I guess the draft board does not forget anyone – I hope Vin and Tom do not go to soon ever if they have to go eventually, because I think once they do get in, they will be in for a long time <u>maybe</u>. It will be nice dearest for you, in going to your cousins wedding, it will give you the opportunity to meet all your cousins together, and to have a little fun dearest.

So glad to hear again how much you like the rosaries I send you Rita dear. You are a good girl. Yes dear it is a good idea about dropping my father and Helen a card. I dropped a letter last Saturday dearest to them, telling them I hope to make it home Palm Sunday. My car is all set to go any time I get to find time to drive it down, either to your house or mind. The Poem was nice, <u>Rita</u>, <u>Bunny</u> Here are three dozen big hugs and kisses dearest, Boy I love my loving Hee dearest.

Rita you are my sweetheart and my fiancée.

Lots of Love,
<u>Walter</u>

Wednesday 12:45 P.M. 4/14/43

Dearest,

Here it is Wednesday and in three more days I'll see you (I hope). I can hardly wait for Saturday to come.

Last night I went to Ann's house. Ruth went too. I met Ann's brother's girlfriend Eleanor, and the four of us had a nice evening. Ann received a beautiful card from her boyfriend (one of those large, fancy ones in a box). She's hoping he gets a pass this coming week-end and if so, maybe the four of us, Ann, Will, you and I could go out. Whenever he does come, he'll probably give her the ring and that will call for a celebration. Ann also received a lot of other cards and some very nice gifts which just shows what a magnetic personality she has. Ann and Eleanor put on an exhibition of jitter-bug dancing to the song "Begin the Beguine" (your favorite). What rhythm! She should go on the stage (Ann). I'll have to stop writing now – will finish it when I read your letter tonight.

6:00 P.M. I liked the letter you wrote yesterday (Tues.) 'way up in your tower. By the way, dearest, you should be complimented on your improvement in spelling. Your letters are very nice – it just goes to show you – when one has lots of patience and desire to learn – also intelligence as you have, you can do almost anything. Keep it up, darling and maybe pretty soon you can throw the dictionary away (ha ha).

Here's a joke Ruth told last night: There were two lady rabbits out walking one day. One lady rabbit said to the other "Have you heard from Peter lately?" The other rabbit said. "Yes I had a <u>litter</u> from him last week." (ha ha). That's cute don't you think so?

I do hope you can get the train you usually do in Springfield, dearest, so then you can be at my house by 6 o'clock. If I knew just what time you'd get in, I'd be at the station – anyway, dearest, I'll be waiting here with bells on.

Love Always,

Rita

xxxxxxxxxx

P.S. I could give you some nice big hugs + kisses, too, dearest.

Thursday Morning 8:30 A.M. 4/15/43

Post 17 A.

Dear Rita,

How is my sweet little irish girl this morning, I hope that you are in the best of health of wealth and happiness dearest this bright morning in April.

The sun is shining bright and it is a nice day all around dearest. I just had my orange that I got for breakfast and I just removed my overcoat and my .45 pistol and belt so that I can write you a nice sweetheart letter. This shift I manage to get good sleep, at least 6 hours at night and 3 hrs in the afternoon, but I do not have the right hours so that I could make the early show nearby, the early show starts at 6:30 P.M. and ends at 8:30 but I have to get ready to go on post at 4:15 PM and start at 8: PM. pounding the <u>beat</u>. On the other two shifts I manage to go to the theatre about five times a week, it breaks the monotony. I washed my weekly wash last night also manage to find some hot water for a good shower, than boy did I have a good sound sleep.

Rita dear you are a very sweet girl, I could give you some nice loving now dearest than you would feel good and I would feel even better than you. Ha Ha, How is my sweet little Jeanie doing these day's, does she keep her mind on her home work or does she make so many eyes at the boys. She will be quite some kid in a few more years, she will have to beat the boys away from her with a <u>twenty</u> <u>foot</u> <u>club</u>. I happened to notice in the Bpt Post that I found in our day room yesterday how, <u>Harry J. Hainsworth</u> is soon to be inducted into the Navy, at least he seems to be the fellow, he will come out of 23 A. board in Bpt. so that must be him. Also noticed the nice picture of your cousin Virginia and her husband leaving Saint Charles Church after the Wedding, they make a nice couple. In our outfit there are quite a few boys from Bpt and they recive the post from Bpt now and than that is how I come to see all this, we have more magazines and books and papers than we can find time to read them.

P.S. Harry J Hainsworth sure does get the tough breaks at least I think that is him that is to go into the Navy soon.

Dearest on our bulletin Board yesterday was put a notice which read, no more passes until all of the 250 men qualify on the range for marksmenship, So that was quite a heartbreaker for all of us boys that would have been eligible for a pass, Palm Sunday or Easter Sunday, but now Palm Sunday seems just like a dream, so that Sunday is out for a pass, than comes Easter, well this may be a possibility but I could not say for sure, I hope that all the man will be through firing by Friday the day before my pass comes due. Maybe this will go on for four weeks. It would be just my luck that they had to start this firing business If they issued passes while they were firing the Louie (?) thinks we would never complete our firing, also they would everyone to qualify as quickly as possible because very soon about fifty or more fellows are due to be shipped out of our outfit into combat units, that will be only for the 1A. fellows, later the louie said it will be our turn to be reclassified that is to pick out the ones that they thinks will be able to qualify to be one A. men, I am in now in 1B non combat unit, of course they would have to pass the physical examination before they could put the one Bs in any other category. But that will not come for months yet. That is what our Louie said, but some day that is what is to come. May be I will be put in Military Combat Unit that is, police Units for over Sea's Service, my duties would be to take care of prisoners behind the lines also direct Military traffic also to handle parachutist <u>that</u> fall <u>behind</u> behind the lines also other MPs duty. but that is just maybe and that is for the future.

I will let you know from day to day how the induction looks. Also over the week end I will call you on the telephone and we will make the best of this induction dearest I hope that next week I will have my turn on the range in that way I will be able to go to the show or nearby Ayer for a beer or browse about the village. This way I can not leave the fort. Be a good girl. Love Walter. P.S. Dearest I recived your Tuesdays letter. So glad that you and Ann + Ruth click so well, you should like my rosaries better, because mine cost $4.00 Ha. Ha. I have good taste, don't I dear. Give Betty my regards, to bad that your club broke up, well girls will be girls. P.S.

Tuesday 12:50 P.M. 4/20

Hello Sweetheart,

I hope this letter finds you well and happy – also doing well on the range.

I don't think I mentioned in my previous letters about where I'm keeping your money, dearest, but anyway I'll tell you now. I have a secret hiding place for it (ha ha). Remember those tin boxes of Chrofts you gave me some time ago? Well, I have one of them in my bureau and I put the money in it. Of course I wouldn't tell anyone where it is (only you) – (ha ha). I can only manage to save a little every week – by December I should have $100.<u>00</u>.

(6:30 P.M.) I didn't receive any mail from you today, dearest, but I probably will get two letters tomorrow. I'll be happy if I get one.

On the way home from work tonight I met Gladys Franke and guess what? She's going to be married June 12th! She just got her diamond last week – she showed it to me. It was on the type of mine but it didn't have the little side diamonds. She's marrying a fellow from the South but who lives at the "Y" here in Bridgeport. He's a college grad and works in the Remington. Gladys was asking for you, dearest.

Well, dearest, since I started to write this letter it has stopped raining and the sun is out now – it's real springy. I hope you like this little poem I'm sending – I do.

Lots of love and kisses,

X X X Rita X X X

P.S. How do you like my new stationery?

Tuesday 7:00 P.M.

Service Club Library

Dear Rita,

How is my sweet little girl doing today, you are my sweet girl Rita, you are nice, <u>Honey</u> <u>Bunny</u>. I recived your nice letters Rita, you write such nice letters. I managed to get a little time to my self and get down to the library at the service club, it sure is a fine library. For the past two days I have been on the rifle range for our trial practice shots, I hope to do all right when we fire for record in a few days, I got 152 out of a 200 possibility in my trial practices, that is enough for me to qualify for markmens maybe I may do much better when I fire for record. I may get a 168 or more which would entitle me to a sharpshooter metal or may be I may get a 178 or better which would be enough for expert. It is a lot of fun firing on the range. I may get a pass for Easter but that is only a possibility, but I will let you know from day to day about that. It looks now as if you will soon have a brother in the Arm Services very soon, well good luck to your brother Tom and I hope that he manages to get in the postal service when he gets placed than it will be much easier than for him, than if he should get placed into some field that he is not familiar on. I am sure that he will do all right for himself if he does get inducted into the service. I am sure that Cele will enjoy the flowers very much. You are a good girl. Give my regards to Peggy and Bill and my congratulations. Your Sweetie Pie <u>Walter</u>.

Monday 4/26/43 5:15 P.M.

Dearest Walt,

The past week-end is now a happy memory which can hold us over until the next time we see each other. We both had such an enjoyable week-end, didn't we, dear?

We were so lucky that I happened to see you on the corner Saturday. It would have been terrible if you went to my house and found that I was gone to the show. It was so nice to go cruising along in your father's car to the Ritz. I know you enjoyed it too, darling. I guess I was the happiest in the world

Easter. The best part of it all was that we both felt the real spirit of Easter – going to church and you receiving Communion.

I hope you had a little sleep on the train on the way back. I didn't realize how early it was when you left until I came back to the house after I left you at the bus. The next time, dearest, let's not leave the house until 5 minutes later or so.

I hope we can always have as nice an Easter as we did this past one.

You said you thought I was extra nice to you over the week-end. I think the reason is, as I mentioned to you Saturday night, I understand you completely now. I've learned tolerance and a better understanding of lots of things since you've been gone. In other words, not to pat myself on the back too much, I've got over my childish, selfish ways a lot.

I was beaming when I went into the office today – everyone noticed how glad I was that you came home.

Your sister Emma's little girl, Dorothy, is a beauty I think. I couldn't help noticing what lovely features – eyes, hair + teeth she has.

Maybe you'll be home again sooner than you think, darling. Be sure and call whenever you do get a pass. If you don't have the money, don't forget you can always reverse the charges. Even if you don't know you're coming until Saturday noon, please call, dearest. Someone will be bound to be here to take a message if I'm not here.

Today is a day that makes one feel like going down to Seaside and walk along the Seawall. It's a beautiful day, real springy. I'll bet it's nice up in the hills where you are.

I'm going to call Dot Smith up tonight and tell her that she + I will surely get together next week. We'll probably use up the film you + I started and I'll invite her here for supper Sunday.

Until the next time you come, dearest, maybe it won't seem too long. I'll be thinking of you and of course our letters will help us feel closer.

Take care of yourself, sweetheart.

Lots of love and kisses
Rita
Your Colleen
x x x x x x

Monday 12:30 P.M.

Dear Rita,

I arrived back in camp safely and managed to get enough of sleep both on the train and in my barrack, got about 6 Hours in all, will make up on sleep this evening.

Rita you are my little sweet heart, I love you devotely dearest, I sure did have a very nice time with you dearest over the weekend.

Rita we both do get along so good, don't we dearest. This morning we had plenty of exercis, lots about two hours of marching lots some teaching in Jui

Jitsu, that's how to handle a person that wants to resist arrest.

Rita you such a good girl, I could give you a few dozen kisses, (large ones)

Lots of Love

Your Sweetheart

<u>Walter</u>

You treat me so nice dearest You are such a sweet girl Rita. Keep up your spirits dearest.

I love your Kisses so much I love you (devotely).<u>Rita</u> dear

(Happy Easter dear! Ha. Ha. Well dont I have to use up this nice stationary.)

Tuesday 6:15 P.M. 4/27/43

Dear Sweetheart,

Received your letter written yesterday at noon and was so glad that you had some sleep on the way back also that you enjoyed the week-end so much.

I guess after the boys get passes in the Army, the officers don't want you boys to be thinking of your girls so they keep you going when you get back to the fort (ha ha). Ju Jitsu must be interesting.

Darling, I knew you would use the Easter stationery this week. I had to laugh when I saw it. Leave it to you, Kleiny, not to waste stationery (ha ha).

I was talking to Dot Smith on the phone last night and she said she didn't have such a bad Easter after all. She went out with Mary, the girl who is going to be her maid of honor. She said Ernie sent her an orchid but it didn't arrive until she had come home from Church. She said he must have been trying to make up for last year because this year he sent her candy, flowers and a card. I asked her if she could go out with me this coming Sunday but she might go to New York with Mary. They wrote to a hotel for reservations for Saturday and Sunday. If I had known they were going I would have planned on going too – that is – save a little money each week for it. She said they've been saving for a long time.

Ann Preston is coming back to work tomorrow. I hope she'll be completely better now.

Dearest, when you write to Helene, your sister, next time ask her to call me up and we can go to the show or she can come here and meet Cele and spend the evening. I asked her Sunday to call me sometime and she said she would but she might forget. I'd appreciate it if you told her to. She could keep me company once in a while, heh, darling?

Well, dearest, I hope everything goes along smoothly for you this week. I'll be thinking of you all the time

Love Always,

Your Colleen

These are big kisses →X X X X X X X X X X X

P.S. Here's a nice poem I marked the parts I liked best. Edgar Guest's poetry is nice

```
                    WEDDING PRAYER
                                    Edgar J. Guest

        God bless them both who pledge today
            The weight of war to share,
        And grant them courage for the way
            Which shortly they must fare.

        Sustain him at his battle post
            Should cruel foes attack,
        And unto her who loves him most
            Soon bring him safely back.

        God bless her now who long must wait
            Beside a lonely fire,
        And strengthen her for any fate
            And grant her heart's desire.

        When victory shall end their fears,
            And war's grim clouds shall lift,
        We pray the boon of happier years
            As freedom's wedding gift.
```

Wednesday 12:00

Dear Rita,

I recived your too latest letters and I am so glad to get your very nice letters, the letter that you wrote Monday sure was a very nice letter. Rita you are a very nice girl. I love my irish colleen so much, I could give my sweet darling some very nice Fort Devens kisses, you know the kind that I like to give. Rita you are so pretty, you are a very femmine girl Darling I feel like I could love you for about a hour dearest. It must be the spring air up here.? Ha. Ha. S glad that you were beaming (over with joy) when you went back to the office, see <u>what I do to you darling</u>.

The Poem sure was a very nice one dearest, you sure do appreciate good Poems. So do I Rita dear. To bad that you can't make it to New York with Dot Smith, well Rita maybe in the near future you can get together with her and Mary. Yes dearest I will ask Helene my big sister to call you on the phone the next time I write to her, She will sure like to go to show or stop at your house for the evening I am sure. You two will make a good pair, my big sister and my sweetheart Love <u>Walter</u>

P.S. This is the last of the Easter stationary Ha. Ha.

Thursday 4/29/43
(Pay Day) – ha ha

Dearest Walter,

I'm glad to hear you enjoyed my letters. I love to receive yours, too, darling – they're such nice ones.

This morning when I went into work I was so surprised – I opened one of the drawers in my desk and there was a package all wrapped up fancy. I thought Ann and Ruth were playing a joke on me at first. Well, I opened it and there were two guest towels (pretty shade of green) with "His" and "Hers" embroidered on them. They were from Ruth for my hope chest. I was so surprised because there was really no occasion to give me a gift like that but she said she just wanted to get me started on a hope chest because I was so nice to her. I really haven't been as nice as I might be I don't think. I think I will buy things from now on, darling such as sheets, pillow cases, towels and personal things for myself. Don't you think I should, dearest?

Tonight after work I stopped in for my watch and it was finally ready so I got it. It feels good to be wearing it again.

Today was pay-day and the $4.00 increase I told you about was in my pay. I now get $36.40 but after all my deductions are made it only amounts to $32.82. Well this is better than before anyway. I'll be able to save a little now, heh, darling?

I hope everything is going along smoothly for you this week, darling. I suppose you are on your school schedule. I also hope you are having as much rest as possible and a little diversion too – as going to the show or something.

It will be nice if you can come home again soon. I'll be looking forward to it, dearest and we can have a wonderful week-end together again. When you get paid I'd suggest that you push enough money aside for your train-fare in case you come home before the next pay-day.

When I got my watch tonight I bought a white gold guard for my little diamond that I wear on the right hand. It was only 75¢ and now I can wear the ring on my ring finger instead of the middle finger.

Did you hear the joke about the moron whose wife was going to have a baby and he brought her to the country because he heard there was <u>rural free delivery</u>? (ha ha)

Did you hear the one about the moron who cut off his hands so he could play the piano by ear? (ha ha).

Also the one who cut off his left side so he'd be all right? (ha ha).

Well, dearest, I guess this is all for now. I'll bet you think those jokes are terrible. (ha ha).

Love Always,
Rita
Your Colleen
X X X X X X X X X X
I love you, darling.

1.

A Woman's Responsibility in Sex Relations

Condensed from You

Louise Fox Connell

"THERE ARE no frigid women; there are only clumsy men." This saying sums up the tendency to put the whole responsibility for sexual adjustment on the husband. A favorite slogan of some authorities on sex is, "The art of love is the art of pleasing a woman."

Unfair to men though this may seem, it is a vast improvement on the belief that a virtuous woman has no sex feelings and that her husband is doing his marital duty if he uses his wife to satisfy his desires without taking the time or trouble to gratify hers.

It is because men have been blind to women's sex needs that good books on marriage are devoting much space to preaching the importance of satisfying a wife. The one danger about this emphasis is that it may keep a wife from realizing that it is just as much her job as her husband's to try to make their unions thrilling and perfect for them both. Some understanding modern psychiatrists go so far as to believe that what they call "emotional nonsupport" by a wife, in daily life and in sex relations, ought to be grounds for divorce.

Of course, sex relations are no more the whole of marriage than the roots are the whole of a tree. Yet, besides being the physical reality of wedlock, the act of mating is the symbol of its spiritual reality. It is a sort of symbolic dramatization of a couple's whole life together. All the faults and virtues which similarly go to make or mar each daily detail of married life are revealed: kindness or selfishness, tact or crudeness, frankness or concealment, confidence or fear, ignorance or enlightenment, patience or its opposite. Learning to become a good lover is more than just mastering a technique; it is the perfecting of one's whole nature. So, after a reasonable time, if a couple have not learned to give and receive happiness and satisfaction in their unions, Heaven help their marriage!

That Heaven often fails to help those who do not help themselves is proved by the fact that there is one divorce in this country to every five or six marriages. An outstanding authority on marriage, Dr. Paul Popenoe, Director of the American Institute of Family Relations in Los Angeles, who has made a study of some 20,000 marriages, says of divorced couples:

"Ten years' study by the Institute has shown that disharmony between husband and wife was, in most instances, associated with failure to make a satisfactory sexual adjustment early in married life. This fail-

92

Sat. Morn. 9:00 AM.

Dear Rita,

To my sweetheart on this fine Saturday Morning goes lots of Love and Kisses. Hows that for a good Starter.

Yes Rita I think that it is a good idea in buying different articals for our future home dearest and different things for your self. So glad to hear that you got your watch dearest from the Jewelers. Now you will be all set. Hee dearest.

Congratulations dearest on your new pay increas. good luck and best of wishes on your good fortune RIta dear. That article dearest sure was very interesting it contained plenty of good information on that good old subject of Sex.

I am fine Rita dear and am getting along O.K But I miss you dearest, I rather be with you than any one in the world. (for the good old days and evenings together dearest). Rita dear, words can not express my Love and feelings for you. You are the finest girl in the universe Rita. You have the best of qualities and finest of character. Love Walter.

P.S. The Jokes were very nice.

Monday 12:45 P.M. 5/3/43

Hello, my Soldier Sweetheart,

How are you this "Blue Monday"? I hope it isn't a "blue Monday" for you, darling. It usually is for the average working boy and girl (like you and I, dear).

Ann Preston, her brother Joe and his girlfriend, Eleanor, came over yesterday afternoon for a little while. They didn't stay long as they were going bowling. Joe expects to be moved this week from New Jersey. He's in the Signal Corps. He had a nice tan like you because he's outside a lot too. He was asking me how you liked Devens, and said he'd like to meet you some time. Ann also sends her regards to you. She certainly is a lot of fun, she's always kidding about something. I'll finish this later.

6:15 P.M. Darling, I received your money order and little note. Yes, dear, our snow ball is growing now ($75.00). I also received your letter you wrote Saturday – the one with all the nice compliments in it. I know it isn't just "your line", darling.

Yesterday I noticed the shoes Joe Preston had on. I think they are the same as what you have in mind to get for the summer. They are plain in the front with the buckles at the side in a nice shade of brown. He had such a shine on them we could almost see ourselves in them (ha ha). If you would like to get them in a week or so, dear, I could send you back some of your money – whatever you think, darling.

Last night I listened to the radio. I was by myself, Cele + Charlie were out. I missed you so much, dearest, I was thinking about Easter week-end, how nice it was to have you home and I was thinking of you being on guard duty all by yourself from 8 to 12. Well, dearest, we can tell ourselves that every day that goes by is bringing us that much closer to the end of the war, then you and I can be together always. I guess that is the thought that helps young couples like you and I to <u>live</u> from day to day and not just exist – if you know what I mean. I've read so much on the two (living and existing) that I'm getting to be quite a philosopher (ha ha).

Be a good boy, dearest and try to keep in good spirits,

Love Always,
X X X X X X Your Colleen, Ritamarie

Monday May 3.

Dear Rita,

So glad to be able to talk to you each Sunday. Rita you are my lifes inspiration. <u>Rita</u> <u>Marie</u>.

I will probably recive your letter this evenning at mail call.

It rained cats and dogs this morning, but I managed to keep dry. I always do alright for myself. I had a post this morning that does not have any shelter, but I used a large pice of canvas for shelter, I manage to get some more pamphlets dearest, I will send them as soon as I read them, they contain some very good information about marrige dearest.

Rita you are my sweet heart dearest.

I could hug you so tight Rita dear, and give you some nice kisses.

Lots of Love to my sincere Irish darling. Keep Smiling <u>Rita Marie</u>

P.S. Rita dear I love you so. Your Soldier Boy

Walter

P.S. Here is one Pamphlet, it got a little wet and dirty I was reading it on post. I read them at night with my flashlight. I will send others later some each day.

Tuesday, 5/4/43 12:45 pm

Darling,

Guess who's getting married! Dot Grant and Jimmy Maguire – June 12th – 10: A.M. in St. Charles. Dot got her diamond last Saturday. Dot Smith met Alice Blake in church last night and Alice said she's going to be one of the bridesmaids – there will be three altogether. They are going housekeeping too. Jimmy got another deferment – six months I think. They certainly are a lucky couple. I wasn't entirely surprised to hear that they are getting married as I mentioned to you before, Dot has been buying things for a long time for a home. Alice will be giving a shower on her soon and I imagine the rest of the "club that used to be" will be invited. Jimmy and Dot seem to be very unsuited for each other but I hope they have lots of luck anyway.

Another bit of news - - Joe and Dot Blake might be married soon too. Joe just came back from Casa Blanca (his second trip) and he has ten days off right now. They wanted to be married during the ten days but Mr. and Mrs. Blake are against it very much as they said Dot and Joe should wait until the war is over. I think they will (get married) anyway soon, as Dot wants to. I hope everything works out for them.

6:30 P.M. I received the little booklet on war marriage, dearest, and have managed to read it hurriedly. It's a good one. This is what I was trying to tell you when you were home – "When a soldier is far away, the thought of love and home waiting for him helps him - - He knows he is not alone, he belongs to someone and someone belongs to him in the clearest possible way. People talk a great deal about the problem of a soldier's adjustment after the war to civil life. The man who can return to his own home has already gone a long way toward readjustment."

I will read it more carefully when I finish this letter but the paragraph I quoted above happened to strike me right away because of you and I talking about it before. Thanks for sending it, dearest. You shouldn't feel as though you have to send a lot of them, dearest, as I think you and I know quite a few of these facts already but of course, it's always interesting to read a lot too.

That was a good idea of yours, dear, using a piece of canvas for a shelter. Leave it to you, Kleiny, to have good ideas.

Going back to the subject of Dot + Jimmy's wedding date - - it's the same date as Gladys Franke has chosen. That's a coincidence isn't it — that we know two people (3 to be exact) who are getting married on the same day?

Well, dearest, you tell me to keep smiling and I'm trying to. I do hope you can come home again oson.

Fr. O'Connell came this morning to take the annual census. While he was waiting for Jeanie to answer the door, he saw your letter in the mail basket and said to Jeanie "Here's a letter from Rita's boyfriend — I see he's in the Army." I guess he must have seen your name in the upper left-hand corner. (ha ha). Leave it to him not to miss anything heh, dearest?

I wish I could give you some nice kisses too, darling.

Love Always,
Rita, Your Colleen
X X X X X X X X X X

235 Reed St.
Stratford, Conn.
May 4, 1943

Dear Walt,

When I say that things happen around here I'm really not kidding. It seems that while we were down in Westport Sunday Emma started labor pains. She was all alone, so she crawled over to old Mr. Burke that owns the house, and asked him to get her an ambulance. He managed that somehow, and Emma had a 1 ½ lb. boy, who died after a few hours. It is very rarely that babies that small ever manage to survive.

If we had any sense at all, we would have been prepared for this, for she has come down at 7 months before, but she seemed to be feeling pretty good so far. In a way it is not the worst thing that could happen. At least Emma is alright, and it wouldn't have been too easy for her to take care of another baby. She has her hands full as it is.

Ruth is staying home from school to take care of the smaller ones, and even if they aren't eating quite the way they are accustomed to, she manages with a helping hand here and there. I'm just wondering how gracefully Gus is going to go through this. He has to do a good deal of the housework now, and that isn't really up his alley.

The paper hangers are finally here, and by the end of the week some of the work ought to be out of the way at least. The sidewalks are also under construction up the other end of the street, and in a few days we ought to have that in, too.

The - - furnace just won't seem to go. It was pretty hot here last night, so I slowed the thing down to a walk. Well, it slowed down alright, and now it just seems to have decided that we don't need it any more and resists all advances with the dogged stubbornness of a mule.

Seems that I had the type of boat all bowled up. It belongs to the "lightning" class, whatever that means. Till I get to know a little more about boats it is just a name – speaking of names, maybe you could think of an appropriate one for it. It's light blue and white. (This is almost as bad as naming a baby.) It's got to be something light, frivolous and odd. That's a big order, but there must be an answer somewhere.

How are you doing with your marksmanship? Or are you on something else now? And you still haven't told me whether there are any bears up there. If there are I think we'll come up and bag one to take home for a pet. I was just dreaming of one the other night. A nice big black one that come up to give me a friendly hug. Crazy? But definitely. Write soon. I'll keep you posted if anything new turns up – which it no doubt will.

Ellen

Thursday 5/6/43 <u>noon</u>

Dearest Walter,

How's my sweetheart today? I hope you're in tip-top shape.

I read the pamphlet through very thoroughly – it certainly was very good. I was wondering what you thought of the paragraph on mixed marriages. It gives all the difficulties that are supposed to be prevalent in a mixed marriage very clearly. – after reading this part I imagine you felt a little discouraged knowing it concerns us so much. It is natural to feel this way, but of course, you and I at least are prepared for mostly all the difficulties – that is, have talked about them and have agreed on all points so we aren't as badly off as if we didn't face them at all and kept all our viewpoints to ourselves. The paragraph entitled "Love's Union" is beautifully written – especially this part "Love, makes a man + woman so important to each other that neither one can any longer live alone. - - - If they are truly in love, they do not need nature or the Church to teach them to make their vows binding for life – that is their natural impulse – their love impels them to promise each other a lifetime of fidelity and mutual help."

You'll probably remember dearest, my telling you some of the things that were in this pamphlet - - it is definitely the Catholic viewpoint on the sacrament of marriage, naturally, as it's written by a priest.

I could go on and on in this letter talking about this subject but we'll wait until we're together, shall we, darling? I only have to work until 5 o'clock tonight instead of the usual 5:30 so I'm going to stop downtown and cash the money order you sent in the main post office – up until today I couldn't because by the time I get to the one on Stratford Ave. it's usually closed.

(6:45) We ate supper out tonight and Charlie brought your letter which you wrote Wednesday afternoon over with him when he met us downtown. I'm writing this paragraph in the car on the way home – notice how crooked this writing is. I haven't read the booklet yet "What to Do On A Date" but it looks good. I did have a chance, tho, to look at all the little notes you wrote in the inside – I had to laugh.

I would love to see you this week-end, dearest, but of course if there is any chance of your coming, you probably won't know until Saturday.

I'm glad that my letters are so interesting to you that you read them over + over when you're on post. This is some of Jeanie's writing paper. I was all out of it when I started to write. I bought some downtown tonight like the kind I sent you once.

I love you with all my heart, dearest, I think of you all the time,
Lots of Love + Kisses
Your Colleen Rita
X X X X X X X X X X
P.S. Keep smiling, sweetheart.

Friday May 7 3:00 P.M.
Day Room

Hello Rita,

How is my little bunny this bright day, I hope that you are in the best of spirits, I know that you are, that is most of the time. <u>Heh</u> darling.

I am feeling fine and I am getting along very good, the weather is getting nice and warm and that helps plenty. Yes the pamphlets contain plenty of good information on the subject of marig. Your a good girl, in going to church so regular dearest, and taking confession. Rita you are my love and life inspiration, you are so sincere, I could travel clear around the world and not be able to find a fine as girl as you, you are the one girl for me. You are the finest girl in the world.

Lots of Love to my sweetheart
Walter.

Sunday 1:15 P.M. 5/9/43
Mother's Day

Dearest, it's a beautiful day – the sun is shining brightly, although it's a little cool. I wish you were here – then we could go out for a nice walk – maybe at the seawall in Seaside or somewhere.

I went to 10 o'clock Mass per usual. The priest gave a good sermon on Mother's Day which was more touching this year than any other year on account of so many boys in the Armed Forces.

I called Dot Smith up this morning and asked her if she'd like to go out for a walk but she didn't feel well yesterday or today so she wants me to go over to her house this afternoon for a visit. I guess I will for a while – Sunday is such a long day. She said she made up her mind to go to live with Ernie when they get married – They will get a small, furnished apartment somewhere near the Camp and live until either Ernie is sent out of the country or until the war is over. Then, of course, they'll come back to Bridgeport to live permanently. I think she should do this, don't you, darling? – as long as Ernie gets enough money to take care of them both it seems the right thing to do. I certainly will be lost when Dot does go down there. – Oh my – this is such a changing world. I'm going to bring the pamphlets you sent me over to Dot so she can read them too – she'll give them back to me when she finishes reading them.

Thomas had to go to Dr. Curran with his ear Friday night. He's had trouble with it for quite a while. The doctor said it was abscessed very badly and that he was lucky it didn't go into mastoids on him which would be very dangerous. The doctor thinks when the Army doctors examine him they won't take him in the Army on account of it. I guess he was glad to hear this although he keeps saying he doesn't care whether he's taken or not. We know he doesn't want to go tho – well, so much for that, you know how I feel about it.

He was telling me that the Fitzgerald fellow's wife (your cousin) had twin boys last Thursday. Imagine, twins! Cele was kidding me saying maybe twins run in your family (ha ha).

Well, dearest, you haven't called up to now (it's two o'clock) so I guess you must be very busy. Well, dearest, right in the middle of that sentence the phone rang and I ran downstairs – of course it was you, darling. I was so glad! You said you probably wouldn't get a pass until the week after next. I do hope you get one then darling. Once a month still isn't too bad is it? I'm glad to hear you're well and everything. Your voice sounded much better than last week.

I'll have to go now as I told Dot I'd be over about 2:30. I wish you were here so I could tell you in person how much I love you instead of just writing it. You're such a good sweetheart to call me up every week – to wait so long for a phone and everything – if I could only express my love so that you'd realize how great it is.

Lots of love and kisses,
Rita, Your Colleen
X X X X X X X X X X X

Tuesday 3:30 P.M. 5/11/43
(Rest Period)

Walter Darling,

We have a ten-minute rest period in the office every day so today I just felt like writing a few lines to you, sweetheart.

Here's a clipping of Peter Plink that I had to laugh at. He thought the "first class" over the gateway referred to his rating instead of class of travel (ha ha).

I met Ruth Sorenson on the bus again yesterday and she asked me if my sweetie pie (you) had been home over the week-end. I told her you weren't.

She said John has gone to Cincinnati this week on business and that the fellow whom you boys call "Hatch" had been home over the week-end. I don't know whom she means but of course you do.

6:15 P.M. – I didn't receive any mail from you today – I hope you are well and that everything is O.K. with you. I suppose you must be very busy this week but I thought this week would be easier for you – that is if you are going to school. Let me know how everything is, dearest, if you can.

I've been wondering lately if you are just as well satisfied being in the Military Police than in some other division in which you could use your mechanical ability. Do you still feel as though you would like to get into something else? If so, I think you could ask for a transfer into another division. The good point I think, about the M.P. is that you are outside a lot, getting fresh air, but on the other hand, the hours aren't regular as far as getting your sleep is concerned, which isn't too good for anyone. I was wondering how you feel about it, dearest. For instance, at first Ernie was in the Engineers Division, then the M.P. and now the Ordnance which he likes best of all, so I think you could be transferred if you wanted – of course if you like the M.P. I wouldn't think of asking for a transfer if I were you.

Dearest, I hope I receive a letter tomorrow – I feel so lost if I don't – I do want you to know, tho, dearest that if you are too busy to write, I will understand. Take care of yourself, darling, I love you.

Love Always,
Rita Marie
Your Colleen
X X X X X X X X X X

Tues. 4:30 5/11/43
Day Room
Post MP.s

It cost you $10.80 per year for stamp dear. funny I just happened to think about all the stamps you civilians have to use. while we do not have to even give them a thought. <u>Ha</u>. <u>Ha</u>.

Hello Rita Marie,

To my Colleen who lives at 1440 Stratford Ave, Bpt and who is my sweet little darling, and the very best girl in the land. I recived your Mondays letter Rita dear

I am going to school as you have said dear, and it gives us boys a chance to relax. we like it very much for a change.

So glad that you had a very enjoyable time at Dot Smiths home. So glad that you met her girl friend Kathleen.

No I dont have very much time to listen to the radio, there are not very many Radios here at the fort, when I do have time, the boys generally do have it all ready tuned to some other program. Give Mr + Mrs Smith my regards. There are sure very nice to Dot, they are sure very nice parents.

Yes dear it sure will be nice when we see each other in a few weeks. We will keep our fingers <u>crossed</u>. Heh dear. Lots of Love to my Sweet Irish Colleen. Rita. M. L. <u>Walter</u>

Wednesday 5/12/43 3:30 P.M.
Rest Period

Dearest,

How are you this very dreary day? It rained cats and dogs here all morning and now it has slowed down to a steady drizzle. I had to practically swim to work this morning. (ha ha).

The office manager put a notice up on the bulletin board that we are to let him know when we're going to take our vacations, that is, which two weeks. I haven't decided yet. It would be nice if you could get about four days furlough sometime in the summer and then I could take part of my vacation at that time, but I suppose you can't tell yet if you will. Dot Smith was saying Sunday if all the wedding plans work out, she would like to have you come home the night before the wedding, if possible, because we'll have to have a rehearsal that night. I told her you'd be lucky if you could come at all. I do hope you can but it's rather early to tell yet, isn't it?

Thomas still thinks he will not be accepted when he goes to New Haven Friday. The doctor gave him some drops to put in his ear which would probably clear the abscess before Friday but he hasn't used them at all hardly. Cele and Charlie think he's doing this purposely so his ear won't look so good when it is examined. If he is accepted he'll get the surprise of his life. I hope he is. I'll finish this letter when I get home, dearest.

6:15 P.M. – I was so glad to receive your letters written Monday + Tuesday. – that you are well and are now able to relax a little that you are going to school this week.

You say you don't have time to listen to the radio. Well, darling, if you go into a place where there is a nickelodeon or some other type of music, listen to the song "You'll Never Know", it's a very nice one – both the tune and words.

Leave it to you, dearest, to figure out how much it costs for stamps a year. I don't care how much it costs, writing to you is worth a lot more than that to me. When you do come home the week-end after this one I'll be so anxious to see you that I think I'll go to the station to meet you. How would you like that, honey bunch? Of course I'd make sure you're coming first. What a wonderful week-end we'll have, won't we, dearest?

I called up Dr. McQueeney to have the ganglion on my wrist taken care of. He told me in February that it would have to be done in the hospital so I thought I'd better have it taken care of as it's been bothering me lately. His nurse answered and said he wasn't in today, it's his day off but she would call me tomorrow night or Friday night and let me know when to go to the hospital. It will probably be done early next week or maybe even this coming Saturday. I will only be in the hospital a few hours I guess – just a little whiff of gas or ether and it'll be all over – it's nothing to worry about at all, dearest. I'll let you know more about it as soon as the doctor lets me know.

Well, sweetheart, get as much rest as possible this week – go to a few shows, service club, etc. and enjoy yourself a few hours.

Love Always,
Your Colleen, Rita
X X X X X X X X X X X

Thursday 12:00 5/13/43

Hello Darling,

I just recived your nice letter Rita dear,

I just got up from bed I was on Ayer town patrol last night, It is a little variety and it gives us boys some time to get about town and see people and sometime to maintain peace and order. between drunks and speeders and wise fellows we are kept pretty busy. It is pretty good experenice I am going on tonight also I work until 1:30 A.M. start at 8: P.M.

Maybe in a few weeks I may start to do train patrol. Maybe. It is a little diffrent than chasing prisoners and doing interior guard duty, and much better.

Rita dear you are my sweetheart.

Rita dear it sure would be nice if you and I could meet each other at the train when I get my next pass. Rita dear I love you I could give you some very nice kisses. You know me. Ha. Ha.

Lots of Love.
Walter.

P.S. Dont worry about that Ganglion dearest It will come out alright dearest.

Friday 6:16 P.M. 5/14/43

Dearest,

I received your nice letter written yesterday noon.

I'm glad to hear you like town patrol. I do hope you'll get enough rest, though. If you do go on train patrol will that mean that you might be sent anywhere in the U.S. or will it be in the vicinity of Mass? I suppose you can't tell yet, dearest. I hope you don't go too far away, darling.

You should see your sweetheart today. I've got a red nose that's running like Niagara Falls (a slight head cold) and I look so funny. – (ha ha). Incidentally, today is my brother Edward's birthday. I sent him a nice card. Tomorrow is Charlie's. I guess I'll get him a tie or something.

Well, Thomas went to New Haven this morning for his physical and by the looks of everything, he will not be accepted, that is, as far as we know now. He called up from there at 3 o'clock this afternoon and said he wasn't finished being examined but the ear specialist thought he could never be taken. I guess he was glad to hear this – of course we won't know the final answer until he comes home. Charlie said the Internal Revenue called up this afternoon and said they might issue a warrant for his arrest as he (Thomas) didn't pay enough income tax for 1941 – he deducted too much I guess. They had sent him several notices but he just disregarded them. Cele is so worried. He'll know all this when he comes home tonight. Such a weak character! I hope everything comes out alright for Cele and Charlie's sake because he's not worth all of that worry. It's too bad he's such a weak character because Vin and Ed are just the opposite – as the saying goes "there's a black sheep in every large family." Well, dearest, try not to be bored by all this talk, but I know you understand. I just felt like telling you – it always helps to tell you things I wouldn't mention to anyone else.

I hope you have a few laughs when you read these moron jokes I've enclosed. One of the girls in the office (the little girl, Virginia) gave this copy to me. Most of them are really funny I think.

About the ganglion, I haven't heard anything from the doctor as to when he can do it so I guess I'll wait a week or so and if he doesn't let me know I'll get in touch with another doctor. I'm not worried about it, dearest.

I guess I'll go to the show with the girls tomorrow night as usual – I like to go once a week at least. Sunday afternoon if it's nice out I'll go for a walk with Ann or Dot.

If you get a chance to call, dearest, could you call around noon as I'll probably go out about 1:30 or 2:00 o'clock. I'll be home for supper any way and most likely Sunday evening too – you can use your best judgment, dearest.

I'll be so glad to see you, darling, in another week (maybe). The days are long (and nights too) sometimes.

Take care of yourself, dear, you're such a good sweetheart. I love you.

Love Always,
X X X X X Rita X X X X X

P.S. Keep smiling!

Did you hear about the moron

Who thought "No kidding" meant Birth Control – I don't get this one
Who thought the word "Asphalt" meant rectum trouble.
Who said of the "Nude Girl", wouldn't she look swell in a sweater.
Who went to the shipyard to find his Blood Vessel.
Who ran around the Bed to catch some sleep.
Who bought a ladder to go to a party because he heard the drinks were on the house.
Who greased himself before going to bed so he could wake up oily (early)
Who kept knocking on the Lamp Post because he saw the light up there and knew someone was home.
Who came home in the rain, put his umbrella to bed and stood in the corner and dripped all night.
Who took the clock to bed with him because he heard it was fast.
Who poked out both eyes so he could go on a blind date.
Who went to his girlfriend's house when she had a little on and a few months later, when he went back, she had a little moron.
Who kept shooting himself in the head with buckshots so his hair would come out in bangs.
Who kept running around the top of a cracker box because it said tear around the top.
Who lost his girlfriend – he forgot where he laid her.

I marked the ones I think are funny (ha ha).

Friday 5/14/43
Fish Day.

Hello Rita Dear,

Lots of Love and kisses to my heart beat and my fiance Recived your letter dated Thursday evening and I am sure happy to recive your nice letters each day. The boys in my outfit and our fellow mailman say's that I sure do have a very nice girl. A girl that writes each day, without missing a day, the say she sure is a very true and good and sincere girl. They say that I am very <u>fortunate</u> in having such a fine a girl as you. So see dearest, what a find and upright girl you are. Congratulations to my lovable and true girl. Rita Marie Lavery.

I had some fun last night on the Ayer town patrol, between chasing speeding cars with the city policeman you see we work and cooperate with the local policeman.

There are always plenty of soldiers even officers drunk, that we have to handle. very seldom do the M.P.s have to arrest them. We try not to if we can get away without to much trouble.

It is a very nice day today I am writing this letter on the near porch, the sun is nice and warm.

Rita dear you are my Love and my inspiration I will give you some nice kisses dear when I get home. I hope to get home the week after this, but with so many fellows leaving and more coming in, it looks pretty bad. But maybe a new batch will be coming in soon. There are suppose to be some coming soon. But I think I will make it tho. Love. Walter.

P.S. So glad that you and Dot can get together on your future vacation

Sunday 5/16/43 – 11:45 A.M.

My Dearest Walter,

I thought I would sit down before dinner and start this letter to you, sweetheart.

Friday night I called up your sister, Martha, and talked to her for a while. She said she hopes you don't think she's forgotten to write to you – she's had a letter all written for the past few days but just didn't get to mailing it. You'll probably receive it one of these days. Martha said Adolph was having a week's vacation this week and they were planning to go up to Poughkeepsie to see the apple blossoms in bloom – just to spend a few days tho, as they were planning to do quite a few things around their house the rest of the week. She said they stopped at your house last Saturday night to see your father and went to Cherry's with him for a while. Martha says your father is lonesome by himself and I guess he'd like Helene to come home, if only for a day or two each week to catch up on the housework. Adolph went to the doctor as his stomach was bothering him and he's on a diet now as the doctor said it really wasn't his stomach but the trouble was due to the kidney that he had removed a long time ago. He's much better since he's been staying on his diet.

Last night (Saturday) I went to the show with Dot Smith and saw "The More the Merrier" with Jean Arthur and Joel McCrea. It was a very good comedy. The other picture "Follow the Band" was a musical and also very good. After the show we went to the "Star" to have a sandwich and we met Ann Preston, Ruth Landry and Eleanor, Ann's brother's girlfriend. We all sat together and talked. I was glad we met them as I was kind of tired sitting with Dot listening to all her plans which I've heard hundreds of times – that is continual talking about Ernie, what a wonderful fellow he is, how considerate + thoughtful etc, etc, etc. I couldn't get a word in if I wanted to. Some girls are like that – I can understand it – they love a fellow so much they can talk for hours and hours about him. That's one thing I try not to do, I think our love is just as strong as anyone elses, (in most cases stronger) and I don't think you or I talk a person's ear off about each other, do we, dearest? (ha ha)

Enclosed is picture of Dot Grant that was in last night's paper – I thought you would like to read the piece underneath it. She's chosen, as you can see, her mother + father's 25th wedding anniversary for her wedding. That's the date I always had in mind, remember, dearest? (June 5th). I'm going to the church but not to the reception.

Thomas was rejected in New Haven Friday. I guess he'll never be taken as his ear is really bad. He said he asked to be put in a non-combat division doing postal work but the doctors there told him they had too many in limited service now, in fact they would not take any more fellows and put them in 1-B, they would either be put in 1-A or 4-F. That doesn't mean that the ones who are in the service now in 1-B like yourself will be changed tho. Charlie had to go over to the Internal Revenue yesterday with him – as I mentioned in Friday's letter, they were to issue a warrant for his arrest, if he didn't get in touch with them. They are giving him until this coming Wednesday to pay for the last half of 1941, so I guess he'll pay it somehow. Charlie told him he'll have to lead a different life from now on or he won't let him live here. I don't think he'll change, though. It seems impossible.

Dearest, I do hope you can get a pass next week-end. I would love to see you and have you home. Please let me know, dear, Friday or Saturday if you do. Then I can meet you when the train comes in and you can come here for supper. We'll have such a nice week-end I know we will. I'd better not count too much on your coming, tho, heh, dearest?

I hope you received the box I sent you by now and that you enjoy all the goodies. Give some to some of the boys too, dear. I have a carton of gum for you but I might save it until you come home. If you need some now, let me know, dearest, and I'll send it during the week. If you need anything in the line of shaving utensils, toothpaste, ties, or anything else let me know, darling I'll send you a few things. I haven't sent you things like these because I thought you had plenty but I'm not sure. I love to buy things for you, I get such a pleasure out of it.

I mentioned to you before I guess that I was going to start buying things for our home (yours + mine). Well, I'm still getting the books from time to time. I have all the sets now but two which I hope they'll send me soon – also the bookcase. Then, darling, what a collection of books you and I will have! They'll be something that will last a lifetime, all types of books, novels, poetry, verse, autobiographies, histories, etc. You + I will always have something to read. Jeanie is still getting those glasses for me. I have quite a few now – all different kinds. I saw a nice pair of embroidered pillow cases and a sheet with a blue border on it that I'm going to buy. Eventually, I'll buy some blankets, towels, linens, etc. – something each week. You and I want to be well prepared don't we, dearest?

I might buy one of those cedar boxes to put the things in – (the type you put your clothes in during the summer) only they are low and wide. You will get a kick out of it, too, dearest, when I show you the things as I buy them from time to time.

Well, dearest, I guess I've rambled on enough this time (ha ha). I hope you're not falling asleep now.

I'll be thinking of you, darling, be a good boy.

Love Always,
Colleen (Rita)

I hope I can give you these in person next week → X X X X X X X X X X X

Selects June 12 for Wedding

MISS DOROTHY IRENE GRANT

Mr. and Mrs. John Henry Grant of 219 Berkshire avenue announce the engagement and coming marriage of their daughter Dorothy Irene to James Henry McGuire, son of Mrs. Mae McGuire and the late James McGuire of 42 Monroe street, Milford. The wedding will take place on June 12, the 25th wedding anniversary of the bride's parents, in St. Charles' church at 10 a. m. A reception will be held from 2 to 5 p. m. in Journey's Inn. No invitations being issued but friends are invited.

Tuesday 5/18/43 12:30 P.M.

Hello Sweetheart,

I hope this letter will find you well and happy. I didn't receive a letter from you yesterday, dearest, but I imagine you were too busy to write or else the mail is slow in coming. I hope there's a letter home waiting for me tonight, tho.

Darling, I'd suggest when you come home that you bring all of my letters that have accumulated and put them in your leather bag. They'll be easy to carry that way. They must take up a lot of room now among your other belongings at the Fort.

A girl in the office lives in Stamford and commutes every day from there. She said that starting May 23rd (Sunday) the train schedule will be changed – so if you do happen to come home this week-end we can inquire Sunday when you're going back what the new schedule will be. I'll inquire about it, darling, I just thought I'd tell you. I do hope you call Friday night or Saturday to say you are coming – I'll be at the station with bells on.

6:15 P.M. I just finished reading your letter written yesterday noon. It's perfectly alright that you couldn't call Sunday, I understand. I know it's hard for you to get a phone on Sunday as all the boys like to use them on that day.

I was disappointed, though, dearest to hear that you might not be home until six weeks from your last pass. Gosh, dearest, I hope you have some luck and can make it this week-end.

Where are you on patrol this week, dearest?

Mr. Patterson (the man Betty worked for) has left our office. He was told to leave as he didn't get along with Mr. Lincoln, our Vice President. Everyone feels very badly as he was well-liked by practically every one. A collection was taken up for him today – we are going to have a luncheon for him this coming Saturday at Wally's in Black Rock. Then we'll present him with the money we collected. So far they have $65.<u>00</u>. As yet he has no prospect of another job – no money and a wife + three children. I guess he'll appreciate the purse we give him.

I have just taken out a hospitalization insurance policy. There was a representative from the insurance company at our office today explaining the whole thing. It has nothing to do with our company, that is, it won't be deducted from our salaries each week, we'll send the money ourselves. For $1.30 per month I'm entitled to $5.00 per day for 30 days, $2.50 per day for the next 150 days + $25.00 for miscellaneous expenses if I ever have to go to the hospital for anything. This will go into effect June 1st so if I have my wrist taken care of after that, the operation will be all paid for by this policy. The operation will probably cost almost $50.<u>00</u>. Maternity cases are also covered by it if it's in force for 10 months. I think it's a good thing to have, don't you, dearest?

Here are a few jokes:

Beaut: "How is it Bill never takes you to the movies any more?"
Cute: "Well, one evening it rained and we stayed home."

(ha ha)

Rookie: "What's on the menu tonight?"
Camp Cook: "Oh hundreds of things."
Rookie: "What are they?"
Cook: "Beans!"
(ha ha)

Passenger "Will I have time to say goodbye to my wife?"
Conductor "I don't know – how long have you been married?"
    (ha ha)

Well, dearest, I'll be keeping my fingers crossed so that you'll have good luck this coming week-end – you'll let me know later about it, as you said.
Lots of Love and Kisses,
Your Rita Marie
X X X X X X X X X X
P.S. I love you, dearest, you're such a good sweetheart.

Thursday 11:25
Post 6A.
Post Laundry
Post tailor Shop
Working from 12 noon to 4:30
12 midnight to 4:30

Dear Rita

    I am on interior guard duty this week, maybe next week I may get on a town patrol again. it take time, a little at a time Yes Rita that hospitalazation insurance is sure a good thing that is useing good <u>forsight</u> dearest.

    Lots of Love to my sweet little irish girl.

    Lots of kisses to my fiance. Rita dear I could give you some nice kisses, I could love you for a bout two hours steady. O. Boy do I feel in the mood for some nice loving with you dearest. I bet you feel the same too dear. Ha. Ha. Well it wont be long now, than I will be able to give you some kisses in person.

    I am fine and am getting along O.K.

    thanks again for the nice daintes and cookies and candy

    ita I could hug to you like a bear.

    I could squeas you so tight dearest. Boy you know <u>me</u>. Boy I am a devil.

    Lots of Love to my fine and upright girl

    Keep Smiling dearest.
Lots of Love from
your Soldier Boy.
Walter J

Friday 5/21/43 3:30 P.M.
Rest Period

Dearest,

How are you today, sweetheart? It has been raining hard all day and is very dreary.

Ann Preston took the day off as her boyfriend called her up from Virginia last night and said he would like her to meet him in New York as he has a three-day pass and wanted to visit his mother in Long Island. Ann left this morning for New York to spend the week-end at his home. I'm glad as she hasn't seen him since February.

Another girl in the office, Eleanor Dalton, who lives in Stamford had a telegram from her boyfriend, who's in the Navy, stationed in California that he was coming home by plane. She was tickled to death as she hasn't seen him in six months. They might be married and then live in California.

It gave me such pleasure to see the happiness on her face as she was telling all the girls in the office about it – also when Ann told me her good news she seemed so over-joyed. That's how I am when I know you're coming home, darling. I'll finish this later (when I go home).

6:15 P.M. I received your letter written yesterday noon. I had to laugh at you dearest when I read what you said about "being in the mood" for a lot of loving. I know you, Kleiny. You're a big wolf with a capital <u>W</u>. (ha ha). If you do happen to come home this week-end I'll bet I'll have to put you in a straight-jacket (ha ha).

The O.P.A. has clamped down on pleasure driving again. People who own cars can only use their cars for work as of midnight last night. Of course when you come home you will not be stopped, darling because you're in uniform.

Dot Smith + I are not taking our vacation together after all. A situation has occurred with Dot that leaves her finances in bad shape. In fact my own finances don't look too good now – income tax is due June 15th ($38.00) and an insurance of mine is due in June ($12.89) so I guess I'll postpone my vacation until Cele and Charlie take theirs. Dot and I have mutually agreed that this will be O.K. so it's alright.

Darling, if you do find out you're coming home Charlie will be here until about 3:30 tomorrow (Saturday) so you could tell him. I'm working until 12 noon, then going to the luncheon on Mr. Patterson, stopping downtown for a short while + will be home about 3:30.

Lots of Love and kisses, dear,

X X X X X X Rita Marie

P.S. I do hope you can come dearest. I know you'd like to come too.

Fish Day
Friday 5/21/43

Dear Rita,

Lots of hugs and kisses to my fiance

Rita Marie Lavery of 1440 Stratford Ave, she is my sweetheart. <u>Heh</u> <u>Kid</u>. Rita I like your walk, I like your talk, I like the very ground you walk upon Give my regards to Ruth and the girls. Thanks for the address Gertrude and Ed. I still do not know any more about the passes, But I hope that I am lucky enough. Heh darling Maybe I will be lucky toget one. I sure will be happy to hear that I am going to get one. Rita here is a nice long kiss, a <u>longy</u>, <u>longy</u> Big kiss.

It will now be pretty tough for Anns Brother. now that he is stationed so far way. But he will get used to it. <u>I hope</u> It sure was so nice when he was stationed so close at Jersey. But that only lasts so long.

Here are three big Hugs and squezes dearest.

Lots of Love Rita dear, Now I have to go to work, I just got up from bed. I manage to get enough of sleep on the double, somhow. You know me if there is a will there is away. Ha. Ha.

Love, Love. <u>Walter</u>

Saturday 5/22/43 9:15 P.M.
(Feast of St. Rita)

Dearest Walter,

Received your letter written Friday saying you didn't know at the time you were writing if you would get a pass this week-end. Well, dearest, when I didn't get a 'phone call from you by the middle of the afternoon I knew you couldn't come home. I know you must have been very disappointed, as I was too, but I have a feeling you'll come home next week which will be five weeks since your last pass. The last time you came (Easter) was the fifth week since your previous one, if you remember. So, darling, try not to be too discouraged. I know the time must seem very long since you've been home, (it seems like months to me instead of weeks) but if you come next week-end it will be extra nice because Memorial Day is Sunday. There's going to be a parade in Bridgeport also one in Stratford in the afternoon. You and I could go to the one in Stratford like we did last year, remember, darling? Let's keep our fingers crossed, dear, and maybe my feeling will be right.

As I mentioned in Friday's letter, I went to the luncheon the office gave on Mr. Patterson this noon. It was very nice. It was held in Nalle's in Black Rock. Almost the whole office went. We presented him with a wallet with $75 in it. He was very touched when we gave it to him. After it was over each one of us went up to him and said goodbye – wished him luck and all that sort of thing. We were all sorry to see him go.

From there I went downtown to buy Dot Grant a shower present. I bought a cake set (a large cake plate and six individual ones with a knife to match). Tuesday is Dot Smith's birthday. I felt like buying her something so I bought her something personal that she can use in her trousseau when she gets married. I know you're dying to know what it is so I'll tell you (I know you,

Kleiny) It's a satin slip (a very fancy one). Ha ha. Guess what else I bought, dearest! Three sheets and three sets of pillowcases for my hope chest. This is only the beginning, darling. I expect to buy a dozen each of sheets and pillow cases before I'm finished, eventually of course, not all at once. Dearest, you can't imagine what a kick I got out of buying them – I guess because it's the idea of buying things for our home, but I suppose a girl would take more of an interest in those things than a fellow would. What do you think, darling?

Well, dearest, I'll sign off now until tomorrow. I wonder what my sweetheart is doing now. My thoughts are always with you, dearest. When you do come home, we'll have such a lot to talk about, won't we, dearest, about all our hopes and dreams – I think talking about these things helps us to keep our courage and gives us a wonderful goal to attain, also gives us confidence in the future which we must have in these trying times.

Good night, dearest – X X X X X X X

Sunday 1:15 P.M. 5/23

Here it is Sunday and it's a beautiful day. The sun is shining but it's still rather cool. I went to 10 o'clock Mass as usual. I wish you could have been there with me, dearest, because the priest (Fr. Brady) gave a very good sermon on Matrimony. He took the marriage vows apart phrase by phrase and said it looks now, in the last decade especially, that couples are forgetting their solemn promises which they make the day they get married. He stressed mostly the woman's place in marriage. He said lots of brides today when they answer "I will" to the vows they mean "they will" until somebody better comes along. When he said that, everybody in church laughed. He believes the woman's place is in the home but now of course he thinks they should work while the war is on – they have to work to do their share in helping to win the war. He also mentioned about men's respect for women. He thinks in the last decade, too, a lot of men have had to lower their opinion of women because the women themselves have acted in such a way as, drinking a lot, smoking too much, dressing like men etc. that this tended to spoil the man's "ideal" of a girl. I think this is all true don't you?

Your sister-in-law, Ellen, called up this morning to ask if you were home this week-end. She was telling me about a boat Al bought last week and said I should get a Coast Guard permit in case you come home some week-end when it's warmer and the four of us can go out in it. You won't need one tho, being in the service. I'm supposed to go to the Coast Guard station on Stratford Avenue and get an application, have my picture taken and then I'll get a pass. It seems like a lot of red tape to go thru just to go out in a boat but I suppose they have to be very cautious in these times. I guess I'll get one soon.

Dot's coming over this afternoon and will stay for supper I guess. She said Ernie sent her a bracelet for her birthday which is Tuesday. It's the stretch-band type in gold. She'll wear it when she comes I guess.

Dearest, I've enclosed $5 that I think you'll need when you do come home for train fare. It's part of your money that I'm saving. I'll replace it myself so don't worry about the money dwindling away. (ha ha). Try to hold on to it so you can use it for train fare. I know you'll need it as you won't get paid until about next Tuesday or so. I hope you have enough for any other little expenses you might have. If not, I can send you more if you want. When you do get paid June 1st I wish you would get those shoes you were looking at before. The rubber soled ones are too heavy for the summer. Please don't go without things just to send money every month. If you can save $15 or $20 every other month it will be O.K. When we do get married we'll have enough money, don't worry, dearest.

It's about a quarter to two now and you haven't called. I know you mustn't have time or you would. It's alright, dearest, I understand. Take care of yourself, darling, I know you'll be home soon.

Love Always,
Rita Marie
Your Colleen and Sweetheart,
Also Fiancée (ha ha)
X X X X X X X X X X

May 26, 1943 – Wednesday, noon

Dearest,

How's my sweetheart this very rainy day? It's a good day for ducks. I hope you aren't out in the rain, darling, getting all wet.

Dot Smith told me last night that Ernie got another rating – Staff Sergeant. Isn't he lucky? He will get $90 some odd a month and $35 to take care of his rent when he and Dot live down there. Dot says he's worked very hard for it and he is satisfied now, that is, he doesn't care if he doesn't get any more ratings from now on.

The shower last night was very nice. There were about 50 people there – quite a few older women, friends of Dot's mother and aunt I guess. The Blakes were there, Dot, Alice and Mrs. Blake. She certainly got some nice gifts. I had quite a time last night before I went. The gift I ordered in Howland's was supposed to be delivered in the afternoon but it didn't come at all yesterday. I had to go to the novelty store near here and buy another gift the last minute. I finally bought salt + pepper shakers in the shapes of peacocks. They are silver plated. Everything turned out O.K anyway. I'll have to refuse Howland's gift when it does come. Getting back to the shower, Dot Smith, Dot Blake + I sat together. Alice had to help Dot Grant unwrap the presents.

Dot Blake and Joe have set a tentative date in July to get married. Joe expects to get a furlough in July. His boat has been in port (in Brooklyn) for repairs for the past month or so and during that time he's been home quite a bit. He wants Dot to go ahead with all the arrangements – getting a gown, veil, go to the priest and all the other details so that everything will be ready by July. Dot says it's hard to do all this by herself but Dot Smith told her that girls have to make most of the arrangements now, with the boys away. Dot Smith told them all about her plans in August, too. Isn't it funny, Dot Grant has picked June, Dot Blake, July and Dot Smith, August – that is, if everything works out for all of them. I hope it does.

Dot Grant asked me to go to the reception in the afternoon but I told her I didn't think I could make it but that I would go to the church in the morning. I'll finish this letter tonight, dearest.

6:30 P.M. Just read Tuesday's letter. It's a nice one, dearest. Gosh, dearest, you flatter me a lot with all those nice compliments. Thanks for those 25 big kisses, too. Yes, I know you, Kleiny and the two hours of loving you would like – I can imagine! (ha ha).

About coming home, darling – as I mentioned before, a new train schedule went into effect on May 23rd. I don't think it will be a whole lot different from the other one, that is, you should get in around the same time as before (5:30 or so). It would be a good idea, dearest, if you inquire what time you could get one in Springfield, then when you call me, you could tell just about what time you'll get into Bpt. and I can be at the station. I do hope you can come this week-end, dearest. I want to see you so much. I know you are anxious to come home, too.

If you call tomorrow night (Friday) to tell me you're coming, could you call after 7 o'clock as we might eat supper out and there wouldn't be anyone here before then? If you call Saturday morning I guess Jeanie will be here to take the good news or I'll be working until 12 noon if you want to call me at the office the number is 3-4175. I'll be home from work about 1:30 if you call after that. I hope you don't think I'm giving you too many instructions, dearest, but I just want to be sure you're coming – you understand.

Gosh, dearest, I can hardly wait until Saturday to see you. I hope we are not disappointed – that is, I hope you get a pass. Try to let me know what train you'll be on so I can be at the station. If you don't see me when you get off the train I'll probably be where the people sit inside – you know, dear. Good luck to you, anyway, honey bunch.

Love Always,
Your Sweetheart,
Colleen and Fiancée
Xxxxxxx

Monday 5/31/43 6:30 P.M.

My Dearest,

I hope you arrived back at the Fort safely, managed to get a seat on the train and have a little sleep on the way. As the train started to pull out, Cele and I ran down on the platform and looked in the first few cars to see if we could find you but we didn't even get a glimpse of you. You must have been sitting on the side farthest from us. I hope you did get a seat.

I had such a wonderful day with you, yesterday darling. I hope the time we had together was worth all your long hours of waiting for your pass, waiting for trains, etc. I enjoyed every minute. I hope the next time you can come at your usual time, so that we can spend Saturday evening together as well as all day Sunday.

There is just one thing that casts a little shadow on our happiness, darling, and that is when we let our emotions get the best of us. In the future we must both try harder not to let this happen. I know it's hard especially since we want so much to spend at least a little time together alone but I was thinking today if we had discussed some subject such as the pamphlet you sent maybe I could have explained a few things that you might not understand so well and in that way, we would forget our emotions for a while and it might not be so apt to happen. I know you understand, dearest, so let's try this the next time.

About the subject of trusting one another that we were talking about last night, I didn't say much but I just want to tell you now, darling, that I trust you implicitly and I know you trust me completely too. You told me you go to the U.S.O. dances and wondered how I felt about it. Well, dearest, it's perfectly alright with me if you want to spend an evening at a dance or any other diversion you might like, dearest, because I know if you are in the company of fellows or girls you will not think any less of me, as you said, our love is so strong it will endure forever, so use your own judgment, dearest. As for myself, I have no desire (as I told you) to go to dances or any other places where I would meet boys. I am content to go out with girlfriends once a week, write to you every day, work, and look forward to your coming home once in a while and to the time when this mess is over and you and I can be together and live normal lives. Let's not ever bring up the subject of trusting one another again, dear, because you and I both know how strong our love is and always will be.

I'm so glad your sister Helene met Cele. Cele thought she was nice. I hope the occasion arises some time when your dad and my family can meet - - before we get married. They might darling, sometime soon, we'll see.

I was so happy today at work, the girls said I was "glowing with happiness". See what you do for me, dearest. You and I have such wonderful companionship and harmony it seems perfect, doesn't it, sweetheart. Let's work together and keep getting close if possible.

Darling, when you send money this month, I don't think it will be necessary to send a money order. If you put the bills in the letter flat so they can't be seen thru the envelope I think it'll come thru the mail O.K. I think it's trouble for you to get to the post office + make a money order out and sometimes it's a little hard for me to cash them too.

Well, dearest, keep well and happy during the coming 4 or 5 weeks, and then we'll have another wonderful week-end together. I'm so happy right now just because you were home yesterday that I feel as though I'll have enough happiness during the next 4 or 5 weeks.

Love Always,

xxx Rita xxx

Monday 5/31/43
Sunny day
Fort Devens Mass.

Dearest Rita,

You and I sure did have a very enjoyable weekend together, dident we dear.

We missed Saturday night but we sure did all right with the time that we had. Parades, good food, plenty of your nice love, my sisters companionship.

Darling I just read your nice letter that you wrote Friday. Darling you write such nice letters.

Dearest you are the finest girl in the world.

You are my fiancee you and I are going to spend many happy years to gether dearest. Arn't we going too dearest thats if you will have me darling.

Darling I love you so much Rita dear. You understand me so much, we get along so well we sure do have a fine companionship and interest, and a strong Love I manage to get a seat on the train right at Bpt. In those front cars that you told me to get into quickly. Darling you guide me so nicely dearest. I had a good trip back. I sleep about 3 ½ Hrs. Darling I love you so much. Love Walter

(Dearest, please excuse the blots on this page. It looks very sloppy but some ink spilled.)

Tuesday 6/1/43 noon.

Dearest Walt,

I imagine this letter will find you well along into your routine again. I hope everything is going smoothly for you.

Today is June 1st, and it's been raining all day. I'm still thinking of the lovely time you and I had together Sunday, dear. I forgot to mention this in my last letter – it was nice of your sister to fuss for us the way she did at noon and in the evening Sunday. I had a very enjoyable time at your house. That certainly was a nice kiss you gave me on the platform when we were waiting for the train, too, darling. I was a little bit embarrassed with Al + Charlie there but I liked it tho. (ha ha).

Last night I read the pamphlet you gave me "When We Go to Confession". You must have found it very easy to understand when you read it as it was written very clearly. Confession is one thing that is very hard for a non-Catholic to understand but as I explained to you once before it was instituted by God Himself, therefore when anyone goes to confession he is telling his sins to a priest, who is God's representative, that is, a priest has the power to forgive sins – he was given this power by God Himself and it's just as though the person is talking to God. Lots of Catholics, as the book said, are afraid to go to confession – they are afraid of what the priest might say to them. It says in the book too, that people shouldn't be afraid because priests have heard all kinds of stories in the confessional and they must forgive even the worst criminal. I was wondering what you thought of this subject (confession). Did you understand more about it after reading the book?

About your reclassification into 1-A – we did decide, dearest, Sunday that it would be better if you stayed in 1-B (if you have any choice). I just want to tell you, darling, if the doctors examine your burn + say they can perform an operation so that you can be put into 1-A, tell them that you would rather not have it done because it really wasn't the burn that bothered you in past years but you did have a <u>nervous</u> <u>reaction</u>, that <u>you</u> <u>can</u> <u>only</u> <u>stand</u> <u>cool</u> <u>climates</u> and that your doctor at home (Dr. Brodsky) advised you that you should stay in limited service in fact, that he didn't even want you to go in the Army at all, wrote a letter to this effect but you were accepted. I asked Dot if Dr. Brodsky meant the remark that he hoped you would not go out of the country as a general remark, that is, one that he would tell anyone + she said definitely not that he really stressed that it was a good thing you are in limited service and that you shouldn't go out of the country if you can help it. He said you know your limitations so, darling, don't think I'm trying to give you a lot of rules and regulations to follow but please try to stick to eating natural foods, if possible, get as much rest, etc. because, dearest, you don't want to have any of your symptoms back again during the coming years. You feel so well now that I know you're apt to forget once in a while and over-eat and drink but dearest, do this for me, will you please? I realize maybe you won't have any choice + might be compelled to go into 1-A in the future but try your best to stay in limited.

6:45 – I just finished eating supper and finished reading your nice letter written yesterday. Thank you, darling, for all the nice compliments.

Yes, dear, you and I will have many happy years together I know – you and I understand each other so well + we both work together – we are <u>kind</u> <u>to</u> <u>one</u> <u>another</u> <u>considerate</u>, our <u>interests</u> <u>are</u> <u>the</u> <u>same</u>, and have everything that makes happiness. From time to time now, as you said Sunday, I'll talk about your future hopes and plans. Sometimes I might pour out all my thoughts on marriage but if I do in my future letters, darling, you don't have to sit down and write long ones too, just think everything over and of course if you disagree let me know how you feel on the subject. Everything will work out when the time comes.

Darling, I was telling Charlie about your brother buying a sail boat + that we might go out in it sometime. He said he wouldn't go in one as he thinks they're dangerous + was surprised when I said I would (with you). Is that right, dearest, would there be any danger?

Walter, when you write to me starting tomorrow (Wed.) – on the envelope when you write Bridgeport, Connecticut put Bridgeport 7, Conn. The <u>7</u> stands for the <u>zone</u>. The post office sent notices to everyone that by putting this zone number on the envelopes, the letters will get to their destination faster – in fact I think it's practically compulsory now. I don't know what number to put for your letters but I'll find out. Don't forget, darling – <u>Bridgeport 7, Conn.</u>

Well, sweetheart, this is sort of a long letter. I hope you don't think I've gone into detail too much on everything. Lots of love and kisses to you, dearest.

Rita, Your Colleen

Wednesday 6/2/43 <u>Rest</u> <u>Period</u>

Dearest,

I hope my sweetheart is well and happy on this beautiful day in June. Well, dear, I guess I'll have to finish this tonight as the buzzer just went for me to take dictation.

6:30 P.M. Just read your letter written yesterday. It was quite a newsy one, wasn't it blue eyes? (ha ha). I was so surprised to hear that Vinny Racky is married. It must have been a quiet wedding because I didn't see anything in the papers about it. Leave it to Vinny to fall in love with his helper, a riveter at that. I wonder if her name is Rosie (ha ha – "Rosie the Riveter"). Well, I hope he has good luck in his new life – he is rather young to be married.

I was glad to hear that Micky is now a corporal. He'll probably go right up the line now as he's such a conscientious fellow.

Darling, I was surprised to hear that you were slated to go on train patrol. I didn't think you would for a few months yet. I imagine you'll like it – you'll be meeting so many different types of people and it won't be as tiresome as if you were patrolling in one place. You also said that next week you might go into Lowell or one of the other nearby towns. Gosh, dearest, you'll be seeing a lot of the state of Massachusetts before you're finished. One place I always thought I'd like to go is Boston. Cape Cod is a beautiful spot – the water and the sand dunes. If you ever have a chance to go there I'm sure you'll think so too.

If I get a chance tonight I'll call up Ellen + explain to her that you didn't have much time on the pass you had over the week-end – that we'll see them the next time.

Every evening I keep very busy. I always seem to have things to do – washing, ironing, reading, talking to Dot once in a while etc. I'm a busy bee, darling.

When you write to Ernie, please don't mention about Dot having a nervous condition, or going to the nerve specialist as she doesn't want Ernie to know. She told me to tell you not to mention it. I know you won't. I think she should tell him in case it interferes with their wedding plans but of course that's her affair. I hope she is O.K by August. She seems much better even in the last few weeks. Dot said things don't look very favorable for Ernie right now. He has the feeling he'll be sent out of the country before August as he had to fill out a "change of address" card which is sent to Washington and then if he did go out it would be sent to someone else to him with his address on it. I told her not to get too alarmed as it might mean only that he's going to be moved to another state. I hope everything works out for them. There's a possibility anyway.

Well, dearest, I have to do the dishes now because Cele + Charlie went to the show so Jeanie + I are chief cooks + bottle washers tonight (ha ha).

Here's a joke:

Why does it take a girl longer to dress than a man?

She has to slow down on the curves. (ha ha).

A girl in the office told me this one (Virginia).

Love Always,

Rita

xxxxxx

P.S. I love you.

Friday 6/4/43 6:15 P.M.

Dear Sweetheart,

I was glad to hear you didn't have much trouble while you were on patrol in Ayer Wednesday night.

I was thinking, darling, when you make arrests, like the other night (June 1st) when the fellow was arrested for carrying a knife, I should think there would be a record kept of those things and that it would help you get a rating. Is this so, or doesn't it make any difference?

I do hope you can get your new shoes soon, darling. Try again soon and they might have your size.

The heat has been terrific here yesterday and today. It was about 90° this afternoon. It's a good thing it keeps cool in Fort Devens because I know you wouldn't like the kind of weather we are having now. If it's this warm Sunday I guess I'll go swimming in Lordship. I'll probably go there – wear my suit and get a little sun anyway. Ann Preston wants to go so she, Eleanor, her brother's girlfriend + I might take a bus out there and spend a few hours. Ann's brother, Joe, is going to give Eleanor, his girlfriend a diamond for her birthday which is in July. He expects a furlough sometime in July. She is only 18 yrs. old and he's 20. They are a cute couple.

Guess what I bought, darling! A cook book. It's called "Victory Cook Book" and has about everything in it – information on food values and meal planning, how to buy food, table setting and serving and all kinds of recipes. A girl in the office, Eleanor Dolton, who lives in Stanford, is selling them for $1.75. They are worth $3.75 but as she is ordering them by the dozen she can get them at the $1.75 price. I think it's a very good buy. I'll put it in my hope chest, dearest. Cele says I should start studying it now and try different recipes out so I can feed you properly when we get married. (ha ha). What do you think, darling? I won't get it for a few weeks yet but I ordered it. Ann Preston also ordered one and a few of the other girls too.

Thanks, dearest, for telling me you think of me so often and that you like to kiss me all the time. Every girl likes to be told that she's thought of so much and a lot of nice compliments and I'm no exception, dear. I never get tired hearing all those nice things. I hope I can <u>always</u> live up to all of the ideals you have of me, dearest. I think of you, too, dear, so much – of all your ways, all the wonderful times we had together and all the wonderful times we will have, darling. I know we will.

Well, I must go now, blue eyes, as Friday night is cleaning night and I'm going to clean my room + do a few other things. Dearest, if you call Sunday, could you call around 12 or 1 o'clock in case I do go to the beach? Of course if you don't have time, I'll understand. I'll be home in the evening too.

Love Always,
xxx Rita xxx

Sunday 6/6/43 12:30 P.M.

My Dearest Walter,

Well, sweetheart, here it is Sunday again and it is a beautiful June day, much cooler than the past few days – everyone is glad of that because it's been so hot.

At this time last week I was at your house, dear, and you and I were just about sitting down to your sister's very good Sunday dinner. Well, we'll have lots more times to be together (I hope).

I'm back to this letter again – you just called, darling. It was so nice talking to you. I'm glad you're well, dearest, and manage to get enough sleep even though your hours aren't so good right now. I hope your bill wasn't too high, dear, we talked a little over 5 minutes. It's nice of you to call me each Sunday. You're so thoughtful, Walter.

Received your letter written Friday. You say you can hardly keep up with my long letters. Darling, I don't expect you to sit down and write long letters, I just want to hear that you're well, that you're thinking of me and whatever else you want to tell me about Fort Devens. I try not to ask many questions so you won't have to answer so much – don't worry about trying to keep up with my letters.

Yesterday afternoon I went downtown with Cele – Ann Preston had lunch with us + did a little shopping with us too. Guess what I bought now, darling! Two beautiful blankets in Read's. One is a lovely shade of blue + the other a soft shade of rose. They are 80% wool and 20% cotton (which is very good for these times). Read's have what is called a blanket club. They keep the blankets during the summer and in fact until October. During that time I'll pay so much a week on them. They were $12.95 each. Cele thought it was a good idea to buy them now as later on there won't be any wool at all in the blankets. They are the Kenwood blankets, just about the best I could buy. I love them, they are bound in satin and the colors are so nice.

Last night Dot Smith, Ann, Ruth + I went to the show. We saw "China" with Loretta Young + Alan Ladd at the Warner. We ate at the Hitching Post, the only place in the city, that has good food now. The picture was good but of course it concerned the war. Ruth made an announcement to the three of us –

she is engaged! Her boyfriend sent her two money orders from Alaska and told her she'd have to buy the ring herself I mean pick it out herself so she + her mother bought it yesterday in Fairchild's. She didn't have it on last night as it was being engraved. She told us about it tho, It's a solitaire (no side diamonds) + she says it's half a caret. She'll have it Wednesday. I'm glad she did get a ring – she wanted one so much and she was in a funny position as she said she was engaged but didn't have a ring.

Yesterday was June 5th, dearest, <u>our day</u> if you recall – or it will be next year if every thing works out for us. It's rather a coincidence, too, Ruth is having June 5th engraved on her ring – it would be my mother + father's wedding anniversary – so it's a rather popular date isn't it, dearest? You remember George Massey I think. His daughter, Ann, was married yesterday too. She married an Irish fellow, Jeramiah McCarthy in our Church at 10: A.M. She had quite a large wedding. He's not in the Army.

This morning in Church I was thinking of you, darling + said a few prayers for you. Remember, when we were on the platform last week waiting for the train + Malcolm Graham's son + his wife (the young couple) were there too? I guess he's stationed in Devens too. He was in church again this morning with his wife. He must come home practically every week-end. I was wishing it was you + I, kneeling there together, but I guess that's rather selfish – I shouldn't expect you home all the time should I, dear?

Well, dearest, Ann will be here soon and I have to get ready. I haven't eaten dinner yet, either. I should get a nice sunburn today. I don't want to get too much tho.

Keep well, dearest, + as happy as possible. I'll be thinking of you. I miss you so much, dearest.

Love Always,
Rita Marie

P.S. Thanks for putting Bridgeport 7. on your letters. If you ever go to the post office you could enquire what your zone number is up there in Ft. Devens, then I can use it. Our letters will then have a better chance of getting there faster.

Darling, I asked you in another letter but I guess you forgot to answer – Are sail boats dangerous to go out in? I still haven't applied for the coast guard pass. Cele + Charlie think it's dangerous. Let me know what you think. I think I'd like to go sometime with you but of course if there is any danger in them maybe I shouldn't.

XXXXXX

5 A.M. Monday Morning. – Monday morning 6/7/43
New Station Hospital.

Dear Rita.

While everyone sleeps I am pening you a line, even the two ward boys are asleep. the two nurses that are suppose to be on duty, lose themselves about the hospital down the hallway. The nurses are very polite both to the patients and us. They are Second Lieutenants in rating.

I am catching up on my mail to all of the boys.

Andy Chonka – Africa

Charlie Chonka – Newfoundland.

Leon Sablofski – Michigan

Micky Racky – Rhode Island

Ernie Smith – Alabama

Mrs. Ellen Klein – Stfd. Ha. Ha.

I am lucky to get a post like this to catch up on my mail, other wise I could not keep up with them. I write to them once each month.

There is a small drizzel out side. It may rain all day. Boy I hated to get up this morning when the corporal called me to get going and go to work I went to bed at 10 oclock and got up at 3: AM. which gave me 5. Hrs. not to bad. all in all. I will get about another 5 Hrs when I get back at 8: oclock. from 8: to 1 oclock in the afternoon Boy some describing. Heh Rita. Darling I could give you some nice kisses dearest. Boy you and I get along so good. We both love each other so much. We both love to love each other so much. don't we dearest.

I hope you had a nice nite sleep darling. Lots of Love

Walter

P.S. It made me so happy to hear your voice yesterday darling.

Monday 6/7/43 – 6:30 P.M.

Dearest,

Received your Saturday's letter tonight. I knew you would get a kick out of my buying a cook book. Darling, I don't think I can be the best cook in the world as you said but maybe when you + I celebrate our 25th wedding anniversary you can say that (ha ha). I had to laugh at the part where you said it's a good thing I bought it – then we won't break our teeth on pasteries etc.

Dearest, I was so sorry to hear you missed Pfc. rating. It's a shame that boy got it who didn't deserve it at all. Yes, it seems to be the same situation no matter what one does – (what walk of life) if one knows the right people or that is, is friendly with the right ones, drink with them etc. he is apt to get further than a person who is conscientious, as you are + tries to do his best. Try not to get discouraged, dearest, keep on doing your best + the next time the ratings come up I'm sure you'll get one. I know how you felt. You probably feel even now that "what's the use of trying to get ahead at all if you have to handshake with people to get ratings". Well, it is natural to feel this way but what do you + I care, darling, when this mess is over, all the sergeants, lieutenants, captains etc. won't be any better off than any other civilian – their ratings won't mean much then.

You said you felt like loving me when you were writing the letter Saturday even if the nurses saw you too. I wish I could have been there so you could, dear. The nurses wouldn't bother me either. (ha ha).

Yesterday afternoon Ann + I went to Lordship. Eleanor, her brother's girlfriend, didn't come. We didn't get a bus until 3:15 they were all so crowded but we finally got to the beach at about 3:45. We wore our suits to get some sun but didn't go in swimming because the water was ice cold. Very few people were in. I looked for the boys, (your boyfriends) but didn't even see their car. That was the first time Ann was ever at Lordship. She liked it. We just laid on the beach for a while + then Ann was hungry so we went over to "Pop's" (Pristini's) + had a hot dog + soda. We went back to the beach then + sat on the wall for about an hour. We left there about six o'clock. Ann came to my house for supper + left here about 8 o'clock. Dearest, it seemed so funny to be at Lordship without you – I felt lost, dear. I showed Ann our favorite spots (at the end of the wall+ told her about last summer how you, Ernie, Dot + I went swimming 'way down at Russian Beach etc. Darling when you come home again let's spend a Sunday afternoon like we used to there. We could go swimming if it's warm + talk like old times.

Here are the pictures. Only 7 came out. I like the one of you, alone, smiling, sitting on the wall the best. I showed it to some of the girls in the office + they liked it too. Your smile is not forced as it is in some of the others. I might have it enlarged. Helene came out nice in all of them. I like the one of you without your hat on too.

Another thing that would be nice when you come home again is to go for a lobster dinner on a Sunday someplace. I don't like lobster but you do, dearest. I often think of the time last summer we went to Wilcox's in Soven Rock. It was so nice there, wasn't it? Of course, we wouldn't have to go that far this year but a lot of the places around Milford Turnpike (Percy's etc.) specialize in lobster. Try to save about $5.00 dear for next time you come home + we can "really do the town" as you would say. O.K?

Well, dearest, it's getting late + I've rambled on for quite a while so keep smiling, dearest.

Love Always,
XXX Rita XXX

P.S. Have you heard about the moron who went to bed eating pop corn + woke up in the morning with a colonel (kernel) in her bed? (ha ha)

New Station Hospital
Post. 5.
6/8/43 Tuesday Morning 5:30 AM.

Dear Rita,

How is my Sweetheart this fine day. I hope that you are in top's shape and that every thing is just <u>Hunky</u> <u>Dunky</u>. Ha. Ha. It sure was a rainy day yesterday, Boy glad that I had this post working inside.

One thing at least on this post I had a good opportunity to catch up on my mail.

Darling you are my love, I love you so much. I could love you for about a hour before breakfast. boy I am some boy, I sure do like my loving from you. Heh Rita. Well we are only young once and boy what a devil I am. Well I like it just the same. what a boy I am. Ha. Ha.

Lots of Love to my <u>fiance</u> – <u>Rita</u>
You have a big <u>kind</u> heart Dear.

I will get your most welcome letter at the 11:30 A.M. mail call darling. Be a good girl Rita.

Love Walter.

P.S. See what extra time does to a boy. Ha. Ha.

Tuesday. 6/8/43 6:30 P.M.

Dearest Walter,

Received your letter which you wrote at 5:00 A.M. Monday morning. I don't see how you can keep your eyes open at that time of the morning to write letters even if you are on duty, darling. I know it isn't a question of wanting to, though, you just have to, heh, dear?

It must be a nice hospital where you are on duty.

You sure have a lot of letter writing to do dearest, corresponding with all those boys. Even if you write one letter a month to each of them – that's quite a bit of writing I'd say.

It's too bad your hours are so irregular when you're on duty from 4 to 8 A.M. + P.M. Try to get as much sleep as possible, dearest.

Last night I was embroidering a little on the apron I told you I bought about a week ago. Cele gave me a beautiful hand-crocheted center-piece for a table for my hope chest. It's one that somebody made for her when she got married (17 yrs. ago) but she's never used it. She just couldn't seem to find a place to use it so she put it away. It's really beautiful. That's one more thing I have for our home, darling.

Ruth was going around today (I couldn't blame her) with her head in the clouds because her ring is supposed to be ready today. Her mother was to pick it up at the jewelers this afternoon so I and the rest of the girls will see it tomorrow. It's too bad that she won't have the thrill of her boyfriend giving it to her but that's war for you.

All of us here, Cele, Charlie, Jeanie + I have been going through a terrible ordeal this week with Thomas. He has come into the house in a worse condition than he ever did. He has to be practically thrown into the bed by Charlie. Vin was told by a fellow in the post office that he is about to lose his job over there because every morning the fellows get a half hour for lunch from 3 to 3:30 but he goes out and drinks during that half hour and comes back to work drunk. I don't know what can be done with him but I do know he's making a wreck out of Cele. She went to the doctor Saturday as one of her legs has been swelling up every night. The doctor thought that it's all her nerves. He called it odeima of the nerves. He said it isn't serious but she should get lots of rest + have no worries. She is going through with him just what my mother had to go through. It's really a shame. I wish he had been taken in the Army but he does such awful things that no decent fellow would want to associate with him – besides he might influence other fellows to drink if he were accepted.

Dearest, I should get down on my knees and thank God you are of such a fine character. I am thankful, dearest! You don't know how wonderful it is to know that you are.

I hope you don't mind my telling you about him. I know you understand the whole thing. I'll try not to talk about it so much any more but oh, darling, sometimes it's so depressing to have to live with a person like that!

Yes, you + I do get along so well, dearest. We love each other so much. I think of you always, dearest. Please take care of yourself.

Love Always,
Rita Marie
XXXXXXX

P.S. I feel better already since I've written this very depressing letter, so don't worry about me, dear.

Wednesday Afternoon 3: P.M. 6/8/43
Second Platoon

Dear Rita,

Those are wooden building at the hospital, they are spread for about 1 square mile. There sure are plenty of them.

I get at least seven hours of sleep out of twenty four.

So I do allright for my self, don't I dear.

In the afternoon I manage to get two hours of that good Sun. Sun bathing up on top of our three story building, I am getting a tan, slow but sure. Boy that Sun feels good upon my back, nearly as good as when you pat my back, while at the beach. Ha. Ha. So nice of Cele to give you that nice crocheted centerpiece for our table. Heh darling. I am getting a big kick out of all those nice things you are buying. It thrill's me so much, it even tickles my spine. It gives me such nice feelings, feelings I did not even have before. good feeling darling. We love each other so much, that's why. I am so happy for Ruth. best of luck to her.

So glad that you think that I have such a fine character. Darling, I like you to tell me those nice things Dearest.

I sure do understand all about your trying ordeal with your big brother thomas. it is so trying on you all at home. I hope that he very soon will start to streghtin out some. I know that the day will come that he will realize his doings and snap out of it. I am sure that he will. Darling I want you to tell me all and how you feel about everything at home. Lots of Love Walter.

Wednesday 6/9/43 6:15

Dear Sweetheart,

Received your letter written Tuesday 5:30 A.M. while on duty.

Gosh, darling, you certainly were in a lovable mood when you wrote that letter. You haven't said anything about receiving any of my letters so far this week, but I hope you are receiving them each day, dearest. Yes, you are a big devil, Kleiny. I had to laugh at the way you wrote half of the letter + printed the other half. Yes, dearest, too much extra time isn't good for anyone but I know you don't have extra time very often.

Today Ruth came into the office wearing her diamond. She was so excited she hardly knew what she was doing (like I was the day after Christmas). The ring is very pretty. It's a very plain one (a solitaire) no side diamonds + the stone is rather large. I guess it's natural for every girl to prefer her own ring – I like mine much better – of course I wouldn't tell Ruth that (just you, dear). She wants to announce her engagement at a tea on Sunday, June 28th. She invited Ann and I but Ann isn't going because her boyfriend, Willie, is coming home on the 20th. I wish you were coming home that week-end, dearest, then I wouldn't have to go – I don't want to go.

I've decided to give that shower present which I bought for Dot Grant to her for her wedding present. I think she'll like it – it's a cake set – large plate + individual small plates. I'm going to take this coming Saturday morning off to go to see her at the Church (10 o'clock). I'll work Saturday afternoon, though. Dot Smith is giving her a wedding present too.

Bill Hughes was moved from Miami, Florida to Salt Lake City, Utah. He sent a telegram to Betty this morning. She's going out there to live with him if she can.

Ann Preston received a beautiful poem from her boyfriend – (a love poem) that he cut out of a paper. He writes very "mushy" letters too, dearest (ha ha).

Well, dearest, I guess this is all for this time except to tell you that I miss you so much, sweetheart. I wish we could be together for the rest of our lives as of now this minute, but of course that's impossible so I'll just go on loving you, wishing you were here, and wanting the best of good luck for you always,

Lots of love + kisses,
Rita Marie
XXXXXXX

Thursday 6/10/43 1: P.M.
Second Platoon

Hello Darling,

Lots of Love and kisses to my sweet little irish colleen.

Darling you are my hearbeat, I think of you each hour and each day, even while I am half asleep on post in the <u>wee</u> hours of the morning, I am thinking of you, and what you are dreaming off. <u>Ha</u>. <u>Ha</u>.

Darling I wish I could give you some nice kisses now, to express myself somewhat. Rita I never tire of kissing your nice sweet face and your kiss able lips.

Rita sometimes I think I am too big of a wolf, but darling you understand me I am sure, I am just trying to show you my love for you Rita, you have such fine qualities.

I droped Gertrude in Long Island a line last night. Just to let her know that I am still at Devens, and that I am getting along alright, and also to tell her how sweet a girl I have, and how proud I am of you. Dearest Rita.

Lots of Hugs and kisses to my fiance.
Love <u>Walter</u>

Friday 3:30 Rest Period 6/11/43

Dearest,

I hope this letter finds you well and as happy as can be.

The weather here is very nice today for a change, I hope it stays this way for Dot and Jimmie's wedding tomorrow – also for Gladys Franke. Weather is really important because if it rains or is even cloudy, it sort of spoils the effect of everything.

As I told you before, I'm taking the morning off to go to Church. Dot Smith + I will go together. Dot Smith is going to the reception in the afternoon but I'm not as I'll have to work. I'm lucky to get the morning off.

Last night my cousin, Father Pat, came over to the house to talk to Thomas. Cele had been telling Irene (Fr. Pat's sister) about Thomas – what an awful time we've been having with him etc. so Fr. Pat decided he'd better give him a good "pep talk", as he hasn't even been to church since last September nor to confession or Communion long before that.

Fr. Pat told Cele that she would be perfectly justified in putting him out of the house if he doesn't change as she has more than done her duty towards him for the past year + a half. Cele always said her conscience would bother her for the rest of her life if she did put him out, but Charlie is getting tired of the whole thing and so Cele has finally come to the conclusion that she'll give him one more chance. Fr. Pat said she should consider Charlie + Jeanie first + made her promise that the next time she has trouble with him that she will make him leave. I don't think the talk did any good – he was just about civil to Fr. Pat but it might have helped a little – that remains to be seen.

6:15 P.M.Gosh, darling was I surprised to find two letters when I came home from work tonight! You must have been in the mood to write, dearest. It's nice to know that you think of me so much, sweetheart. I'm so glad.

Glad to hear that you're getting a nice tan – you always did look well with a tan. Also glad to hear you're getting such a thrill out of my buying different things for my hope chest (and our home).

You don't know how wonderful it is to know that I can tell you about my difficulties at home (Tom). It helps me to tell you once in a while – sometimes it's unbearable. Thanks a lot, dearest for being so understanding.

I'll tell you about the wedding in my next letter, dear. I might go to the show with Cele tomorrow night. Dot Smith can't go – she's going to confession, Ann is going with Eleanor, her brother's girlfriend + I don't know about Ruth. I wouldn't enjoy going with Ruth, she's too catty + high + mighty. I'll be thinking of you, sweetheart. I hope you have as pleasant a weekend as possible. Darling, if you call Sunday, could you call early like last week because if it's nice out I might go to Lordship with Dot Smith – I'll ask her to come over here.

Darling, if you don't mind my telling you, try to hold on to as much of your money as possible because you'll need it for train-fare + when you do come next time we could go out + "do the town" as I suggested once before. What do you think about it, dearest? What I mean is, that we could go someplace nice for a lobster dinner (you like it) – go someplace dancing, wining + dining or whatever else you'd like to do. Let's follow the song "Let's be foolish while we're young" – (ha ha). You know what I mean, dear.

Well, sweetheart, I'll mail this now so you'll get it tomorrow (I hope)

Love Always,
Rita
X X X X X X
[Image of two hearts labeled Walter and Rita with an arrow
drawn through them]

Sunday 6/13/43 2:00 P.M.

My Dearest Walter,

Here is the piece about Dot's wedding. I also found this picture of both Dot + Jimmie in the Post after talking with you on the phone. The picture is very nice of Dot but I guess the sun was shining on Jimmie and it's not too clear. The description of the wedding says that his brother who's in the Navy was best man but that's a mistake. He couldn't get any leave to come home so Dot's brother, Ed, was best man. Everything about the wedding (at the Church) was perfect down to the last detail. The altar of the Church was banked with red + white roses + gladioli. Father Gloster, the pastor, married them but the other priest, Fr. Dwyer, sang the Mass which was beautiful. The music during the Mass was very good. They sang the "Ave Maria" and "Mother At Thy Feet is Kneeling" (that's the hymn I'm going to have sung at our wedding, dear). Alice Blake looked very nice. You'll notice when you read the piece in the paper that Alma Kaeser, Jimmie's cousin, was also a bridesmaid. If I recall, you said you knew her. She's a very pretty girl. After Church of course, both Dot + Jimmie had to stand in the vestibule of the Church and accept everyone's good wishes. Jimmie was really funny. When Dot + I went up to congratulate him he kissed both of us. He had lipstick all over his face from everyone kissing him. He seemed all excited but very happy. Dorothy was very calm, cool + collected as usual. She looked lovely – as you can see from the picture. They are certainly a lucky couple. They have a rent in Bridgeport in the North End, Beechmont Ave, a very nice section. I hope their luck continues through the years.

Dot Smith went to the reception at Mary Journey's in the afternoon. She said everything was nice – there was plenty of liquor of all kinds floating around the place. It was over at 6 o'clock then Dot Grant (Maguire) went home to her house + she + Jimmie left from there on their wedding trip. They were to stay in a Hotel in New York for one night + then they were going to the place they went last year in New York state "Sugar Maples", a summer resort. Well, dearest, so much for the wedding – I thought you'd enjoy hearing about it.

Yesterday I went into work from a quarter to one until a quarter to five. Then I met Cele + Jeanie downtown and we had dinner and then went to the show. We saw "Forever and a Day" – as usual a depressing war picture. Well, we passed a few hours anyway. This morning I went to 10 o'clock mass and this afternoon I was going to go to Lordship for a while with Dot Smith but the weather isn't nice at all. It's very dull, the sun isn't shining + looks like rain so I guess I'll catch up on some things I have to do.

Darling, it was nice talking with you today on the phone. It has only been two weeks since we've seen each other but it seems so long, doesn't it? Your call each Sunday helps so much, darling. It's nice to look forward to every week. I'm sending you a magazine "Army Laughs" which you'll probably receive Tuesday. I thought seeing you'll be going to school this week you might have a little time to look it over and have a few laughs. Cele was glad to hear that you liked the box she sent.

Ann Preston's boyfriend, Will, came home from Virginia unexpectedly Friday morning. Ann was working of course + didn't know he was at her house until she went home at night. He came at 9 in the morning + had to wait until 6 at night for her. If he had called the office for her to come home, she probably wouldn't have been able to get the time off anyway. He was to go back at 4 o'clock this morning. He is giving Ann a diamond in July – he expects a furlough then (about 10 days) + will buy it in New York. I'm glad – Ann is what one would call a "regular" girl. She has a nice personality. From all I've heard about Will, her boyfriend he is nice too. I've seen pictures of him + is very good looking (he's Italian tho, + I know you don't like them much, dear) but he comes from a very well-educated family. He's one of 7 children – 6 boys + 1 girl. He's a corporal + is trying for sergeant's rating now.

Darling you've probably been wondering why I mentioned in Friday's letter that I don't enjoy going out with Ruth because she is high + mighty. Well, as I told you before, when you met her at Christmas time you sized her up right away as being very much the "I-love-me" type. You were perfectly right but at the time I didn't know her too well + thought she was nice. I've changed my mind since then, in fact, all the girls in the office have all they can do to be civil to her as she puts on so many airs. For example, the day she came in with her ring on, she started to compare it with mine to see which one was larger. She decided that hers was larger – as if the size of a diamond means anything! I told her that if a girl was given a ring from the 5 + 10 she'd think just as much of it than the largest stone a fellow could buy – the ring is just a symbol of the engagement. It is the engagement itself, the knowledge that the couple is closer to each other during the engagement period is what really counts. For the past week Ann, I + the rest of the girls have heard nothing only what a wonderful ring she has – it's the best blue-white diamond the salesman has ever sold (for the money). Every time some one comes near her they get her hand stuck in their face. She's having a picture made of it to send to Alaska to her boyfriend. She's also announcing it next Sunday at a tea + her picture will be in the paper the following Sunday – all of which I suppose is alright if one likes a lot of fanfare. Please try to understand, I don't mean to be catty, I just want to explain to you an example of what she's like. I do like her ring, + wish her the best of luck but I can't really consider her a real friend.

Well, sweetheart, I do hope you can come home in a few weeks. I miss you so much. Keep well + as happy as possible and my thoughts will be with you, dearest. I know you miss me too, darling, but our day will come + when all this is over, you + I can make up for all this separation during the coming years.

Love Always,
Rita
X X X X X X

Wed in St. Charles Today

MR. AND MRS. JAMES H. M'GUIRE
Mr. and Mrs. McGuire, photographed as they left St. Charles' church after their wedding yesterday morning. Mrs. McGuire is the former Dorothy Irene Grant, daughter of Mr. and Mrs. John B. Grant of 219 Berkshire avenue, and Mr. McGuire is the son of Mrs. Mae McGuire of 42 Monroe street.

Dorothy Grant Wed to James M'Guire

Ceremony Held in St. Charles' Church, This Morning.

Miss Dorothy Irene Grant, daughter of Mr. and Mrs. John Henry Grant, of 219 Berkshire avenue, and James Henry McGuire, son of Mrs. Mae McGuire and the late Michael McGuire, of 42 Monroe street, were married this morning at 10 o'clock in St. Charles church by the pastor, the Rev. Thomas B. Gloster.

The altar was banked with variegated garden flowers in a background of ferns. Albert Tordorf, at the organ, and Margaret Tallon Morris, soprano, offered the musical program.

The bride who was escorted by her father, wore a floor-length gown of white marquisette, made with a heart neckline having a deep tucked yoke outlined with a frill, bishop sleeves, and full skirt shirred to a long torso bodice. Her fingertip veil of tulle was caught to a pompadour bonnet of shirred tulle with a cluster of pearlized orange blossoms, and she carried a prayerbook with white stock and streamers dotted with stock florets.

Her sister, Miss Jean Grant, was maid of honor and the bridesmaids were Miss Alice Blake and Miss Alma Kaeser. They wore gowns of marquisette with scallops of val lace, matching bonnets similar to that of the bride with net streamers, the maid of honor in pink and the other attendants in ciel blue. Their old fashioned nosegays of variegated flowers were tied with pink and blue streamers in contrast to their gowns.

The bridegroom's brother, M. Raymond McGuire, Seaman 2c, U. S. Navy, served as best man and Edward Grant, brother of the bride, Henry Mijares of Hartford, and Robert Sennett ushered.

A reception is being held this afternoon from 2 to 5 o'clock at Mary Journey's after which the couple will leave on a trip. The bride will travel in a dusty rose frock with navy and white accessories. They will live at 692 Beechmont avenue.

Monday 6/14/43 6:15 P.M.

Dearest Walter,

How's my sweetheart today? I hope you're in tip-top shape. It is lovely out today, there's a nice breeze and the sun is shining brightly.

Last night (Sunday) I got caught up on a few odds and ends – washed my hair, listened to some good programs on the radio and read a very good story in the "Redbook". I listened to "Manhattan Merry-Go-Round", a musical program at 9 o'clock. Frank Mund at 9:30 and Inter-Sanctum, one of those hair-raising mystery thrillers.

Ann Preston was telling me all about the nice week-end she had with Will, her boyfriend. They didn't go any place special but talked about their coming engagement + their ideas on marriage. She said he bought the ring (diamond + wedding band both) in New York Friday but left it in the store until he comes home again in July. He knew that she prefers the diamonds on the side like mine so that's the kind he picked out. After she receives the ring she's going to start buying things for their home (just like you + I) dearest. Ann is only 19 yrs. old + Will is 27 + will be 28 in July. That's quite a big difference in ages but

Ann acts much older than 19. She's such a nice girl, Walter, I know you'd like her – she has a wonderful sense of humor and one could listen to her talk all day as she has a pronounced New York accent.

Dot Smith wants Mary (the girl who's going to be her maid of honor) and I to get together with her soon and talk over her wedding plans. The time is drawing closer and we'll have to start looking for gowns etc. She said as far as Ernie knows now he thinks everything will be in their favor in August. Dot told me to tell you that she hopes you understand about what you'll have to wear (if you can make it) in August. She said you, Ernie + the best man will have to wear your winter uniforms because they have a coat. I know it will be very hot then but you'll only be in Church about 15 or 20 minutes + after you come out of Church she said she won't care if you take your coat off then, just as long as you can keep it on during the ceremony. Ernie is sending his uniform up here about a month ahead of time so Dot can have it cleaned for him. I told Dot that she should have someone else in mind to ask in case you can't make it – just so she won't count on it too much. She understands – she knows how the Army is just as I do too. I was thinking, Darling, if you are due a pass on the 21st anyway, maybe you could ask if it could start Friday afternoon instead of Saturday afternoon + then could go back Saturday night because if you come at all, you'd have to be here Friday night for rehearsal. I know it's very early yet to know just what you can do, but when the time comes, dearest, try your best to make it – that's all you can do.

Dearest, I wish you were here close to me so I could talk to you – and you could talk to me too. It's hard to write about lots of subjects in letters, it's better to talk to each other personally. I have the feeling you get discouraged sometimes, although your letters seem cheerful but if you were here, you could tell me just how you feel about everything. Am I right, darling? Please try not to get too discouraged, the main thing is to keep <u>well</u>. Sweetheart, maybe I'm all wrong thinking this but let's talk everything over when we see each other.

Love Always,
X X X Rita X X X

6/14/43 Monday 12:05
Second Platoon
Fort Devens Mass.

Dear Rita,

Lots of Love to my sweetheart on this Monday morning. I hope that you are in the best of spirits and health darling.

I want to thank Cele for that nice box of assorted fancies cookies and candies. So nice of her to remember me darling, they sure are nice, I passed some of the candy around to the boys. They said I sure do have some good friends to get such nice boxes of sweet's every now and than. I said well it pay's to have a good girl friend and her family to remember you each day of the year. Someone who is so sincere and kind + nice. I am up on the roof top of our three story building Sunng my self. just after diner, for about a hour of that good old Sunshine.

So that account's for this pencil, (my pen just ran dry) <u>Ha</u>. <u>Ha</u>.

Rita dear you are so sweet, I could give you some nice kisses now dear, about three dozen nice big one's, you know the kind I like to give. <u>Heh</u> <u>Darling</u>

Saturday + Sunday and tonight I am on lowell town patrol with another fellow, a irish boy, his name is <u>(Torney)</u> that's his last name We get along quite well. Lowell is a big textile city. Boy they sure do all like to drink in that city. the population is about 100,000 people, quite large. The Soldiers behave quite well. the hardest time of the month to get along with the service men is just after pay day. thats when the boys feel pretty <u>frisky</u> So happy to hear that Jimmie and Dorothy's Wedding day was so nice. I am so happy for them both. Yes dear Maybe now Thomas will catch on to him self. May be. I hope so, for his benifit + Cele's Jeanie, Chick's and your's. Dearest.

Lots of Love
<u>Walter</u>.

Tuesday 6/15/43 Rest Period 3:30

Dear Sweetheart,

As I won't have time to write before 7:15 this evening, I thought I'd write these few lines to let you know I'm thinking of you, dearest.

If you recall, in one of my letters about three weeks ago I mentioned that I wanted to buy a set of silver from a woman who sells it – from whom Dot Smith bought hers last year. I wrote the woman a letter telling her I was interested and didn't hear from her for about two weeks – then she called to say she'd get in touch with me soon – that she had been away. She called me up last night and asked if it was alright to come tonight so I told her to come. I don't know if she'll have anything I might like but she represents a very reliable silver house in New York. I'm interested in the silver plated sets not the Sterling because silver plated ones are much more lasting + don't turn color like the Sterling. She's coming at six o'clock tonight and I know I won't have time to write to you until about eight o'clock – that's why I'm writing this in the office, dearest. I'll tell you whether I bought a set of silver or not in my next letter and give you all the "ins and outs" – (ha ha).

So you see, darling, you are always in my thoughts even when I'm working.

Well, dearest, rest period is over now and I have to get back to work – I'll write a nice long letter later.

Lots of love and kisses
Rita, Your Colleen

Tuesday Evening 6/15 9:00 P.M.

Dearest Walter,

Received your most welcome letter written Monday at noon.

I thanked Cele for you for the box she sent you – in fact I read the whole paragraph to her in which you gave her all the nice compliments – she said she's glad you enjoyed it – also some of the boys. She also said you have a very nice way of expressing your thanks, dearest.

I noticed that the pen I gave you seems to run dry quite a bit when you write. If you'd rather use your own pen, darling, I could send it to you. I use it all the time, it writes nicely but I could use some of the other pens we have here in the house if you'd like yours. Let me know, dear.

As I told you in my last letter, dear, I expected the woman to come to the house with her line of silver at the time I wrote that letter. She came about 6:30 this evening and I bought the Sterling silver after all. She showed me only Sterling as she didn't have any silver plated with her. The set I bought is beautiful. I bought six forks, six knives, six teaspoons, six salad forks + six soup spoons also one sugar spoon + one butter knife. The price (don't collapse when you read this) $117.<u>16</u>. A silver plated set would be $85.<u>00</u> – so you see the difference in price isn't too great and sterling lasts a lifetime while the silver plated is only guaranteed for 25 or 35 years. I asked her about Sterling turning color very easily and she said when it's delivered (in five weeks) it will come in a chemically treated flannel cloth that will have a little pocket for each piece so that it won't turn in color.

I have a confession to make, dearest. I had to make a down payment of $19.53 tonight so I had to take $20.<u>00</u> of your money which I'll replace as soon as possible. I hope you don't mind my doing this but I didn't have that much money myself as I just paid my income tax. Dearest, I will put it back very soon. When it's delivered in July – July 5th to be exact, I'll have to pay $19.53 more + from then on I will pay $12.<u>00</u> monthly. The first two large payments is really the 1/3 of the entire bill $117.16.

Cele thought it was a very good buy. If I bought it in the stores downtown it would be $169.<u>00</u> at least. The make of the silver is "State House Sterling" and is advertized in most of the well-known magazines. It's really very beautiful. Let me know, dearest, what you think of it. I'll send you a picture showing the design of it in my next letter. By the way, the first of July the price is going up 30% so it looks as though I bought it just in time.

Darling, don't worry about my going into debt or anything buying things for our home – I'll manage well. If I thought I would run into debt I wouldn't buy so much.

I forgot to mention – I had to give her three girls' names and if one of them buys a set of silver I'll get a placing (one) free – that is one each of what I have already bought. I gave Ann's name, Ruth's and Betty's. Maybe none of them will buy any, but I don't mind anyway as I have the service of six which is plenty to start with.

Well, dearest, I certainly have gone into detail about the silver, haven't I? I want to explain fully about everything I buy because all these things will be for <u>our</u> home, dearest (in the future) and I know you are just as much interested in having a nice home as I am.

Well, sweetheart, it's getting late + I'll have to be going to bed soon so this is all for now except that I love you, darling - + think of you always,

Goodnight, darling

Lots of love + kisses,

Rita Marie

X X X X X X

Wednesday 6/15/43 12:10 P.M.

[Wed. was the 16th]

Dear Rita,

Recived you nice letter dearest. You keep my pen dear, I am manageing to get about 12 letters off with this, (your) pen. So that is alright, Heh dear. I'll use it until I wear it out, and it is rendered useless. <u>Ha Ha</u>.

Boy that Sterling Set sure must be nice dearest, I know you have good tastes.

It is alright that you used our money dearest. You can replace it any time. For that matter you can just forget about it. after all I can pay a little something to help out. Heh Darling But darling you spend so much for the Set. Well I suppose it pays in the long run.

I always though one could get a good set some what cheaper. But now days everything is so high. And than again the Sterling you bought must be the best. Right darling. I know if Cele said it was a good buy, I am sure she and you have good judgement and tastes.

Darling I miss you so much. I could give you some nice big Kisses Lots of Love to my Sweet heart and <u>fiance</u>.

Love Walter

Thursday 6/17/43 6:00 P.M.

(Pay Day)

Dearest,

I just came home from work and finished reading your letter. I only have to work until five o'clock on Thursdays.

I'm glad that you like the idea of my buying the silver but I'm surprised that you thought it rather a lot to pay. Sterling silver is the best kind of silver one could buy – it always did cost quite a bit even before the war and starting July 1st it's going up 30% more. I think it's worth the $117.16 since it will last a lifetime.

Darling, you said I could forget about the money I borrowed from your savings. It's very nice of you to say that you'd like to help pay for it, but I'd rather buy the whole thing myself. I intend to put the money back in your account just as soon as possible in fact, today is pay day so I'll put $5.00 of it back tonight. I don't like to touch our little "snowball" (ha ha) at all, dearest, but that was an emergency the other night. As soon as I replace the $20.<u>00</u> I'm going to put all of the money in the bank. Darling, you'll need it when we get married for the wedding ring, the priest and a trip. (our honeymoon, dearest – ha ha).

Today during rest period some of the girls in the office were discussing the subject of whether boys in the Army, those who are going steady or engaged go out with other girls near the camp or the nearest town. One girl said (kiddingly) (but she wasn't kidding) "I'll bet Walter has a girl in Boston he goes to see the times he doesn't come home." Ruth was in on the discussion too and she got a big kick out of that remark. Ann, who hardly knows you said "Walter isn't that kind of a fellow, he thinks too much of Rita to go out with anyone else." I said "Well, (to all the girls) there is such a thing as trusting a person completely but some girls (meaning them) wouldn't know what trust means." I said I hoped if you ever did have time off to go to a nearby town that you have a good time in whatever way your good judgment tells you. I also told them I wouldn't go with anyone who didn't have a fine character as you have, dearest. So I guess I told them what's what heh, darling. Girls, sometimes, are such cats aren't they? I would rather have them pass remarks about myself rather than you, darling, because I "can't take it" very good when they do. Well, so much for that subject. Talk is cheap as you always say.

Darling, I miss you so much too. Also your nice kisses. It will be so nice if you can come home next week-end (June 26th) but I suppose I shouldn't plan on it. I know you'll let me know if you can come. Kissing and loving you (as much as I like to) is only a minor thing – if I could just see you, talk to you, maybe dance a little, or whatever else we might feel like doing together, it would be wonderful. I know you're looking forward to seeing me too, sweetheart.

Lots of love + kisses,
Rita, Your Colleen
X X X X X X X X X

Thursday Noon
Day Room
Post. M.P.

Dear Rita,

Hows my sweetheart this fine day. I know you must be very happy today knowing you are the owner of that beautiful Sterling Set. Heh darling. Nothing cheap about you or me, dearest, the best is none too good for my Sweetheart and <u>Fiance</u>. It sure is beautiful Sterling darling, you have good taste. Yes I think that the Short handles and long blades are the best.

That sure is nice that Betty bought a set too. Thats good for her and also good for <u>us</u>. Ha Ha Yes dear I take very good care of myself, as well as I can under the circumstances. So glad that you think that I am the nicest

Sweetheart. I want to be <u>darling</u> Rita. So glad that you like my letters each day. I try to express myself the best I know how. (<u>Bunny</u>)

I still didn't get my shoes, the supply did not come in yet. I will get them eventually darling. I hope if not this month than the next. <u>Ha</u>. <u>Ha</u>.

Our first Sergeant gave us our metals about two weeks ago, so I am all <u>metaled</u> <u>up</u> <u>now</u>. Ha. Ha.

Rita I could give you some nice big kisses. You know those nice big ones.

Lots of Love,
<u>Walter</u>

P.S. Inclosed is the Pattern <u>dearest</u>

Saturday 6/19/43 10:30 P.M.

Dear Sweetheart,

I just felt like talking to you (in writing) so I thought I'd sit down and write a few lines before going to bed.

I went to the show with Dot Smith this evening and we saw "Lady of the Burlesque" with Barbara Stanwyck and "Leopard Man" – a mystery picture. The pictures were just "fair". Dot and I were roasting in the show it was so hot. The weather has been exceptionally warm today and the Polis does not have air-conditioning. We stopped in the "Star" before coming home to get a cold drink.

Dot's not getting along as well as I thought she was. She said she was very depressed all day and went to the doctor for another injection (she has them once a week now). The doctor weighed her + she lost four pounds. Even while we were in the "Star" she had a crying spell which I guess goes with her nervous condition. I didn't know what to say to her to cheer her up – as all I could tell her was to try not to worry about everything so much – just try to put herself in the doctor's hands and give herself time to get better. The doctor told her it would take him a good three months to cure her but she's losing patience. I told her it took you a number of years to get over yours (thinking that would make her feel better). She's going to give up her job the last week of July and take a rest before she gets married. Maybe she'll feel better if all her plans work out – that is if Ernie comes home, they are married etc. as she's worrying so much over her plans. Incidentally the fellow Ernie was to have for his best man can't get a furlough in August as he's getting one in July so he can't come here for the wedding. Dot says he's going to ask a fellow he used to work with in the Brass Co. Bill May – he's not in the Army. I hope everything works out for them, as I said before, it might help Dot a lot.

I'm all alone, dearest, writing this letter. Cele, Charlie + Jeanie are out and except for the radio going it's very quiet. I was thinking about you a lot today, darling. I always do think of you but today I let my thoughts go back to the first night we went out together – and then thought of all the different happenings from that time on – of all the nice times you + I have had together – right up until the last time you were home, dearest. I was thinking of different things you said when we used to have little talks on our opinions, our feelings, hopes, plans, etc. It's nice to review all those happy times once in a while, darling. Of course, now we must think of the future and although one can't plan from one day to the next in these uncertain times, we can at least tell ourselves that we will be together some time in the future, and that we must be ready for a little sorrow in our lives and a lot of joys – at least that's what we hope isn't it dearest? Do these thoughts run through your mind too, darling, during the long hours when you're on duty? Well, it's 11:30 now so I guess I'll go to bed. I'll finish this letter tomorrow, goodnight sweetheart.

Sunday – 12:30 P.M. Here it is Sunday and when I came home from 10 o'clock Mass this morning Charlie said you had called. Darling, I'm so sorry I missed your call. If you had only called five minutes later I would have been here. Charlie said you had to go on duty at 11:30 so I know it was the only chance you had to call. He said you thought I went to 9 o'clock Mass on Sundays but I guess you forgot – I always go to 10. Charlie said it was too bad you had to spend 50¢ to talk to him instead of me, (ha ha). Well, sweetheart, it was nice that you thought of me anyway. I hope I'm here the next time. You said on the phone that you hope you can come home next week. I hope you can too, darling it would be so nice. I could meet you at the station if I knew what time you'd be in – that is, approximately what time. Well, we'll see anyway + keep hoping.

Darling when Dot + I were walking down main street last night on our way to the show we were looking in the Shoe Store windows. They had those light-weight brown shoes with the buckles at the side (the kind you want) in McAnn's. I got a good idea when I saw them in the window. If you still can't get them at the Fort by the time you come home next time – you could get them in McAnn's when you get off the train if it's before 6 o'clock. The trouble is I don't think the 17th coupon is any good now but I could bring my 18th + you could use that if you have to. What do you think of the idea? The ones I saw in the window were $6.50 – they were very nice I think. That's just a suggestion, darling, if you can get them at the Fort it will be all the better.

Well, dearest, I'm going to give myself a manicure now so my hands will look pretty holding a tea cup this afternoon (ha ha) or should I say cocktail glass? That's what these parties usually turn out to be – a cocktail party. If so, I'll have one cocktail to be sociable but that's all.

Lots of love and kisses,

Blue eyes,

Your Colleen, Rita

[Walter + Rita written in a V-shape of X's.]

Aren't I artistic, sweetheart? (ha ha)

P.S. Notice how crooked the writing is on the first page. No, I wasn't drunk when I wrote it, darling – just tired I guess. (ha ha).

Sunday 9:15 P.M. 6/20/43

Dearest Walter,

I'm home alone again listening to "Manhattan Merry-Go-Round" on the radio. Right now the song "Don't Cry" is being sung by Marian McManus + Alan Hung. It's very nice – in fact the whole program is always very good. Cele + Charlie have gone out to Ethel and Bob Greene is in Lordship, Jeanie is at the movies with her girlfriend and so that leaves yours truly (me) home by myself. Thomas is upstairs in his usual "state" but I really consider myself as being alone.

I came home from the tea at about a quarter to eight. The tea at Ruth's house turned out nice except for the heat. She lives in the apartments (Black Rock) on Haddon St. and I think it's always hot in the summer in an apartment. Walter, I don't think I was ever so warm in my life as I was this afternoon at the tea. So help me, between the wine that was served and the heat I wasn't worth two cents. (I'll bet you're laughing your head off at this). After two servings of wine Mrs. Landry served iced tea but by the time she did we couldn't feel its cooling effect from drinking wine. Well, anyway aside from the heat everything was nice. They had a large cake in the center of the table with two hearts (made of the frosting) on it with Ruth and Don written in each heart, also little sandwiches, olives, stuffed eggs, + the iced tea. There were about 15 people there altogether counting Ruth + her mother, also Ruth's boyfriend's mother. I met Ruth's cousins + some friends. All the girls there seemed to have done a lot of traveling since the war started, some of them visiting their husbands, their boyfriends etc. Two of the girls had been on cruises (before the war) and told the rest of us about Panama, Havana, Haiti + other places. One girl since last June had been to half a dozen different states visiting her different boyfriends. I felt like a child amongst them as the farthest distance I've ever been from home is Cape Cod + Atlantic City. When we left there Ann said she felt like a green horn too. (ha ha), although she has at least been to Canada once. Are you glad I'm the "stay at home type" darling? Traveling once a year (and not too far) is enough for me I guess. (ha ha)

Speaking about traveling, Cele, Charlie + I have our vacation all in the same week, starting the week of July 4th. Cele + Charlie were considering Atlantic City as they've never been there. I'd like to go there again too. I liked it very much the year I went with Mary Connell. It's changed a lot since then though as the Army has taken about ½ of it over – practically all of the hotels on the boardwalk are used by the soldiers + the two large piers are open only week-ends now. I'm not sure if we will go but we will go someplace for at least part of the week. I'm trying to hold the second week of my vacation off as long as possible in case you get a few days, darling. Then I could be with you – we could go to N.Y. for a day to a good play or something. I guess this is only wishful thinking heh, dear?

Tuesday night at 7 o'clock I have an appointment with Dr. McQueeney. I called up to make an appointment to have my wrist taken care of – thinking I could go right to the hospital + have it done but he wants me to go to his office because he wants to look at it first. Then he'll tell me what time to go to the hospital – what day and everything. I'm quite anxious to go + get it over with now. I only hope he doesn't have me go next Saturday as if you do come home next weekend I might not feel 100%. I'll only have to stay in the hospital a few hours anyway + won't be bed-ridden or anything so it won't be too bad I guess.

I called Dot Smith before writing this letter to see if she felt any better than last night + to see if I could cheer her up a little. She seemed better – at least she wasn't crying like last night. She says I understand her better than anyone else – when she tries to explain to other people how she feels they tell her it's just her imagination. You + I know only too well what she's going through don't we dearest? You know from experience + I know from seeing the same condition practically, in my cousins (Fr. Pat – Judge Lavery) + of course you. She seems to think the doctor is just taking her money + is not really interested in her case any more but I told her not to lose confidence in him yet – to give herself more time. I also told her that you helped yourself a lot more than all the medicine in the world could by complete rest – months of nothing but lying on the beach. I guess it's impossible for her to do just that but she is going to give up her job at the end of July. Then she'll have practically 5 weeks of rest before the wedding. I think she's making a terrible mistake by not telling Ernie, at least that she's under the doctor's care but I won't say anything to her – that's her personal affair. Cele + Charlie think it's very unfair to him too because if she has a recurrence after she's married it will be harder to explain then especially to the type of a fellow Ernie is. He never makes allowances for anyone who's sick as he's never been himself. I can understand this tho, but if Dot tried to explain the whole thing now, he might understand it + it would make it easier for the both of them later on.

Well, dearest, this is turning out to be a long letter isn't it? I hope all this descriptive detail isn't too boring. I just feel like talking to you, blue-eyes + tell you that I'm thinking of you + love you so much – I'll finish this letter tomorrow dearest, so for now, goodnight, sweetheart.

Monday 6/21/43 – 3:30 (Rest Period) Well, honey bunch here it is Monday again and another very warm day. We have a large fan here in the office which helps a lot though. I went without stockings today for the first time but I feel very sloppy. It really looks better to wear them I think.

Ruth didn't come into work until this noon today – she was sick this morning. Everyone was kidding her about drinking too much tea (they mean high balls) but she said it was just from all the excitement + heat.

Cele + Charlie had an awful time with Thomas yesterday while I was at Ruth's so when I go home tonight I won't be surprised if he's left the house for good. If Charlie has his way he will be. Cele + Charlie both have been wonderful to him – they really can't stand him any more, but you know how Cele is – she'll be worrying about him even more if Charlie does make him leave. Well, let's hope for the best anyway. Well, dearest the ten minute rest period is over so I'll finish this later.

6:30 P.M. I came home from work tonight + guess who is here now! My brother, Ed, from New York. Gosh, I was glad to see him. He was on business in the Devon Plant + stopped in here for supper. I haven't seen him in a long time – he looks very well, has gained a little weight. He'll be going back to New York in a little while I guess.

I guess you didn't have any time to write yesterday, darling, as I didn't receive any mail today. I hope I do tomorrow, sweetheart – I miss your letters when you don't find time to write.

Well, darling, I'll close this lengthy letter now as I have to eat supper (Fried chicken, incidentally) – that's a luxury now.

Love Always,
Rita Marie
xxxxxxxxxxX

Monday 6: P.M.
Second Platon

Dear RIta,

I recived your two nice letters, the last one a good long one.

Yes I am sure in time Dorothy Smith will manage to overcome her fears and doughts, too bad Ernie could not pat her worried brow. Thats probably what's would help plenty. I am sure. I am sure time will do the job for her. It takes plenty time sometime because the nervous system takes too times as long to repair <u>and</u> <u>tone</u> <u>up</u> as it does to wear down.

Yes I do hope I get my monthly pass this coming weekend. I could use a little time off, especially with you darling dear.

We could go down to Lordship for some of that good old Salt water and Sun. Remember the good old days. Ha. Ha.

Rita dear you are the Sweetest girl in the world. Bunny you are my <u>Love</u>.

Lots of Love.
<u>Walter</u>

Tuesday 6/22/43 3:30 P.M.
Rest Period

Dearest,

As I have to be at Dr. McQueeney's at 7 o'clock this evening I thought I'd write to you during this 10-minute rest period, just so you'll get a letter tomorrow telling you that I'm thinking of you and love you, dearest.

Enclosed is a poem that I think is very nice – I cut it out of the magazine "the St. Joseph's Messenger – Advocate of the Blind" which I think Cele subscribed for. I hope you like the poem too, darling. I imagine hearing the taps played would give one the feeling as described in the poem but everyone can't express himself in writing like that.

Edward took the 9:45 train back to N.Y. last night. It was nice having him at the house for a while. We had quite a conversation. He saw my diamond for the first time (I haven't seen him since before Christmas). He thought it was exceptionally nice, seemed to like it a lot. He asked me if we had the date set yet – of course I said "no" – Cele said "Well, she'll be having a job for you to do when the time does come + that is to give her (meaning me) away. Ed said he'd be glad to do the "honors" (ha ha) when the time does come. I said "Cele surely is preparing you away ahead of time." He said well, I'm glad you told me in advance. (ha ha). I showed him the pictures we took the last time you were home and he thought you looked very well – he could tell you've gained weight. I also showed him the Rosaries you sent + he thought you had very good taste in picking them out. He told me about you writing to Gertrude. By the way, did she answer your letter yet? Ed didn't know. They've put their car up as they don't use it any more. Whenever he goes away on business now he goes by train. He certainly gets around a lot. He was telling us about his different experiences – that is, of people he's met, about the swanky hotels he has dinner in when a lot of his business acquaintances from Pittsburgh come to N.Y. He had a lobster dinner at the Waldorf Astonia in N.Y. last week. There were eight men and the bill was over $40.00. Darling, don't get the impression that Ed talks about himself all the time – we were asking him a lot of questions that's how I know these things (ha ha).

Betty Hughes had a telegram from Bill yesterday. He was moved to New Mexico. She's going there on her vacation the week of July 11th. If she can find good living accommodations, she said she'll stay there. I guess he thinks he'll be stationed there for a while because he'll be going to a school at the Air Base there.

Ann Preston was telling me in the Camp where her brother is in Missouri there are forty fellows in the hospital suffering from a wood tick bite. I never heard of a wood tick bug before but she says they get under the skin + leave sores on the skin + can poison one's whole system. Her boyfriend (in Virginia) said one fellow died from them. Isn't that awful? They come from bad wood – I guess when the fellows are on maneuvers they can get them. Are there any of these in Fort Devens, darling? If so, my Walter better be careful, heh, darling?

Well, dearest, I'd better close now and get back to work. I hope everything is going along smoothly with you – also that there's some mail from you when I get home. Keep smiling, sweetheart.

Love Always,
X X X Rita X X X

P.S. 6:15 P.M. – Since writing the above the doctor's nurse called up + cancelled my appointment. I should be used to it by now – it seems to be a habit with him. I'm supposed to call tonight + let him know if I can make it Thursday afternoon but I don't know whether I will or not yet.

I received your most welcome letter dearest – gosh. I was glad to hear from you, sweetheart. I hope you don't find it too hard to write every day – I know you must, sometimes when you're very busy. I do appreciate your letters a lot.

None of us have seen Thomas since Sunday night. I guess he left the house Monday morning early and hasn't been home since. We don't even know if he's working. Of course Cele is worrying her head off. In fact there's a lot of friction here between her + Charlie over it. I imagine he'll be back one of these days as all his clothes are here. I can't imagine where he could be staying.

Dearest, I love you so much – keep well and we'll keep our fingers crossed so you'll get a pass this week-end. I'll try not to count on it too much though.

Love Always,
Rita
X X X X X X

FOR ONE WHO WENT AWAY

My days still run their even course
With many things to do
To keep me occupied and calm,
But when each day is through
And dusk steals down the quiet street
And stars ride up the sky,
Then loneliness, like sea birds lost,
Becomes a haunting cry.

I stand beside my door each night
With eyes too dimmed to see
The little gate, so silent now,
Through which you came to me.
Here I shall wait, dear heart, for you,
And hope will ever burn,
As bright as any star until
That hour when you return.

Tuesday 11:30 AM
On duty at Mess hall. Guarding <u>Prisoners</u>

Dear Rita.

I recived your nice long letter that you wrote Sunday. Boy it sure was a good long one. Darling you sure do write nice newies letters.

Yes dear you are a nice Stay at home girl, thats good dearest, In that way I know just where to find you Ha. Ha. Darling you are sweet. I could give you some nice long kisses some nice ones. Boy darling I sure do miss your nice kisses, and Loving and companionship. I wish I were with you <u>Bunny</u> now. We could go to the beach at Lordship, for a good swim and some of that good Sun and some good <u>Smoching</u> Dorothy Smith is such a sensitive girl and so serious minded. That accounts for her condition somewhat and the fact she is so small and delicate and the worrying type, So that makes her a easy target for that perticular ailment. But as time goes on, time will heal, plus as time goes on, she will get to understand herself so much more, also she will get to know her capassaties (misspelled Ha. Ha.) and limitationes. She will have to know that she can not keep up with the crowd and this Worldly pace. She will and does require plenty of relaxation and rest, More than the average person. She is about the same type of person as I am. We are what they call a Introvert typ of person, always thinking inwardly, instead of outwardly.. And we are to active for our own good. So that's the story somewhat, dearest, Ha. Ha Love Walter

Wednesday 6:15 P.M. 6/23

Dearest Walter,

I hope you are well on this beautiful June day. It's nice and cool today – not like the past three days which were too hot.

I just read your letter written yesterday and was glad to hear you like my long "newsey" letters – as you call them. I miss your companionship too, darling – also your nice loving (ha ha). Yes, darling, I do often think of the nice days that we spent at Lordship last year, lazying in the sun, swimming, talking, etc. Those days will come again soon, dearest – then you and I can resume our wonderful companionship that we had in the past only then (maybe) we'll be Mr. and Mrs. And it will be even nicer, don't you think so, dearest? Anyway, when you do come home we can spend a few hours at least at Lordship (I hope).

You were right, darling (practically) in your opinion of Dot Smith's condition. She is a very very sensitive and serious minded person, also the worrysome type but I think you're mistaken when you say she's too active for her own good and tries to keep up with people whether she can or not. She probably was like that when Ernie was home, wanting to go out a lot and not having much relaxation but since Ernie has been away she's been very inactive, only going out once a week and getting loads of sleep. I think the whole thing in a nutshell is she's been alone too much leaving her too much time to think about herself + to worry, which is bad for anyone. Well, as you said time is what she needs more than anything – I think by August she'll be her old self again. The doctor thinks so anyway.

Lately I've met so many people who are suffering from "nerves". This morning on the bus I met Ruth Sorenson (Swede's sister) + she is also doctoring for a nervous condition. She said she can only work about 35 hours a week and has been going to bed every night for the past few weeks at 7 o'clock and sleeps until 7 in the morning. She also said at one time she weighed about 140 lbs but now weighs about 105. I guess these uncertain times gets everyone down at some time or other. I'm still surviving it though, darling, so don't worry about me (ha ha). Ruth said she remembers when you spent months at Lordship when you were doctoring yourself, dearest. She said she used to envy you with all that time that you were lying in the sun but she realizes now what you went through.

Well, dearest, I suppose you are anxiously waiting to see if you can get a pass. I am too. Whenever you find out that you are, could you call – Friday or Saturday – whenever you can, dearest? If you call here I'm sure someone will be here to get the call if I happen to be out. Saturday morning I'll be in the office until 12 noon. (3-4175).

If you do come, sweetheart, it would be a good idea to bring all my letters home in your leather bag so they won't take up room at the Fort – also anything else you might want to leave here or at your house.

Love Always,

X X X Rita X X X

P.S. I sent you a half carton of gum. I kept half of it myself, dear because gum is so scarce now and you know how I like to chew it.

6/23/43.

Robbins Pond

Fort Devens Mass.

Dear Rita,

I am now writing while at robbins Pond Suning my self, I have no bathing suit but I am never the less getting some Sun. It is some fun watching them all frolicing about in the Pond and on the beach.

There are about 2 dozen of the boys here with me, trying to keep cool. We managed to get some time off this afternoon, some thing <u>unusual</u>. for us to be off. Boy we could use plenty of afternoon's off. Ha. Ha. I hope to get a pass this coming weekend. I hope so very much. I will surely be happy to see you dearest. Boy it seems so long since I was home to see you. We will have to make up for lost time. We can go swimming ahd have a lot of fun in <u>general</u>. like old times. You know dearest. <u>Bunny</u> Rita you are a good girl I love you Rita Marie <u>Lavery</u>

P.S. I will call if I do get a pass. <u>Bunny</u>.

Lots of Love,

<u>Walter</u>

Thursday 6/24/43 5:00 P.M.

Hello Sweetheart,

Charlie just called the office to tell me to meet him and Cele downtown to eat dinner out tonight so I thought I'd write a few lines now while I have a chance. He'll bring your letter downtown with him (if there is one) and then I can read it for dessert – isn't that nice? (ha ha).

Cele and Charlie have decided not to go to Atlantic City on their vacation but to New York instead for three or four days. I'll go with them, also Jeanie. We are going to stay at the Hotel Taft and see "Sons o' Fun" and maybe a good play. As I mentioned before our vacation starts July 4th, the week after next. I wish you could get a little time off, darling, during the summer and you + I could go for a day to N.Y. and see a musical comedy or something. Well, maybe you will be lucky, dearest.

No one has seen or heard from Thomas since last Sunday so I guess he finally did take Charlie at his word when he told him to leave. We don't even know whether he's working or not. Well, he'll be back for his clothes I imagine as they're still here. Since he's been gone these past four days we don't have that tension in the house like we did before although Cele is worried about him. She is afraid he has no place to sleep but we keep telling her that it is foolish to worry because he always thinks of his own comfort first. I hope you don't mind my mentioning him in my letters, darling, since all the trouble started, but I know you'll understand and know what Cele + Charlie have been going through.

I'm alone in the office now. Everyone goes home at 5 o'clock on Thursdays but I have to make some time up as I have a 5 o'clock appointment with the dentist tomorrow. It's very quiet here now – the office boy is here putting up all the mail. Well, sweetheart, I'll finish this later.

Here I am home again – we ate in the "Star" per usual. There wasn't any letter from you today, dearest, but it's perfectly alright – I know it must be hard to write every day when you're busy – as long as I know you're well and everything's going as smoothly as possible I don't mind so much.

Since writing the above about Thomas we found out from a fellow who works with him that he hasn't been into work all this week and is staying with a fellow (who drinks a lot) on Iranistan Ave at his house. Isn't that awful?

The fellow who was telling Vin this said that Thomas + the one he's staying with (Dick Bassett) are going to be told they are out for good when they do come into work. Cele is all upset over this as she says if he could only keep his job it wouldn't be so bad. If he's let go he'll never get another one. I can't imagine how anyone could go on like he does not caring whether he loses such a good position. Hundreds of people would give anything to have one like it and would do everything in their power to keep it. You would, wouldn't you, darling? Well, dearest, I just thought I'd tell you this new obstacle – so much for that.

I hope you call Friday or Saturday saying you are coming, sweetheart, I surely would love to love you and I know you are anxious to come home, too, darling. I would love to meet you at the station when you do come – when you call, you could let me know about what time you'd be in Bridgeport.

Love Always,
Rita, Your Colleen
xxxxxxx

Monday 6:15 P.M. 6/28

Dearest,

We now have a lot of happy thoughts of the past week-end to hold us over until next month when you come home again. We both had such a wonderful time together, didn't we, dearest? (in spite of the hot weather).

I hope you didn't find it too hot on the train going back last night. I'm glad I went to the station with you, dear, although saying goodbye is getting harder each time. We need each other so much – I need your companionship and love more than anything else in the world – you're so kind and understanding and thoughtful. You helped me so much even over this past week end by talking to me, giving me good, sound advice on my little problems also the big one (Thomas) which the rest of the family has too. It's nice to talk over about the things we'd both like in the future too.

Your sister, Helene, always makes everything so pleasant for us, doesn't she? She's going to call me up tomorrow night and I'll let her know what time I can meet her Thursday to have dinner and go to the show. We should have a nice time. See, darling, I'm trying to take your advice about going out once in a while during the week (with girls – ha ha). I'd like to treat Helene to dinner and the show because she's been so nice to us – that's the least I might do.

Darling, I'd like to explain what I meant last night when I asked if you would want me to work when we are married and the war is over. I've always thought that I couldn't work and keep house at the same time – that is to do it right. You asked what I would do all day at home. Well, washing, ironing, cooking + cleaning + most important of all making everything pleasant for you would be a day's work – if the war continued I would want to work as it wouldn't seem right to stay home under those circumstances – so that's what I meant when I asked your opinion, darling. Of course that's a problem for the future and we don't have to give it much thought now.

Next week at this time I'll be on my vacation – oh boy! Today everyone in the office received a nice surprise – a bonus of a week's pay – mine amounted to $28.00 (40 hrs pay) minus victory tax + social security so it came to $26.32. Now I can replace all of the $20.00 I borrowed from your account, dearest, also buy a bathing suit. It surely comes in handy.

Speaking about money, dear, when you send the money to me this time I'd rather not have a money order. If you send the bills, laid flatly within the letter I'll get it O.K. I think, but keep enough for yourself as you won't get another pay for five more weeks. Buy anything you need, hat, a few shirts + ties + keep some for incidentals. If you don't mind my telling you, darling, try not to loan any more money or go out drinking with the fellows. I know you don't ordinarily, but if you get very lonesome as you said you do sometimes, it would be better for you to go to a dance, show, read or to the Lutheran Center. Don't think I'm preaching, darling but I just want you to take care of yourself. If you send $20.00 I could send your trainfare back to you a few days before your next pass but you use your own judgment, dearest.

Well, sweetheart, my hand is tired from writing so I'll get this out now.

Lots of Love, darling,

xxxx Rita xxxx

Keep smiling, dearest!

Monday 11:30 AM.

Dear Bunny,

I sure did have a very enjoyable weekend with you darling.

Darling you treat me so nice, you are so thoughtful and sweet. I managed to get some sleep on that old chung chung. I got in at 5:15 in the morning, the train was about two hrs late It stops at every hick town. I guess the engineer got thirsty at every little berg. So he must of stoped in to get a good shot of whiskey and beer. Ha. Ha.

This morning the lieutenant gave us a good work out on the drill field. He always gives us the toughest work out on each Monday it seems. Tonight I will manag to make up for lost sleep darling. I will get about ten hours sleep. So that will fix me up some. Darling I could love you for about a few hours now Rita dear. You know me. dearest. Darling we sure did have a good swim at Lordship, I sure did enjoy it plenty with you darling.

I am sure Helene enjoyed herself also. That nice diner and that nite life at Champs and that nice fun at Lordship

Rita darling I love you so much darling we do not have enough of time to express ourselfs, but we do the best we can with the amount of time we have, Darling I gave you some nice kisses, did'ent I dear

Lots of Love. Walter

Tuesday 6/29/43 6:30 P.M.

Dear Sweetheart,

Here is a little poem that I came across last night in the paper. It seems to be just what we were talking about Sunday – that one can never really plan ahead especially in these times. As it reads in the last stanza – the couple Edgar Guest is talking about planned to be together another way but everything works out sometimes anyway (for the best). I guess the best thing to do is just to hope for the best possible future – that's what you + I will do heh, darling?

I called Ellen up last night and told her that it was too late Sunday when you remembered to call her so you told me to tell her you received her letter + writing paper. She said it was alright you didn't call – she realizes time is short on a week-end pass. She said they were out in their boat Sunday but stayed near Short Beach as there wasn't enough wind to go around to Lordship. They went out in it about 3 o'clock + stayed until about 6 o'clock. They're getting a lot of enjoyment out of it. I told her about you, Helene + I being at Lordship swimming and said maybe the next time you come home we could get in touch with her + your brother.

Ann Preston is on her vacation this week. When she comes back to work next week I guess she'll be engaged. I miss her so much in the office. She always livens everything up a bit – that is, between the two of us, we manage to have a little fun in between all of our work (ha ha).

Thomas is still here + hasn't gone back to work yet. He's been sick since he came home Sunday night (of course you know what from). I'll just have to try not to let him upset me too much but it's certainly hard, you understand, dearest.

There's a little girl who lives across the street from me – I went to school with her. She's very tiny (smaller than even I) + is married. Her husband is in North Africa + she is expecting a baby any day now. She's been married about a year. Her name was Helen Callahan + now is Pavone (Italian fellow). Well, what I started to tell you is her husband wrote her a letter + told her to keep her chin up as well as she can because he thinks, from all he's seen, that this whole mess will be over by December of this year. This seems impossible and improbable to me but is nice to hear that much optimism from anyone isn't it, dearest? I like to hear things like that even if they might not be so. I'll bet you do too, dearest.

Hearing that made me think of what you said at the station Sunday. "How nice it would be if you were home, had a job and we could be together like we used to." Darling, let's hope we can soon, then I could begin to show you just how strong our love is + you could too.

Love Always,
Rita, Your Colleen
x x x x x x X

Just Folks

BY EDGAR A. GUEST

PLANS

Never give your heart to plans,
Life is never fixed or set.
No one tomorrow clearly means,
Change may suddenly be met.

Dreams you follow and pursue
With the hope that lures you on,
And the thing you'd planned to do
In a moment may be gone.

Now together here we stand
As we started, she and I,
But there's little that we planned
In those yesterdays gone by.

For in uniform is he!
She a soldier's bride away!
And that's right as right can be,
But we'd planned another way.

Thursday 11:30 A.M.

Dear Rita,

I just got through finishing reading your nice letter that you wrote Wednesday at rest period. Darling you are such a fine and upright Irish

Colleen, I could kiss you so nicely right now <u>Bunny</u>.

Yes darling you should keep your hair looking nice and get your permanent now and than. Darling you know how to keep yourself looking pretty. Leave it to you <u>Darling</u> Yes I am sure every thing with Dorothy Smith will work out for the best, I do hope so much, for Dorothy and Ernie are two swell person's.

So glad to hear that you and my big sister Helene are to go dineing and wineing and to see a good movie. So happy to hear of the good news, that you two finally are getting together for a evening of diverson.

Rita dear you are so swell, I Love you so much. Last nite I was on train patrol, from Ayer to Boston. Boy is Boston a boom City now. something Like New York, but on a smaller <u>scale</u>

The <u>nite</u> before I went to Lowell on patrol doing Town <u>Policeing</u>. It is not a to bad of a town textile City. <u>Ha</u>. <u>Ha</u>. <u>Greeks</u> and <u>French</u>

Lots of Love
<u>Walter</u>

P.S. Yesterday I <u>purchased</u> my new <u>shirt</u> and <u>Hat</u>. <u>Tie</u> Some class. Heh.

Friday 7/2/43

Dearest,

I was so glad to receive your two letters written Tuesday and Wednesday, also the money. They were waiting for me when I came home last night from the movies. Darling, when I send you $5 at the end of the month we'll have $100 – our "snowball" is getting bigger all the time. It gives me a thrill, dear, when you send the money every month. I'm going to put it in the bank in a week or so in my account but any time you need some of it, just say the word, dearest, and you'll have it in a jiffy.

There were so many nice compliments in your two letters – I hope I can always live up to them. I read your letters over several times too, dearest, they're so nice – just like you.

I had a very nice evening last night with Helene. We went to Jeannettes' (across from the "Star") to eat and after a lot of persuasion on my part, Helene finally let me treat her to dinner and the show. I was very insistent about it because she's been so nice to us before. We went to see Judy Garland in "Presenting Lily Mars", don't miss it, dear, if it plays at the fort. It's a musical and there's nothing about the war in it at all.

Last night Helene + I did talk about you, darling, as I said we would. Helene thinks the Army has done you the world of good. You look so well and don't pick when you eat like you used to (ha ha). I'll bet you don't like me to say that, do you, dear? We talked about everything – our likes and dislikes, etc. I told her I'd get in touch with her maybe next Friday (the end of my vacation) and we could go to the beach or downtown or someplace, depending on the weather.

Cele made reservations at the Taft in N.Y. for next Tuesday. We might stay two nights, I'm not sure yet. I'll write to you from there, dearest.

I'll add to this letter when I get home tonight, sweetheart – it's time to go back to work now. X X X X X X

6:15 P.M. I just read your letter written yesterday morning, dearest. I'm glad you bought a hat, shirt + ties, you'll look very nice when you come home next time, darling. I think it's better to be over-fussy about clothes than to be sloppy + not care how one looks. It was hard for you last week to be all dressed up spic + span on account of the heat, everyone was wilted. Some class to you, dear.

Well, sweetheart, I'll be thinking of you all the time over this week-end. If you call, could you make it about 11 o'clock Sunday morning (if you have time, if not, it'll be O.K). I might go to the beach (maybe). As the song says, darling
"When you're away, dear
 How weary the lonely hours"---

That's how I feel sometimes, dearest, but we'll just have to make the best of everything, won't we?

Love Always,
Rita, Your Colleen
X X X X X X

Sunday 7/4/43 1:00 P.M

Dearest Sweetheart,

I was so glad you didn't call up while I was in Church – that I could talk to you, darling. I love to have a 'phone call from you each Sunday. The 8 to 12 guard duty isn't too bad, is it dearest? You can get a little more sleep than when you're on the 12 to 4 shift. Interior Guard Duty must be tiresome tho, it is a good thing you get a break in between going on train patrol and going to school. I hope your good luck continues, dearest, being so close to home – being able to come home once a month and calling up each week. You and I surely have had everything in our favor so far, haven't we darling?

I have quite a bit of news since my last letter. First of all, let's start with Friday night. Ann Preston + "Willie" her fiancé now, came over and spent the evening. I saw her diamond and it's pretty if one likes fancy settings. The only word I can think of to describe it is elaborate. The center diamond is about the same as mine as far as size goes – it has two very large side diamonds, they are so large that you can't see the yellow gold band at all. Just between you and I, darling, my ring is 100% over Ann's but I wouldn't tell anyone that – only you, dearest. As I said before if a person likes fancy settings + extra large diamonds I guess it could be called a nice ring. Willie bought it in Jamaica, Long Island where he lives (that's where Ann used to live). I think if you met Willie you'd like him, dearest. Of course you can tell he's Italian right off the bat – he's very dark complexioned, also his hair + eyes but he's very nice, a lot of fun, always joking just like Ann. He'll be 27 yrs. old this month + looks about 20. Cele met him + thought he was very friendly. He talked to her as though he knew her for 10 years. He said he'd like to meet you sometime Walter, maybe in the future, the both of you might be home the same week-end and the four of us could go out. He has a 10-day furlough right now + doesn't have to be back until Wednesday, is in the Coast Artillery + is a corporal – (wants to try for Staff Sergeant). He thinks he + Ann should be married soon but Ann wants to wait awhile, she's very young yet (19). I bought some ice cream, cookies + soda + we had sort of a party.

Yesterday morning I went into the office + got a surprise - Betty told everyone she was leaving (yesterday noon) for good. She gave up her job entirely + is going to New Mexico to Bill Tuesday night at nine o'clock. I knew she'd go sometime but didn't think she'd leave in such a hurry. She said Bill called her up Friday night + told her to come at once if she could. He has a room for her to go to and can stay with her every night. He said the quicker she got there the better because he had something to tell her but couldn't tell her over the 'phone. Betty thought what he meant was that he thinks he's going out of the country very soon. She's going to stay with him as long as she can anyway. Everyone in the office hated to see Betty go. Within a half-hour a collection was taken up and we gave her $40. Immediately of course there was the question of who would get her job. Everything happens fast in that office. The office manager said he doesn't want me to take it because in the future they are going to fire the Jewish girl who's Secretary to Mr. Lincoln + said he'd rather have me wait until this happens + then I could have the job. Mr. Lincoln is being moved back to Asme (?) Shear + a new man, Mr. Butler is coming in his place Tuesday. Eventually he'll need a secretary (it might be me). If I took Betty's job, although it would be secretary to the Purchasing Agent it would be no advancement at all so I told the office manager I'd wait then + not take it. They might ask Ann Preston if she wants it but I don't think she will as Mr. Trefry, the purchasing agent is an awful person to work for. Betty said she was about to leave anyway as she couldn't stand the job any more. I hated to see Betty leave because, although at times she would get streaks + not speak to anyone, I guess it was because she missed Bill so much + worried over things so much. She + I on the whole got along very well considering that. We always worked together during the 2 – ½ yrs. she was there. Mr. Trefry wrote a wonderful letter of recommendation for her in case she looks for an office job in New Mexico. Some of the girls in the office are taking her out to dinner Tuesday night but I won't be there as I'm going to N.Y. Tuesday morning. I said goodbye to her in the office. I hope she has the best of luck + happiness. She is the one who has kept their marriage as fine as it is (75% for Betty + 25% for Bill) if you know what I mean.

My cousin Eileen (who is married to Dr. Sekarak) had a baby girl last Wednesday. They were living on East Main, had 3 rooms up over his mother but now they're in their own apartment in some new ones that were built away up East Main St. I'm glad everything is over for Eileen she was quite sick during the past months.

You asked me on the phone how Thomas was behaving. He hasn't drank hardly at all this past week as he was recuperating all week from the week before. He hasn't worked in over two weeks + is supposed to go in tonight. He has no money at all. Cele has been giving him money all week + will have to continue giving it to him until August 1st until he gets paid again. She also had to buy medicine for him for his stomach + ear. How anyone can accept a home, money + a lot of other privileges + not give anything in return is beyond me. Last Sunday night after we left to go to the train, he was going out again but Cele called him back + made him stay. She is still feeling sorry for him + he certainly loves all the attention. Well, dearest, you must think I'm very bitter (which I am) but at least I try not to say a word to anyone in the house. It wouldn't do any good if I did so from now on no matter what he does I'll not say anything in approval or disapproval. So you see dearest, in the future when you + I are together + have our own home (rent), you can't realize how happy it will make me to be away from this tension and have you to confide in + help me in my problems.

As I told you on the phone Dot bought her wedding gown + veil yesterday. She bought them in a little store on Main St., the Chain Apparel. I met her at 6 o clock + we went up to the store + she showed it to me. It's beautiful, has a train too. There's one there in Nile green, a beautiful shade, that she wants me to try on next week. Dot also had her picture taken at Brignolo's for the paper. She's going to the priest this week with her mother to make arrangements. She finally explained her nervous condition + about going to the doctor to Ernie in a letter. She skipped writing to him one night as she was very tired + didn't feel well anyway. He wrote a very fresh letter to her saying he didn't see any reason why she couldn't write every night as he did when he was tired etc., etc., etc. Dot sat down + wrote him a long letter + explained just how she felt, about doctoring but told him not to worry because she'd be alright by August. I'm glad she finally told him. She won't get his answer until the end of this week but he'll probably understand somewhat anyway. Dot looked better last night than the week before. She gained another pound back so maybe now she'll improve + won't have any more setbacks. She said she felt better yesterday than she had in a long time. The doctor thinks she'll snap right out of it as soon as she gives up her job.

Well, sweetheart, this is turning out to be a long letter isn't it? As I told you, if you don't find time to write Tues. Wed. or Thurs. it will be perfectly alright as we'll be in N.Y. anyway. Of course, darling, I can get your letters when I get home anyway + I'd love them if you do happen to write. I'll write in N.Y. but the mail might take a little longer to go to Ft. Devens from N.Y. You'll understand, darling.

I'd surely love some of those nice kisses you felt like giving me when you were talking on the phone. We like our loving, don't we, dearest? Maybe in three more weeks we'll have some, heh, dear? (if you come home). I hope you do.

Love Always
Rita Marie, Your Fiancée +
Colleen + Bunny (ha ha).
X X X X X X X

Sunday Morning 8: A.M.
Post. 6 A. Post <u>Warehouse</u>
Interior guard (third Relief 8 = <u>12</u>)

Dear Rita,

I recived your latest letters and also the nice pictures that we took at the beach. Darling I could love you so nice this morning. You know me, Sweetest. So glad that you had such a good evening with my sister Helen, you both should get together more often.

Yes dearest our Snowball is really growing. Before we know it we will have two hundred Dollars. We know how to do it. <u>Heh</u> <u>dearest</u>.

I sure do hope you and Cele and Charlie and Jeanie do have a good and enjoyable time at New York, while on your first week vacation. The Taft Hotel must be a nice place. That Poem or little Joke you sent the other day I had to laugh. The girls in the office sure do alright for themselfs They are devils. I bet there is not a thing they dont know about <u>boys</u> and all the humorous Jokes.

I think the title of that Joke was. (<u>Would</u> you) I do not have it with me, it is in my other shirt with that letter. But I happened to remember about it as I was writing this letter.

You bet I read it first, especially after seeing that tittle. <u>Ha</u>. <u>Ha</u>.

(Would. I.) (you bet I would.) <u>Ha</u>. <u>Ha</u>. Leave it to me, dearest. I am a big wolf. Ha. Ha.

Lots of Love to my Sweetheart and <u>Fiancee</u>

<u>Walter</u>

P.S. Nothing to good for you dearest.) Heh <u>dear</u>.

Monday 7/5/43 1:00 P.M.

My Dearest Walter,

Well, here it is Monday, the first day of my vacation – also Cele's + Charlie's. We all slept late this morning – it was wonderful not having to get up + rush off to work so early in the morning. Darling, I wish you could have a little vacation too, so you could get up when you want to, eat etc. and have some time you could call your own. Maybe before the summer is over you might have a few days at least – I hope so, dearest.

The weather isn't very nice – it rained during the night and now it's very damp + chilly (no sun). We expect to leave for New York tomorrow morning about 9:30 + then will get into New York about 11:00. We'll go right to the Hotel (Taft). Cele reserved two rooms there. We haven't planned every hour but we'll go to a few shows, "Sons o' Fun" – maybe to the Music Hall, maybe go in a few stores as I'd like to get a bathing suit + will most likely eat our meals in the hotel. I guess we'll be back Thursday night. I'll tell you all about it in my letters, darling.

Yesterday I spent a quiet day at home because the weather wasn't good for the beach. We went to 11 o'clock Mass, I wrote you that long letter, darling, + read a good story in "Redbook". The afternoon went by fast. Last night, Cele, Charlie + I took a bus out to Fairfield to visit the Neary's (my cousin Loretta) + had a nice evening out there. They always ask for you, dear, if you were still in Ft. Devens, how you like the Army etc. They think you're lucky to be stationed there.

Today Cele, Jeanie + I will spend the day getting some clothes ready to take with us. Jeanie wants to take so much, you'd think we were going to Europe for a year (ha ha). We'll take one suitcase, a large one, - we'd better not put too much in it because Charlie has to carry it. Last year when we went, he carried it + was weighted down. (ha ha).

I hope you are not kept too busy, dearest. I think about you always, I miss you so much. I wish we could be together so we could tell each other our every-day happenings, etc, like we used to, dearest. Of course I do write all those little things in my letters but it isn't the same as talking to you in person, darling. Well, letters are the next best thing to seeing you, sweetheart, they help us both a lot.

When I'm in N.Y. I'll be thinking of you too, + will be wishing you could be with us for a little diversion.

Love Always,
Rita, Your Colleen,
X X X X X X X X X <u>X</u>

Monday Morn 9: A.M.
Mess Hall
Prison Chasing

Hello, Rita My Little Bunny, I am now at least out of the rain on this Rainy Monday morning. Ha. Ha. I am getting so I am getting to chow the right people that accounts for every thing. <u>Heh</u>, other wise I would be chasing out in the rain, about the fort. Darling you are my <u>sun shine</u> and my sweet little girl, I could give you some nice loving now Rita, you know me. I am not a wolf. am I dear. not much. Ha. <u>Ha</u> I hope you have a very enjoyable time on your trip to New York.

Darling I wish I were with you now, this very minute to give you some nice loving. Boy how I like to love you. <u>Bunny</u>.

It was so nice hearing your voice yesterday darling, you are so nice <u>Rita Marie Lavery</u> you are so intelligent and swell.

Lots of Love
Walter.

Tuesday 1:00 P.M. 7/6/43

Dearest Walt,

Here we are at the Taft on the fifth floor – Cele + Charlie have one room and Jean + I have another right across the hall. The rooms are very pleasant, have a bath, radio, desk although aren't very large.

We arrived in Grand Central about 12 o'clock + took a taxi to the hotel as it's quite a distance. It was so hot on the train + a lot of people had to stand. We managed to get separate seats. I agree with you, darling, they should have <u>all</u> air-conditioned trains.

Well, dearest, Cele, Charlie + Jeanie are relaxing while I'm writing this. We are going downstairs in the Grille Room to eat lunch now so I'll finish this later.

9:45 P.M. Sweetheart, we are back in our rooms now after a very enjoyable day – boy, you should see us all lounging around we're so tired from the hustle-bustle of this N.Y. whirl. This noon we had lunch downstairs here in the Grille Room + during luncheon Vincent Lopez + his orchestra played + broadcasted for one-half hour from 1:30 till 2:00. After he broadcasted he still continued playing until 3 o'clock. His orchestra is very smooth + I could have listened to him play the piano all day. The Taft Grille Room is like Zimmerman's (remember, dearest where you + I ate dinner Labor Day) but on a smaller scale. It's certainly beautiful. Also during lunch a lot of couples danced – we watched them for quite a while. There were so many soldiers, darling, with their girlfriends + wives, also a lot of couples who looked as though they were on their honeymoon. I was wishing you were with us, dearest, so you + I could have danced.

We left the Grille Room about 2:45 + then bought our tickets for Sons o' Fun for tomorrow night. ($3.30 per seat). After that we went to Radio City Music Hall + saw the picture "The Youngest Profession" (not very good) but the stage show was very nice. We didn't get out of there until 7 o'clock. Then we ate dinner in Child's, walked around a little more + then came back here to the Hotel. We were going to another show but that will wait until tomorrow, we are all so tired. Cele says she likes N.Y. just for one day + night that's all – She said she wouldn't mind checking out of the Hotel late tomorrow afternoon + going home but we have seats reserved for Sons o' Fun for tomorrow night (Wed.) so I guess we'll stay until Thursday.

Everything is so expensive, especially food. Our rooms are $6.50 each + you can see for Cele, Charlie + Jeanie it amounts to quite a bit – I don't mind so much – it isn't so bad just for me. Darling, I had $31.00 this morning + tonight I have $21.00. Trainfare (round trip ticket) lunch + dinner, the show + $3.30 for tomorrow night's show accounts for $10.00. It's a good thing I only have a vacation once a year isn't it, darling? Oh well, I don't mind – You know me don't you, dearest? (ha ha).

Darling, I've certainly given you all the details on our trip so far haven't I? I know you like to hear all about everything.

Dearest, I think about you all the time even in N.Y. Maybe some day you + I can spend a few days here (when we're married) would you like that, sweetheart? I'll write more tomorrow, guess I'll go to sleep now.

Love Always,
Rita, Your Colleen.
X X X X X X X X X X

Tuesday 4: PM.
Military Police

Dear Rita,

I recived your two nice long letters and I am so glad to hear from you dearest each day.

Yes Jeanie sure must be very happy, I can just picture her picking all of things with great enthusiasm, she is a great kid.

I hopd you all do have a very enjoyable stay at New York. I am sure you will dearest Rita.

I just came down from the roof after haveing a nice sun bath, than I took a nice warm and later a cool shower, So now I feel nice and comfortable, so nice I could love you for a few hours before I fall out at Seven oclock to do a little guard duty. Heh dear. Boy I am quite some lover dearest. I never tire of loving you Bunny dear. I lost my old pen somehow, It was no good any how, I am going to buy a cheap one at the P.X. this one I am useing is a cheap one I borrowed from my next bunkie. It is pretty good and only cost about .75 cents of a dollar.

Boy that letter you wrote Sunday was a good long one also a nice newsie one.

Darling lots of Love, to my Fiancee Rita Marie Lavery.
Love
Walter

Wednesday 7/7/43 5:15 P.M.

Dear Sweetheart,

We are in our rooms right now relaxing a little after going through a lot of stores since noontime.

The weather here today is very windy + it has been raining off + on. It didn't dampen our spirits much though.

We didn't get up this morning until about 9:30 + left the hotel about 11 o'clock. We ate breakfast in the coffee shop downstairs – then took a taxi over to Macy's Store as Cele wanted to buy some dresses for Jeanie. We looked around in Macy's, Gimbel's + Sak's but didn't get any. We ate lunch in Child's about 1:30 then took a bus down to Fifth Ave. + went through Kresses' 5+10, Woolworths', Arnold Constable's Dept. Store + a few others. Darling, you'd just love to go through these large 5 + 10¢ stores (Kresses' + Woolworth's) they have so many things that you don't see at home – all kinds of novelties to wear + for a home, really nice things – they are huge stores, one could spend a whole day in them + still not see everything. Charlie likes to go through them but not the regular Department Stores – he always leaves us when we do + meets us later.

I think we'll be starting for <u>1440</u> tomorrow afternoon. As I told you in my last letter, dearest, we're going to see "Sons o' Fun" tonight + after maybe a little wining + dining (ha ha). Tomorrow for the rest of the time we'll be here, we'll go to the Paramount to see Bing Crosby + Dorothy Lamour in "Dixie" and the Andrews Sisters in person on the stage. We like stage shows better than movies, you do too, heh, darling?

I'll bet you're wishing you could be with us, dearest. I wish you could too. You'd certainly enjoy yourself – well, maybe in the future. My thoughts are always with you, sweetheart.

Lots of Love, hugs + kisses,
Rita, Your Fiancée.
X X X X X X X X X X

Thursday 7/8/43 10:00 A.M.

Dearest,

I got up about an hour ago and right now we are waiting for Jeanie to get dressed so we can go out to breakfast. She's had one of her sick headaches all during the night – she gets them every once in awhile from too much excitement. She's a lot better right now tho, so I guess she'll be O.K.

Last night we went to see "Sons o' Fun" and the funniest thing happened. Our seats were on what's called the second mezzanine (it's really the balcony) – we were a little disappointed because we thought for $3.30 we could at least get seats downstairs. Anyway, we were sitting waiting for the show to start + all of a sudden I turned around + saw your sister Helene + Ellen also another girl whom I didn't know. Was I surprised! Helene said they had just come to N.Y. for the day + were going home right after the show. It seemed so funny to meet someone from home – especially Helene + Ellen. The show was very long. It started at 8:30 + was over at 11:30, but was really a riot. Ten minutes before it started the ushers played jokes on the people coming in. They brought quite a few of them right up on the stage + as the girls were going up the steps they pulled a little trick so that their dresses went away up almost over their heads. (ha ha). You never could tell when they'd do that + was it funny to see the expressions on people's faces! The usher showed one woman to her seat, went to help her take her coat off + then started scratching her back (ha ha). There were a lot of other jokes – I'll tell you later. There was a lot of music in it + dancing. You'd like it, dearest.

Well, it looks now as tho Jeanie won't be able to go out with us for breakfast after all. Cele + I will go downstairs to the Coffee Shoppe + Charlie will stay here until later.

I've been wondering how you've been, sweetheart, I hope everything is hunky dory. I miss your nice letters, darling. I'll write later, dearest.

Love Always,
X X X Rita X X X

Thursday 12: AM.
Post. M.P.

Hello Rita,

How is my sweet little irish darling today, I hope you are feeling fine and that you had a very enjoyable time in New York with Cele, Charlie and Jeanie, I hope that you stayed <u>sober</u> Ha. Ha. <u>Heh</u> Rita dear. I am a devil am I not dearest. Dont mind my kidding Rita Marie Lavery.

I could Love my sweetheart so nice right now dearest. you know me Rita, Darling I could hold you so tight to my <u>busom</u> and kiss you tenderly. I would kiss you until I would be all out of breath and ready for a good long rest or sleep. Boy I am such a big wolf and devil. But you know me dearest dont you. I heard from Ernie yesterday, I get a letter from him each month, he is so happy now because in seven weeks or so he will be a married man, he can hardly wait. He wants me to try my utmost to try to be at his wedding, I will do my utmost to get a three day pass, because I want to be at his Wedding so much.

I hope that Dorothy is now feeling much better, she is such a good girl, I think when she is married she will feel much better. <u>Heh</u>, <u>dear</u>. I often think of your brother Vincent and Eleanore, I hope there are doing allright for themselfs and that he continues to work for the C.P.L. Co. They make such a nice couple and get along so well.

I bet Betty Hugh's is now so happy to know that she can now stay with her Husband Bill, at least for a few month's any way. She is sure very good to Bill and sure does her share of the marriage. I am sure you will do just as good and even better – Heh dearest Rita.

Rita you are so sweet and delovley.

Lots of Love to my Fiancee.

Love <u>Walter</u>

Saturday 7/10/43 11:30 P.M.

Dearest,

I came home from the show a little while ago, found myself alone (Cele + Charlie are out) so I read your last two letters over (Friday's + Thursday's) + thought I'd sit down and answer them. They were such nice ones, dearest. I had to laugh at them Walter, I can imagine the mood you were in when you wrote them – you must have felt very "wolfish" (ha ha). No, darling what I really mean is you must have felt very affectionate (that sounds better doesn't it?). Anyway, dearest, I surely would enjoy some of that hugging + kissing you felt like giving. I wouldn't mind some of it right now.

I went with Dot Smith this afternoon to try on a gown she thought would look nice on me for the wedding. They didn't have my size but they fitted a larger size of exactly the same style as the one she had in mind + it looked good as it has a lot of fullness to it. We decided to take it so they're going to order it in my size. It's a beautiful shade of Nile green. Just six weeks from today is the wedding (if everything turns out alright – I hope). You said in your letter that Ernie wants you to try your utmost to come. Well, I know you will, dearest, you + I both want everything to be fine + dandy. Dot said to be sure and try to get here Friday night for rehearsal – so everyone can practice at least once to know what to do. I do hope you can get a three-day pass at that time but I'll be more than satisfied if you can just be here for the wedding. You'll have to ask pretty soon won't you dearest? I don't doubt that Ernie is very happy thinking about all his plans. Dot is improving very slowly she's beginning to look a little better now so I guess by August 21st she'll be her old self again. Incidentally, she went to the pastor of St. Charles Church to make arrangements. Fr. Gloster, the pastor, has the reputation of being definitely against mixed marriages + tells people so in no easy terms. Dot said he was very nice to her, though, he asked her quite a few questions about Ernie – where he was from where he was stationed, how old he was etc. He gave her a form to be filled out + to be signed by the Chaplain of the Camp whom Ernie will have to go to for six instructions which are necessary in case of mixed marriage. Then Fr. Gloster will get the special dispensation from the Bishop.

When Dot brings this form back to the priest, signed, then he can tell her what time the wedding will be + make all arrangements – music, flowers on the altar etc. Dot said Ernie was to go right away to the Chaplain for the six instructions so there won't be any delay I guess.

Well, dearest, I just felt like talking to you for a while – now I don't feel so lonesome. I'll finish this letter tomorrow, darling so for now good night, pleasant dreams X X X X X X

Sunday 12 Noon 7/11/43

Hello Darling,

It was so nice talking with you (on the phone) – the three minutes went by so fast tho, didn't they, dearest? I was so glad to hear you had so many hours sleep last night. I hope you have time to go to the show tomorrow to see Judy Garland because it's a good musical, you'd like it. The one we saw last night "Mr. Lucky" with Cary Grant + Lorraine Day was good too although it wasn't a musical. It was at the Warners' – Dot + I went after I bought the gown.

It was a coincidence meeting that fellow who knew Vin wasn't it? Yes, they are taking bus drivers now. Vin will probably be going within the next six months or so.

My vacation is almost over (one week). I don't know whether I mentioned it to you before but I'm taking my second week the week ending Aug. 21st. (Dot's wedding). If you do happen to get three days, darling then I can be with you. Dot + I will probably go a few places that week – it'll be the last chance I'll have to be with her because she + Ernie will be going down to Alabama the following week. Gosh, I'll surely miss her. I'm going to give her a small shower in about 3 or 4 weeks. I might ask Mary (the maid of honor) if she wants to give it with me. I'll only have about one dozen people there + will have it out someplace – maybe the Hitching Post. It's always customary for the attendants to give a shower on the bride-to-be. Darling, by Sept. 1st. I'll have to file bankruptcy (ha ha).

I saw Dot Grant (Maguire) + Jimmie Maguire downtown together yesterday. Jimmie doesn't look well at all, he's so thin – I guess he must be working extra long hours. Dot looks the same. Jimmie was very friendly but Dot just gave us a very cold "hello" + kept on going. I saw her alone the week before downtown + I was with Cele. She rushed right by when I stopped to talk to her + just said "hello". Cele even noticed that unfriendliness too. She certainly doesn't act very happy for a bride. Oh, well, that's how she's always been – never friendly with anyone.

I hope the next two weeks go by fast, dearest for you + I then maybe you can get a pass the week after next. We could have another nice week-end together, dance a little maybe at Pleasure Beach, go for a swim etc. Darling, keep well + happy as possible, I want to think of you that way all the time – don't give yourself too much time to get lonesome, sweetheart – then it won't be long before you'll be giving me those nice kisses you've been talking about in your letters.

Love Always,

Your Colleen, Rita
X X X X X X X X X **X X X**

Monday 7/12/43 6:15 P.M.

Walter Darling,

I hope my sweetheart is well + everything is going along smoothly for you today. It's been a very hot day here.

I went back to work today and everything is so changed in the office. In fact every day there are so many changes made we don't know whether we're coming or going. They are always getting new people in and continually moving the desks around. Someday I expect to go in + find myself having to sit on the roof. Wouldn't that be funny, dearest?

I went over to Dot Smith's yesterday afternoon = she was in the midst of one of her very depressed spells over letters which she keeps receiving from Ernie over some certificate he thinks is necessary for her to send to him pertaining to getting married. He says he has to have it so that when the Army doctors give him an O.K. on his blood test he must have it so the doctor down at Camp can fill it out. For the past month he keeps asking Dot to get it + she inquired different places + there's no such thing when a couple gets married in Conn. Even Dr. Brodsky inquired about it + found it isn't necessary at all. Ernie won't believe the doctor nor Dot nor anyone for that matter. The last letter he wrote was so insistent about the whole thing, Dot is all upset over it now. Mrs. Smith says if he keeps writing such letters she'll have to sit down + write him a good stiff one. You know Mrs. Smith, Walter, she's so outspoken. They kept kidding me saying when you + I get married I'd have to go through the same thing – I know they're mistaken, tho, because you wouldn't write such letters, darling. Mary, the girl who's to be the maid of honor was there yesterday + she's going to give a shower the week after next on a Sunday for Dot. I guess it didn't occur to her that I'd like to give it with her – I mentioned this to her but she seemed to have all the plans made. She's inviting the club (that used to be) + is having about sixteen there altogether, so now I'm just going to have a few girls, Ruth + Ann, Mary + Dot + myself get together a few weeks before the wedding + have a dinner party at the Hitching Post (my treat) + we'll all chip in + give her one present. Cele thinks this is a good idea too, also Mrs. Smith. Of course Dot will be surprised.

Well, dearest, my letters from now on will probably contain a lot of information about the wedding. I hope you don't mind my talking or rather writing about it so much – I know you're interested tho, aren't you, darling?

Darling, I wish you were here now so I could tell you how much I love you.

Love Always,
Rita, Your Colleen
X X X X X X

Monday Morning 11:30 A.M.

Dear Rita,

How's my sweet <u>Bunny</u> Rabbit this warm July day, I hope you are fine and that you are saving those nice kisses you said you would like to give me on the phone yesterday, Bunny Rabbit. Ha. Ha. <u>Dearest</u>. So glad to have been able to talk to you yesterday on the phone, you are my sweetheart and fiancee, I could give you some of my nice kisses, some of my nice big one's, those nice loving kisses, those very <u>hot</u> ones dearest, Boy am I a devil, I am a big wolf, but you know me, It must be the hot weather, I better keep out of the <u>hot</u> <u>Sun</u> Heh <u>Bunny</u> <u>Rabbit</u>.

This is my school week, so I will probably go to see that movie, Judy Garland in <u>Lilly</u> <u>Pons</u>, it is playing at the NO 1 Theatre so I will go to see it, dearest. Bunny.

P.S. I still feel like being kissed very much?

Darling I wish I could hug you close to me and kiss you passionately until you and I would be hasbing for our breath's, Boy I am in a bad way. Heh Rita. But I will <u>cool</u> off eventually. wont I Bunny, like I always do. I am a <u>big</u> <u>love</u> <u>bug</u>.

I am pretty passionate, but not to much, I hope. Ha. Ha. Darling when I get home to see you on my next trip home, I am going to love you until, I will have enough to hold me for a month, and you will also have enough to keep you happy also. Heh Rita dear. See Rita dear I am saving all my Love for you and you alone, I have not been out of the fort for a evening of fin two weeks, so you see I am sincere.

Lots of Love to my Fiancee
Walter.

Tuesday, 7/13/43 7:00 P.M.

Dearest,

Received your funny letter written yesterday morning. I had to laugh at you, darling, describing about the lovable mood you've been in lately and while you were writing the letter.

You said when you come home next time you're going to kiss + hug me enough to hold you over until the next month. Darling, confidentially, (don't tell anybody) I had that same thought in mind today. (ha ha). We never seem to have enough loving do we, dearest? Yes, darling, Walter, we will make up for lost time the next time but we mustn't go too far. We must let our heads + conscience rule us somewhat.

I'm glad you're going to school this week, sweetheart, it might give you a few free evenings to yourself. Two weeks of confinement in one place is quite a long time. Darling you said you were going to see "Lilly Pons" – The name of the picture is "Presenting Lilley Mars". I had a good laugh when I read that. You're so funny, darling, sometimes when you get all mixed up.

You remember Ann Hughes Christenson who worked in our office? Well she left the office last April as she was expecting a baby. Well, last week she lost the baby. It was born prematurely (8 months) + was born dead. The doctors can't seem to find the reason for it as she was so well all thru her pregnancy. It certainly is a shame as she wanted a baby so much + with her husband away (in the Navy) it would have been a blessing for her. That's a terrible thing to happen to a girl I think.

I received another bond today – which makes five I have now. You + I will be wealthy in ten years, dearest, with all our bonds (ha ha).

Our Company is starting a new type of insurance with the Aetna Life Insurance Co. I've decided to take a policy out (40¢ a week deducted from my pay) for $1,000.<u>00</u>. I really haven't enough life insurance now. If I leave the company at any time I can still continue the policy on a 20-year endowment basis or payable on death either one – that's the good part of it – being one that can be continued if I ever leave the Company (which I hope I will some day – ha ha). I think this is a good idea, don't you, dearest? Then I'll have $2,000.<u>00</u> insurance altogether. I think that's enough don't you, darling?

Well, darling, it's getting late so I'll mail this so you'll get it tomorrow. I still feel like kissing you too, darling. Is that bad or good?

Love Always,

X X X X Rita X X X X

P.S. I hope you get the letter-opener I sent today O.K.

Wednesday 7/14/43 6:30 P.M.

Hello Walter Darling,

I just finished eating supper and thought I'd sit down and have my little conversation with you (on paper) – (ha ha). How is everything going with you, sweetheart? – fine, I hope.

Dearest, when you were home last time you mentioned that most of the time my letters are rather conservative. On the whole, I guess they are – I don't usually tell you how much I love you – just once in a while, heh, dear?

I'll tell you in this one just what I've been thinking lately about you + I, dearest. I guess you know without my telling you how strong our love is. As you + I both said a short while ago, one of the reasons why our love is growing stronger is because we have both had time to think of different incidents that happened in the past + in this way reached a better understanding of one another, darling. We always did get along together very well in the past but since you've been away as I said before, I've had time to think of all your characteristics and understand you so well now, darling.

Another reason that I think why our love seems so complete now is because for the past six months since you've been away I've tried to treat you the same way that I want to be treated + you do too darling in your feelings toward me. Do you see what I mean? If two people like you + I, dearest, try constantly to think of the other person's feelings first, give that person consideration, be courteous, show respect etc., naturally, then, our love is so strong it will endure all through the coming years.

I suppose I shouldn't mention the physical part of our love – what I mean is our desire to kiss + be close to one another all the time but you + I can both understand, can't we, dearest, when we don't see each other for four or five weeks at a time it's only natural to let our emotions run hay-wire in the few hours we're together when you do come home. It's really hard, isn't it, when we love each other so much to let our minds rule us, but that's what we have to keep trying to do as I said in yesterday's letter – let our conscience + minds rule us somewhat.

We have a lot of things in our favor as far as marriage is concerned when the time comes. Dearest, I don't want you to think that I've painted a picture for us that our life will be a bed of roses when we are married. You know, too, that we'll have plenty of sorrows, obstacles, disappointments, along with happiness but I know, or I should say, I'm very confident, you + I love each other so much we'll be able to meet each joy or sorrow equally as well without too much trouble. As far as money is concerned, darling, I guess you + I won't have much of it but we'll enjoy life anyway won't we?

You are so sincere, dearest, + frank with me in everything – that's one of your outstanding qualities, - you have a lot of other fine qualities too, also another one is your over-confidence in yourself (in some things) – I would rather have you go on thinking that you want nothing but the best for yourself + for me than to lack self-confidence. You know all of your abilities, dearest, but at times you lacked confidence in yourself to carry them out (before you joined the Army) but now you have gained it I think since you've been away.

I hope all these thoughts aren't boring to you, sweetheart, I just want to tell you once in awhile how I feel about everything. I love you so much, dearest. I want everything the best for you throughout life. You will be my whole life in the future I hope + I'll be yours, dearest.

Lots of love + kisses,

Ritamarie

X X X X X X

P.S. All these thoughts seem rather complex now that I've written them down but if you don't understand what I mean, we can talk when you come home about them. They all mean just one thing – how much I really love you.

Another P.S. – This is what you call a love letter isn't it, dearest? (ha ha).

Thursday 7/15/43 12:45 P.M.

Dear Sweetheart,

I may as well start this letter by telling you about the poem enclosed because I know you'll read it first anyway (ha ha). Do you think it's funny? I'll bet your mind was away down in the gutter until you read the last paragraph (ha ha). Ann Preston's boyfriend sent it to her so I made a copy of it to send to you.

Today is pay day + everyone here is down in the dumps as the new 20% tax was deducted from our pay, also social security + bonds. In my pay all the deductions come to $7.96 + will be that amount each week from now on – as you can see it surely is quite a dent in my salary. I don't think everyone will mind so much, though, as long as the war is over in the near future. I'll never be rich anyway so what's the difference? (ha ha).

Ruth said she received $140.<u>00</u> from her boyfriend in Alaska to put in the bank for him. There is no way in Alaska that one could spend money so he can save a lot. He says there's a chance he will get a furlough in Sept. or Oct, if so they'll get married while he's here. He's never had one since he's been in the Army – he went in last September, so see how lucky you've been, dearest (so far). I'll finish this letter when I go home from work tonight.

6:15 P.M. I just read your letter written yesterday at chow time as you said, dearest. Your 85¢ pen writes good but, darling, I'd rather have you use your own (the one you let me keep) so when you come home next time, please take it back with you – I know you always liked it + I don't think you'd lose it. We have quite a few pens here in the house that I can use when I write. O.K., dear?

Today I received an invitation from Mary Buccino (Dot's maid of honor) to a shower that she's going to give a week from this coming Sunday in the afternoon. That will be the week-end that you'll be home but I have it all figured out, dearest. I'll just make an appearance there, just stay until Dot opens the gifts + that won't take long. Everyone will understand if I don't stay because they'll know you'll be home then (I hope). I do want to spend every minute with you if possible + I'm sure Dot won't mind. Darling, I've been thinking – you no doubt will want to give Dot + Ernie a wedding present so you + I could go in together on one. I could pick it out here in Read's or one of the stores + put both of our names on the card. I wasn't quite sure that we should do this seeing we're not married but Cele says it's perfectly alright, that's just what we should do, so dearest, the next time you send money to me I could take $5.00 out of it put $5.00 of my own + get them something very nice for their home. Mrs. Smith says she hopes people don't think just because they won't be going housekeeping right away that they shouldn't give them things for their home – she said she'll put everything away + save them until they can use them. I'll look around from now on + find something nice that you + I could give. What do you think about this, dearest?

Gosh, darling, as you said in your letter, you certainly were in a bad way for wanting some hugs + kisses. I understand, sweetheart, tho, we'll both have a lot of loving together when you come home – we'll make up for lost time. I wish I could have some of your nice loving too, darling. It won't be so long now before you're home – another week, I hope, but I'll try not to count on it too much – I know how the Army is – let's keep hoping anyway, dearest.

Lots of Love and Kisses, dear,

Rita Your Colleen

(I wish I could give you these in person --> X X X X X X X X X X X

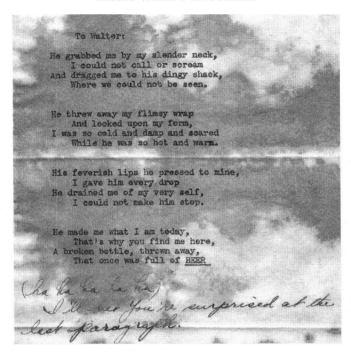

Thursday 12:30
M.P.s.

Dear Rita,

Lots of Love to my sweetheart and Fiancee, I love you Rita Marie so much, I could love you so nicely right now, give you some nice big kisses, Some of my extra big nice ones. Boy Rita I am still in that kissable mood, I am a healthy normal boy or something, Heh Rita. All this week I have felt very wolfish. Ha. Ha. Is it good or bad, Good of course. Heh Darling dear. Rita. I saw Lilly Mars darling, with Judy Garland, it was very good I thought, I also saw that picture with Abbot and Castello in that ice skating picture. That was very good also, it was very funny, I laughed my head off, <u>dear</u>. To bad about Ann's Christenson Baby, I feel so sorry for her, especially now that her husband is in the army.

Those bonds sure will come in handy. Heh dear. We sure will have plenty of use for them in our later years, dearest. Yes dear $2,000 is a just nice sum of insurance for you Bunny dear. Just a nice comfortable sum in any <u>emergency</u>. So glad that you still feel like kissing me dearest Bunny, I hope you still feel like it when I get my monthly pass be prepared dearest because I am going to love you so nicely I am going to love you (In <u>moderation Dear</u>) until you and I are satisfied and contended in showing our Love for each other and to express ourselves. Boy dearest I am surprised at myself. Boy o. Boy. what a Boy. thanks for that nice Lovely Letter opener dearest. Love Walter.

Sunday 1:15 P.M. July 18, 1943

Dearest Walter,

I was so glad you called up a little while ago. Cele + Charlie both told me not to hesitate in reversing the charges when you call – it's perfectly alright any time at all. When they pay the bill I'll give them the price of your call anyway, and even if I don't it's still O.K.

Darling I'm sending you $3.<u>00</u> that I hope will carry you over until Saturday. I'll send you $5.<u>00</u> more Thursday or Friday for your trainfare. It's too bad that you run short of money so often but I think the reason for it is, there are five weeks in most of the months and that makes it quite a long time until your next pay day. We'll work out a system when you come home, dearest, so you won't run short from now on. After sending you these $3.<u>00</u> + $5.00 at the end of the week, then we'll have $97.<u>00</u> in our "snowball" but that still leaves us a tidy little sum, don't you think so Walter? Let's try not to touch it any more tho, I guess I better put it in the bank.

I worked until a quarter of five yesterday afternoon + then met Dot – we ate in "Ye Olde Tavern" and went to see "Stage Door Canteen" at the Majestic. It was one of the best pictures I've seen in a long time. If you get a chance, darling, go to see it.

As I mentioned to you on the phone, it's very very warm here today and I wanted to go for a swim although it is cloudy but Dot called up and said she was too tired – she was going to sleep this afternoon. Her job is really the cause of all her nervousness + everything – she really looks very bad + weighs only 85 lbs. She's leaving work for good next Friday + Dr. Brodsky says he can't help her much until she does leave. He gave her a Wasserman blood test yesterday + keeps telling her she'll be alright by Aug. 21st.

Her plans for the wedding are practically completed. She + her mother made arrangements at Roseland Friday night to have the breakfast + reception there. They're having about 25 people at the breakfast. It's really a dinner – there will be one cocktail served to each one first + then a half a chicken, vegetable, potato, rolls, coffee + dessert. In the afternoon the reception will be from 2 until 6 + I guess they'll have quite a few people there. The owner of Roseland said they'd have the whole place to themselves, would furnish the Nickelodeon for dancing + a keg of beer. They have to buy ginger ale there but can bring their own liquor, so it looks, darling, like the Smiths are really going to "make a day of it." You + I could both have a good time too, dear, if you can come. Dot's inviting the ex-club girls to the reception too – also Ann + Ruth. If I were Dot I'd be worrying about Ernie going to the chaplain down at Camp for his six instructions – he hadn't gone up until last week. If he doesn't have the six instructions they won't be able to get married. Fr. Gloster of St. Charles said to tell Ernie to go right away because it takes about 2 or 3 weeks to get the dispensation from the Bishop in Hartford. Instead of giving all this some thought Dot is worrying about all the little details. The wedding is four weeks from yesterday. She hopes you can let her know if you can make it in plenty of time in case she has to ask someone else to usher. I told her not to worry – that you'd find out soon.

I do hope you come home this week, darling. I know you want to so much too. We could go out to Pleasure Beach + have a few dances in the ballroom – it's always nice + cool out there. Next Sunday is Dot's shower but I'm only going to stay for a very short while so you + I can spend as much time as possible together – maybe you could go for a swim while I'm there or something – we'll see anyway, dear. I bought 8 cocktail glasses for Dot's shower – each one is a different color – in Read's. They are beautiful – I hope she likes them.

Do you still feel like kissing me, dear? (I do).

Love Always,
Rita (Bunny)
X X X X X X

P.S. Ann Preston's boyfriend came home again (72 hr. pass). He was home about 2 weeks ago for 12 days – that's when he gave her the diamond. I hope their good luck continues.

PART III: The Courtship Continues

Religion Could Keep Them Apart

The culture in the 1940s was intensely ethnically divided. Rita's letters reveal her preference for the Irish—along with her contempt for the Italians. Rita was fond of the Irish, as I assume the Lavery family had Irish origins. Each immigrant ethnic group distrusted the other, especially ethnic groups that refused to speak in English, groups that looked different, or that held different religious views. My father, Albert Klein, intensely disliked several of his Swedish co-workers at Bullard's. These co-workers, according to Pop, spoke in Swedish to each other. My father, in his paranoia, assumed they were talking about him.

The ethnic distrust was, in my opinion, rooted in the larger economic struggle as the immigrants strived for a better standard of living. The everyday culture was permeated with an atmosphere of us versus them. Each immigrant group trusted its own people; and generally held others in question and suspicion. Racism existed and was a part of the language and culture in America. Yes, racial tones become evident in the Walter and Rita letters.

Walter and Rita had many issues to resolve. One prominent issue was the matter of church affiliation: Rita was a devout Roman Catholic whereas Walter was raised as a Lutheran. This church background dichotomy was discussed and reappears at length throughout their many letters. In their correspondence during this time period, it became apparent that Rita feels she would be the last of her friends to get married. She believed Walter may have been hesitating to firm up wedding plans because his family might object to their "mixed marriage."

Letters: July 19, 1943 – September 19, 1943

Monday 6:45 P.M. 7/19/43

Hello Sweetheart,

I hope this letter finds you well and also $3.00 richer than you were yesterday, (ha ha), in other words, that you received the few dollars I enclosed in yesterday's letter. I also hope you are not finding the hours on duty too long and tiresome – just this week (what's left of it) and you'll be at 1440 at your little bunny's house. (oh boy!) – at least I hope that's where you'll be on Saturday night at 6 o'clock, dearest. I know you do too.

My silver set was delivered today and oh, it's so beautiful. I can hardly wait to show it to you. I haven't unpacked all of it yet, just a few pieces, but I'm going to look it all over tonight and make sure each piece is perfect. It was packed in a corrugated carton + then in a blue box. Each piece is wrapped individually in tissue paper + is in a chemically treated blue flannel cloth that will keep it from turning color. From now on I'll pay $12.00. per month. ($3.00 per week) on it + it'll be paid for in about four months. I've paid $39.00 on it already.

Yesterday afternoon I was rather lost by myself. As I told you on the 'phone I wanted to go swimming in the worst way – it was such a hot day but Dot was too tired to go, Ann Preston was with Willie as he was home for the week-end, Ruth was visiting people someplace so that left yours truly alone (me). I didn't want to go to the beach alone, even Jeanie wouldn't go + of course Cele doesn't like the beach at all. I managed fairly well home here, catching up on a few things anyway. Charlie went to work at 4 so Cele + I went up to Hollister Ave. + tried to get a bus out to Lordship after supper but they were all so crowded we couldn't even get on. We wanted to go just for the ride to get a breeze. Finally we gave up + came back + sat on the front porch for the rest of the evening. So you see, dearest, if you were home everything would have been perfect – you + I always had such grand week-ends together. Well, I know we will again sometime in the future, in the meantime, we can still look forward to seeing each other every four or five weeks (I hope).

Ann Preston said her brother was home just for a few hours over the week-end and the place in New Jersey where he's stationed now, is an embarkation center. He expects to go out of the country but doesn't know exactly when. He went into the Army the Saturday after you did.

Dearest, I meant to tell you that I notice you've been putting your serial number on your letters lately. Is that so your mail won't be so apt to get lost?

Darling, if you do get a pass this coming week-end I'd like to meet you at the station but on second thought I know you always like to stop in Shonda's or someplace (mostly Shonda's – ha ha) and have a beer or two, also talk to "Sully" and a few of the others, so I guess it'll be just as well if I don't meet you, just try to be at the house by 6 o'clock O.K., darling?

About letting me know if you're coming let's leave it this way. If I don't hear from you at all, that will mean that you're getting a pass + will be here at the usual time, but if you don't get one, could you please call, dearest + let me know? Let me know what you think of this arrangement, darling.

Well, dearest Walter, I guess I'd better sign off for now + get this letter out in tonight's mail. Be a good boy, sweetheart.

Love Always,
Rita, Your Colleen
X X X X X

Tuesday 7/20/43 6:45

Walter dearest,

I just read your letter written at 6 o'clock yesterday morning. You surely are an early bird, dear, with your "penning" as you call it.

Yes, dearest, we'll make up for lost time when we see each other this coming week-end (if you do come), loving each other. But, dear, if we keep hugging + kissing like you say we're going to do, we'll be exhausted and then we won't be able to enjoy the week-end. (ha ha). No, I'm only kidding, we'll try to express our love in moderation. I know you wouldn't want to embrace me so much that I'll be all out of breath (you might want to, but then you'll remember that I'm a little girl compared to you, dearest Walter). I like I mean love all your hugging + kissing tho, dear, I miss it a lot too.

When I unpacked the silver last night I was surprised to find that I did get the extra placing after all. If you recall, I told you Betty cancelled her order + the lady who sold me the silver told her that I couldn't have the extra placing on account of that, but I guess seeing Betty didn't get her deposit back they let me have the extra. I didn't take the paper off each piece, just one off each type. It's surely beautiful – wait till you see it, darling I know you'll like it a lot.

Do you remember the fellow Cele + Charlie asked if you knew him – who was in the hospital in Ft. Devens recuperating from wounds received in No. Africa? Well, he was sent home from Devens Hospital to convalesce at his own home now. Vin + Eleanore went to see him Sunday + they said it was pitiful all he's gone thru + is still going thru from the shock. He's suffering from amnesia, shell-shock + shrapnel wounds in his back. He saw four of his buddies killed right before his eyes. He says they expect him to go back in the Army in the future but he knows he'll never be the same again. He says they'd have to drag him + beat him before he'll ever go out of the country again, that the people here don't realize what the boys who are across are going thru. He says anyone who's in 4-F is lucky – also 1-B – so, see darling, it is best for you to stay in 1-B as long as you can. Of course this seems to be an extreme case, although there are hundreds of other fellows who have gone thru a lot more even than Vin's friend, but it's just that when you know the person, it seems more terrible. Well, dearest, I'll mail this as it's getting late. Take care of yourself, sweetheart.

Lots of Love + Kisses

Your Colleen

X X X X X X X X X X

P.S. I love you so much, darling

Tuesday 10: A.M.

New Station Hospital

Hello Darling,

I am now at the prison Ward with one of our boys from the <u>Hotel</u>, the guard house, but us boys call it the Hotel. Ha. Ha. (Some place). all the boys come here where they can get a nice long <u>rest</u>. It seems as tho the same boys come back at least a half a dozen times. I took one of our boys down to the operating room about a hour ago for a hernia operation. I saw part of the operation the way they give them spinal injection and later I help to lift the patient on those so called wagons or <u>buses</u>, as the ward boys call them. They sure do plenty of operating here at the hospital. The Ward boy said this was the seventh one already – and it was only nine oclock than, boy some business thanks Rita for those nice ties. I sure can always use them. Rita you are so nice. I could give you some nice big kisses dear. I am sure you could also stand some nice kisses. You know some of my extra good Loving and kissing. Dear I am still in that very nice loving mood, I hope you still are also, so when we get together over this coming weekend we sure will make up for lost time, I will love you Rita like you were never loved before by me while home on leave. Boy it must be the hot sun.? Ha. Ha.

I am writing this short letter while sitting on the hospital porch, the sun is shineing so nice, I will be through at 11:30 for the day. I will probaby get some of that good sun being on the roof top later on our barracks. Dear send that train fare early enough so I will <u>have</u> get it for Saturday noon. Because I will be ready to get the bus at 12: noon Sat.

Darling I am still feeling so much like loving you. Boy I am a old <u>hot</u> <u>tomato</u> alway, rareing to go. Darling be prepared for me, because I feel like loving you so much. Ha. Ha.

Lots of Love Walter

P.S. thanks Rita for sending the three dollars. Boy you are right on the Ball. very prompt you are Rita. You are the <u>Sweetest</u> <u>girl</u> in the <u>world</u>.

Wednesday 7/21/43

Dearest Sweetheart,

I enjoyed your letter written yesterday very much. It must have been quite an experience witnessing part of that hernia operation. I got a big kick out of you calling the guard house the "hotel", (ha ha).

I'm glad you like the ties I sent, dearest. You can wear one of them home maybe.

Yes, I'm still in the mood for lots of loving, darling + will be Saturday too. Be careful of staying in the hot sun too long, dearest, if it affects you like that (ha ha). I wouldn't say it's the sun, Walt, let's just say it's because you haven't seen me for quite a while.

I'm so glad you seem quite sure you'll get a pass Saturday. I'm enclosing $5.00 – I hope it's enough until you get home, dearest. The trainfare is over $5.<u>00</u> though, isn't it? Walt, maybe you have enough left of the $3.00 to add to it. I hope so, darling.

All of us in the office had a letter from Betty today. She's living in a little town near where Bill is stationed by the name of Clovis. She likes it there a lot. Bill only works eight hours a day + can stay with her nights. She doesn't know how long he'll be there + is trying to get a job but says the chances are very slim as it's such a small place + there are very few offices or even stores for that matter.

We had a lot of excitement in the office this morning. Ruth's mother called her up + said Western Union had called her home + said there was a Cablegram for Ruth but they couldn't give it to Ruth's mother over the phone + not even to Ruth herself unless she was in her own house. Of course Ruth thought it was from her boyfriend in Alaska + got all excited. Everyone in the office thought that too. Well, anyway, she went home about 11:30 called Western Union + they said it was from her boyfriend's brother in North Africa congratulating her on her engagement! Imagine, what a disappointment! She was so upset she could hardly work for the rest of the day. We all felt sorry that it wasn't from Don saying he was coming home. Ann + I tried to cheer her up. We bought her a "good humor" – (ha ha).

Well, sweetheart, I can hardly wait until Saturday until I see you. I hope nothing happens to prevent your coming. Please try your best to come, dearest. I'll expect you about six o'clock if I don't get a call from you by then. O.K., dear?

Lots of love + kisses,

Rita, Your Colleen

P.S. Your sister Helene didn't call me up at all – I don't know why. Well, I'll see her over the week-end (I hope).

<u>10:30</u> AM. July 22. 1943

Military Police

Fort Devens Mass.

Dear Rita,

How my sweet little irish colleen this fine day, I hope you are in the best of spirits.

I am writing this letter from the New station hospital, I am useing the nurse's desk and pen and ink, she is not to bad of a nurse, some of them are to strick.

I just took a patient down to the operateing room to have a ingrowing toe nail removed. I saw just how to remove one, just in case you <u>dear</u>, have to get one removed. <u>Bunny</u> I am so glad to get this job of chasing in the hospital, that keeps me out of the rain. Ha. Ha. I guess I have been <u>polishing</u> <u>apples</u>, <u>Ha</u>. <u>Ha</u>. as the boys put it. Lots of Love to my Fiancee and Sweetheart. Hope to see you dear at 6: oclock Sat. nite I will keep my fingers crossed. tho dear.

Rita lots of Love to you, and <u>you</u>, and <u>you</u> <u>alone</u> you are a very intelligent girl, with your money and my brains we should go very far. Ha. Ha. Bunny dear.

I wish I could Love you for a bout a half hour dear. I am just in a loving mood. (<u>Something new,</u>) <u>Heh</u> <u>Rita</u> (Love Walter)

Friday 7/23/43 6:15 P.M.

Dearest,

As I'm writing this letter I'm very worried about you, darling. I just read in tonight's paper about the fellows who were killed and some hurt on the way home from a U.S.O. dance in Ayer. All the fellows were from Fort Devens too. I guess you can't imagine what an awful feeling I had when I was reading the piece – I was so afraid I'd find your name. I do hope everything is alright with you, dearest. It said that a lot of the Military Police were called to the scene of the accident so I guess there must have been a lot of excitement + work for all you boys. Cele seems to think the accident will interfere with your getting a pass this week-end. Gosh, I hope not, sweetheart.

I received your nice letter written yesterday morning while you were on duty in the hospital. I had to laugh when I pictured you removing an ingrown toe nail for me (if I ever had one) – you'd look funny, dear, and so would I. Yes, dearest, you're lucky to get the job in the hospital "that keeps you out of the rain" as you said. It does pay once in a while to "polish apples" I guess.

I was talking to Dot Smith last night on the phone and she said the girls in her office gave a shower on her Wednesday night at the Fairway and gave her a beautiful set of crystalware (glasses) – a dozen of each kind. She was surprised. She said she had received Ernie's Monday letter yesterday + he couldn't locate the Chaplain of the Camp at all. He said he tried all day Sunday + just couldn't find him. This seems almost impossible to me that a priest couldn't be found in the whole camp because they have to say a Mass every morning. Well, maybe by now he's located one to have his six instructions, otherwise Fr. Gloster here in Bpt. won't be able to get the compensation + they can't get married. Everything will turn out alright in the end because Dot keeps stressing all this in her letters so I guess Ernie realizes the importance of getting the instructions. Dot says she hopes you know this week-end (if you come home) whether you can make it for the wedding or not. I keep telling her you'll find out as soon as you can, darling.

Dearest no news from you will be good news between tonight +

tomorrow at 6 o'clock. If I don't hear from you, as I said before, that will mean you're coming. I hope you don't have any trouble getting a pass. I'm so worried about you, darling ever since I read about the accident.

If you do come home, dear, have a nice trip down on the train, if you haven't any company, have a little snooze for yourself.

I surely hope you come, darling.

Love Always,

Rita, Your Bunny

X X X X X X X X X X

P.S. See you at 6:00 or before (I hope.)

Monday 7/26/43 6:15 P.M.

Dearest,

I hope this letter finds you well and rested after your long and tiresome trip back. I felt so sorry when you were on the train and couldn't find a seat. I hope you didn't have to stand long. One woman who was seeing her son off was standing next to me on the platform and said it was terrible that all the soldiers had to stand and civilians never offer their seats. She saw me waving to you + said "the poor boys have to get up at a quarter of six in the morning, they at least deserve a seat, they're fighting for us," and so on and so forth.

We did have a wonderful week-end together, dearest − I enjoyed being with you so much. The next time you come, though, we'll make sure we get our Sunday afternoon swim + some nice sun at Lordship.

Darling, I guess I didn't tell you enough yesterday how happy I was when you went to Mass with me. It's a wonderful feeling to be close to you spiritually as well as other ways. Maybe since reading the pamphlet on the Mass you gave me Saturday you understand a little more about it. Sometime when you come home again, we can sit in the front of the Church + see the priest better + then I could answer any questions you might have. I guess it must be quite hard for a non-Catholic to realize the beauty of it all. I'm going to read the pamphlets you gave me tonight, dearest.

Sweetheart, about your physical exam this week − you asked me if I thought you should try to stay in 1-B + I told you I did. Of course I don't know if you'll have any choice or not − it might depend on what the Army doctors think entirely. I'd like you to stay where you are as long as possible (I know you would too, dear) + I suppose people would say (if they know) that we're very unpatriotic not wanting to go out of the country or not wanting to be put in a Combat Division but I think from all you've told me about the Army, the smartest thing to do these days is to be strictly G.I. to all appearances (let people think we're all for it) but you + I will keep our thoughts to ourselves, heh, dearest? We both know there's no glory (no matter what anyone says) in going in a Combat Division + going right into the fighting. After the war is over all the boys will be civilians anyway unless they make the Army their career (I'm sure you wouldn't). What I'm trying to tell you, dear, is that your chances of staying "on this side of the pond" will be much better if you stay in 1-B. As soon as you know, could you let me know the outcome of your exam, dearest?

Enclosed is a four-leaf clover that I always believed was good luck. I thought you might like to keep it in your wallet, dearest. Eleanor Dalton in the office brought it in to me. She found it in her yard. Also enclosed is a little bit of philosophy in the form of verse. I hope you like it, sweetheart.

Well, keep well and try not to be too lonely, sweetheart.

Love Always,
Rita
X X X X X X X X X X

Monday 4:30

Dear Rita,

Rita dear I sure did have a very enjoyable weekend with you dear. you and I sure do get along so well. I sure did enjoy your nice kisss. I love you Rita dear, and you love me too dearest so much. I am so happy to know that you do love me so much Rita dear.

I had a good trip back dear. I managed to get into a air conditioned car. I got a seat when I got to New haven. Rita I hope you enjoyed being with me over the weekend just as much as I enjoyed myself. My sister (<u>Helene</u>) treats us both so good, also my father, also your sister Cele, and your family, See Rita dear they all like us Dont they dearest.

Lots of love to the sweetest girl in the World. Rita you mean so much to me. You (<u>have</u>) put a joy in to my life since I have found you Bunny dear.

Lots of Love
<u>Walter</u>

(P.S. I sure did enjoy going to church with you darling.)

Tuesday 7/27/43 3:30 Rest

Walter Dearest,

How is my best beau today? I hope you're in tip-top shape – going to school and managing to have a little free time to yourself.

I hope you will know by Thursday or Friday if you can make Dot's wedding because I was talking to her last night on the phone and told her you'd know by then. She said Bill May said he'd be glad to be best man for Ernie + is supposed to stop over to her house to meet her + talk over what he + Mr. Smith will wear. Ernie is now taking his instructions, and likes them very much. He says the priest is very nice – he's been going to see him every night for the past week + looks forward to it each night because the priest is a regular fellow. He's going out of his way to explain a lot of things in the Religion that Ernie doesn't know, so I guess everything will all work out now for Dot + Ernie as long as his furlough isn't cancelled or something. I hope so. Dot is feeling much better since she left work + has had a chance to rest a lot. By Aug. 21st. she should be entirely well. Dr. Brodsky guarantees that she will anyway. Her nervous condition must be an entirely different type than yours was, heh, dearest?

Well, sweetheart, rest period is over now so I'll finish this letter tonight.

6:30 P.M. I just finished eating supper, darling. I had potatoes, string beans, meat loaf, ice cream, cake + tea. – pretty good for a little girl like me, heh, dearest? I have a very good appetite when I come home from work at night but don't eat so much in the morning or noon. We only have a half-hour at noon so I don't have time to eat much.

Darling, today I was thinking how much you've changed since you went in the Army last January – but it's practically all for the better so don't worry. Each time you come home I can see so many changes. You seem more carefree now, don't worry about anything which is very good. You are not tense like you used to be at times, that is, are more relaxed + sure of yourself now. You look so much better too, dearest. The Army has helped you quite a bit so far – there's just a few things in your personality that I suppose is natural when you're in the company of fellows so much – one is your language – I guess you forget when you're with me, darling, swearing + using rather uncouth words like "blowing your top", + a few others. A lot of it is Army talk but it sounds kind of ill-mannered + tough (in talking to girls). I hope you don't mind if I tell you about it, dearest, I know it's just that you forget. I did mention it to you Sunday but I thought I'd like to ask you again to watch it from now on. We talked about a few other things Sunday that you were going to try + check too – you knew I guess what they are without my going into detail – (example – when we were up to Jack's + Lil's Sunday). Darling, please don't think I'm trying to change you over to my liking – I love you as you are but if you try to please me the best you can by being courteous first of all, considerate etc. + I, too, try my best to follow your ideals, then we'll really have a 50-50 basis relationship. Do you understand, darling? I hope so. Let me know what you think, dear. You might see a few changes in me too that you'd like to tell me about.

I forgot to tell you Sunday – when I was leaving Dot's shower Dot Grant (Maguire) told me to go to see her + Jimmy sometime soon when you come home (the both of us). They are pretty well settled now in their home + I guess would like to have company. I told her we'd stop in sometime to see them. She said it's near the Merritt Theatre on Beechmont Ave.

Love Always,
Rita, Your Fiancée
X X X X X X X X X X X

Wednesday 6. P.M.
Post M.P. Second Platoon Second floor <u>Ha. Ha.</u>

Dear Rita,

I recived your two latest letter, and I am so happy to recived them each day. Rita you are the most prompt and <u>Sincere</u> girl in the land. I am so happy to have you as my future <u>wife</u> Rita dear. Because you posess the finest of qualities, you have a very keen mind and you are very feminine.

I will let you know more on that reclassification of men just as soon as I get more loop on the subject. I got my physical on Monday after noon, It was not to much to it. I think that I will stay right here for some time. even if I am put in 1 A. I and men like me will get the preference of Service Unit work and get the easier work. See I rate, at least I think so. <u>Heh dear</u>. than again some of the men who have been a liability and not a asset to the army, will be honorable discharged from the Service but there will be very few discharges, that will be men who have not been able to preform there duties (and fellows that have been on sick call to often) So I do not think that I will be in that category. But no one knows to much about it as yet.

I sure did enjoy going to church with you Rita dear Sunday, Darling I got a great joy being so close to you while in church and shareing our spiritually life together.

Thanks Rita for that nice four leaf clover, Maybe it will bring us more luck. Heh dear. Those verses sure are very nice Rita dear. I like them very much. I am now quite rested up after that very nice week end with you dear. I am getting along very good considering, and am feeling tops Yes dear I will let you know by Friday or Saturday if I can make the Wedding (I hope so) I will see about it tomorrow. Rita dear. So glad that Ernie is prepareing himself for the Wedding. I know that he sure will have a fine married life with Dorothy. Darling I feel sometimes that I wish you and I were now married, but that again we do not want to rush to fast We are getting there slow but sure. Heh dearest Darling. Yes dear that service Mens news letter which I get from my church each month sure is a nice new's letter, I look forward for it, because I get the dope on the where abouts of my other friends from the church Yes the Army has cured me of my funny spoiled way's It has helped me quite a bit the Army has its good points as well as its bad ones. Heh dear. yes dear I will watch my Army <u>Slang</u> and language from now on dearest, its just that I form that habit since being with the boys here, but I will not say any more of thae sayings, Darling <u>Rita</u>. Yes dear I will alway's try my utmost to be courteous and be considerate at all times to you Darling, because I love you to much to be otherwise. Its just that us soldier boys forget ourselves and sometimes I guess its just to be funny or something, but sometimes I guess we do not know why we are like that, But I know that you understand. Rita dear. Because you are tolerate and intelligent and matured enough to know me. Heh <u>Rita</u>, <u>bunny Darling</u>. Dear. Rita you deserve the best that life has to offer, I am so sure and I will try my utmost of my capasities and limitations to offer you the best that's in me. Dear.

Lot of Love Walter

P.S. No I do not know of any consturited [constructive] suggestions to make to you, dearest, because to me you are top just the way you are at present.

P.S. (A Hundred big <u>Kisses</u> to my Love.)

P.S. I sure would like going to visit Dot + Jimmy Maguire at their newly furnished Home.

Thursday 7/29/43 3:00 P.M.

Dear Sweetheart,

This is my afternoon off this week as I'm working all day Saturday.

I left the office at 12:30, brought my gown from the store to a little shop that does alterations for the store. The bottom of it has to be cut as it's much too long. It should look very nice when it's fitted to my size – I'll pick it up about Aug. 17th.

Dot's mother is giving her a shower tonight at the house of one of her friends. Cele + I are going. Dot will be surprised again – she doesn't know a thing about it. Cele + I bought one gift between the two of us – eight dessert glasses (each one a different color) to match the cocktail glasses I gave her last Sunday.

I went over to Dot's house last night for a while + had a nice visit. She has all the gifts she's received so far on display in the living room. They certainly are beautiful. The sterling silver set that the office gave her is gorgeous. It consists of a tea pot, coffee pot creamer + sugar bowl also the tray all sterling silver. It must have cost a small fortune. Quite a few people in her office contributed towards it. Another nice gift she has is a set of dishes (service of four) that's called "Fiesta Ware". Each plate, cup + saucer is a different color + Dot says when Mr. + Mrs. Klein (you + I) come to visit the Smiths' she'll use that set. There are four colors, bright red, green, blue + yellow. She said she'd serve you food from the green dishes, me the red, Ernie the blue + her the yellow. (ha ha). To me all that planning for the future seems so far away, it doesn't seem possible that we'll be visiting the Smith's home + they'll be visiting our home, but I guess I should try to see the future the way Dot does that we'll all be back to normal living in the near future.

Ernie is having twelve instructions instead of six, the Chaplain down there thinks he should + besides, he's very much interested himself. He sent his winter uniform to Dot + she had it cleaned already. I saw it hanging up last night – 3 chevrons + all. Dot bought her going-away outfit, a pretty suit in a very nice shade of blue. Everything is practically all arranged now as far as the wedding's concerned, even to the kind of flowers Mary + I are going to carry – I'm going to carry peach color gladioli + Mary – orchid ones. Dot's going to carry the usual bridal bouquet – white roses. Now if only you can come, dearest, everything would be complete. I didn't receive any mail from you today – I hope I do tomorrow telling me that you can come. I know you'll try your best + that's all you can do.

The Singers (Ed + Mary + Joan) came to see Cele + Charlie last night. When they come to visit here they always stay so late. Cele + Charlie were so mad because they didn't leave here until 2 o'clock this morning. Ed didn't have to go to work until 1 this afternoon so they didn't have to get up until late this morning. One other time they stayed until 3 in the morning. Cele didn't feel well when she got up this morning + besides was so tired she just stayed home from work, in fact she didn't go in at all today. You'd think they'd have realized that Cele + Charlie have to get up early for work.

I suppose by now, darling, you've had your physical. I hope you make out well. (stay in 1-B).

Dearest, here's a suggestion – When you get paid Saturday or Monday + send some money, if you could send $20 then I could take $5.<u>00</u> of it for Dot's + Ernie's wedding present (your share) + if I could keep $5.<u>00</u> of it to send back to you for your trainfare, then we'd still have $10.<u>00</u> saved – added to the $97.00 it would be $107.<u>00</u>. Do you think you'd have enough left then for the rest of the month if you did this?

Well, sweetheart, I'll be looking forward to a letter tomorrow. Take care of yourself, dear.

Love Always,
Rita, Your Fiancée.
X X X X X X X X

Thursday 4:30 P.M.
Second Platoon
Post Military Police.

Hello Darling,

Lots of <u>Love</u> to my Fiancee on this quite rainy day, I hope dearest that you are feeling well and that you are in the best of spirits.

I hope to stop in to see if I will be able to get to Ernie's Wedding. I will go to see the first Sergeant this evening at 6: P.M. I hope that I can make it. But it is hard telling dearest. I may get three <u>3</u> days. but maybe not at the right time. I may get the three days starting from Saturday noon, which will be to late for the Wedding, but it will enable me to get to there reception, in the evening dear. Yes Waldo Pierre is a swell fellow, we go out now and than, whenever we can get together, he has his girl friend that lives in Jitchburg [?] Mass, which is about <u>30</u> minutes ride on the bus, Yes dear, when we are Mr + Mrs Walter J. Klein it will enable us to express ourselves to the utmost of our capacities Heh dear. Darling I am just rearing to go, I feel that I just want to be near and with you at all times. Darling it will not be long and than we will be able to be <u>one</u>. Heh darling. On this rainy afternoon I wish I could be with you to express my Love to you darling. To Kiss you and caress you nicely, Darling I am in such a nice mood now to Love you so nicely. We will save all of our Love for each other, so than the next time I am home we can enjoy our Companionship so much, Heh dear.

We sure do Love each other so much. I Love you more now than ever before, our Love is growing stronger as the time goes on darling, just think as the years go on, our Love will be so strong it will be impregnable and nothing will be able to <u>Mar</u> or injury our Love for the least. Heh Rita dear. Rita I am now reaching a point, slow but sure where I think how nice it will be when we are one. Mrs + Mrs. Walter J Klein. See Darling it thrills me as I think about it so often as I lay on my bunk or while on post. It must be that we are now reaching a point where our love is now reaching its highest peak, while still in our single state. Its hard to explain, but you understand, <u>dont</u> you Bunny. Gee dear. but it feels so good, as I'm writing this letter, I never did know that God would bestow upon us that happiness that comes from finding such a <u>extra</u> <u>super</u> Love with each other. O Darling, what <u>extancy</u> or happiness you and I are deriveing out of our Love for each other. First we have our companionship, next our future home, next our Sexual happiness dear. which you and I like so much, especially me. Heh dear. I sure do like Loving you. I could Love you so nicely right now. just pictureing in my mind of you and your sweet smile. darling. Than later which should come first, so the good book says is our children Because that is suppose to be the main reason people get married to perpetuate the human race. but darling I will leave that up to you as far as the children are concerned. But of course I wouldint like to many children, one boy and one girl I think is enough for you and me, but the prist and the good book says to have plenty of children, (Boy I am sure the <u>one</u> that could make plenty of them). <u>you</u> to Heh dear. Because you will be the one to have them. not me. <u>Ha. Ha.</u> darling Boy I am a Big <u>Devil</u>. Heh dear.

Love Walter.

As I reread all I have al ready writened, I find that I am still unable to express myself, but I feel I want to continue to write, and than maybe I will satisfy my self. On our companionship, we will have each other to keep us from getting lonely and feeling lost in this great universe. Heh dear. With each other to comfort each other in time of stress and pain and sickness. We will find happiness, also to share each others great joy's and sadnesss. [sadnesses] than in our home, we will find home a place to find warmth and comfort. Than our sexual angle again. Boy <u>o</u> Boy that's what I am going to like Darling with you I know once we get ajusted to each other, which I am sure will not be to hard, we will find great enjoyment, and also a way of nature to express our Love and also to perpetuate the human race. Boy darling I am sure getting the desire to get married I am so happy to be reaching that stage, and I am surprising myself. I am sure you and I will find life so much more beautiful even than now, when we <u>are</u> one. Heh dear.

Friday 7/30/43 6:15 P.M.

Dear Sweetheart,

I just finished reading your long letter written Wednesday night. I was very much surprised that you wrote such a long one. I enjoyed it so much, darling. Thank you for all those nice compliments, Walt, it makes me very happy that you think so much of me.

I was very glad to hear that your chances of staying at Devens for some time are very good (as far as you can tell now). No, you certainly would not be given a medical discharge as your record has been so good ever since you've been in the Army, that is never being on sick call. The prospect of being a civilian at home, coming and going as you please probably seems wonderful to you now but you really would never want to get a medical discharge. You can always look forward to being home after the war is over anyway, dearest.

I do hope I will know from the letter I'll receive tomorrow whether you can come for Dot + Ernie's wedding or not. Dot really should know by tomorrow at the latest in case she has to ask someone else. If I don't receive any letter tomorrow then I'll count on knowing when you call Sunday.

You say you wish sometimes that you + I were married but at the same time you think we shouldn't rush things. Well, dearest, I can understand somewhat how you feel but I wouldn't say we'd be rushing things by being married since we've been going together over 2 – ½ yrs – it will be three years in December. That certainly is not rushing anything. I guess this waiting is a good test of my love for you – in the end it should show how strong it really is. I just hope that when you're moved from Ft. Devens and we don't see each other for months at a time that you won't regret that we waited so long – I think you will but I won't say "I told you so" It makes me feel very badly when people keep asking me when we're going to be married. If I ever said we didn't want to rush things it would be a joke to them because most people think 3 years is too long to go together + not be married. Well, dearest, I could tell you a lot more about the way I feel on this subject but I won't because I don't want you to think I'd force you into anything or try to change your feelings to my way of thinking – I want you to have the desire to get married of your own accord.

I went to Dot's shower last night. She received some beautiful gifts + was surprised. Mary, the maid-of-honor was there. She doesn't go with any fellow steady + she seems to be looking forward to having a very good time with Bill May at the wedding. In other words, she's hoping she makes a hit with him. She's a very nice looking girl but is definitely Italian in her ways.

Well, dearest, I'll mail this now as it's getting late. I hope you have some free time over the week-end + enjoy yourself as much as possible. I'll be looking forward to a call from you around noon Sunday.

Love Always,
X X X Rita X X X

Sunday 8/1/43 12:30 P.M.

Hello Darling,

We hardly had time to say "hello" on the phone the three minutes went by so fast heh, dearest?

I explained the whole situation about your coming for the wedding to Dot – that you went to your first sergeant and he told you he didn't see any reason why you couldn't make it but at the same time you shouldn't count on it either because with fellows being moved out all the time you might be needed at that particular time, that you couldn't tell from one day to the next just what will happen. I said that the first sergeant told you the best thing to do was to tell the people (Dot + Ernie) that they should ask someone else whom they could really count on. Well, Dot was very disappointed after I told her all this, but at the same time she says she won't give up hopes of your coming. She is going to ask someone else but with the understanding that if you do come the last minute that person will realize the whole situation. She said it will be up to Ernie as to whom he wants to ask – maybe someone he worked with in the Brass Co. but anyway, dearest, if you do find out the last minute that you can come on a Friday, you'll still be in the wedding party. It would be a good idea to have your clothes all ready just in case everything is in your favor the last minute even though right now the possibility might seem very slight. In any event, you'll probably get your usual week-end pass, could get here by 6 or 7 o'clock at night + at least see Ernie + Dot for a short while before they go away. Let's leave the matter that way, then, dearest, that you still have a very slight chance of coming, O.K.? The day won't seem complete, dearest, without you there. I'll feel so badly to go through the day – be in the wedding party, at the breakfast, + reception without you, darling Walter, but if it has to be that way I'll try to make the best of it, it surely will be hard tho, dear.

Yesterday I worked until 4:30, then met Dot + went to the Warner to see "The Constant Nymph" which was very good. After the show we stopped in "Ye Olde Tavern" upstairs in the Arcade + had a sandwich, so you see, I had a nice evening with Dot. I can't imagine how I'm going to spend my Saturday nights when she goes – not only Saturdays but how I'll miss talking to her on the phone + visiting her. She is really the closest + best friend I have – I hate to think of her going away because even though we will correspond our friendship will not be on the same basis when she is married + I'll be single, our interests won't be the same because Dot's life will be Ernie then – which is the way it should be of course.

Darling, just last week at this time you + I were together at your house having a nice time.

I received the letter you wrote Thursday last night when I came home. It surely was an extra special one, dearest – it was very touching, the way you expressed your love for me, darling. You must have been in a lovable mood when you wrote it, dearest, because it contradicted somewhat the one you wrote the day before (ha ha). It's the first time you ever told me that you had a desire to get married. When you gave me the diamond it was just sort of understood that we would marry sometime but we didn't talk about it very much. You often did tell me what your idea of a real marriage was but not in regards to you + I – if you understand what I mean. I had reached a point where I was almost afraid to bring the subject up (except kiddingly) because you never seemed to want to talk about it. I'm glad now that you told me just how you feel about marriage – my hopes, feelings + desires are the same as yours, dearest – that companionship will be first with you + I – of course our love will be enduring, our home even if it's only a few rooms will be a home not just a house to live in, as far as sex is concerned I don't know if I'll get as much pleasure out of that phase of marriage or not as you will, but I'll at least do my best to see that you do. Yes, as you said, marriage is primarily to perpetuate the race but I can see your desire – not to have too many children, that you think two will be enough. I can't tell about that yet either, it will all depend on my health after we get married. As far as I can see I don't see why we couldn't have just two children, dearest. Darling, you're mistaken about the priest + the "good book" as you call it saying that couples should have a large number of children – that is the main purpose of marriage to have children but the Church says it's the Will of God as to how many children a couple should have. It might be that some couples could never have any, or just one or two but a couple should leave it to nature + God – take Eleanor + Vin for instance, they had triples born + then lost them. Ever since Eleanor has wanted a baby so much but can't seem to have any. They are following the Marriage rules of the Church but it just seems as if it's God's will that they can't have any. Eleanor is perfectly healthy + normal so maybe they will in time. Then again there are some couples who could have about ten children if they wanted to but who just can't on account of health, financial reasons – they have one or two and do their utmost to bring up their children with proper food, clothing, love etc. There is nothing wrong in this as long as they don't prevent life to a child, see darling?

Whenever we do get married, dearest, I realize that your father would never welcome me into the family as though I were a non-Catholic. I don't expect even to be close to your family, that is, that I'd like to be considered one of them. Of course they would always be welcome to our home (yours + mine) + I would like to visit them sometimes but that's all I'd expect, dearest. Can you understand Walter dearest? I'd like Cele + Charlie to meet your father, Martha + Adolph + Emma sometime soon if possible. Maybe when they take you up home next time they could stop in your house + meet your father. I'd like to have Martha + Adolph down here some night – I've asked them several times to stop in on the way to your house but I guess I'll just have to set a definite time.

Cele + Charlie visited Catherine + Frank Sarnicky the other night + they said Artie is awfully mad at you because if you'll recall, when we were going by in your father's car last Sunday, Catherine, Frank + Artie's mother were on the porch + you unconsciously passed the remark that Artie's division Battalion or whatever he's in was moving out soon. Artie never tells his mother anything like that as she worries herself sick over anything like that. I don't remember that his mother was on the porch when you said that but anyway she overheard somehow + asked Artie + told him that you said so. He was wild – he said to Catherine + Frank "I guess Walt Klein is no friend of mine – I always thought he was tho," Cele + Charlie said if you did make a remark about his being moved they're sure you didn't mean for his mother to hear it + you probably passed it unconsciously without thinking. I'm telling you this just so in case you ever meet Artie you can have an answer ready for him. Cele + Charlie don't like him anyway they said he's a sucker + a wise Pollock. Frank said the reason he got Corporal's rating is because he worked almost every night in the office until 10 or 11 when everyone else would be gone. He sticks around all the sergeants + officers (commmissional) too. In other words he's an apple polisher. So darling, please don't worry about saying that in front of his mother but I would be a little more careful if I were you when you're talking to them, it just shows you what trouble an idle remark can cause. From what I've heard about Artie – I've never met him, he's got more nerve than brains + is typical of his nationality. Am I right, darling?

I love you so much, dearest Walter.

Love Always,
Rita, (Colleen).
X X X X X X X X X X

Friday 8/6/43 – 12:30 P.M.

Dearest Walter,

My lunch hour is over – or I should say my half-hour (that's how long we have every day except Thursday) so I thought I'd take a few minutes from work and answer your letter (Tuesday's) that I read last night when I got home from the show.

Gosh, darling, you sure do like to write "mushy" letters don't you? Oh, don't misunderstand me Walt, I like them but I also would like you to tell me a little about what you're doing (about your work etc.) – what hours you're on duty, about the news of Ft. Devens (if there is any).

You said in your letter you could hardly wait to come home on your next pass so you could show me how much you love me by kissing, hugging etc. Darling, I know just how you must feel while you're writing all those things but let's not forget there are lots of other ways you + I can express our love. For instance just by a look – a kind word – a nice compliment we can express ourselves, sweetheart. Remember you + I always said we would consider the physical part of our love <u>after</u> every other part. Dearest, I do miss your nice kisses so much but as I said before, let's not think that's the only way we can show how much we love each other – understand, dearest? I know you do. So Walter, from now on, if it isn't too much trouble, could you answer my letters (if I ask any questions) + tell me more about how everything is going with you?

I had a nice evening with Helen last night. The show was funny – we laughed + laughed. I felt much better when I came out of the show (not as depressed as when I wrote you yesterday noon). Helen insisted on paying for my dinner + my way into the show. I treated her to a sundae afterwards anyway – that was the least I could do.

I never realized before how interested Helen is in horoscopes + fortune telling. I know you've often said she was but didn't give much thought until she was telling me about all the books she's read on the subject + about the fortunetellers she's been to. Darling, remember the one I went to last year? I told Helen about it but said I didn't believe in them at all – I just went for the fun of it. Helen says she keeps telling herself that she shouldn't but after she's been to one she just can't help thinking about what the fortune teller told her. I guess those things would be apt to stay in one's mind after a while.

Darling, there's a shortage of beer here in Bpt. You'll be out of luck I guess for a glass of beer when you come home again unless your father gets stocked up a lot. There's hardly a drop left in the city. Taverns, drug stores etc. are out of it + I guess will be for the duration. I don't know whether this is the case in other states or not but don't worry Walt, your pappy probably has enough on hand to last a while (ha ha) + besides, you can get used to going without it if you have to heh, dearest?

Walt, I was thinking, if you could send me one of those insignias for your area (number 1 in a diamond) I could sew it on the new shirt I bought you + you could wear the shirt whenever you get your three-day pass. Do you think this is a good idea?

Tomorrow afternoon Cele, Ann, Ruth + I are going to pick out a present to give to Dot next Thursday at the party I'm going to have on her. I'm not sure just what we'll decide on – maybe a nice mirror for a living room (about $12.00) or a nice end table or something. Ruth's father works in Nothnagles (furniture store) so we'll go in there + look around. After that I'm going to look at lamps + pick one out – it will be from you + I. I'll pay about $10 for it. Then, except for the cost of the party next Thursday, my expenses for the wedding will be over. Am I glad! So far it's cost me a small fortune + although I don't mind because it's for Dot, still, there is a limit, don't you think so, dearest? Oh, well, after the wedding, I can save something for myself I hope.

7:00 P.M. We are home now, dearest – we ate in the "Star" – I guess we won't go there any more – their food is getting worse by the day. While we were in there, there was a couple sitting near us – the fellow was a Coast Guard Office + the girl was very attractive. They were eating their dinner + talking + all of a sudden the fellow took out a little box wrapped up fancy + gave it to the girl. By that time I was fascinated because it reminded me of the times you + I were together + you'd give me gifts, dearest. Well, the girl opened it + it was a beautiful sterling silver pin in the shape of a horse shoe with a horse's head inside. I couldn't help but notice the expression on the fellow's face – he got such pleasure out of giving it to the girl (just like you, dear) + of course the girl was surprised (just like I used to be). She put it on right away.

Charlie brought your Thursday's letter down town with him so I had to read it for my dessert (ha ha). You're so thoughtful, dearest, to drop me a short letter when you had a few minutes Thursday. Thanks, dearest. I enjoyed your letter a lot. You must have been "in the mood" when you wrote it (ha ha).

Dearest, I'll be thinking of you over the week-end. I'd like to go to the beach this Sunday (I always want to don't I, dearest but I never seem to get there). I think Ann Preston will go with me. I know Dot won't want to she doesn't like the beach, so darling, could you call around noon Sunday?

It won't be so long now + you'll be home again, dearest, the week after next if you're lucky so, dear, try to keep your spirits high until then.

Love Always,

"Bunny"

X X X X X X X

August 9. 1943

Post M.P.

Fort Devens Mass.

Dear Rita,

Hows my sweet little irish girl this fine day. I hope dear that you had a very enjoyable week end, maybe went for a swim or for a nice walk in the park.

Hope that you are not working to hard at the office these days, Ann, Ruth and you sure do make a good three O Ha. Ha. they are such nice girls.

I had a few week end duties, this week I am on school detail, so that will give me some time to myself. Saturday as I was telling you on the phone, I was on detail at the Wac Area, at there farewell Gala show and party. Boy the show was very good, eats drinks, and of course Mary Martin sure was very good and especially very sharp. Ha. Ha. She is a very good singer. there were about three thousand soldiers (or more) and Wacs there. the party was held as a farewell party to the Wac's, because very soon all the Wac's are soon to leave they are to go to different states to recive farther training. the goverment as you probably heard is discontinueing this 4th Wac training center. the Wac's are now part of the army. They took the oath the other day, they had quite a ceromony – here at the fort. I was doing traffic duty all that morning right there (near) at the parade field. there were governors, Senators, Generals and all kinds of big shots or something Ha. Ha. I am feeling fine and I am getting along very good considering everything. I am sure looking forward to getting home to see you Rita Marie Lavery. and to Love you so nicely. Heh dear I hope that Dorothy Smith is feeling well also Ernie. Boy before very long they will be well on there way down the aisle and they will be one more of our swell couples gone and done (get) it. I do hope that Dorothy and Ernie have the finest that life has to offer, they should do very well. So lets give them the best of wishes. hope and luck. Heh Rita dear.

I could Love you so nicely right now. Gee but I alway's feel like Loving you. I am thinking of you all the time Bunny dear. I miss you so much. Darling

Lots of Love

Walter

P.S. those two Wac's also were on duty at the War Party thing and about Six more, there were four of us. Some class at least they think so. Ha. Ha. We kid them along plenty, abut they can take it. I guess they get us to it. Heh Rita

Left to right, Private Josephine Selnick of Lawrence and Private Grace Fisher of Newton Upper Falls, WAC MP's look keen and alert as they patrol area at Fort Devens.

Tuesday, 8/10/43 3:30 Rest Period

Dearest,

How's my sweetheart on this very rainy Tuesday? I hope when I go home from work tonight there will be a letter from you saying everything is going along smoothly with you, sweetheart.

Here's some very good news – Ernie called up Sunday from Alabama + said he was definitely coming home for Aug. 21st. He'll be here by the 18th. He said he had a hard time getting the O.K. on his application for the furlough but seeing he's getting married, they said it would be considered an emergency furlough. All the other fellows who were supposed to get furloughs at the same time had theirs cancelled – so you see Ernie just made it "by the skin of his teeth". You can imagine how happy Dot is now that she's sure he's coming. She said if only you could come everything would be complete.

Here's the situation about your part in the wedding now, dearest: Mrs. Smith went to N.Y. + asked her nephew if he could substitute for you if you can't make it. He said he'd be glad to – if <u>you</u> <u>can't</u> <u>come</u>. So now Dot says the only thing we can do is wait until about Tuesday of next week – that if you could tell us one way or the other + then she can send a telegram to her cousin to tell him to come or not to – If he isn't in the wedding party he won't come until Saturday morning – if he is he'll come Friday, but he'd like to know by next Wednesday. Do you think, dear, that you could call me up next Tuesday night + let me know definitely?

I'm sending you Dot's picture – it was in last night's paper. It's a very nice one don't you think so? I'd like you to send it back to me, darling, as I'd like to keep it. She had it taken a few weeks ago.

Well, sweetheart, rest period is over so I'll finish this later.

6:30 P.M. Just read your letter written yesterday + received the picture of the Waacs. The way they posed for the picture was odd I thought. They look as though they're the type to have lots of tricks up their sleeves – maybe I'm wrong tho.

You must have had fun at the party last Saturday from what you've told me. I did know that the Waacs are now part of the Army but I didn't know that the 4th Waac training center was being discontinued. Well, I guess it's just as well there won't be any more of them up there where you are because then you boys won't get into trouble (ha ha).

We now have a new addition to the Lavery-Monohan clan – a puppy. Charlie got her (it's female) from a fellow he knows + it's the funniest looking little dog you ever could see. It's so small that Jeanie can hold it right in the palm of her hand. You'll probably laugh your head off when you see it. Cele + Charlie are going to give one of the cats to an aunt of mine. If Charlie + Jeanie keep on taking in animals we'll be living in a zoo.

I've asked you several questions in the letters I've written in the past month or so but I don't ever get any answers from you. I shouldn't say anything to you about this – I should be glad to receive the ones I do from you but I don't see how it could be any trouble for you to have my last letter in front of you as you write + just follow right along. Cele remarked last night that she thinks your correspondence is falling off some as lately I don't get any letters Monday or Tuesday or Saturday but I explained how you said you were going to write Mondays, Wednesdays + Fridays.

Well, darling, it looks as though this letter is beginning to be a lecture so I guess I'd better sign off for now. You can use your own judgment about the things I've mentioned – after all – I feel if you really have the desire to write you don't have to be told to – you are the one who's supposed to be "courting" me not vice versa. (ha ha).

Love Always,
Rita

Selects Aug. 31 for Wedding

MISS DOROTHY MARIE SMITH

MISS DOROTHY SMITH
PLANS HER WEDDING

Miss Dorothy Marie Smith, daughter of Mr. and Mrs. Alfred T. Smith of 298 Harriet street will become the bride of Staff Ernest Smith, son of Raymond Smith of Augusta, G. on Saturday morning, August 21 at 11 o'clock in St. Charles' church. No invitations have been issued but friends are invited.

Thursday 5:30 Nite

Hello Rita Bunny,

Hows my sweetheart this fine day. I hope you are in the best of spirits dear and feeling your best. Bunny Because in a week or so your love will be at your beck and <u>call</u> at 1440 Stratford Ave. Heh, dear. I will let you know tues. if I can make it or not.

15 men are being discharged for being unfit for duty, in our outfit. Hundreds from all over the camp. and in about a few days some more are to be trasfered to other Post. (that is Men to be shipped). So it is hard telling Rita dear.

So happy to hear that Ernie is all set to arrive in Bpt at the given time. It sure was hard for him to get away. good thing Weddings are considered Emergencys. That's the only reason I guess he is making it all right So nice you and <u>Ann</u> get along so well, she is a good girl with plenty of humor. <u>Heh</u>.

Lots of Love to my Fiancee. I love you Bunny so much, you are the best girl in the world. I am so lucky to have you for my girl.

Last nite I was on super Numeries. Tues nite I went to the Ayer U.S.O. dance they have very good dances there.

Lots of Love. Walter.

P.S. Dorothy sure does look very nice. Boy she looks best ever.

Friday 8/13/43 6:00 P.M.

Dearest Walter,

I came home fifteen minutes earlier from work tonight than usual because I worked over last night – it seems good too, the buses aren't so crowded + it gave me a chance to read your letter fifteen minutes earlier than other nights (ha ha). Really, tho, dearest, I look forward to your letters so much.

You said you expect to be at my beck and call here at 1440 next week. Gosh, I hope so, Walt. The past three weeks went by so slowly + I'm starting my second week's vacation tomorrow + I imagine the week will seem very long until the wedding which will be the climax of it – your coming home will be the best part of it, sweetheart.

I know you won't be one of the fifteen men who are going to be discharged, dear, because your record has been so good. I can see where all these changes men being moved – discharged – etc. will affect the handing out of passes – but let's keep on hoping for the best, dearest.

What I wouldn't give, Walter, to have you call up Tuesday or Wednesday + say you're coming Friday! I could meet you at the station any time during the day or night as I'll be home.

Well, the party on Dot turned out very nice last night. She really was surprised. We gave her the mirror + she's crazy over it. The Fairway is a good place to have a get-together because there's music practically every minute – never a dull moment. They have a woman who plays an accordion + sings, besides the orchestra. We told her Dot was a bride-to-be + she played the wedding march right at our table ("Here Comes the Bride"). She also sang a few songs that we requested. We all had a cocktail + a turkey dinner + after that we danced with each other. It didn't look out of place because there were so many other girls there dancing together. The party broke up about 11:15 – Charlie came + took the mirror to Dot's house which made it nice. It seemed so funny to go to a place like the Fairway without you, dearest. I felt strange dancing with the girls. If only all of our boyfriends were there everything would have been complete. I hope we will all be together soon (out of uniform).

Ernie finally managed to get a room in Ozark, Alabama 35 miles from his camp. That's the best he can do for the time being but he has a few good prospects nearer the camp but will have to take that for the time being. There is no stove for cooking in the room so that means they'll have to go out to eat every night. Dot will be by herself all day + will have to eat breakfast + lunch alone. Dot said the room was $10.00 a week + considering everything this is very expensive – going out to eat etc. I guess she'll work if she can get it after a while. Camp Rucker is so far South it's right near the Gulf of Mexico which makes it so hot (106°) in the daytime. I don't think I'd like being so far away from home – the heat, or the idea of being alone all day but of course I'd never say anything like that to Dot. (just you, dear).

Well, Walter dearest, next Friday at this time I'll be going to rehearsal at St. Charles + then back to Dot's for sort of a party. I hope you'll be with me, too. If you could only come, we'd have a wonderful time at the wedding even though we wouldn't know hardly any people but if I'm alone – that is, you can't make it – I'll feel so strange – well, I will try to make the best of it that's all.

Darling, I'm enclosing $2.<u>00</u> for pin money. You must be low in funds by now (ha ha). This should help you out a little at least. You can buy yourself some ice cream, go to the show + use 50¢ of it to call me Sunday (ha ha). Leave it to me to think of that, heh dearest? This is your money, darling – I took it from what you have saved – in other words – as you would say "I tapped the till." (ha ha ha).

Well, dearest Walter, just tell yourself tomorrow night that only this coming week-end + you'll be at 1440 (Friday I hope) but maybe Saturday anyway. Gosh, sweetheart, it'll be wonderful seeing you again, being close to you, talking to you + maybe sharing each other's pleasure at the wedding (I hope).

Well, 'bye now, my husband-to-be.

Love Always,
Rita Marie

P.S. How do you like my calling you "husband-to-be"? (ha ha) I'd love to see the expression on your face. (ha ha).

These are long ones, honey bunch → X X X X X X X X X X X

Saturday 12:00 Midnight

My Dearest Walter,

I'm writing this letter, or that is, starting to write it in my room – half asleep. I'm all ready for bed but it's so warm tonight I just can't sleep so I'll just keep on writing until my eyes close. I feel like talking to you anyway, dearest Walter.

Cele + Charlie are out yet – they are up to Katherine + Freddie's house – you remember Freddie, dear, we went to their wedding reception at Champs + Katherine is Charlie's niece. They invited all the Monahans up to their apartment for the evening so I guess they're all having a "bang-up" time.

The little puppy we have is downstairs in the kitchen crying, incidentally its name is "Curly" because it has black + white curly fur. I was playing with him a little while – it's just beginning to use its teeth quite a bit + likes to chew things – especially Cele's + Jean's + my toes when we have toeless shoes on. He's so used to getting a lot of attention that when we are out of the room or out of the house altogether, it cries + cries. He really is cute tho – wait 'till you see him – you'll have a good laugh just looking at him he's so small.

I went to the show tonight with Ann Preston. We saw "Heaven Can Wait" with Gene Tierney + Don Ameche. It was in technicolor + was good. After the show Ann + I went into the Barnum Coffee Shoppe to have a sandwich. It's air-conditioned in there + we felt so nice + cool we hated to go out again into the heat so we stayed there for about two hours talking. We decided we'd have a cocktail while we were talking so we proceeded to order Manhattans. The waitress took one look at me + didn't want to serve me because she thought I was a minor – can you imagine! She asked me how old I was so I told her the truth (24) – she just shook her head + looked very disgusted. I know she didn't believe it because she took a long time serving the drink. She didn't question Ann at all (who's 19). Ann could very easily pass for 23 or 24 anyway. I used to be questioned quite a bit about a year ago but thought I was doing well for a while – until tonight. If you were with me you probably would have laughed your head off. Well, we had a nice evening anyway. I might go swimming with her tomorrow – depending on the weather.

Darling, I hope this time next week you'll be at 1440. I'll be so glad to see you, sweetheart – you can't imagine how happy I'll be. I hope this coming week goes by fast.

Well, sweetheart, I'll write more tomorrow – my eyes won't stay open another minute – but if you were here now, dearest, I'd give you some nice big kisses – I wouldn't be sleepy then would I, darling? X X X X X X X X X X

Monday 8/16/43 4:00 P.M.

Dear Sweetheart,

I hope this letter finds you well and in good spirits. I felt so badly yesterday after I had talked with you on the 'phone because you seemed so depressed – "down in the dumps". I can understand, tho, how you feel, darling, Army life would get anyone down at times – especially when you can't tell from one day to the next what's going to happen – then being lonesome all adds to your feeling of depression.

I wished, after talking to you yesterday, that I could have been with you to give you a little comfort but, dearest, the only way I can help you (and it's just a little way) is by writing. When you feel blue + depressed, Walt, just try to tell yourself that you have me back home here waiting for you + loving you constantly. I, too, am waiting for the time to come when this whole thing will be over + you + I can be together always. In fact, all of us home here, your family + mine + all the other fellows' families are just living for that time. We, too, often feel depressed, lonely, + discouraged, that is, all the wives, sweethearts, sisters, mothers etc. You + I have been lucky so far seeing each other once a month, we at least have had that much to look forward to. Now, in just a matter of days, we'll be seeing each other, if everything goes along alright for you. This time of war is a good test of one's character. If we can take all the hard knocks in their stride, then our character can stand any test. I know you never complain (to me anyway) if things bother you but I can always tell by your voice, + once in a while by your letters. Don't be afraid to write just the way you feel, dearest – I'd rather have you tell me than to keep everything from me because then I'll feel closer to you + will understand you better. You don't always have to make your letters cheerful if you really don't feel that way. In that way (telling me just how you feel about different things) I probably could give you some suggestions or advice + that goes for me too, you could help me out if I felt "down in the dumps", see, dearest?

Everyone is anxiously waiting to see if you're coming Friday for the wedding. Mrs. Smith wants you to come so much she's been praying that you will. Dot says Ernie will feel very badly if you can't make it too. As for myself, you know how much I'd love to have you come – nothing would make me happier, so you see, dearest, when I get your call, Tuesday, you'll know how much your answer will mean. I have a feeling that your commanding officer won't tell you definitely until Friday, but if this is the case, Mrs. Smith will tell her nephew to come + then if you do come the last minute you can still be in the party because they'll have two ushers instead of one. It's really customary to have two anyway. I know you'll try your best to come, Walt, we all know you will. As far as I can see, you have two things in your favor – one is that you still haven't had your three day pass + the other is, you're usual pass comes every 4th week + the 20th is the 4th one so maybe if you mentioned this to your first sergeant, you could get it. Well, dearest, it all depends on the Army's way of thinking + planning but let's hope for the best anyway.

Yesterday afternoon I went to Lordship with Ann Preston about 2:30 + came home about 6 o'clock. We didn't go in the water but we lazied in the sun. We went into Peggy's for something to eat + I think it's getting to be a regular pick-up place. It isn't safe for girls to go in there alone any more. The few fellows left who aren't in the Army, pass all kinds of remarks about every girl who goes in there. Ann + I didn't stay long, you can bet on that. We went back on the beach again + then went home.

Dot came over last night + we just talked. I thought her nervous condition was improving a lot for the past few weeks but she said she went to Dr. Brodsky Saturday + cried for an hour in his office because for the past few weeks she's had crying spells again + had those "urges" again. The doctor thinks getting married will be good for her because she won't have time then to think about herself so much but still, he says, this condition might continue off + on for about six months yet, he couldn't tell. He said he's treated 17 or so people for the same condition exactly + they're perfectly O.K. now – it just has to take its own course. Dot says you'd understand better than anyone as you've been thru practically the same thing yourself + it's something that can't be explained to people – they just think it's silly. Well, I didn't say anything to Dot except to try to encourage her – saying that she'll feel better when she is married but personally, I don't think being alone all day will be any good for her and being so far away from her family, friends etc. I do hope everything works out for the best.

The lamp that I bought (that <u>we</u> bought) her from you + I was sent to her today. She called up this morning to thank me + told me to thank you too. She loves it. I'm glad she likes it so much. You'll like it too when you see it. I put a nice card in the box too – with yours + my name on it. It has a very nice verse on it. She has all her gifts on display in the living room. You can see them when you come, darling.

They are staying at the Taft Hotel in N.Y. That's where we stayed. Dot made reservations + they're having a double room – a bedroom + a sitting room with chairs, desk, etc. I think – for $6.<u>00</u> less 10% for soldier's discount. This certainly is cheap for two rooms. We paid $6.50 for each of our rooms.

Well, dearest, this is turning out to be a long letter isn't it? I'll be looking forward to your call tomorrow night (Tues.). If you want to reverse the charge go ahead – don't hesitate + if everything isn't clear about your coming at the end of 3 minutes let's talk until it is. O.K.?

Dearest, won't it be wonderful seeing each other this coming week-end? I'll be so glad to see you, sweetheart.

Lots of love and kisses,
Rita "Colleen"
X X X X X X X X X X

1 P.S. The 'phone rates are cheaper after 7 o'clock at night – so a few minutes after 7 would be a good time to call, darling.

2. If you were here now I'd give you some nice kisses, dearest, I'll bet you're just "in the mood" for some too, heh, darling? Oh boy - - - - - - - - - (ha ha).

Monday 11. AM.
Interior guard Post 17 A
Magazine <u>Area</u> 30 foot tower.

Hello Rita Dear,

Hows my sweet little irish girl this fine day I am now up in my little <u>nest</u>, up in that 30 ft tower that over looks Fort Devens. It is quite a nice view, with the tree and countryside all shaded in greens, it looks <u>nice</u>.

I was taking a sunbath for about two hrs. So you see I manage to get my share of sunlight. Heh. dear.

Sorry for the pencel. It's the best I have with me.

Hope that your swim with Ann was very good.

Hope you diddint swallow to much of that good old salt water at Lordship.

I miss you dear so much, and your nice kisses.

I could go for some right now, say about a dozen good big ones. Heh dear.

Hope that I can get away in time for Dots' and Ernies Wedding But we will have to keep our fingers crossed.

Hope that all your family are well and that everything is going O.K. with them all,

Lots of Love,

Walter
(P.S. Had the Same post in April. Remember me telling you.)

Tuesday 8/17/43 3:30 P.M.

Hello Walter Darling,

I just finished reading your letter written while you were in the 30-foot tower, or in your little nest as you said.

Yes, dearest, I remember when you were on duty in April up there. At that time you said everything was just starting to turn green + looked so nice. There certainly must be a beautiful view from way up there. I'm glad you can get sun while you're up there – you must look nice + tan now.

I'll excuse your writing in pencil, darling, I know you wouldn't use pencil if you had ink with you.

You said you miss me so much, sweetheart, + my kissing. I feel the same way, Walter dear. The time until we see each other seems to be dragging by – it seems so long that we've seen each other. Well, it won't be long now + we'll be together – for a while.

Dot called me up this morning + said Ernie had just arrived in Bpt. station. At the time she called he hadn't reached her house yet but was to take a taxi from the station. She was so excited she could hardly talk. One can hardly blame her – not having seen him in six months + then all their plans being realized on Saturday. She didn't expect him until tomorrow noon but I guess he left Alabama Sunday night instead of Monday night. She wants me to call her tonight just as soon as I know whether you're coming or not. Oh, dearest, all day today I've been wishing + praying that you'll call tonight + say you can come Friday night or at least have a good chance of coming. I can hardly wait until you call tonight.

Yesterday I spent most of the day lazying around. Cele, Charlie Jeanie + I slept late yesterday morning. In the afternoon I washed my hair + got caught up on a lot of little odds + ends. We all went out to eat last night + then went to the Merritt Theatre to see "Spitfire" with Leslie Howard, an airplane picture + "Alaska Highway" with Richard Arlen. They were both very good. This morning I slept late again – until about 10 o'clock. Cele went to New York today with Sarah, Charlie's sister-in-law for the day. I went to the post office + mailed you the three pairs of socks I bought you. I kept the tie I bought here with your shirt. You can wear it if you need it or you can take it back with you. I hope the socks will be O.K., the size + everything. Maybe I should have sent you garters so they won't be all stretched out + fall down (ha ha). You should get them Thursday at the latest.

I went downtown about 1 o'clock this afternoon with Jeanie to get my gown – it was supposed to be ready today but it wasn't. I left it in the Handy Shop for alterations about three weeks ago. They told me it would be ready tomorrow surely. I hope so. Wait 'till you see me Saturday, darling, you might not know me all dressed up. The gown is a pretty shade of green + is made very full. The hat matches it + has a veil on it. I'll wear white satin sandals + carry gladioli. Mary will be dressed exactly the same only in yellow. I managed to get some film for your camera to take pictures + use up the rest of the film we have left yet but your camera looks as tho it's broken – it doesn't click right + I think there's something covering up the view (in the inside). You could probably look it over + fix it if you can come – if you don't come I'll have to take a chance on it the way it is.

I'll send you the $5.00 trainfare in tomorrow's letter + you'll get it Thursday. O.K. dearest?

I called Marino's (next door to you) + asked if I could speak to your sister Helene but she wasn't home. They asked if I'd like to leave a message + I told them I'd like to have Helene call me when she comes home. Maybe she's over to your sister, Lil's for the day + will call later – this evening or tomorrow. I'd like to go out with her Thursday night to the show.

I changed my mind, dearest, about sending you the money tomorrow. I'm putting it in this letter so you'll get it in plenty of time. I hope you'll have enough with this $5.00 to hold you over until you get home. If not, let me know, darling, + I'll send more.

Well, dearest, Walter take care of yourself so you'll be in tip top shape by Saturday so we can have another wonderful week-end together.

Love Always,
from
You know who,
don't you, dearest?
(ha ha).
X X X X X X X X X X X X

Wednesday 8/18/43 12:30 P.M.

Hello Sweetheart,

I'm writing this letter lying across my bed. I'm the laziest girl imaginable this week but I guess I might as well rest as much as I can this week 'cause I won't have another vacation until next year.

Well, darling, according to what you said on the 'phone last night everything looks unfavorable for you to say the least as far as your getting a pass is concerned but darling, you are so pessimistic about everything. I know your chances of coming are very slight but I won't give up hope of your coming until late Saturday night. After all, your first sergeant didn't say "no" definitely so something might turn up in your favor the last minute. You said you'd be lucky from now on to get home every other month. This might be so, but, Walter, why cross your bridges until you come to them? I'll admit it will be pretty awful seeing each other about every two months or so – it's bad enough now, your getting just a pass each month, the time in between seems so long, but if you're going to be so pessimistic about everything, our future (yours + mine) will seem very dismal + dark. Remember, darling, it's the <u>hope</u> in everyone's heart for a bright future that keeps people from breaking down under the constant strain they're under. Take the girls who have husbands + boyfriends out of the country for a long period of time – it's just the thought in their minds of "well this can't go on forever or he will be home soon (whether he will or not)" that keeps those girls from breaking down completely. Dearest, can't you see how lucky you + I have been compared to other couples. Ernie + Dot are good examples of what I mean. It seems right now as tho all their plans are being realized getting married + Dot going down with Ernie. Of course they both realize Ernie might go out of the country in the future but they are at least hoping for the best.

Dearest, I'll finish this letter later – I have to go downtown now to get my gown.

5:00 P.M. Here I am, dear, back again. My gown was finally ready. It fits very well now so I guess I'm all set for the wedding.

By the time this letter reaches you, you'll probably know about your uncle Gus dying. I knew it when I was talking to you on the phone the other night but I didn't want to make you feel any worse than you did. Helene told me just before you called + said she had written to you. I felt very <u>sorry</u> when I heard it but he's really better off after suffering for so long. It must have been hard on your aunt taking care of him all that time. Then, it's too bad one of his sons who's in England couldn't be here when he died. Helene said, she, your father, Al, Ellen, Adolph, Martha, Mr. and Mrs. Fisher + your uncle, Bill were all going to Hartford today.

Darling, please try to keep your spirits up. Everything might not be as bad as it looks right now. I'll be thinking of you, dearest, + I do hope you can at least get your regular week-end pass. If you find Friday by some miracle that you can come Friday, call up – reverse the charges – please call, darling if you do come so I'll know. If I don't hear from you I'll know you can't make it. As for your regular pass, if you do manage to get one, just come as soon as you can. If you get into Bpt. about 5:30 or 6:00 you could probably still get in touch with me at Roseland, if it's after 6 I'd probably be at Dot's or at 1440 so use your own judgment, darling. If you call when you get into Bpt. someone could go to the station + get you + bring you to wherever we are. O.K. darling? It would be so nice if you could see Dot + Ernie before they go Saturday. They said they're going to wait as long as possible for you. They'll probably leave for N.Y. about 7 o'clock.

They were sure of getting Dot's cousin to substitute for you up until yesterday but then his mother called + said she didn't think he could get the time off. He works in a butcher market + I guess even if he does get the time off, it'll be quite a loss of money to him – he's only 17 yrs. old. Ernie said he'd see if he could ask some of the fellows he used to work with. Don't worry, darling, I guess they'll get someone by Friday.

Dearest, this letter seems to be a lot of instructions to you doesn't it? It's just that I want you to be straightened out on everything. I love you so much, dearest Walter – keep your chin up + try not to worry about anything.

Everything will work out in the end.

Lots of love and kisses, dear.

X X X Rita X X X

Wed. 10. A.M.

Post 17. A. FORT DEVENS

Hello Rita,

So happy to hear your voice on the phone last nite.

So sorry that I could not give you a defenat anser about me coming home for the Wedding. Hope that it all works out O.K. So nice of Dots' cousin to come to Bpt from Jersey for the Wedding.

I am well and getting along O.K. the nite's are getting cooler while on post here at the fort. Some of the boys are packing <u>today</u> (24) of them and are being trasfered to Camp Edwards Mass. Last week Sat. (13) were discharged out of the Army because of some defect that had saped them to much to perform their duties. Boy who they Happy to leave. they were drunk for two days some of them. Some felt pretty bad about leaving <u>tho</u>. I think that will harm our passes that were due us boys. But time will tell. We will hardly have any one in school now that (35) boys have gone and left us. There were only about 40 in our school each week so that may mean very few passes each month.

Hows my sweetheart darling this fine morning. Lots of Love to my girl Rita.

Walter

Thursday 8/19/43 1:30 P.M.

Walter Dearest,

Received your letter dated yesterday written while you were on post 17-A.

I'm glad to hear you're feeling well, darling. You said the nights are getting cooler up there at the Fort. They're cooler here too, in fact the days are too. Today it's rather chilly.

I don't think the fellows who were moved to Camp Edwards will find it any better than Fort Devens do you, darling? I supposed they like the idea of being moved just for the fact that'll be something new — new surroundings etc. The 113 fellows who were discharged might feel happy to leave but wait until they get back into civilian life + have to do a lot of explaining to people. The adjustments will be much harder for them now while there is still war than if the war were over.

Well, dearest, it looks as though yours truly (me) will have to walk down the aisle alone Saturday morning — and walk back alone too because Dot + Ernie still haven't an usher. Dot's cousin called up from Jamaica + doesn't think he can get the time off because the fellow who works with him is sick. If he does come at all it might not be until Friday night late or Saturday morning.

Of course that would be O.K. because he really wouldn't have to rehearse – there's nothing much to ushering. They have another fellow in mind but they're not sure of him either. We'll just have to see how everything works out tomorrow. If only a miracle would happen + you'd come, darling but I suppose that's impossible + improbable. If you did come you'd probably have everybody pouncing on you + kissing you, we'd be so glad (ha ha).

Last night Cele, Charlie, Jeanie + I went to the Stratford show + saw "The Fleet's In" with Dorothy Lamour. It's an old picture (about the Navy) that was brought back by request. It was very very good – a lot of laughs + music. I've been going to a lot of shows lately it seems. Well, it's as good a way as any to pass away an evening.

Dearest Walter, I can hardly wait to see you. I miss you so much. If you don't get your pass this week-end I'll be so lost. I know you want to come so much, too, dear. I'll say a prayer for you, Walter dear - + let's hope for the best. I'll be thinking of you, sweetheart.

Love Always,

X X X X X Rita X X X X X

P.S. (1) I hope you've received the nuts Cele sent + the socks I sent by now. Did you, dearest?

P.S. (2) Would you like some nice kisses as much as I would right now? I hope so, darling.

Thursday 4. P.M.

Second Platoon

Dear Rita,

HOws my sweet little irish girl this fine August day, I hope that you are in the best of spirits and that you are in the best of health. I am sure that you are. Heh dear.

Give Cele my thanks for that package she sent. I did not get it as yet, but the boys said I had some mail and a package down at the mail room. I missed mail call at 12 o clock, but will be at the five o clock mail call to recive it dear.

I am feeling fine and I am getting along O.K., just as long as I miss those shippments. twenty more are to leave next week. but the first Sergeant does not think I am on it. that will make about fourth five men going with more placements, that looks bad for passes. it looks tough. Heh dear, but maybe not. Give Ernest and Dorothy and Dots family my best regards. If I do not get a pass over the week end I may call Ernest at Dots home to wish him and Dot the Happiest and best of life in there marrige. Rita dear I think about you at all times, while on post with another fellow I tell him how nice my girl is. He says boy you sure must have a good girl. I say I sure have.

Lots of Love

Walter

P.S. I bet Rita dear you sure will look very pretty in your nice new Wedding gown.

Friday 8/20/43 12 noon

Dearest,

I was so glad to receive your letter written yesterday, it was a nice one, darling.

I'll just get started on this letter because I have an appointment at 1 o'clock to have my hair washed + set for tomorrow. At this time tomorrow Dot will be Mrs. Ernest Smith. Think of us about 11 o'clock tomorrow morning, darling, going down the aisle. I'll be thinking of you, dearest, wishing you were beside me and wishing you could be there to see the whole thing – so that you'd have a good idea of what your wedding will be like when the time comes – our wedding I should say. I'll be lost without you there, sweetheart but I must try to make the best of everything + smile if it kills me. If I could only see you tomorrow night everything would be perfect.

It's very nice of you, dearest, to say you might call Dot + Ernie at Dot's house (if you don't come) to wish them happiness, but Walter, I don't think anyone will be at her house all day. From the church we'll go to the photographers + then to Roseland until about 6 o'clock – I guess if you called after that you could get them. It would be cheaper if you send a telegram to Roseland Restaurant 3320 Fairfield Ave. Bpt. to Mr. + Mrs. Ernest Smith between 1 + 5 in the afternoon (if you find you can't get a pass). When you call Western Union on the phone you'd just say you want to send a telegram to a newly married couple wishing them luck + happiness etc. + the telegraph office will word it for you but darling, use your own judgment about this – this is only a suggestion. I'll finish this later, darling.

4:15 P.M. I just came home from downtown after having my hair set. Cele is all curled up too. I'm supposed to be at rehearsal tonight at 7 o'clock – it isn't until 7:30 but Dot wants us to be at her house at 7. I don't know whether they have an usher yet or not. She said if they did get someone she'd let me know but I haven't heard anything yet. I have avoided calling her since Ernie's been home because I know she doesn't feel like wasting time talking on the 'phone while he's there. I hope I don't have to walk down to the altar alone nor come back alone but maybe they'll have someone the last minute. I hope the weather tomorrow is as nice as it is today – it's perfect today – not too warm + the sun is shining.

I met your sister at 4:30 yesterday + had a very nice evening with her. We ate before going to the show in "Ye Olde Tavern" + then saw "This is the Army". Don't miss it, dearest, because I think it's one of the best pictures of the year. There's lots of music in it + a good story too. After the show we went in the "Star" + had a sandwich.

Helene said there were quite a few people at your uncle's funeral, that she hardly recognized him laid out, he lost so much weight – of course this is natural after what he went through. She said your aunt is keeping up very well considering everything. Your cousin, Earl + his wife were there. She said he was laid out in a very nice funeral parlor + the cemetery where he was buried was beautiful. (as funeral parlors + cemeteries go).

Dearest, if you find you can't get a pass tomorrow (Saturday) try not to be too discouraged. I'll be thinking of you + maybe in another week you'll get one. I'll be wishing every minute you were here + whenever you do come, dearest, we'll make the most of every minute. If you don't come I'll tell you all about the wedding in my next letter + will send you the piece from the paper. Keep your chin up, darling, (I know things are bound to seem pretty bad at times) but if we try our best not to get "way down in the dumps" everything will work out in the end. Gosh, dearest, I'd love to see you this week-end tho.

Love Always,
These are big ones, darling. →X X X Rita X X X

Saturday 8/21 8:30 P.M.
(Ernie + Dot's Wedding Day)

Dear Sweetheart,

The day for which everyone has waited so long is practically over now. I've enclosed the piece that was in this evening's paper that I think you'll like to read but I'll give you the little details that I know you're anxious to hear.

The wedding was beautiful, darling, everything went off very well and oh, dearest I can't tell you how much all of us – Mr. + Mrs. Smith, Dot + Ernie + of course myself wished you could have been here. I couldn't help but think of you, dearest, throughout the day. I know how badly you must have felt, too, not being able to get a pass even for the week-end. Several times during the day different people remarked "If only Walt was here, everything would be perfect."

I'm home alone now, sweetheart + I guess you know without my telling you how badly I feel to think that you can't even come home tonight. Darling, I just have to keep telling myself that you + I must have lots of happiness in store for us and that we'll see each other soon, no matter how bad everything looks right now.

Let me give you a little description of the wedding.

Last night (Friday) we all went to rehearsal of course + afterwards went back to Dot's house + had sort of a party. There were Dot + Ernie, Bill May = Mary Buccino + I. Incidentally, the piece in the paper reads that Charles Farrell (Dot's cousin) ushered. He did usher but he didn't walk down the aisle. They had another fellow by the name of Ray O'Kane who ushered too + who walked down the aisle with me. He couldn't come to rehearsal last night but he knew just what to do this morning because the priest explained everything to him this morning. Getting back to last night we had a nice time at Dot's (of course it could have been a lot nicer if you were there, dearest). Mrs. Smith served a lunch + had the dining room all decorated in red, white + blue. We got home from Dot's about 12 o'clock last night. This morning we had one of those large cars with the two seats in the middle – they hold six people – take the whole bridal party to the church, photographer's + Roseland. It made it very nice because then we could ride all together. Dot hired the car from

Hayden's Taxi Service.

The wedding ceremony itself was beautiful. First I walked down the aisle with Ray O'Kane, the usher, then came Mary (the maid of honor) alone + then Dot + her father. When we reached the altar Mr. Smith gave Dot to Ernie + then went in the seat. (While we were coming down the aisle Ernie + Bill May walked out from the sacristy (at the side) + stood together until we came down). Then we all genuflected together + stood while the soloist sang "Ave Marie". Then Ernie + Dot went to the top step (outside the altar rail) + the priest read some prayers, they recited their vows, Ernie put the ring on Dot's finger + then they were Mr. + Mrs. The priest read some more prayers + it was over – we all walked out with our partners – Ernie + Dot first, Mary + Bill, Ray + I. Ernie was a very nervous bridegroom much more so than Dot. Mary was also nervous going down the aisle – as for myself before I got to Dot's house this morning I wasn't very calm, but once I got started down the aisle I didn't mind it at all.

After the Church we all went to Brignolo's to have pictures taken. We spent about an hour there. By the way, darling, we'll have some developed of the group too besides one of Dot + Ernie alone. I had one taken all by myself, darling for you – with all my regalia on – gown, hat, flowers etc. It's taken sitting down. He took two poses + there will be six pictures altogether. They won't be very large so you might like to keep one, sweetheart. The proofs will be ready Thursday + as soon as I get the picture I'll send it. Of course I'll have one of the group as well as one of Ernie + Dot too.

From the photographers we went to Roseland, + the dinner was served promptly at 1 o'clock (chicken dinner). After the dinner there was dancing + everyone had a wonderful time. There must have been about 65 people there Dot Maguire, The Blakes, Joe was home + came with Dot, Ruth + Ann came + of course Cele, Charlie + Jeanie. Everyone seemed to have a good time. It was over around 5:15. Dot threw her bouquet + guess who caught it! (I did). You know the tradition – whatever single girl catches the bride's bouquet she is the next bride. Of course I don't believe it but lots of people do. Everyone seemed to take it for granted that I will be (except me).

After the people left we went back to Dot's but no one went to the station with her as there were no more cars available by that time. I managed to get a ride with one of the fellows who was there – he took pictures of the ceremony in Church, he used to work with Ernie. Dot + Ernie took a taxi to the station. They got the eight o'clock train to N.Y.

Gosh, I felt so badly when I had to say good-bye to Dot. You can't imagine how much I'll miss her. They'll be back from N.Y. about Monday or Tuesday but won't have time to see anyone because they'll have a lot to do before they go to Alabama which will be about Thursday. She said she'll miss me a lot too but of course we can at least correspond.

I saw Ernie for the first time since he's been home last night at rehearsal. He looks good, has a nice tan but keeps very thin. They were so tired after the day was over – between the excitement + rushing around last week. He's such a quiet fellow. Dot's Aunts, cousins, uncles etc. kept remarking that they never met such a quiet fellow. As many times that you, he Dot + I have been out together in the past I can't say that I know him. He's very hard to approach. Today he looked anything but a happy groom – Dot says he thought everything was too long-drawn out. I guess it was because he didn't know hardly anyone there + doesn't mix well. He should have been more pleasant because Dot's relatives + friends will have to be his now, too, in fact Mrs. Smith told him this. Mr. Smith says he can talk to you much more at ease than with Ernie. Oh well, as long as he's kind + considerate to Dot, that's all that matters I guess.

Dearest, writing all the details of the wedding has made me feel a little better. I miss you so much, darling. I'd give anything to see you right this minute. I know you must be anxious to get home soon too – maybe you can next week-end, darling. I'm so tired now, Walter, I'll just have to go to bed. I danced quite a bit today – with the ushers, Bill May, Warren, the fellow who took all the pictures + some others I didn't know. I was just thinking, if I feel this way (so tired) after someone else's wedding, imagine how I'll feel after my own. (ha ha). I'll finish this tomorrow, sweetheart (X X X X X X).

Since writing the above I got myself ready for bed but found I couldn't sleep – I guess I'm over-tired. I still feel like talking to you, dearest – I'm writing this in bed so excuse the writing, please.

Ray O'Kane, the usher who was my partner is a fellow you'd like to meet, darling. He's only 18 but looks much older. For the past three summers he's worked in the Brass Co. where Ernie worked + during the fall + winter goes to St. Thomas' Seminary + is studying to be a priest. He's starting his third year there next month + has six more years of study ahead of him. He will make a wonderful priest because besides being so interested in his studies he has a wonderful personality – is a "regular" fellow, one of the nicest anyone could meet. You'd enjoy holding a conversation with him, darling, he's exceptionally intelligent + told me quite a bit about Seminary life + some of the good times he has had too. He stayed for the breakfast but had to leave right after as a friend of his who's in the Marines was home on pass + is going to be shipped out of the country so he wanted to say goodbye to him. He managed to dance with Dot Grant, Alice + Dot Blake while I wasn't there + the question came up as to who would be the next bride from the ex-club girls. Dot Grant said she surprised everyone by being the first – Dot Smith is the next + Dot Blake said she might be next. They asked Cele when you + I were getting married + guess what she told them! She said we had no plans yet but that you would like to be married this year but I hadn't decided yet. I guess she just made this up because a short while ago she asked me if we (you + I) were going to be married this year or next. I told her as far as I knew it would be next year. Imagine! That's just how people take things for granted which is really a joke because if anyone would like to be married this year it's I not you.

Dearest, I hope you find time to call up tomorrow. I'd love to talk with you just for three minutes. It's the next best thing to seeing you, darling. Lots of love + kisses, sweetheart – I guess I can sleep now.

Sunday 1:00 P.M. 8/22

I'm so glad you called me this noon, dearest. You sounded quite cheerful in spite of the bad breaks you had – not getting any pass. I felt so much better after talking with you, darling – after I saw you didn't let it get you 'way down in the dumps'. I know you'll try hard not to let those things get the best of you in the future. I know it's so hard for you, dearest because you've been used to coming home practically every four weeks + then yesterday when you couldn't, you were bound to feel depressed. As I said on the phone it's better to take a pass whenever you can get it – whether it's during the week or not, what difference dearest, as long as we can see each other some time. I can always take time off from work to spend with you. Don't forget, sweetheart.

It must have been an awful place to be on a Saturday night as you said on the phone – in Ayer station. If it were a busy station like Bpt. with people coming + going all the time it wouldn't be so bad. I know you must have been thinking of the wedding all day yesterday, dearest, but we were all thinking of you, too + wishing you could be here.

Cele said Ellen called up yesterday early in the afternoon + asked if you would be home for the week-end. Cele explained everything to her – how you were supposed to come for the wedding + that you still might get a week-end pass but still Cele thought there was just a slight chance. Ellen said she'd like to see you – I guess the four of us go out or something – she + Al + you + I. Whenever you do come, you could call her up at least if you didn't have time to see her.

Ann Preston called this morning + I'm going to her house later this afternoon – then we'll take a walk down to St. Mary's – I guess Ruth will go too. Then we might go to a show early this evening. I don't know. It will pass the day away for me. I try to think of Dot as married – Mrs. Ernest Smith but it seems unbelievable even after the wedding + everything. I guess you'll know how much I'll miss her. Everything (our friendship) just can't be the same as it was before – we won't have the same interests any more – Mary Buccino feels the same way. She's known Dot since they were 5 yrs. old – they grew up together + were always the best of friends. Of course we'll write to each other + maybe by the time you + I get married the four of us, Dot, Ernie, you + I can resume our friendship the way it was before. When the war is over they'll come back to Bpt. + the Smiths + Kleins can visit each other. Don't you hope it all works out this way, dearest?

Dot's mother + father surely will be awfully lonesome too. She's always been very close to them. Mrs. Smith said she'd like to see you whenever you do come home so let's make a visit over there, heh, Walt? They said in losing Dot they've gained a son (Ernie) but Mr. Smith still feels as tho he doesn't really know Ernie as he's so quiet. I called Mrs. Smith up this morning + talked for a few minutes. She was very blue + was glad I called. Dot gave Mary rheinstone earrings + gave me a pin of rheinstones with a small blue stone in the center for being attendants. Ernie gave Bill May + Ray O'Kane tie clips of sterling silver – one had a dark blue stone in it + the other a ruby. They were very nice.

Well, darling, it'll probably take you quite a while to read this volume I wrote (ha ha). Don't strain your eyes. After today I won't have anything to talk about with the wedding all over + Dot gone. Well, I'll still keep writing anyway to tell you I'm thinking of you always + loving you so much. Take care of yourself, dearest + we'll see each other soon I hope.

Love Always,

X X X Rita X X X

P.S. This is the longest letter I've ever written – 14 pages

Monday 8/23/43 6:00 P.M.

Dearest,

I hope this letter finds everything going along smoothly for you – after your week-end disappointment of not coming home.

I went into the office today after my vacation all rested up and ready for the old routine again but instead found everything changed so much it took me all morning to get over the shock. The changes, as far as I can see, are not for the best. I'm now Secretary to K.N. Trefry, Purchasing Agent. Ann Preston is going to do my work (stenographic) + Ruth is coming downstairs again in the outside office to work for a Mr. Morrison who was sent to our plant to push production ahead but who has left his position entirely from the government + is now working for E.W.C. In a few days I'll be moved into a small office where there are just Irene Noonan, Assistant Secretary of the Company, Mr. Trefry + myself. I will be alone practically – that is I won't be in contact with the rest of the girls (which I don't like), the position doesn't pay any more – it's just that it will be secretarial work instead of stenographic that I did before. I told them I'd rather continue doing the work I do now as Mr. Trefry is a very very hard person to work for but they want me to give it a two-weeks trial at least, then if I don't like it I can be put back on stenographic work in the outside office, so I guess I'll give it a trial but I dread it. Darling, I hope I'm not boring you with all these facts about myself but I just felt like telling you.

Yesterday afternoon I went to Ann's house + Ruth was there, also Eleanor, Ann's brother's girlfriend. We all went for a walk to St. Mary's By the Sea + it was beautiful down there. We walked along the wall + then sat down on a bench awhile + watched the water – the sailboats + people fishing. It's surely one beautiful spot. Then we went back to Ann's house, had something to eat, took a bus from there downtown + went to the show. Ruth, Ann and Eleanor wanted to see "This is the Army" so I went too even tho I saw it with Helene last Thursday. I didn't mind seeing it twice it's such a good picture + one I would like you to make it a point to see because there is a girl in it, Joan Leslie, whose name is Eileen in the picture + she's in love with Ronald Reagan, a corporal in the Army. We (you + I) are in the same position they are in (in the picture) + Joan Leslie's opinion on marriage is the same as mine – I'd like you to see it, then you'd know just how I feel.

Dearest, ever since I wrote you the letter asking you to tell me more about yourself + less "mushy" stuff, your letters have gone to the other extreme, altho you probably don't realize it. Now, I miss all your endearing words. Do you think you could write in a happy medium, tell me about yourself, how everything is going with you + also how you feel about me? The letters you wrote before were more like yourself than the ones I get now. (ha ha).

I miss you so much Walter, dear, I'll be so glad to see you (soon I hope). Maybe you'll be lucky + come home next week-end.

Love Always,

X X X Rita X X X

Monday Nite 5: P.M

Dear Rita.

Hows my sweet little irish girl feel after walking down the ailse as a bridesmaid.

I recived your letter that you wrote Friday and I am so happy to hear from you each day. Huh Rita

I just missed getting a weekly pass by a hair. I was on duty at the Ayer Railroad station over Sat - Sunday So I was kept quite busy. Tonite I may get off, the first in about ten days, I may go for a ride to Fetchburg [?] to say Hello to a fellow that operates a <u>Grill</u>. For Pat Marino that is now in Sicily Italy, In his last letter he was saying how he would like me to get in touch with that perticaler fellow.

Pat and Andy Corka are now both in Sicily. I hear from them both each month, they are both well and getting along as well as could be expected under <u>combat</u>.

Lots of Love to my Sweet irish girl, you are so sweet RIta dear.

I Love you <u>Rita</u> <u>Marie</u>.

So happy to hear that the Wedding worked out O.K. Give my regards to Dot and Ernie and Dot Family.

Lots of Love Walter

Tuesday 8/24/43 6:00 P.M.

Hello Darling,

I hope you are well today and are managing to have a little free time to yourself – I didn't receive any letter yesterday or today but there must be one on the way (I hope).

I started my new position today – my desk, Dictaphone, etc. were all moved into Mr. Trefry's office. He was away on business today in New Jersey so I had a chance to get caught up on everything + get used to my new surroundings somewhat. He'll be in tomorrow so the fireworks will begin then I guess. It's very lonesome in there tho, without all the girls. Well, I'll try to make the best of it anyway.

I received a card from Dot + Ernie saying they have a lovely room at the Taft + that they were going to see "Sons of Fun" + also to the Hawaiian Room of the Hotel Pennsylvania + were having a swell time. I called her mother last night + she says she dreads to see Dot go down to Alabama with Ernie, she'll be so lonesome without her. I talked with her for a few minutes about the wedding + she said whenever you do come home for you + I to stop over to see her + Mr. Smith. I told her we surely will. She's to let me know when Dot + Ernie get back from N.Y. as I'd like to see Dot before she goes.

Do you think there's any chance of your coming home this week-end, dear? You never did have to wait six weeks for a pass (it will be six weeks after this week-end) but I suppose everything is different now with all the fellows gone.

Ruth thinks her boyfriend will come home soon from Alaska now that the Japs have left Kiska. It will be a year next month since she's seen him – I hope he does come. If so, they'll get married.

I'd feel much better tonight if I had mail from you today – I just can't seem to get used to going so many days without a letter. I haven't had one since last Thursday. So darling, can't you give me a break + throw a little ink this way, it's not rationed + it only takes a few minutes to write a page just to let me know you're thinking of me. I don't think I'm unreasonable, do you? I love you, dearest.

Love Always,

X X X Rita X X X

Wednesday U.S.O. 9. P.M.

Ayer Mass.

Dear Rita,

Hello Darling, I have been quite busy so far this week, traffic duty prison guard tues + Wed from 5 A.M. to 6:30 P.M. So that accounts for the fact that I am slipping in, on – Corspoundac [correspondence] you understand, dont you dear.

Darling you are so good and so prompt with your letters. P.S. thanks Rita for the stockings they were the right size. Dear. I enjoy them, so much, and I look forward to each day for your letter Darling Rita Rita Marie you are the <u>Sweetest</u> <u>finest</u> girl in the World

Bunny you are so sweet and so nice, I will kiss you so nice when I get home.

This coming week I think, I am going on interior guard, so I will not be able to get home for a another week. Dearest.

P.S. I could love you so nicely right this moment Bunny.

Love

Walter

Thursday 8/26/43 6:00 P.M.

Hello Darling,

I hope you're in tip-top shape and everything's going along smoothly with you. Dot Smith called the office about 5 o'clock this afternoon and said she + Ernie were practically on their way to Alabama – they were leaving for New York at 5:30 + would get the 9:15 train out of N.Y. for Georgia + then change trains to bring them right down to Alabama. They wanted to be in N.Y. at least an hour ahead of time because it's so hard to get a seat on the trains now. Her mother or father were not going to the station with her – they feel so badly – it would only be worse for them. Mary Buccino said she wanted to go tho but I decided I'd rather not. I said goodbye last night at her house + I guess you can realize how badly I felt – even now, after talking with her on the 'phone I have a very desolate feeling. She's the best friend I ever had. It's a terrible feeling to say goodbye to a very dear friend + not know when you will ever see them again. I certainly wish both her + Ernie all the luck in the world + told them you did too.

As I told you in yesterday's letter I went over to her house last night + Bill May, Mary + Warren (I don't know his last name) were there + of course Mr. + Mrs. Smith. Ernie looks very well – he's gained five lbs. since he's been on furlough + they both looked <u>very</u> <u>happy</u>. I spent a nice evening there – we played records, sang while Dot played the piano. She brought me back a lovely hand-made luncheon set (small tablecloth + napkins) from N.Y. for my hope chest – also one to Mary but not the same kind. It was certainly nice of her – I don't know why she did it. Warren, the fellow who develops pictures as a hobby, made up about 4 sets of the pictures he took with a flash bulb at the wedding. They are quite large + came out pretty good. I didn't come out so good in one of them but that was because I didn't even realize he was taking it. I was going to send them to you but I think it would be better if I didn't send them thru the mail because they might get all bent. You can see them when you come home, dear.

Getting back to the subject of last night, they told us about all the places they went. They liked the Taft Hotel very much – they said they had a lovely room. They went to see "Sons o Fun" (the one I saw), also went to some swanky night club near Central Park (the bill for the two of them was $15.00) – they went to RCA Building to view N.Y. from the 75th floor. They also saw the Normandie which is being brought up a little more each day. They had a wonderful time but they said the time went by too fast. When you write to Ernie from now on, by the way, you can use their home address which is: Staff Sgt. Ernest Smith, c/o Mrs. Holman, 126 Brood St. Ozark, Alabama. Ernie said it's in one of the large, old, houses the South is well-known for + they have a large room. I misunderstood about it being so far from the camp – it's only a half-hour's ride on the bus. Mrs. Smith served drinks, cake + ice cream + we didn't leave there until about a quarter to twelve.

I happened to be upstairs with Dot alone last night + she said she + Ernie were talking about you + I when they went away + decided that you + I should get married + asked me why we don't. It certainly was embarrassing – I didn't know what to say. I told her we might next year and that it would be hard now as you're a private + would most likely have to stay at the barracks + I probably wouldn't see you very much so we were going to see how everything would be next year. She thinks we are silly + Ernie can't understand why we aren't. They both said we'd be better off if we were. I don't know what they mean by saying that – it could mean lots of things + I don't like the implication. I don't see why people say things like that – I'd never think of saying anything like that to a single couple – after all it's our business. I guess they don't realize how everything is that's all. They also kept asking if I told you that I caught the bouquet – I told them I did tell you – along with all the other details of the wedding. They said they hoped you knew what that meant. I guess one reason why Dot + Ernie would like you + I to get married is that then we'd have everything in common again (the 4 of us).

I wish I knew if you were going to get a pass this week-end or not, dearest. How I wish you could! Let's leave it this way – If I don't hear from you by six o'clock Saturday, that'll mean you're not coming +I'll probably go to the show with Ann if I don't hear by that time O.K.?

Darling, I miss you so much – I wish I could see you.

Love Always,
X X X X X X Rita, "Colleen"

P.S. Did you ever receive those socks I sent you? Also, did you like the nuts?

Friday (<u>fish day</u>) 11:30 A.M.

Dear Rita.

Lots of luck in your new job Darling Bunny, I am so sure you will use your utmost ability to progress more and more as time goes on. Heh. dear, with your mentality and your nice personality Dearest your will reach the highest mountain peak. <u>Rita</u>. dear. I <u>am</u> <u>sure</u>.

So nice that you could go over to Dots home to see Ernie and Dot before they left for Alabama. I wish them both the utmost of happiness and success. they are both such nice person's. P.S. I sure did enjoy that nice long letter that you wrote Sunday and Monday. Bunny you must of gotten writers grimp or something he dear. I bet you had to take a break every half hour. <u>Ha ha</u> I am feeling fine and I am kept quite busy. especially now that we have just enough of men to preforme our duties about the Fort and nearby towns. last nite I was on the alert, that is to be ready to go on duty just in case I am needed for any thing that comes up on the spur of the moment. I and three others were on duty this coming week I think I am going on another week of interior guard duty. I bet as far as I can see.

Lots of Love,
<u>Walter</u>

P.S. Bunny dear I Love you so much I can hardly wait to get home to hold you in my arms and kiss you nicely <u>Heh dear</u>.

Sunday 8/29/43 12:15 P.M.

Dearest Walter,

I was so happy to receive a letter from you yesterday (Saturday). I like to get mail on Saturday because then the week-end doesn't seem so lonely.

Darling, I think you over-estimate my ability when you say that I'll progress in my work to such an extent that I could reach the highest mountain peak. I had to laugh when I read that, dear. Anyone who can hold a job at E.W.C. is lucky. Yesterday they fired Mr. Sweeney (you've heard me mention his name before). He had been with the company for 24 years and knows more about the company, its operations, accounting, etc. than anyone. The reason they fired him was because for the past year or so, he hasn't been well, has a heart ailment and has stayed out of work once in a while. He felt so badly when he was told, he cried + everyone in the office hated to see him go. They also fired the Jewish girl who was secretary to Mr. Butler, the Works Manager. Everyone was glad to see her go because she had been getting paid for doing nothing. Mr. Butler came into Mr. Trefry's office (the man I work for) + said Mr. Trefry had just taken me for his secretary in time – that if I had been in the outside office Saturday he would want me himself but now that I'm working for Mr. Trefry he wouldn't have me moved again. That made me feel good. Working for him would only take about 3 hrs. a day so maybe I'm just as well-off to stay in with K.N.T. (that's what I call Mr. Trefry – his name is Kenneth Norman Trefry) – ha ha.

Darling, I hope I don't bore you talking about the office – I never did tell you much about my work did I? Maybe I will from now on – you might get a kick out of the goings-on of E.W.C. (ha ha). It's surely a funny office.

I imagine Dot + Ernie are in Alabama by now – they expected to get there by Saturday noon. I'll probably get a card or letter from Dot this week sometime. I miss her so much – especially over the week-end. I used to go to the show with her Saturdays + go over to her house Sundays – then during the week we always called each other up. I called up her mother yesterday + she said the house seemed so empty + that she was very lonesome. She hadn't heard yet from them but expects to soon. I told her when you come home we'd surely go over to see both her + Mr. Smith. She said she'd be tickled to death to have us + was going to have some pickled herrings for you, darling. How would you like that?

Dearest I laughed my head off when I read the part of your letter where you said I must have had writer's <u>grimp</u> when I wrote that long, long letter last Saturday + Sunday. I guess you meant "writer's <u>cramp</u>" (ha ha). You say you think I had to rest every half hour while writing it, well I didn't. I wrote half of it Saturday night + half Sunday morning – with no breaks in between (ha ha).

It must be hard for you now, Walt, with so many fellows from your outfit moved. I don't know whether I should say this or not, but Cele + Charlie said that if you can't work all those hours, why not tell them you just can't keep the pace + go on sick call once in a while. In fact, they think you should have done that right from the beginning. I think there were lots of times since you've been in the Army that it was quite an effort for you to keep going on those broken hours. It was hard before with all the fellows there, but now it'll be harder seeing they aren't going to be replaced. What do you think about this, darling? Maybe we're wrong – you might be so used to broken hours now, you don't mind it at all. In any case, don't wear yourself out trying to keep going if it's too hard. For instance, if you find yourself getting headaches + dizziness – that would be from lack of sleep + I don't see why, if you explained to your commanding officer, you couldn't be allowed an easier routine. Ever since the 1-B fellows were reclassified there have been quite a few discharged because they couldn't keep the pace, as you know. I'm not saying that you should be but it doesn't hurt to give in once in awhile, do you think so, darling?

In the Sunday Post's Magazine Section today, there are a lot of pictures of M.P. girls. It shows the different duties they have to perform, knowledge of "Judo" which is knowing the leverages + vital nerve centers, truck convoy duty, traveling on the Troop trains, giving commands to carelessly groomed W.A.A.C.s etc. If you can get the paper in the Service Club or wherever they have them, you might enjoy the article + pictures.

I do hope you can get a pass next week-end, dearest. It will be six weeks + it seems so long. I suppose it would be impossible for you to get a three-day pass over Labor Day – you'll be lucky to get a regular one, heh, dear?

Last night I went to the show with Ann + Ruth – We saw "The Sky's the Limit" with Fred Astaire + Joan Leslie (the girl who played in "This Is The Army"). Incidentally, did you see "This is the Army" yet? I'm sure you'd like it.

Darling, Jeanie is sending you some cookies that she made. They have raisins in them. She's sending them tomorrow so you should get them by Wednesday. I hope you don't find yourself in the hospital the next day (ha ha ha). She had a half-year of cooking in school last year so they should be pretty good. She'd love it if you wrote her a little note letting her know what you think of them, O.K. dear?

This is turning out to be another volume isn't it sweetheart? It's 1:15 now so I guess I'll close + eat my dinner – it's ready. Since you didn't call up you must be quite busy, dearest. I hope everything is alright with you, sweetheart. I miss you so much, darling + love you so. I'll keep on hoping that you can come home next week.

Love Always,
Your Future Wife
X X X X X X X X X X.

P.S. Your sister Helene just called me + was wondering why you didn't come home this week-end. She thought you were coming because in a letter she received from you during the week you said you expected to see us all this week-end. She baked a cake + your father bought duck thinking you were coming. It's a shame that she fussed like that. I told her I didn't expect you this week. Helene wants me to go up to your house for a while this afternoon so I guess I will. I told her I'd be up about 4 or 4:30. Darling, it would be better if you didn't write in letters to her that you expect to come (even if you're sure at the time) because Helene fusses + everything for nothing. O.K. dear. I'll probably have a nice visit at your house this afternoon dear.

Sunday 4: P.M.
Second Relief
4: to 8.

Hello Darling,

Hows my Sweetheart this fine day. Darling I wish I were with you on the Sunday afternoon, I hope to see you this coming weekend dearest, I miss you so much, I miss your Loving and companionship and your kind understanding (ways). Rita you are the Sweetest and most cheerful girl in the World. Keep up your good spirits. Bunny Sorry I did not call today, I got up late and than I said to myself I would write instead of calling. In that way I would save fifty cents. See darling how much Jewish I have in me (<u>Ha</u>. <u>Ha</u>. or something) wanted to keep the few dollars that I have until pay day – Thursday.

Rita do you feel sometimes the way I do. I bet not quite so romantic or passionate Heh dear. Leave it to Kleiny, that's where I shine. You know me. Dont you dear.

Lots of Love
Walter

Rita what a big wolf I am Heh dear. Ha. Ha. But I love you so much dear – I can not help it Bunny

Monday 8/30/43 6:45 P.M.

Walter Darling,

You don't know how happy I was tonight when I found your letter written yesterday waiting for me.

It's perfectly alright that you didn't call up Sunday – I realize you must sleep as your hours are so long – it was nice of you to write – as long as I know everything is O.K. with you I don't worry when I don't get a call from you. You say you saved 50¢ by not calling + that it must be the Jewish in you. It's a good thing you wrote "ha ha" after it or I'd think there <u>is</u> some in you, darling. I'm surely glad you aren't – I can tolerate any nationality but that one.

You certainly were in a devilish mood when you wrote that letter, dear. You say I probably feel that way sometimes too. Well, dearest, I don't think I have such strong desires as you have but I often do wish I were a part of you + that you were a part of me – in other words, that we could belong to each other physically as well as every other way – thru the sacrament of marriage of course. You and I always tell each other that the physical part of our love comes last + companionship is first. This is true but we can't overlook the physical expression entirely can we, dearest? Along with so many other things about you, I also miss your kisses, darling. I guess it's only natural. I was just thinking today – it seems so long since we've been close together. I hope you can get a pass next week-end, dearest I miss you so much, your companionship + advice + nice long talks we have sometimes.

Yesterday I went to your house, darling. It makes me feel very good to be able to say that – at last. Your father was there but went out to Cherry's. He said "hello", how are you – etc. + then said they expected you home – I told him you'll probably get home next week-end. I had a very nice visit with Helen. I stayed for supper. We ate the duck + salad + all the other good things that were especially for you, darling. Helen said if you do come next week you'll probably have to eat <u>chicken</u> (ha ha). We talked awhile then when it was time to leave about 8:30 Helen + I took a Barnum + State bus downtown instead of her walking down with me to Bruce Ave. (it was too dark). We had some ice cream downtown + then I left her + went home + she took a Barnum + State bus back home.

Helen is a very nice girl – she likes to fuss when you come home – really looks forward to it. Her birthday was Aug. 24th + I didn't know it or I would have sent a card. She received quite a few of them.

She wants me to go with her to a fortune-teller this week Wed. or Thurs. I told her I'd go just to keep her company but I wouldn't have mine told.

Dearest, it's getting late so I'd better mail this letter.

I love you so much, dearest – try your best to get a pass this coming week-end.

Lots of love + a million kisses

X X X Rita X X X

Tuesday 1: o'clock.

Second Platoon

Hello Bunny,

I just took a nice warm shower and washed all of my cloths, undershirt, shorts. <u>Ha</u>. <u>Ha</u>. stockings, handkerchiefs, and shaved, cut my fingernails, and toenails. see darling I am kept quite busy. Ha. Ha.

Darling when you are my Loving wife, you can maybe do a few of those things for me, Heh dear. and I will do a few chores for you, of course we do not want to slave and work our selves to death, but doing some of those things sometime for each other will be a lot of fun, wont it dearest.

When you take your daily bath, maybe you will want me to help you wash your nice back, Ha. Ha. and viesa and versa. O. boy dear we will work together always. Heh dear. Rita be prepared for a lot of Loving Bunny, because I miss you so much and your nice companionship, and kisses, and Loving. I will Love and Karess you dear so much, that we both will enjoy it very much. I hope that you feel like Loving me also Rita Marie. It must be that good climate up here that makes me want to hold you so close that we will not want to part but stay embraced for hours.

O Rita it will be so good when we are one (<u>one</u>), so we will be able to express ourselves and show our Love to the fullest, and share each others feelings. Rita how do you feel about it, dear. I bet you are rearing to go, once we get <u>married</u>.

See Rita how much I want to be with you. Rita what a big wolf I am, the irish are suppose to be very hot tomatos, but I do not think they can be any more sentimental than the people like me. <u>Heh</u> <u>dear</u>.

Rita do you feel like you could hold me tight and hug me for hours too. I bet you do too sometime.

Hows my fiancee and Sweetheart. I hope to see you this week end and will we make up for lost time. You bet we will, but only in moderation. Bunny so you do not have to worry you know me, dont you dear. I dont care much for to much smooching or loving do I dear Ha. Ha. (<u>not much</u>)

Lots of Love.

<u>Walter</u>

P.S. Don't let any one see this letter dear.) its too spicey.

P.S. I hope no one sees this letter. Heh dear. It is to (mushy)

Tuesday 8/31/43 6:30 P.M.

Dear Sweetheart,

Just read your long letter that you wrote yesterday. I was so glad to receive it, darling, + surprised too – after getting a long one from you yesterday. You must be in the mood this week to write (ha ha).

Don't worry about my ever letting anyone see that letter, Walt, I'd collapse if anyone did. What a mood you must have been in!

Yes, dearest, when we're married you + I will enjoy doing things for each other – one thing I think I'll like to do for you is wash your hair. Isn't that funny? I'd like you to wash mine once in a while, too, dear (when we're married). I guess all this working together – helping each other comes under companionship. It'll be a lot of fun I think.

You say you are doing fairly well controlling your feelings seeing we haven't seen each other in so long. The time to do your utmost to control them is when you come home, dearest. We have no right to lose control of our emotions when we're together + I do know, it's very hard, but we are not married yet + should try to be careful. If we were married it would be wonderful, as you said, + could express ourselves to the <u>fullest</u>. From what you've said, not only in this letter but before, + from the way I feel too, we are certainly both ready for marriage emotionally. When two people love each other the way you + I do + find it so hard to restrain ourselves when we see each other, then there is no question but that they should be married. I love you so much, darling. I do hope you'll be home this coming week-end.

I suppose there's no use of your trying for a 3-day pass. If you only could get one it would be wonderful with the holiday (Monday) – I don't have to work.

Ann Preston invited me to her house for the evening (tonight). Today is her brother's girlfriend's (Eleanor) birthday + Ann is having a few people at the house. Her brother has been shipped out of the country but they don't know where he is yet. Before he went he left enough money for a diamond for his father to buy it as he never had time when he was home on pass. So Mr. Preston will give Eleanor the diamond tonight for her birthday present from Joe (Ann's brother). I wouldn't like to get one that way but I guess there's nothing else Joe could do. He's a very nice fellow + Eleanor is a nice girl.

Well, dearest, just 3 – ¾ more days + you'll be home (I hope). I can hardly wait to see you.

Love Always,

X X X Rita X X X

P.S. I feel in the mood for loving – myself, darling. If you were here now there would be two dents in the divan (you + I would be there (ha ha).

Thursday 9/2/43 12:45 P.M.

(Pay Day) – Lunch Period

Dearest,

Your letter written Tuesday was waiting for me when I got home last night. It was such a nice one, sweetheart.

Post 8c, the pumping station where you were on duty sounds like a very pretty spot with the trees, lake etc. all around.

It surely makes me very happy, dearest to hear you say that you think about me so much while you're on duty there – about all the happy days we have spent together and all the happiness we will have together in the future. Thanks, dear, for all those nice compliments.

I'm also very glad to hear you don't find the hours too much of a strain + that you're now managing to get in some "good rackets" as you call the different jobs. I still think tho, darling if you do find sometimes that the long hours bother you, it wouldn't do any harm to go on sick call or explain to your commanding officer that you just can't keep the pace. I'll finish this when I get home tonight, dear.

5:45 P.M. Here I am at home – we only work until 5 on Thursdays. As I told you I was going to, Helen + I went to the fortune-teller last night. Of course I didn't have mine told – I think it's silly. I don't believe in that stuff at all (I didn't want to discourage Helen too much tho) + above all it's definitely against the Catholic religion to believe in fortune-tellers. Well, I guess Helen was rather disappointed in the whole thing. The fortune teller didn't tell her very many good things – I'll let Helen tell you about it when you come home.

Yes, dearest, as you said in your letter Helen + your father have been very good to you. She likes to fuss when you come home. You say I'd better see if I can find her a boyfriend (ha ha). Well, darling, it is a shame that she isn't married – she'd be a very good wife for some fellow. She seems to be a very unhappy and disillusioned person but of course I'm just telling you this, dear, I don't want you to repeat it – it's just my opinion. I think if she were working she'd be much better off – I mean doing something she'd be really interested in – then she wouldn't have time to think of herself. Also, if she worked she'd be amongst people + could make friends. I'd never say anything like this to her, Walt, I'm just telling you so let's keep these opinions to ourselves. I wouldn't hurt her for the world – she's been so nice to me. I know she thinks a lot of you, darling, even tho you might think she didn't show it so much before you went in the Army. Also your father – don't ever think he doesn't miss you or worry about you – he does. I wouldn't tell him things that might worry him if I were you.

I get those poems I send you from different places – yes, darling, they are typed by me, some of them at least. I sent away for a book of poetry – some of them came from that book, others I cut out of magazines, some from girls in the office. I'm glad you like them. I like poetry very much. A lot of what I sent you is very sentimental isn't it, dearest?

Darling, you certainly are a "love bug" this past week or so. I am too – it's been so long since we've seen each other. I don't doubt that you will shower me with hugs + kisses but, dearest, we don't want to wear ourselves out – we want to enjoy the week-end don't we, sweetheart?

When I wake up Saturday morning I'll say to myself "At last, this is the day my dearest is coming home." Maybe I shouldn't count on it so much tho, heh, dear?

I'm going to call Mrs. Smith tonight. I haven't heard from Dot yet – Mrs. Smith must have heard by this time. They have been gone just one week tonight. I miss Dot so much. I wonder how she likes Alabama.

Here's a joke, dearest:

Physican: "Lady, if you want a health examination, you'll have to remove your blouse."
Kitty – "Oh, no, doctor – no"
Physican – "Come come - Don't make mountains out of molehills" (ha ha).

Do you like it? – it's spicy.

Dearest, just two more days + I'll see you – I hope. You were lucky you weren't moved from Ft. Devens with the other fellows, I think.

Lots of Love and Kisses, dear.
XXXXX Ritamarie XXXXX

P.S. I love you.

How would you like riding in this contraption and being kissed by me dear Ha. Ha. Ha.

Dear Rita,

I recived your Nice card Bunny, It is so nice of you to think of me so much, cards, nice letters, and gum, cookies, stockings, candy, and all those nice kisses that you are going to give me when I see you this coming Sat. Sept 4th (I hope)

Bunny you are the Sweetest Irish Colleen in the world. Keep up your good works and I am sure you will be repayed for all that you do for me. dear. kindness and cheers are the best and do not cost to much. Lots of Love Walter

P.S. NO MORE INK. Ha. HA. HA. (Keep Smiling) <u>Bunny</u>

Friday 9/3/43 6:15 P.M.

Dear Sweetheart,

Received your Thursday's letter and also the postal card. The card was a cute one – especially the way you marked it. I wouldn't mind riding in that "contraption" as you called it – with you, darling.

I'm glad you enjoy the things I send you from time to time, cookies, candy, cards, ties, socks etc. It gives me a lot of pleasure to buy things for you, dear, you deserve everything the best.

Jeanie said she had a letter from you today telling her you enjoyed the cookies but she won't let me read the letter – imagine that! She says I never let her read the ones I get from you, that's why. (ha ha). I'm glad you liked them, dearest. I was afraid they'd be stale by the time they reached you.

Dearest, I do hope nothing prevents you from getting a pass this week-end. I want to see you so much. I need your understanding + companionship right now. If you don't come I think I'll stay away from this house for the week-end. Thomas has two weeks off – he started last Tuesday + well – you can guess how everything has been since then. He's been drinking ever since + has everyone in the house on edge. I try not to let myself get upset but I can't help it – I feel very depressed when he's around here like that. The worse he gets, the nicer Cele + Charlie are to him – it seems that way to me. Well, dearest, I hate to even mention these things to you but right now I feel so depressed I wish I were a hundred miles away from here. Your coming home this week-end will certainly help me a lot, dearest. By the time you get here Saturday (if you come) he'll probably be half-way sober + you'll wonder how I could feel this way. Well, dearest, I think you can understand my position anyway – also Jeanie's. We hate to ask our friends here to the house when he's here – it's so embarrassing. There's no saying anything to Cele – she feels sorry for him + would never say a word to him.

Last night I called up Mrs. Smith + she wants us (you + I) to come over Sunday afternoon. She'll have pickled herrings for you – she made them herself. Mary (the Italian girl who was Dot's maid-of-honor) will probably be there. She visits Mr. + Mrs. Smith quite a bit. I told her we'd surely stop over. She said she had two letters from Dot + she loves Ozark, Ala. She said they have a beautiful room, very large with a fireplace, big chairs, lamps, a desk etc. + is in a lovely house. Dot has gained weight already so I guess married life was what she needed – to overcome that nervous condition she had. She said Ozark is a town just full of soldiers + their wives to be near the Camp – there aren't many civilians. I'm so glad everything seems to be working out so wonderful for her + Ernie. It makes it nice for Ernie too – he can come home to Dot every night. Well, dearest, maybe our day is coming? Do you think things could work out like that for us?

Well, dearest, I'll expect you tomorrow if I don't hear otherwise from you. I hope you can manage to get into Bpt. about 5:30. If you can't get a pass, I just dread to think of the week-end but I'll just have to make the best of everything that's all. If you do come, dearest, have a nice trip down + rest, if possible, so you won't feel tired Saturday night.

Lots of love and kisses, dearest.

X X X Rita X X X

P.S. Good Luck, dearest – I'll be so glad to see you.

Tuesday 12:00 Noon

Dear Rita.

Hows my sweet darling, Gee Bunny I had such a good time over the week end with you. Rita I love you so much. You are my lifes inspiration and my lifes companion to ease each others joy's and happiness. Heh dear. I worked all day yesterday from 5. A.M. to 7 P.M. Tuesday from 5 A.M. to probably 6 P.M. So I Well I may get some time to my self. I had no time to write last nite. I got 4 hrs sleep last nite. Boy was I tired after all that trip, days work and all.

Lots of Love. To my Future Wife, <u>Rita Lavery</u>

P.S. I can hardly wait to be your husband

September 8 '43, Wed. 6:30 P.M.

Hello Sweetheart,

Your postal card was waiting for me when I got home from work tonight. Leave it to you, Kleiny, to pick out a card like that with a hula hula girl on it + a picture of you (the wolf) in furs. It was cute tho, darling.

You sure must have been awfully tired Monday night after such a long day + the week-end too. I don't see how you will be able to work those long hours for any period of time. Darling, please don't try to keep going if you find it too hard – it won't hurt to give in to yourself once in a while – in fact, I think you'd be better off if you did. After all the Army isn't going to worry about your health either now or after the war, so it's up to you, dearest.

Everyone here was glad to hear the news about Italy surrendering (unconditional). That's one of the axis powers gone anyway + people seem to think this is the beginning of the end. Maybe Mr. Smith is right after all – saying this mess will be over by Christmas – that is, as far as the European mess is concerned. As for the Japs, well, we can't afford to be optimistic on account of them.

I read the little booklet titled "Your Wedding Dreams" written by Oscar C. Hanson (one of the ones you brought home this last time). I don't know whether Oscar Hanson is a Minister or a layman but I think the booklet is very good. I do know he is a great Advocate of the Luther League. There is a paragraph about it in the book. It says the Luther League is the best place to meet genuine Christian friends + that every pastor thanks God when two Luther Leaguers unite in marriage. This is very true I think – it's the same thing as the clubs the Catholic Churches have like the Regis Club (St. James) + the "Stella Maris" (Blessed Sacrament). That's really the purpose of these clubs to bring young people of the same religion together.

All this brings me to what we were talking about Saturday night, darling. Ever since Sunday I have been worried over the things you said Saturday nite (about you + I). I didn't want to appear over the week-end as tho they did bother me because I didn't want to prolong the subject + spoil your week-end so dearest, later on this evening I'm going to write you another letter that will cover the whole subject. I haven't time to write everything in this letter – I want you to get this tomorrow + it's getting late now. You'll probably get the letter I write this evening about Friday.

I just want you to know exactly how I feel on the subject of Religion as far as you, I, the Catholic + Protestant Religions are concerned when we get married. Don't worry, sweetheart, everything will work out I'm sure. I love you, dearest.

Lots of love + kisses
x x x Rita x x x

Wednesday 8:45 P.M. 9/8/43

Dearest Walter,

You've probably received the letter I wrote earlier this evening by now. I hope so at least. I just want to talk further than what we did Saturday night on the subject of Religion.

Sunday morning when I was in church all the things you said Saturday (about you + I getting married in the future + how religion would enter into it) struck me all of a sudden. You know how it is, darling, sometimes things don't strike you until a day or two later – then you begin to think + you might get everything straightened out in your mind then or you might not. Well, that's how it was with me Sunday, the more I thought about what you said, the more confused I was.

First of all, let's take your position from the time you met me until now. You said your brother + sisters always told you to try to go with someone of your own Faith but you were always somehow attracted to Irish Catholic girls. Then you met me – you saw we were beginning to care for each other + the first New Year's Eve we went out together you brought the subject up of Religion but at the time I didn't realize you were trying to tell me it wouldn't work – you + I loving each other. You probably don't even remember the conversation now but I do – you said you didn't think I knew what love was, there are so many things that enter into it – Religion the most important. Well, as I said I just didn't give it much thought at the time – we kept going together until the following June + then you said (one day down on the beach) that we should let our hearts rule us + not our heads + that you'd like to go "steady" with me. By this time we both loved each other. From that time on the subject of Religion came up once in awhile + you explained just how you felt about mixed marriages – you believe the children should be brought up in whatever religion the mother was although you didn't say much in regards to you + I until about the beginning of last year. Then you said you admired the Catholic religion – some things about it but a lot of things you didn't agree with. It wasn't until the night before Thanksgiving that we talked seriously of being engaged. By that time you knew surely that I would never marry you unless it was by a priest + in the Catholic Church – I think I made that understood right from the beginning. When we became engaged it was with the understanding that we wouldn't be married for at least a year + a half + you agreed that we'd be married by a priest, in Church + if there was any children they would be brought up Catholics. Up until this past Saturday night, darling, I thought that was understood but now you say since you've been away + have had time to think of everything, you are sometimes doubtful as to how everything could work out. You say you can't imagine your father even going to our wedding (in a Catholic Church) nor the rest of your family. You also say you should have given more thought + straightened everything out when you gave me the diamond but now that the time is coming closer, you can't help but feel badly that we aren't the same religion. You say your father + the rest of your family probably would go to our wedding – that they'd go for your sake. I don't know what you mean by that, dearest. I think what you mean is, although they'd be against the whole thing, they'd go just to make an appearance. The thing that really hurt me, darling, was when you said our difference in religion is what has been holding you back – that if we had been both the same right from the beginning, you probably would have been married long ago. Also somehow when you were talking you said something about if you + I should be separated – neither of us could stand it. I don't know how you could even think of such a thing – how could we stop going with one another for no reason? I don't understand what you were trying to say there either. I'd like to give you my position. To say a few words: I'm not asking you to give up your religion. I realize it means just as much to you as mine does to me. Don't you know I regret just as much as you do that we are not the same + probably never will be the same religion? As far as your family is concerned, they too must realize my religion means just as much to me as yours does to you. You say there'll always be that coldness – I don't think it will be as bad as you say it will. The two things I am asking you to do are: that we are married by a priest in the Catholic Church + that in case of children, they are baptized Catholics. It would have to be this way or not at all. If we are going to be married in the future, Walter, you know this is the way it would be – you have known it for the past two years so, dearest, I can't understand why all these thoughts are just occurring to you now.

We have a lot of things in our favor, to have a happy marriage – I'm confident everything would work out. We both love each other very much, we are both broad-minded, understanding, each of us willing to help the other + if we both pray + do our utmost that God will bless our marriage – I don't see why we couldn't live in complete harmony.

I guess you don't realize it, but that conversation of Saturday night has caused me so much heartache. I have been thinking ever since – suppose you find you just couldn't marry me (in the future) in the Catholic Church + that you just couldn't consider bringing our children up Catholic – I'd hate to even think of the outcome of a decision like that. Of course, if you find that is the way you feel, you should tell me right away – not keep going with me. If it had to come to that, it would be better to break off entirely than to keep on + on with all those doubts in your mind. Oh, dearest, it hurts me to write this but I don't understand all this uncertainty in your mind. I have the feeling sometimes + have had it lots of times before you went in the Army that you are pushing me away from you. It's hard to explain – but you know what I mean.

When I read on the postal card you sent me that you could hardly wait until we're married I thought – well, maybe you just felt depressed Saturday night + didn't realize how awful the things you said sounded.

Dearest, when you read this long letter, don't feel that you have to write a long one in answering it – I just wanted to let you know how I feel about our chances for a happy + holy marriage. I would like you to tell me, though, whether you think I should go on assuming our understanding will be the same – that we are both working towards marriage at sometime in the future or not. I'll always love you, dearest no matter how you feel about me. I'd like you to "put all your cards on the table" as it were + be frank with me.

Love Always,

x x x Rita x x x

Wed. 11:45 A.M.
Post M.P.

Dear Rita,

Hows my Fiancee and my Love Darling. Rita I Love you so much. I wish I were with you always. the more I am with you the more I want to be with you. See Bunny dear. you are my little girl, and the best in the land. I recived your nice letter yesterday nite and I am so happy to hear form my Rita, the best Sweetheart in the world. (Dear.) (Bunny) Yes Mr + Mrs. Smith sure did make us feel at home, we sure did have a very enjoyable time at there home. Those pickled Herring sure were good. Ha. Ha.

Rita I sure did have a very enjoyable week end with you Darling. It could not have been any better, spend, that nice walk home to your home sure was very nice, I enjoyed it too. Bunny. Heh. Dearthat nice soft hammock on my porch was very comfortable, was'ent it dear. We have a very nice time swinging together, I though about how nice we both enjoyed swinging there. It just tickled my spine, Boy we are two Love birds. Heh dear. But I like it very much. I would not part with it or anything. Bunny. that Ending dear sure did meet my approval. Rita I like when you finish your letters like that. See Rita I am getting the desire, more and more. Before you know it I will be pestering you all the time, about getting Married <u>Ha. Ha</u>. No Rita it does not scare me <u>very</u> much., it just tickles my spine when you End your letters, <u>Rita</u> <u>Marie</u> my <u>future wife</u> and the future Mrs Walter J. Klein. <u>O. Boy</u>. Today I am on school, so it gives me time to rest tonite I am on patrol at the Wac Area to make sure what Wac's are left will not be pestered to much Ha. Ha. I go on at 4: P.M to 12. P.M. Midnite.

Lots of Love
Walter

P.S. Yes dear I think I sure did have enough of hugging and kissing dear to hold me until I see you in four weeks I hope. I like your loving so much. O. Boy.

Thursday 9/9/43 5:45 pm

Dear Sweetheart,

Your Wednesday's letter was such a nice one. After reading about how much you love me + that you are getting the desire more + more to get married etc. I'll just consider Saturday nights' conversation a bad dream + try to forget the whole thing. I know you were very tired + probably depressed too + everyone is bound sometimes to say things they really don't mean when they feel "down in the dumps". I know you love me, dearest + you know I do – it will take all the rest of our lives together to show each other our love won't it, dear? I'm going to do my utmost to make you happy. We won't have to have a lot of money either, dearest. As the saying goes, "We haven't a lot of money but we have a lot of fun" – not that I expect only fun out of our lives together – what I mean is – just sharing the simple things of life together will be wonderful.

I called up your sister Helen last night and she wasn't home so I called Ryan's – across from your sister Lil's + Helen was still at Lil's. She intended coming home today. She + I are going to the show Saturday night, to eat first, then to the show. She said Lil is feeling better now that just the baby was home, Joan + Carol are staying at Jack's mother's for a week or two. Joan can't go to school for a few weeks anyway as she has the whooping cough.

Ruth Landry is so sure her boyfriend is coming home from Alaska that Saturday she + the girl who's to be her attendant are going to look at bridal gowns, veils etc. to get an idea of prices + how long it would take to wait for it after it's ordered – so that when he does come she can do everything in a week. I think this is awfully foolish for her to be looking at gowns etc. because her boyfriend never said he was coming – he thinks he'll be there for quite a while yet, in fact, but Ruth thinks just beause the Japs left Kiska that the Army won't need all those fellows up there now. If he does come I guess Ruth will hog-tie him (ha ha) + rush him to the priest. Well, I hope he does come home soon both for his sake + Ruth's — they haven't seen each other in <u>one year</u>. Just imagine, dearest, what would you + I do if we didn't see each other for a whole year? I can't even imagine it + don't even want to think of such a thing. You + I are lucky, dearest, seeing each other once a month.

Ann Preston hasn't heard from her brother in about 3 weeks now so I guess he's gone out of the country. Her boyfriend Will, thinks he might go out soon too he's been in a year + a half.

Dearest, take care of yourself — get as much rest as you can. I think about you all the time. I want my sweetheart to feel in tip-top shape all the time. I love you, Walter dearest.

Lots of love and kisses
Rita, Your Future April, May or June bride
(I hope). (ha ha)
X X X X X X X X X X

Friday 11:30 A.M.
Fish Day at Fort Devens

Dear Rita.

Sweet kisses to my Love on this Nice September day, It is nice and cool up here in these hills, I prosume it is cool also in good old Bpt Me and my friend driving around in a cruising car is all right, at least we did not have to walk this time on that Wac patrol last nite, we got through at 12: Midnite, started at 4: P.M, So that was a pretty good detail, we get plenty of hot coffee and Sand wiches + and desert. O Boy, See we do all right Some time. Heh dear. I feel fine darling, I am all rested up after that strenous week end. I think I will live through it O.K. leave it to me. <u>Ha</u>. <u>Ha</u>.

Yes dear, <u>Italy</u> <u>unconditional</u> <u>surrender</u> is some good news, all the boys were sure happy to hear the good news. that helps plenty in getting italy out of the way.

That poem sure was nice, it fits us two to a <u>tee</u>. Heh dear.

Dont worry Rita dear about the Religion angle dear to much, it will all work out I am quite sure.

I sounded so Saturday as if you and I had a mountain in front of us that could not be passed, but we will manage to clib over that obstacle gradually, Heh dear.

We Love each other so much and I am sure we will manage to handle all difficuties as they arrive. Heh dear. RIta I could hold you close to me right now. I never get enough of hugging and Loving from you. We Love kissing each other so much. We are meant for each other, thats why.

Rita I am always in the mood for your nice kissing and close embrase. I am a old Love bug. Rita I wish you and I were together now, I hope that in early 1944 we will be Mr + Mrs <u>Walter J. Klein</u>. Heh dear.

Lots of Love
<u>Walter</u>

Sunday 9/12/43 1:00 pm

Hello Sweetheart,

It was so nice talking with you on the phone this morning – we talked about five or six minutes but it seemed like a minute – I could have talked to you for an hour, dearest – but as it was – it must have cost you almost a dollar. I could tell by your voice that you have a cold – that's too bad. Dearest, please take care of it won't you – dress as warmly as possible when you're on duty from 12 to 4 – try to get as much rest as you can in between times. You probably think I'm concerned about you a little too much, but, darling, I worry about you a little because you always try to keep going and never give into yourself even a little bit, so sweetheart, won't you please both for your sake + mine take good care of yourself?

Walter, I didn't mean to upset you when I wrote that letter last week on the subject of Religion but I was upset myself the more I thought about our conversation last Saturday so I thought I'd better be very frank about everything. I understand now, tho, dearest – you were tired + depressed + lots of times when you feel that way you paint a very, very black picture for the both of us. Darling, when you come home next time we'll iron out all the little kinks in the whole situation so we will be straightened out <u>once</u> ± <u>for</u> <u>all</u>. In the meantime, Walter, let's both pray for + look forward to a wonderful life together – I am sure everything will work out – we love each other so much and at least we can both pray to the same God to ask Him for his blessings on our married life (in the future).

Today is a beautiful September day. It's very cool but when I was out this morning going to church I felt that "September tang" in the air – you know what I mean, Walt. Incidentally it's Ernie's birthday too – he's 28 today. Today I was reminded of the days last fall when you + I went to the football games in Longbrook Park, Stratford – remember, dear? Oh what nice Sundays we spent together! You used to wear your corduroy jacket sometimes + looked so nice. Dearest, when you come home next time let's go to one if they have them this year, heh, Walter. I miss you so much sweetheart, especially when the seasons change, I think about all the things we used to do – I know you think of them too. The fall is a lonesome time of the year anyway, don't you think so, Walter? The month of September is especially bad for me because of losing my mother. It will be 2 years ago, September 27th. Christmastime is lonesome too because my father died two days after Christmas. This year it will be 7 years.

As I told you on the phone, darling, your letters are so nice. I like to hear about what you do – the hours you're on duty, where, if you go anyplace new + of course most of all I like the parts of your letters where you write "mushy" – you know, dear. As you said in Friday's letter you + I were meant for each other – I'm sure. <u>We could never be happy with anyone else</u>.

You say you hope we can be Mr. + Mrs. W. J. Klein in early 1944. I hope so too, Walter dearest. We'll be much happier when we belong to each other in every way. It doesn't seem possible that I will be Mrs. W. J. Klein in the near future. I guess I'll never feel grown up. I'll always have these kiddish ways even as the years go on but you won't care will you, darling?

I met your sister, Helen, at 5:15 yesterday. We went to the "Hitching Post" + had dinner then to the Poles' to see Claudia. It was good but I liked the play better. Then we went to the "Star" for a snack but first we had a slo-gin-fizz. It's the first time Helen ever had one. She liked it I guess. Then we had a B. L + T. sandwich + coffee – after that we staggered home (ha ha ha). Helen had to help me on the bus + I finally found my way home. Goodness knows how Helen got home. Maybe she hitch-hiked (ha ha ha). If you believe all this you ought to have your head examined (ha ha). I'll bet you could kill me if you had me near you now. Oh well, dearest, we haven't any money but we have a lot of fun.

I'm going to invite Helen to the house to spend the evening sometime soon. We can play cards or something. I hate cards tho – in about a week or two I'll ask her. I always enjoy going out with her – we talk a lot + of course your name creeps into the conversation quite a bit. Helen looked nice yesterday – she had a bluish-green suit on. By the way, Walt, I bought a new dress myself yesterday. It's an American Beauty color velveteen that's between a red + a rose shade. It's a two-piece + is quite cute I think. I hope you like it – I'll wear it when you come home. I'm going to wear it to the shower Wednesday.

Yesterday I also told Read's to send out those blankets I bought. I don't know where I'll put them tho. They'll be in great big boxes. You see Walt, when they're paid for the store won't keep them any longer + I made the last payment yesterday. You'll see them when you come home I think they're beautiful.

Well, dearest, now I'm going to wash my hair + dry it out in the sun. I don't know what I'll do tonight – maybe go visiting with Cele + Charlie. Ann Preston is in New York over the week-end + Ruth has a girlfriend visiting her from New Jersey. Ann has been acting awfully odd all this week – I don't know why unless it's because she's worrying over her brother, Joe. They haven't heard where he is yet. She has been snapping peoples' heads off (mine too). It's very unusual for her to act like that. When I told her Thursday that I was going to the show with your sister Helen Saturday she hollered + said "That's a fine thing to do – leave me alone over the week-end." That was before she planned to go to N.Y. She said "I hope you don't have a good time that your conscience bothers you all night." Isn't that silly? I asked her to come with us but the answer I got was "No thanks" very emphatically you'd think I didn't have any right to go out with anyone except her. Honestly, Walter, sometimes it's awfully hard to understand girls – they are jealous + gossip all the time about everybody. I think fellows get along much better amongst themselves than girls do.

Well, darling, I certainly write a long letter when I get started don't I? I hope you don't get eye-strain from reading them (ha ha). You're such a good sweetheart – I like to write you all my little problems + like to tell you everything. You're so understanding + kind, dearest. <u>Maybe</u> in three more weeks we'll see each other again. I wish with all my heart that we will.

Love Always,
The future Mrs. W. J. Klein (Rita)
P.S. I wish you were here so I could kiss you + you could hold me in your arms tenderly. X X X X X X X X X X – these are nice <u>long</u> ones, sweetheart.

Monday 9/13/43 6:45 pm

Hello Darling,

How's my sweetheart this beautiful September day? I hope your cold is better – that you are in tip-top shape.

Dearest, you'll never guess what I did last night! I baked a cake. Yes, sir I did – and besides it came out very good if I do say so myself. Cele + Charlie went out last night visiting + Jeanie + I were here alone. I looked through all the recipes in my new cook book for cakes + came across one that sounded good + made it. Jeanie wanted to help me but I wouldn't let her. It's a chocolate cake – plain – no frosting. We didn't have enough butter to make a frosting. I brought a few samples of it into the office + the girls liked it but they kidded me all day. They said "poor Walter". (ha ha). From now on I'm going to try different recipes in that book. There are some very good ones for salads, cooking meats, cakes, cookies etc. next week I'm going to try some cookies + if they come out good I'll send you some, sweetheart. I think I'll like cooking once I get started. What do you think, dear?

Ruth picked out her wedding gown Saturday in Reads. She showed us a picture of it in "Brides" magazine – it's white satin. I think she was foolish to order it because she hasn't the slightest idea if Donald will be home or when, but she said the reason she bought it was that it takes any of the stores at least a month to order a gown + if he does come, she can have that much accomplished. Boy, she sure is anxious to get married!

Ann Preston is back to her old self again – I hope she doesn't get into any more of those "moods". She had a nice week-end in N.Y.

Darling, I think about you all the time + wish we could be together. Isn't it odd, you'd think as time went on I'd get used to your being away + not miss you so much but it's just the opposite I miss you more + more each day + wish more + more we could be together. Our lives (yours + mine) are anything but complete without seeing each other isn't that so? Well, let's keep our spirits up (if we can) + wait patiently for the time when we can go back to normal living. We love each other so much don't we, dearest?

Love Always,
Rita, "Colleen"
Here are some nice big kisses for you –
X X X X X X X X X X

Monday 7: P.M.

Dear Rita,

Hello Darling, O. Boy how I wish I could have you with me, as I am getting ready to go to the theatre next to our quadrangle, here on the post. The Naome of the Picture, is (I have never been licked) If you were here with me dear, you and I could hold hands and have a nice time together, Heh dearest Rita. Later may be a few nice kisses. I recived your very nice long letter. Gee dear how I long for your mail each day It is so nice of you writing each day, you are very sweet. Today I got to bed at 4:30 A.M. in the morning, Sleep until 11: A.M. that gives me 6 Hrs. sleep. not to bad, had chow, chased prisoners until 5. P.M. Had chow again for my self, later chased the prisoners to chow, So I got through at 6: P.M. took a nice shower, shaved So here I am finally writing to you Rita my Love. O rita I love you so much. Yes Rita when I get home we can get a few nice kisses again, and Have a nice chat on a few small details Heh dear. So glad that you and my sister Helene had a good time together.

The show starts at 7 seven oclock so I better get going

Lots of Love, Walter

I will get out of the show at 9:30 = and get. 2 Hrs sleep before going on post 12 oclock midnite What a nitelifer, Heh dear

Tuesday 9/14/43 6:30 P.M.

Dearest,

I was so glad to receive your Monday's letter. I like your letters so much + look forward to each + every one of them.

I was so glad to hear that you manage once in a while to have a little time off to go to the show. I couldn't make out the last word of the title of the movie you were to see (ha ha). – "I Have Never Been - - - it looked like licked. It must be a new picture that hasn't played in Bridgeport yet.

Dearest, if you don't mind my saying, it's much better for you to go to a movie or to the service club, Lutheran Center or U.S.O. than to go out drinking when you have any free time. I know you realize it too, darling. I don't want you to pull yourself down by drinking or keeping late hours. I love you so much, dearest. It will be better for you in the end to "stick to the straight + narrow path" because then you can always have excellent health even in the years to come.

Walter, dearest, I'm enclosing some parts of that booklet you gave me on "Problems of Courtship + Marriage". I read the book the first time you brought it home + the last time you came you brought another copy of it so I read it thru again. These are the parts that are outstanding + that apply especially to you + I. It made me feel so badly, darling, when I read these parts over a few times – so ashamed to think that I could be so weak to let you touch me in any way that you shouldn't. As it says in one part, one might wish to be pure, pray, go to Church, novenas, confession + Communion but still knowingly put themselves in danger of losing it. (their purity). As it says in one part, these rules don't apply only to Catholics but to every form of religion. I have known all these facts since I was about 12 or 13 yrs. old + still with all my high ideals when you + I are together I forget everything. Read these pages carefully, dearest + you'll see why I am anxious to get married. You probably think I'm over-anxious but all these things are what I've been trying to tell you for quite a while. I guess if you were to compare our courtship or engagement period with other couples' we have a much finer love but we really have no right to compare ourselves with anyone else. We have tried somewhat to keep our love up to the highest level but at times we get mad at ourselves, don't we, when we lose control of our emotions? I know I could always trust you to the fullest that you would never go to <u>extremes</u> (you know what I mean) but even now I feel so badly when we forget sometimes — you understand, dearest. Especially since you've been away, it seems as tho we're both under a strain + when you do come home we have, up until now, made a habit of letting ourselves go too much.

According to this book, we are supposed to avoid being alone — you might as well say altogether, shouldn't kiss too much nor be too close to one another. You know how impossible that is when you + I see each other so little. Well, dearest, let me know what you think about all this — I guess you must feel the same way as I do — we would be better off married — we wouldn't be committing sin + wouldn't be making our love common as it will become if we keep on the way we are now.

Isn't it odd, that when couples are single sex seems so important + after marriage it becomes a minor thing after the couple is adjusted?

Although I hate to even mention it, each time I let you touch me in <u>any way that</u> I <u>shouldn't</u> I have to tell it in Confession — you can imagine how awful I must feel. It's so hard to understand — my ideals are just as high as they were when I went to Blessed Sacrament School but I can't understand how I can let you touch me the way you do sometimes. When you read these pages you'll see, dearest, why I think next June or even next spring seems so long to wait for marriage. To me it's wrong to keep putting it off but I know you just can't see it that way, dearest.

Well, dearest, I'd better mail this — it's getting late. Take care of yourself, sweetheart. I love you so much.

Lots of love + kisses,

X X X X X Rita X X X X X

Tuesday 6:30 P.M.

Dear Rita,

just got though reading your nice letter dearst.

O Boy how I just wished I was there when you took that cake out of the oven. I bet it was. <u>very</u> <u>good</u>, Heh dear, I bet you will be the best cook and pastry girl of your family.

I hope that those cookies will come out good, than I will eat, <u>Heh</u> <u>dear</u>.

I am still on the same schedual as yesterday, that <u>Moon</u> sure was very nice last two nites.

Lots of Love to my future wife, how do you like that title dearest. Rita It just thrills me so much to just think about how we are going to be husband and wifeie.

O Boy that will be just swell. I think we have been missing all the best part, but we will catch up, wont we dearest, after all we had to have our courtship period, <u>and</u> it was a very good courtship, Heh dear.

Rita I could Love you so much, right now, but I guess we can not satisfied our desire's all the time. Heh dear.

I am now going to the No. 6 theatre, to see 'He dooth it, that comedy show its that new movie.

Last nite that movie, We are never beaten was O.K.

Lots of Love <u>Walter</u>

Wednesday, Sept. 15th, 12:30 P.M.

Dear Sweetheart,

I just finished my lunch and thought I would say hello to you now and let you know I'm thinking of you (as I always am) because tonight is Dot Blake's shower and I'm supposed to be over to Mary Buccino's house by 7:30 – we are going together.

I don't know whether I mentioned in my other letters what I bought for Dot's shower. I bought a lovely vase – it's a very nice shade of blue and is an odd shape. I'd like to have one like it in our home (yours and mine).

Mary, (Charlie's niece) finally heard from Ralph. He's in Camp Gruber, Oklahoma and is in the Infantry. This is sort of a bad break for him being so far away and that camp isn't a good one either because Frank Collins, Vin's boyfriend had his basic training there and was only too glad to be moved from there. He says it's the worse place anyone could be. Well, maybe Ralph won't be there so long. Everyone feels sorry for Mary – she's finding it so hard to adjust herself. They were always together and Mary is the type of a girl who never bothered with girls, never cared to go out with them. It's too bad that she is that type because it makes it all the harder for her now.

Ann Preston's mother just called her up and said they have a "V" mail letter from Joe, he's in North Africa. The letter was dated Sept. 4th. That looks bad don't you think so? He's having combat training now and Ann seems to think they'll push the unit he's in right up into the "hot spots" as she calls it soon. Joe says the place he's in is filthy and there is so much disease they have rigid rules they have to follow. They have to carry a gun at all times when they leave their tents and if they are caught without their dog tags they are severely punished. He's so lonesome too. All the boys in the camps throughout the United States should thank God they are still here when you hear such things don't you think so, dearest? I was just thinking last night how awful it must be for our boys in Salerno, Italy right now. I guess you realize how lucky you are don't you, darling? You probably get discouraged in Fort Devens sometimes, Walt, but just think what the fellows are going through who are right in the midst of all the battles. So, dearest, if you go on fighting the "War of Devens", you'll be alright (ha ha).

I hope and pray this mess will be over soon and you and I will be together. I think about you all the time, sweetheart. It will take the rest of our lives to show our love for each other won't it?

Love Always,

Rita

Your Future Bride

XXXXXXXXXXXX

These kisses are great big ones. I wish I could give them to you in person. Oh boy!

Wednesday 5.P.M.

Relief Barracks

Dear Rita,

Hows my Sweetheart and fiancee today, I hope that you are in the best of cheer and spirits. Heh dearest.

I did not get to mail call as yet today, but will get your letter in twenty minutes.

I am still on the same schedule today I witness a general courts martial, it was quite a experiance, the soldier was charged with desertion, he was gone from his post for four 4 months, it was his second offense, there were twelve officers and one girl clerk. for Jury the soldier was given Seven 7 years at hard labor, all pay that is due, and becomes dues is lost, and at the end of Seven 7 years he is dishonable discharged from the Service. of Course if he is good he may only do about 1 one year, and reinstated into the army, thats the usual proceduare. every day at least one soldier is given a general court's martial, so that is not anything new. That Show last nite, (he dood it, showing Elenore Powell and Red Shelton was very funny good. Tonite I may see another movie, what's cookin, another comedie.

Lots of hugs and kisses to my Love. Rita you are so sweet.

Love Walter.

Saturday Night 9/18/43 11:00 P.M.

Dearest Walter,

I just came home from the show – I went with Ann Preston + Eleanor (Ann's brother's girlfriend). We went to the Warner + saw "So Proudly We Hail" with Claudette Colbert, Paulette Goddard + Veronica Lake + I might say it's probably the best picture of the year – that is, as far as giving realistic scenes of Bataan and Corregidor – you know, darling, it brings the war's horrors right before your eyes – into your mind – there's no story-book stuff about it. After seeing that picture you feel as though you've been through it yourself, it plays on your emotions so much. Well, when we were going into our seats in the show I gave the girls a good laugh by falling on the floor (ha ha ha). I thought the seat was down + it was so dark I couldn't see well. I landed on the floor instead of in the seat + the three of us laughed for the next half hour. If you were there dearest, you probably would have laughed your head off too. I guess I looked awfully funny sitting on the floor (ha ha ha). After the show we went to "Ye Olde Tavern" + had a sandwich.

I received your two letters today – one written Thursday + the other Friday. Dearest, that picture "I dood It" must have been extra specially funny for you to see it twice. It hasn't played here yet but when it does I'll see it. I'll bet the stage show you saw Wednesday night was good – pretty girls + all – as you said. You + your eye for the beautiful girls, Kleiny (ha ha ha). I know you, darling. You must have had a grand time for yourself admiring all those girls (ha ha).

About that philosophy I sent you - - I hope you don't think all preachers don't practice what they preach. I'd say about 90% of them do follow strictly what they preach. As far as you + I are concerned, dearest, let's try our utmost as long as we are still not married to keep our love on the highest possible level. I know we both have a strong desire to be very close to each other when you come home but as long as we're single we really have no right in the world to let our emotions go so far. I do realize tho, darling that all the preaching of rules on what to do + what not to do + all the reading about it in the world won't stop either of us from at least wanting to share our love in a physical way. The only thing we can do when you come home is to try not to be alone too much (and that sure is hard when we see each other so little). Well, anyway, darling, let's try our best from now on until we are married to give ourselves a real test of character by not going too far.

Dearest, it's 11:45 now so I guess I'll go to bed. Lots of love + kisses, darling.

Sunday 9/19/43 12:15 pm (noon)

Here I am again, dearest writing to my wonderful sweetheart. It's a beautiful day but the weather is very cool for September. I went to 10 o'clock Mass as usual, did a few little jobs in the house + now am waiting for dinner to be ready. You haven't called up yet but you are probably having chow or else on duty or something. I hope you are not working too hard, dear. I haven't answered your Friday's letter yet so here goes.

You asked me if I get as sentimental as you. Well, Walter darling, the only way I can answer that is more + more lately I wish we could get married. When I think the whole thing out there are more advantages to getting married than disadvantages. If you are worried about finances, darling, don't worry because as far as expense of the wedding are concerned I would have most of the expenses. The bride always does. I would pay for the reception and of course gown, veil, flowers for the altar + a gift for the attendant. You would pay the priest (which isn't very much) buy the ring (plain gold bands are cheap) buy the attendant's flowers + give a gift to the best man + then of course if there would be a wedding trip (I hope there would be) you would pay for it. So when it comes right down to it we can't use money (lack of it) for putting off getting married because even now, your $115.00 would cover your expenses easily. I think what you are concerned with most of all is that you wonder how your family would feel about it especially your father. Well, Walt, he knows we will be married sometime I'm sure, so it isn't as tho he would be stunned over the idea. I really don't think he'll mind too much. When we do get married we'll be better off financially I'm positive we would. I could save your entire allotment for our home + could live on my pay. The only disadvantage to our being married would be our being separated but if we don't think the sexual part of marriage is the most important part, everything should work out. Dot + Joe will be in the same situation that you + I would be. Joe will be away quite a bit but when he comes home he'll stay at Dot's house it will really be his home until the war is over + they will both save for their future home.

It seems logical to think if we wait until next June '44 it seems almost impossible that you would still be stationed at Ft. Devens. Of course no one knows about those things but as I said before it seems logical to believe that you won't be. I don't think the war will be over by then but that's my personal opinion + again no one knows.

Well, dearest, I'd like you to think all these things over + when you come home next time let's talk about them. I'm very anxious to know how you feel about everything. Please don't think I'm pushing you along by writing all these facts. I certainly wouldn't want to consider marriage at all if you feel entirely different than I do about it. So, dearest, let's get straightened out on everything when you come home next time. I mean tell me how you feel about the whole thing. I don't know why we evade even talking over the whole thing.

Dearest I hope you get the pictures I sent + also the fountain pen tomorrow or Tuesday. Charlie thought I was awfully silly to send you the pictures to have you pick out whichever one you wanted. He says the fellows will think I sent them as a hint that we should get married + that they'll keep kidding you all the time. That thought never even entered my mind. I realize that the picture would be kind of large for you to keep there – if you want you could take the picture out of the folder + send the folder back to me. Then it wouldn't take up so much room. You can use your own judgment, darling.

This week I'm going to put your $115.00 in the bank in my name. I have $13.00 in there from about 5 yrs. ago so then we'll have $128.00. I don't like to leave it around the house. From now on I won't keep any more than $50.00 in my bureau. Is this alright with you, dearest? By the way, how are your finances now? Are you managing to hold on to some money or are you broke? I hope you have enough until payday because if you haven't, it will be a shame to keep taking money from your $115.00. Let me know tho, dearest, if you haven't enough + I'll send you some.

I miss Dot so much – we always used to visit each other on Sunday. I've only had one letter from her so far + she's been gone four weeks. I know she doesn't like to write. I guess I won't hear from her much.

I have to eat dinner now so I'll close. Darling, what I wouldn't give to see you right now. I love you so much, dearest. It's awfully hard sometimes to keep our spirits up, isn't it, this war gets everybody down sooner or later. Let's hope + pray we'll get back to normal living soon.

Love Always,

X X X X X Rita X X X X X

PS – maybe in two weeks I can give you these in person heh, dear? I hope so. You haven't called up, its 2:15 now. You must be awfully busy, darling. It's perfectly O.K. Keep well + as happy as you can.

PART IV: The Reality of Combat

Family Tragedy in the Midst of War

As the war plodded on, Rita became more affected by it and disillusioned from it. In her letters from these months, Rita expressed her opinion that the war was futile and only served to disrupt lives. This point really hit home—and on a very personal level—when the boyfriend of her co-worker was killed in action.

Rita and Walter also had to deal with family tragedy. On November 21, 1943, Walter's sister Lilli (Lillian) Augusta Klein Bridges succumbed to cervical cancer at age 29. She left three young children: Joan, Carol, and John. The letters describe the grim events and how the larger Klein family was impacted. The story as told in the letters was not always pretty, but it was told in the black and white of daily letters.

Through the letters of this time period, the reader can also get a feel for life in 1943 as Rita mentions that Helene has been prescribed a new sulpha drug that works quickly to cure her sore throat. Of course, sulpha drugs are widely used today to treat bronchitis, pneumonia, and other bacterial diseases. Rita also tells Walter that their rental house is going up for sale, with an asking price of $5,800, which she feels is horribly over-priced.

Letters: September 20, 1943 – November 12, 1943

Monday 9/20/43 6:15 Pm

Dear Sweetheart,

I hope this letter finds everything going along smoothly with you. As you didn't call yesterday and I didn't get any mail from you today, I'm a little worried about you, darling. You are probably very busy tho.

Our little dog "Curley" was in the dog hospital (Dr. Pickett's in Stratford) over the week-end. She was sick for a few days last week + Charlie brought her to the doctor + he said to leave her with him for a few days. Charlie brought her home this afternoon + she's much better but awfully thin. The doctor said she didn't have enough calcium in her system (that sounds funny doesn't it for a dog to be lacking in calcium). I guess she'll be alright now. They've become attached to her now + wouldn't want anything to happen to her especially Virginia – she's crazy over the dog.

Darling, I wore the little yellow handkerchief you gave me today in the pocket of my skirt. It looked nice because I had a yellow blouse on. You have good taste, Walt.

Remember Virginia, in our office – the girl you danced with at the Christmas party last year? Well her boyfriend (he's Italian) went in the Army about two months ago + came home yesterday with a medical discharge. He's supposed to have a bad nervous condition but everyone thinks (from what Virginia says) it's just an act. He was stationed in Georgia + went in as a 1-A man. All of a sudden he wrote home that he just couldn't take Army life any more. I guess he must have been like some of those fellows in Ft. Devens who just won't eat, or do their work + finally are discharged. When Virginia was telling some of the girls in the office today about him they came right out + told her what they thought of him – that he's just a weakling. They even brought your name into it, darling. They said they could understand if a fellow like you who went in as a Limited Service man found he just couldn't stand the routine + that you would have every reason in the world to give in to yourself – but they couldn't see how a fellow of 21 who's in perfect health all of a sudden develops a bad case of nerves. Well, Walter, you hear about all kinds of people these days isn't it so? It seems to be mostly the Italians + Jews who just won't take it. What do you think about it, dearest?

Yesterday afternoon Eleanore + Vin came over + stayed for supper. They hadn't been here in a long time. They are both well. Eleanore is working yet but Vin thinks he might be drafted soon. He says if he is he hopes he passes his physical – he would feel bad if he didn't. I don't see any reason why he shouldn't pass. He really hasn't any idea when he will be called but says they are taking the married fellows so fast now, it will probably be soon. Eleanore is very anxious for you + I to get married. She says she doesn't understand what we are waiting for. (ha ha). She knows when the time does come that she will be the matron-of-honor. She + Cele were having a grand time talking about the kind of a wedding you + I will have. You know — they were giving their opinions on what I should wear, what kind of a reception we should have + so on + so forth. Eleanore said she'd give a shower on me. Well, darling, it seems as tho every one is awfully anxious to get us married. (ha ha).

Well, dearest, I guess I'd better mail this letter. It's almost 7:15. Take care of yourself, dear. I love you so much. You're such a nice sweetheart. I sure do miss you, Walter darling.

Love Always,

X X X Rita X X X

P.S. Do you think you will ever get a three day pass, dear? I suppose it's hard to tell. Let me know if you still have chances of getting one, heh, sweetheart?

Monday 12:10 P.M.

Post. M.P. Co.

F. Devens Mass

Dear Rita,

Hello Rita dear, how's my Fiancee and my Love today, I hope dear that you feel in the best of spirits and that you had a very enjoyable week end. These fall day's sure are very beautiful, even more so up in these hills, each day when I am on duty I think of you and the nice times you and I had during the fall days. How I <u>pray</u> and wish that you were with me on these beautiful fall nites, and days. I am now doing another week of interior guard duty, it should be my school week but now with less men, it is nothing but a <u>work</u> <u>house</u>, O well thats the way it goes, maybe we will get some replacements soon, so than we fellows can get some time off. I am going to keep after them for my three (3) days pass, thats the only way a fellow can get a pass, is to <u>hound</u> them and give them a <u>cry</u> story. <u>Ha. Ha</u> <u>Ha</u>. I did not have the <u>money</u> to call you yesterday, and I did not want to reverse the charges, so that accounts for me not calling yesterday. <u>Bunny</u> dear, Send me that five (<u>5</u>) so if I should get my (3) three days off next week I will have money to get home, if I do not get a pass I will have money until next pay day which comes in about ten (10) days Even after I buy care fire if I get a pass I will have a dollar for spending money to go to the show. I saw last nite the movie, (<u>Best</u> <u>Foot</u> <u>Forward</u>) it was a good musical, stareing Loucille Ball, and some new actors. I also saw the movie. phantom of the opera, staring Nelson Eddy and others. I also saw Edward G. Robinton in <u>Destroyior</u>, I am seeing plenty of good movies lately, I am not going out of the fort so much lately, See <u>dear</u> admittance 15 cents. Cheap. <u>Heh</u> <u>dear</u>, I am learning how to do it in passing a good evening of <u>diversion</u>. Rita I think about you all the time, especially at nite while on post. I am on the second relief. 4-8, it is very cool in the morning at (3) three oclock while (going) on post. We are wearing our overcoats allready at nite. Ha. Ha. <u>some</u> <u>fun</u>. Rita I always feel as thou. I could hold you close to me and hold you forever in my arms, and kiss you, O so nice. Rita. I _Love_ you so much. Rita I can hardly wait to get home, to see you darling. Rita I am always in the mood for your nice kisses and Loving. O Boy. Rita I sure do like my hugging and kissing I can hardly wait to get home to see you Bunny.

Love. Walter.

P.S. Rita, I wish I could hold you close to me, and maybe later go to bed with you. O. Boy. I am in the mood. It must be the Sun. _Ha_. _Ha_. _Ha_. O Rita I am such a hot _tomato_, always wanting to hold you tight and embrace you until we both are lost in _our_ _Love_.

Rita I still feel like writing to you darling, Rita I am a old divil as far as smoching and hugging in concered, Rita I think when we get _married_ we will be far better off, Heh dear, than we can express ourselves to the utmost. Heh dear. Rita I feel like I would like to hug you close to me and stay with you until I would feel all out of breath. Rita I am getting so I think marrgige will be good for us both, of course the War does not help it any, of everything is so uncertain and the money angle of the thing, But we will be able to express ourselves to the fullest both, physical, mental, and spiritial, Heh dear. _O_ I guess there are addvandges and disadvadages in all undertaking's...

O Boy I can hardly wait, to give and to take what marriage has in store, We will keep working together and not just think marriage will be the End of Endings, it is all hard work. One has to give something, in order to derive any happiness, Heh dear. We will give plenty to Keep improving our happiness together, Heh dear, - As I am writing this here letter I am getting a tickle right up my spine, O Boy. Rita dear, I am slowly arriving at that stage that we have been working for a long time. Bunny, _Marriage_, _companionship_, home, children, physical satisifaction, and to walk hand in hand through life together.

O Boy Rita we are now going places, Heh dear. We will get there. Won't we dear, a little late but never the less we will achive our _goal_ and _distanation_. Rita I feel now and have felt for months and weeks, like I would like to hug you close to me for hours, and hours. I keep thinking at different times how much we will defive from marrige. Rita I am so happy now as I am writing this letter. Rita beware the next time I am home, I will hug and kiss you so, we will have enough to hold us for a few weeks, Rita I do not get enough of your Loving it seems, just cant seem to get enough. Rita I feel in the mood for some right now. O Boy, I am a hot tomato. RIta we are not satisfied it seems just hugging, we want to even go further. O. Boy. Love Walter

Tuesday 9/21/43 6:15 P.M.

Darling,

I was so glad to get your nice long letter in today's mail. It was such a nice one, dearest.

Here is the $5.00. I didn't realize you were out of money. Gosh, dearest, it went fast this time didn't it? I hope this will hold you over until you get paid. It never occurred to me Sunday that that could be the reason you didn't call.

Yes, Walt, I think it's a good idea to keep hounding your officers to get a 3-day pass. You certainly deserve one – you have never had any time off since you've been in the Army except your week-end passes once in a while. Try your best to get one, dearest.

I saw the movie "Best Foot Forward" too, dearest. I liked it a lot. I've heard a lot about "Phantom of the Opera". It hasn't played here yet tho. Don't overdo going to the shows, dearest, you might get awfully tired of them – once or twice a week is enough, don't you agree?

Dearest, you seem to agree with me on the subject of marriage, except as far as money is concerned but, as I told you in Sunday's letter, your money that you have saved so far will cover your expenses easily, dearest + as for my expenses by Dec. 1st. I'll get $100.00 Christmas Club check that I intend to put right in the bank and besides Cele always told me not to worry about the reception – there is some money set aside fot that. You say the war doesn't help it. Well, I agree with you, dearest. We won't have a real marriage in every sense of the word – what I mean is – it will be hard to be separated from each other once we are married but when we are together (when you get home) we'll be able to be together in every way – we can express ourselves to the fullest as you said – physically, mentally + spiritually.

Yes, dear, we will both be working together – I realize our lives won't be a "bed of roses" at times but if we both try our best to think of each other – in all things – I'm sure we would have lots of happiness. Really, dearest, I'll do my utmost + I know you will too, to make you happy.

You said when you come home we never seem to be satisfied just kissing + hugging – we want to go further. That's true, darling + that is definitely wrong. We can never express ourselves to the fullest – there is always in the back of my mind that I am committing sin + my conscience bothers me for days after. So, dearest, if we both see all the advantages + disadvantages + there seems to be more to be gained by getting married, what are we waiting for? I really don't know. Why don't we talk everything over when you come come + try to compromise on something? It's hard to put all of our thoughts in writing.

I called Mrs. Smith up last night + she said Dot + Ernie are moving again. She said they went in with another couple + when the people who owned the house found out that there were two couples living in the house he raised the rent from $45.00 a month to $60.00 so Ernie + Dot won't pay it – neither will the other couple. Besides, Dot said they have found out that they'd be better off by themselves – the couple is nice but there is no privacy. They are moving at the end of this month + are going to try to find a place in Dothan, the nearest city to where they are now. Mrs. Smith said Dot is gaining weight + feels fine. So I guess married life has helped her a lot. Well, I hope when they get settled in their new place, they won't have to move any more. It must be hard moving all the time.

Darling, I'll have to close now it's getting late. I love you, dearest.

Lots of love and Kisses

Rita "Bunny"

X X X X X X X X X X

P.S. I hope you have received the pictures + your fountain pen by now. Let me know, please, dear.

Tuesday 12:13 ½ P.M.
(Roast Beef for Diner it was good. Ha. Ha.)

Dear Rita,

Loads of Love to my Sweetheart on this fine tuesday noon. Rita I recived your two beautiful pictures also my fountain pen, thanks ever so much for sending my pen, it sure comes in handy, I am sure this time I will not lose <u>it</u> (<u>this pen</u>) or damage it. Both pictures are real nice of you Bunny, you look so sweet and Lovely in your beautiful gown. Rita you will look ever <u>more</u> beautiful in your Wedding dress. (<u>gown</u>) Heh dear. Because you will be over bubbling with happiness and Joy on our Wedding day. Heh dear. Rita I <u>Love</u> you so much, Rita you are so <u>sweet</u>. Gee but this pen makes a difference at last I do not have to fill it every five (5) minutes. Ha. Ha. Rita Marie Lavery you are so nice and (<u>oh</u>) so <u>femmine</u>.

So happy to hear that Vin and Eleanore are both feeling fine and that everything is just fine and <u>dandy</u>. <u>Virginia</u>'s boy friend, just knows how to <u>buck</u> as we boys call it, well thats the way it goes. There are quite a few like him in the army. If being discharged from the army after only being in two months does not borrered him, well he is a fellow with a light concience or something.

Give your good looking pupie my regards and a speedie recoverery. <u>Ha. Ha. Ha.</u> Yes Eleanore sure will be a sweet girl to be your Matron of Honor. Heh dear. Rita I Love you so much. I could love you for hours and hours (<u>at a time</u>). I will not ever get tired of your hugging and <u>tugging</u>. <u>Ha</u>. <u>Ha</u>. Yes Rita we will try are utmost to refrain from going to far in our way of expresstion, and of our emotions, and feelings. That will be a good test of our <u>character</u> Heh Bunny. But I do not know how I will be able to stay away from you Bunny, especially after not seeing you weeks at a time, BUT we will manage somehow. right Rita Marie Lavery. Marie I could squeeze you so tight right now, Marie I am a old <u>Bear</u> always wanting to <u>hibernate</u>. <u>Ha</u>. <u>Ha</u>. Oh darling I think about you all the time, and review all the good days you and I had together. Rita you are the finest girl in the U.S.A. Rita. <u>Oh</u> Rita How I could Love you. <u>O</u> <u>Boy</u>.

(your Soldier Boy)
Lots of Love
Walter J. Klein

Wednesday 9/22/43 8:00 p.m.

Hello Walter Dearest,

When I came home from the dentist tonight your nice letter was waiting for me. Gosh, darling, your letters have been extra special lately – It's so kind and considerate of you to write such nice letters. I noticed the writing in this letter (written Tuesday) was very small compared to the way you write sometimes. I like it that way, dearest, it looks nice + neat.

Yes it's true what you said about Virginia's boyfriend – he certainly did know how to back as you said + has a light conscience to say the least. Everyone is still talking about it. Since he's been home – he's perfectly alright Virginia says – they go out together every night + he's having a grand time. He's going back to work in a week or so. You'd think his conscience would bother him but it doesn't in the least. You'd think too that Virginia would see what a weak character he has but that's how love is I guess – "Love is Blind" as the saying goes.

Dearest, you say you don't know how you will be able to stay away from me when you come home. Well, when I say that we should try our utmost to control our emotions from going too far I mean we should try to have a medium – that doesn't mean we can't even kiss one another. You understand, don't you, dearest? We'll manage somehow, Walt, don't worry.

I told "Curley" the dog that you hoped he would have a speedy recovery + he said "Tell Walter, thanks + I'm feeling much better now" (ha ha ha). Really, Walt, he's getting better, he's his own lively self tonight – biting everything he can get hold of.

Next Tuesday is Virginia's birthday (our little Virginia). She isn't very little any more tho. She'll be 15 yrs. old. I don't know what to give her – maybe a pair of novelty pearls + some cologne or something. She's a nice kid – she does a lot of favors for me – has a good heart. She's really growing up to be a nice young lady I think. Cele + Charlie get a lot of compliments about her. Darling, if you think of it, you could send her a birthday card, she'd get a kick out of it I'm sure.

I think Dr. Mac Callo (the dentist I went to tonight) is very nice. He's colored you know but he seems to know his business. I have a wisdom tooth that has a cavity (you know how sensitive they are to fill). Well, he put something in it – a sort of a foundation so that when he fills it (Friday) he can drill away wild + it won't hurt at all. It's something new in dentistry. He said I haven't much to be done + if you remember, dear, I told you I had trouble with my gums bleeding a lot – well, he gave me a prescription for it + said that scaling the teeth every once in a while should clear the condition up. He said the bleeding is not due to a faulty diet but because my teeth are out of alignment quite a bit (that means they don't meet the way they should) + also due to malocclusion – an irritation under the gum. He's sure the condition will clear up shortly. The reason I'm telling you all this is because sometimes you say to me "let me see your teeth" + a few times have asked me if I brushed them. It makes me feel bad because I've always taken care of them + no matter how often I brush them they never look good. The dentist said they are not white naturally. He said he can tell they have had very good care so, see, darling, I really can't help how they look. Some people don't know what a dentist's chair looks like + their teeth are beautiful – that's the way it is. You understand don't you?

Well, Walter darling, I hope I'm not boring you with all this history of my teeth (ha ha). Before I close I just want to tell you that I can hardly wait until you come home. If you don't feel tired, Walt, let's really "go to town". Maybe you might like a nice lobster dinner or if not, we could go to the "Hitching Post" + have a good dinner – that is on Sunday we could. Saturday we could go to the Ritz or if we are flushed with money (ha ha) we could go to the Gables or someplace nice, but of course if you're too tired we don't have to go out at all. Whenever you do come we should make it a point to visit your brother Al, + Ellen – we haven't been there in a long time. We'll see, dearest. I do hope you can get a pass next week (Oct. 2nd). I love you so much, dearest. I want you to know too that I appreciate all of your fine qualities – you're a grand person, Walt. You understand me better than anyone ever has in my whole life except my mother. I don't know what I would have done these past two years if it wasn't for you helping me along the rough ways. I guess we bring out the best that's in each of us don't we dearest? Your happiness will come first with me always, Walter. I'll consider it an honor to love a person like you for the rest of my life.

Love Always – Your future bride

x x x x x x x x x x Rita

Wednesday 12:05 P.M.

Second Relief

4 A.M.- 8 P.M. – 4 A.M. – 8 A.M. [?]

Dear Rita,

Kisses galore to my Love on this quite rainy day. It is a good day to stay home and make <u>little</u> <u>ones</u> Ha. Ha. Ha. Thats of course when we are married. Than we can tickle each other a bit. I am feeling quite fine and manage to get enough of Sleep now and than, I look at <u>the</u> <u>your</u> beautiful Wedding pictures, they are so nice, you look just as fresh as a (<u>Red</u>) Rose in blook. I did not get your letter today, I missed your letter today, I did not get to mail call early enough, but will get the letter tonite. (<u>Bunny</u>) I saw that Picture, <u>How</u> <u>proudly</u> we hail, also it was a very good picture of that piticular type.

Rita you <u>are</u> my Love and my <u>Fiancee</u> I Love you to the top of my head and the bottom of my feet. I <u>worship</u> the ground you walk <u>upon</u> Rita, <u>Marie Lavery</u>. Rita you are so nice to me, you think of me all the time. Sending me things and spending about $15.00 dollars a year for stamps. See <u>Honey</u>, I think of everything.

Last nite a boy that lives in (Pvt. Ward is <u>his</u> <u>Name</u>) Lowell Maww, and who is in my outfit, He and I went down to the Service Club for some of that good Strayberry and Vinella icecream. Us soldier's get a <u>big</u>, <u>big</u> scope for ten

10 cents. it was real good. See us boys even like ice cream. Ha. Ha. Ha.

Rita I feel like loving you so much, I always think about you, and I tell the boys how nice you are, and how nice you treat me, they see me alway's reading your letters and see me writing to you, they call me the (great Lover), Ha Ha. Ha. They say to me, why dont you marry the girl, and give her your Love. They say I am old enough. See how the boys watch out for me. Here are some squeeze's for you Bunny. Some of those nice ones. You know how we Love so nice. O. Boy.

Lots of Love
Walter.

Thursday Night 9/23/43 8:00 pm

Walter Dearest,

I just read your Wednesday's letter it was such a nice one, darling. I'm glad you are getting as much sleep as possible – keep on trying to, sweetheart, keep rested up as much as you can. I know it's hard tho when your hours are broken.

Dearest, you flatter me when you say the pictures of me in my gown are beautiful. Thanks, Walter. I didn't think they were beautiful – I'd say they're O.K. I had to laugh at Eleanore when I gave her one Sunday – she liked it so much she kissed it + said "you look so young and innocent in it" (ha ha). I gave her one of the serious pose.

Sweetheart, sometimes I have to laugh at your spelling. If you don't mind my telling you – the other night you wrote the word puppy – you spelled it pupie, also scoop (of ice cream) you spelled it scope (ha ha) + vanilla not vinella as you wrote it. Don't think I'm laughing at you, dearest – I'm really laughing with you if you were to see the word correctly + then the way you write some of them, you'd have a good laugh too. Dearest, when you + I are married I'll teach you all the fundamentals of spelling. There will be lots of evenings when we'll have time on our hands to do things together like that. There are a lot of things you could teach me too, sweetheart.

I have to laugh too at the boys calling you "the great lover" (ha ha). They certainly keep track of you watching you read my letters + write to me. When they kid you, darling + say "why don't you marry the girl" you say – "don't worry I will + you'd all like to have a nice girl yourselves" It's true, dearest, the ones who do all the talking are the ones who'd like to be engaged or married to a nice girl but they won't admit it. Isn't that so?

Cele + I went to Case Clothes tonight. They sure have some good bargains there. Cele bought a nice two-piece suit + I did too. I didn't intend to but the ones I tried fit so well I decided I'd better take advantage because I take such a small size (size 10) + it's hard to get fitted in the stores downtown. Cele's is a black + white tweed mixture + mine is a light beige tweed, double breasted coat with pockets. It was only $12.95. Downtown it would be at least $25.00. The reason they can sell so cheaply is because they have no overhead to pay.

As soon as the clothes are made, they're put right out on the racks. Cele's was $16.95. We didn't take them home with us. I guess we'll get them in a few weeks.

Darling, when I was downtown I bought you something nice in Read's. I hope it fits. I want you to be surprised so I won't tell you what it is. If it isn't the right size, send it back + I'll get the right size. I heard you say you could use one when you were home the last time. Be on the lookout for the package either Saturday or Monday, O.K., dear?

You say you feel like loving me so much. I feel like it too, Walter. It seems so long, doesn't it since we've had any kisses. Well, maybe we'll make up for lost time when you come home, heh, dearest? I hope you can get a pass next week-end. I suppose it would be impossible that you could get a three-day one. Gosh, wouldn't that be wonderful? I could easily take time off from work. Well, dear, let's keep our fingers crossed.

Love Always,
Ritamarie
X X X X X X X X X X

P.S. Have you decided on our wedding date yet? (ha ha ha). I'll bet if I were to see your expression now, I could knock you over with a feather (ha ha). I don't really expect an answer to this question, dear – I'm kidding (ha ha ha).

Thursday 12:30 P.M.
Back Porch
Second Platoon

Dearest Rita,

Kisses galore to my Love on this fine Sunny day, I am writing this letter out on the near porch, where the Sun is shineing so bright, <u>Oh</u> that Sun feel's so good. I just got though eating diner, we had <u>meatloaf</u> and everything that goes with it. even pumpkin pie.

Last nite a special detail of men, I was one of them, were sent out to derect traffic, to give the right of way to all the abulances, that were bringing in the wounded from the hospital train, down at the railroad sideing. There were about nine (900) hundred of them. I think they just got in on a boat from Sicily Italy. They were mostly shell shock cures, I saw quite a few of them, up at the hospital, they could walk and get along O.K. but they would just stare into space. I guess a little rest and they will feel much better. They feed them very good food up at the hospital, because us M.P.s had chow there last nite at 1:30 A.M. in the morning, I was out on the intersection for four (4) hours, but the time went by very quickly from 9.P.M. to 1: AM.

Thanks Rita for sending me that $5.00, it sure will come in handy, I had to have all my O.P. cloths cleaned, so that used up that other money up that I had before you send <u>reinforcements</u>. <u>Ha</u>. <u>Ha</u>. Darling you are so considerate. I could kiss you, <u>oh</u> so good, very, very, <u>nice</u>

Yes Rita we will have plenty of that folding money, by the time we are

ready to walk down the aisle, we have nearly enough now, Heh dear, with my
saving <u>unsticks</u> We will have plenty. O Boy, you and I, will be one. Heh darling
that will be so nice. Loving and shareing each others joy's and sorrow's Heh
dear. No I will not go to the theatre to much, dearest, other wise I will over do
it. So glad that you like my letters <u>Bunny</u>, I try to write a happy, <u>dappy</u> <u>letter</u>,
somewhat, <u>you</u> <u>know</u> <u>me</u>.

I look at your most beauiful Brides Maid's pictures each day, Boy you have
some class dear. That's the old irish spirit, always smiling. I will bring one back
with me – probably the one where you are not smiling. <u>Ha</u>. <u>Ha</u>. <u>Ha</u>. Yes I
though about Ernie and Dot living with that other couple, would not <u>pan</u> out
yes no privatcey, thats not so good, especially for a newly Wedded couple. Heh
dearest, I know that you and I would not like that, Heh dear. We would always
want to be Wooing and <u>Cooing</u> and sneaking into the bed room to make Love
and to tickle each other. O. Boy thats where I shine. right dearest, you know
me. Dot and Ernie are to Love bugs too, I bet they will have a <u>baby</u> before you
can say Jack rabbit. Ernie is nearly, if not as bad as me, in as far as Loving is
concerned. Heh dear. And you girls are no ice Bergs by no means, you both
may be <u>hot</u> house girls, meaning working in heated offices, and alway's being
cold when out doors, but beware. <u>Oh</u>. <u>oh</u>. I am a big Devil. Heh dear.

Lots of Love <u>Bunny</u>

Your Future Husband

Walter <u>J</u>.

Thursday 2:00 P.M.

Day Room.

Post M.P.s.

Darling Rita.

I still feel like talking to you in writing, so I am now in our cozy day room,
our day room is painted up in cream, and white, with green broader, the floor
is all waxed, oh it is so slippery, if I do not watch out sometimes I start to do a
half Nelson. <u>Ha</u>. <u>Ha</u>. We have a piano, one of the boys is now playing (<u>Moon</u>
<u>beams</u>), on it now. <u>Not</u> <u>Bad</u>. We have ten large easy chairs, it is a beautiful
lounge, the money comes out of our company funds. This here pen (<u>eversharp</u>
<u>pen</u>) that I am useing is also furnished by our company, not bad – Heh dear.
We even have three (3) (large) rugs on the floor, two wine color, one <u>Red</u>,
Some class. We also have a Combination, Radio and <u>phonegrafter</u>, it play's very
good, also have two nice writing desk, with two nice writing lights. On the
windows, is nice <u>irish</u>, green, and white <u>Kurtains</u>, we have one Soldier boy,
who taks care of the day room each day, thats not a bad job, he will be very
handy when he gets married. Heh dear. That would be good practice for <u>me</u>.
Als have a very good pool table, I play on it once in while. also have a show
case with plenty of good books to read. I was alway's wanting to tell you about
our nice cozy <u>day room</u> at different times, so at last I have arrived at its time.
<u>Oh yeh</u> we even have Six large ash trays, as I notice, as I am looking around,
just that I do not miss any thing, to important to miss mentioning. So you see
we have one of the finest day rooms that money can buy.

Lots of Love
Walter.

P.S. Here are a dozen large Squeezes. Those nice ones, that make us both gleam with Joy and happiness. <u>Oh</u>. <u>Boy</u>

Sunday 9/26/43 1:00 pm

Dearest Walter,

I hope everything is well with you today – that you are not too busy and have a little time to yourself. As you haven't called up I guess you just haven't the time – I hope it isn't because of lack of money – if you don't want to use some of the $5.00 you could reverse the charges. Well, in any event, I hope everything is going along smoothly for you, dear.

I have your Thursday's letters in front of me now – one written at 12:30 pm + the other at 2 o'clock, also your Friday's letter. I have a lot of answering to do, haven't I, sweetheart?

I'll start with the 12:30 letter, here goes. You said you had meat loaf + all the "fixins" also pumpkin pie. Dearest, I think you are getting much better food in the Army than we, here at home are. It's awfully hard to get good meat now. I'm glad you are getting good food, Walt. You need it when you work long hours.

It must have been awful to see all those wounded soldiers who were in the Sicilian Campaign. It must be like heaven for them to be sent to Ft. Devens to recuperate after all they've been through + the awful sights they've seen. 900 seems like such a large number but it's only a "drop in the bucket" compared to the number of casualties there will be I guess.

Your letter written while you were in the day room was nice. I was picturing you while you were writing it – taking everything in while you were writing. It must be a nice, cozy room. I'm glad you have some place like that you can go when you have spare time. It must be nice to listen to the records, read, play pool, or just lounge in there.

I had to laugh at Friday's letter where you said you had just combed your beautiful black hair + were all dolled up (ha ha). Gosh, dearest, you sure were in a loving mood when you wrote that letter. You said that you save all your love for me that's why you're over-flowing with vitality + zip. Well, Walt, you're lucky you can control your feelings until you see me. It must be hard on your system to be aroused so much + not release your pent-up emotions. It's best to try not to think too much about it – try to keep active when you have free time – that might help, dearest. Don't you think sometimes it's more a state of mind than anything? I hope when we do get married, dearest, you will have full satisfaction of your desires. As we both said before, once we get adjusted it won't seem so important. Right now it does seem important because we are both keyed up to such an extent that it bothers us. Maybe I shouldn't write so plainly about these things, dearest, but I do want you to know that I understand how it must be with you sometimes.

I went to the show last night with your sister Helene. We saw "The Fallen Sparrow" with John Garfield + Maureen O'Hara. Also "Footlight Glamour" a "Blondie" picture – you know Blondie, Dagwood, Alexander + the puppies in the funnies. "The Fallen Sparrow" was very good – it was about the Nazi spies. After the show Helene + I went to the "Star" to have something to eat. We talked for quite a while. Helene said she's been going to Lilly's quite often lately – that is for a day or two at a time because Lil has bad days sometimes. Yesterday she went to the hospital for examination + Helene went over there to take care of the children. She called me up from there in the afternoon to say she would go to the show – if Lil didn't feel so good when she came home from the hospital she would stay with her but Lil felt pretty good – in fact I was talking to her on the phone + she said she had a letter from you on Friday. I'm glad you write to her, dearest, try to write every two or three weeks at least to her. Helene said she hadn't had mail from you since before you were home the last time + your father was asking her if she had heard. Please drop them a line, dear, because I think your father worries when he doesn't hear from you.

Helene + I had sort of a heart-to-heart talk last night about you + I getting married in the future. I told her we haven't any date set but that she shouldn't be surprised next spring if we do get married + that you might mention something about it home sometime soon. Helene said she didn't think you would – that you never say much about yourself at home. I told her what you said about your father not liking the idea of it so much + also that you thought Al wouldn't be so keen about being best man. She said you're foolish – she sees no reason in the world why Al wouldn't be best man + why your father should be so much against it. As for herself she said she'd never advise you or anyone what to do – that you + I should both know our own minds by now + her belief is if you are a Catholic be a good one + if you're a Protestant be a good one too. She said if she met someone who wasn't her own faith + she thought she'd be happy with him, she wouldn't hesitate in marrying. She said she's gone with plenty of fellows of her own faith + never had any luck. Well, Walt, to sum it all up, she thinks you're worrying too much about the whole thing. She said she didn't think it would be wrong for you + I to get married while we are still in the war because you + I have been going together for a plenty long enough time but thinks it's foolish of these couples who just meet + get married + of course I agree with her. She asked me what kind of a wedding we would have, a very quiet one or a large one. I told her what I thought I'd like – a Church wedding but a simple one. I told her I had so many relatives that it would have to be a case of inviting no one or everyone that I couldn't have one family without the other if you understand what I mean. I said I hadn't planned exactly what I would have or wear or anything else but just that you + I have been talking of marriage more + more lately.

I had a letter (finally) from Dot Smith Friday. She said they can't wait to get out of the house they're in now – away from that couple they're with. They have a chance to get an apartment in the city + expect to be out by the end of this month. She realizes their mistake now in going in with a couple. She's feeling fine + is gaining weight. Ernie is losing weight + has an awful cough – it's a cigarette cough! If you write to him tho, Walt, don't say anything about this. Dot didn't tell me about Ernie getting so thin but Mrs. Smith did. He has 30 colored fellows under him + worries about his job a lot because according to the Smiths, it's a very responsible one. He says he has to watch the colored fellows all the time – it's hard to get any work out of them + working with all those explosives, he can't tell from one day to the next what they'll do. Dot says she's very happy in spite of everything but will be glad when the war is over so we can all be together again.

Well, dearest, I hope you are well + that I hear from you tomorrow or next day saying everything is O.K. Tomorrow (Monday, the 27th) [my mother] will be dead two years. It seems much longer than that sometimes. Every once in a while I go back to that week before she died + think of it all – it's awfully hard to forget how awful the whole thing was – the Saturday night she was taken sick + from that day on kept getting worse each day. If she had lived she would have been an invalid + that realization would have killed her anyway because she could never resign herself to that, she was always too active. Darling, you were wonderful to me all during that time, if it wasn't for you I don't know what I would have done. You were so kind, comforting + understanding it was at that time that I realized what a fine character you had. Another fellow might have been disgusted at the way I used to have those fits of depression + crying spells but you helped me a lot. I hope I can help you as much some day when you might need someone to help you along.

I do hope you come home next week-end I want to see you so much. We'll have lots to talk about won't we, dearest? I love you so much – it seems a long time since I've seen you. Right now I wish I were in your arms just resting quietly – just knowing you were close to me would make me very happy. We don't even need words sometimes, do we dearest, to assure us of our strong love – we know it – can feel it all the time. This war will probably make people realize how futile, + silly little arguments are. People all over the world will be so glad to be together again when this mess is over, they'll appreciate peace when it does come.

Dearest, this sure is a long letter isn't it? I guess I'm all talked out now.
Lots of love and kisses, dearest.
Love Always,
X X X X X Rita X X X X X
↑ I hope I can give you these in person next week.

Tuesday 9/28/43 7:30 pm.
Hello Darling,

We ate supper out tonight so I'm too late for the 7:15 mail. Maybe if Thomas takes this letter to work with him tonight you'll get it tomorrow. I hope so, dear.

Received your Sunday's letter today. It was nice of you to write Sunday, dearest – I know you don't usually but you did because you didn't call.

That post patrol duty you were on over the week-end must have been sort of tiring – 11 p.m. to 7 in the morning. I'll bet you wouldn't want to work those hours all the time, heh, dearest? What hours are you working now, darling, + for the rest of the week?

Don't worry about my making eyes at the boys while out walking on a Sunday afternoon, dear. I would like to go out walking on Sunday afternoons when the weather is nice but I can never find anyone to go with. With Dot gone I sure am lost. Ann Preston goes to N.Y. quite a bit lately over the week-end (she's going again this week-end) + of course going out with Ruth is out of the question. So darling, I usually spend Sundays alone – writing to you, catching up on little odds + ends, reading, etc. I don't mind being alone tho, dearest, I'm getting used to it now.

Right now I'm rather discouraged about my job - + disgusted. You don't mind if I tell you about it do you, dearest? If you'll remember I told you quite a while ago that when Betty left the office the Office Manager (C. Thibault) said it was just as well I didn't take Betty's job because he thought if I stayed in the outside office that I probably would be working for Mr. Butler, the Works Manager as they were going to fire the Jewish girl he did have for his secretary.

Well, the way everything finally turned out was this: They did let the Jewish girl go (everyone was glad). + naturally I thought I'd get the job – it's the best one in the place I think. What did they do then but tell me the day I came back from my vacation that from that day on I'd be working for Mr. Trefry – the hardest man in the office to work for. I told them I didn't think it would work out – my working for him but I really had no choice altho they didn't come out + say that. They said I should at least give it a try so I did. Now you're wondering who did get the job of being secretary to Mr. Butler – well, Walter, of all people Ruth Landry. You might think this is hard to believe but here's the truth – she can hardly type – when she does – she has no speed at all + no accuracy – she can't take shorthand <u>at all</u> – she writes all his notes in long hand. She can't use a comptometer. Now you're probably wondering what she can do. Well, before she worked on production records - + that's all. Do you blame me, dearest, to resent seeing a person like her get a job like that? Besides, she's getting the same amount of money I am - + I've been there three yrs. + she hasn't been there quite a year yet. I don't mind seeing anyone get a good break who really works hard + deserves it but to see the way she bluffs her way along kills me + then to think she got the job when it was practically promised to me. You used to say the people you worked for before were a bunch of sneaks + liars. Well, they couldn't come up to the ones that run E.W.C. You never met such two-faced people in your life. They'd tell you black is white if you didn't argue your point. They sure do put everything across us girls. I get along better than I thought I would with Mr. Trefry. Some days. he piles me with work + the next day I haven't hardly anything to do. All the rest of the girls in the place think it's awful that Ruth even considered taking that job + does she take advantage of her position! You know how high + mighty she is anyway – well now it's twice as bad. Some of the things we have to listen to from her are really a joke. Once in a while my sense of humor comes to my rescue + I see how funny the whole thing is – watching her strut around + blunder her way along. You think you can't spell very good – your mistakes in spelling are nothing compared to the Miss Landry's. Well, I guess I'll just have to make the best of everything. You know if you leave a place of employment now, if the factory won't release you, you have to wait 30 days before you can get another job + starting Oct. 15th it'll be 60 days that anyone will have to wait before they can go to work anyplace else so you see they have us cornered alright. Cele said I should ask for a release + if they make a fuss tell them my capacities aren't being used as they should be. You probably never did know how much I get a week – well it's $36.40 + with all the bond deductions, withholding tax, social security + insurance I get $27.99. Isn't that awful? Then you wonder why I can't save every week. I'm lucky to meet expenses with the way prices are today.

Well, dearest, I certainly sound awfully disgusted don't I? Well, I hope you can understand a little now why. I don't mind working hard but I think everyone should be paid a decent salary these days – everyone has to work hard enough – 48 hours a week, but what gets me down is when I think of doing my work every day the best I can + then to be lied to by a lot of sneaks + chiselers who wouldn't trust their own grandmothers. (ha ha that sounds funny).

Well, Walter darling, I won't bore you any more with my troubles but I felt like having your understanding. You've probably worked with the same types of people plenty of times. Would you advise me to stay there or get out in a hurry?

Dearest, I miss you so much, do you think you'll be home this coming week-end? I love you, sweetheart. You're so kind + understanding. Lots of love + kisses Walter, dearest.

Love Always,

X X X X X Rita X X X X X

(big ones ↑)

Wednesday 12: Noon

Second Platoon

School Week.

Dear Bunny,

I just got through reading your very interesting letter, about your work at the famous E.W. Carpenters, Ha. Ha. Ha. and about your very nice Co, Worker Ruth Landry. Oh Boy. Heh dear. Didn't I tell you from the very first time, what type of a girl she was. I guess right, Heh Bunny.

She means well, but I guess, it must be her egnorence or something Hold on to your work at E.W.C. I am quite sure that in time, everything will work out. Changeing now, in these times is sure a lot of trouble, and you have to go through a lot of Red tape.

Bunny today, I had a little <u>calissedics</u> or exercise as one would call it, after <u>that</u> we had a little close order drill, later a little cleaning up, in our barracks and, and than a little bunk fatiege. Oh Boy Thats where I shine, when ever I do get the <u>chance</u>.

Bunny I was just kidding you aboyt making eyes at the boy's, when every you might go for a walk. <u>Ha</u>. <u>Ha</u>

I am a old <u>hot</u> <u>tomato</u>. I need to be married. Heh Bunny. We will be. Heh Bunny, just as soon as we talk about it a little more and accumalate a few pennies more. Right <u>Bunny</u>.

So happy to hear that you and my sister Helene get along so well. She sure does know how much we Love each other. I dropped her and my Father a letter yesterday. <u>Oh</u> Boy, pay day tomorrow. We will have a few more pennies for our funds to get married with, <u>Oh</u> Boy we are getting there, slow, but sure. <u>Oh</u> Bunny you are the sweetest girl in the World. <u>Oh</u> you <u>Darling</u>, Irish Colleen. <u>Rita</u>.

Lots of Love. From your (<u>good</u>-<u>looking</u> <u>HA</u>. <u>Ha</u>. <u>Ha</u>.)

Future Husband, Walter.

Thursday 9/30/43 12:45 pm.

Dearest Walter,

I just came back from lunch. Ann + I went out this noon for a change as we have an hour on Thursday. We ate in the "Palms" on State St. + had chicken chow mein (yum yum). It was good.

Last night I went over to Mrs. Smith's for a while. She gave me two pictures that were taken the day of Dot's wedding at Brignolos. They are large ones – one is of Dot alone (it's beautiful) + the other is of the whole wedding party which is very nice too. I'll show them to you when you come home, dearest – I'm sure you'll agree that they are beautiful pictures.

Mr. + Mrs. Smith are so lonesome without Dot – I feel sorry for them but Mrs. Smith says she never lets on to Dot that she is when she writes to her. Dot would only worry + she is so happy down there with Ernie that Mrs. Smith wouldn't want her home for the world as much as she misses her. Mary was at Smiths' too and told me to tell you she was asking for you. She thinks you're very nice, darling, + that you're full of fun. She said when this mess is over you + I will have to get together with her + some other fellow + go out together. Don't be surprised someday, dearest, if you get a funny card that will be signed "guess who" – it will be from Mary. She said she'd like to send you a funny card – as you're just the type who would get a big kick out of it.

Here is a little philosophy enclosed, darling. I cut it out of last night's paper – it's by Fannie Hurst. It wouldn't apply to you so much, sweetheart because I know when you + I are married you'll be considerate of me + will do your utmost to make our marriage a happy one but I think it's a good bit of philosophy for any fellow to read. I think you'll find most girls can overlook a lot of faults (this goes for me) but they like to be treated courteously at least + they like to feel as tho their husbands are proud of them – you know, dearest. I have to be at the dentist's tonight at 5:30. I'm going to Confession tonight too because tomorrow is the First Friday of the month + I'll go to Communion at 6:30 (in the morning). I'll say a prayer for you, dearest, in Church tomorrow – in fact for the both of us.

8:30 P.M. Well, Walter, since writing the above in the office this noon I've accomplished quite a bit. First of all, I went to the dentist at 5:30. He cleaned my teeth + filled a very bad cavity. He also treated my gums for the bleeding + for all that work charged only $3.<u>00</u>. I think he's a very good dentist – the best one I've been to. My gums have stopped bleeding almost entirely + my teeth look much better since they've been scraped + polished.

I came home from the dentist's at 6:30 + your three letters were here waiting for me. Gosh, darling, I was so surprised + glad to get them! You must like to write lately – writing two letters in one day. I surely love to receive so many. After eating supper + reading your nice letters I went to Confession. Now I feel good, dear, you know – so close to God and much stronger spiritually you know how you feel, dearest, when you receive Communion in your church you've told me lots of times how good you feel after – well that's how I feel tonight. Dearest, it's very cold out tonight – so windy – I almost got blown apart. Walking down to church in the wind I was thinking of you + I, dearest, how happy we'll be when this war is over + we're married and then I thought even further ahead to the time when our children will be growing up – how wonderful it will be to teach them their prayers – we can both help them to get their religious education. You can teach them prayers you might like them to know + I can too, dearest. It will be so wonderful bringing up two children, dear, even if we never will have much money, we'll manage somehow won't we, Walter darling? Well, that's thinking a long time ahead isn't it, Walt? Now let me go back to your letters.

In Tuesday's letter you said it will probably be Oct. 9th before you'll be home. Well, dearest, I feel better now that I know definitely what week-end you will be here. As much as I would like to see you this coming week-end, maybe it's just as well you have to wait until Oct. 9th because then you might have a chance to get a three-day pass. Yes, darling, if you do get a 3-day pass we can have a wonderful time together. If you could get Sat. Sun. + Mon. it would be so nice. I wouldn't hesitate taking a day or two off from work no matter when you get it, dearest, so take it whenever you can. I can get time off easily. Gosh, dearest, I can hardly wait to see you. Let's make the most of every minute, dear. If you have 3 – days you'll have a chance to get a little rest too away from Army routine.

Yes Walter darling, I guess you're right about E.W.C. I might as well stay there + try to make the best of everything. It'll take more than a girl like Ruth Landry to get me down – after all I have a lot of good old Irish spirit in me + I guess I can take a few hard knocks. At least I can console myself as the job I have as secretary to Mr. Trefry requires a person to have tact most of all, patience + plenty of intelligence + I'm sure Ruth couldn't handle it. That probably sounds very egotistical of me, doesn't it, dearest but just between you + I, it's true, Walter. She wouldn't speak to Ann or I all day today because we went out to lunch + didn't invite her. The reason we didn't was because Ruth is very friendly with Eleanore Dalton (which is perfectly alright) but we thought she'd be eating lunch with her so we didn't ask her. Well, if she wants to be so silly, let her. You certainly know how to size people up the first time you meet them, dear, you're usually right too.

Yes, dearest as you said in Wednesday's letter, we will be married soon – we must talk everything out tho, dearest, when you come home. Again, dearest, don't worry about the money. As far as your expenses are concerned, you have enough now but let's talk over a few things about the type of wedding, + a few other details. I think we should decide when too, darling, it seems hard right now to set a date but I don't think we'll be any more sure of things six months from now than we are now – as far as the war is concerned. Well, we'll see, dearest.

I'll give this letter to Thomas to mail – I hope you get this tomorrow.

I love you so much, dearest.

Lots of love + kisses,

big ones → X X X X X Rita Marie X X X X X

P.S. I bet you were glad to get paid. Keep enough out to hold you until you come home. If you send me $10 or $15 you'll have plenty for yourself won't you, dearest?

Saturday 10/2/43 2:30 P.M.

Dear Sweetheart,

I thought I'd be different this week-end and write to you on Saturday. I don't think I've ever written to you on a Saturday, darling – I usually tell you about Saturday's happenings in Sunday's letter + make it long, but I just feel like writing to you today.

I met Cele + Jeanie downtown this noon and they brought your Friday's letter down so I could read it for dessert for lunch (ha ha). Mostly every Saturday we eat lunch downtown + Cele always brings your mail with her. I always like getting your letters so much, dearest. First I read them thru once – sort of skim thru and then I read it over carefully the second time – then I read them a few more times – you know, dearest, all the "mushy parts" (ha ha). I surely do enjoy them.

The $10 you enclosed in Friday's letter was received intact and handled with good care (ha ha). Yes, dearest, you have quite a tidy little sum for your expenses for our future wedding - $120.<u>00</u> now. I am wondering how much you think you will need for your part of the expense, dearest. I know that $150.<u>00</u> will more than cover your expenses, dear. I guess you must feel that you need a lot more but really, darling, you don't, so you see, you mustn't use lack of money for a reason that we can't get married. If we were planning on buying furniture for our home now well then of course $150.<u>00</u> would only be a drop in the bucket but to cover expenses of any fellow's wedding it's plenty.

You say you get all a-flutter just by writing to me. I do sometimes, too, dearest. Sometimes as I'm writing about how I love you so much I wish so much you were here so I could give you some nice big hugs and kisses. I hope next week at this time you'll be on your way home. You know, dearest, I've never met you at the station + I'd love to, so maybe you could call me up when you get in Springfield + then I could tell just what time you'd get into Bridgeport + could be there to meet you. What do you think of that idea, dearest? Let me know, heh, darling?

I had a letter from Dot Smith this morning. She + Ernie are still with that couple but expect to be by themselves soon. She seems very happy. I had to laugh, darling at her letter. There was one part marked "personal" and when you come home I'll let you read it. She says that I shouldn't let the thought of the sexual part of marriage stop me from getting married. She says that a girl wouldn't have to know hardly anything about that part – but should just have faith in her husband + the adjustments all come very easily. She said "remember how you + I used to talk about that part of it + wonder if it was bad or good" well, she told me not to worry about it at all – she + Ernie seem to be getting along fine + dandy in that respect. She said Ernie has been very considerate of her + she knows you will be too. She's gaining weight all the time but says it's because she's married – she calls it "natural" weight.

Darling, I hope when you + I get married everything will work out as easy for us in that respect as it has for Ernie + Dot. Gosh, they've only been married six weeks (a little over) + they seem to be pretty well adjusted already. Darling, remind me when I'm home + I'll let you read the letter. Dot + Ernie seem to be very anxious for you + I to get married (ha ha). It's natural tho, that it would take much longer for you + I to adjust – as you wouldn't be home much. Gosh, darling, after reading this letter up to this part I'm surprised at myself for writing about all this (ha ha). I'll bet you're surprised too.

Well, dearest, I guess I'll close now. I'm going to the show tonight with Mary Buccino. Then when I get home I guess Cele's party will be in full swing. (ha ha). I wish I could see you, dearest I miss you so much. Well, I'll keep on hoping you can get your pass next week. We'll have such a nice time won't we, Walter darling?

Here are some big hugs + kisses for you, dearest - - - -

Love Always,

Rita

X X X X X X X X X X X

P.S. I can write the kisses but I don't know how to draw a hug (ha ha ha). Keep smiling, sweetheart.

Sunday 10/3/43 1:45 p.m.

Dearest Walter, (My Wonderful Sweetheart)

I feel so happy as I'm writing this letter because you called me up today – it was so nice talking with you – you sounded good, dear – in good spirits and everything. I hope everything goes along smoothly for you, dearest, during this week so you can get your three-days over the week-end. Gosh, Walter, it will be so nice having you home for three days – even a regular pass is nice but three-days oh boy (ha ha).

As I told you over the 'phone the party last night on Bud didn't break up until about 2:15. It was in full swing when I came home from the show at 11 o'clock – you know, dearest, plenty of drinks going around + sandwiches, cake + coffee later. Cele had a cake made with "Good luck buddy" on the top in fancy frosting + a few little flags on top. Then there were red, white + blue paper plates + napkins (very patriotic). They also gave him a card with a nice verse on it (about going in the service) + $24 in it. Buddy hates to go in the Army tho. You know he's been married for two years now + has a nice home (they rent a place on E. Main St), have nice furniture + now Arline (his wife) will have to carry on herself. She is going to try to keep the rent up but it'll be hard for her alone. I felt sorry for both of them last night – when they gave the card + money to him Arline felt so badly she cried + Bud couldn't say a word either. Mary (Ralph's wife) was there too + she had an awful time adjusting herself with Ralph away. They have been married 7 yrs. I couldn't help but think last night as I was watching Bud + Arline trying to keep up a good front how this awful war is affecting everyone's lives. Homes have to be broken up in a few weeks – everything one works for has to be given up and for what – nothing – this war can never end all wars – you + I both know, don't we, dearest, it's silly to think that – that's why this whole mess is all so futile. Everyone just has to go on the best they can putting on a false front + keep hoping + praying it will be over soon. Isn't it a shame tho, darling? Bud is going Wednesday + I can imagine how they will both feel at the station Wednesday morning – it will be the old scene – everyone trying their best not to let the other know how badly he or she feels. Well, dearest, I could go on + on couldn't I about the awfulness of the whole thing but I'd better not – it's too depressing.

Last night I went to the show with Mary. We tried to get in to see "Wintertime" with Sonia Henie but it was too crowded so we went to see "Phantom of the Opera." This is the second week – it was held over. I know you saw it + liked it, Walt. I thought it was very good. The music was especially good – Nelson Eddy was at his best + Suzanna Foster surely has a lovely voice. The other picture "Dangerous Blondes" was funny. Mary + I went to the "Star" after + had a bite to eat. We had a nice evening together.

Dearest, I hope this week goes by fast. Next week when you come home I'm going to wear my new suit. I'm having the skirt fixed at the tailor's + it'll be ready Saturday. I hope you like it, dearest – it's a beige color – double-breasted jacket. I have a velveteen dress that you haven't seen yet too – I'll wear it Saturday (if you come). Let's make the most of every minute, dearest +

if you want to visit your sisters + Al we can try to make all the visits in one afternoon – O.K. darling? I think we should make sure we visit your brother as we haven't stopped there for a long time, also Lil, Emma + Martha if we have time. If you get three days, Saturday we could go out – have a few dances, a little snack + a little wine. (wine, dine + dance (ha ha). Sunday we could make all the visits + Monday we could spend by ourselves. What do you think, dearest? I know we'll have a wonderful time.

Darling, I wish you were here now I'd give you some hugs + kisses I know how much you'd like it, Walter (I would too). Next week we'll enjoy some nice loving, won't we, Walter, dearest? But we mustn't let our emotions go too far. I know what a job that will be with a big, healthy, raring to-go boy like you, darling, but let's try our best, sweetheart. We'll have lots to talk about so our minds won't keep dwelling on that.

I love you so much. Walter, + I hope I'll be able to show you how much when we're married. I want you to be happy with me always + I know you want me to be too. We'll both do our utmost to make our marriage a happy one by being kind to each other, considerate, having each other first in our thoughts, having faith in each other. All these things will make our love fine + enduring – as it is now – only as the years go on we can make it even more wonderful than it is now.

Lots of love and kisses, dearest Walter,
How do you like that? → Your Future Life Partner
X X X X X Rita X X X X X

Monday 10/4/43 5:15 pm.
(In the office)

Hello Sweetheart,

I thought I'd start this letter now as I have a few minutes to myself. My boss is in Hartford this afternoon and I'm all caught up in my work. In ten minutes the buzzer will go – that means the day is over and it's time to go home. At 5:25 everyone makes a mad dash to get out of here (myself included) – ha ha.

Last night I made some cookies – tole-house cookies. I sent you a few samples darling – they came out fairly good for my first attempt at baking cookies. I only made a dozen and sent you only four because they are rather large + I figured they are equivalent to about 8. (ha ha), so Walter dear, don't think I'm stingy. By the time you get them (about Wednesday or so) they'll probably be hard (hard tack – ha ha). Maybe you'll like them, dear, I don't know but anyway as long as they don't give you indigestion, everything will be alright (ha ha). There goes the buzzer, dearest, so I'll finish this later.

6:15 p.m. Walter dear, I was so glad to receive your Saturday's letter – I don't usually get one on a Monday so it was a nice surprise.

Yes, Walter, we're getting away ahead of ourselves when we talk about our children – we have to think about a lot of other things first – when we'll be married – is the most important thing right now – then once we decide that – the next thing is talking to the priest – that is, you would take your six instructions that are necessary in the case of mixed marriages. Those instructions are really given by the priest to you alone – Ernie took them but he took more than he really had to – he had about 12 altogether. Any chaplain in any camp can give them. As far as the details like the reception, flowers, what I'll wear, etc. they will be all up to me so don't worry, darling. As all you'll have to worry about is buying the ring, getting your instructions + getting home at the right time + of course paying the priest + giving your best man + usher something + oh, I forgot the trip too – (paying for it). Darling, don't think I'm telling you all this because I have all these plans in my mind – I haven't – but I just want to give you an idea of what your part will be like when the time does come, see darling? I know the kind of wedding I'd like but naturally we should both talk all these things over – I would never make all arrangements (in the future) without talking every thing over with you first.

Only 4 + 3/4 more days this week + I'll see you, sweetheart (I hope). Gosh, I hope you have good luck getting a pass, dearest. Don't you think by Friday you'll have a good idea whether you will or not? Usually the week-end after you're on 8 to 12 you do get your usual one anyway. I sure would like to meet you in the station if you do get one, dearest.

Lots of big hugs + kisses, Walter, dearest

X X X X X Rita X X X X X

P.S. I wish you were here now, dear, I'd give you some nice big, big hugs + kisses some extra big ones. I know you'd like them, honey. bunch. (ha ha)

Tuesday Nite 6: P.M.
Post. M.P. Co.
Day Room.

Dear Rita,

Hello Rita, Marie Lavery. hows my totsie, Wodsie, this fine day: in autumn.

Tomorrow I am going in to see the first Sergeant, about my weekend pass, and ask for (3) days. Here's hoping. I will let you know about it, just as quickly as possible. Oh boy. Keep our fingers crossed.

I am now waiting up in arm's, for those soft cookies oh Boy, I will be waiting for them tomorrow or the next day. Here's Hoping dearest that I Survive. Ha. Ha. I bet they will be good. Heh dear.

Yes dear we will talk, more about marriage and all the details that acompany marriage yes dear we will always talk over every thing over together. Heh. Bunny.

You will look just as vergin like as a angel dear, on your Wedding day. Rita you are a very fine and intelligent girl. You are very cultured and refined. Thats so good and how, I like your very nice hugs and kisses, oh boy, thats what I like, I could eat, kisses for breakfast, diner, and supper, oh Boy instead of food to survive

Keep Smiling Bunny.

Walter J. Klein, your future Husband

P.S. A boy likes to use that other Pen I just had, that accounts for the change. Ha. Ha. I gave it to him seeing I was nearly finished. See how considerate I am.

Wednesday 10/6/43 6:15 p.m.

Hello Walter Dearest,

I'll bet you have to wear your red flannels these chilly days (ha ha) – or are they strictly G.I. – white or khaki color?

Received your Tuesday's letter – Dearest, it's so nice of you to write every day – I love to get them (your letters) – they are so like you – you write just like you talk.

Don't worry, darling, I expect a lot of kidding about those cookies I sent you but I'll improve as time goes on – I'm going to keep on trying out different recipes each week so by the time you + I make our home together I'll be able to give you a variety.

Mrs. Smith called me up a little while ago + said she met Madge Blake + Madge said Dot + Joe's wedding has to be called off – it's supposed to be Saturday but Joe got his shipping orders – he's going out to sea but will only be gone six weeks so they'll be married then (if he comes back safe + sound). It's a shame isn't it? Joe had 10 days off in July + wanted to be married then but Dot didn't want to – it's too bad they didn't I think. Oh well, maybe everything will turn out alright for them – I hope so. It must be awful for two people to have their wedding all planned + then have to postpone it – I hope that never happens to you + I, dearest but one never knows, heh, dear?

You said in your letter you could have my kisses for breakfast, dinner + supper + never get tired of them – they'd be better than food. Sometimes I feel that way too, dearest. A big kiss would be nice for dessert (ha ha).

Gosh, dearest, I hope if you can't get three days you can get your regular pass at least. It seems so long since I've seen you. We'll have a wonderful time together.

Love Always,

X X X X X Rita X X X X X

P.S. I'll give you some nice hugs + kisses when you come home, sweetheart. mmmm! (ha ha)

Thursday Nite 6: P.M.

Day Room

Dearest Rita,

Yes Rita I do have to wear my G.I. winter undies, that is part of them, the top's of them. Ha. Ha. Ha. You will be needing to wear your's quite soon too. Heh Bunny. So nice to know that you and my sister Helene are planning to go to the movie Friday. <u>thats</u> <u>good</u>. <u>Oh</u> Boy, I write just like I talk, thats me, all over. Heh <u>Bunny</u>. Bunny I did not recive those much talked about cookies, but I am quite sure they will taste good, and that you will improve as time goes on, and you will become the best little cook in East Bpt. <u>Ha. Ha</u>

It is to bad that Dorothy's and Joe's Wedding has to be posponed, for a half a dozen weeks, but I am sure it will all work out.

About that happening to us, I dont think we would be so unlucky. Yes Bunny, I sure would like your nice big hugs, and kisses for <u>Bk</u>. <u>Dn</u>. <u>Sp</u>. Boy, that would certainly be excellent desert. Darling I think about you all the time. I dream how I will hold you, so nice in my arms, and kiss you so devinely, until we both are bubbling over with Joy. Heh Rita. Yes Bunny, I will bring my bag, and all my extra things, your letters, picture, and wear your nice sweater. I am going to keep the picture of you where you are expressing that irish smile. <u>Oh</u> Boy Bunny What class. You look <u>Oh</u> <u>so</u> <u>nice</u> I have not gone in as yet to see my quite sensitive friend, the first Sergeant. Everett E. on Holtz is his name. what a German name. But he does not show me any favoritisem only <u>sometime</u>

Love <u>Walter</u>

(I wrote this letter before I went in for my pass. I was keeping my fingers crossed.) He was not in his office at first.

P.S. I. Bunny, I have good news, the first Sgt. just said O.K. all I have to do now tomorrow is get the captain's O.K. which will be easy <u>Oh</u> Boy Be seeing you I am so happy I am jumping up and down <u>Bunny</u>. I am lucky.

P.S. If you do not hear tomorrow that means I will not have the time <u>to call</u> <u>Oh</u> Boy Oh my and yours. Irish <u>luck</u>. <u>Oh</u> Boy.

P.S. I will be getting through late Sat morning, so I can not say right now what time I will get into Bpt So I will try to call you from Springfield O.K.

Friday 10/8/43 – 12:45 p.m.

Dear Sweetheart,

I hope this letter will find you getting ready to leave Ft. Devens hills for home. I do hope you have good luck getting a pass, dearest, even if it's just a regular week-end. If there is a letter from you today at home I won't see it until I get home from the show tonight.

Today I don't feel so well – I feel as if I'm getting a cold. Practically every person in the office has one or did have one + Cele, Charlie + Jeanie did too, so leave it to me to get one too. I called Marino's house (next door to you) to see if I could call off the show tonight with Helene but there was no answer. I really should stay home + doctor it up so I'll feel "in the pink" when you do come home, darling. Well, I'll try later on again but if I can't get any answer I'll meet Helene + go. I can stay out of work tomorrow morning if it isn't any better. Mr. Trefry won't be in tomorrow anyway.

Ann Preston is home sick with a cold too. Everyone is bound to get one I guess, the weather is so changeable. It's like spring today – really beautiful.

Well, dearest, I'll make this a short letter today. I hope you can tell me whether you're coming or not in the letter that's home now or in the one I'll get tomorrow. Don't forget to bring some extra things to wear if you get three days. Gosh, it looks as if I'm giving you a lot of "dos" + "don'ts" heh, dear?

If you can't get home this week-end darling, try not to be too discouraged. I'll be thinking of you, Walter dear,

Lots of big hugs + kisses, sweetheart,

X X X X X Rita X X X X X

P.S. 4:30 P.M. I guess I'll meet your sister Helene after all – there is still no one home in Marino's + besides I feel better now.

Love Always, dearest

Rita

Friday Nite 6. P.M.
Day Room.

Dear Bunny,

Hello Bunny, hows my sweet little irish girl today, I hope you are in the pink.

The Captain O.K.ed my pass for (3) days. So I will see you. Bunny dear. <u>oh</u> Boy. I will see you before you get this letter I think. I will not be able to get away until 5. PM. Sat so I will see you later Sat nite. It looks like St. Louis Cardinals are due to win the World Series, So all the boy's think, at least thats where all the money is being placed on they would have had the Series all in a <u>bag</u> already if the fielders had not made so many errors. I think they are both very good things. No. (<u>Bunny</u> I <u>do not</u> <u>bet my</u> <u>money, you</u> <u>know me</u>. <u>I am a</u> <u>old thrifty boy</u> Yes Bunny, I saw the Boston common twice, it sure is very nice. Boston is not to bad a place, once a person gets to know, where to go.

Bunny, how I long to love you and hold you in my arms and kiss you so nicely. <u>oh</u> boy. I will like that very much.

Bunny I love you so much Bunny I could hold you, <u>oh</u> so tight, right now, until I would be all out of breath Darling, be a good girl.

Be seeing you.

Lots of Love

<u>Walter</u>

Tuesday 10/12/43 6:15 P.M.

Hello Walter Dearest,

I hope when this letter reaches you, you'll be all rested up after your trip. You must have been very tired after the few miserable hours sleep you had at my house and after all the train-riding back to Worcester. The next time you get three days (it'll probably be quite a while from now) you'll know which is the best train to take. I think it's just as well you took that train tho, dearest, it's always better to be a few hours early than late – you probably realize that yourself.

I went to work this morning after all (at 8 o'clock). I woke up at 6:45 as usual so I thought I might as well go but oh how I wished I didn't go in, darling. I was completely exhausted – you must have been today too from letting our emotions get the best of us. Isn't it foolish of us dear, when we know our systems can't stand being all keyed-up all the time. Well, I hope we've both learned our lesson now (I know I have). I guess it's natural to want to crowd everything into three days, but the next time you get a pass, dearest, let's not keep rushing around here and there. We could go for a dance or two Saturday + Sunday go to a football game like we used to. Don't misunderstand me tho, I enjoyed the three days with you very much – it was so nice having you home + up until the time you came back to my house last night, we had a wonderful time. I guess I spoiled our last few hours together by bringing up what Helene said about your sister, Lil + going all to pieces myself. I'm awfully sorry, dearest, I don't blame you in the least for getting mad the way you did.

Dearest, please don't think I'm making excuses for myself but the only way I can account for my being upset is because I was overtired + because I hated to see you go – you know, darling, I still get spells of depression – just once in a great while now + last night it was brought on because I was so over-tired. I realize now what a mistake I made by bringing up the subject of the way your sister, Lil, feels but dearest, let me explain a little now what I was trying to last night. Helene went out with me to the show one night + somehow started talking about how she's been going to Lil's lately to help her out + was very discouraged because Lil doesn't seem to be improving – she has some bad days + some good ones – of course you knew that – since she came out of the hospital last year she has been having bad + good days but the reason Helene was so depressed was because Lil says when she goes to the hospital now the doctor just examines her + doesn't tell her whether she's improving or not. When she goes to Dr. Thomas in Stratford he just gives her vitamin pills to keep up her resistance. You can understand why the doctor who examines her in the hospital wouldn't give Lil the details of her condition + Helene thinks it's up to either her or Jack to go to the doctor + find out how everything is. Helene says it's really Jack's place to go but you know how he is (no sense of responsibility) + Helene hates to go herself. I know all this is none of my business, dearest but the only reason I thought I'd mention it to you is because you wouldn't want to go on thinking she was getting along fine when she isn't would you, darling? All of your family naturally keep all this to themselves + Helene, when she goes to Lil's tries to be as cheerful as she can but of course worries a lot about her so don't think darling, Helene is going around talking about it – she isn't – I guess that night she just felt like telling me. I can't understand how you could get so mad at Helene for worrying – she's just that type + can't help it. It's natural isn't it, darling, when someone close to you is sick + doesn't seem to improve much. Lil herself gets discouraged but when anyone asks her how she feels she says "good". So, dearest, as far as you're concerned, I know you must think of her quite a bit but don't worry – just write her once in a while – cheerful letters. That's the situation Walter dearest + again I'm awfully sorry I brought the subject up last night when you were so tired especially since you understood how everything is (as you said) without my telling you. I won't bring it up any more – it's none of my business anyway. With Helene helping Lil out as much as she does + Lil taking care of herself the best she can, she'll probably improve as time goes on.

Darling, tell me that you understand about everything now – I did make such a mess of everything. Take care of yourself, sweetheart – get as much rest as possible. During the next five or six weeks I'll think of all the happy hours we had together this past week-end – before you know it you'll be home again.

Love Always,
Rita (Bunny)
X X X X X X X X X X

Wednesday Nite
Post. M.P.
Day Room.

Dearest Rita,

Lots of Love to my <u>Future</u> <u>Wifie</u>. Heh Rita Dear.

Rita, dearest, you are so sweet, and so nice to me. I Love you so much. you are so intelligent, RIta you have a very <u>keen</u> <u>mind</u>. You have so many extra fine qualities. Today I had a good day at school. I sleep slept Ha. good last nite, boy did I need <u>sleep</u>, I was all <u>played</u> <u>out</u>, <u>Ha</u>. <u>Ha</u> just like you were, <u>Bunny</u> rest up, all week, wont you dearest. That's a <u>good</u> <u>girl</u>.

<u>Bunny</u>, I understand you to the utmost, you are not to hard to understand. Yes you and I were very tired, thats accounts for us being so <u>cranky</u> the last few hours. Darling I know just how my, <u>sweet</u> Sister Lillian feels. She is such a good kid, she has a very good sense of Humor. Her three children are real <u>cute</u> Jack is a good fellow in his <u>own</u> <u>way</u> considering he was the only <u>child</u>. You and I will have to pray for a quick recovery for Lil. We will buy her something real nice, to give to her on our next visit. Heh Bunny. to <u>cheer</u> her on for good <u>Health</u>. and Happiness. Helene is a good kid She is very sensitive and High String So is my Father. he is very kind in his ways.

Last nite I went up to the reception center and looked up, Bud Monahan, Boy his is quite some Boy. his is fine, and ajusting to army life quite fast. he was very surprized to see me. he reconized me right off. He and I had a few beers <u>near</u> at the P.X. later we took a bus ride to the Service Club, for coffee and pie, Later I took him up to my barracks, to phone his wife, <u>Eileen</u>, he talked for <u>28</u> minutes. <u>Boy oh</u> Boy. Some kid. Later we saw Humphy Bogard [Humphrey Bogart] in Sahara. <u>Desert</u> (<u>picture</u>

He give you all his Love. (<u>Love</u> <u>Walter</u>)

Thursday (Pay Day) Oct. 14th 12:30 P.M.

Lunch Hour

Hello Sweetheart,

How are you today? – Well – I hope. I thought I'd just write these few lines now during my lunch hour because Ann Preston's mother invited me to the house for dinner (after work) so I won't have a chance to write tonight.

Ann had her tonsils out Tuesday – as you know + has to stay in bed a few days until her throat heals. Mrs. Preston called me here yesterday at the office + said she was quite sick as yet. Well, that's to be expected – it's harder when an adult has them out than a child.

Last night I wrote a long letter to Dot Smith + told her what a nice week-end you + I had together. It was such a long letter I had writer's cramp when I finished (ha ha).

Dearest, I haven't had a chance yet to read the book you let me take but I will have time over the week-end. I'm sure I'll learn quite a bit about everything (you know what I mean by everything – ha ha).

I hope you are managing now to get enough sleep + that you have a little time to yourself too. I think about you, always, dearest. You're such a good sweetheart – so kind + understanding of all my childish ways. Yes, I guess as we both said the other day God bestowed on us this fine love we have. We both have a lot to be thankful for in finding each other. Let's keep it this way when we get married too, dearest by each of us doing our best – our utmost towards making our marriage a very happy one. I know it will be.

Well, Walter dear, I have to go back to work now. Take care of yourself, darling. I love you.

Love Always,
X X X X X "Bunny" X X X X X

Thursday Nite
Day Room.

Dear Rita.

Lots of kisses to my Love. Recived your nice letters, Bunny you are my love and Future wife. Heh dearest. Yes Bud Monahan is sure a regular fellow. I also saw him last nite, we had some near beer and eats, together at the P.X. Later a chat at his barracks, at O – C Barracks 8 R.R.C. Tonite I may meet him at the No 1. Theatre Betty Grable is playing in a musical, it appears to be good, I hope I (Posey o'Grady) is the Name of the Picture meet him then, I just got through, chasing prisoners all day. He is suppose to be on a truck detail today, according to his scedual yesterday. Thats Bud. I am talking about Jeanie is a good girl. Boy your cat family is sure growing. Ha. Ha. Ha.

Lots of Love,
Walter,

P.S. I have to get to the early movie.

happy (dreams) Rita.

Love Walter

Friday 10/15/1943 12:30 pm
(Lunch Time)

Dearest Walter,

I hope this letter finds you in the best of health and rested too.

There wasn't any mail from you when I got home from Ann's last night but I know there will be some tonight – it takes a while to get mail now the post offices are so rushed with people sending their Christmas packages to the boys.

There is a girl who works in the office here (her name is Irene Mandulak) + her boyfriend's mother got a telegram yesterday saying that he was killed in action. Irene has been crying all day – all of us felt so badly to hear it. He was on a destroyer in the South Pacific. I guess we'll be hearing about a lot of those happenings from now on. I couldn't help this morning but think of Al Hammer – I certainly hope and pray he is lucky enough to get out of this mess alive and well – it's a good thing he has that "easy go lucky" personality that he has got – it gives him an equilibrium that will help him a lot thru all this.

I have to be at the dentist's tonight at 6 o'clock. I was supposed to go Tuesday night but had to cancel the appointment I was so tired.

Last night I went to Ann's for dinner. Her mother had Italian spaghetti (yum yum) – you know how much I like that, darling. Ann is getting along very well considering how bad her tonsils were. She managed to eat a little last night but I guess it will take another week before she's herself again. I spent a nice evening at her house – I can always be sure of a few laughs when I go there.

Dearest, I'll be thinking of you over the week-end. Have as nice a week-end as you possibly can. I'll try to keep busy. I'm supposed to go to Ann's again Sunday afternoon + Sunday night I'll see if Mary would like to go to the show, if not I'll stay home + find plenty to do – read or something.

Dear, when I get those pictures I sent away (the roll of film) I'll send them to you. I should get them next week some time. I'm still thinking about the nice time we had together last week-end. It's nice we can have all those happy thoughts when we're apart isn't it, dearest?

I was figuring this morning just about the time you'll get your next pass (leave it to me, heh, dearest, to figure that). It should come about Nov. 13th or if not then, Nov. 20th. It's so nice too, we can both look forward to seeing each other every five or six weeks. I hope you will go on continuing to be so lucky – I know you hope so, too, Walter dear.

Lots of love and kisses to you, sweetheart.

Love Always,
Rita (Bunny).

Here are some big kisses for you, Walter
X X X X X X X X X X X X (1 dozen).

Saturday Oct. 16th 3:00 P.M.

Dearest,

I have your Wednesday's and Thursday's letters in front of me as I'm writing this. They're such nice letters, dear – I was so glad to get them when I got home from the dentist's last night (at 8 o'clock).

Thanks, dearest, for your kind understanding (in Wednesday's letter) of the way I got so upset just before you left Monday night. I'm glad you understand too about how your sister, Lil, feels. Yes, she sure is a swell girl – also – her children are all so nice – she has a lot to be proud of in them. I'm sorry I can't feel the same way as you do about Jack tho, but I'll keep my opinions to myself as far as he's concerned. Yes, dear, that's a good idea of yours to buy something for Lil but I think she'd get a kick out of it if you brought something home with you from the fort. Maybe you could see something at the P.X. – a nice pin – compact (one with the insignia on) or something in the line of cosmetics – whatever you think, dearest, these are just a few suggestions.

Darling, I'm glad you got in touch with Bud Monahan + managed to go to the show etc. a few times. He certainly appreciates your getting in touch with him. He sent us a card yesterday + said what a nice evening he spent with you Tuesday night. Gosh, dear, you must have been awfully tired Tuesday night – after the week-end + then going all day + then to the show with Bud at night. I know how you are, dearest, you never think of yourself when you can do someone else a favor. I know you always go out of your way lots of times for people when you're tired. If you don't mind a little advice, dearest, don't over-do it. I mean try not to keep late hours – get as much rest as you can. As long as Bud is there, of course, I suppose you feel as if you want to keep him company – teach him the ropes as you would say but take it easy, dearest, don't go so much that you'll tire yourself out. I love you so much, sweetheart, I want you to keep the good health you have now. It was hard for you these past five years to get yourself up to where you are now, so now you want to try to stay in excellent health. As you're reading this I'll bet you're thinking I'm worrying too much about you + it's all unnecessary – but dearest, I'm thinking of our coming life together – we'll have a very happy life if you take care of yourself now. You know, dearest, good health is one of the most important factors in happiness. You know all this, Walter, I know you do but I think you forget sometimes – you feel so well – you go off the "straight + narrow" (ha ha). So dearest, won't you be careful for me if you don't want to think of yourself – about drinking + smoking? – even just beer too much of it can be harmful in your case.

I worked until noon today as usual. Tonight I guess Cele + I will go to the show – Charlie's working from 4 to 12 so that leaves Cele alone. We'll go early about six o'clock so we can get a seat – then we'll be home early.

I stopped downtown this afternoon and met Mrs. Franke + Gladys. They were asking for you + thought you were lucky to be stationed in Devens. Mrs. Franke asked when we were getting married so Cele said in the spring (I didn't even get a chance to answer). Ha ha. Mrs. Franke thought that was very nice +

said "I suppose Walter can hardly wait until the time comes" (ha ha). I said well, we have to depend on the Army's decision as far as the time to get married is concerned – that we can't plan too far ahead but as far as I could see now, it would be in the early Spring – that's what I've been telling people when they ask – I hope that meets with your approval Walter J. (ha ha).

As I told you when you were home Mrs. Singer (Eddie's wife) always said she would make my wedding gown when I got married. Well, she asked Cele if I was planning to get married soon + Cele said she thought next year (in the spring) so Mary said I'd have to let her know two months ahead if she is to make it because there's a lot of work to a gown. She has some ideas of her own on the style so I can see I'll have to buy the material in February or before if we get married in April. The gown is nothing to worry about but the wedding, as far as the Church is concerned, is what will take time. Oh well, time enough for all that later, heh, dearest?

Darling my Christmas Club will be paid up the first of November ($100.00). As soon as I get the check I'm going to put it in the bank with your money – I'm not going to use it for Christmas presents at all this year. Don't you think that's a good idea, dear? $100.00 towards my expenses of the wedding bill will sure help a lot.

I've decided what I'm going to give you for Christmas + your birthday too. I won't tell you what I've decided on tho, dear except that they will both be things you can use now – while you're in the Army. I think it's foolish to buy you things you'll have to save – for instance – when the time does come for us to get married you'll need a nice robe + a traveling bag but it would be silly to buy these things for Christmas – you'd only have to save them so I was thinking when you are ready to buy those things you can use some of our money we have saved. Is this alright with you, dearest?

Walt, I miss you so much but at the same time I know it's best that you come home only every five or six weeks. These fellows who come home every week or <u>every</u> <u>other</u> <u>week</u> are really the unlucky ones because as you said, they are shipped out sooner or later – that only lasts just so long. Of course I'd love to see you all the time but I guess it's just as well the way it is.

Darling, this is turning out to be a long letter isn't it? I'll write more tomorrow, dearest + in the meantime I'll be thinking of you.

Love Always,

"Colleen"

or Bunny (if you prefer) (ha ha)

X X X X X X X X X X (big ones)

Saturday 2: P.M.

Second Platoon

Dear Rita,

I recived your Friday's letter today, and I read it in bed for a nice relaxer. <u>Oh</u> Boy, it felt good, Bunny to read your nice letter, Darling you are so sweet. I

Love you, so much. Bunny. one of the boy's in my squad calls his sweetheart, (Sweet Pea) Ha. Ha. Ha. I though I was the only one with a funny name to call a sweetheart. oh Boy, but I see I have compatistion. Have a good weekend Bunny and enjoy yourself what you can do, a nice walk in the park with your girl friends and may be a good show. Sweet Posie Ogrady with Betty Grable, starring in that light musical is a very good light humorous show, I did not meet Bud Monahan that nite, as I had planned, he must have been bush or something and could not make it. I hope his gets home this afternoon as he had planned, thats if he did not get shipped before today.

I am going on the Second relief. 4 – 8 – 4 – 8, it's not the worst relief, even if I have to get up at 3 in the morning. This relief I do not have to chase prisoners. It is a 24 hours post. where the other time has to be up and with prisoners, which is long hours.

I am all rested up now, bunny, and I hope I had enough of Loving to keep me for 4 or 5 weeks, Ha, Ha Ha you too. Heh Bunny, yes we learned our lesson to not key ourselves all up continueous all the time together Heh Bunny. So glad to hear that Ann is getting and feeling much better, and that you had a enjoyable time at her home.

So sorry for Irene Mandulak and her Boyfriend killed in Battle.

Lots of Love
Walter your Future Hubie

Sunday 10/17/43 1:00 P.M.

Hello Sweetheart,

You called a little while ago in the nick of time – I was just about to hop into the bath tub for a nice, hot bath. Wouldn't it have been funny, Walt, if I had to run downstairs to the 'phone dripping wet? (ha ha). It's so nice of you to call on Sunday, dear, it makes me feel close to you hearing your voice.

I'm glad everything is hunky-dory with you in spite of the fact you're on second relief – (4 to 8). As I said on the phone, dearest, it's just as well if you don't go out too much this week – being on that schedule you need your rest. I know you won't over-do it, Walt.

Cele + I went to the show last night. We saw "A Lady Takes A Chance" with Jean Arthur + John Wayne at the Warner – it was very good. After the show we ate in the Barnum Coffee Shoppe. We had a nice steak (you know how I like steak, dearest). You want to see that picture if you get a chance it's awfully funny.

When we came home I started to read that volume of the encyclopedias you let me take but didn't get very far. You really have to take your time reading that subject. It'll probably take me about three weeks reading a little each night. So far, it's very good but it stresses the physical part of marriage too much. I'll quote you one part tho, dear, that you + I have said very often + it's this "Everyone knows the gloriously rejuvenating effect of love upon the whole personality – If he does not he's to be pitied. Lovers look their best +

try to behave their best – they think + act in a manner new to them. To be sure they do this to win the object of their affections. But they do not consciously deceive. On the contrary they think ± feel just what their actions ± words indicate. Love calls out the best in them. It casts out the demon of selfishness. It erases coarseness ± vulgarity. It refines ± elevates the personality."

You + I know the above is true don't we, dearest, it (love) certainly has brought out our best points. I'll let you know what I think of the book as I read more, dearest.

Dearest, I asked Cele if she had any idea how much a cedar chest would cost (in mahogany) – I thought about $65.00 but Cele said you should be able to get a good one for $50.00 at the most. This seems like a lot of money to spend all at once, doesn't it, dearest especially with money so scarce this year but another way of looking at it is that it will be something we'll need in our future home – they hold a lot of things – blankets – linen etc. + besides look nice in a bedroom. I'll leave it up to you, dearest. I don't know what you plan on using for money – is it that silver you have saved? Well, dearest, if you do buy one I hope it won't take your last penny – it shouldn't if we can manage to hold on to the money we've saved so far (your $120.00 + my $100.00). If you do decide to buy one, you can send or give the money to Cele + she can pick it out. I won't like to see it until Christmas. She has very good taste anyway, but it's up to you, dearest – whatever you want to do.

Darling, I love you so much. You mean everything to me – you'll always be first in my thoughts. It'll be so wonderful, won't it, when this mess is all over + we can enjoy many happy years together – first of all adjusting to married life – then working together for a happy home + children. Gosh, dearest, just thinking about it thrills me + I know it does you too. Let's start right in the beginning of our marriage to work towards a rich + full life together – I'm sure with God's help we'll have a bright future.

Love Always,
Rita, Your Future Life Companion
X X X X X X X X X X X

Monday 10/18/43

Dearest,

How's my sweetheart today? I hope everything is fine with you, Walter.

I had a nice time at Ann's house yesterday. I was only going to spend a few hours there but in the end I spent the late afternoon + evening with Ann – until 10 o'clock last night – didn't get home until 10:30. Preston's house is something like your brother Al's – once you get there they never want you to go – although Ann, Eleanor (Joe's girlfriend) and I did have a lot of fun. We played a lot of records + danced. Ann is getting along fine + will probably be back to work Wednesday or Thursday of this week.

Tomorrow (Tuesday) is Cele + Charlie's anniversary. They'll be married 18 yrs. Imagine that! They might go to New York over next week-end to celebrate or maybe just for a day. I hope, dear, when you + I are married that long we'll be as happy as they are – I'm sure we will be aren't you, Walter?

Mrs. Smith called me up yesterday and said the colored snapshots that were taken at the wedding are ready – they are postal card size + are colored – the pictures were taken outside of Roseland + she said the colors of the gowns, trees in the background etc. show up very nice in the colored pictures. It's very expensive tho to have a roll like this developed. I'm having a set made + it will cost me $2.40 for 4 pictures (60¢ each). I want to have them to add to the collection I have now tho.

Jeanie had the funniest thing happen to her. Her girlfriend, Jean Buckley (the girl you saw on the porch when you were home) has been writing to this boy in the Army – a boy she grew up with. She asked him for the fun of it if he had any boyfriend that her girlfriend (meaning Jeanie) could write to. He answered that he did have + gave Jean Buckley his name (Floyd Walters) + described Jeanie to him. She must have given him a good description because Jeanie got a letter from him Saturday. He's a P.F.C. in the Air Corps in Lincoln, Nebraska + has had two years of college (the university of Ohio) believe it or not. She let Cele + I read the letter + altho I wouldn't be so quick believing he has had some college education, the letter was written very nice – he seems quite intelligent. Cele + I laughed our heads off over the letter. He addressed it as "Dear Miss Monahan" + went on to say he's from Ohio but has no relatives to write to him + would like to hear from Jeanie – wants to know all about her – what she's interested in (sports etc.) + also wants her picture. The funny part of it is he knows she's only 15 yrs. old. Cele said she could answer his letter but that she shouldn't send her picture, then she can tell when he writes more what kind of a fellow he is. If he's the real McCoy it will be O.K. to write to him (impersonal letters). Don't tell Jeanie I told you about this because she gets mad if we laugh about it + kid her too much. I'll let you know later if it's alright to kid her about it. (ha ha).

6:45 P.M. Dearest, I received your nice letter written Saturday. I especially like to get mail from you on Monday – you know – blue Monday isn't so blue if you receive mail.

I had to laugh at that name "sweet pea" (ha ha). Bunny is a nice name compared to that. I'm getting used to "bunny" now, dear – it isn't so bad.

Bud told Cele + Charlie over the week-end he couldn't meet you last Thursday because he was so tired he could hardly move – at the end of the day. He just fell into bed I guess. Cele + Charlie said he looks very good – he seems to like Army life so far. I hope he gets a good break – gets into something he likes. He thinks you're a "regular" fellow, dearest. He sure is right, darling. I never met anyone yet who didn't take a liking to you, Walter dearest. You make friends so easily + with your gift of gab (ha ha) you can hold your friends. You're a likable fellow to everyone, dear, but to me you're a lovable one.

I'm glad you finally got rested up after our strenuous week-end together (ha ha). I finally did too but it took me a few days. Gosh, I was exhausted! No, Sir, darling, we'll never act like that again, we know better now.

Dearest, I was thinking – do you think you could manage to save $15 out of each pay instead of $10? Because figuring our finances – if you save $15.00 each month from now until next April, you'll have $210 besides what I'll have saved. That will be a nice sum of money to meet every emergency for the wedding – <u>our</u> <u>wedding</u>, <u>dearest</u> (for your expenses). By the way, darling, how are your finances holding out for this month? You won't get paid for two weeks more Walt, so you'd better try to hold on to a few dollars at least because I can't send you any (it's all in the bank). Let me know how you're making out, dearest, because I wouldn't want you to go without anything for lack of money.

Cele told my cousins that you + I were getting married sometime next year (early in the year). Irene was asking her about you + I so Cele thought she'd better say we are because they are the closest relatives to us + should be the first to know those things. I don't like to tell people we are <u>definitely</u> because you never know how things will work out. Eleanor said she would like to know by the 1st of the year just when we are going to because she will have a lot of planning to do. I told her we should know by that time, is that alright, dearest?

Well, dearest, it's getting late so I guess this is all for tonight, except to say that I'm thinking of you, dearest, all the time, and love you so much. Take care of yourself, Walt.

Love Always,
Rita "Bunny"
Your Future "Little Mrs" (ha ha)
X X X X X X X X X X

Second Relief
Monday 1: P.M.

Dear Rita,

Recived your Saturday's letter – Bunny today. Hows my Sweetie Pie today. I bet you are in the pink after a nice weekend of rest and relaxation. Yes Bunny, adding that $100.00 dollars to our funds, Boy that will help things. <u>Ha</u> <u>Ha</u> Bunny. Boy that Christmas Club funds is sure not a bad way to save. <u>oh</u> Boy. You Bunny in the <u>spring</u> or in June will be the time for our marrige, depending on the outcome of the army. of <u>course</u>. But I am quite sure it will work out all O.K. Heh Bunny.

Recived a letter from Ernie today, he writes a very nice letter. he is fine and also his Sweet <u>wifie</u> Dot. He is kept quite busy, they are still looking for a place to be all by there solitude, <u>oh</u> Boy. Yes Bunny, I will keep my eyes on the alert, for some nice gift for my sister Lil they have. very nice things in the line of cosmetics, leave it to me. Heh <u>Bunny</u>. dearest. I bought Lil a nice compack, just last Christmas so I will have to buy something else. She is a good girl. Heh Bunny.

Bunny I Love you so much, you are my Love. <u>Oh</u> Bunny, <u>oh</u> Bunny, how you can Love. <u>Oh</u> Boy. I do all right for myself too. Heh dearest. <u>oh</u> Boy. But I like it. No Rita dear, I will not drink or smoke or keep late hours. This week I am managing to get plenty of sleep, I go to bed just as soon as I get into the barracks and manage to get Sevens (7) hours at a clip. Thats not bad for this kind of work. 8:30 at nite – to 3: A.M. and from 7. AM. To 2: P.M. not bad, heh Bunny for getting sleep. Those are my sleeping hours.

Lots of hugs and kisses to my future Irish <u>wifie</u>. and to the Sweetest girl in the land, who will be the best wife in the good old, U.S.A.

Love, <u>Walter</u>

Tuesday 10/19/43 5:15 p.m.

Dearest Walter,

As you can see by the top of this letter, I'm not finished work yet – I'm still in the office. It seems that for the past half hour I haven't had anything to do – I'm all caught up in my work. Mr. Trefry noticed this and said "why don't you write to Walter" so I didn't have to be told twice (ha ha).

How are you, dearest? It's a very bleak + dismal day + very cold. I hope you aren't freezing 'way up in Ft. Devens hills, dear. Well, there goes the buzzer to go home – I didn't have time to write much did I?

6:45 P.M. Here I am home again, Walter, - I've been looking over Cele + Charlie's cards they got on their anniversary (today). They got some funny ones – I sent them a humorous one. Charlie gave Cele a dozen of red roses. They are going out tonight (visiting Sadie + John).

I just finished reading your nice letter (Monday's). I'm glad you're getting plenty of sleep this week, darling. I know it doesn't give you much of a chance to go out to the show or anything but when you're on some better reliefs you'll have more time to go out, heh, dearest?

Dearest, you say in the spring or in June will be the time for us to get married (depending on the Army, or course). I think the best time would be when you get 10 days (if you do). If you get ten days + we <u>don't</u> get married it will be practically impossible I think to get more time off later. Everyone here in the family (Cele, Charlie, Eleanore + Vin) think that we will be married if you get 10 days early next year (Jan. Feb. Mar. or April). It would seem more logical to want as much time as you could get for our wedding wouldn't it, dearest? Ten days would be perfect – time to go away for a few days + time to spend at home, too – without having to rush around so much. Well, dearest, it's hard to tell now just how this 10-day business will work out but you'll be able to tell better at the end of the year, won't you, dearest?

Yes, Walt, I remember now you bought your sister, Lil, a compact last Christmas. Well, you use your own judgment, dearest, about what you'd think she'd like. You always have good taste.

Thomas got all of us upset last night. He has three days off (started Sunday) + of course has been drunk all the time he's been home. He told Cele he had the time coming to him but last night the fellow he pals around with all the time (Dick Bassett) called up + told Cele the reason he was given the three days was because he was supposed to learn some kind of a new system that the post office put thru about two months ago but he never took time to learn it. Dick Bassett said all the fellows in the post office had learned it a long time ago except Thomas, so they told him to stay out until he did learn it. Well, he's made no attempt to learn it but has just been drinking continually. It's really a miracle he's been able to keep that job — they have given him every chance in the world to straighten himself out but he doesn't even try to stop. It's really discouraging — he gets worse all the time. I think the only way he could ever stop drinking is to go away for one of those drink cures in some hospital — but then I suppose it would be the same thing all over again when he came home. Cele waits on him hand + foot (Charlie too) but he would never thank them — he expects it. I have all I can do to be civil to him + poor Jeanie is embarrassed to tears when she has her friends here + he comes in like that. I wouldn't even write some of the awful habits he has but you can imagine, dearest. He has no self-respect at all. He gets pleasure out of it if he can destroy anyone's peace of mind. Fr. Pat told Cele she's more than done her duty towards him — that she should put him out of the house, definitely, but of course Cele never will altho Charlie would if it wasn't for Cele — she'd only be in a worse state of mind if he did than she is now. I try not to let him bother me at all but, oh, it's certainly awfully hard. Sometimes when we all sit down to the table to eat I have to choke the food down when he is at the table — it's so disgusting just to watch him, sometimes I don't eat at all (until he finishes) with the rest of the family. I guess it's hard for you to believe these things about him, dearest, because you see him so seldom. When you're here he's either in bed, out, or just getting up so you see him at his best. I'm ashamed to say he's my brother he has such a low + weak character and if I live to be a hundred I'll never have a bit of respect for him. I know that's an awful thing to say, Walter + you're probably shocked but I can't help it. Of course I never talk about him to anyone (only you). Jeanie feels the same way I do but she tells him right to his face but I never say a word to him. Well, dearest, I could go on + on but I've bored you long enough with this subject. I even hate to mention anything about him when I write to you but tonight I just felt as tho I needed your kindness + understanding. You see, darling, I doubly appreciate all your fine qualities when I see him + all his weaknesses. You can't realize how much you mean to me, dearest. I just thank God all the time, that I'm going to spend my life with a type of person like you, you are so sincere, kind, understanding + are such a clean-living, upright person, darling, honorable in every respect.

I feel better, dearest, since writing all this — I have to pour my heart out to you, dearest, once in a while — you are the only one who understands me so well.

You will probably answer by saying that Thomas will change eventually but he won't, dearest, he's been drinking every day now for the past two years — unless maybe if something drastic happened to him (it would have to be something very drastic) he might change. Well, anyway, dearest, writing all this has helped me — I don't feel so depressed now so don't worry, darling.

I love you, Walter dearest, and think of you all the time.

Love Always,

"Bunny"

X X X X X X X X X X X X (big ones)

Tuesday 2: P.M.

Post. M.P. Co. Second Relief. 4 – 8

Our Main gate where I come in after pass. <u>Ha</u>. <u>Ha</u>. <u>Ha</u>.

Dear Rita,

<u>Hello</u> <u>Bunny</u>, <u>Bunny</u> <u>Honey</u>. You are my Sweetheart and the best girl in the World. <u>Heh</u> Rita. Yes Bunny we will know just about how things will be by January, so we can let Elmore know just how to plan. <u>O.K.</u> <u>Bunny</u>, I have still seven dollars $7.00 left, so I will have plenty until pay day. Yes <u>bunny</u>, I will try to save $15.00 dollars per month, I think that will not be to hard.

On my way back from duty, last nite at 8: oclock after I got relived from duty, I stopped into the R.R.C. section, and at Bud's Monahan Barracks to see how he felt after that ride back on that State of Maine train, we call it the cattle train. <u>Ha</u>. <u>Ha</u>. <u>Ha</u>. I found him O.K. and just were I thoughI would fine him – in bed, he was quite tired, after working all day at the Whitmore Ordnance plant here on the post, working around cleaning up and so. He and the other boys sure did have a good time at home and in Bpt. I may stop into his barracks to see him tonite again on my way back to my outfit. We may go to the movie, chorvette's, the picture about those boats that knock all those german Sub's off its those English boats, you read so much about that's if he does not get shipping orders for Wed. Morn. Yes Jeanie is quite some girl. Boy the Boy that gets her will not get cheated in no way. Heh Bunny. She is a very intelligent girl.

Boy 18thteenth wedding anniversary for Chuck and Cele. Give them my congradulation's, and I wish them many more <u>18th</u> eighteen's years together and plenty of happiness and prosperity.

Give Ann Preston my best of wishes and quick recovery. Heh Bunny. She is a <u>good</u> <u>humorous</u> <u>girl</u>.

So happy to know <u>Bunny</u> that you derive so much from Church and Mass. I sure like going to Church also, you and I can go together on my next trip home. <u>Heh</u> <u>Bunny</u>

(Love Walter)

P.S. How do you like my new stationary. Some Class. <u>Heh</u>. <u>Bunny</u>

P.S. II I am now writing to Ed, and Gertrude Lavery in New York. Mr. + Mrs will address it.

Thursday, October 21, 1943

Dear Sweetheart,

How are you this beautiful fall day? I hope everything is going along smoothly for you, Walter dear. It surely is nice today - - the sun is shining and the leaves are so pretty in all their different colors. How I'd like to be with you up in the Ft. Devens hills!

Last night Cele, Charlie, Jeanie, Eleanore, Vin and I went to Case Clothes – Eleanore bought a suit. Then we went out to their house for a while. It was the first time I'd been out there since last Christmas, imagine that! They have a very nice home I think – just the type I'd like for you and I, dear. Since Eleanore's been working she's been able to get quite a few nice things for the house that she couldn't get otherwise. They have a new coffee table (mahogany) something like Cele's and also a nice ash tray of mahogany that is quite large. They are a good example of a couple who got married without hardly any money but they both worked together so they could have a nice home and now they have about everything as far as furniture is concerned. They also bought a used washing machine lately. I hope if Vin goes in the Army Eleanore will be able to keep the rent going somehow – it would be a shame to have to put their furniture in storage or something.

Eleanore asked me what I'd like for my birthday this year. She never gave me a birthday present before but wants to this year – she wants to give me something for my hope chest. She said to tell you that just because she doesn't write to you, don't think it's because she doesn't want to – she doesn't write to anyone – finds it awfully hard. She told me to tell you she thinks of you and that's another reason she wants to give me something for my birthday – it will really be for you too, Walt, giving something we can use in our home (in the future). I told her not to bother but I suppose she will anyway.

Ann came back to work today and looks very well. We are going out to eat lunch this noon together. It's 10:30 in the morning as I'm writing this to you – I should be working but I haven't much to do as yet today so it doesn't make any difference.

Our other cat started having kittens yesterday morning and had two so far but they were born dead. The poor cat is in awful pain there is one or two more to be born but we think they are dead too, that's why she's having such a hard time. You'd feel sorry if you could see her – but there's nothing we can do to help her – she might die herself if the other kittens don't hurry up and come, - us and our animal trouble, heh, dearest?

Well, darling, I'll have to go back to work now. Before I go, though, I want to tell you I'm thinking of you and love you so much, dearest. Take care of yourself, Walter and before you know it you'll be home again soon (three or four more weeks I hope).

Lots of Love, Walter dearest,

"Bunny" – Your Future "little wife" (ha ha.)

X X X X X X X X X X X X

Thursday 6:30 p.m. 10/21.

Dearest,

I find I have time to write a few more lines to you after all. I went to the dentist but he wasn't there – his wife said he was called away unexpectedly on an emergency so now I have to go Monday night.

Received your Wednesday's letter (a short one). Even if you only write a few lines dearest, I appreciate it a lot – I know it's hard to find things to write about sometimes – just as long as we let each other know how we are + that we're thinking of each other + love each other, that's all that really matters, isn't it, Walter dear?

I'm glad to hear that you see Bud so often – it makes it nice for the both of you but again, dearest, let me ask you, please don't overdo it – try to get your proper rest – I mean don't stay out too late with him or drink so much.

Darling, you always have a good laugh about all my beautiful curves, don't you (ha ha). Well, I know I haven't any and probably never will but it doesn't bother me in the least as long as you love me (ha ha). I can take all your kidding, don't worry, Kleiny. I'd rather be the way I am than like some girls – for instance, Ruth Landry + Eleanor Dalton, (another girl in our office). Ruth calls her curves her "personality" + Eleanor makes it a point to wear extremely low-necked dresses to show off her curves so you see, dearest, some girls have no shame in them. No matter how tight their clothes are, they don't care as long as they attract the boys.

Thomas is still going strong – if you know what I mean. He hasn't gone into work yet + hasn't made any attempt to learn the job he was supposed to. Oh well, the only thing that has to happen now is that he might lose his job – that's up to him.

I miss you, dearest, so much. It's been two weeks since we've seen each other. I hope the next three weeks go by fast. It's so nice when you're home.

Lots of love, Walter,
Your Future "Little Mrs." (ha ha)
X X X X X X X X X X X (big ones).

Thursday 12:30
Post M.P. Co.
Second Relief

Dear Rita,

Your <u>Sweetheart</u> <u>Walter</u> <u>Boy</u>, recived your two nice letters, they are so nice, <u>Bunny</u> I enjoy your letters so much, I also recived a letter from Ellen my Brothers wife, also a short letter from Donald, my little nephew. He is quite some kid.

Bud Monahan is still at the R.R.C. the lieutenant asked for four (4) volunteers for four (orderlies) <u>Mess</u>) <u>hall</u> jobs, so bud useing that good old irish head voluntered for the job, before the lieutenant could get him trasfered from shipping list to the, Head, quarters Co. thats the <u>(Cadne)</u> in the R.R.C. the ones that are stationed at the R.R.C. steady he was ready to board the train ready to go for a nice long train ride, with the rest of the boy's when, Low and Behove, his Name was scrached off the shipping list. So it looks like he will be at the fort for a while. he was at the Movie last nite when I sptopped in to see him at 7:45 P.M. I may see him tonite on my way back from duty.

Yes Bunny, on my ten (10) day's furlough will be the proper time for our marrige, oh Boy. Heh Bunny. yes I will be able to tell better at the first of the year, I dont think I will be able to get my furlough be fore the spring or after that, but we will see. Heh <u>Bunny</u>. Yes Bunny, I will buy, my sister Lil, something real nice. Leave it to me. Heh Rita. Perfume, handkerchiefs, powder, lipstick, rough. I understand Rita dear, how you feel about your brother Thomas, I know it is no fun living with a person that indulges in to much drink, cause I had to live with my pa, when he was at his worst way back in the depression day's and I have some uncles also that, take of the spirits to much, and it is no picnic, living with them. Dont worry <u>Bunny</u> dear, I know it is no fun. But just <u>hope</u> and <u>pray</u> that he will someday, be released of his hold, and not be a victim of that much dreaded alcohol tendence Moderation in all, I say. <u>Heh</u> <u>Bunny</u> Bunny I hope and pray I never become a slave of Alcohol. I know I never will, at least I will try my utmost not to be. Heh Bunny.

My brother brought another automobile Sold his old one for $6.00 dollars and brought a 1941. one year newer. Ellen and Al like fooling around with different car's, it seems. No flies on them. Heh <u>Bunny</u>.

So happy for Cele and Chuck, they deserve all the happiness that life has to offer. They do so much for, you, Jeanie, and Thomas. they sacrifice so much for you all so that you will all be happy and contented and live a good clean life. I know you and Jeanie appreciate all that they are doing for you both. Heh Bunny. Keep up your good work. Rita dear. I understand <u>oh</u> so much, cause I went through the same fraze of experince. Keep Smiling, Keep that good old Irish spirit up oh boy. Thats the girl. and I know you will be rewarded in the end. Yes dear, your hope chest will be plenty full, by the time it is ready to be filled thats good. Bunny At Christmas time. <u>Oh</u> Boy. <u>Rita</u>, <u>dear</u>. Yes dear, we have a strong Love, So happy to know that you like my letters.

Loads of Love to my Future Wifie. (the Best irish Colleen in the World.) Oh Boy Walter J.

I bet those red roses are nice just what you like. <u>Oh</u> Boy.

Yes Bunny on my ten day's fourlough will be the appropriate time for our Wedding. <u>Oh</u> Boy. It just tickles my spine just thinking and writing about it. <u>oh</u> Boy.

P.S. I had short arm, inspection this morning. <u>Ha. Ha. Ha.</u> I made it O.K. <u>Ha. Ha. Ha. Ha.</u>

Friday 10/22/43

Dearest Walter,

By the time you get this letter, another week will be practically gone by and the week-end starting. I hope you have as nice a week-end as you possibly can but I suppose it will be the usual routine for you – being on duty, Saturday inspection (maybe) + a lot of other things to do. Well, dear, if you do happen to have time to yourself, go to the show or something. I'll be thinking of you, Walter as I always do. I'll probably go to the show Saturday night with your sister, Helene if she wants to go. I haven't heard from her yet but I might call her up tonight.

Cele heard from Bud's mother (Sarah) about the good break he got – that he was all ready to be shipped from Devens + was called back + is now attached to Headquarters + will probably be in Ft. Devens for about three months. His mother said he was glad to be stationed there – he likes it + might get home once in a while. I'm glad he will be there for a while at least. He's lucky because he said he was almost in the Infantry (a good outfit to stay out of).

Last night I read a little more of the book you let me take. I understand a little more now about what you + I were wondering about the last time you were home (if you know what I mean). There are quite a few long medical terms tho, that are hard to understand. Darling, I think the more one reads on that subject, the more complicated it seems – it's just as well not to read too much I think as long as I understand the fundamentals it's alright, don't you think so, Walter? I'll keep on reading different parts of the book tho, the parts I think I should know. I don't understand the colored chart at all but you probably do + can explain it sometime.

As I'm writing this letter we have quite a few men here in the office in conference on our war contracts. Some of them are engineers, a Captain of the Ordnance District (Capt. Goff Smith) + some other men who represent companies that are sub-contracting for us. It's funny to listen to them – one is trying to out-talk the other. Most of them really know what they're talking about tho, they have to because if what they manufacture is .001 out of the way it's rejected by the government inspectors – every company (including E.W.C) have to stick to extremely close tolerances. I've learned a lot about such things, dearest since I've been working in this office for Mr. Trefry. If you were working on this type of work, Walter, I mean where such precision is required, you'd probably shine – because I know your nature – perfection (practically) or nothing – that German characteristic of yours would come out (ha ha). I hope all this "shop talk" isn't boring to you, Walt.

Charlie just called me + said we're going to eat dinner out tonight – I hope I have time to finish this later, Walter dear.

(7:00 P.M.) Dearest, I'm finishing this letter in Charlie's car. We ate in Kitless' on E. Main (near Boston Ave.) + now Cele + Jeanie are in a little store across the street buying a sweater for Jeanie. Charlie brought your <u>very nice long</u> letter that you wrote yesterday, but Walter dearest, I'll have to close this letter very shortly because it's almost time for the last mail pick-up. It's a very nice letter, darling. I enjoyed it a lot + I'll answer it tomorrow. I want you to get this letter tomorrow (Sat.) because then maybe you won't feel so lonesome over the weekend. If you find time to call, Sunday, Walt, it will be nice to hear your voice – I'll be home.

I love you, dearest, + think of you always. Lots of big hugs + kisses, sweetheart

Love Always,
"Bunny"
X X X X X X X X X X
(great big ones)

Saturday 10/23/43 3:00 P.M.

Dearest Walter,

I've just come home from downtown and have your Friday's letter – also Thursday's long letter in front of me.

Yes, Bud is lucky being stationed at Ft. Devens. As you said, he used his head in volunteering to stay – now he can come home once in a while + even if he is there for only three months, it's better than being in the Infantry + going so far away. Three months from now will be a little nearer to the end of this war. He likes Ft. Devens anyway – was tickled to death when he found he was going to be there for a while. He must look cute in the Cook's outfit he has to wear (ha ha). His wife, Arline, + the rest of the family are all glad he's stationed in Ft. Devens.

I'm glad you agree with me, dearest, that the best time to get married will be when you get your 10-day furlough and as you said by the first of the year you'll probably know better just how everything will be. It gives me a thrill, too, dear, writing about our coming marriage. I know when each of us takes the marriage vows, we'll really mean them, will fully understand them and will do our utmost to live up to them. We don't want just a wedding, do we darling, we want a marriage that will endure for the rest of our lives. We have both given a lot of thought to the subject of marriage, we aren't children + won't be like some couples taking their vows lightly + going into marriage without a thought of the future. We know each other so well + understand each other so much that I know ours will be a beautiful relationship – we have high ideals + will live up to them + most important of all, we'll both work together – by work I mean we'll live for each other – try to make each other happy. So, dearest, when you think it all over, we have a lot in our favor + we certainly have a lot to be thankful for in finding each other.

Thanks, darling, for your kind understanding of how I feel about Thomas. You say you had to live with your father when he was like that during the depression. It must have been hard on all your family then but I don't think your father's drinking was a daily occurrence – day in + day out because if it was he wouldn't have been able to stop – you'll have to admit, he doesn't drink hardly at all now. Getting drunk once a week is bad enough but when a person drinks continually, every day, something is bound to happen sooner or later. Well, that remains to be seen. Thomas still hasn't gone into work (since last Saturday) – and is still going strong – he won't stop until his money is gone entirely + then will get money from Cele from time to time until next pay day

+ then he'll start the same thing all over again.

I called Marino's last night to talk to your sister, Helene, but Helene wasn't home so I called Ryan's next to your sister, Lil's + Helene was at Lil's. She's been there since Thursday helping out as Lil didn't feel so good. Helene said she'd like to go to the show but didn't want to leave Lil + said she'd call me today to say whether she could go or not. She called a little while ago + said she couldn't make it as Lil didn't feel good + was having the doctor (Dr. Thomas). Helene said Jack's mother + father were there visiting so Helene thought she'd better stay + get supper etc. I told her it was perfectly alright – that she should stay there. The doctor will probably give Lilly something to make her feel better – something to give her an appetite – she didn't feel like eating at all. Helene is going to give me a ring during the week – Lil will feel better by then + we can get together some night. Helene had to have the doctor herself – the week after you left – she had an infected throat + the doctor gave her that new sulpha drug that acts so fast. She's all better now tho. Walter, drop Lilly a few lines if you have time + also Helene or your father. They're all good to you when you come home + I know they like to hear from you.

Some class to your brother buying another car – yes I guess he + Ellen like to keep changing their cars from year to year. You're right about Cele + Charlie being good to all of us – they certainly are doing everything to make this home a pleasant one + it could be if it wasn't for that tension that always exists when Thomas is around. Charlie would like to move into an apartment – put Thomas out + go into 4 or 5 rooms but Cele will never do that, although she'd like an apartment too. This house is so hard to heat + is so old + besides it's hard to take care of it – up + downstairs – an apartment would be just the thing – heat supplied etc. in the winter.

About our kitten family, dearest, we still will only have two cats – the two little ones that were just born are promised to people. Ann Preston is taking one + a fellow Charlie knows, the other so we'll have Mother + daughter + Curley, the dog (ha ha).

If only you were here, dearest, we'd have such a nice evening. I'll be thinking of you, anyway, sweetheart. I wish you were here now so I could just be close to you – just knowing you'd be near me would be so nice, dearest. You're so kind + understanding of all my problems. I'll try to keep smiling as you said, dear, after all if I try hard enough not to let things bother me, it shouldn't be too hard seeing I have that Irish fighting spirit in me, heh, dearest? (ha ha).

Lots of love + kisses, dearest Walter. I'll write more tomorrow.

Love Always,

Rita Marie

X X X X X Your Future Colleen Wife X X X X X

Sunday 10/24/43 12:20 p.m.

Hello Soldier, (My Sweetheart)

How are you on this Sunday afternoon? I hope you don't have to work too hard. You must be quite busy, darling, as you haven't called up.

Buddy came home again this week-end + last night Cele + Charlie went up to Bud's mother's house (Sarah + Garry) so I went with them as I couldn't seem to get anyone to go to the show with. Bud + Arline were there. I think Bud looks very well – it was the first I'd seen him since he went in the Army. He's so glad he's going to be in Devens for a while + expects to come home every other week-end from now on. He told me he saw you Friday night + considers himself very lucky, dearest, to have you for a friend while he's there. He said you + he have spent some nice evenings together so far + from now on will see each other often.

Frank Sarnicky called Cele up this morning + said Catherine had a baby girl at 11 o'clock last night. He said Catherine had an awful time – had to be operated on + the baby almost died but everything is all over now + both Catherine + the baby are getting along good. I guess Frank wanted a boy but doesn't care much now – I mean, he said as long as Catherine is alright, he isn't disappointed.

I might make some cookies today, dearest if I have time. If I do I'll send you some – they won't be like the last ones – I hope. I'm going to try another recipe + maybe they won't fracture your toe like the last ones did (ha ha).

Walter dearest, I miss you so much – sometimes the weeks seem so long until I see you again. I hope you can get a pass on Nov. 13th (3 more weeks). It seems a long time since you've been home. I guess I'm rather selfish wanting so much for you to get passes, heh, dearest? But, Walter, you know by my letters this past week I've been "way down in the dumps" with Thomas drunk continually + I wish you were here just to be near me, dearest, just to have you put your arms around me close – I'd feel so much better – you're so kind + understanding + I'm always happy when I'm with you but again I suppose I'm being selfish + self-centered – then again maybe I make you very happy too when you're with me – I hope so, dearest.

Charlie saw Thomas last night out in front of Lupe's drug store leaning up against a pole + with a bottle in his pocket. He was so drunk he was hardly able to stand up + didn't even recognize Charlie. That was about 8:30 + Cele + Charlie wanted to go up to visit Sarah + Garry so I hated to stay here by myself. I knew he'd either have to be taken home or would stumble his way into the house + didn't want to be here when he did, so I was glad I could go with them. He just got up a little while ago + rushed over to Farrells (across the street). He usually gets a double alka selzer for his head + then rushed down Wilmot Ave. to Burn's on Connecticut Ave. (his usual hang-out) to start the same thing all over again. That's the way it's been every single day this past week. It's a wonder he's living but maybe that saying is true about "being preserved in alcohol." He might out-live all of us. The post office must have told him to stay out of work because he's been out all week + we don't know when he's going back. If he would only be man enough to tell us he really wants to stop drinking Cele would probably pay all expenses to do something to get him cured of the habit – send him to a hospital or something but we can see he has no desire to stop at all – he makes no attempt to stop just keeps getting worse all the time.

Well, dearest, here I go again talking about the awfulness of the whole thing – I always start to write to you with the intentions of not mentioning him at all but I always end up telling you don't I, dearest? It helps a lot to tell you, tho, Walter.

Darling, Bud told us last night that sometimes when you go on the schedule of chasing prisoners you ride in a cart with them – the cart is drawn by two donkeys + you go with the prisoners to see that they do their work. I don't remember your ever mentioning this, dearest, it must be funny to go riding along like that (ha ha). Cele said to ask you how it feels to ride behind two asses (donkeys) (ha ha ha). She would say a thing like that, heh, dear?

Take care of yourself, dear + remember I'm thinking of you all the time + love you, dearest.

Love Always,
Rita "bunny"
Your future "little Mrs"
X X X X X X X X X X

Monday
Day Room
6: P.M.

Dear Rita,

Hello Bunny, hows my Sweetheart today, I hope you are feeling fine.

Today I was on Division Patrol yesterday prison chaseing. Tomorrow I will be on division patrol again, with another M.P. It is a very good job, rideing in a 1942 Cruseing Car. Hours. from 7 A.M. to 3: P.M. good hours. Heh dear with the nites off to go to the movies. Yes dear, buy some film, but not to much. I rode in the wagon with the donkeys, _twice_, it is a lot of fun. They only use them for small detail's (<u>with</u> <u>the</u> <u>prisoners</u> <u>driving</u> <u>them</u>) only the summer time (<u>mostly</u> <u>use</u> <u>trucks</u>) Some. FUN. Ha. Ha. Ha. Bunny I Love you, you are my Love and Sweet darling. I miss you so much. I would of called you Sunday, at Noon, but just as I was going to the phone booth, I had a detail of prisoners to bring over to chow. Boy and do they eat. They get a good appetite, working outdoors, <u>Oh Boy</u>, some fun they have about <u>75</u> here, right at the present time I though by two (2) oclock when I got through work you might not be home. It feels so good in this day Room, with the raw, raining weather outside that joke sure is good. There are no flies on that particular boy. <u>Heh</u> <u>Bunny</u>. the little boy's and girls know all the angles how day's, Heh <u>Bunny</u> <u>Ha Ha Ha</u>

Love. Walter.

Wednesday 10/27 6:30 p.m.

Hello Walter Dear,

I was so happy to get your Monday's letter today. Your letters mean so much to me, dearest. I was glad to hear you're well and that you've been on Division Patrol. The hours 7 a.m. to 3 p.m. are very good, darling, as you can have the evenings to yourself.

Walt, I did buy one dozen rolls of film after all and we have 3 #620 too, that I bought just before you came home last time. It will be good to have some next spring (when we get married). The rolls are good for at least a year + each time you come home we can use some, dearest so in the end, we won't have too much of it.

I finally got the pictures I sent away – you remember, dear, the roll I sent to be developed + enlarged + I'm enclosing them. They're all very good except the one of the group (all of us taken on the wall). It looks as tho there was too much light. You came out very nice in all of them, dearest. I like the one of you + Helen together, also you + Al Hammer + then there are some good ones of you + I, too. If you'd like to keep any of them, go right ahead, Walt but send the rest or all back because I want to show them to the girls in the office + then put them in our album.

It's alright about your not calling, Sunday, dearest, I know you didn't have time but if you had called at 2 o'clock I would have been home. I'm usually – practically always – home on Sunday afternoon.

Yes, dear, it's nice you can stay in the day room when the weather is so bad. I often wonder if you enjoy reading like you used to. Remember, dearest, you always used to like to read "Life" magazine + a lot of other educational magazines + books. I imagine it must be hard for you now to keep up with your reading, but darling, try to as much as possible. It's not only good relaxation but it's a good idea to be well-read – even if a lot of it is light reading.

Gosh, dearest, again I want to tell you how much your letters mean – I enjoy them so much – (they help to fill that "empty" feeling), especially since I miss you so much. Darling, confidentially, I'm in one of those loving moods. If you were here now I'd give you some nice kisses. I'll bet you'd like them too. (ha ha). Now I'll bet you're saying "What a little devil Rita is, heh, darling?"

Lots of Love and Kisses, sweetheart

X X X X X X Rita X X X X X X

(big ones) ↑

Wed. Nite 6: PM

Day Room

<u>Keep</u> <u>Smiling</u> <u>Bunny</u>

Dear Rita.

Bunny, Dear, lots of Love to my <u>Love</u> on this quite rainy day. I hope you are in the best of spirits today. even tho the weather is not to good. Heh Bunny.

Last nite I went to the movie to see Robert Cumming's and Olivia De Haweland, <u>in</u> Princess <u>ORourke</u> It was very <u>humorous</u>. I enjoy it very much. I also saw the other nite, the movie, with all that supersiction in it, and all a lot of bad dreams, staring Charles Boyer and Barbara Stanwick In the, Flesh and Phantences [Fantasies] I did not like that one, too, much, it had to many people dreaming in it. Ha Ha Ha.

SO happy to know that you think of me so much and <u>Love</u> <u>me</u> so much. <u>Thanks</u> <u>Bunny</u>, <u>you</u> are so sincere and so good to me. Bunny. I Love you also Bunny, so much. You are so sweet and so feminine. Rita you are the Sweetest girl in the land. <u>Reminiscing</u> (<u>your</u> word) <u>Ha. Ha. Ha.</u> thats how come it is spelled right. Ha. Ha. Ha. is so much fun especially all the fun you and I had together <u>Heh</u> <u>Bunny</u>. I know <u>Rita Marie Lavery</u> that you will do, more than any other person in the World for me. You have such a fine Character, the finest that a person could pocess, Bunny you are the <u>apple</u> of my <u>heart</u>.

Lots of Love and Hugs
From You <u>Darling</u>
<u>Fiance</u> <u>Walter</u>

Thursday 10/28/43 6:00 p.m.

Hello Sweetheart,

I got out of work at 5 o'clock and stopped downtown to pay a little bill in Read's and then came home and found your nice letter waiting for me.

I'm glad you are finding time this week to go to the show. I didn't see Princess O'Rourke but I imagine it's a good picture. I like Olivia de Haviland.

Here's a little poem enclosed that I like. It was in the Saturday Evening Post and it caught my eye so I copied it for you, dearest. The title "When You Return" of course means after the war is all over. I like the last few lines don't you, dear?

Thank you Walter dearest for your telling me all those nice things you think about me. I think <u>you</u> will do more than anyone in the world for me too, darling. I surely will do my best to make you happy always. I was just thinking the other day, Walter, I can't remember your ever criticizing me in any way – I know I have a lot of faults but you never tell me about them – as far as you're concerned I have no faults. If you do notice some bad ones I wouldn't mind if you tell me once in a while, Walter.

I was also thinking, Walt, the next time you come home let's go to the Ritz for a few dances like we used to and have a snack too. Then maybe Sunday we could go to a football game if there is one and if it isn't too cold. By the way, dearest, do you think there's a chance of your coming home in two weeks or don't you know yet? (Nov. 13th I mean)

If you want to call me up Sunday + haven't the money, reverse the charges, dearest. You probably will have money, heh, dearest if you get paid Saturday. In any event, I'll be home Sunday, dearest all day.

They are lifting the dim-out regulations all over the United States

November 1st. Even in New York around Times Square all the big signs are going to be lit just like they used to. It will seem good to "have the lights go on again" as the song goes. I think it's odd tho, as the war isn't over yet. Well, one never knows just when it will be over (I think not until 1945) but a lot of other people think before that. It can't be over too soon, heh, dearest?

I love you so much, dearest and I always will. You + I will have a wonderful life together I'm sure. I wish I could show you just how much.

Lots of love + kisses, sweetheart.

Rita, Your future

Mrs. Walter J. Klein

X X X X X X X X X X X X

P.S. I feel just as much like loving you tonight as I did last night, Walter dearest. Do you think I'll still feel this way in two weeks? (You hope so, heh, dear? – ha ha).

When You Return

When you return I shall not question you
  On all your little deeds since that far day
Time wedged our paths apart. I shall not say,
  As others might, who missed your presence, too:
How do you like the town of so and so?
  Or some such phrase friends utter unconcerned.
What use are casual words to those who learned
  One day, in silence, all they need to know?

I shall abide my time, and when, at last,
  The clamor and the greetings all are done,
Our eyes shall meet, and silently as one,
  We shall relive one moment in the past.
And you shall know, though lips let no word fall,
  That in my heart you did not leave at all.

Friday 12:30 Noon time

Steak for diner <u>Oh</u> Boy It was good.

Dear Rita,

(That <u>in</u> <u>my</u> <u>heart</u> <u>you</u> <u>did</u> <u>not</u> <u>leave</u> <u>at</u> <u>all</u>,) that sure is right. Bunny, that poem is right <u>100</u> percent.

Bunny, you are my Darling, I miss you so much. Bunny I Love you so much. Rita Marie Lavery, you are such a sweet person. Yes Bunny I will let you know, if at any time you need construction criticizem.

Yes Rita, the Ritz and than a football game, sure will hit the spot, on my next trip home which incidentally might come in one week, thats after I finish my next week of Interior guard duty. <u>Oh Boy</u>.) But time will tell. Heh <u>dear</u>.

I will call you dear Sunday, we get payed Monday, but I will have some money than I hope. If not I will reverse the chargs. <u>Ha. Ha Ha</u>.

Last nite I had off. I went to a Halloween party dance, a <u>formal</u> at the Ayer U.S.O. It was a very nice dance. quite a few of the boys attended. I think I will go on the first relief. 12 – 4 – 12 – 4. Yes Bunny we will have a wonderful life together you and I. Thats to start with, and than maybe a boy + girl. <u>Ha</u>. <u>Ha</u>. <u>Ha</u>. <u>Oh Boy</u>

Bunny, you still feel like loving me so much, thats good, very good <u>indeed</u>. I hope you still feel like that on my next trip home. But I am not so sure you will feel quite so much. But you + I always do alright for ourselves. Heh dear. <u>Ha</u>. <u>Ha</u>. <u>Ha</u>.

Love Walter.

Saturday 10/30/43 4:45 p.m.

Dear Sweetheart,

Received your nice Friday's letter when I came home from downtown early this afternoon.

I used my 18th coupon and bought a pair of shoes. Gosh, dear, everything is so expensive. I had to pay an atrocious price for them - $9.<u>95</u>. Isn't that awful? The same shoes last year would be about $6.<u>95</u>. I have a very narrow foot and can never buy cheap shoes. I never paid that much tho, before. I can see I'll do <u>very</u> <u>little</u> Christmas shopping this year – the stores downtown haven't much stock + what they have got is junky but expensive – in other words when you buy things this year in the line of clothes – you're paying an awful price and getting practically nothing for your money. All this probably seems unbelievable to you, dearest, in the Army, not having to <u>buy</u> much but really you would have to buy things yourself to believe it. You're lucky you don't have to <u>buy</u> clothes.

Dearest, you say there's a possibility you might be home in a week. It would be so nice if you could come but I doubt it seeing you're going on from 12 to 4 unless you can get your pass at 5 o'clock next Saturday. Well, we'll see, darling. You'll probably get one on the 13th (I hope).

I'm glad you had a night off to go to a formal dance. Did the girls have nice gowns on, dearest? Gosh, it must have been nice. I wish I could go to another formal dance with you. Remember the one we went to on Feb. 14th last year in Stratford (the Masonic Temple). That was a semi-formal but was nice. I like to wear a gown once in a while + go formal.

I called your sister Helen last night. She's still at Lil's and will be there for a while yet. Lil is getting along fairly good now but Helen is staying there to help with the housework + taking care of Johnny, the baby. She says he has to be watched all the time – he's just at the age where he gets into everything + it's better that Lilly has someone there to take care of him. Helen said she went home (to your house) one day last week + said she didn't see any mail from you + thought it was funny you haven't written.

Darling, if you haven't written home since you went back on your last pass, please write the first chance you get to your father. He + Helen are so good to you when you come home – giving you money + letting you take the car – you should write as often as possible. I know your father would like to hear from you once in a while at least – especially now that he's alone + you could write to Helen + send the letters to White Street. Writing to all those other people, Charlie – Ernie – Micky Rocky + Pat Marino should all come after you write to your family no matter what, dearest. I don't want you to think I'm preaching, dearest, but, I just want to remind you how important it is for you to write home once in a while – please dearest, show your appreciation a little at least.

You say you hope I still feel like loving you a lot when you come home next time. Don't worry, dear, I will only remember we're not going to tire ourselves out like the last time. I think all that loving the last time was too much for you, dearest, you don't seem to be "in a mood" the way you were before, or maybe I'm wrong. Maybe you are still "raring to go." (ha ha ha).

I'm really only kidding, dearest, what I would like when you do come home is moderation in everything – companionship – nice, wholesome fun – a little dancing, football, etc. + a <u>little</u> <u>loving</u>. That's the <u>real</u> <u>thing</u>, dearest, a happy medium to strive for.

Lots of love + kisses,
X X X X X X Rita Marie X X X X X X

Sunday 10/31/43 12:20 p.m.

Dearest Walter,

As I'm writing this letter you are probably on duty (12 to 4). I hope you are in good spirits.

I went to the show with Mary Buccino last night + we saw "Young Ideas" with Susan Peters, Mary Astor + Herbert Marshall. It was funny + also "My Kingdom For a Cook" which was a comedy too. After the show we went in the Star + had a bite to eat. It was a nice evening.

I invited Ann Preston over to the house tonight for supper but she wouldn't come because Eleanor, her brother's girlfriend was coming to her house. Sometimes I don't understand girls at all – last week Ann was so mad at Eleanor because Willie, Ann's boyfriend, was on pass + came Tuesday night just to spend the evening. He had to spend the rest of the time with his family (in Long Island). Well, the night he came Eleanor was there too for dinner + Ann said she sat in the living room all night + wouldn't leave Ann + Will alone for even a minute. Willie was mad too because he only had about 4 hrs. with Ann anyway, + thought Eleanor was very ignorant to stay in the room all evening. She even went to the station with Ann + Willie. What I'm trying to tell you is Ann talked + talked about Eleanor for the rest of the week – how awful she was etc - - - but when I asked her to come over here she couldn't because Eleanor was coming. That's how 85% of the girls are, dearest, they gab their heads off about other girls – say everything about them + then fall all over them when they see them. That's the way it is in the office too – one girl is talking about the other continually behind their backs. A group of fellows get along much better together than girls – in business – socially etc. I listen so much to all the gossiping that goes on in our office + sometimes I'm afraid I'll get like the rest of the gossipers. Well, I hope not, heh, darling?

A "For Sale" sign was put up on our house by the Housatonic Land + Title Co. It has been on private sale for a long time but of course now, with the sign up, it's on public sale. I don't know what they're asking for it now – the last time we heard – it was $5800.<u>00</u> (isn't that a joke with all the repairs it needs etc?). I think someone will buy it eventually tho + then we'll have to move. If we do, I don't know where we'll ever find a rent – there is no such thing as a rent any more in Bpt. with all of the out-of-towners here. Well, I hope we won't have to move for a while at least, as much as I hate Stratford Ave.

Thomas still hasn't gone into work – it's two weeks now + still hasn't learned the job he was supposed to. Cele + Charlie haven't any idea when he is going back. Evidently the post office told him to stay out because since he's been home they haven't called up once so I guess they don't care if he ever goes back. He's still drinking heavily (every day). He certainly is a disgrace.

Bill Hughes' brother-in-law works in E.W.C. factory + gets mail from Betty once in a while. He said she's working in a 5+10¢ store in Clovis, New Mexico. She works 48 hrs. a week + only gets $14.<u>00</u>. Isn't that awful? She could get a job easily at the Air Base there (office work) but would have to sign a contract for at least 6 months + is afraid Bill would be moved if she did. She says by making $14.<u>00</u> a week she can pay the rent ($12.50 a week for light housekeeping) + as long as she keeps on working can stay with Bill. Betty is sure a wonderful wife to Bill – she would work her fingers to the bone to be with him. That's real love, I guess, isn't it, dearest? I guess too, I'd do the same thing if I were in her position. Betty + Bill are good examples of money (lack of it) being no obstacle. They stick together + work together no matter what – most of the credit goes to Betty I think. Love is a beautiful thing, isn't it, dearest, when it can keep two people together like that? Maybe they are only existing tho, darling + not really living, I don't know.

I wish you were here now, dear, so I could be close to you + tell you how much I love you but most of all I wish we were married so we could express our love to the fullest + by that I mean not only physically but in every other way. I think if we wait any longer than June to get married (preferably April) we will have waited too long + might grow further apart from each other. There is such a thing as waiting too long and when two people do, their love becomes commonplace + ordinary - + then it's impossible to remain close to each other. I don't know whether you feel this way, darling, or not. Besides, we are not getting any younger. Of course this doesn't make any difference as far as you're concerned but with girls it does. One thing that is in my favor, in a way, is that even tho I'm going to be 25 soon I'm not as matured as a 25 year old girl is usually – physically nor mentally. In our case, this is a good thing because if I were equivalent to a girl of 25 I'd be a lot older than you. Girls mature much faster than boys. So you see, dearest, when people take me to be

19, it's just as well they do – I'm used to it. By the way, Mr. Trefry, the man I work for thinks I'm still in my 'teens. Some day I'm going to surprise him + tell him how old I am. (ha ha).

Dearest, take care of yourself until I see you – keep well + happy.
I love you.

Love Always
Rita
X X X X X X X X X X X X

Monday Nite 6: P.M.
Post. M.P.

Dear <u>Bunny</u>,

I recived all of your nice letters, and they are so nice. I like them very much.

Yes Bunny, we will have to attend another nice formal, again. The girls wore very nice gowns. All styles. Some very exceptional. <u>Oh</u> Boy, they had all the boy's, in a <u>whirle</u>

If I do not get a pass this week, I would <u>will</u> have to wait until Nov. 20th the passes now start at 5: P.M. Saturday, instead of at 12 noon. Something new, started by the new Post Commander of the Post. Yes Bunny, 25 years old is plenty mature for a girl to contemplate marrige. 28 years of age for a boy is O.K. also, Heh dear. <u>Bunny</u> <u>dear</u>.

P.S. I dropped my folks a line yesterday at home. to Pa. + Helene.

To bad about thomas. it makes it so hard for you all at home, especially after treating him so good.

I am feeling fine and I am getting along. O.K. Bunny.

Post <u>21</u> is the Commuacation Bld. all the telophones and tellagraft are recived there, It is a inside post. civilian girls in daytime Wac's at nite operate the swich Board. Boy they are some pep's <u>Ha</u> Ha.

Today is pay day, so I am a little richer than for the past few weeks, <u>ha</u> <u>ha</u>. I got $39.95 <u>Oh</u> <u>Boy</u>. We will now be able to add to our fund's now, heh dear. $10.00 <u>more</u>.

Bunny I miss you so much. I love you dearest. last nite I could of <u>eat</u> you up for after supper desert <u>Oh</u> Boy. Ha. Ha. Ha. I am always hungry, <u>hungry</u> for you. Bunny. Love, Walter.

P.S. passes come after a week of guard duty, not after a week of school. I will be finishing 2 weeks of guard and already two weeks of school. So if I dont get my pass after finishing guard. I will have to wait two more weeks. passes do not come after school week, because we have to go on guard duty at Saturday Noon after a week of school. <u>Ha.</u> <u>Ha</u> Ha. either a pass this coming week or on Nov. <u>20th</u>

Tuesday 11/2/43 4:30 p.m.
(Election Day)

Dearest Walter,

I'm writing this letter in the office because Mr. Trefry is in Worcester, Mass. on business. Some days I have lots of work to do (tomorrow I will) + other days, I haven't much.

How's my sweetheart today? Well + happy – I hope.

Darling, you know the package I told you I was going to send you? Well, I told Charlie when he brought it to the post office to send it first class mail because there's a little note in it. He sent it third class tho because he said first class would be too expensive. The fellow in the post office asked him if there was any writing inside + Charlie said "No." You know, Walt, it's a federal offense to have writing in the inside of a third-class package – it's O.K. tho if it's sent first class. Now I'm just hoping the package won't be opened before it reaches you or I'll end up in jail. (ha ha). Remember, Walt, if you have to visit me in jail I like flowers (roses) – ha ha. I'll never put any more notes in your packages again, dearest, unless I'm sure they're going first-class. I hope you get that one alright.

Things with Thomas sort of reached a climax yesterday. He still hasn't gone into work + two fellows who work with him in the post office came over to warn him that his bosses were giving him only the rest of the week to learn the job he's supposed to + get back to work. If he doesn't learn it while he's home this week, there is a notice going thru to Washington whereby he'll lose his job + will be out once + for all. They told Charlie he was supposed to learn it when he first started working regular hours 7 yrs. ago in the post office but never would so his bosses told him to stay out until he did + in the meantime are disgusted with the way he's been drinking + want him out of there altogether. The fellows said he goes into work lots of weeks + is drunk 4 nights out of 5. They think the same as Cele + Charlie do that he should go away for a cure. Poor Cele is a nervous wreck over the whole thing. It seems as tho he just can't learn it now – the last few days he's been spending a half-hour or so a day + then goes out + gets drunk. He can't concentrate at all + I suppose if he does study a little it just doesn't penetrate. Well, I don't know what the outcome of the whole mess will be. Even if he does learn the work, I think he'll be fired eventually on account of his drinking. He's been drinking a little less in the last few days because he spent all his money + hasn't a cent. Cele has to give him a quarter + fifty cents at a time.

Today is Election Day in Bridgeport. I'm going to stop in (at Lincoln School) on my way home from work + vote. No doubt McLevy will be elected again. I was surprised today to know that quite a few people never vote at all – quite a few girls here in the office. I think everyone should don't you, dearest, it really is a privilege.

6:15 p.m. Here I am home again + have just finished reading your nice letter (Monday's).

It was pouring rain when I got off the bus to vote but being in a very patriotic mood decided it was no excuse not to vote (the rain) (ha ha). It's just coming over the radio now – McLevy was elected again. This will be his sixth term.

You said in your letter that your passes from now on will start at 5 P.M. instead of 12 noon. That isn't so good is it dearest? But you + I will have a nice week-end anyway, Walter, dear, I do hope you won't have to wait until the 20th. If you do get it I could meet you at the station at 10:30 or whenever you get in if you call me when you're in Worcester or wherever you change trains, then I'd know just what time you'd be here, dearest.

Let's leave it this way: If I don't hear from you (up until 5:30 in the afternoon) that will mean you're coming – then if I don't get a call by then I'll wait until you call me from Worcester or Springfield – if you can't call until you get into Bpt. it will be O.K. dearest but come right to the house won't you? We can have a few hours together Saturday night at least. O.K. dear?

You say you could have eaten me up for dessert last night at supper (ha ha). You're funny, darling. You wouldn't get much <u>meat</u>. (ha ha).

Lots of great big hugs and kisses, dearest.

Rita Marie ("Bunny)"

x x x X x x x

<- This one is a half-hour long. (ha ha).

Wed. 11:30 A.M.

Squad Room

Second Platoon

Dear Rita,

Thanks every so much for the very nice shower bath shoes and also for the swell ties, I recived them last nite with your nice letter. They are the right size. Bunny you are my <u>Belovedy</u> Darling.

I will have to give you some very <u>extra</u> long and nice kisses, on my next trip home, which may be this Saturday. I will hold you tight, and embrace you close to me, until we are lost in our world of Love, than we can hold hands and I will put my head close to your's and we will fall off, to a <u>oh</u> such a beautiful sleep or would you call it a hours' or two of wonderful happiness. <u>Oh</u> Boy. Yes Bunny that poem, sure was a very nice one. <u>Bunny</u> you know nice poem's, when you see them. Bunny, my Sentamental girl. I like you that way. Heh dear.

So good of you dear to go to church yesterday. Rita. thats it, be a good girl. <u>ha</u>. <u>ha</u>.

I understand how, <u>shy</u> you are when ansering the phone, when I am giving you some kisses over the phone. or when I am embaring you in front of some of your folks. I understand Bunny. I am <u>shy</u> also. <u>Oh</u> yes, <u>Ha</u>. <u>Ha</u>. <u>Ha</u>.

Bunny, I alway's feel like Loving you, but just in moderation, Heh dear. Bunny, I would like to be close to you and maybe squeez you, <u>oh</u> so tight, and than just drift off to a nice snooze in your arms, or may be while lieing in <u>bed</u>, close to you, just holding you close to me. <u>oh</u> Boy, what a devil I am. Bunny, I will be <u>good</u> – very good <u>Boy</u>.

Love. Walter.

Sunday 11/7/43 12:15 pm

Dearest Walter,

I really shouldn't be writing to you now – I'm in such a bad mood. It isn't bad enough that we both have to be so disappointed over your not getting a pass (the last minute) but we can't even talk to each other for three minutes – we were cut off when we were talking only about two minutes. If you only stayed in the booth for a few minutes we could have been connected again. I hung up + dialed operator + told her we were disconnected + she tried to put another call through and locate you but you had left the pay station. Oh well, I suppose you were mad too. If you had told the operator she could have connected us again – but I know just how you felt. While I'm on the subject of phone calls – when it comes right down to it – it's just a waste of money for you to call every week, don't you agree, Walt? After all, what can we say in three minutes – the usual – "Hello – how're you, what did you do last night – I miss you + goodbye" – that's all it really amounts to + we can say a lot more than that if we write. So, Walter, from now on, it's up to yourself if you want to spend $.50 a week on phone calls ($2.00 or $2.50 a month) I think it's foolish I'd rather get a letter on a Monday from you.

I guess you know without my going into detail that I was just as disappointed as you last night when I knew you couldn't make it home. That's the Army for you – We'll have to learn to take things like that, that's all.

As I mentioned on the 'phone I went to the show with Ann Preston + Eleanor (her brother's girlfriend). We went about eight o'clock + by that time the shows were all crowded. I wanted to see "He dood It" with Red Skelton + "Doughboy in Ireland," both comedies but we couldn't get in so we went to the Majestic + saw "The Man Down Under" with Charles Laughton – It was rated as a very good picture but I didn't like it at all.

I was talking to your sister Helen on the phone Friday night (she called me) + told her you might be home this week-end + that we'd stop at Lilly's (Helen is there all the time now) but if we weren't there by 5 this afternoon she'd know you didn't come. In that case, she was to call me + we'd both go to the Stratford movie tonight. I guess I'll go with her if she calls. She hasn't been out to a show in ages. She told me you sent Lil a card + were going to send perfume + handkerchiefs. Yes, Walt, Blue Grass Cologne + handkerchiefs make a nice gift to send. I'm sure she'll like it.

Last night while I was waiting for Ann at Main + Fairfield I met Charlie Krolides + Irene. They stopped + talked for a few minutes. Irene is expecting a baby in December (six more weeks) + Charlie thinks he'll have to go in the Army in January – that he won't be able to get deferred any more. They both wanted to know why you never wrote to Charlie since you've been away. I said I didn't know + asked Charlie why he didn't write to you + he used the excuse that he didn't know your address. I said I'd give it to him right there but Irene said no, it was up to you to write first. If he really wanted to write why didn't he get your address from the fellows who hang around the store or from Pat Marino? Charlie writes to him all the time. Oh well, that's how he is – he wants everyone to cater to him. They wanted to know why you + I don't get married – that we should be – Irene said "You'd be much better off when Walt comes home on pass or furlough then you wouldn't have to say good-night at a certain time etc etc." Charlie said yes, Irene's right - look at us – "we aren't even married a year + we're going to be a pappa + mamma" – you + Walt had better hurry up.

Walter, it just goes to show you – they both are ignorant – to say things like that. Charlie (+ Irene too) are typical of their nationality – nervy + ignorant both. I always thought they were + still feel the same way. I told them we might get married in the Spring but didn't know for sure. Irene worked up until two weeks ago – imagine that! You'd think she'd be ashamed in front of the fellows + girls she worked with in that condition. Well, I guess those kind of people think nothing of it. Charlie told me not to forget to tell you that I met them + said to be sure + write to him.

Walter, I've been thinking about that Manicure set that I told you I'd like for my birthday. I don't know what I was thinking of when I said I wanted one. I really don't expect anything this year – you haven't money to be spending on things like that – so darling, forget about the present. I don't think I'd have any use for a manicure set anyway as I haven't used nail polish in quite a while now. If you just send me a card I'll be happy. I mean this, Walter, don't buy anything at all – just a card. You should try to save as much money as possible from now on, anyway, Walt.

There were some hope chests advertized in the paper the other night for $35.<u>00</u>. I don't know how they are for that price but I think for $40 or $45 they might be pretty nice. I'm just telling you this, dearest so you'll have an idea of the price. That's another reason why you shouldn't buy a birthday gift – Christmas is so near my birthday. Think this over Walt, you'll see that I'm right.

Last night there was a beautiful moon (a half-moon) + it was so warm it was like spring – and today is a perfect day too – for football or a nice walk. Well, dear, we'll have to make up for lost time when you do come home. The next two weeks will seem so long but I guess I'll live thru them, heh dearest?

Cele saw Bud last night and he said he hasn't seen you in two weeks – he's gone several times to No. 1 theatre to see if he'd see you but didn't. Cele said you've probably been busy. You could get in touch with him once in a while, Walt, if you have a chance.

Take care of yourself, Walter dear, until I see you in two weeks (I hope).

Lots of love, sweetheart,

X X X X X X Rita X X X X X X

Monday 11/8/43

Dearest,

I hope everything is well with you on this rainy Monday.

Are you all settled in your new barracks yet or am I mistaken – was it just the day room that was moved? I still can't get over the fact of your pass being cancelled the last minute – as if you couldn't move on a Monday or some other day, heh Walt? The Army always talks about the civilians keeping up the morale of the soldiers but they, themselves lower it by doing things like that, don't you agree, Walt?

I went to the show with your sister, Helen, last night. We didn't go to the Stratford show after all – we went downtown + saw "I Dood It" with Red Skelton + "Doughboys in Ireland" with Kenny Baker. Those are the pictures that Ann Preston + I wanted to see Saturday but couldn't get in. They were both swell pictures I think. It did Helen good to get out for a few hours + have some laughs. She almost couldn't get to the show – Jack wanted to go out last night but Helen said she made the date with me Friday (if you couldn't come home) so he had to stay home. By the way, I was talking to Jack (Bridges) on the 'phone yesterday afternoon. He called up for Helen to see if you had come home. I told him why you couldn't + he was kidding me saying you probably decided to go someplace else this week-end (ha ha).

I also talked to Lil. She's getting along fairly well I guess but has to have someone there with her all the time as she has her bad days once in a while.

I had a letter from Dot Smith today + she + Ernie have finally found a place by themselves. It's in the same town (Ozark) + Dot says it's a two-room cabin has hot + cold water + electricity. She wrote the letter on Nov. 3rd + they're supposed to move in the 8th (today). She said they were tickled to get it. I guess I'd better not write to her until I get her new address. Dot says Ernie helps her a lot in the house – with the dishes etc. I guess the Army has taught him all that, heh, Walt? Would you help me with things like that when we get married, dearest? I can't imagine you. (ha ha). Dot says they are still going without coats down there, it's so warm. I wouldn't mind living in the South for the winter – you know me – I hate cold weather.

Thomas still hasn't gone into work + hasn't learned the job yet either. A little while ago a fellow who works in the post office called up + said he was supposed to report today + take a test on the job but he didn't show up at all. Cele or Charlie don't know where he is – he's been out all day. I don't know what he thinks he can do if he loses that job – I know Charlie won't let him stay here if he does – Isn't it a shame? Cele has been home from work today sick – I think it's her nerves more than anything. Ann Preston got a letter from Willie her boyfriend + he expects to get home again this coming week-end. He was home three weeks ago. Wouldn't it be nice if you came home, too, dearest, then we could all get together + you + he could meet? I know this is practically impossible for you, tho, Walt. Darling, if you have a chance to get one (a pass) during the week sometime within the next two weeks, take it. I can take time off from work + we could have a day together.

I miss you so much – it seems so long since we've seen each other, heh, dearest? I think of you all the time, Walter, + love you so much. Take care of yourself, sweetheart – try to stay in tip-top shape.

Love Always

big long ones → X X X X X X X X X X X Rita "Bunny"

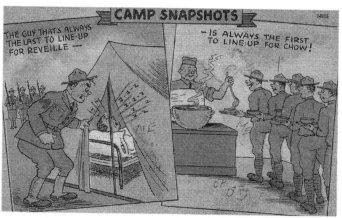

Dear Rita,

Hows my Bunny today. So glad to be able to talk to you yesterday. Bunny, I could love you so nice. <u>oh</u> Boy. Darling I Love you Today I am chasing prisoners it is quite <u>Raw</u> out Hope you had a nice time over the week end, dear. Rita, I wish I could hold you in my arms now and Love you oh Boy.

Tuesday 11/9/43 3:30

Rest Period

Hello Sweetheart,

I'm eating a Milky Way and writing at the same time – in the office at my desk. I have quite a bit of time on my hands today because Mr. Trefry went to Worcester last night + won't be back until tomorrow. I've finished up all the work I'm supposed to do + just have a few odds + ends now to work on but would rather write to you, dearest.

I never told you much about my work did I, Walt? I will now – if you don't mind.

First of all, I'm in an office called the Purchasing Department. It's rather small – Miss Noonan (you met her) is the Sales Manager + her desk is over in the corner facing mine. Mr. Trefry, the man I work for is Purchasing Agent + his desk is right near mine. Next to my desk is a big table with large books full of government drawings, a Dun + Bradstreet Reference book (gives information on different concerns all over U.S.) also Thomas' Register, another book of the same type. There are six filing cabinets, 3 contain catalogues that different customers send us from time to time. The other three files contain Sales Correspondence + Purchasing correspondence. On top of the files there are different books with records in that I keep up to date. Between Miss Noonan's + Mr. Trefry's desk there is a display case (made of glass) showing the different parts of what we are manufacturing for the government (a secret – ha ha). I have to dust these parts + the case once a week (what a job!) Then there are a few extra chairs in here for company – (salesmen etc). Mr. Trefry kids me a lot about my corner of the office being so neat + his + Miss Noonan's being so sloppy. Sometimes he says, "Poor Walter, he'll have to put everything away in its place + be neat with you for a wife" (ha ha). I told him you were neat too – you didn't like a sloppy house either. Am I right? (ha ha) Oh yes, there are two maps on the wall – one of the U.S. – it's very large + the other of North Africa, (all colored) Europe + the Mediterranean.

As far as my work's concerned I try to follow a schedule – each day, but it's hard to because (Tref) that's what I call him behind his back (ha ha) dictates whenever he feels like it – not at a certain time each day.

In the morning I file a lot of correspondence first of all (after dusting his desk + my own). Then I keep some records up to date – in pen + ink. Each day a certain number of parts come in from sub-contractors + I keep a record of them. Then Tref usually dictates or sometimes there's a roll left from the day before + I do that. The time that I'm not taking dictation or transcribing it – I work on all different records – one that has to do with Sales + the rest purchasing. I make little notes + put them on Mr. Trefry's desk to remind him to follow up different things like dictating to companies when he wants to follow up different subjects. This is probably all very boring to you, darling but it just gives you an idea of what I do. Some days I'm rushed with work + others I haven't much at all. I'd rather be rushed – it isn't so tiresome.

Mr. Trefry just came back – we didn't expect him until tomorrow. Oh, well, it's 5 o'clock now – only another half-hour to go. I'll finish this later, dearest.

6:15 Received your funny postal card, dear. Yes, the fellow sleeping (the last one to get up in the morning) is just like you (ha ha) – also the first one at chow.

You said you were chasing prisoners – Darling, I thought this was your school week – maybe if you're on guard or detail this week, you might get a pass at the end of the week – is there any chance at all, dearest?

Yes, Walter, I wish I could be in your arms too – give you some nice long kisses. I miss you so much – the time has gone by so slowly these past four weeks – I guess because we've been all on edge here – you know over who.

Charlie is sick right now – upstairs over Thomas – he went over to see his boss (Charlie went over to the post office this afternoon) to get the real facts of Thomas' job + Mr. Kearns sure gave them to him. He said he was giving him until Thursday + if he doesn't show up then for the test or if he does take the test + doesn't pass he's out altogether from the post office. Charlie came home + had such a fight (argument) with Thomas that he's all upset himself now. I don't know what the outcome will be but he doesn't want the job – he admitted it today – doesn't care if he is put out.

Isn't it awful? He's been living here for 4 weeks without contributing one cent but Cele has been giving him money (a little change now + then). If he keeps on the way he is, he'll cause one or all of us to break down – but he'll go on most likely in the best of health. Charlie can't believe a word he says, he lies so much. I hope God will punish him some day for all the wrong he's done – maybe me, too, heh, Walter dear, for talking about him like this to you. Well, I don't talk about him to anyone else + you understand me so well, I just have to once in a while to you.

Well, dearest, take care of yourself – eat properly + get as much rest as you can + before you know it you'll be at 1440 with me in your arms. Go to the movies once in a while etc + the time will go by. I love you so much, dearest Walter – you mean everything to me.

Love Always,
Rita Marie
X X X X X X X X X X X X
(great big ones)

Tuesday Nite Post 21.
Post Communication Building. Hrs – 8-12

Dear Rita,

Hello Bunny, (Main Gate), hows my sweet little girl today, I hope you are feeling fine, and getting along O.K.

Tonite I was going to the movie, but at the last minute, the first Sergeant put me on duty, to replace a boy on this post. It will only be for tonite, I will get finished at 12: midnite. This is my school week, so I should not be doing this work, but thats the way it goes. hum. hum. Bunny, I miss you so much, you are such a sweet girl. You are my darling.

Rita, I could, wrap myself around you and hug you galore, oh Boy. You know me.

Bunny, we will have the finest of companionship. Some taste and some interest, sports, plays, education, Spiritual life and oh such a good warm life together. Heh dear.

Yes dear, talking for three (3) minutes is not hardly worth it. But we like to talk to each other on the phone sometime Yes dear, some of those Hope chest sure are very nice, but nothing is too good for my girl. Rita Marie Lavery. Oh Boy, tell Cele not to work to hard. Thomas makes it so hard for her. It is to bad. Cele is such a nice person. She tries to please every one so much. Bunny be a good girl. I hope to see you in a few weeks.

Love
Walter

P.S. Next week I have my usual week of Interior guard duty. So I hope to see you on the 20th of Nov. (Bunny)

Wednesday Nov. 10, '43
3:30 Rest Period

Dearest Walter,

I'm writing this letter during the afternoon rest-period because I promised Mrs. Smith I'd go over to see her tonight. Mary will be there too. If there is any mail from you at home I'll answer it tomorrow, dearest.

Mr. Trefry brought in this cartoon I'm enclosing to me this morning. He laughed his head off over it + asked me if I could phrase those words better + send a letter out if he dictated that way. I told him I could (ha ha).

I've been quite busy today – usually am after "Tref" takes a trip.

Cele + Charlie are both home from work today. Charlie was sick all night (something he ate I guess) + Cele feels better but she took another day off to keep him company.

Darling, I was thinking – The next time you come home, let's see if we can have Cele + Charlie meet your father somehow. Maybe if they drove you to your house they could stop in + be introduced to him – it's certainly about time they've met, don't you think so? The only ones they've met in your family are Helen + Albert + Ellen. It's too bad they weren't home that time when you were home + Adolph + Martha stopped in at my house. I wish Martha would stop again + then they could meet + that Cele + Charlie could meet Lilly + Emma too. Oh well, maybe they will soon, but in the meantime I hope they can at least meet your father. If you have any suggestions about this, please let me know, Walter dear.

I think about you all the time, dearest + hope everything is going along smoothly for you. When you do come home, I'll give you some nice kisses.

Lots of love, sweetheart

X X X X X X Rita X X X X X X

STRICTLY BUSINESS   By McFeatte

"Uh—'Herschel, Crovny and Wort—uh Gentlemen: Go to the devil! Yours very truly!'—phrase that a little better and get it out in the next mail!"

Wednesday Nite
Lowell Mass.
Merrimack Hotel.

Dear Rita,

Tonite I am with a half a dozen of the boy's from my outfit. We all though that we would come to Lowell tonite, one of the boys' is being shipped to Maine tomorrow, So we are to have a last nite together. enjoying a few drinks and some fun together. Tomorrow and Friday I am on patrol in Ayer Mass. and Saturday I am to go on Interior guard duty.

I hope that thomas gets on to him self. It makes it so hard for you all at home, especially, Cele and Charlie. Its to bad he is so weak, But that's the way it goes in life. We all have our weakness's. Heh dear. I sure do understand every thing Bunny. you can <u>confine</u> in me at any time.

Bunny, I miss you so much, Rita you are such a sweet girl, I am sure happy to have you for my near future wife. Rita you are so intelligent, you have a very good job, and carry it out so eficent. It is very nice work. See Bunny how capable you are. Thats good. <u>Rita</u>. <u>Marie</u> <u>Lavery</u>. Hope that you and I can get together on the <u>20</u>th of Nov. Bunny, I Love you So much. I wish I had you in my arms this fine, full Moon Nite. <u>oh</u> <u>Boy</u>

Love. Walter

Thursday, November 11, 1943

Dearest Walter,

I'm sending this letter to you Special Delivery and darling, please try to get a grip on yourself for some very bad news.

Your sister, Helene, just called me up at the office and said Lilly was taken to the hospital this morning and Helene was just notified that she is on the danger list in the hospital. The doctor thinks that it will just be a matter of days or maybe just hours that Lil will live. Jack and your sister, Helen were up all night as Lil was in terrible pain so all the doctor could do was give her morphine to ease the pain.

So dearest, try not to be alarmed if you receive a telegram that the end has come. I hate to tell you this way (writing) but Helen told me to write so you would know the truth. I wish I could be with you, dearest, I know how you feel about it – being away from home and knowing that you can't do anything to help. The doctor said Lil will be much better off if she goes because she is suffering so.

Helene will let you know if anything happens. Darling, please keep up the best you can. If you want to call me tomorrow (as soon as you get this) you can call at the office (3-4175) and by tomorrow I might have some more information.

Love Always,
Rita
Thursday 11/11/43 Armistice Day 6:00 p.m.

Dearest Walter,

I hope by the time you receive this letter you will have received the special delivery one I sent earlier today. I know how you must feel, sweetheart, and I wish I could be with you to give you my understanding at least.

Here are the few little details I got from Helen over the phone. As I told you, the doctor brought Lil to the hospital early this morning. Helen said both she + Jack talked to the doctor last night + he gave them the real facts that it was just a matter of time for Lil but Helen thought maybe it was just one of her bad spells and that she might rally + feel better as she has when she had spells before but the doctor said it was practically impossible for her to pull out of this attack as she's hemorrhaging + of course that's very weakening.

I called Ellen a little while ago to see if there was any change in Lilly's condition + she said she was just about the same + told me she wrote to you + said she'd call me tomorrow if there was any change.

Helen was going to send you a telegram for you to come home but then, on second thought, she (+ I) didn't think it was wise. If you came now, dearest, you'd be as helpless (as much as you would want to do something) as the rest of the family.

If her condition changes for the worst, Helen will send you a telegram + then you can come <u>immediately</u> – when you show it to your commanding officer.

Darling, I know when you're on duty you'll probably have time to think a lot of the whole situation but please try to keep in mind that if anything happens it will be much better than having Lil linger + suffer. No one would want to see that happen.

As far as the children are concerned – it certainly is pitiful – they are three grand children but God will surely take care of them somehow.

I know, dearest, when you're away from home as you are, you can't help thinking a lot of the awfulness of it – you feel so much as tho you should be home here doing something to help but you can help a great deal if you pray that Lil, if it's God's will, will have a <u>speedy</u> <u>recovery</u> or a <u>happy</u> <u>death</u>. I'll pray for her + the children too, dearest.

Dearest, try not to let your mind dwell too much on the whole situation (I realize only too well how hard this is). I understand you, Walter, so well – I know once you face the situation, + take it in hand you'll be <u>sensible</u> <u>enough</u> <u>to</u> <u>realize</u> <u>that</u> <u>whatever</u> <u>happens</u> <u>is</u> <u>God's</u> <u>will</u>.

I wish you were here now so you could be close to me, sweetheart, but as it's impossible I just want you to keep up that wonderful spirit that you've always shown when you experienced hard knocks before. I love you, dearest + will be thinking of you all the time. Please take care of yourself – if you want to call me when you get this letter I'll be home, dearest (after 5:30).

Love Always,
X X X X X X Rita X X X X X X

Friday 11/12/43

Dear Walter,

I hope you are managing to keep your spirits up (fairly well at least) in spite of all the bad news you've been receiving about your sister's condition.

Helen asked me to send you that telegram, darling, this afternoon, as she thought it was best that you come but when I explained the situation to her after you called the second time she agreed with you – that it would be best not to come now. If you came today, Walter, there would be nothing you could do anyway – but of course see Lil.

The last time I talked with you on the phone I told you the doctor wanted Lil to have a transfusion. Well, when I talked to Helen again she said the doctor had decided not to give one – she said one doctor wanted it + another one didn't so up until about 4:15 this afternoon they didn't give her one.

Jack stayed at the hospital most of the day, today, I guess because Helen said he took Joan + Carol up to Trumbull to his mother's + left the baby with Helen.

According to what the doctor told Helen + Jack yesterday, he's positive Lil won't pull thru but couldn't tell exactly how long she'd last – in his opinion it wouldn't be very long so that's the story, dearest. The only thing anyone can do is wait now + pray. I know how you must feel, dearest. I understand exactly – it's a shame that you have to be away from home now but as I told you in yesterday's letter I know you'll be sensible enough to take everything in its stride.

Dearest, here's $5.<u>00</u> that I'd like you to hold on to in case you do have to come unexpectedly, (for trainfare). Please try not to spend it. It's $5.<u>00</u> of the $10.00 you sent last time.

About calling me – tomorrow (Sat.) I'll be in the office 'till 12 noon + after 2 in the afternoon will be home so if you want to call don't hesitate + reverse the charges if you want. Cele said to tell you that. I'll try to tell you just how everything is.

I couldn't hear you very well when you called the second time but from what I could hear you said something about having to take a Vocational Aptitude Test. I hope you make out well, dearest. I wish you could have a chance to use your mechanical ability in some line but then maybe you'd be moved from Ft. Devens + that wouldn't be good would it, Walter dear?

Dearest, please try not to think too much – I know it'll be awfully hard for you – go to the movies or something to keep your mind occupied on something else.

I'll be thinking of you over the week-end + as I said before will be home <u>tomorrow</u> <u>afternoon</u> + Sunday too, so if you want to call, dear, don't forget you can reverse the charges.

Keep your chin up, sweetheart, everything will work out for the best.

Love Always,

X X X X X X Rita X X X X X X

P.S. I love you so much, darling.

PART V: Planning for the Future

Concerns About Walter's Career Path

Walter served in varied support capacities; notably as an MP and then in the Quartermaster Corps. He did not like being in the Military Police. He wished to demonstrate his mechanical skills with vehicles and engines. Walter felt, as evidenced by his letters, that the MP duty was a dead-end as he wouldn't be able to get an advance in his rating. He clearly felt that showing his skills would lead to a promotion and better pay.

Rita shared Walter's dislike of the MPs. On the other hand, she tried to encourage Walter in her letters, pointing out that the MP duty wasn't all that bad, especially as Walter would remain at an Army camp closer to home. Rita clearly liked Walter's ability to come home on weekend passes.

After being in the Military Police for a year, Rita's letters reveal her great joy that Walter could switch out the ensign on his blouse (shirt) collar from crossed pistols to the Quartermaster Corps. That switch came just months prior to their marriage on April 22, 1944.

Letters: November 25, 1943 – January 17, 1944

Dearest,

I hope you arrived back safely after your long and tiresome train-ride and that you aren't finding it too hard getting back into routine.

I thought it was nice of your folks, dearest, to come to the station last night – I'll bet you were surprised to see them. I rode back with them on the bus – as far as my house – they were all going back to Al's house for coffee.

The weather is beautiful today for Thanksgiving – it's ideal for football. Virginia went to the Harding Central game – Harding won – 6-0. Stratford won too but I don't know yet what the score was. Remember, dearest, last year when you + I went to the games – the weather wasn't as nice – it was much colder but we enjoyed it so much. It was just a year ago today, too, that we talked about being engaged – you decided you'd give me a diamond for Christmas, remember, darling? We decided we'd be engaged for a year + a half before getting married + now everything seems to be working towards that point, heh, dearest? As you said it was God's will that you + I should meet – love each other + marry to spend the rest of our lives together. He knows that we could never be happy with anyone else.

You and I couldn't be together this year, dearest, but we were very close to each other in spite of this, weren't we? In the ten days that you were home, it made me so happy, dearest, to be able to share your sorrow and it made me realize all the more what a wonderful person you are. I know God will reward you for everything you did for Lilly. You did your utmost in every possible way + now, darling, I hope you have peace of mind in knowing you did everything. If we had people in the world with half of the character you have, there wouldn't be any war.

Dearest, during the long hours between now and the next time you come home, I know you'll realize in all your loneliness, that everything that's happened is for the best – as hard as that may seem.

Last night, after you went + we were all waiting for the bus Helen + I had a few minutes together while waiting in a doorway. She thought your father made a mistake in bringing up the subject of the children last night when everyone was so upset. I told her that Jack said he'd carry out whatever decision she would make regarding them + Helen said she's going to let everything ride for just a little while. By this she means she'll stay at White Street with the three children until some agreement is reached about everything. She said she knows her place is home with your father + will go home soon – as soon as everyone in your family gets their bearings. At first I thought she'd be making a mistake by doing this because then Jack might let things go on indefinitely – that is, stay at White St. without bothering to decide anything but Helen said she'll see that this won't happen. I guess Helen is right don't you, dearest? Everything will work out in time but I guess it will take time. I'm sure that's the way Lilly would want it – Helen making the decisions – because Helen was always such a big help to her + always so capable.

I'll call Helen up from time to time + stop to see her too. Darling, please, for your own sake + mine take care of yourself – get as much rest as possible, a little diversion once in a while. You have been thru an ordeal for the past two weeks + if you balance your life (the best you can) you'll be able to take this sorrow with clear thinking + reasoning.

I'll be thinking of you always, dearest. You'll be home soon again (after Christmas). I love you so much, dearest Walter.

Love Always,
Rita Your "future Wife"
X X X X X X X X X X X X – (12 great big ones.)

Thursday Nite 6:30 P.M.

Dearest, Rita,

I arrived safely at the Fort, I managed to get five (5) hrs. of sleep, so I feel O.K. (dearest).

I chased prisoners this afternoon, tonite, at midnite I am going on interior guard. I will sleep from, 7. Seven P.M to 11:30 P.M. That is I will get some shuteye right after I finish this letter. I just got through eating supper, We had turkey and all the fixens also mince pie and cider. <u>Oh</u> Boy, and even those nice Olives, also ice cream. Here on the post, the thanksgiven meal, was served at 5:30 P.M, not at 12: oclock <u>Noon</u> like you and I always had it. <u>Heh</u> <u>dear</u>.

I am quite sure <u>God</u> is being good to my Sister <u>Lillian</u> on this <u>Thanksgiven</u> <u>day</u>.

Bunny you are such a nice girl. I Love you <u>Bunny</u> so much. My pappy and all my family think you are so nice and posess such a fine charactor. Rita you are my girl and my Life's <u>insparation</u>. God will watch out for my Sisters Lillian's children and I am sure <u>Jack</u> and all my family will do there utmost to do as Lil would want them to do, (in such a case) you Rita and I and your family will also do as <u>God</u> wants us to do in trying times as this. Too <u>feel</u> right from the <u>heart</u> and <u>mind</u> and do without to provide for My Sister Lil's Beautiful children. and I know you and I will watch them and give them a helping hand, as they will certainly need plenty of <u>guidence</u> and <u>Love</u> and cheer incourage while going through life.

Your Loving Boy
<u>Walter</u>

P.S. I thank your family for being so good during all my advesities and trials. They are all so kind and good. <u>Walter</u>

Friday Nite

Dearest Rita,

Hope you Darling had a very enjoyable Thanksgiving, and I know that you had good food and all the cheer, that goes with a holiday It sure was very nice of my folks to come to the station, I sure was very surprised to see them.

That was very nice for Jeanie, to attend the Harding + Central High Football game. 6-0 in Harding's favorite, Boy not bad. Good old Stratford High did alright too, I was wondering just how they made out. Thanks for sending me the results. (Bunny) Dear.).

Yes dear one (1) year ago we were making our minds up as to getting engaged, Boy that was a very happy day Heh dear. Yes it is God's will and you and I are so happy to know that God wants us to be lifes partners together for life. Oh Boy thats so good. Right Bunny dear. God will reward my Sister Lillian, I am sure for all her suffering while on this earth. he will also reward you and I and all our folks also for trying our utmost to ease her pain and suffering.

I know in my heart, that God will watch out and care for my Sister Lillians Beautiful children. Jack Bridges I am sure will do his utmost, I think he relizes now his past Sinful ways, he confesed them to me and my family and the pastor. So I have faith in him to care for the children

Love. Walter.

P.S. Yes dear every thing will work out O.K. in time.

Saturday 11/27/43. 4:45 pm

Dearest,

The nice letter you wrote Friday was waiting for me when I got home from downtown about an hour ago. I like your letters so much, sweetheart.

I went downtown from work this noon + tried to do a little Christmas shopping (just for the family). I have your gift + Cele's bought. I bought Cele a rheinstone bracelet + earrings to match – I hope she likes it. We met Eleanor downtown + we happened to be in Outlet's near the lingerie counter + Eleanor asked the salesgirl if she could see some bridal sets (nightgown slip + underwear). I was standing there with her (Cele too) but didn't think she was planning to buy one for me – the salesgirl showed her a white Satin one – Eleanor asked if I liked it + when I said "yes" didn't she decide to buy it! Isn't that awful? It was so expensive ($12.95 for the whole set). Cele + I told her not to think of buying such a thing but she wouldn't listen to us at all – no amount of persuasion on our part would stop her. So that's my Christmas present from her + Vin. I can't imagine why Eleanor wants to spend money like that – but she says as long as she's working she can't see any point in saving it – her motto is "spend it while you have it." It certainly is a beautiful set - + if I know you, Walter dear, you'll be dying to see it on me (ha ha). While I was downtown I went into Clark's + told them I had decided to take the cedar chest. They are sending it out sometime this week. It's beautiful, dearest, wait 'till you see it.

11:30 pm. I'm upstairs now, darling, sitting on the bed – I just feel like writing a little more. Mary + I went to the Warner to see "Old Acquaintance" with Betty Davis + Miriam Hopkins – I liked it a lot. After the show we stopped in the "Star" (as usual) + had a snack. Mary told me to send her regards to you + also her deepest sympathy over Lil's death.

Dearest, as I'm writing this, you are probably on post walking out under the stars. I hope you are not too cold (it is cold tonight) or too lonely – I can't help but feel lonely too, dear, when I think of you now. I wish I could be with you – be right with you, hand in hand, darling. I miss you so much, Walter. I know you do, too. I was just thinking today – on Dec. 6th we'll be going together three years – I must remember to send you an anniversary card (ha ha). Really, dearest, they were the three happiest years of my life – knowing you – having all the happy + sad times together – I never knew I would ever care for anyone as much as I care for you now – it always seemed impossible to me that two people could love each other as much as you + I. Thank God we do, heh, dearest? Just think, Walter dear of all the wonderful years we'll have together in the very near future – that is, starting in the very near future.

Well, dearest, I just wanted to tell you a little how I feel before going to bed. You're such a wonderful sweetheart. I remember you in my prayers every night – I always like to say a special one for you (the "Memorare") – prayer to the Blessed Mother. Here are some kisses, dearest. X X X X X X X X X X X

If you don't have time to write between now + Christmas, send them a card, dearest. I know it's hard for you to write to so many people. As long as you write to your father (once a week if you can) + the rest of your family, that's all who matter, and of course your little bunny too (me) ha ha.

Well, sweetheart, this is quite a long letter isn't it? I miss you so much today (+ everyday). The weather is so nice. I'd love to be with you out for a nice, long walk or something. Keep well, dearest Walter + as happy as you can.

Love Always,
big ones → X X X X X X Rita X X X X X X

Saturday 1: P.M.

P.S. I am on Supernumeris [Supernumeraries] over the weekend. That's a extra man for interior guard just in case a man has to be replaced on guard, so I should get plenty of rest just waiting around. <u>Oh</u> <u>Boy</u>.

Hello Bunny,

Just finished reading your nice Friday's letter, Bunny Dear.

Rita you are such a nice girl. Gee I am so <u>happy</u> in having you for my girl and Sweet heart and future <u>wife</u>.

Yes Dear, we will have a wonderful life together, <u>God</u> is guiding us each Day of our lifes, he means that we are to be lifes partners. I pray for <u>Lil</u> each nite, that God will reward her for all her goodness on this earth and I am quite sure he will.

Bunny, you have already helped me so much, and I know that you would do so much for me, always doing without, just to please me.

So nice to hear that you are resting up so much dear, thats good. You must have been quite tired, after doing so much for <u>Lil</u> and me and my family.

I am getting plenty of rest and I will go to the theater for some deversion, if I feel like it over the weekend. <u>Bunny dear,</u>

I droped the Nurses at the Hospital, a appreciation card, they were so nice in treating Lil and us kind. Especially, Mrs. Ford + Miss Strong, Miss Mulligan.

I also droped Jack a letter too, once again reminding him of our obligations to <u>Lil's</u> <u>Children</u> and never to lose Heart and Mind in them. I have faith in him. <u>Jack</u> and all of us that are to do our duty for God and Lil.

I also dropped my father a letter, saying everything is O.K. with me.

Love <u>Walter</u>

Sunday 11/28 – 1:30 p.m.

Here it is, dearest, a beautiful Sunday afternoon. I was so glad when you called Walter and to know that everything is well with you – your voice sounded good over the 'phone. I'm so glad, too, dearest, that you managed to get so much sleep last night + that you had time to go to Church this morning. I was thinking the other day about you getting to Church Sundays – I know sometimes you don't have time at all to go but, Walter, will you please from now on, if you have any time at all on Sunday morning, please try to go? Even if you can't stay for the whole service – as long as you make an attempt – that will be a whole lot. You'll feel much better if you do, sweetheart. You know yourself if you don't go for weeks at a time you almost forget there is a God – you just forget (unconsciously) that you have a soul too as well as a body. I don't mean just you, dearest when I say this – I mean everyone who gets into the habit of staying away from Church. That's the way I feel if I don't go to Communion at least once a month – this coming Friday is the first Friday of the month so I'll go to Communion then.

As I told you on the phone I called up Helen Friday night + everything was going along fairly well with her, the children + Jack. It was 8 o'clock when I called + Helen said Jack hadn't come home yet – she said he probably stopped someplace first. I didn't say anything to Helen but I'm a little afraid he'll go on now thinking she'll stay there with the three children indefinitely – I don't know where he could go if he moved anyway – rents are so sparse. Well, we'll all have to give him a fair trial, won't we, Walter – I guess no one can pass any opinion about him until they see in time just how he carries on. I hope Helen realizes that her place is with your father after something is worked out in regard to the children. I can't understand why Jack's mother couldn't take at least one of them. It seems almost inhuman to me – I don't think his mother + father ever said they wouldn't – it's just Jack's idea in not wanting them to. Naturally, he feels as tho he couldn't get along with his mother + father if he

went with them – it's easy to see why – they would have to keep consistent
watch on him + he wouldn't like living like that – having to give account of
everything he does + everyplace he goes. I'm sure he will live up to his promise
that he made to you + the rest of the family – that is – that he'll never let them
go in a home – so don't even think about that, dearest, but what your family
will have to be careful of is – that he might let all the responsibility fall on
Helen's shoulders – that is – taking care of them during the day, etc.

Well, dearest, I hope you don't mind my saying all this to you – it's just the
way I feel about it – don't worry, Walter, I'll never say anything like this to any
of your family – these opinions are just between you + I.

I think it would be a good idea if you wrote to Helen + tell her just how
you feel about things – she's probably in a muddle herself – if she has to make
all decisions. What kind of a letter did you write to Jack, dearest?

Walter, you know my cousin, Elwood Lavery, who went up to Devens
with you? He's now in England somewhere – has been since October. He was
at an embarkation point for quite a few weeks in New York + his wife + baby
came east while he was there + saw him a few times before he sailed – he
couldn't come home while he was in New York but his wife could go to see
him. His aunts (Judge Lavery's sisters) were here for a visit last night + told
Cele. As far as we know he hasn't even a rating. Isn't that awful? It seems a
shame that he's had such bad luck so far with all of his education – I guess it
doesn't help anything as far as the Army is concerned.

Dearest, I'm going to write Dot Smith a short letter this afternoon. I'll tell
her about the happenings of the past weeks with you + tell her to tell Ernie
you'll write when you get a chance – O.K.?

Monday 11/29/43

Dear Sweetheart,

I was so glad to receive your Saturday's letter when I came home from
work tonight. I like to get a letter on Monday. It takes the gloom away from
"blue Monday."

Yes, dearest, being on Supernumeries [Supernumeraries] over the week-
end gave you a chance to get a little rest. I hope if you have a little time to
yourself that you'll go to the show, read or something for diversion.

Dear, the cedar chest came late this afternoon. They didn't waste any time
in sending it out, did they? It's all covered with a heavy paper – tonight we're
going to look it all over to make sure it's in perfect condition. It's a beauty,
dearest, I can hardly wait until you see it. We're going to keep it upstairs in my
bedroom – move the sewing machine downstairs. There is really no room for it
downstairs + even if there were, it might get scratched.

Darling, you told me to save your Christmas present until you come home
but I hate to do that because if I do – Christmas day will go by + you won't
have anything. I'd like to send the presents to you from all of us with Bill when
he comes home before Christmas. Do you see, Walter dear? It's bad enough

for you to be away on Christmas Day but if you have a few little gifts you might not feel quite so bad. I'll do whatever you say tho, Walter.

Let me know, please, dear.

Dearest, I say a prayer every night for your sister too – there is no doubt Lil will be rewarded for the good, clean life she led + for all her hard work + suffering so don't ever doubt that, Walter dear.

Darling, I wasn't tired last week when you were home for what I did for Lilly + you (that wasn't much)... [water damage] from an upset routine. You know me if I don't get rest. I'm getting rested up now – Cele is still worried about the way I look – she keeps telling me I look tired out + too thin but it's just her imagination I think. I would like to gain some weight tho, if I could but on the other hand – as long as I feel alright I guess it doesn't matter much. You'd probably like me to be a little roley poley when we get married tho, heh, dearest? (ha ha).

Well, sweetheart, take care of yourself now – keep well I love you so much, dear. You know I ... I like to tell you over...

Love Always,
X X X Rita X X X

Monday 2:00 P.M.

Hello Bunny,

Hope that you had a very enjoyable weekend, and that everything went along <u>O.K.</u>

Darling Rita, I love you so much, I am so happy in knowing I have you as my future wife. Bunny I am thankful to <u>God</u> in having you dear as my life partner, you are the finest person one could know or find. I <u>thank</u> <u>God</u> again for finding you for my future wife. We were both born and ment for each other, I am so happy to know that in my heart.

Yesterday afternoon I had some extra time, so I took a walk up to the R.P.C. and looked up <u>Bud</u> Monahan, he just got through working at 1:00 o'clock noon, so I was fortunent in finding him in his barracks. He is feeling pretty good, We later took a ride on the bus to the Service Club, We had Pie ala Mode and Coffee, also had a nice chat. about himself and his wife and family also you and your family. He thinks you <u>Rita</u>, are one <u>fine</u> <u>girl</u>, he thinks the world of your family, Charlie, Cele, Jeanie, and the others.

I could not go out of the fort because of my work – Super Numeri? But Bud had a pass, so he ? went to Ayer to the U.S.O. He is a nice fellow.

P.S. I also told him how we plan to get married this coming June. <u>Oh</u> Boy, he said, that's swell, he said he likes nothing better than going to a nice wedding. He said he hopes he will be around in the spring.

Darling I love you so much. I think of you al the time.

Be a good girl like you always have been. I pray for <u>Lil</u>, and her Beautiful Children each nite. God will take care of Lil and the children with our <u>help</u>.

Love <u>Walter</u>

P.S. I am working Second relief. 4-8 – in the afternoon. 4-6 in the morning.
Not Bad. Heh dear. Next week I will be in school. I <u>hope</u>

Tuesday 11/30/43

Dearest,

How's my nice sweetheart today? I hope everything is fine + dandy with
you.

I called up your sister Helen last night about 9 o'clock. The children were
in bed. Helen said everything is going along pretty well. She said everyone in
your family went to Church Sunday + the flowers were still on the altar +
looked nice + fresh. Sunday night all of your family went to your brother's
house for supper – Helen + the children – I don't know whether Jack went or
not – I think so, tho. Helen said everything was nice. She said she'd like to get
out some evening for a change – she's been confined to the house for such a
long time now – so she said maybe she could at the end of this week – go to a
movie or come to my house for the evening. She said she's going to do a little
Christmas shopping for Joan, Carol + Johnny if she can too – after all
Christmas should be as pleasant as possible at least for the children.

Darling, I have a good idea – if it's alright with you + I know it will be, I
could take $5.00 of the money ($15.00) you told me to save for you + give it to
Helen to buy some things for Joan, Carol + Johnny – some little toys for Carol
+ Johnny + whatever Helen thinks Joan would like – or maybe she could buy
them things to wear if she wanted. They would be from you, dearest, for
Christmas. I could buy the things but I think Helen would know more about
the size they wear + what they'd like – O.K.? Let me know what you think,
dearest. Helen wants me to go up there next Sunday for a visit but said she'd
let me know later in the week.

I got quite a surprise in the office today – in fact everyone did. Ann
Preston + Virginia (the little girl you met last year at the party) were both fired.
The excuse the office manager gave them was that there just wasn't enough
work for them, everything is getting rather slow now with all the cancellations
+ cutbacks of orders. It wasn't fair at all that they should be laid off because
they were both there much longer than Ruth + Eleanor Dalton. It's a shame
right before Christmas too – I know they won't have any trouble getting a job
once they get their release but it's just the mean way they have of doing things.
I think one of the reasons Ann was told to leave was because she spent a lot of
time talking in the office I'm in – talking with me + Irene Noonan. She was
told about it twice but didn't pay any attention – kept coming in + Mr. Trefry
even told her to stay outside + not to bother me. Ann never bothered me but
that's the way Mr. Trefry felt about it. Well, she'll probably get a much better
job anyway – maybe they really did her a favor.

Dearest, I'm so glad you found time to get together with Bud. Cele,
Charlie, Jeanie + myself think a lot of him too. He's a good fellow + deserves
the best. I hope if he is moved from Ft. Devens that he'll get a good break +

get into something he really likes.

So you told Bud we are going to be married in June, Walt. I thought it was going to be in the Spring – April or May. Well, dearest, that's something we can decide when you come home in January – it's practically impossible to plan anything I guess until the last minute.

Cele, Charlie + I looked over the cedar chest last night + it's in perfect condition as far as we can see. We're going to move it upstairs tonight. It sure is beautiful. I love it. I told your sister, Helen, about it last night + she thinks they're very useful + is glad you gave it to me.

Take care of yourself, dear.

Love Always,
X X X X X X Rita X X X X X X

Tuesday Noon

Dearest Rita,

I just got though eating diner, we had steak + all the fixins also apple pie + coffee.

That letter that I send to Jack was about what we had already talked about, but I just felt liked writing to him to ask him again to never let the Children down, for the kids + Lil's and his own sake, if he wants to find happiness in the World. I told him never to lose heart and mind ever for his Beautiful Children. I also send him a nice card, a cheerful, sympathy card, I also send my sister Helene one she deserves all the happiness that <u>God</u> can bestowne upon a person.

I went to see that movie that you saw. <u>Old</u> <u>Acquaintance</u>, it was a very good picture of that type, very heavy dram. Heh dear, Both good actresses.

Mary Buccino is a nice girl, you alway's choose nice friends Dear.

So happy that you selected that very nice cedar chest. Thats good Bunny dear, I want you to have the nicest things. You deserve the very best in every thing dear. So glad that it arrived at your home already. quick service I should say so.

Yes dear I will try to get to Church as much as possible, it is so good for a person, and I like to attend Church

Elwood Lavery is moving fast these day's. I did not know he was in England He should have a rating by now. to bad he has'ent. thats the army. He could use the extra money, for his wife + child.

So happy to know that the three (3) years we have been going together have been happy years for you It has made me very happy to have a girl like you and to plan for our future life together. Oh Bunny, I am so glad that period was the happiest years of your life, same goes for me. I got paid today. I was not redlined for not taking my physical. My Corporal fixed it up so I would get paid. Cpl. Bryant. enclosed is $20.00 for our fund. <u>dear</u>

Love your <u>Fiance</u>
<u>Walter</u>

P.S. Yes dear sending my gift with Bud is a good idea he know's where I stay, because I had him up visiting my barracks.

Wednesday 12/1/43 7:00 p.m.

Dear Sweetheart,

I'm writing this rather hurriedly so it can go out in the 7:15 mail. We went up to Nadeau's to eat + just got back.

I'm glad you got paid for December, dear and the $20.00 you sent will be added to our fund (which is a nice sum now). I received my Christmas Club check in the mail today ($100.00) + am not going to use any of it for presents — I'm going to put it in the bank until we get married.

We took up a collection in the office for Ann Preston + Virginia who are both leaving Saturday. We collected $12.50 for each of them so another girl + I were given time off today to pick out a gift for them. We bought a nice bracelet for each of them — also earrings to match. Tomorrow we're all going out to lunch + present them with the gifts. Gosh, I'll sure miss Ann.

Yes Mary Buccino is a nice girl + Mrs. Smith tells me I should feel honored that she goes out with me — she has no real close friends except the Smiths but told Mrs. Smith she'd rather go out with me than any other girl she knows. I always have a nice evening when I go with her.

Darling, you always give me so many compliments — thank you, Walter dear, it's so nice of you. All the nice things you say to me apply to you, too, dear. You mean everything to me. I want the best for you always. I love you so much.

Love Always,
X X X X X X "Bunny" X X X X X X

P.S. Don't worry about anything at home, dearest, everything is going along smoothly now + everything will work out in time for the best.

Wednesday 1: P.M.

Dear Rita,

Just had chicken all the work's that go with it, also pumpkin pie. Boy they are feeding us boy's the best lately. It seems the good food comes in spells.

Yes dear, giving my sister Helene either five or ten dollars to buy for the children is a very good idea, I will say that is a good suggestion, I was just wondering what to buy them, but you and Helene can figure that out Heh Bunny.

So Sorry to hear about Ann Preston and Virginia, Boy that was very sudden and quite a surprised, that's to bad, Ann is such a fine girl, also Virginia.

I was going to ask you about the flowers at the church, I ment to ask you about them, and about my family attending church. So happy to hear that the flowers held up beautiful also that all my family attended church, to pray for my sister Lil that <u>God</u> will be good to her.

Received a letter from Ellen, she is a good girl, So happy to hear that they all got together at her house for supper She asked me if I got a seat on the train. After a while, I got one in New Haven, that's not bad considering all the Holiday traffic. Heh dear. So glad to hear that Lil's children are well and getting along O.K. also Jack, Helene, I sent Helene a nice cheerful card, also Jack.

I got my watch out of Hock, I paid the five I owed on it plus a few cents interest, with what money I brought up with me, which was $20.00 and my pay. I will have $25.00 left after paying all my debts. Enclosed is another five $5.00

Love
Your <u>Fiance</u>
<u>Walter</u>

Thursday 6:00 pm. 12/2

Dearest,

I'm glad to hear that the food has been so good lately – you must have a new chef in your kitchen, darling (ha ha). I wish the Army would send some of that good food along to Bridgeport – it sure is hard to get anything very good here. I guess none of us mind it so much tho, as long as you boys are getting it.

Gosh, darling, you must really be getting very enthusiastic about saving now for our wedding – sending the extra $5.00 plus the $20 I received yesterday. You now have $155.<u>00</u> (after I take out the $5.<u>00</u> for the children for presents). That's very good dearest, before you know it you'll have $200.<u>00</u>. You'll surely have plenty of money by the time we get married to take care of your expenses – more than enough, I think. I'll have enough too, dearest, so don't worry.

All the girls in the office took Ann + Virginia out to lunch today (the Palms in Black Rock) + we gave them the gifts – they liked them a lot. I'll sure miss Ann in the office – she's always been my pal. It's a shame they're letting her go – she's really a good worker...

I received an acknowledgment card from your family today – signed with Jack's name, your father + Helen's name (for the flowers). Helen must have had quite a job acknowledging all of the flowers – there were so many.

I'm glad you got your watch out of hock – now you can wear that when you're working + the one I gave you when you get dressed up (if you ever do these days, dear).

Last night Cele + Charlie brought the cedar chest into my room. What a job getting it up the stairs! It's rather heavy + the stairway is narrow + then they had a job fitting it thru the bedroom door. They finally managed to get it in... I put my blankets + sheets... in it. After Christmas I'm going to get some more things.

Dearest, it would be so nice if you could come home for Christmas – even if you couldn't get here until Christmas night. I know you'd like to if it's possible at all but of course that depends on the Army.

I miss you so much, dearest. If only this mess was all over + we could be together. Wouldn't it be wonderful? We'll just have to go on trying to make the best of everything I guess. That's hard sometimes, isn't it, dearest?

Please take care of yourself, Walter dear – I think of you all the time. Don't worry about anything, darling. I love you, dearest.

Lots of love and kisses

X X X X X X Rita X X X X X X

P.S. Here are a dozen big kisses for you. I wish I could give them to you in person, dear.

Thursday 12:30 <u>Noon</u>

Dearest Bunny,

I just received a very nice assortment of handy little articles from my Church, gum, cigarette, writing paper, fruit cake, candy, razor blades, shaving paste, soap, tooth paste, a very nice assortment, Heh Rita. Boy the boy's way out in the Pacific Islands and Europe sure will appreciate these gifts. We fellows here in the U.S.A. appreciate them plenty also. The Church is sending out about <u>60</u>, all around the World that's nice of the folks.

Each nite for the past week, I and two other fellows take the colors, (flag) down, we fire a 3 in. cannon, and than let the flag down as either a bugle or band plays, either a retreat number or the Star spankle Banner. It is quite colorful. Later I finish out my time on post for a few hours. hours 4-8, two of those hrs are spend on the parade ground taking care of the flat and other details.

I am going up to the dentist to have a few fillings taken care of, this after Noon. at 1:30. they do a very good job of it, dear.

Next week I think I will be on school, It looks as tho I will not be able to get home until two week end after New Years, but that is hard to say right now, we will see as the Days go by. Heh <u>Bunny</u>.

Bunny I ran some very nice Manicuring sets at the P.X. I think tho, that I will wait until after Christmas to buy one, that's if you think you would like a set. what color do you use, I think you said natural. But Bunny I think I will let that Set go until a later date. What do you think, they have some very nice sets from five, $5.00 up to $8.00 eight, some for even $2.50 up to five.

the first chance I get I wan to get to Ayer to buy some very nice Christmas cards to send out the ones that they have at the P.X. are not very nice, that's the Christmas cards, the ones that they have are those painted ones. I don't like them as well as the Spiritual ones Bunny I hope you like that nice Birthday card I sent. I tried to get a smaller one, but I could not find the Ideal one for you <u>Bunny</u> in the smaller size.

Love, Your Fiance

<u>Walter</u>

(Bunny I love you so much)

Ann + Virginia sure will appreciate the gifts — Bracelets and earrings. that's so nice of you girls — Bunny
Bunny you will see too it that Lil's children have something nice at Christmas. Use $10.00 of my money. My folks will also buy them something also.
That Christmas Club of $100.00 sure will come in handy when we say I do Heh dear.

Tuesday 5:30 P.M.
Second Platoon

Dear Rita,

Received all of your nice letters + the Sympathy Card that Betty + Bill sent to you, So nice of them to think of me, they are such a swell couple.

We were in a hurry to catch the bus in that way I forgot the phone call to you

Sunday I was all set to call you as I usually do, than I had another hr of works, so I let it go for a hrs, in the mean time the boy's were asking me to go to Lowell with them, Some were going to the show and Bed and, that boy I stayed with, we had some good food + good beer and then came back to the fort at 8:30, I thought of calling you, while I was in Lowell, but than I remembered you saying in your letters how it doesent hardly pay to call for just (3) minutes, but I sure regretted it later, especially on your Birthday. Heh Rita dear. I am so Sorry I wont forget next time.

Yes dear, we will start to make some plans as to our coming marrige, Before we know it, we will be Husband + Wifie. Heh, dear Rita.

So glad to know that Ann liked your nice cedar chest. that's good, Bunny dear. I want you to have nice things.

I sent my Soldier friends that are overSea's my Christmas + New Years greetings, I bought some very nice cards, so now I am all set. I sent the long distance on, so they will get there in time. I bought a very nice one for my Father and Sister, also some other very nice ones for the others in my family, some very nice ones also for my friends.

I also have a very especially nice Christmas Card for you, Bunny dear.

Bunny forgive me for not calling you Sunday. You understand Rita. Dear, I am sure. Don't be mad at me, will you Bunny. Me being not out of the camp for 2 weeks or more, I must have been hurrying so fast to catch the bus, I did not remember the phone call until I was on my way to Lowell.

Love Walter

P.S. I think of you all the time, Bunny, I miss you so much

Wednesday 11:55 Post - M.P.Co.

Dear Rita,

I just finished reading your Tuesday's letter, I am so glad to get them so prompt each day.

Yes dearest, it's the small things that count. Bunny I think of you all the time.

Rita I was so shocked to hear about Catherine Mogner's condition at the hospital after her having her baby. I meant to mention this in my other letters, but somehow did not at the last moment. I know of cases like hers, where it was only temporary, it lasted on six months, a slow relief coming after a month or two and with treatment at a Sanitorium in Norwich Connecticut. She got home after six months and had a full recovery after one (1) year. That is all. Racbeiwicy, Vinny Praelsy's Brother's wife

Depending on the individual and circumstances, some recovery even after a few shock treatments, and ? right out of it, just as fast as they got into that state. It sure is pitiful. Rita dear, sometimes I wonder why <u>God</u> makes innocence people suffer so, for no reason at all. But I guess thats his will and way of doing things, I sure do and ? for all his family feel, It sure is hard for all ? It is a great sorrow for Freddie , but I am sure that with ? fine medical science today she will regain her health, and will be repaid for her suffering. Give my regards to Chick and his family, I am so sorry for her, because I know what it is to be stricken so.

Yes Ann is a very nice girl, that's nice that you two stay in contact with each other and that you are going to her house for supper Wed.

Yes my sister Helene will enjoy going to a movie with you (Gala?).

Love, Walter

Thursday 12:01

Dear Rita,

yes dear going out to a nice movie will be just the thing for my sister Helene and you to do, its good for you both to get out now and then.

I met Bud Monahan at the Ayer U.S O. last nite unexpected. We both had a few dances those nice polka dances. Boy Bud is quite a Jitter Bug. Later we had a good sandwich and coffee + pie up at the diner than rode back to camp at 10:30 P.M.

This afternoon and tomorrow I am working on post patrol, hrs three (3) P.M. to 11. P.M at nite not bad hrs.

We ride around in those cruiseing car the police up the speeder and the boy's, but we have very little to do, the boy's behave very good. We had Chicken for diner. not bad, heh dear. <u>Sent</u> a note Ernie and Dot a nice Christmas Card. getting the long distance ones off early enough because of the rush.

Bunny, I love you and Miss you so.

Love

<u>Walter</u>

P.S. Bud and I hope and pray for a quick recovery for Katherine Magns.

Friday 12/10/43

Dear Sweetheart,

I hope this letter will find everything going along smoothly for you.

Just think, dear, Christmas Eve is two weeks from tonight – it hardly seems possible. I guess it won't be a nice Christmas this year for most people – We'll be engaged one year Christmas Eve. Remember, dear, last year you + I went + picked out the ring, then you gave it to me with a card – you were so excited putting it on my finger. I didn't want you to kiss me because Cele was in the room. (ha ha). Next year at this time we'll be married (I hope) + I hope we'll be together then, don't you, dearest?

Last night I met Helene downtown about 7:45 + we went to the Globe + saw Micky Rooney + Judy Garland in "Girl Crazy" + "The Vampire Returns" (a spooky picture). They were both good. After the show we stopped in the little sandwich place near there + had a snack.

I'm glad Helene finally managed to get a night out – it did her good – she should get out once a week from now on. I gave her the $10.<u>00</u> but she wants me to buy the children some toys – says she hasn't time to get downtown as Mrs. Ryan is working in Leavitt's now for the holidays + Helene has no one to stay with the children. She's going to call me up + give me a lot of suggestions as to what to get. I hope I can get whatever she suggests – since the war started they aren't making all kinds of toys like they used to – also I hope I have time. Saturday afternoon is the only time I have to go downtown + if anyone can buy anything with the awful crowds downtown this year – they're good. Well, I'll try my best. Helene herself is going to buy them clothes they need right now. She's been holding on to some money that was given to the children at the time of the funeral – also some from a friend of the family + from Bullards – they took up a collection – so all in all, she can get what they need with it. It's nice that they did give money instead of flowers I think – it comes in handy now for Christmas.

6:30 P.M. Received your nice Thursday's letter tonight.

Glad you met Bud at the U.S.O. + had a few dances + a snack after.

I had a letter from Dot Smith today – Gosh, I envy her – she + Ernie are very happy. Everything certainly worked out beautifully for them. I'm glad. They are in a little furnished house by themselves now. Dot says she's met a lot of nice girls down there – she belongs to the Catholic Women's Club + goes to Red Cross a few times a week too. She told me to tell you she was awfully sorry to hear about your sister, Lil.

Ernie is taking some subjects (I don't know what ones) + Dot says he wants her to study with him – nights I guess. She says she wishes you + I were married + living down in Ala. near them. Wouldn't that be nice? Well, it's all impossible but nice to think about anyway.

Well, dearest, I guess this is all for now. Have a nice week-end (as nice as you can). I don't think I'll go to the show tomorrow night seeing I went Thursday with Helene – I'm flat broke anyway – with all the Christmas shopping I've had to do (just for the family).

Love Always,

X X X X X X Rita X X X X X X

P.S. I miss you awfully. It seems so long since I've seen you. Being separated for so long is discouraging I think. I feel it more + more all the time, dear.

Tomorrow is Ellen + Al's wedding anniversary (10 yrs.). Ellen asked Helene to go to their house – I guess they're having a party but of course Helene can't (no one to stay with the children). I guess those 10 yrs. were happy ones for them – even if things were hard for them at times.

Lots of love and kisses, dear.

Rita

Saturday 11:15 <u>Noon</u>

Dearest Rita,

I just eat early chow, Beef + carrots, cold slaw, potatoes, gravy, dressing, coffee, phim's, pastry, Pretty good chow, <u>heh</u> dear, no wonder that we boy's gain weight, ten and fifteen pounds.

Over the weeks end I am going to chase prisoners, from – 1 – 6 today and tomorrow from 5:30 A.M. to 1:00 P.M. in the afternoon Monday I have no duties, so that nite I am going to Ayer to buy my Christmas Cards and a few things that I can use.

Tonite I am going to see that movie, <u>Stage</u> <u>Door</u> Canteen. The boys said it was very good, the last time it played here I missed it than.

I am getting plenty of <u>sleep</u> <u>Dear</u>; I went to bed at nine 9 last nite, until 3 A.M. Than I got in bed at 6:30 A.M. and sleep until 11 A.M. Went on post for three 3 hrs. Post <u>Commissary</u> Not bad heh dear considering

The weather here has been very good, I would say beautiful on this time of the year.

Hope <u>Bunny</u> <u>dear</u> that you have a very good weekend, and that you find plenty of time for some good diversion, maybe a good movie, or a nice walk in the park with Mary, or Ann or my sister Helene.

Wish I could go to <u>Church</u> with you each Sunday, tomorrow I may not go to Church because I will be working, unless I take the prisoners to church like we do sometimes. Some fun <u>heh</u> dear, going to Church with our guns. <u>45 pistol</u> Happy Birthday, Boy how the time sure flies by, you are now a grown girl; <u>25</u> years old is that right, Bunny dear, and what a Swell girl, the best that they come.

Love,

Your <u>Fiance</u>

Walter J.

Hope you got my Birthday <u>Card</u>. <u>dear</u>.

Dear Rita. (first relief(I am on the <u>12</u> – <u>4</u> relief. Recived your very nice letter, was so happy to look back with you at the time just one (1) year ago that you and I got engaged, that sure was a very happy moment of our life, Heh dear, <u>yes</u> and in another year we should be one happy Married couple. <u>Oh</u> Boy that will be very nice. Remember I got a little excited putting the ring on your nice engagement finger. <u>Ha</u>. <u>Ha</u>. And we were both a little bashful before <u>Cele</u> to kiss each other. <u>Oh</u> Boy. You + Helene both get along well, toy's will be nice for the children. Send Betty + Bill Hughs a card from you and I. Heh dear. I just though about that. <u>O.K.</u> All the rest of people I took care of. Dearest. Bunny, I miss you so much. last nite I was thinking about you as I lay in bed. Nice though's dearest of the past and present. I wish I could keep your feet <u>warm</u>. (help to)

Ha. Ha. Ha. Love Walter

December 14th – Tuesday – 2:30 P.M.

Dearest,

I'm writing these few lines in the office because I won't have a chance tonight when I get home from work. Helene is coming to my house at 6:30 and we're going down to the Lincoln Hardware to look for some toys.

How are you these days, dear? I hope everything is well with you. I think of you often especially in the afternoon from 12 to 4 o'clock – I hope you don't find the weather too cold while out on duty. It must be awful when you're out from 12 to 4 midnight. (12 midnight to 4 in morning) 6 degrees above zero here this morning and it was probably much colder 'way up in the hills. Well, dearest, dress as warmly as possible so you won't catch cold.

There is quite a feud here in the office among the girls today. Some of the girls want to have a Christmas party in the office Friday noon (Christmas Eve) and some want to go out someplace to eat at noon. Eleanor Dalton and Ruth Landry asked me for my opinion and I said I'd rather go out because if we had it here in the office each of us would have to bring sandwiches and salads in and everyone can't eat meat on Friday. If we brought in tuna fish or cheese it takes a lot of points for those things. I could never bring any in because sometimes home we haven't enough points for the week.

I guess the way it will wind up will be half of us will go out Thursday noon and half of the girls will have a party here on Friday anyway. Isn't that awful? Oh well, you know how girls are heh, Walter? (ha ha). I don't see how anyone could feel like going to a party this year anyway – it's hard to have any enthusiasm, heh darling?

I can hardly wait to see you – I miss you so much, sweetheart.

Please take good care of yourself. By the way, how is your money holding out? I haven't any on hand to send you – it's all in the bank but dear, if you really need some in case you come home, Charlie could take some out for you (maybe he could). On second thought I don't know if he'll have time to get to the bank either because he's going to work in the post office for the Christmas rush – the hours he isn't on the bridge. Thomas still isn't working. He was supposed to go in and take a test Monday morning but the last minute wouldn't go. We don't know now when he will go. He hasn't worked in nine weeks. If you do need some money, dear, let me know and I'll send you some of mine, or/if worse comes to worse you could put your old watch in the pawn shop again (ha ha). In any event, dear, let me know.

Lots of love, hugs and kisses, dearest

Ritamarie

P.S. Did you ever use those shower shoes I sent you, Walt? I hope you can get some use from them.

X X X X X X X X X X X X (over)

You'll notice I left some words out – I typed this in an awful hurry. I have quite a lot of work to do, You understand, heh dear?

Wed. 6: P.M. <u>December 15. 1943</u>

Dear Rita,

Hope dear that you and Helene found some nice toy's last nite for Lil's children for Christmas, Rita you are a <u>good</u> <u>girl</u>.

I am feeling fine dear and I am getting along O.K, even tho the weather is quite <u>cold</u>. I dress very warm dear, so I am plenty warm. Bunny you are a good girl, worrying about me, if I am warm enough and etc <u>dearest</u>.

Yes dear it is very nice having a party at Christmas Eve at the office. Sancwiches, etc. but of course the <u>points</u> is another thing. They are so hard to get. I think the best thing also is to eat out. Have a good time dearest, and <u>don't fight Ha Ha.</u> Ha You know how <u>girls get along</u>.

Boy, I sure would like to be able to, slip in bed, to help to keep your little toes'ies warm. <u>Oh</u> Boy, that would just thrill <u>me</u>.

Darling, how I wish I could hold you close to me and tell you how sweet you are and kiss you on the cheek'ies and your <u>nice lippers</u>. <u>Oh</u> darling I am in such a Lovable Mood. <u>Boy, Oh Boy</u>.

Bunny, I have (6) Six dollars so that is enough to carry me along, either until I get home or get paid.

Chuck is so ambitious, he is alway's <u>on the ball</u>.

Hope that Thomas get's on the Ball, soon, he has had a quite long rest. <u>Ha Ha</u> he must be quite rested up by now and rareing to go.

Yes dear, I use those very usefull shower shoes, when I take my usual shower. because I dont want to catch that much dreaded <u>athlete foot</u> that is so easily caught.

Bunny, I would like to hug you and Squeeze you, <u>oh</u> so tight

Love.

<u>Walter</u>

Rita dear, I Love you so much, and miss you so much. Wish I could be close to you right now. But we will be soon. Heh dear.

Thursday 12/16 – 10:30 p.m.

Dearest Walter,

I'm writing this letter in bed before I go to sleep. I received your two nice letters that you wrote Tuesday. Darling, you've been writing a lot this week haven't you? You wrote Sunday night even tho you called me at noon + then two letters on Tuesday. I love to receive them, dearest, they make me very happy.

I had to laugh at the one you wrote Tuesday morning – it was so "mushy" (ha ha) but I liked it, dear – it sounded just the way you talk.

Yes, dearest, as you said – when we get married it will be very strange at first – sleeping together in the same bed but I don't think it will take long to adjust ourselves. At first I'm liable to run in the closet to get undressed or dressed (ha ha). I'll bet you'd laugh your head off if I did, heh, dear? Well, I don't know yet just how it will feel but don't be surprised at anything I do. (ha ha).

I'm enclosing this clipping about Dorothy's + Joe's wedding. It was in tonight's paper + the wedding is to be this coming Saturday. I didn't hear anything about it – Joe must be getting a furlough – I'm glad their plans will surely work out now. I can't take any time off to go to see the wedding but I know it will be very nice.

I wonder where the "Candlelite" is – where they're having their reception. I don't think it's in Bpt. It doesn't mention in the piece what Joe's rating is – that's unusual don't you think so? It looks like you + I are the last ones of the crowd to get married, heh darling? I don't think when the war is over that any of the crowd will be friendly with each other except maybe Ernie, Dot – you + I. Oh well, we'll have lots of other friends anyway. I feel kind of funny about not sending a wedding gift but I really can't afford it now with all the expense of Christmas. Ernie + Dot sent one when Dot's + Joe's plans were announced the first time. Mrs. Smith bought it + sent it from them. I hope they have lots of luck + happiness.

Tonight Cele + I picked out a tree + carried it home between us. We also went to the Lincoln Hardware + picked up the toys Helene + I bought the other night. You should have seen us trying to carry everything. We managed O.K. tho. I bought a few more toys for Johnny tonight I have about $2.00 now out of the $10.00 so will get about one more thing with that Saturday. I called Helene up tonight + told her what I bought etc. She said everything is going along O.K.

Dearest, I'm getting writer's cramp + my eyes are closing so I guess this will be all for now. How I wish you could come home this week-end but I suppose you won't know until the last minute. Good luck, dearest. I'll be thinking of you.

Love Always,
Rita.
X X X X X X X X X X X

P.S. The mail is (slow) this week on account of the rush. If you write tomorrow (Friday) I might not get it until Monday; that is, even if you say you are coming I might not know so if you do get a chance to come, dearest, it would be a good idea to call up Saturday – either in the morning at the office (3-4175) or home late Saturday afternoon. If I don't hear from you, dear, I'll know you can't make it. I hope you do, sweetheart – also hope your money is holding out.

Friday Nite. 12/17/43

Dear Rita,

It looks as if I will be home with you my Darling on Sat. Dec. 18. 43 I am not listed for any detail, so that makes me eligible for my pass. So that means that I will be working, Christmas and New Years day Well that's the way it goes. Heh dear.

Bunny, I will be so happy to be with you. Boy I will hug and tug you dearest. But I miss your Loving, and Sweet kisses.

But darling, we will make up for lost time, heh dearest.

I guess it is best to take the passes when ever I can get them, without trying to get them at a certain date.

Bunny, I Love you and miss you so much.

Rita I think of you each day and especially at nite. During the day I am kept quite busy, and do not have to much time to think of you and dream of my little <u>wifie</u>. Rita Marie Lavery.

Love From

Your Husband

<u>Walter</u> Ha. Ha.

Bunny, How I wish I could warm your little toes'es Oh Boy Your little <u>Hot Cross Bun</u> Walter. Ha. Ha.

Monday Nite 6:30 A.M.

Dear Rita.

I recived your Fridays' letter, also the nice gifts in that package that you sent. Cele's + Chick's nice stockings, your gum, and nice candy. Thanks dearest. I recived a about ten (<u>10</u>) cards today, Boy , I am getting plenty of them this year. Even one from Mr + Mrs Charles Krolides. <u>Ha. Ha.</u> What a surprise? I also recived your very pretty Christmas Card, dearest. It is a pretty one Bunny. I <u>love</u> you Rita dear so much. You are going to be my pretty Bride this coming Spring. Bunny you are going to make a very Beautiful Bride. Dressed all in White. Bunny. I had a very enjoyable weekend with you. Tonite I am going to be in bed by Nine (9) oclock, I will get plenty of rest. I chased prisoners today.

Love Walter.

I met Bud Monahan and three (3) other of the boy's (at the station and, on the train coming back. We had quite a chat as far as New London and then had a Snooze We found seats O.K. on the <u>TRAIN</u> We got into Ayer at (4) four A.M. and had a 1 ½ Hr. sleep before going to work.

Give Cele + Chick my thanks for everything. They are so good to me and you dearest.

Your Sweetheart +

Fiance. Walter.

Tuesday 12/21/43 – 4:30 p.m.

Dearest,

I have a few minutes right now to write you because "Tref" (Mr. Trefry) is in Springfield today and I'm pretty well caught up in my work.

I'm going to meet Helene downtown tonight at 7:30. She has to get some clothes for the children – ones they really need. I talked with her on the phone last night + she thought then she might not be able to go because Carol had a swollen glazed + ear ache but I called her this afternoon + she said she's going – Carol feels better today. It really isn't necessary for me to go with her but I guess Helene just wants someone with her. I really haven't anything to buy. I spent the $10.<u>00</u> you gave me + a few dollars besides on the children. I think they'll have enough toys.

All of us here in the office got a bonus today (40 hours pay) minus 20% withholding tax + social security. After all the deductions mine amounted to $24.<u>52</u>. I'm going to buy you a birthday present with some of it + the rest I owe. It'll come in handy, heh dear?

The office is going to close Friday (Christmas Eve) at noon. I'm glad – not that I have anything special to do but no one feels like working on Christmas Eve.

6:30 p.m. I didn't receive any mail from you today, Walt, but I know it must be on account of the rush – I will tomorrow (I hope).

I received lots of Christmas cards – one from Dot + Ernie sent "free" with Ernie's writing on the envelope + his Camp address in the corner. I guess that was Dot's idea – to send all the cards for free – you know how she is about money.

Dear, I hope you will have time to get to Church on Christmas Day but I suppose as it isn't considered a holiday you are supposed to go on with your duties as usual. It would be so nice if you could have time to go to either a Mass or your own Church, dearest. After all, that's the real true way to observe Christmas no matter where you are.

I feel so bad that we can't be together this year but I know there's nothing to do but try and make the best of it – that sure is hard tho. I hope this time next year you are home with me – with all of us here who think so much of you, dearest. I know you hope so too.

Love Always,

X X X X X X Rita X X X X X X

P.S. Don't worry if you can't get those scarfs for Norene + Ann – Gertrude is nervy asking you to get them – she can buy them in N.Y. – after all, you haven't much money to spare. Not one of us here have received any cards from her. I sent Ed some books + Gert some stockings but they probably won't even acknowledge them. Next year I'm not going to bother sending them anything.

Tuesday Nite. 6:30 December 21. 1943

Dear Rita.

Recived your nice letter that you wrote last nite, it got here quite quickly considering the Christmas rush, usually your letters take two (2) day's to get here lately.

This nice new pen that you gave me for Christmas sure is very nice. I just filled it and I managed O.K. dearest. Bunny thanks so much for it dear. The Boy's that bunk next to me, think it is the finest of pen's. They noticed it right away. See dearest how shiney it is. <u>Ha Ha Ha</u>.

I recived a very nice Christmas Card from my Sister Helene, it is very pretty. I also recived a nice card from your, Sweet girl friend <u>Ann</u>, Preston. <u>Thank</u> her for it <u>dear</u>.

Today I have been to classes, we were familryzing ourselves with the Machine gun, we are going on the range to try to qualify.

We are also going to go through the infratration course, thats the place were there are trenches and landmines going off, Nothing harmful.

They fire a machine gun over us, while we crawl on our hands and knee's, and all the while the explodtions are taking place. One can not get hurt, unless one stand's up while going through, it will be a free weeks until we go through it. We are also going to qualify with the Pistol also like we did with the rifle, the lieutant said.

Bunny, so happy to know that you had a very enjoyable weekend with me. (Ha. Hee. Bunny you said you get all up in a cloud, the next day after you see me. Thats good dearest. The girls in the office notice the expressions on your face, the picture of Love and Happiness, See dear. So nice of <u>Cele</u> and <u>Charlie</u> and <u>Jeanie</u> in letting us have privaty Sunday Nite, It held up putting up the Christmas tree, See dear, how we hold up things, Ha. Ha. Ha. They know two Lovers when they see them. Bunny we have a fine Love. I am so happy. I am going over the No I theatre to listen to Christmas <u>Carols</u> <u>Now</u>,

Love

Walter

So glad that you liked that <u>Mass</u> <u>Christmas</u> <u>Card</u> <u>dear</u>. Bunny, dear I think of you alway's. I Love you So much. Wish I had you in my arms now + Miss you

Thursday 12/23/43 4:30 p.m.

Dearest Walter,

Received your little card last night – the one with the picture of the airplane on it – written Monday night. It's a nice little card, Walt.

I'm glad you received the candy, gum + socks – also my card + that you like everything. Are you using your new pen yet, Walt? I hope so.

I thought I'd at least start this letter here in the office while I have a little time – Mr. Trefry went home about an hour ago sick. He'll probably be in tomorrow tho.

Last night I wrapped the children's gifts – the toys, games, etc. It's a hard job to wrap some of them they are so clumsy. I hope Jack comes after them tomorrow. I bought Helene a pair of stockings + a little set of nail polish + remover for Christmas – hope she likes them.

This noon all of the girls in the office went out to lunch (15 of us) to the Palms in Black Rock. We had a nice time – Ann Preston stopped in there + said "hello" + had a drink with us. She lives right near the Palms. Willie is home for 10 days, has to go back next Monday. Lucky, heh? Ann said she sent you a card. I sent one to Willie too. Willie gave Ann a cedar chest for Christmas also. It's one of those modernistic styles – rather light wood + stream-lined. It's lower than mine. I like mine better, the Mahogany is richer looking wood I think. Of course I wouldn't say that to Ann.

We only have to work until 12 noon tomorrow – that will be nice getting thru at that time.

I thought you might like to see this picture of Dot Blake + the description of her wedding. Isn't it a nice one of her, dear? She must have looked lovely – also Madge + Alice. I sent a card to Dot + Joe – one wishing them luck + happiness. I guess I really should send a gift too – maybe I will in a few weeks I don't know yet.

6:00 p.m. I didn't get any mail from you today – I hope the mail will catch up with me tomorrow. I guess they are giving Christmas cards preference this week. I received a lot more cards today one from Dot + Joe Pavlick too.

We're going to start trimming the tree tonight – at least putting on the lights + finish it tomorrow. It's too bad you won't see it, Walter dear. I don't know whether you'll receive this letter by Christmas or not but anyway, dearest, have the nicest Christmas possible. I'll be thinking of you all the time + we'll miss you so much.

Lots + lots of love + kisses,

X X X X X X Rita X X X X X X

P.S. **X** – this is a great big one for Christmas day.

Dorothy M. Blake, a Bride Today

MRS. JOSEPH PAVLICK

Dorothy Blake Wed to Joseph Pavlick

Remington Nurse Married in St. Charles Church This Morning.

The altar in St. Charles church was banked with white chrysanthemums this morning at 11 o'clock for the wedding of Miss Dorothy Mary Blake, daughter of Mr. and Mrs. John Blake, of 26 Hayes street, to Joseph Pavlick, son of Mr. and Mrs. John Pavlick, of Easton. Albert Tordoff offered a program of organ music and Margaret Dillon Morris sang.

The bride was escorted by her father. She wore a gown of white satin, made with a fitted bodice trimmed with inserts of Chantilly-type lace, long sleeves pointed at the shoulders with deep pointed cuffs of lace, and a long full train. Her fingertip veil of illusion was draped from a coronet trimmed with orange blossoms and she carried a prayer book with white orchids and bouvardia.

She was attended by her two

Thursday Nite 8:15 P.M.

Dear Rita,

I just got through shaving and taking a shower after being on K.P.

(working in the dining room) which was Started just two weeks ago. The Prisoners use to do it. I was on from 5:30 A.M. to 6:30 P.M. So I guess I will sleep very good tonite. Tomorrow I am going to school and at Christmas Eve I have off, so I may go to Church if there is any, which I think there will be, Services held.

I was Bud last Nite at the U.S O dance. We had a few dances and got back to camp at 10:30 P.M. Had a good time.

Christmas I am slated to work half a day. Chasing prisoners. In the afternoon. Sunday I am to chase a half a day also, in the morning.

Love Walter

It looks like I am going to have another week of school and not be on guard duty. Have a Merry Christmas Dear. I received all of your letters, even Wednesday.

Friday, Christmas Eve. 5:30 p.m.

Dearest,

I was so glad today when I received your Tuesday's + Wednesday's letter. Now that the mail rush is over in the post office you + I will probably get our letters each day, heh darling? I hope so.

In your Tuesday's letter you said you're going to have a course in school where you would have training as to landmines, trenches etc – also that you were going to have to qualify with the pistol like you did with the rifle. Dear, it looks as tho all you boys are being trained for combat units - - that is, if you all qualify going thru all that training – your group (called 1-A-L) might be put in the regular 1-A classification + then transferred to another division. I'd hate to see that, Walter dear, if it did happen. You + I both know you are better off fighting the "War of Devens" (ha ha). As it is now I hope by this time next year you'll be home even if this mess isn't over. What do you think, Walter? I guess I shouldn't write these things, heh dear? Let's hope for the best anyway, sweetheart.

In your Wednesday's letter you said you had seen "The Messiah". I'm glad you did, dearest. That's a musical oratorio I've always wanted to see. It must have been swell. I'm familiar with some of the parts of it. I like the "Hallelujah" especially. I wish I could have been with you, dearest I would have enjoyed it so much (you too).

Well, today is Christmas Eve, darling + I find myself feeling so lonesome for you. I can't help but think of the other years we had together at Christmas. Remember the first Christmas you gave me the dresser set but I didn't know you very well then + I didn't see you Christmas day. The next year (after my mother died) you gave me that nice phonograph + you didn't come down here until late in the afternoon – then last year – the best of all – the beautiful ring + the engagement. I wouldn't want it to be this time last year now, tho, dearest, because then I'd have to go thru a year with you away (like the past year). The best thing to do I think is to look ahead towards the future. Every day that goes by brings us that much nearer to being together (when you come home).

I miss you so much right now, dear – it doesn't seem right that you or all the other boys should be separated from their families + those you love now or any other time. It's all so futile.

The tree is all trimmed (lights + all) + it's a shame you can't be here to enjoy it. I'd enjoy it a lot more if you were here, dearest. Tonight we'll exchange presents here in the family. When you come home next time, dearest, I'll show you my presents.

I called up your sister Helene last night + she was waiting for Jack to come home. He was supposed to come home early because Helene wanted to go to Stratford Center to get a few more things but wasn't home when I called at 7:30. Helene was mad. I wrapped all the toys for the children but he hasn't come for them yet. I hope he does tonight.

Mr. Trefry gave me a box of Schraft's candy for Christmas. I haven't opened it yet – it's wrapped so fancy I hate to. He sent me a card too. I sent him one too.

I love you, dearest, + will be thinking of you over the holiday. Keep your spirits up as much as you can. I know you must be awfully lonesome too – but we'll make up for all this some day.

Lots of love, hugs + kisses, dearest
X X X X X X "Bunny" X X X X X X

P.S. If you have any money left of what your father gave you, get whatever you need for yourself – if you don't need anything, treat yourself anyway, dearest – you won't be any richer by not spending it on something worthwhile. You could stand a good pair of shoes (dress ones with the buckles at the side) – some nice shirts or dress gloves. Go ahead, dear, splurge a little for a change (ha ha).

Saturday Christmas Day 3:30 pm

Hello Sweetheart,

Happy Holiday Season to you, Walter dearest. I hope you experienced <u>real joy</u> on this Christmas Day – being close to God and being happy in knowing everyone here is thinking of you – wishing you were here + also remembering all the past Christmases we spent together. Even tho we aren't together today we are very close in spirit anyway, dearest. Maybe with God's help you'll be home next Christmas = you + all the rest of the boys.

We have all spent a quiet Christmas home here so far. Last night we exchanged presents among ourselves, Cele, Charlie, Jeanie + I + then about 11 o'clock Eleanor + Vin stopped in + we exchanged presents with them. We all sat + talked a while + then Eleanor + Vin left. They went out with Fran Collins, Vin's friend who's home for the holiday. Remember last year when Eleanor + Vin came over, darling, + you were here + everyone was looking at my ring? We went to bed about 12:30 or 1 o'clock. Last night Eleanor + Vin stayed out all night – visiting everybody + went to 6 o'clock Mass this morning.

Jack didn't come to pick up the children's toys. I called up Helene about 9:30 + she said he wasn't home + didn't expect him to be all night. He must have gone out celebrating. Helene asked Mr. Bridges (he was helping her trim the tree) to come down after them but he didn't have enough gas. Everything is still here. They were all supposed to go to Trumbull for dinner today – maybe they'll stop on their way home tonight. If they do I don't think I'll be here – we might go out to Fairfield visiting Loretta + John Neary. Maybe I can leave a note on the door to go in + pick them up – leave it open. It certainly is a shame they couldn't have them this morning under the tree when they got up. Well, what can anyone expect from Jack Bridges – Nothing. Helene said some of the people in Armstrong's sent them toys – they had quite a few things I guess. I'm going to ask Helene here some night next week. Tuesday or Wednesday – also Mrs. Smith + Mary Buccino some night.

I got some nice gifts for Christmas, dearest – a beautiful chenille aquamarine color robe from Cele + Charlie. It's too pretty to wear – maybe I'll save it till later. Eleanor + Vin gave me the beautiful white bridal set that I told you about before. I also got some slippers (wine color) from Cele + a nice scarf (a head scarf) from Jeanie – also some writing paper from her. I got some stockings + a nice slip from Irene + Florence, my cousins. I did very well for myself, heh, Walt? (ha ha). Cele + Charlie got some nice gifts too + Jeanie got so many things – it would take me ages to tell you about them. One thing is a pair of ice skates (white shoes + all). She's been wanting those for a long time.

This morning we went to 10 o'clock Mass. It was so nice – the choir sang the carols + the church was all decorated with poinsettas + holly. The crib was on the altar. I don't know whether you've ever seen the crib with all the images in it – the Blessed Mother, the Infant, St. Joseph + the animals. It's really a stable. You'd like to see all the decorations, dear.

I'll send along your birthday present this week, dearest, you'll probably get it about Thursday or Friday. I hope you like it. I want you to use it too, don't save it, Walter.

I was looking over all my cards today that I received. I got 40 of them – that's quite a lot, heh, darling? I'll bet you have a lot of them too. You + I know a lot of people + you have many friends too, heh, sweetheart?

Well, dearest, I have to eat now. I love you so much + am thinking of you all the time.

Love Always,
Rita "Bunny"
(great, big ones) → X X X X X X X X X X X X X

Christmas Nite December 25. 1943
Ayer U.S.O.

Dearest Rita,

Lots of Love to my Sweetheart on this Christmas Day. Hope that you and your family are managing to have a happy Christmas. Last Nite Christmas Eve I was at the No. I Theatre I should of gone to the Midnite Mass, but I did not go, somehow I could not find any of the boy's to go. Most of them had gone to Boston or else where or out getting drunk. I am here at the Ayer U.S.O. now, later they may have a Formal dance, with the entertainment from Worcester Mass. I may attend some church somewhere tonite yet, if I find one that is having Service tonite. Bunny, I miss you so much, especially now at Christmas day. Bunny, you are the Sweetest girl in the world. It sure does feel funny not being home with you at Christmas dear. (Its my first Christmas away from home) Rita dear. I wish I could be with you now, just like old times. Heh dear. I bet the Christmas tree at your home is a pretty sight. Today I chased the prisoners to chow at diner and at supper, as we did not do any work other than that today. very little work was done here at the Fort, but we had to be here, just the same.

Tomorrow – I have to get up at 5:30 A.M. and chase the prisoners to Breakfast and to diner, than I will probably get the afternoon off. Monday, I am not listed for anything, I am suppose to go to school for another week.

Bunny be a good girl, like you always are. Give my regards to Cele + Chuck, Jeanie + Thomas

Love, <u>Walter</u>

P.S. The food here at our Mess sure was good, turkey, and all the fixins, ice cream cider, cake.

Monday 12/27/43

Hello Sweetheart,

Enclosed is a little joke that I thought you'd get a kick out of. One of the girls in the office gave me this copy. (Margaret Anton – a very quiet type person). It's funny I think – don't you? (ha ha).

I called up your sister, Helene, this noon to ask her to come down and spend the evening tomorrow night but she said she felt as tho she had the grippe – she ached all over + was coughing. Isn't that too bad? It's hard for her to take care of herself with the three children to take care of – she really should stay in bed for a few days. She called Mrs. Bridges this morning + asked her to take Joan + Carol for a while till she feels better but that leaves the baby who has to be watched. She's taking some pills the doctor gave her once before for a cold so I hope she'll be alright in a few days. It's a shame that she's sick. She has so many cares + worries as it is – without getting sick herself. I'll call in a day or so again + see how she feels. There's a lot of grippe + flu around now.

I didn't go out at all last night. Cele, Charlie, Jeanie + I stayed in. It was pouring rain anyway. We listened to the radio + enjoyed the tree for a while. I got caught up on quite a few little things – wrote a long letter to Dot, washed my hair, took a bath (ha ha) + pressed some clothes.

My father has been dead seven years today, the 27th. It seems much longer than that. He died in 1936 when I was going to Normal School. Time flies, tho, doesn't it dearest? Especially when you think of all that can happen in one year.

I received your Thursday's letter + your Christmas Day letter today, dearest. It's too bad you had to go on K.P. Why don't the prisoners go on doing it as they used to? From 5:30 A.M. to 6:30 p.m. is an awfully long day. When you have a hard day like that, dearest, go to bed right after so you won't be so exhausted.

Yes, dearest, it's too bad you couldn't go to Midnight Mass Christmas Eve or even go to your own Church Christmas Day but that's the way it is sometimes, dearest, as you said, most fellows like to go out and drink at that time + don't think of Church at all.

Well, dearest, I have to go and eat supper now. I hope you are well and everything is going along smoothly. Please take care of yourself, dearest. Don't get the grippe or flu – stay good + healthy as you always are. I love you.

Lots of Love, Darling
X X X X X X Rita X X X X X X

Tuesday Nite 6:30 December-28-43

Dear Rita,

Hello Bunny, Dearest. So glad to recived all of your very nice letters, Bunny, you are the most sincere girl and the finest girl that a Boy would want for his life partner, Bunny, you have such fine qualities and such a keen mind, your Mentality is above the average person especially the women.

Thanks Rita dear for the very nice Wallat, it is such a good one dear, you have such good tastes. Bunny you treat me so good.

Bunny, you are way ahead of me dear in giving me presents. I own [owe] you so much. I hope that I may get you something nice for you too, <u>soon</u>, Marie. <u>Rita</u> <u>you</u> <u>are</u> <u>exception</u> <u>Sweet</u>. (<u>Sweeter</u> <u>than</u> <u>Sugar</u>)

So glad that Lil's children finally recived all the nice gifts that you and Helene purchased for them. Lil's children are so nice. I sent Joan some of those nice Handkies with the insignas on them. I think that she might like to wear them with her Bloues to school.

That Poem was quite the thing, Leave it up to those quite girls to get literture like that. Ha. Ha.

So happy to know that you Cele + Chuck + Jeanie had a very quite Christmas Eve together, thats the way it should be. Because that's the way I alway's liked to spend Christmas Eve, which I and you think is right, Heh dear.

Bunny, I miss you, just as much as you miss me. Try to go out to the Movie with the girls and my sister now and than. Bunny I want you to have some diverison too, It is not right to stay in all the time. I get most of mine at the good old U.S.O. and at the theatre or a train ride to Boston.

Love. Your Fiance <u>Walter</u>

Bunny, I sure will be a fine life when you and I are going to live a normal life. Heh dear. <u>Keep</u> <u>Smiling</u> <u>Rita</u> <u>Dear.</u>

Thursday 12/30/43 5:45 p.m.

Dearest,

I only have to work until 5 on Thursdays + when I came home a little while ago your Tuesday's + Wednesday's letters were here. I was so glad to receive them, dear. I'm glad you received the wallet I sent – you got it awfully fast – I didn't send it until Monday morning thinking it would take three days or so to get to you. Do you really like it, dearest? It's hard to get ones with zippers in them – in fact it's impossible here in Bpt. but the part about yours I like is the ising-glass in the inside for pictures – you can really fit 8 pictures in the different sections – that is, if you cut them down to size. I'd like you to go right ahead + use it now, dearest – the other one I gave you three years ago is awfully shabby by now. I noticed it when you were home.

Your sister, Helene called me last night + said she had to have the doctor (Dr. Thomas). He said the cold was all in her head + throat + had laryngitis + that the house was too cold for her + the baby. It is an awfully cold house. Helene is so disgusted with Jack. He's been staying out nights + makes no attempt to sit down + have a talk with Helene as to what they're going to do. Helene said the only solution she can see is that your family (your father, Al + you, if you were home) go up + talk to his mother + father + see what they think about keeping the two girls. Helene said if she keeps leaving everything to Jack nothing will ever be decided. It makes Helene mad to see him out night after night – it just shows how little he's grieving for your sister. She said something will have to be worked out within the next month or so. I don't blame Helene for being disgusted with him – she's like a slave for him – washing + ironing his shirts, getting his meals + keeping his children together. Of course she's really doing it for them but after all, there is a limit. I hope everything works out for the best – it's surely an awful problem.

Yes, dearest, I know you want me to have some diversion – I will go out once in a while from now on to the show at least. I might go out Saturday night with Mary. I'm glad you go out once in a while.

I had to laugh at you when you said you hoped you won't break your teeth over the things I'll bake in the future (ha ha). Well, dearest, I hope you won't – I think I'll be able to get a plain, ordinary meal together – no fancy stuff (ha ha). I don't think you'll have to worry about losing your teeth over my biscuits, etc.

Well, darling, Cele just came in from work so I have to set the table etc. for supper. I wish I could be with you on your birthday to celebrate it with you – not that you'll do any celebrating but just to be with you would be so nice. I hope you have _many_ many more birthdays when we can be together. Take care of yourself, sweetheart. I'll be thinking of you tomorrow – as I always do. You deserve such a happy life – I hope I will make you so.

Love Always,

X X X X X X Rita Marie X X X X X X

X – Here's a great big kiss for your birthday. I wish I could give you a lot of them in person, dear.

Thursday Nite 6: P.M. December 29 [Actually December 30.]

Dear Rita,

Take care of your cold dear. I know how you must miss me, it is so hard, waiting for a whole month to see each other.

Bunny you are a good girl, I Love you so much, and miss you so much also. Today I recived two cards for my Birthday, Boy I am almost 28 years old. Boy, See <u>dear</u>, I am quite a big boy. Martha + Emma sent them, Martha also sent a nice assortment of cookies. Also heard from Leo Sablofski my cousin he is now on the U.S.S. Colorado, he is Now on the West Coast, at San Francisco.

Today all the M.P.s went through the, Infiltration Course, that's the course where they fire, Machine guns over us boy's while we crawl through Barb Wire, also they have diamite explodtions going off, at the same time. I was one of the first ones that finished first. We finnish up by Falling into a big trench. It was a <u>lot</u> <u>of</u> <u>fun</u> but at first we were all quite <u>frightened</u>. But once we started through it was not to bad.

Love Walter

Thanks for the Nice Wallet you Sent. Tonite I am on Station duty. also New Years Eve Hrs – 6: P.M. – to 3 or 4 in the morning. I will be able to get a little rest while on duty. It is quite quiet at the wee hrs of the morning. But tomorrow will Keep us very Busy with drunks.

Friday Nite. December 31 – 43

Dear Rita,

I recived your very nice Birthday Card also the one from Cele with the two dollars $2.00 inclosed, Boy. Cele treats me so good. See Bunny I rate with her and Chuck. Thats good. I am happy for that.

I also recived cards from Helene + Martha, very nice one's also.

Martha Sent me another package, as yet I did not open it. That fruit cake that Helen gave me for Christmas is real good. Boy it does not take long for it to vanish once the boys hear you unwraping the package.

Your box of candy I did not open as yet. I dont want to open everything at once.

Yes Rita dear, we will work out some thing as far as Jack is concerned when I get home, Hope Helene's cold gets better, she works so hard.

Bunny, you are the Sweetest girl in the whole World. I am so fortinate in having you as my Fiancee. <u>God</u> has a way in having young people meet and eventually get married and Live a happy life together. Rita you have a <u>extra</u> <u>Super</u> <u>Character</u>. See what fine upbringing you had. The Lavery are a fine family. You should be very proud of the Name and I know that you are. Rita Dear. Thanks for the very nice <u>large</u> <u>kiss</u> that you sent me for my <u>Birthday</u>

<u>Bunny</u> <u>I</u> <u>Love</u> you So much and miss your companionship so much. We get along so well. and never do we <u>fight</u> Ha. – Ha. – Ha.

Bunny – How I wish I could be with you on my Birthday and on New

Years Eve to Celebrate the occations. and to Love each other oh so nice. Heh dear.

Love <u>Walter</u>.

P.S. I am Sweet Twenty Eight (28). See Bunny, I am a big Boy. Ha. Ha.

Saturday – Jan. 1st '44 1:00 pm.

Hello Sweetheart,

A very happy New Year to you, dearest. It doesn't seem possible, does it, that another year is beginning. I hope it'll be much brighter for everyone than the last one. It will if the war is over in Europe this year.

How do you like my fancy writing paper? It's one of my Christmas presents. I don't like large sheets like this unless I'm writing a real, long, letter. I know you don't either dear – you like small ones – then you don't have to write so much (ha ha ha).

Last night I spent a very, very quiet new year's eve – I went to bed early – the reason I did was because Johnny Connors (the fellow you've met from New Jersey who has an Irish Brogue) was here. He came yesterday afternoon and stayed at Brooklawn for a few hours and then came over here about 8:30 last night. You can imagine, Walt, the kind of an evening that was spent with him here. The only thing he likes to do is sit all evening, drink + talk about the war continually. Of course Thomas stayed here because there were drinks + Cele + Charlie had to sit + talk to him. He's the biggest bore of anyone I know. I went to bed about 10 o'clock. It was the most lonesome New Year's Eve I ever spent. It would have been alright if he hadn't come + there were just Cele, Charlie Jeanie + I here but you know how it is when Johnny comes. He hasn't been here in over a year – works in some airplane factory in New Jersey + works about 7 days a week. I guess he'll stay here tonight too + will go back late tomorrow afternoon. We'll all be glad. Cele + Charlie aren't so keen on having him here either. Well, dearest, if I don't stop talking about him you'll think I'm awful heh, Walt? (ha ha).

Tonight I'm going to the show with Mary Buccino. It'll be such a relief to get out of this house for a change.

Bud's mother said he's been on sick leave for the past few days. I guess he's having his old trouble again (kidney). It's too bad that condition doesn't clear up.

Tomorrow I'm going to see if Helene will come down here for a while in the evening. I guess she'd like to if Jack would stay home and take care of the children for a change.

The weather is beautiful here for this time of the year – not too cold. I hope you are managing to keep warm, dearest, 'way up in Ft. Devens. I wonder what you are doing today, dearest, right now. You're probably going on about your regular duties. I hope your mail catches up with me Monday. I didn't receive any yesterday + of course there are no deliveries today.

I went to 10 o'clock Mass this morning as today is a holy day of obligation (the same as Sunday).

Dearest, I guess you know from the depressing letters I've been writing lately how much I miss you. It's only two weeks since we've seen each other + it seems like two months. I hope you can come home again in two or three more weeks.

As I'm writing this Vin just came in to say "hello." – he's working today. He's so different from Thomas – thank God – he + Ed aren't like Thomas. He still isn't working + guess he doesn't intend to. I guess there's no reason why he should when he has good meals here – nice room + a little pocket money (provided by Cele). It's so disgusting + discouraging having him around here day in + day out. He's waited on hand + foot by Cele + Charlie + when they ask him when he's going to work he won't answer. No one is supposed to bring up such a subject. He hasn't worked since October. I don't see how anyone can be civil to him let alone doing anything for him. I never talk to him at all nor even sit in the same room with him. I guess God will punish me for hating anyone so much but I just can't help it. I'll never feel any different as long as I live – not just because of the way he's been for the past few months but it goes much further back than that – to the time when my mother was living + I saw how he treated her. I guess I shouldn't write to you when I feel like this, Walter, but you understand so much better than anyone else. I'll get over this feeling when I go out tonight (I hope).

Well, dearest, I guess I'd better close and set the table for dinner. Cele is so mad that she has to cook + do dishes all day because Johnny's here. Ordinarily when we're here alone we just have breakfast + one big meal in the middle of the afternoon. She says just when we can have a few days off + can take it a little easy we have to cook + work all day long. He has such an appetite he's liable to eat the kitchen table.

Keep well, dearest + as happy as you can. I love you so much.

Lots of big hugs + kisses

X X X X X X Rita Marie X X X X X X

Monday 1/3/44

Dearest,

I hope you didn't mind the train ride back too much last night – that you had company + that you don't have to work too hard today.

I can't begin to tell you how happy I was when I saw you Saturday night. I was so surprised, dearest. You probably received the depressing letter I wrote Saturday afternoon by now so you can realize a little how glad I was to see you. You brought me right out of the gloom + made me feel so good, dear. You know your little old spinach face, heh, darling – I'm always so happy when you come home but sometimes – just sometimes, Walter dear I get so lonesome that I'm very depressed.

We had such a nice week-end, dearest. We weren't alone hardly at all yesterday but now I'm glad because you know if we were what would have happened – (the same as Saturday night). I would like to have talked with you more tho, Walter about our marriage – not that I don't know + understand your viewpoint but I wanted to tell you a few things that are a little hard to explain in writing but we'll let things go until you come home again – we should come to a definite understanding by that time – that is about telling your father – the date, etc.

Right now you probably can't help thinking about the situation on White St. – about the children, etc. It really isn't your problem but I know how you feel, dearest, you want the children to have someone take care of them who will have real affection for them + not some strange woman. It certainly is an awful mix-up right now but if your father, you, Helene, + Jack could get together up in Trumbull I think something could be worked out. Jack has to have someone make him wake up + act – not just talk – someone like your father who would come right down to brass tacks, so that he wouldn't just promise this or that – his promises aren't worth anything. Your family will have to watch him closely (and I know you will) + insist on some decision.

6:45 p.m. I just came home from work and your Thursday's + Friday's letters were here. They were nice ones, dear. You didn't have any idea at the time you wrote them that you'd be home. I always like to get mail on Monday.

The weather is terrible here right now. It's raining + snowing at the same time + is very slippery. I don't know how I'm going to get across the street to mail this letter it's so slippery. I'm going to see if I can bribe Jeanie with a quarter to mail it for me (ha ha). Leave it to me, heh, dear – I can be a gold-bricker when I want to.

Ruth Landry said she saw you last night when you were crossing the street going to the station but I guess you didn't recognize her.

Your sister Helene stayed 'till about 11:15 and then Cele went to the bus with her. While they were waiting for the bus Emma Castlelot (I think that's her name) got off a bus + Helene introduced Cele to her.

Well, dearest, I'll have to close now as it's almost 7:15 + I'll have to start bribing Jeanie. Take care of yourself, dear, go out for a little diversion – show or U.S.O. but try not to drink too much – I know you don't usually.

Lots of Love, Dear.

X X X X X X Rita X X X X X X

Tuesday 1/4/44

My Dearest Sweetheart,

How do you like that salutation, dear? You are my dearest sweetheart – you know it too, heh Walter?

The weather is awful today to say the least – worse than last night. It's been pouring rain + snowing all morning and very windy besides. You should have seen me this morning, dear, trying to buck the wind coming to work. I almost got blown off my feet – I'm so light + the wind was so strong. I had boots on, raincoat (reversible) umbrella, babushka on + everything. I guess this is only the beginning of the bad weather. I hope you aren't out on duty in this miserable weather, dear. If you are, please dress real warm.

Last night Cele + I took down the Christmas tree. What a job! Those big trees are a lot of work both to trim + take down. Then we had to clean the house – after getting it down + put all the images, lights, ornaments + presents away. Cele said she'll never have a big one like that again. Table trees are less trouble + are just as nice.

Dear, remember my telling you about the girl in the office whose husband has such a bad nervous condition? She called me up at the office this morning + said she made an appointment with Dr. Brodsky for him. She has to stay home from work with him – he was up all night – can't sleep or eat. I don't think he's on the verge of breakdown but I think he's right in the midst of one. She asked if she should mention your name but I told her I wouldn't if I were she because you only went to him once + he probably won't remember – it's quite a while since you were there. I think her husband's condition is an extreme case + probably will have to go away for a rest. It's a shame. The girl is only about 23 or 24 + seems very nice – she's only been working here a few weeks. Her husband's name is Bill Auer (pronounced like hour). The reason I'm telling you about it is so that you can realize a little how lucky you were that you weren't as far down as he is when you went to Dr. Brodsky + it just shows you how quickly you can go down. It's been 3 yrs. since that fellow had a complete breakdown + since then hasn't taken good care of himself – kept late hours, worked 12 hrs. a day etc. I know you will take good care of yourself, tho, dear – you wouldn't be so foolish not to.

I'm writing this during my lunch hour (1/2 hr.) + will write more later – when I go home tonight – that is, if I'm not blown away by the wind (ha ha).

6:15 p.m. The office manager (Charlie Thibault) took me home from work. I had a talk with him about the raise I asked him about last week + I am getting one but it will only be 5¢ an hour more. According to the way I'm classified under the War Labor Board (Stenographer – Secretary) that's all I can get – I'm getting the maximum salary I can get (75¢ an hour). So you see it's a question of "take it or leave it". If I don't take it I'll have to leave + wait 60 days before I can get an availability slip to work any place else. It looks as tho I'll have to take it. I can't say that I'm satisfied with it but one thing that I'm learning from working for Mr. Trefry is tolerance. If I can get along with him I will be able to get along with any one. So far, it's been an awful effort but maybe by the time you + I are married I'll learn to be tolerant + will make you a better wife. What do you think, dearest?

You were inducted one year ago tomorrow into the Army, heh, dearest? (the 5th). It seems longer sometimes but I suppose it doesn't to you because it was an entirely new life. I hope by this time next year you'll be home (permanently).

Well, dear, I have to mail this now. It's late. I'm thinking of you all the time, sweetheart + miss you. You're such a good boy, dearest.

Love Always,
X X X X X X Rita X X X X X X

Tuesday Nite January 4. 1944
Day Room

DearRita,

Hello my little Spinach Jack, hows my Sweet Irish girl. Bunny I hope that you are feeling in the pink and I bet that you are still feeling at your high, after seeing your Swell heart and Fiance Walter J. Klein. Ha. Ha. Ha. Bunny I miss you and your cheerful Smile and Sweet disposition. Rita dear. I love you, Oh, you <u>dear</u> are so nice to me.

God meant that you and I were to be Hubbie and wifie, heh dear.

Rita, you have such a fine <u>character</u>. I cant help but want to repead that, time and time again. Bunny, I feel like a good <u>hug and tug</u> night now. Bunny just writing to you, makes me, <u>oh</u> so excited. It makes my heart do extra beats. See dear, what you do to me. But, oh dear. I love it. Ha. Ha. Ha. Today I attend school. Tonite I am not slated to work, so I will go up the R.G.C. to see Bud Monahan and maybe take in a show, thats if he is not working tonite, as he sometimes does.

Yes dear you know how to bribe Jeanie. Leave it to you Dearest.

Yes dear, we will get all of our plans straightened out, on my next trip home – <u>Oh</u> Boy dear. It just <u>tickles</u> me to write about our, <u>marrige</u>, Yes dear. On my next trip home, I will talk to Jack about his plans, I only hope he does not run off with some of those <u>wild</u> <u>women</u> until than. Each Nite I pray that the children get into blood relation families, either our family or his. Some one to <u>Love</u> and encourage them and be close to them In heart and mind and not only in natural possessions.

Love Walter.

A sensible girl will think of so much. wondering if she could love the children and do everything for them even when they are tired and sick or when trouble comes. Jack's women are not even thinking of such things, So when she comes of them she will abuse them and not care for them. Those women of Jack's, sure are no good. I know as well as you do. Because only one in a million girls will ever let themselves fall for a married man. So his women have no Character. They did not care of Lil's and the children happiness or else they would not bring misery to a happy married family. If they were like that than, I am sure they are the lowest type of person one wants to know. Anyone who thinks of there happiness first is no good for any one, never mind the person to bring up Beautiful Children I may write to Jack but I think I will wait to see him in person. I will see that those children of Lil's get the love and cheer and close family relations that a normal child needs, they need a family who will think of there welfare first and happiness Also someone who they can go to when problems come up. My Father and Helene will watch him very closely too.

Wednesday Jan. 5th 6:45 pm.

Dearest,

Received your Monday's letter tonight – it was such a nice, long one, dear. I'm glad you enjoyed the week-end so much. We always have nice week-ends when we're together.

You give me such nice compliments all the time, darling – saying that you just like to look at me – thanks, dear.

I'm glad you received so many cards for your birthday + those nice handkerchiefs from Martha.

It's a good thing you left my house early + caught the 10:10 train to New Haven + got up to the fort at 3: AM. That's much better than the train you usually take – glad you managed to get enough sleep too, sweetheart.

Yes, dear, it surely will be wonderful if you are stationed in Devens for a while so you can put in for a furlough so we can get married.

What do you think of the suggestion I made about meeting each other half way + getting married in May? I think it would be so nice – about the middle of May – the weather will be warm by then + seeing that June 5th isn't so good – if we waited 'till the middle of June or the end – it might be too hot. By that time your father will understand everything fully (I hope). As I don't have a chance to talk much about these things when you're home, I guess we'll have to write our thoughts on the subject.

That fellow (the husband of the girl in our office) who went to Dr. Brodsky has to go away for 3 months + have treatments besides that will cost $250.<u>00</u> alone. The doctor said he was in a very bad condition (his nerves). It's a shame but it's a good thing he didn't wait any longer to go to the doctor.

Dearest, that training you were telling me about that you have to go thru – crawling on your knees while the sub-machine guns are going off is called <u>infiltration</u>. Every time you wrote the word you spelled it differently so I looked it up in the dictionary + it means – passing thru into enemy territory (as in the midst of battle etc.) so I guess that's the right word. (ha ha ha). Let me know if I'm right, heh dearest?

I was so busy today in the office. I was going every minute taking shorthand + transcribing.

Take care of yourself honey bunch 'till I see you again (I hope it will be soon). Darling, in a few weeks even if you aren't scheduled for a pass – if you find yourself (like you did last Saturday) without any duties – apply for a pass anyway, even if it isn't your usual week to come home. Confidentially, I think this is a very good idea (ha ha ha). Leave it to me to think these things up. (ha ha).

Love Always,
X X X X X X Rita X X X X X X

Wednesday Nite January 5 – 44

Dear Rita,

Bunny, I got your letter that you write the nite before each Day at <u>Noon</u>. So your letters come very prompt. Bpt + New York also Boston had plenty of Snow and Slush and rain, but here at Devens, just twenty (20) miles from Boston was no rain or snow, but it looked like we would get some. I was surprised to hear that you had the snow and Slush in Bpt.

Yes. Dr. Brodsky is just the man for your friends, Husband to treat him and overcome his (<u>fears</u>). which is 75 percent of his Definite and trouble He will sure do the tricks for that man with the mans own help of course.

Bunny congradulation on your newly increase in pay. Bunny, See what <u>earning</u> power you have. You are such a intelligent girl. Stick to E.W. Carpents. Good old E. W. <u>Corp</u>.

<u>Ha</u>. <u>Ha</u>. <u>Ha</u>.

Today I attended School again, tonite I am going to the Ayer U.S.O. Barn Dance that they hold each Wednesday. About ½ dozen boy's M.P.s attend each Wednesday Nite, if possible. I Saw <u>Bud</u> <u>Monahan</u> last Nite at his Barracks. Had a nice <u>chat</u> and I also attended a Movie. (Jack London) was the title of the picture. Bud is going to be at the U.S.O. Dance also. He goes, now and than he likes the <u>polko's</u> <u>dance</u>.

Tomorrow I may have to chase prisoners – (<u>Yes I do</u>.) the boy's just came up from downstairs and I am the New Scedual on the Bulitian Board. So Friday I will be back on school. Next Week I guess I may go on Interior guard.

This week has been a good <u>easy</u> week for the boys that worked over the Holidays, the First Sergaent treated us very good. Heh dear. That is a very nice Saluation dear I like it very much. dearest Rita Marie.

Yes dear, working for Mr. Trefry is a good way to learn tolerance, Its so good for any person to acquire. But dear you were pretty tolerant, but the more the better. <u>Heh</u> <u>dearest</u>. Ha. Ha. Ha. Ha.

Yes Dearest. Today is (one) year for me in the Army, See dear. I am a <u>old</u> <u>Soldier</u> and I can take it too heh dear. See dear I can take more than I though I could take. See Bunny, what a Big Soldier Boy you have for a <u>Fiance</u>.

Bunny, I Love you so much. you are such a good girl. Rita dear. I feel as tho I could Love you for a hr or two just before I go out <u>to</u> <u>the</u> <u>usual</u> <u>ornal</u> <u>retreat</u>, that we have each Wednesday. Nite. At 5:00 P.M.

<u>Oh</u> <u>dearest</u>. just think, by this coming June 15 we will be <u>Mr. & Mrs.</u> <u>W. J.</u> <u>Klein</u>. Bunny, I Love you so, we will spend and have each others <u>happiness</u> and <u>sorrows</u>.

Love <u>Walter</u>

P.S. You have pretty <u>writing</u> <u>paper</u> <u>dear</u>.

January 6th – Thursday 6:00 p.m.

Hello Darling,

I worked 'till 5 tonight + received your Tuesday's letter when I came home. The writing was so crowded I could hardly understand it – is there a shortage of writing paper at Ft. Devens, dear? (ha ha).

Yes, dear, it's nice to get in touch with Bud once in a while but I wouldn't make a habit of it because he likes to go out a lot + doesn't mind late hours or drinking. He's a nice fellow but not good for you to make a steady companion. I understand tho, dearest, you haven't seen him in quite a while.

Yes, dearest, I think you're right about not writing to Jack – it'll be better to see him – it wouldn't do any good to write anyway – in fact I don't think it will do any good to talk to him either. He's capable of taking care of the children in a physical way – that is – he's able to work to give Helene money every week for their support but he's not capable mentally. He doesn't talk sense at all. What right has he to say he doesn't want the children split up – as far as I can see that's the only way they can be taken care of. If only someone in your family could take the two girls or even Jack's mother + then Helene could take the baby they would be taken care of in the right way – that is – would be given affection + would live in a home-like atmosphere but if he marries some stranger this would be impossible (you've said the same so many times). I think what he really has in the back of his mind as Helene said Sunday is for her to marry him + then he could still be free to run around + at the same time the children would be taken care of – or one other things he might have in mind – that is that he might marry someone but expect Helene to stay with him anyway figuring that she'd do it for the children's sake. This would be a terrible thing if it did happen. He'd make Helene's life miserable to say the least. This probably seems unbelievable to you that he could have such things in the back of his mind but don't forget his brain is working every minute but all the thoughts concern himself – Well, darling, don't worry about it between now + the time you come home again – I don't think he'll run off with any of those women in that time. I still think your father would be a good one to straighten everything out. You are inclined to agree with him – once you start talking to him + would be very easily swayed by what you think is the truth. You know by now you can't take his word for anything – you have to have (on demand) proof right before your eyes. But, dearest, God will see a way for the children – you'll see. Please don't worry – you know dear, it doesn't do any good for <u>two</u> <u>people</u> to worry about the <u>same</u> thing (ha ha ha). – good philosophy heh, dearest? Remember that when you start worrying and you'll have to laugh.

Last night Cele, Virginia + I took the bus + went out to Eleanor + Vin's. They still had their tree up – it was nice. We had a lot of laughs out there.

Tonight I'm going to bed early – I'm awfully tired.

I hope everything is well with you, lovey (I like to call you that, dear – "lovey" – ha ha). I think of you so often, sweetheart. You're such a nice person – such a good, clean, upright character – I'm very proud + happy to know you'll be my husband soon. I'm going to do everything possible to make you happy.

Love Always,
X X X X X X Rita X X X X X X
X – good luck
X – lots of happiness
X – Good Health
X – God Bless You.

Thursday Nite January 6. 1944

Dearest Rita,

Here at Mass. the snow began to fall at 12: Noon and now at 8: P.M. we have about 5 inches of it. This morning it rained for a half a day. So the weather is begining to get, just like winter.

Today I chased prisoners, but managed to keep dry. leave it to me. Heh dear. the hrs were from 5:30 A.M. to 6:00 P.M. So after I fininish this letter to you darling. I am going right into the good old <u>Sack</u>. Ha. Ha. Ha. Be a good girl. Bunny.

Tomorrow I am going to school, maybe shovel Snow too, for awhile.

Bunny. Tonite would be a very exceptional good evening for you and I to crawl into bed, and try to keep warm. Heh dear. You know Bunny how I like to try to keep your feet warm on these cold Snowie nites. Oh Boy. Bunny. I would like that so much.

But I guess you and I will have to only <u>dream</u> until we can get married and make it ligetimate. Oh Bunny dear. It just tickles my spine, writing about our coming Marrige this coming, May or June. Yes dearest. the Middle of May, would be a nice time for our coming Marrige. Oh Boy Bunny. I get old excited just writing about it.

Bunny. on our next weekend home together we will talk more on our coming Marriage. Heh dear. and we can also continue to write about it also and work our little problems out. Heh dear. Tough for that M of the girl's at your office, that had to go away for a short break and rest from every day routine.

<u>Infiltration</u> is right dear. yes dear, I will take advantage of every opportounity to get a pass. Leave it to us. Heh dearest Rita.

Love <u>Walter</u>

Friday 1/7/44 – 12:30 pm.

Dear Sweetheart,

I just finished eating lunch and thought I'd at least start my daily letter to you.

I feel very good today because I received Holy Communion at 6:30 this morning – today is the first Friday of the month. I went to Confession last night. I don't know whether you ever heard this before, dearest, but if a Catholic goes to Communion on the first Friday of the month for nine months (consecutive months), he or she is always sure of having a priest to anoint them before they die. I made the nine Fridays before but I'm going to try to go this year each month for nine months again (just to be sure I'll have a priest when I'm dying) – not only for that reason but it's a very good practice to follow. I offered up the Communion for you + I – for our future – so that everything will work out in the best way for us.

As I'm writing this letter there's a man in here by the name of Mr. Fry who smokes cigars continually. I'm almost choking here from the smell (ha ha ha). Speaking about smoking, I often wondered if you'd like to smoke a pipe. I have the idea (maybe it's silly) that a fellow looks nice smoking a pipe. I'd buy you a nice one if I thought you'd like one. Do you, dear? I'll bet you're laughing your head off at this.

6:45 p.m. Received your Wednesday's + Thursday's letters – your mail finally caught up with me, dear.

I was surprised you got the snow + rain later than we did. The weather here is nice + clear now but a little cold.

You make me laugh when you say I have earning power – that's a "joker". I can't see why you want me to stay at E.W.C. I don't see myself how I've been there this long.

I had a letter from Dot Smith but I haven't had a chance to open it yet.

In Wednesday's letter, dearest you said we will be Mr. + Mrs. This coming June 15th. In Thursday's letter you agree with me that May 15th is a good date. I don't want you to agree with me just to make me feel better – I want you to have the desire yourself to be married in May – even April – that would be better.

Please excuse the mess of this paper – This is spaghetti sauce on this side – on the front is water. I'm writing this on the kitchen table. Thomas is at the dining room table (where I usually write) + I can't sit there because I'm liable to collapse from the smell of him. (I'm not fooling, either). It's too late to re-write it – I would if I had time, dear, tho, it's awfully sloppy isn't it?

Yes, I think we can talk about our marriage in our letters – we never have any time alone when you're home so maybe in writing about it we can come to some decision.

I'll be thinking of you, dear over the coming week-end. If you get a chance to call Sunday, I'll be home but if not, it will be O.K., darling. You'd better try to keep a little money on the side in case you get a pass before next pay day.

I miss your kisses too, dear, it seems a long time since we've had time for any, heh dear?

Lots + lots of Love, dearest

X X X X X X Rita X X X X X X

Saturday Night 11:30 pm. 1/8/44

Dearest Walter,

I'm starting to write this letter in bed – I probably won't write much tonight because my eyes won't stay open long enough but let's see how far I get anyway.

I went to the show tonight and saw "As Thousands Cheer" (in technicolor) with Gene Kelly, Catherine Grayson (a new actress), Mary Astor, John Boles + a lot of other well-known stars. If you haven't already seen it, dearest, don't miss it – it's an Army picture + there's a lot of music in it (something like "This is the Army"). I went with Mary Buccino + we had a nice evening. We went in the "Star" after the show and had something to eat, one drink of wine + talked for a while.

In Dot Smith's letter that I received yesterday she said they are saving money to come home in February – Ernie expects 10 days furlough. It'll be nice to see them. Just think they've been married almost 5 months now. Dot said she was sending me a gift for my cedar chest – two hand-embroidered dish towels + a guest towel. Isn't that nice? Everyone must be very anxious for me to fill it – giving me gifts for it.

I didn't get any mail from you today, Walt, but I guess it's because they're so short of help in a lot of the post offices – it takes longer for your mail to come than it used to. You said the last time you were home that Connecticut still has lots of single men eligible to be drafted. Maybe this is so but at the same time they are taking an awful lot of fellows now with 1, 2 + 3 children. We know of quite a few. It's certainly a shame. We haven't heard yet how Ed Singer made out – he was trying to appeal his classification at the draft board but it probably won't do him much good to appeal. We know of another fellow who has two children + another on the way + he has to go in a few weeks.

As I'm writing this letter, dear, I wonder if you're outside on duty or are you in bed sound asleep by now. I hope you're not outside – the weather is so cold. It's only a week since we've seen each other but it seems so much longer – but then – the time always seems long to me 'till I see you again.

Dear, I guess I'll go to sleep now – I'm tired + have to get up for Church tomorrow at 9. I'll write more tomorrow. Lots + lots of love, dearest.

X X X X X X

Sunday 1/9/44 12:30 noon

Hello Dear,

I was so glad when you called, Walter. I think the operator let us talk more than three minutes – it seemed a little longer than usual.

It's too bad you're on those awful hours, dearest. (12 to 4). Those are the coldest hours in the morning. It's been very cold here too, Walt, about zero. If you're outside all week, dear, on duty, please dress real warm – especially your feet + chest.

You sounded a little discouraged on the phone at first, Walt, but then as we went on talking you sounded a little more like your usual self. I guess being on duty in such cold weather would get you down.

I meant to tell you when I wrote last night – I called Helene up Friday night. Everything seems to be going along fairly well with all of them – altho she didn't say how Jack was behaving + of course I didn't ask her. She said there was to be some sort of a party up to Martha's in Easton – last night. Harry Eisenman + his wife – your father – Helene + I don't know about Ellen + Al. Martha told Helene to tell Jack she was going + to stay home with the children but up to the time Helene talked to me she hadn't told him. She seemed really afraid. She said he might have made other plans to go out + in that case she'd have to ask Ruth to come over + stay. She certainly is foolish to take that attitude – hesitating to tell him she's going out. But I didn't say anything. Martha told Helene if I happened to call to ask me to go but I had already promised Mary to go out with her when I talked to Helene and anyway Helene said it was really a family get-together.

Cele has been telling me that I should be looking around a little for material for my wedding gown. Mrs. Singer is going to make it + Cele was talking to her on the phone the other night + Mary (Mrs. Singer) said I should be looking around too. She gave us two suggestions as to where to go for material. One store is here in Bpt. on Main St. + the other is in New Haven. She'll be willing to go with Cele + I any time to help pick it out. Cele also thinks I should be starting to buy a trousseau – slips, etc. + also if I see a nice light color suit (to wear going away) that I should put a deposit on one + leave it in the store. I don't know whether it's too early or not to look around. Then too, I'm rather discouraged that you haven't told your father. We haven't even set a date yet so I guess it's foolish to go ahead with anything yet till you + I get straightened out as to how your family feels.

If I were you (this is a suggestion) the next time you come home – when you can be alone with your father – tell him that you + I want to get married in the spring (probably May) – that you have no intention of giving up your own religion but that we'll be married in Blessed Sacrament Church, that you realize that being in the Army is one of the things that isn't in your favor (as well as Religion. (difference of religion) but that you + I have been going together over three years + you feel that you (+ I) would like to get married + save for the future after the war. If your father says he isn't in favor of your getting married in the Catholic Church tell him that I said it has to be that way or not at all.

I don't think your father will be as much against it as you think because you said yourself the day of your sister's funeral you talked to him a little about me + he said well, sometimes it's God's will that you meet, go with + marry someone of the opposite religion + you can be happier sometimes than if you married someone of the same religion. If Cele + Charlie can be broadminded about our marrying I don't see why your family can't at least try to be. I'm not asking you to give up any of your beliefs.

Cele has even asked Bob Green, a friend of hers + Charlie, to sing at the wedding already. Of course she said she wasn't sure just when it would be but it would be in the spring sometime. He said he'd be glad to. He has a grand voice + would sing at the Church + reception both.

It makes me feel so badly that Cele + Eleanor are so enthused over our getting married + there's such hesitation on your part that I'm getting so I don't even want to bring up the subject lately.

So, Walt, won't you please face facts the way they are + not make obstacles when there aren't too many? It's certainly not my place to tell your family but so far I've had to tell Helene, Al + Martha. Last week when I told Martha you were so afraid + embarrassed you'd think I was telling about a crime we'd committed.

Well, dearest, you probably don't like the idea of my writing about these things but it is the way I feel + don't see you alone very much when you come home. It really isn't funny to joke the way you do about fellows putting marriage off 'till the last minute. I think we'll both be much happier when we're married knowing that we belong to each other in every way — we won't have to lower ourselves like we do now letting our emotions go, + most important of all can have that wonderful companionship that comes more fully with married life + can get our home together — save + plan for a real home — not just a house.

Dear, I miss you so much + hope + pray each day that you can be stationed in Ft. Devens or someplace near till after this mess is over. I'm counting a lot on the war with Germany being over after the major invasion of Europe + then maybe you will have a chance of being released + we can live a normal, happy life together.

Love Always,

X X X X X Rita X X X X X X

Sunday 5: P.M.

Day Room

Bunny, I have come to the conlcution's that no other person will ever take your place or could ever, dear.

Hello Bunny dear,

I enjoyed talking to you on the phone so much. I wished I could have been going out with you Bunny dear, on this Winter afternoon, instead of going on post. But duty comes before, enjoyment, pleasure, and Love. phooee I say. Ha. Ha. Ha. Heh dear.

I say, being with my Love on Sunday, all Day. comes first. Heh dearest. Leave it to us. Rita Marie Lavery. By the way, Rita, you have such a very nice full Name. Rita Marie Lavery Good old Lavery's. Long May they Live and Live a healthy and happy Life.

Bunny. I think of you each hour of the day. especially while on post at Nite when I have lots of time, to my Self to let my Mind wander Back to you dear and our past day's of happiness, and all of those very happy day's ahead. Our coming Marrige dear, is being looked forward with, so much in those, and happy though's.

Bunny, we have such a fine Love.

Rita dear. I am getting the Desire More and More to be together and be Hubbie and Wifie. See Bunny, dear what you are doing for me, to make me happy.

Bunny, I Love you so much, you know so much you are so intelligent, extra intelligent dear. Bunny, I actually right now think it is going to be the best thing for us to be happily Married, in that way we can proceed on with life, to reach a full and lasting life together. We did not go to long before we reached this point or have we reached a decession to soon. I think it is working out just as it should. Heh dear. depending on us as indevedual's and circumstances.

We do not want to wait to long, and in that way, we would waste a year or two. Heh dear. Bunny, it is working out just fine dear, as far as our plans for our coming Marriage is concerned. I hope that, it just works out, so that May. 15th or around that date will be our Wedding day.

Bunny. Boy I am surprised at my Self. Talking so freely of our coming Marriage which I should not refrain from planning Heh dear. Bunny. I am so happy you make me that way dear. Bunny. I want to help you make the plans also dear and not have it all up to you.

Rita we can ajust our self to the Marriage state, for about two (2) years before we plan to consider having an addition to our family, which will start, just with you and I. – Ha. Ha. Ha. Bunny, See how Sentimental I can be at times. See what you do to me. I like it so <u>much dear</u>

Rita, I just can picture you walking down the aisle dressed all in <u>white</u>, a Beautiful Wedding gown. Bunny you will look, so Beautiful and exceptionally pretty.

Bunny be a good girl. Rita. I still feel like writing some more to you. Rita, I am writing all this, just as it comes from my heart. I and you, have had a long Meditation over our <u>Love</u> and how much we <u>love</u> <u>each</u> <u>other</u>. Our good points, and our bad points. and the few defferances of our Back grounds, religion and Nationality. You know that you <u>love</u> <u>me</u> very much right from your <u>heart</u> and <u>Mind</u> and I know it <u>also</u> that you ove me, as much as a person can show from the heart. I come to the conclution that I also Love you so deeply and with no doughts about it. I Knew it from the very Start., the time we just had gone for a few months, But time has made it even a hundred times stronger.

<u>Rita</u>, <u>Marie</u> <u>Lavery</u>. You are the Girl of My Life. And We are going to be Married this coming May. And be life partners for our entire lifes together, while on this earth.

Bunny you know how I am, also making so sure that everything is just one hundred percent in your Mind, before we make a decision. SLOW POKE I AM HA. HA. <u>God</u> ment it so, that you Rita, and I would fall head over heals in Love and eventually get Married, and have a home and to live a full life, having maybe one or two children if its God will that we have them. I love children and I know you do too. But of course only a few. That's because that's all I and you will be able to handle and to provide Education, and all the other things possible, to a happy life, for them.

Rita, I want to <u>thank</u> <u>God</u>, for giving you to me, to live a full happy normal life together. So that you and I will not be lonesome or all alone, during the day's that we need some one to comfort us and to Love and encourage us to

Keep up our spirits and Keep going, when the going gets tough. Thank God that you come from such a fine family. Cele, Chick, dward, Thomas, Vincent, Jeanie, you had such a fine Mother and Father. Thank God for that fine upbringing dear

Love Walter

Monday Nite 8: P.M.
Day Room

Dear Rita,

Hows my Sweet little irish Colleen today, Hope that you are in the best of spirits, and managing to keep warm during this cold weather dear.

Just got finished reading your letters that you wrote Sunday afternoon.

Yes dearest, we will try to get all of our plans made as well as we can, considering the circumstances of the Army.

Yes dear, on my next trip home, I will have a <u>chat</u> with my Father, and get his opinion of our plans in getting <u>hitched</u> <u>Ha</u>. Ha. <u>Ha</u>, this coming Spring, On May <u>15</u>th if everything works out as we plan.

Bunny, you are such a sweet girl. I <u>Love</u> you so much. Bunny you make me see <u>double</u> when I read that blunt letters. Leave it to you dearest to write and drive home to me, just what you mean. Good old Rita Marie Lavery.

Rita, I am sure that on my next trip home which I hope will not be to long away, we will iron out all the Bend's in the line,so to speak. Heh dear. Bunny, I Love you so much, and Miss you so much.

Tuesday Jan. 11th 12:30 pm.

Dear Sweetheart,

I hope you are not finding it too cold being on duty from 11:30 p.m. to 3:30 in the morning. If you can go into a shelter (if there is any) it wouldn't be so bad. Every morning when I get up I think of you hoping you didn't freeze during the wee hours of the morning.

Yesterday I received the two dish towels + one guest towel from Dot – the ones I told you she was going to send. They're very nice – I'll show them to you next time you come home. They're all hand-embroidered.

You know what, dearest? This morning Mr. Trefry was talking to a fellow from N.Y. on the phone at Youngstown Sheet + Metal in N.Y. + the man told him he'd have to call back later. He said if he wasn't there, to ask for "Walter Klein". Mr. Trefry was kidding me all morning saying you are probably fooling me – you're not in Devens at all but you're working at the Youngstown Sheet + Metal Co. in N.Y. (ha ha ha). Isn't that a coincidence tho? Mr. Trefry hasn't called there yet but will this afternoon + I told him when he does to ask him if his middle name is "John". (ha ha).

The other day Mr. Trefry asked me what your job was before you went into the Army. I told him you worked for a Construction Company but that you just took a job like that because it was outside work + it built up your nervous system. I told him you were a good mechanic also that you always felt as tho you'd like to sell but felt you didn't have enough education. I told him you had a very good personality for salesmanship – in other words you had a "gift of gab". He says an education isn't really a necessity in selling – he knows lots of fellows who haven't had much at all but who are very good in that line. He used to sell cars himself. Miss Noonan (you met her, dearest) got into the conversation + said you were foolish to feel that way too. After the war is over there will be loads of opportunities along that line. For instance, we had an agent who used to sell harps (for lamps) for us. He not only had our line but sold things for other companies – was out on the road all the time between here + N.Y. He made quite a bit of money this way as his percentage was 5% of what he sold (just for this company). Since the war he bought out all of our harp business + now will make himself a nice sum of money if his post war planning works out.

The reason I'm writing all this is because being in the M.P.'s doesn't give you much chance to learn much – to keep your brain "sharpened" (ha ha). Before you went in the Army dear, remember how much you used to read + learned quite a bit that way. Well, now, you don't have much time + the new things you do learn pertain to Army life so, dear, I'd suggest that every chance you get, you read up on any subject that interests you so you won't lose your perspective. Of course there is no use worrying about what you'll be doing after the war – that will straighten itself out in time – you don't have to feel that you'll have to go into some factory just for the sake of making money.

Remember, dear, before you went in the Army you said you'd like to get a mailman's job – you'd be outside + everything. That's another possibility after the war altho the civil service exams are quite stiff.

I think the idea you had from the time I met you until you went away about storing up knowledge is very good – you won't lose your keen-ness of mind. I'm not worrying about what you'll do after the war, dearest – I know between you + I we'll work something out – but one thing I do know working in a construction company like you did before doesn't equal your abilities at all. Don't you agree dear? If I were you I'd grab every bit of knowledge I could thru reading – then at some time of your life you'll have that excess knowledge to fall back on. Don't lose your ambitions, darling – you won't be in the Army for the rest of your life + if you can just keep that in mind + the thought that after everything is over you can start out + find out what you're best suited for, I'll help you adjust (if I can). See what I mean, darling? Let me know how you feel about this – you don't have to go into detail in your letters but just let me know if you think I'm right about not letting your mind become dull, etc.

6:45 Dearest, I received your Sunday's + Monday's letter tonight. I was so surprised you wrote Sunday. You usually don't when you call – and such a long letter too! I enjoyed it so much.

I was so happy when I finished reading Sunday's letter knowing you really have a desire to get married now. I'll answer it more in detail tomorrow or late tonight – it's getting late. About your Monday's letter – I'm sorry that "you saw double" as you said when you read my Sunday's letter. Please don't think I'm a little tiger – I do mean every word I said in that letter. If you tell your father on your next trip home he'll be used to the idea by the spring. I don't think he'll object too much anyway. I have to be blunt with you at times – if I wasn't sometimes you wouldn't think things out clearly – everything would be in a muddle. I'm not mad at you, dearest, you know how much I love you – after all – all the planning we'll do for our marriage will be for your happiness as well as mine. Please don't think I want you to do things if you really haven't the desire – you must want to agree to everything because you want to – not just for me. From what you said in Sunday's letter you really do want to get married now – it's the first time you've openly admitted it – I mean agreeing to the date + everything. May 15th is Charlie's birthday but it's on a Monday. Maybe you'd prefer Saturday – it doesn't make too much difference to me – Mon. or Sat. – maybe we won't have any choice, heh, dear, it will probably have to be whenever you can get a furlough in May sometime.

After your next trip home I'll have to start looking around + getting an idea of what I'm going to wear, etc. As you said, dearest, the next time you come we'll straighten everything out once + for all + from then on everything will take it's own course. We'll have a grand wedding if everything goes along in our favor. I'll tell you just what I'd like + then you can give me your opinions too. Don't worry, dear, or be afraid, just think of our new life with happiness + ask God to help us. I'm sure He will. I know everything won't go along smoothly for us all the time but when we have each other – we'll have a lot – we'll both do our utmost best to have a wonderful marriage.

Take care of yourself, dearest.

Love Always,

X X X X X X Rita X X X X X X

P.S. I'm still in a very lovable mood, darling – you know why too, heh? I would just like to be close to you + to tell you how much I love you.

Wednesday Jan. 12th 2:45 pm

Dearest Walter,

I'm fairly well caught up on my work + Mr. Trefry isn't here right now – he went upstairs to the Engineering Department for a short while. I've been sitting here at my desk thinking of you, dearest, wondering what you are doing right now. I hope everything is going along smoothly for you this week even if you do have to be on duty from 11:30 to 3:30.

Sometimes during the day even while I'm working I think of you and if I have a few spare minutes I like to write to you. I agree with what you said in Sunday's letter, dear – phooey on that belief that work should come first + pleasure after. You + I like – or I should say would rather be with each other all the time, heh dear? Well, maybe we will be soon.

Dear, you said in Sunday's letter that it wouldn't take us long to adjust when we're married + that we should wait at least two years before raising a family (having one or two children). Yes, dearest, if the war continues for a year or so it might take us a little longer to adjust to each other than it would ordinarily because we'll only see each other once in a while but even so, dearest, we'll adjust in time + during this time we can be saving for our future home (I don't mean owning a home) but saving for furniture, etc. Then when the war is over + you are home + we're settled – we'll have some children I hope. So you see there will be three stages that we'll go through. The first is the adjustment period, 2nd saving + planning for our home during this time + then having our children. It probably will take two years for all this – but no matter how long it takes, just think of all the happiness we two will have together – working together. All these thoughts are about the future, dearest.

For the next four months we will be concentrating more on the wedding itself + the next time you come home, dearest, as I said in my other letters, you can tell me just how you'd like everything + between both of us we can plan a nice wedding. I won't mind, darling, taking care of all the details – it would be nice tho if the both of us could go down to see Father O'Connell (about in Feb. or March) + ask him about the procedure that is if you should go to see the priest at the Fort or not. As time goes on, dearest, everything will work out – don't worry.

Yes, dearest, as you said God was very good to us in having us meet each other. I'm very thankful too. I know too that I could never be happy with anyone else. I knew it almost from the first time we met at the Ritz – of course I didn't realize it right at the first meeting but I always felt that we belonged together somehow. Life sure would be miserable + empty, dearest, without you.

Tomorrow (the 13th) you'll be at Ft. Devens one whole year. Remember last year, darling when Cele, Charlie + I went to the station to see you off? I felt so badly, but tried not to let you know, Walter dear. You've been lucky, tho, so far, being stationed at Devens for a whole year. Look at Elwood – he's been in England since last October. I hope you stay either in Devens or the New England states at least for the duration. During the past year, I've missed you so much, sweetheart + I know you must have wished lots of times you were home with your honey bunch (me) – ha ha.

Received your Tuesday's letter tonight – I like your letters so much, Walter dear. It must be hard for you to write each + every day – I realize it tho, dearest + appreciate your efforts so much.

Glad you enjoyed the candy I sent (as much of it as you were able to get after the fellows had some – ha ha). I hope the fruit cake won't be stale by the time you open it.

Yes I suppose it's too much to hope for – that you can get a pass again this coming week-end but if you don't happen to be listed, apply for one, heh, dearest, I won't count on it at all – I usually go to the show on Saturday + am home by 10:30 so even if you do happen to come, I'll be here. Darling, whenever you do come home from now on, no matter how late you get into Bpt. stop at 1440 – we're all usually up late on Saturdays anyway + I'd love to see you – I mean any time in the future that you happen to get a pass.

I'm glad you did so well firing the 45 pistols – I'll bet it was fun.

I wish you could be with me too, dearest, when I feel in this lovable mood. I still feel that way + probably will 'till about Friday or Saturday. I'm surely an old love bug, heh, dearest. I'd just like to be close to you + have you hold me in your arms – you understand, darling.

Dear, you're so sincere in everything you say + so frank about everything. I know you hesitated up till now to talk much about marriage because it takes you longer than I to think everything out + make decisions – you think very slowly + decide on things very slowly but once you make up your mind, you're sure heh, dearest? This isn't any fault – dear, a lot of people are like this. You want everything to be "100%" right as you say. In a way, Walt, it's a good thing one of us is this way. I am very impulsive but together we'll make a very good pair, heh, dear? (ha ha).

I love you so much, sweetheart, you're such a good boy.

Take care of yourself, sweetheart, + lots + lots of luck in your second year in the Army. I want the best for you always.

Lots of big hugs + kisses

X X X X X X Ritamarie X X X X X X

Wednesday Nite

Day Room

Dear Rita,

Hows my Sweet little irish Colleen today Bet you are feeling in the pink, and in a Lovable Mood also, Heh Dear. Bunny, you are so sweet, that's better now. I mean the pen that I am using, furnished in the day Room. I just filled it up with some ink.

Bunny, yes dear, I will try my utmost to continue to progress with my reading and also keep my ambitious desire's up to par. Heh dear. Just as you say, they will pay devedents later, as they alway's do.

Today, it was quite cold up in these hills, but I got my long John's, on and my nice warm socks on, that Cele sent to me for Christmas, they sure do come in handy.

Cele is such a Nice person, She is so understanding and has aquired, quite a wisdom, and knowlege of people for her age.

Bunny, you will even do better, just give you a little more time. Bunny, you are a, chip off the old Lavery Block. And what a honor. Yes dearest, on my next trip home, we will accomplish so much more towards our coming Marriage. Heh dear. Bunny, I bet you are still wishing that I could be with you right now, so you and I could snooze and hooge and oh be so happy in each other's arms. Bunny, you and I have such a fine Love. You and I get along so well. We never do fight like a lot of other couples. do we dear. Thats because of your ingenewatey and fine Mentalitiy.

So nice of Pat Smith to Send you those nice inbroidered dish towel's. Maybie, you will have such a nice selection of gifts, by the time we are, two little pigies. Ha. Ha. Ha. Married and all happily Married. Bunny. you will make such a good little Wifie, you and I will make each other so happy. Making, someone else happy and doing Something for some one you love that in turn makes you and I happy. thats the way God have planned things. If a person just Seeks his own happiness and desires and good times he never, finds much Joy and goodness out of life. Heh dear. What philosph.

Love Walter

Thursday, Jan. 13th.

Dearest,

Today is pay day for all E.W. Carpenterites (ha ha). That big raise I got went into effect today. Now I get $39.00 gross pay + after all deductions are made it amounts to $29.96. You + I will never be rich I guess, heh, darling? (ha ha). Having money is nice but not one of the most important things in life – I don't think – You + I can be happy without a lot of it, heh, dearest?

Do you remember I told you Bill Hughes had been moved from New Mexico? Well, now he's in Virginia at Langly Field + Betty is living with him too. His brother-in-law works in the factory here + he said both Betty + Bill said they'd never want to "stay-put" in one place again. They like to keep traveling all the time. It looks from this that Bill must intend to stay in the Army even after the war is over. He's been moved a lot since he went in – I don't see how they could like that kind of a life after the war, do you, dear? They can never have a home or even a family that way.

Mr. Trefry was talking to John Sorenson on the phone this morning about some inquiries we sent them on screw machine work. The inquiries were sent in this morning from Ellsworth Steel + were signed by him. We're not going to have them do the work tho, the prices are too high. I told Mr. Trefry that "Swede" was a friend of yours + he asked me how old he was. I said in his early twenties + Mr. Trefry said he sounds much older over the phone. He must be smart, heh, darling? I don't see how he's stayed out of the Army this long, do you? I'm sure he could be replaced in his work. Maybe he's a 4-F. Ruth, his sister, doesn't work at the Remington any more – she left there + now works in Casco's. I meet her once in a while on the bus. She always asks how you are. I told her we were planning on getting married in May (if everything worked out) + she seemed very glad. She's a nice girl I think but is extremely nervous + inclined to be self-centered. She calls John her "kid brother" – says he's a Mama's boy (ha ha).

5:45 pm – I only had to work till 5 tonight, dear, + now I'm home + just finished reading your Wednesday's letter.

I'm glad you're managing to keep warm in spite of the cold weather 'way up in Ft. Devens with your long Johns on (ha ha) + the socks Cele gave you.

 Yes, dearest, I still feel in a lovable mood – I wish I could be in your arms + kiss you for a long, long time but probably we won't see each other 'till about the 29th of this month, but whenever you do come home again, dearest, I'll be glad to see you – not just because I miss your loving, kisses etc. but I miss just being with you, talking, + our fine companionship.

 I know tho, dearest, that you might want to straighten out some things with Jack about the children the next time you come – those things are really more important right now than the desire of you + I to be together. Don't think, dearest, that when I talk about our coming marriage, I've forgotten about your sorrow – our sister, Lil. I think of her every day – all the suffering she had in her life – not only when she was sick but all she had to go thru with Jack. Please, don't think will you, dearest, that I'm thinking of myself only in talking about our marriage + that I think getting that straightened out is the most important thing right now. If you do have to talk to Jack the next time you come, you can go up there by yourself – or if you go to Trumbull – I don't think it would be right for me to go with you – after all, it's something personal between your whole family + I'd feel out of place being with you. But maybe by the time you come, everything will be pretty well straightened out. I haven't talked to Helene since last Friday night I don't know how things are now. But by spring, dearest, I think we'll be perfectly justified in thinking of our own happiness (getting married) don't you?

 I'm sure your sister, Lil, is in Heaven now that she's getting her reward for all the goodness in her life. I think of her + also of you – I know when you're on post during the long hours you think a lot about her, the children, etc. but don't worry, dearest, everything will work out for the best.

Lots of love, dearest
Rita "Bunny" Rabbit (ha ha).
X X X X X X X X X X X X

Saturday
12:30 Noon
Day Room

Dear Rita,

 Just had my diner and am now in the day room relaxing and writing to my Sweetheart, you Bunny dear. Bunny hope that you have a very nice weekend, and that you are not to lonesome.

 Rita, wish I could have you in my arms, and hold you, <u>oh</u> so close to me. Bunny you are so sweet, what a nice feminine girl you are.

 Bunny, It will be so nice when we see each other again soon. Hope that it is very soon. Heh dear. I miss you so much. just as much as you miss me.

 Wish I could, attend church with you on Sunday.

 I enjoy going with you so much. You are a real religious girl. thats so good. <u>dearest</u>.

How I would love to hug and tug you dearest. Bunny I am alway's in the Mood to Love you. <u>Oh</u> Boy.

Love From your Future Husband.

Walter

Bunny, dear, I still feel like writing to you. See Dear hos much I enjoy writing to you.

I wrote to Ernie and Dot yesterday, they are so happy, now that they are married, I told them you and I hope to catch up to them real soon, In <u>May</u> if every thing works out as we plan. Heh dear. Bunnny.

Bunny, how I wish you and could be together tonite to go out for a nice evening of fun and have a nice time together. Talking and Dancing, and just being together in generally.

Be a good girl dear. Rita dear.

Love

From your Future Husband

Walter

Saturday Night – almost midnight

Dear Sweetheart,

I'm writing this letter in bed just before I go to dreamland for the night (hope I dream of you, dear).

Your Thursday's letter was waiting for me when I got home from downtown this afternoon (you seem to be getting my letters faster than I do yours).

You said you enjoy my letters so much. I'm awfully glad you do, dearest, + I've noticed too, that you've been writing longer letters lately yourself + as you said, you're getting used to writing now + really like to. I love to receive your letters whether they're long or short – they make me very happy. From now on, dearest, my letters will probably concern thoughts that I have about our coming marriage. The way I figure it, I most likely won't see you until about the end of this month + then after that – the end of February, March + April so I think we can get a few things settled (little details) in our letter-writing in the meantime + then when we do see each other, we can decide on the important things. So, dearest, from now on, if I ask you any questions that I have in mind or ask your opinion about some little things, will you please answer them? I know you won't mind will you, darling, because I want your opinion + answers – it'll be your wedding too, dearest (ha ha ha – as if you didn't know it, heh, Walt?)

Dear, you're always telling me I treat you so nice. Why shouldn't I, dearest, you're such a fine person + I love you so much. You know I want your happiness first – you surely deserve lots + lots of kindness + good treatment.

Glad you heard from Ernie – when you answer his letters, darling, would you be careful of your spelling, etc. because Dot reads them + a few times before, she passed remarks about your writing + spelling (in a kidding sort of a way) but I don't want her or Ernie to think you can't spell correctly — you can, dearest, if you take your time writing + think, or use the dictionary as often as you have to. O.K. dear? I hope you don't mind my telling you this, but I imagine you feel the same way yourself about it as I do.

I'll write more tomorrow (Sun.) dearest, I'm falling asleep (almost). How I wish you were next to me here (in bed) just so I could fall asleep with your arms around me. Do I shock you, dear, saying things like that? I'll bet I do.

Lots + lots of love, sweetheart. X X X X X X

Sunday 12:30 pm. 1/16

Hello Dearest,

I just finished doing a few chores here in the house, (making beds, dusting, etc.). I hope everything is going along smoothly for you, today, Walter. You're probably busy — you haven't called up but maybe you will later on.

Last night when I wrote I didn't tell you about what I did yesterday afternoon or evening.

Mary + I went to the show last night + saw "Jack London" with Michael O'Shea (a new actor) + Susan Hayward. It was very good — you'd like it, dear. After the show Mary + I had our usual snack + chat in the "Star". I like to go out with Mary — she's a nice girl — very hard to know but after you do know her you can't help like her. I think when you met her, Walt, she gave you the impression she thought a lot of herself but I don't think she really is that way.

Yesterday afternoon Cele + I (also Eleanor) went to look at some bridal material just to get an idea of the price. We only went in one store (the one Mrs. Senger recommended) but they didn't have just what I wanted. They did have some white taffeta that was rather nice tho + it wasn't too expensive by the yard. They expected to get the kind I'm looking for in about a week. I tried to get the "Brides Magazine" that comes out every three months to give me an idea for a pattern for a gown but every magazine store I tried was out of it already. It must be a popular magazine. So you see I didn't accomplish much just by looking around, did I, dearest? Oh well, I think there's lots of time yet but Cele doesn't. She says we only have a certain number of Saturdays to look for anything + it's almost February. I tried on a few suits yesterday too — the new spring ones are in already. There were a few nice ones but what prices! I'm getting so I hate to go shopping on Saturdays — it's so crowded + you get so tired out going from one store to another + then the prices are atrocious — you feel as tho you're getting nothing for your money. That's just another one of the effects of the war.

If you can give me $15 each time you get paid, darling from now until May, you'll have $235.<u>00</u> by then. You'll have to have a trousseau too, Walt (ha ha ha). Really, tho, dearest, you'll have to use some of the money you have saved to buy a nice pair of shoes, a robe, slippers, + I was thinking you'd look better if you wore one of those blouses without that belt effect in the back (the straight fitted style) – what do you think about it, dear? Maybe you could borrow one for the occasion. Then the ring that you'll buy + the paying of the priest + for a little trip – also flowers for Eleanor + a gift for the best man. You'll probably spend about $150.<u>00</u> for your expenses – maybe more I don't know.

I was wondering if you'd like a wedding ring too, Walt. If you do I'd buy it. Some fellows do like them + some don't. It's up to yourself, dear. The only reason I think you might like one is that seeing we won't be with each other much it might make you feel a little closer by wearing one. But it's entirely up to you, sweetheart, whatever way you feel about it – if you'd rather not wear one, it's perfectly alright.

These are all little details, dearest, that you can think about – you don't have to decide everything right now – they will take care of themselves.

I just finished talking with you on the 'phone, dear, I was so glad to talk to you. You sounded as tho you were in good spirits, dearest, I'm glad. It's a good thing you're on town patrol for a few days, dear – it relieves you a little from the interior guard duty. I had to laugh at how excited you got when I asked you if you were on from 4 to 8. (ha ha).

You said you were going to write a letter after your call – I'll bet it'll be a nice mushy one, dearest. I know you (ha ha).

Darling, I miss you so much – I do hope you can come home the 29th (two more weeks). You asked me if Thomas was working. Well, as I told you he isn't + is supposed to go in Wed. morning to take the test on those cards but I imagine it'll be the same as the other three times he was supposed to take it. He won't go over there when Wed. comes.

He's certainly making this house miserable (everyone in it). There's always that tension when he's around. Jeanie is getting so she's out all the time – either at the show or her girlfriend's just to get away – so she won't be here when he is. I'm in every night but stay either in the kitchen or in my room. He just sits in the living room by the hour reading or staring into space or talking to Cele + Charlie who both sympathize with him a lot. I can't sit at the table + eat when he does – I almost get sick. It's all a state of mind I guess but I just can't be tolerant or understanding as far as he's concerned, he's so low.

Well, dearest, I always seem to be telling you about this, don't I? It's something that's hard to explain to anyone. Cele + Charlie get mad at me + Jeanie + that's the way it is – continual tension + friction. I hope my nerves don't get the best of me – it's getting harder all the time to keep my self-control. This would be a much happier home if he wasn't here. I know it.

Dearest, I'll be thinking of you + maybe the next two weeks will go by fast. I hope so. I love you so much, dear. I have to go downstairs now + see if I can eat some dinner (if Thomas is finished). I had to leave in the middle of it – I just couldn't stand eating while he was there. Don't worry, darling, things might work out – I can still hold my own.

Love Always,

X X X X X X X X X X X X Rita

X – Here's a great big kiss for you, dear. In a few weeks I'll give you some nice ones in person (ha ha).

Lots of love, Walter dear.

Rita

Sunday 1:25 P.M.

Day Room

Darling Rita.

It was so nice talking to you over the phone. The operator was either new, or very nice, as they are some times. I mean very leanient to us boy's as far as the time is concerned while talking. She let us talk at least four minutes, heh dear. She must have been new. because she only told me to drop 40 cents in for three minutes. Ha. Ha – Ha. I told her she must be cheating her self or something. Ha – Ha. I should of not said anything. Heh dear. I would of saved 10 cents Ha – Ha – Ha.

Bunny. So happy to know that you and Mary Buccino get along so well and attend a Movie each weekend. Give my regards to the Smith's when ever you visit them. At any time, Heh dear.

I Bet little Jeanie is quite a kills with all the Boy's on the Avenue. She is a cute kid, Heh dear. Bunny. I was dreaming about you last nite. I dreamed I had you in my arms, and that we were married and I was Kissing you and loving you oh so nice. All this took place while we were in bed thats the way my dreams were. Bunny. See I even dream about you in my Sleep. See what you do to me. Oh Boy. In my dreams, I was tickleing you and holding you. oh so close to me.

Bunny, I must be a big devil, when I even dream about you while sleeping. Bunny. I Love you so much. Wish I were in your arms and Kissing you, oh so nice and being close to you. Talking about our Future and coming Marriag. Bunny. We are so much in Love with each other. Heh dear. Be a good girl, and don't make eyes at all the Boys. Ha. Ha. Ha.

Last Nite, I and three other M.P.s where on duty in Lowell. There were more drunks then usual in town. Because of a Suplementary pay and the fact that Some of the boy's most be due to be shipped in to other ports that's the other outfits I am talking about. So they wanted to have there last fling in Lowell before they leave.

Before we through at Nite. There were eleven (11) total, locked up in the Loose Cow. If they are to tough and wise, we leave them cook in the cells for a few day's the others we take back to Camp. It sure is a Mad House here in Lowell. There are about twenty thousand women running around Loose. There are twenty thousand Men from Lowell in the arm forces alone. So that accounts for the number of women running Loose they even Start to try and hug and tug us M.P.s So you can see, how lonesome, or Something those women are. They are just like wild. Bears. just let out of the cage. Ha Ha Ha. They drink pretty heavy also.

We saw two pretty good floor shows. The people here go for that short of stuff. you think Bpt. is bad you should see this place. its like a Mad house. You know how it is around a army camp. We got plenty to eat also had plenty of nice <u>french</u> <u>fries</u> and nice hot coffee. There is also a nice long Ball Room (Commandore Ballroom) that we go into now and then, to make sure there is no ruff stuff. As if we could do much to prevent it. with only three M.P.s and two or three civilian cop's to help at the time, that's until we get re inforcements. the Radio cars that the cops have Radio's in, that's how when we have to much to handle we get help.

Ha – Ha – Ha.

What fun. <u>Oh yeah</u>.

Love <u>Walter</u>

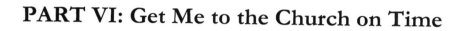

PART VI: Get Me to the Church on Time

The Wedding Date (Sort of) Draws Near

In early 1944, Walter transferred to Camp Edwards on Cape Cod, when he was finally assigned to motor pool duty.

In Walter's letters, he expressed at one point his reluctance to come home every weekend. During the war, society looked down on shirkers typified by 4-F types. Many men were overseas and in combat, including several of Walter's cousins. His cousin Leo Sablofski was at sea serving in the U.S. Navy. Coming home too frequently suggested shirker status, which Walter wanted to avoid. Rita, on the other hand, was glad to see Walter as often as possible. She encouraged him to come home whenever he could, arguing in her letters that there was no shame on a soldier coming home on pass. In one letter, she commented that the cost of coming home, such as for train fare, would be balanced because if Walter stayed at Army camp, he would inevitably spend money there.

Rita carried the burden of all the wedding planning, with the uncertainty of when Walter would be allowed a 10-day furlough. She hesitated to purchase fabric for her wedding dress as she couldn't be sure of the furlough date. She also worried that their friends Dot and Ernie would not be able to attend as it would be difficult for Ernie to coordinate his leave at the same time.

Along with the wedding planning stress, Rita continued to deal with the tension created by Thomas, and the worry over Lillian's motherless children.

Letters: January 18, 1944 – April 14, 1944

Tuesday Jan. 18th '44 noon

Hello Sweetheart,

I've just finished eating lunch + have a few minutes so thought I'd start my daily letter to you.

The weather is beautiful today – for January – it's not too cold + the sun is shining. This month is going by rather fast. Before we know it, dearest, it'll be May + that nice couple by the name of Walter Klein + Rita Lavery will be walking down the middle aisle (I hope) + will be Mr. + Mrs. Walter J. ten minutes later (ha ha). Kleiny will have to have a few drinks before, to calm his nerves + maybe Rita will too (ha ha). Won't we be the happy couple tho, dearest! Of course we will.

Last night I called your sister Helene + everything seems to be about the same on White St. The children are well – Helene still has a cough from her cold but is taking medicine for it. She said she's been staying in the house on account of her cold but thought she'd like to go to the show at the end of this week but said she'd call me later + let me know what night she could make it.

Dearest, tonight I received three letters from you all at once written Saturday, Sunday + Monday. They were nice ones, darling – very mushy (ha ha).

You said in yesterday's letter that you had written to your father, Helene + Emma. I'm glad, Walt because when I was talking to Helene she said you hadn't written – I told her you probably didn't have time but I guess she thought I was making excuses for you. It would be a good idea, dearest if you wrote to Helene + your father once a week + the rest of the family once in a while (once a month) just short letters, dear, to your father + Helene to tell them how you are etc.

Yes, dear, I've wished so much as you do too that I could be in your arms – in bed too. It will be so much better for us when we're married – we can express our love to the fullest + it will be right in the eyes of God + everyone. The way it is now – when we're together we always get aroused but have to restrain ourselves because naturally our conscience tells us it's all wrong. After we're married, darling + you are away + get aroused as you do now at least, you'll know that when we are together we can express our love to the utmost but when you look forward to your visits home now, you know we can only go so far – if you understand what I mean. It doesn't seem right to me to go on much longer the way we are – single + having to hold our feelings in all the time.

Don't worry, dearest, about my "making eyes at the boys". You are the only boy I would want to "make eyes at" (ha ha). Anyway, as I told you before – even if I did want to (which I don't) the cream-of-the-crop is in the Army or

Navy now – so you see, darling, you needn't worry. (ha ha). The only place I ever go is to the show anyway, or visiting someone.

I don't suppose there's any chance of your coming home this week-end heh, darling? I do hope you can make it the 29th tho – it will be 4 weeks then.

I finally managed to get a copy of the "Brides Magazine" Mrs. Singer told Cele about. There are only about 2 gowns in it that I could wear – that are nice + full.

I'm really afraid to go ahead + buy material or anything for the wedding because there is no assurance whatsoever that you will get a furlough in May. I don't know what to do. Cele thinks I should go ahead + get everything I need anyway + I can always use the things whenever you do get it (furlough) whether it's in May or any other month. Mrs. Singer said she should have the material for the gown a few months ahead at least because she has to sew for other people too. I think I should wait 'till March before I buy anything. What do you think dearest? I was thinking last nite where are we going to get liquor or beer for drinks if we have a reception there's such a shortage? (ha ha – what a thing to think about, heh dear?). Cele said maybe my cousin James (downtown) could get some – I don't see how tho, it's against the law to sell it outside of taverns. Oh well, I guess we should be sure there is going to be a wedding before we think about those things, heh, dear? (ha ha).

If you were here now I'd give you some nice big kisses, darling. I just feel like it. I'm an old love bug – ha ha.

Love Always,

X X X X X X Rita X X X X X X

Tuesday Noon

Day, Room.

Dear Rita

Just finnished my diner, we had a nice steak and the works, that go with it. Yum yum, it was good. Also nice desert and coffee. Last Nite, was a nice quite nite on patrol in Lowell. Saw plenty of good entertainment had good food. Got in bed at 2:30 got up at 11:30 – good Nine hours of Sleep. Oh Boy. I feel so good now. I feel as tho, I want to hug and kiss you dearest, for a whole hours or two. Bunny, I miss you and your nice Loving. Bunny on my next trip home I am going to spend, two whole hrs, kissing and hugging, you.

Received your very nice long letters that you wrote Friday – Sat and Sunday dearest.

Bunny. I Love you So much. you are my Future little Wifie, and what a nice Wifie you will make, Oh Boy. Dearest Bunny.

Tonite I am not Slated for any duty. So I think I will go to the Ayer U.S.O. maybe See Bud Monahan. Love Walter.

Wednesday 1/19/44 6:30 pm

Hello Sweetheart,

I just finished eating supper (really my dinner) + also finished reading your Tuesday's letter for the second time.

Yes, dearest, you do get good food in the Army — that is, all the boys in this country. There's a girl in my office who's brother is in No. Africa + he writes home all the time saying he's half-starved — says he hasn't had a decent meal since he left the United States which was in October. See how lucky you are, dearest. I know you must realize it, tho.

Glad you manage to get plenty of sleep when you're on town patrol. I'll bet you'd love to get 9 hours every night, heh darling?

Dear, you sure were in a lovable mood when you wrote yesterday's letter. I know you save all of your love for me, dear + that whenever you go to the U.S.O. + fool + kid all the girls it doesn't mean a thing. I know it'll always be like that with you, dearest, even after we're married — so you see, darling, I trust you completely all the time — don't ever think I haven't complete trust + confidence in you.

Dearest you said you received the long letters I wrote Sat. Sun. + Mon. but you didn't answer any of them. Maybe you intend to straighten out our little problems on getting married when you come home next time, dear, I don't know + that's why you didn't mention anything on the subject. In any case, dear, I hope you are giving some of the things I'm writing about lately some thought. Maybe you don't what to talk much about the wedding 'till you tell your father — it's alright with me, dearest, if you don't want to answer but would rather wait 'till you come home. Just let me know + if you'd rather not have me write about our wedding we'd surely better decide everything when you come home.

You say the next visit home you're going to spend two whole hours just loving me — kissing etc. Dear, I wish we could have a week-end together like we used to — when you go around visiting we have no time at all to ourselves. I know your father expects you to if he lets you take his car + I suppose you do have to visit to a certain extent but since you've been in the Army you've never given me an entire week-end. Think back + you'll see I'm right, dearest. Now I know you will want to go visit White St. until things are straightened out there — it's perfectly alright with me if you do, dear, but I hope after we're married + you come home week-ends we can have more time to ourselves.

Dearest, I miss your loving too. I hope you can get a pass in a few weeks (the 29th). We have so much to talk about.

Love Always,
big ones → X X X X X X Rita X X X X X X

Wednesday Nite 6: P.M. 1/19/44

Dear Rita,

Here I am again dear, alway's bothering you with my chatter. Heh Bunny. Rita dear. It seems as tho I have the desire to write to you twice, each day.

Bunny. See how I am falling so Madly in Love with you, that I could not Love you any more than I do. I Love you so much Darling that we have the Strongest Love that two young people could attain. Tomorrow I am Slated to work on that, <u>must do</u>, K.P. – Ha – Ha. Hrs from 6 A.M. – to 6 P.M. with a little time off in between. Tonite, I am going to take in a movie and later get to bed early, to, <u>charge my</u> Batteries. Bunny wish I could get Some very nice long Kisses from you, Say about for two Hrs of Kissing. Hum – Hum. <u>Oh</u> Boy. dearest.

Separation only finds and makes our Love grow stronger. Our Love is <u>100</u>. Hundred percent. The finest that God can bestowe upon us dear.

No I dont think that I stand a chance of getting a pass this coming weekend. But one never knows.?

<u>Cele</u> is right dear. go ahead and buy what you will Need dear for Our Wedding. Early is Better than being to late. And one Never Knows when I will be able to get off on exactly what day our Wedding will be on. Yes dearest, we will be a happy couple, very happy couple. Oh Boy. It it chills me dear to even write or think about our Marriage.

Yes dearest. after we are Mr + Mrs Walter J. Klein, we will be able to express ourslevs to the Utmost. Both physically + Mentally, Spiritually, emotionally, and live a rich and full life. Oh Boy. Bunny. You make me so happy. dearest.

I Love you Bunny more.

Love <u>Walter</u>.

Thursday 1/20th.

Hello Darling,

Here it is – pay day again but with each pay day it seems as tho I have more + more financial problems. I'm always "in the red', dearest, isn't that terrible? I figured out a budget for the next 5 weeks for myself + it looks as tho I won't be out of debt until Feb. 17th. I'll be so glad when we're married, dearest – then you can keep our money intact – you're a good manager, dear. I suppose you're wondering why I have so many bills right now + what they are.

Well first of all I charged some things in Read's for Christmas (total $13.79) which has to be paid by Feb. 10th – then I have to save for a big insurance that I pay every 3 months ($12.89 due March 5th). Besides these bills I have an appointment with the eye doctor for an examination on Feb. 1st. (He'll charge $5.<u>00</u> + if I have to get rest glasses they'll cost about $15 or $20.) Then, if you'll recall a week ago I was supposed to get a permanent (last Friday) but when I went to get it they didn't have any record that I had made an appointment + couldn't take me that night because they had 2 other people for permanents so I had to make another appointment for Jan. 27th – a week from tonight which will cost $7.<u>50</u>. Isn't that an awful price? They are much more expensive than they used to be. (they use the war as an excuse for the increase). Besides all of these bills I borrowed some money from our fund too, darling, but don't be mad at me – I'm putting it back – I've put some of it back already.

So as you see, darling, I'm just n.g. (no good) as a manager of money. But as I said before, by February 17th I won't owe anything providing I can stick to the budget I've figured out. I forgot – March 15th my income tax will be due – I haven't figured it out yet but it shouldn't be as much as other years as they've been deducting a withholding tax every week. Oh me! I do get myself into some awful messes, heh, dear? It's a good thing you can manage money, heh, dearest 'cause if you couldn't we'd end up in the "hotel". (ha ha). Don't worry, dearest, I'll get straightened out soon.

About my going to the eye doctor – for a long time my eyes have been bothering me – that is – they water a lot + are always tired so that I feel like rubbing them all the time. It's just that they're strained – there's nothing wrong with the sight so if I do need them it will only be when I'm working or reading – I won't have to wear them on the street. Maybe I won't need them at all – who knows? I'm going to Dr. Gildea in the Professional Bldg. on Lafayette St. – he's an eye specialist not just an optometrist + couldn't get an appointment with him 'till Feb. 1st.

Last night I read a good story, dear. The name of it was "Never Forget the Spring" + it was about a young couple who were married + had a little girl + when the war came the husband enlisted in the Army + his wife + little girl followed him from camp to camp. The story ends where he's accepted for O.C.S. + his wife + child go back home. Then he's sent to No. Africa when he gets his commission. It was a good story because it told about all the heroine's experiences in going from one town to another with her husband – all the hardships she endured etc. – very true to life.

5:45 pm: I'm home now from work, dearest + just finished reading your Wednesday's letter. Gosh, dearest, you certainly are in a bad way these days for want of some loving. I wish I could be there, dear, to give you some. I'd like some nice kisses too. You know me, heh, Walt? Yes, we'll have to make up for lost time when you come home – but definitely! (ha ha).

When the boys kid you about "how could I go with you," etc., just tell them they don't know you like I do or they'd love you too (ha ha). Tell them when you turn on that personality of yours I fall like a ton of bricks (ha ha). That's the truth, dearest tho, they couldn't know you the way I do.

Dearest, you said you were off Tuesday night + went to a show + expected to go to a movie Wed. nite. What schedule are you on now since you finished town patrol duty? That is, what are you doing during the day time (besides thinking of me – ha ha).

Darling, you say you can hardly wait 'till I'm your wife. Why not get married in April then as I wanted in the first place? (Ha ha) Leave it to me to suggest this – heh darling – just as soon as you admit a thing like that. Well, this is leap year you know so it's my privilege (ha ha). Really, dear, you'll be more apt to be in Ft. Devens in April than in May – I have the feeling you'll be moved – I don't know why. It just doesn't seem possible that we could plan everything for May + then have it all work out. We might have a better chance of it working out in April – you were supposed to get a furlough in the spring anyway weren't you, dearest? May will be alright with me – that is if we could only be halfway sure you'll be in Devens then. By April, I mean towards the end of April. Darling, that's just one of the things we have to get straightened out when you come home (the date).

Well, sweetheart, I guess you know how happy it makes me to think of us being married. It isn't that I think that everything will wonderful then – that we won't have any problems or anything but the wonderful part of it is that we'll be able to face all the joys, sorrows etc. <u>together</u>. That's the wonderful part of being married. There is something beautiful + a lot of other words that I can't express – something that isn't tangible anyway, about two people getting married + working together, planning + living in complete harmony together – even when the two people are separated (as you + I will be) we can both work together in making our marriage fine + lasting – I'm sure it will be everything that we hope for. I am much more confident than you are, dearest, - what do you think? Is it only because of the difference of religion that you are so hesitant? If we are both so willing to meet each other half way or even further, why should there be such a lack of confidence on your part, dearest? Is it because you're afraid you will fail me in any way or because I might in some way fail you? Don't feel hurt at my asking you these questions, dearest – it's just that if you feel that there's something holding you back – I'd like you to tell me frankly – there is no reason now why either of us should keep our thoughts locked up.

Well, dear, I'm not worrying, I just thought I'd write what I'm thinking so we can iron everything out when you come home. I love you so much – you know I want your happiness first, dearest.

Hope we see each other in another week – don't you dearest?

Love Always,

X X X X X X Rita X X X X X X

X ← (half hour long) yum-yum (ha ha)

Friday Nite 9:00 P.M.
Lutheran Service Center
Ayer, Mass

Hello dearest,

Received your nice long letter and I am so happy to hear from you – each day. It was a nice letter dearest. Boy. I look forward for them. Ha. Ha. See how you spoiled me. Yes dear, I am quite a fair Budgeter. leave it to me dearest.

Hope your eyes are O.K. and that they only need a little rest. Heh dearest. Dont work so hard.

So glad that you – read nice store's [stories] now and then to enjoy and pass the time. Yes dear I have a pretty fair personality. Ha – Ha – Ha – I Love my Self. heh dear.

Tomorrow I am Slated to go on Interior guard duty. Probably tho <u>2</u> or <u>3</u>th.

I think relief. This passed weeks I have been on my So called School week. But it is really a work weeks. – Heh dearest.

Dearest, <u>April</u> is not a Bad Month for our Marriage. Thats a good Idea. Heh dear Leave it to you for some good suggestion's. Bunny we will talk and Straighten out our little problems, Heh dear. Religion, has played a big part, the biggest part of all in not having our Marriage sooner.

I wanted my people to get used to the idea, and so they would not be so surprized to the idea.

No I never though of any other fact, that would hinder us, and not be worked out with a little time.

No dearest. I belive you will make the finest of a wife, that any girl could make. And never fail me.

Bunny you are the Sweetest girl in the World. Talking with my Daddy will anser a lot of our problems.

On my next trip home will <u>Settle</u> a lot. Date of Marriage, type of Marriage, What my Father thinks of the Idea. and everything in general.

Dont worry dear. Every thing will work out. I am sure dear.

yes dear, Marriage is the best bussiniss that two people can Unit into. It's a good bussines that pay, es divindients. Big Friede to:

This coming, Saturday. January, 30th, should be the date. Oh Boy. Dear, I can hardly wait, until that day.

Bunny, I love you so much. You are such a sweet girl. Be a good girl. Like alway's. Heh dear.

Love From Your Walter

Lear <u>year</u>, oh Boy Bunny thats a good idea. Ha – Ha – Ha. Yes, dear, we will meet each other alway's half way. In that way we will alway's make a go of our Marriage. Bunny, you are a good girl. A Hundred percent, with me alway's.

Love Galore To my Fiancee
From Your Fiance Walter.
Be Good – Bunny Dearest.
Rita Marie Lavery

Saturday 1/22/44 – 6:00p.m.

Dearest,

I'm writing this just before I eat my supper.

How's everything with you, sweetheart? I hope you are rested up by this time after your K.P. duty that you had Thursday. It was nice of you to write Thursday, dear, I know you didn't have much time – I received the letter this morning. It sure was a "mushy" one, darling.

I guess I'll spend Saturday evening at home because Mary Buccino can't go to the show she has to visit one of her relatives with her mother. I called your sister Helene last night + she thought she could go tomorrow night (Sunday) but this afternoon she called me + said she didn't feel well enough. She had Dr. Thomas again during the week as she couldn't seem to get rid of her cold –

had aches + pains all over her + a cough – I think she feels the way I did last year (after you went away) – all runned down. The doctor told her she was runned down + too thin, that she should try to get out of that house + go home where she could get plenty of rest. She was very discouraged when I talked to her this afternoon – said she would have to do something very soon – didn't think she could stay there much longer as she's all tired out. She gets up at a quarter to six every morning, gets Jack's breakfast + does up his lunch sometimes – then during the day she always has housework – washing, ironing, cooking etc. Helene said too your father is discouraged + disgusted – being alone all the time + I guess he knows Helene doesn't feel so good + worries about her. It's certainly a shame that Helene can't go home + take care of herself – she's in an awful mess – staying there day after day + no one making any attempt to make some arrangements about the care of the children. You seem to be the only one in the family who can get things straightened out. I can't see why your brother can't go up to Trumbull with your father + have a talk with Mr. + Mrs. Bridges seeing you're not home. I suppose he feels as tho it's none of his affair but someone should get going + do something – after all – leaving things to Jack, Helene will be there for the rest of her life.

If I were you, dearest, when you come home next time suggest to your father that the both of you go up + either have a talk with Jack or go to see his mother + father. Your father probably would go with you – even if it means spending a whole Sunday afternoon – it will be worth it – Helene would have a peace-of-mind anyway. Everyone in your family seems so helpless. You seem to be the only one (+ your father) who are "up + doing" – if you know what I mean. Don't worry, dearest, everything will work out somehow. As far as taking Jack's word that he'll be out of that house by March 1st, I don't see how he could be – where will he ever find a place to live – a rent – they're so scarce – so no one knows what he has in mind to do.

Dearest, please don't think I want to tell you what to do – it's up to you – it's your family's concern + not mine but it would be a good idea I think to go with your father + either talk to Jack or to his mother + father when you come home.

This afternoon I looked at some samples of material for a gown that the man in the store said I could order + he'd get it if I liked it. I thought I'd better have Mrs. Singer look at it first before buying anything. In the meantime I looked in Read's at some gowns ready-made + there were a few nice ones but I didn't try any on. There are so many pretty ones that I could choose from all ready made that it seems foolish to have Mrs. Singer make it. Then too, she's upset about Eddie going in the Army + said she might not be able to do it later on, as she might have to break up her home if he passes his physical for the Army – he's going to N. Haven in a few wks. for his exam. Eleanor looked around a little bit too for a gown. She won't have any trouble buying one – she's easy to fit.

I met your sister Emma + Dorothy + Eileen downtown this afternoon + Emma said she got your letter but the reason she didn't answer is that she really has nothing to write about. I said you really didn't expect her to write – you know she's busy etc.

Dearest, how I wish you were home tonight so we could enjoy each other's companionship + stay close to each other + talk - + of course have some nice kisses in between (ha ha). I miss you so much, dearest, I hope you can come home next week. When you do, I'll give you some great big hugs + kisses.

Well, dearest, I'll close now + try to get this letter out in the 7:15 mail so you'll get it Monday.

I love you, Walter J.

Love Always,
X X X X X X Rita X X X X X X
X X X X X X – (extra big ones)

Saturday 9:30 A.M.
Day. Room.

Dearest, Rita,

Hello Bunny dearest. Hows my Sweet little Irish girl today. Bunny. How I wish I were able to be coming home to see you dear over this weekend. But, I guess, you and I have to be patient and just wait until next Sat. Heh dearest. Rita. Bunny, I am still in that Nice Lovable Mood. Oh Boy. If I were coming home today, I would just hachet and hurry right down to 1440 to See my Darling Rita, and would I hug and kiss you dear. Bunny. I would do, my Love making, just like old times.

Bunny. I think of you each day.

Be a good girl Rita dear. Wait for me dear, and I will See you next week. We can Love each other, and talk about our Marriage. Bunny, you will make such a fine Wifie. Won't you dearest Rita. Bunny wish I were in your arms Hugging and Kissing you right now.

Bunny, you and I probably would have been Married a few Months sooner had our Religion been the Same.

But being different, it takes time for ajustment and a true understanding of each other's belief's. Other from that the other thoughts come second. I also think of my past work and future vocations after I get out of the Army. Married and Starting out again to provide for you and myself. But that comes only Secondary. Third thing I also alway's want to take care of my physical well being, which now is fine.

Other from that, we have no problems at all. And these problems are only Small ones in one sense of the word. You have not hardly any small problems, So you are all set for, our Matraimonial Jurney to a happy and Rich Life.

Each day Rita dear my Love for you Seems to grow, and grow, ever more stronger than ever, - it seems hardly posible that our Love could be any Stronger. But that's how it is dear. See dear what you do to me and I love it. Oh Boy.

Love Galore – from your very Soon <u>Groom</u>. Love – Walter.

Sunday 1/23/44 – 1:30 pm.

Dearest Walter,

I'm always so happy after talking with you on Sunday over the 'phone. I've come to the conclusion lately, dear, that it's worth 50¢ to call – really worth a lot more than that to talk to you, even if it is only for 3 minutes – remember darling, a short while ago we thought it wasn't worth it? – that we didn't have time to say much etc., but when you stop + think it really is nice that we can talk to each other once a week. The few Sundays you didn't call (a while ago) I felt lost. Just to know that you're well + everything is going along alright with you makes me happy.

Dearest I was only kidding you on the 'phone when I said you'd better start buying your trousseau (ha ha ha). I just wanted to see what you'd say. (ha ha). You have lots of time to buy the things you'll need.

I'm glad you have enough money to hold you over 'till next pay day. It was a good idea to buy your ticket ahead of time because if you didn't you might have spent the money. Try to hold the $6.00 this week, dear, as long as you can – I mean if you go to the show or anyplace use it sparingly (ha ha). because I haven't any of your money on hand now – it's all in the bank. Sometimes I keep some of it in my bureau in case you need it but Saturday Charlie took it to the bank + deposited it. I have to put some back, tho, that I borrowed from our fund but don't worry, dearest, I'll put some in every week. You now have $175.00 + I have $100.00 which is pretty good, heh dear? The $100 that I have, will buy my gown, veil + suit to wear away. The other things I'll need can be bought each week. As far as the breakfast + reception are concerned Cele has some money in the bank that's to be used for that – that's the way my mother would want it. Everything is awfully expensive now tho – gowns, veils, + clothes in general – also dinners the type that is served after a wedding. Most places now can only serve a small number of people as they can't get waiters + they can't guarantee enough food – the restaurants themselves are short of food. That's why sometimes I think it's foolish to bother with a reception in these times – maybe we should just have a breakfast (really a dinner) just for your family + mine + that's all, but we can decide those things as time goes on, dearest – we'll figure out something. In my family there are so many cousins, aunts, + uncles that we'd have to invite all of them or none of them – we couldn't have some + not others, see, darling? Just for the fun of it I figured out one day just about how many people we'd have to invite if we have a reception + there would be at least 75 people – mostly all of them Laverys – then of course you would want some of your relatives + close friends (like the Fishers) too. That just gives you an idea, dearest, of what we have to decide on – then, too, we have to be sure you can get time off to get married – that's the most important thing. (ha ha). Well, as I said before, as time goes on we'll straighten everything out I hope.

I told you on the 'phone I might go down + have a talk with Fr. O'Connell some night soon. The reason I was thinking about it so soon is because if you take the necessary instructions up at the Fort, I don't know how long it will take to complete them – maybe the priest couldn't take you each week, so I thought I'd better inquire from Father O'Connell just what procedure you are to follow + if he wants to see you, I'll go with you some Sunday when you're home. There's also a question I'd like to ask him – something I thought I was sure of but now I'm not – that is – will it be alright for your brother, Al, to be your best man as he is a non-Catholic? You see in the case of baptizing a baby in the Catholic church both people who stand up for the baby that is, who are to be the godparents, must be Catholic + some people say this is true also in case of marriage by a priest. Both attendants at a marriage are supposed to be Catholic. I knew this was so if there was a Mass but in our case there won't be a Mass so I can't see why it wouldn't be alright if your brother was best man but that's something I'll have to find out. I sure do hope he can be – I would like him to be + I know you would too. If I find out that it will be impossible, it'll be awfully hard to explain it to him or your family. I know you'll understand, dearest, that the rules of the Church aren't made by me or the priests but by God Himself + I can see where a person outside of the Religion would find it hard to understand. Well, we'll see + hope for the best.

Eleanor + Vin might be over for supper later this afternoon. Charlie is going to work at 4 o'clock so it'll be nice if they do come because Cele + I will be alone. Jeanie has gone to the Mosque this afternoon skating with about six or seven other girls. She has a lot of fun for herself – she started to go roller skating about a month ago at the Mosque + now she goes Friday nights + Sunday afternoons, she likes it so much. I kid her all the time + say it's probably not the skating she likes as much as the boys (ha ha). I think quite a few of the boys ask her to skate out there – you know, they're all high school kids out to "make a hit" as you would say. I think Cele + Charlie will have their hands full in another year trying to keep the boys away. As it is now she gets a lot of attention. She's full of wit – some of the things she says are really funny. Sometimes she has us laughing all the way thru supper at nite + you know how Charlie is – he's so serious – he gets mad at Cele + I because we get silly streaks at the table (ha ha). Jeanie is the one who makes this house livable – you know how it is with Thomas around. It's a good thing we have some sense of humor left. He's still not working – said he went over to the p.o. to take the test but they were too busy to give it to him (that's what he says). Now he says he's going over tomorrow + take it. I'll believe it when I see it. He hasn't worked since the first week in October – isn't that awful?

I hope this week goes by fast + that you get a pass. You probably won't know tho, 'till the end of the week. We'll keep our fingers crossed, heh dear?

I'll keep in touch with Helene thru the week + see how everything is + let you know. She'll probably feel better when she gets away from that house + can rest. She's had it so hard not only since your sister Lil's death but long before – all the time Lil was sick – that was quite a strain on her – worrying all the time, etc. I wish someone could help her now – could make her see that she's got to take care of her own health. I wouldn't write to her tho, dear, about her not feeling good – she'll think you're worrying – just see if you can't get something straightened out when you come home + knock some sense into Jack's thick head. (ha ha). That's practically impossible now, heh, dear?

Take care of yourself, darling,

Love Always,

X X X X X X Rita X X X X X X

Sunday Nite 9: P.M.

Post. M.P. Co.

Day, Room.

Dear Rita,

Enjoyed talking to you on the phone so much dearest. This was a good time for us both, to be able to have a short <u>chap</u>, I mean <u>chat</u> dear. Ha – Ha.

Bunny. I Love you dear, you are my Nice Sweetheart.

Rita dear, you are such a very Intelligent girl. See how Smart you are Bunny. you know and have such a broad Knowledge of Every thing.

Bunny, dear, how I wish you and I could be curled up in each others arms. To have some nice Kisses and to be very close to each other, May be I would tickle you a little. You know me, Heh dear.

Bunny, So glad that you prayed for me at Church this Morning dear. See I seem never to get to Church, like I used to.

I love to go and attend Church, especially with you dearest.

Hope you had a very enjoyable weekend, in spite of the bad weather, at least you could relax and listen to the good program's on the Radio. Bing Crosby and Good old Frank <u>Sinatra</u> and the other, <u>Slippery</u> Fellow's that play the <u>Women</u>. Heh dear.

Bunny. Wish I could sneak into Bed with you, to try and help you keep your little toesies warm. OH. BOY.

Love –

From Your Fiance - Walter

Monday 1/24/44 – 6:45 pm.

Hello Dearest,

Received your Friday's letter when I got home from work tonight + I was especially glad to get it, sweetheart, because it was the first one in a long time that really answered my last letter. It seems lately, darling, that I've been writing so much about our wedding but you didn't answer any of them – that is up until Friday. Well, anyway, dearest, as you said, we can get things straightened out when you come home – date, type of wedding etc.

Darling you said you like yourself because you agreed with me that you have a nice personality. Well, I'd rather have you feel that way than feel inferior + have no initiative or nerve at all. I like you to be the way you are – sure of yourself. There's no reason why you should feel inferior.

You agreed with me that April is a nice month for our marriage. I think so + Cele does too. She said Easter Monday would be a good day or the Saturday after (the 22nd). What do you think of the 22nd, dear? Cele + Eleanor asked me last night when you were going to put in for your furlough. Maybe you should ask for it the first week in February so you'll have a chance of getting it by the end of April or middle of May. Incidentally, I had a letter from Dot Smith + she + Ernie expect to be home in two weeks – that will make it about the 5th of February. It looks now as tho you are going to miss seeing them by one week. Oh well, one never can tell.

You said you wanted your family to get used to the idea of our getting married. Well, dear, I can see your point but they all know we are planning to except your father + that should be settled when you come home.

As I mentioned before, Eleanor + Vin came over yesterday + Eleanor + Cele gabbed all day about our wedding. (ha ha). They certainly are enthused over it. I am too, now, but I'm afraid to go ahead with anything yet until you ask for a furlough – also until you tell your father. They were talking about a shower that Eleanor will give me where would be a good place to have a reception (if we decide to have one) where they could get liquor – whether I should buy my gown or have it made etc, etc, etc. Well they have a good time talking about it, heh dearest? It would be nice if everything did work out, tho.

Dearest, I miss you so much. I hope you can come this week-end – but you can tell later in the week better. Keep well + happy, dearest, 'till I see you.

Love Always,

long ones for you, dear → X X X X X X Rita X X X X X X

Monday Noon
Post. M.P. Co.
Day, Room

Dearest Rita,

Just had my diner and just finished reading your very nice letter that you wrote Saturday. Bunny So happy to know and being told so many times, that you <u>Love</u> me. I Love you also, <u>oh</u> so much, So much that I can't express my Self on paper. Heh darling Rita, <u>Marie</u>.

Yes dearest they do have a nice selection of ready made gown's. It doesent' hardly pay to trouble Mrs Singer, in making one, especially now that Mr Singer is due to go into the Army. But use your own good, judgement, Bunny dear.

Yes, Eleanor, will not find it very hard in finding a nice gown to fit her. She has those nice feminine curves Ha – Ha – Ha. Just like you dearest. <u>Oh</u> Boy. <u>Dear</u>. I will keep my eyes open for a nice Blouse for my Self.

Yes dearest, this coming Saturday, I hope to stop at Bridges to have a chat, with him and Helene, to see just, how we can plan things, So that Helene can be relived of some of all those duties. I am sure that we will work out something, for Lil's children.

Bunny I am quite sure, that <u>God</u> will watch over Lil's Children, He has left us as guidance for them, to help them, and consider there happiness first, So that they will not ever become hungry for want of Love of parents, for someone to share there problems, and when they want companionship, - they should have it. Companionship, Love, Incouragement, Cheer, Humor, Laughter, and a warm family Invironment, plus plenty of good nurishing food, warm clothing, those I consider, come last and least important if they have Love they will surely get the latter. My Father must be quite Lonesome, But it will work out. I am quite sure. He has a super, Super Will Power and has a fine Character with very few flaws in it. He can take adversities, right on the chin and come up fighting. He has a very strong Constitution. That has been tested, time and time again during his life. So he will make out. I am sure.

Bunny I am looking forward in seeing you this Sat. I am due my usual pass. But nothing is sure in this army. The minute I get into your arms I am going to Kiss you for a full hour Oh Boy. Darling, I am a old love bug for you. See what you do to me. I love it tho. Ha – Ha.

Love Walter

Tuesday 1/25 – 12:30 pm

Hello Walter J. (My Dearest),

How's my sweetheart this week? I hope everything is going along smoothly for you.

Thomas finally took the test with those cards he's been studying for the past 3 – ½ months but he failed the test – said he almost made it but not quite so they told him they still couldn't take him back to work if he didn't know it. Now he says they'll have to take him because he's "pulled some strings" with someone who'll get him back without taking the test again. Leave it to him! Some other fellow in the same predicament wouldn't know who to turn to for help but he always seems to have good luck – oh well, I hope he gets the job back for Cele + Charlie's sake.

7:00 p.m. Darling, I guess I won't have time tonight to get your daily letter out by 7:15 – quite a few things detained me tonight + I had to eat supper – but you'll understand, dearest, you'll probably receive it Thursday.

I received 4 letters from you tonight, dearest – I'm so happy – two you wrote Saturday, one Sunday + yesterday's letter. Gosh, dear, you like to write to me, heh, darling? I'm so glad. Yes, sometimes it does make us feel closer when we write. It really is the next best thing to seeing each other.

Yes, dear, I know if it wasn't for the difference in religion we probably would have been married sooner. But everything should work out very well after you tell your father + we talk to the priest about the procedure you'll take - - that is about the instructions (I think there are 6 you have to take). Dearest, I'll never interfere in any way with you practicing your own beliefs after we're married. As long as I can be free to live up to the Catholic religion + in case there are children I can be sure they will be baptized Catholic, then there will be no obstacles. You'll be entirely free to follow the Lutheran Religion. When you tell your father about our planning to get married be sure to stress that, dearest. I don't want him to think I'm trying to change you because I'm not.

You said you often think of your past work + what you will do after the war + want to make sure that you can provide for me + yourself. It's natural + right for you to think of these things, dear, but don't think about the past - the most important thing in your case (you said it was secondary) but I think it's the most important, is that you keep physically well – keep yourself built up the way you are now – because as you know yourself, you are at your best now + you don't want to start sliding down the hill again. If you'll keep this in mind – be careful of what you eat + try not to drink much + of course get lots of rest (as much as you can in the Army) you won't have to worry about your work after you get out of the Army. Don't forget, dearest, I'd always try to help you – not be a worry to you. If worse came to worse I could work – if it meant that we wouldn't have the necessities (ha ha). I wouldn't want to work tho, dear, after the war, because it would be more important to have a pleasant homelife for you than a few extra dollars. So, dear, don't worry about those things – I have a few little obstacles to overcome myself that have nothing to do with you – I'll explain when you come home – they are things you might have noticed yourself but anyway, I think when we're married they'll be overcome. I might as well mention them while I'm on the subject. Well, dearest, if you'll recall Cele is always kidding me about gaining weight after we get married – I think I probably will + my whole physical system will improve 100%. You know, dearest, you always had to be careful of the kind of life you lead with your nervous condition – well, I've always had to be careful too – it was always more of a physical run down condition with me if I wasn't careful. Remember last year at this time, dear, I became all run-down? Well the doctor gave me a tonic to get built up which I did take + have been very well for the past year – not just from taking the tonic but from eating right + sleeping right but then I cut down on the amount of vitamin pills I had been taking + cut out the tonic entirely + as a result – today for the first time in a year noticed that old runned-down feeling again. It's a feeling that's hard to explain – a tired out feeling + aching all over + a weakness with it. Today in the office I was in a cold sweat for a few minutes – it went away + tonight I feel fairly good again. Cele made me get the tonic filled again so I guess in another few weeks I'll feel my normal self again. It's nothing to worry about, dearest, Cele thinks it will be overcome after we get married. I just thought I'd tell you about it so you'd understand maybe I told you once before. Starting tomorrow I'm going to get lots of rest, eat properly + take the tonic. I'll explain more later, dearest, when you come home but don't worry, dearest, if it was anything to worry over I wouldn't even think of getting married.

No, dear, I probably won't have Mrs. Singer make my gown after all – I'm not quite sure yet but I think I can buy one in the store just as nice. You said I shouldn't bother her with her husband going in the Army + everything. Well, dearest, it isn't as tho she'd make it for nothing I'd pay her well for making it. We'll see, dear.

You say you intend to go + have a talk with Jack + Helene when you come home. I do hope something is arranged so that Helene can go home + take care of herself. I called her tonight + she still doesn't feel well – can't seem to get rid of her cold + said herself she hopes you come home this week-end + talk to Jack. She'll be looking forward to seeing you. When you do go, dear, you should have your father go with you because I know you – once you start talking with Jack you'll agree to what he tells you – the best thing to do is say that you think Helene should go home + rest + <u>stick</u> <u>to</u> <u>your</u> <u>point</u>. If Helene gets real sick so she isn't able to take care of the children at all – he would have to make arrangements pretty fast then. There would be no "ifs ands or buts."

I don't think I'll go to the show this Saturday, dearest. I'd just as soon stay home + maybe you'll be able to get into Bpt. by 9:30 or so (if you get a pass) + I'd be here. It would be a good idea, dearest, to call me up on the way – when you're in Worcestor or wherever you change trains – then I could tell just about when you would be home. I would hate to be at the show if you came.

I can just imagine you grabbing me as soon as you get to 1440 + kissing me for an hour as you said you were going too (ha ha). Aren't you going to wait 'till you get your breath? (ha ha). Dear, I love you so much. Hope I feel better by Saturday than I do now tho.

Lots + Lots of Love

long ones → X X X X X X Rita X X X X X X

Tuesday Noon

Post M.P. Co

Pay, Room

Dear Rita,

Yes dear, I guess a reception would cost too much. yes, may be just having a breakfast for our families is better as far as the finance is concerned dearest.

Long <u>Live</u> the Lavery's. Heh dearest. The Lavery's always's do all right for themselves.

Carl Wallat my cousin married a Catholic girl at your Church, remember, with a <u>Mass</u> and his Brother was his Best Ma, with Leo. Sablofski my cousin usher. the girl's name was Murial Siebert Sifred.

Jeanie, is quite a cute Kid, She sure does slay the boy's. Oh Boy – she just drives the boy's Mad, with those pretty sweaters she wears while skating at the Mosque and going to school Ha – Ha – Ha. Especially next year, she will be quite a devil, Bunny, she will sure give you plenty of competition at 1440 – <u>Ha</u> – <u>Ha</u>.

Tomorrow, Thomas will straighten out eventually I am quite sure. People like him and in such a state of <u>fear</u>, take lots, and lots of time to get a grip on themselves. So glad that you still <u>Love</u> me Dear. Oh Boy. See how I rate with you dear.

I <u>Love</u> <u>you</u> <u>passionately</u> also dearest. Wait until we are on our Honey Moon at that Nice Classic Hotel in New York. Bunny, I will tuck, you into bed and let you Sleep <u>oh</u> so nice. you know dear you and I will need a nice snooze after that Nervous Walk down the Middle Aisle.

Oh Boy. Bunny I wont ever be Nervous a bit, you know me and the Same goes for you. Especially dear, I know you wont be Nervous undressing at the Hotel. Ha – Ha – Ha – I am a big devil. Heh dearest. (I wont even look at you dear, while you are preparing to have a nice Snooze. Will I dearest? I might take a little peek tho. Ha Ha. Yes dear we will keep our fingers crossed as for me getting my usual monthly pass. I am quite sure tho of getting it. Boy, Bunny will I hug and kiss you and stay nice and close to you. Bunny I miss you so much, I am so hungry for your pretty kisses and loving. You know how much I hate it. Ha – Ha – Ha.

Yes Helene is such a good girl, I am quite sure that she will be rewarded for all her goodness. I won't worry her dearest. I will stop up to see them all on my visit home, to have a chat.

Enclosed is a phamflet [pamphlet], explaining the use of the Rosary. It explain's quite clearly how to use them and what they mean. Here at the Ayer U.S.O. they have phamflets concerning all faith's. I have quite a few on the Catholic Religion, that I read quite often. especially when I have time on some of the posts.

Love,
Walter

Wednesday – 1/26/44 – 2:30 p.m.

Dear Sweetheart,

I'm writing this letter in bed – didn't go to work this morning. I have that "achy" feeling again so I'll probably stay home from work for a few days or maybe for the rest of the week. Don't worry, tho, dearest. I'll be fine + dandy again after a few days' rest.

Darling, you said when your cousin, Carl Wallat got married his brother was his best man. Yes, dearest, I remember now. Well, I guess there is no reason why your brother, Al, can't be best man at our wedding then. I'm glad you reminded me of your cousin's wedding, dearest. I sure do want Al to stand up for you + I know you do too.

I'll tell you the type of wedding I have in mind, dear. I'd like to be married at 11 o'clock in the morning – in white with Eleanor + your brother as our attendants + not send out invitations but just tell everyone in your family + mine – cousins, aunts, uncles, etc. to come (if they want to). From the Church we could go to the photographers + have a few pictures taken of the wedding party + from the photographers go to wherever we decide on for a nice dinner just for your family + mine. Just counting the immediate families there would be about 25 at the breakfast. It would cost about $50 for 25 people. Then after the dinner we could come back to the house + any of the relations who wanted to could come back to see the presents (or am I being too optimistic that there will be quite a few gifts – ha ha). Then we could go away about 4 in the afternoon to N.Y. Now, darling, don't think the wedding has to be just the way I've just outlined it to you. If you would really like a reception, we can talk it over when you come home + might compromise in some way. I think Cele + Eleanor are in favor of a reception, altho Cele says it's entirely up to you + I – whatever we decide on will be alright with her. To me the most important part of the wedding is in Church when we are, or will be I should say reciting the vows. I can't see much sense in providing a lot of drinks for a reception so people can get feeling good. Eleanor + Vin said for a crowd of 75 people we'd need at least one case of liquor ($40.00) – (if you can get it) + also beer for those who like it. Imagine spending that amount of money on drinks alone. Wow! Oh well, we can decide on those things when you come, dearest, I want you to tell us what you want too. I like plain, simple weddings with no fuss – they are the nicest for people like you + I in moderate circumstances. Even the type of wedding I've outlined to you, darling, will be rather expensive but it will be worthwhile I think to spend the money on the ceremony itself and a nice dinner afterward.

I'm so glad, darling, you are quite sure of getting your monthly pass – I'll be all better by Saturday, dearest, + will be waiting for you at 1440 with bells on. (ha ha).

Gosh, dearest, we have such a strong love – I'm so glad. I want to do everything to make you happy, sweetheart. You're such a good boy + so deserving of the best. I'm not as matured as I should be, dearest, but give me a few more years + lots of patience + kindness + I'll come thru. I haven't half of the tolerance + understanding you have but I know I have a lot to learn yet + you'll help me just as I'll help you, dearest.

When you come home, dear, I'll give you some nice, big hugs + kisses.

Lots + lots of love, dearest

X X X X X X Rita Marie X X X X X X

Thursday 1/27/44 11:15 p.m.

Hello Walter Dearest,

I'm a "lady of leisure" today too, dear – I didn't go into work. I'm like a piece of broken-down machinery heh, dearest (ha ha) – I get all worn out + tired – but lots of rest fixes me up again (ha ha). I feel a lot better than I did yesterday, tho, darling. I got up at 10 o'clock – had some breakfast + read your nice letter for dessert.

Yes, dearest, our bank is growing. You said I can always borrow some pennies from it – you won't mind. Well, Walt, I did borrow – but it was more than pennies (ha ha). I won't tell you how much but anyway I'm replacing it – some each week so don't worry, dear.

Mrs. Smith called up last night + talked to Jeanie – said she had a letter from Dot + now Ernie can't get his furlough 'till the first week in March. Dot said they'd love to be here when you + I get married but of course Ernie will have to take the furlough whenever he gets it – just as you will too, so that seems almost impossible. It's too bad tho that they won't be at our wedding.

I'm so glad you think April 22nd would be a good date. We won't have so much time in which to get nervous, heh, darling? If we don't get married until May – we'll be worrying about everything but if we can be married in April we can spend the next two months preparing for it + won't have so much time on our hands (ha ha). It should be rather warm by that date too – we should be having a little spring weather at least + that's better than having the weather too hot. We'll keep our fingers crossed, darling.

I had a letter today from Betty Hughes too. She said all the fellows in Bill's squadron "have an appointment with the dentist" as she put it very soon (they're going to be shipped out) + Bill is getting a 15-day furlough starting the first of February. It's a shame he's being shipped he hasn't been in the Army a year yet. Betty said she is thankful they were able to have the past 7 months together – she's glad she followed him around. She said if we get married in April we should make it the 11th – it's their anniversary. It will be 2 yrs. this coming April. It doesn't seem that long does it? Gosh, dearest, if we were to listen to everyone's advice as to what day we should get married, we'd have to be married about 6 different times (ha ha).

Yes, dearest, I know the way you write letters. As you said you answer what you can remember of my letters – sometimes you don't have time to answer everything. It's alright, dearest, but as time goes on – we'll be writing about all the little details of the wedding + then it will be very important that you do answer them – so you'll be all straightened out on everything. I know you have to get a fast letter off sometimes, darling + I do appreciate your writing every day.

I love you so much, Walter. You're a good boy. You're the apple of my eye, dear. You mean so much to me – I couldn't begin to tell you everything, dearest but you know how much I care for you, heh, darling?

I might go into work tomorrow I don't know yet.

Take good care of yourself, dear, 'till I see you.

Love Always,

X X X X X X Rita X X X X X X

Saturday Night 8:15 p.m. 2/19/44

Hello Sweetheart,

Here it is Saturday night + you, dearest, are 'way up where the sand dunes are on Cape Cod + I'm 'way down here at 1440.

I hope you didn't count too much on getting a pass this weekend, darling. I didn't count on it too much this week – I wasn't sure really whether you would or not but figured they wouldn't give you one so soon – that you'd be given some detail + then I didn't hear from you + as it's about 8:20 now, I don't think you'll be home tonight. Well, dearest, maybe you will next week. I hope so.

I received the letter you wrote Thursday night this morning. Yes, dear, that certainly was good news about your being put into limited service + that there's a possibility you might be attached to the Camp there. Gosh, Walt, they can't seem to make up their minds what to put you in — first you were in 1-A-G.S. + told you that you might be put into the construction engineers or Combat M.P.s + now you say you might be put into the M.P.'s up there or possibly the 2.M. Corp. Well, dearest, I hope you are stationed at Camp Edwards for a few months anyway + kept in a S.C.U. of some kind — it would be a very good break for you + besides then you would have a chance to get a furlough — maybe in April.

Here is the news I wanted to tell you. Today I bought my gown + veil, your ring + mine + Eleanor also bought the gown she's going to wear + hat. We surely accomplished a lot didn't we, dearest?

We bought both Eleanor's + my gown in Miller's (on Stfd. Ave. — where you + I saw the satin one last week). They had the best selection of gowns than any other place I tried. When I say I bought it, darling, I mean I paid a $10 deposit on it — they are going to order it in my size + then I'll have it fitted. It'll take about 10 days for my size to come in. The one I tried on was size 12 but they pinned it on me to see how the right size would look. It's much prettier, dear, than the one that was in the window, is made of Chantilly lace (around the shoulders — from the shoulders to the hips is satin + from the hips down (the skirt) is marquisette — a very sheer + soft material — with a train. I don't know whether you can picture it in your mind from my description or not, dearest but it's really lovely — wait 'til you see it! You can't see it 'til the day of our wedding. The veil is a fingertip + has a pretty headpiece on it. The gown was $39.50 + the veil $12.50. The gown is definitely one to be worn only in the spring or summer so, dearest, I hope you can get a furlough before the summer is over — you can see how important it is that you do get one, heh, dearest? Eleanor's gown is lovely too — it's an orchid net + she'll wear a yellow net hat (quite a large one — with streamers on it) — it's a very nice combination yellow + orchid. I also bought the rings — in Fairchild's where you bought my diamond. They are both very plain ones — the one I picked out for you was size 10 ½ but they are putting a piece in + it'll be size 11 ¾ - the size of the other ring I gave you. Mine doesn't have to be sized at all — they had my size (5 ½). Mine cost $7.50 (cheap, heh) + yours was $12.50. The man's ring is always more because it's heavier. I'm not having our initials put in because it would take too long — they have to send them away for engraving. They can be engraved later if you really want it, darling, but it's unnecessary, I think. I paid $9.00 on the rings + will pay the balance when yours is ready.

I bought some other things I need, too — you know what, dear, those little frilly things — I won't go into detail about them. (ha ha).

Next week I'll pick out a coat, etc. to wear when we go away + then I'll be all ready — as all I'll have to do then is wait for you to get some time off, heh, dear? There will be a lot of little details to take care of such as announcement in the paper, gifts for Eleanor + Al, flowers, but I can take care of them in time. It would be nice, heh, dearest, if we could be married in April. (the middle or so).

I miss you so much, dearest. I guess I'm spoiled – having you home for the past three weeks. I hope you're not out in the cold tonight, dearest, on guard duty or something. Please take care of yourself, dearest – keep well + as happy as you can. Maybe you'll call up tomorrow – I hope so. If you need any money, dear, let me know + I'll send it to you. I hope there are some kind of amusements in Camp Edwards – shows at least.

Bud came home this week-end. Cele was just talking to him on the 'phone – we told him you were in Camp Edwards – he was glad you didn't go far – says he hopes he stays in Devens for a good long while (haha – you know him, heh, Walt?).

I gave Ellen your new address so maybe she'll have Al tell your father – Helene knows it too but it would be a good idea if you dropped Martha + Emma a line giving them your address.

Well, dearest, Cele, Jeanie + I are going to have a snack now before we go to bed. I'll be thinking of you, dearest – I love you so much, Walter dear. Hope we'll see each other soon.

Love Always,
(big ones) →XXXXXX Rita XXXXXX

Feb. 21st – Monday

Dear Sweetheart,

I hope you made good train connections in Providence + got into Camp so you could have at least three or four hours' sleep.

I enjoyed being with you so much yesterday, dear, even tho we didn't have much time – we did have such a nice afternoon + evening ('til 8 o'clock).

Dearest, I can hardly believe that everything seems to be working in our favor now – your being put into Limited Service + being stationed in Camp Edwards for a while (as far as you know).

I hope when you are assigned that you'll be put into the 2.M. Corps. As you put it you'd be "fooling around with trucks, motorcycles, etc." By this I guess you mean repairing equipment (motorized equipment). This'll give you a chance to use your mechanical ability. If you were put in an M.P. outfit, dear, it might not be too bad. Of course the hours wouldn't be good but as Cele says, if they were too bad you could start to "buck a little". It would be better to be put into the M.P.s + be stationed in Camp Edwards than to be moved, wouldn't it, dear? I'll go on praying for you, darling, so you won't be moved from there.

Yes, dearest, I guess it would be too tiring for you to come home every week (if you have the chance while you're unattached) – so use your own judgment. I'd love to see you as often as possible. I wish you wouldn't feel the way you do – about people seeing you every week. Cele + Charlie think you're foolish to feel this way. As long as you're not scheduled for any detail I think you have a perfect right to come home as often as you can get a pass. Please don't feel that way, darling. You know how much we all like to see you. You'd probably spend the amount of money it takes for trainfare anyway – if you stayed at Camp. Try to keep as much money as you can that your father gave you, dearest because it might be a while before you get paid.

Charlie + Thomas brought the – "you know what" back to the post office last night. There is only one fellow who works on Sun. night + he replaced the three "things" that were missing from it (you know). So everything is O.K. in that regard but we don't know when he's going back to work. Some fellow is coming here tomorrow to help him learn the system.

Someone who works in the American Chain wants to look at our house some night this week (a prospective buyer). He's willing to spend quite a bit in repairs – is a Carpenter + can do a lot himself – so that looks bad, heh, dear?

Well, dearest, please take care of yourself – get as much rest as possible – go to the show if you have a chance. I'll be thinking of you, sweetheart.

Love Always,

xxxxxx Rita xxxxxx

Wednesday 2/23 – Rest Period

Dearest,

I thought I'd write my daily letter now – during rest period because tonight Mary is coming over early + we're going to Church – so I won't have time to write then.

I called up home this morning to see if there was any mail from you but Jeanie said there wasn't. Well, maybe there will be in this afternoon's mail – or maybe you didn't have time to write Monday.

I sent a pair of white satin shoes (sandals) to the cleaners this morning. They are ones that I used for both Eileen's + Dot's wedding + as they are practically new – just soiled I thought I'd have them cleaned + wear them for my own wedding. They are nice ones + I couldn't buy a pair as good now – it's almost impossible to get white satin now (in shoes).

Darling, when you come home next time I wish you would tell your father more about our wedding plans. Couldn't you at least mention to him that you are going to try + get a furlough soon + that when you do get it that you + I will be married? You said Sunday that you want to tell him everything slowly – a little at a time. I can understand that, Walter, but I don't see why it would hurt to bring the subject up each time you come home – tell him a little more each time. In that way he'd get more used to the idea + would accept the fact that we are going to be married in Blessed Sacrament Church. If you keep silent on the subject week after week – you'll have to tell him everything in the end anyway + it'll be much harder for you. If you left it for me to tell him our plans, dearest, I certainly wouldn't hesitate – you know me, dear, I don't believe in wasting time nor words.

I imagine you won't know whether you'll get a pass this week-end 'till about Saturday noon or late Sat. afternoon so there'll be no way that I will know if you're coming, heh, dear? You see I never know whether I should go to the show with Mary or not, darling. I'd hate to be at the show if you did come. Well, dearest, we'll trust to luck like we have in the past week-ends. Maybe you can let me know when you write Friday's letter – you might not know definitely but you could give me an idea anyway whether I should expect you, heh dear?

It's very windy today here – I'll bet it is 'way up on Cape Cod too, dearest. I hope everything is going along smoothly for you in spite of the coldness. Dress warmly, darling + take care of yourself.

When I go to Church tonight I'll say some prayers for you.

Love Always,

xxxxxx Rita xxxxxx

Thursday 2/24/44

Dearest Walter,

It looks as though you're giving me the "silent treatment" this week – not getting any mail from you, unless I get a letter in this afternoon's mail. I called up home again today + Jeanie said there wasn't any this morning. Well, I suppose you must have a good reason for not writing – or maybe you did write + the mail is extra slow in coming.

Mary didn't come over last night after all – she is always making dates with me + then breaks them. Last Saturday she was supposed to go to the show with me + the last minute called up + said she couldn't make it. This coming Saturday she's going to N.Y. for a week so we won't be going to the show this week either. So, darling, I'll be home Saturday night. I do hope we'll see each other this week-end. Right now, tho, dear, I don't know how things are with you – whether you're still unattached – I hope you won't have to go on K.P. for a week.

I might go downtown tonight to the show with Cele + Charlie – I'm not sure tho – to see Spencer Tracy + Irene Dunne in "A Guy Named Joe" – it's supposed to be good.

I called your sister, Helene, last night to see how she was. She says she's going home a week from this coming Sunday – definitely + that last Sunday – in the afternoon Jack brought his <u>girlfriend</u> to the house while Ellen, Al + the children were there. Isn't that awful? The girl's name is Jean (I don't think Helene knows her last name) + Helene says she's blond, wears glasses + is Hungarian. She thinks it's the one whose husband is in Iceland but isn't sure. Imagine the nerve of him bringing her to the house! After supper Helene went to Ellen + Al's house + when she came home again – they were still there. She said they acted kind of mad because she had gone out + left the children with them – they wanted to go out themselves. Can you beat that? She said she told Jack she intends to leave there definitely, but he won't say one way or the other what he intends to do about the baby. Mr. + Mrs. Bridges are taking Joan + Carol but they don't say anything about the baby. Helene says she made up her mind she's not going to take him. She doesn't see why she should bear any of Jack's responsibility.

I think Helene should have gone home right after the funeral – she's not getting even a thank you for staying there this long – in fact he's insulting your family right to their face by bringing a girl to the house when Lil has only been gone 3 months. Helene says everyone in your family (you too) talk about how weak he is + get mad at him but no one says anything to him – that the family leaves all the "dirty work" to her. Well, she certainly was all upset when I talked to her last night – I don't know why she's waiting 'til a week from Sunday to leave – she should have gone long ago. (my opinion). I guess things will work out when she goes home – but they won't straighten out as long as Helene is there. I mean as long as he has her to lean on.

Well, dearest, I have to get back to work now. I hope you are getting my letters regularly now + that I receive some mail from you this afternoon or tomorrow.

I'll be thinking of you, dearest.

Love Always,
xxxxxx Rita xxxxxx

P.S. If you have a chance at all to come home this week-end, dear, take it – even if it is for a short time. I do realize that it's tiring to go back + forth each week but I'd like to talk to you – not this "I love you" business + "When are you going to marry me?", but some real sense – (ha ha) – about our wedding.

Lots of love, dearest.
"Bunny"

Friday, February 25th

Hello Dearest,

I can't tell you how happy I was to receive your three letters last night when I got home from work; two of them were written Tuesday (I think) and the other Wednesday.

I'm glad you were assigned to the Quartermaster Corps, (the Service and Supply Co.) In Wednesday's letter you said you expected to start working at the Motor Pool in the afternoon but weren't sure if you would be there permanently. Well, dearest, it would be nice if you were – I think you'd like it. If you are eventually put into the Engineers of the Quartermaster's it would be good, too, dearest – I think you'd have a good chance to get a rating in that outfit. I just hope they don't decide to move you from Camp Edwards, that's all, dear. You said that you and the rest of the boys get dizzy trying so many different things before you are finally placed – I can understand that, Walt – you don't know what to expect from one day to the next, but when you are told definitely just what kind of work you'll be doing, it will be much better.

It's a very good break for you, dearest, being in the Q.M. Corps., don't you think so? I remember when you first went in the Army you wanted to get into that. I hope you'll be kept in Limited Service for the duration – you and I both know you'll be much better off than being in 1-A and put into a Combat Division. I hope your good luck continues, dearest.

That was good news about your passes too – if you can get one about twice a month, it'll be wonderful.

This is just a little detail, dear, but I hope you will take out the cross pistols that you've been wearing on your blouse and replace the button with the Quartermasters' Insignia; also when you come home next time bring one for the blouse you have at my house – the one you are going to wear for our wedding, o.k. dear? Maybe it would be a good idea to save the cross pistols for a remembrance of the M.P. (ha ha).

I don't know whether I should expect you home this week-end, dearest. I'll be home Saturday night anyway and if you don't come home at all over the week-end I might go to the show Sunday with Helene (if she can make it). It would be so nice to see you, tho, dearest but maybe I expect too much – I'm spoiled, heh dear, after seeing you for the past three weeks? If you have a chance at all to come, darling, take it – don't worry about what people might think about your coming home every week – you have a perfect right to if you are not listed for any detail.

Cele and I are going to inquire some time soon in Champs about what they would charge for a wedding breakfast, how many people they would accommodate, how far ahead we would have to let them know, etc. That would be a nice place for the breakfast, don't you think so, dear? That is, providing it isn't too expensive. Well, we'll see.

I'm glad you're getting my letters regularly, dearest. I think yours were held up this week on account of the holiday.

Dearest, if I don't see you this week-end you'll probably call up Sunday if you get a chance. I'll be thinking of you, darling. Keep well and happy 'til we see each other.

Love Always,
Your future "little wife"
big ones→X X X X X X X X X X X X X

Monday 2/28th 6:45 p.m.

Dearest Walter,

I hope by the time this letter reaches you that you'll be pretty well rested up after your trip back to Camp + that everything is going smoothly.

After your train came in last night Helene + I went to the Pickwick + had a sandwich + coffee – I was home by 10 o'clock.

Well, we didn't "click" so well this week-end, did we, Walt – due to the fact that you started off on the wrong foot by drinking too much – and talking too much. Your tongue is your worse enemy, Walt, as you probably realize by now. I hope if you come home next week-end that you'll know enough to come to 1440 as soon as possible from the train + also bear in mind not to talk so much. There was one remark you made when Sarah, Garry + Mary – (also Cele + Charlie) were here Sat. that I had to do a lot of explaining to Cele. That was when you said "you realized you had a little too much to drink during the evening – you shouldn't drink so much because then you get fresh + I get mad." Cele said she just hoped Sarah + Garry (+ Mary) didn't take it up the wrong way. I told her I thought you meant talking too much at Roseland – I had to tell her about it. She said she knew when you came in Sat. night you had too much to drink. It's a good thing it doesn't happen hardly ever because you talk a lot even when you're sober but when you have a few drinks you're twice as bad. Well, Walt, as you've said yourself many times – you won't get in trouble if you don't talk – so you'd better get on to yourself. I don't like the idea either of your being so apologetic to people (Al + Ellen yesterday) about the difference in our Religion – I thought it was an accepted fact - + that we were both going to be broadminded about it – that it was settled a long time ago. Al even told you yesterday he didn't see any reason why you have to explain to everyone about being married in the Catholic Church + discussing the difference in our religion – that it was your business – that's the second time I heard you tell people you're sorry – that you wish we were both the same. Don't you think I feel the same way? But I don't tell people it's too bad etc. – I want to meet you half way + make the best of it. You told Ellen + Al yesterday that we both knew + recognized the difference right from the beginning but we didn't stop going together – that these things do happen etc, etc, etc. You act as tho you're sorry. Well, Walt, think all this over + we can talk about it if you want, when you come home next time. There's no reason why we can't be happy together if you would get over those ideas you have.

I hope you can get some information this week about the procedure you are to take in asking for a furlough. As far as I'm concerned spring or summer will be alright – even if it runs into the middle of the summer – the only thing is – you never can tell where you'll be by that time + the only thing to do I think is take your furlough as soon as you can get it.

Well, dearest, after reading this letter you probably feel that I put everything too strongly – that I don't really mean all that I've written but I really do – I'm not in a bad mood either – I'm just giving you a few facts. In the past few weeks that you've been home I've had to use a lot of effort so there would be harmony between us – (it's been approximately a 60-40 basis) – so remember if you want to get along – not only with me but with other people don't talk so much.

Love Always,
xxxxxx Rita xxxxxx

P.S. I would have told you all this last nite but Helene was with us.
Don't write back + say you're sorry either – really <u>act</u>.

Tuesday, 2/29/44 – Rest Period

Hello Sweetheart,

I hope everything is going along well with you this week – your work, etc. + that you're getting plenty of sleep + diversion too.

We're having Lenten Devotions every Tuesday + Friday nights during Lent in our Church + I'm going to try + go to them. I went last week twice + expect to go tonight too. On Tuesdays we have Rosary, sermon (by a priest from outside) + benediction. On Fridays we have the Stations of the Cross + Benediction. A lot of people go at the beginning of Lent each year but towards the end the crowd tapers down to a few people. I like to go right thru twice a week until Easter Sunday because I usually don't give anything up for Lent in the line of sweets like some people do – I think you can sacrifice in lots of other ways. If I stopped eating sweets I'd lose weight + you know, heh, darling, I can't afford that (ha ha).

6:15 p.m. Received the letter you wrote yesterday noon in transportation barracks. From your letter I can see you really enjoyed the week-end – well, I'm glad you did, Walt. I guess you didn't feel as I did – that we didn't click so well. You said when we were waiting for your train that I missed our usual "smooching" – well, you're entirely wrong – I didn't miss it – but I missed the companionship that we share – most of the time. I think you + I better have a little talk when you come home next time – there is some feeling between us that I can't put my finger on – there just seems to be something lacking – maybe we are both changing.

You said in your letter that by talking to Helene + Al about our wedding + doing a little more each time you come home towards working out our plans is good. I don't think any more talking about them is necessary – except to your father – just to tell him what type of a wedding we were planning, Church etc.

I'm glad you're going to make a few inquiries about your furlough – it won't hurt to inquire + put in an application anyway.

You probably think, dear, while you're reading this letter that it's very depressing + contradictory – tho I feel that way as I'm writing, I don't really – what I'm trying to say is that a lot of things you've done + said in the past few weeks are very annoying + I've had to use a lot of control so I wouldn't argue with you. We did start to a few times if you remember, but everything was O.K. by the time you left. I can't understand why the things you say + do upset or bother me – they didn't before. Since you went back this time I've been going through all the happenings of the past week-end especially in my mind - + as it's hard to explain the way I feel in a letter let's have a talk when you come home + reason everything out. There's no use being mad – we'll talk everything over reasonably. You'd think with our marriage so close that we'd be very happy - + enthused about it but when we do talk about it – it's always about the physical part of it, somehow. Oh well, I'll get this "mixed up" feeling straightened out when you come home next time (I hope).

I do love you, dearest, don't ever doubt it + I know you love me but as you've often said yourself, love isn't like it's written in books – it can make people feel all kinds of ways, heh, dear?

I'll be thinking of you, dearest + I hope you'll be lucky again this week-end

+ come home.

Love Always,

xxxxxx Rita xxxxxx

Thursday 3/2 – 6 o'clock

Dearest Walter,

Received your Tuesday's letter tonight – I was awfully glad I got some mail today from you.

No, dearest, that's true – you can't seem to get away from prisoner chasing – they would make that system now, heh, dearest? Oh well, doing it in the beginning of the week is better than having to do it over the week-end. I do hope you can come home this week-end, dearest, + that you can get into Bpt. about the same time as you did last week. I'll be waiting for your call about 6:45 or so.

I'm glad you liked the wedding rings I picked out – I like them too – they are very plain, but nice. I'm glad yours fit you, dearest.

I guess you thought I was mad at you, dearest, telling you in the letters not to talk so much, etc. I wasn't mad when I wrote them – I was just telling you how I feel. As I said in my other letters, darling, let's have a talk when you come home this week – I'll tell you how I feel about this mixed up feeling I have – I can explain better when I talk to you, dearest.

I think of you all the time too, darling + of our future together. I wish it was time for you to get a furlough + that we could go thru with all our plans – that they'd all work out perfectly. It would be nice if you could get some time off around the 22nd of April or the second or third week in May. I'll pray that you will, dearest.

I should be getting a ring from Miller's one of these days telling me that my size came in – in the gown I picked out. Then I can go + have it fitted. I got my shoes today (the white satin sandals) from the cleaners – they came out pretty good. Next week I'm going to take my suit + coat from the store. I just have to get accessories now to go with them – hat, gloves, blouse, bag + shoes. I can get a little each week. Well, I guess everything will work out.

I don't know whether you know this or not, dearest, but I can't get the marriage license unless your signature is on it so that means you'll have to come a day or two ahead of time so we can go down together + you can sign it. They are really fussy about it. I thought maybe I could send it to you to sign but we can't do this either – we both must sign it in the presence of one or two witnesses. So whatever date we decide on – or rather what ever date you can come – you'll have to say a few days ahead at least, see, dearest?

Well, darling, I have to eat my supper now. Please try to come this week-end – we'll have a perfect week-end together – we'll really enjoy a nice companionship this week.

Lots + lots of love,

xxxxxx Rita xxxxxx

Tuesday, March 7th

Dearest Walter,

How's my nice sweetheart on this awfully rainy day? I'll bet it was gloomy 'way up on Cape Cod, dear, cause it poured cats + dogs here all morning but has stopped now.

I received your Friday's letter last night, Walter — it was a nice, mushy one (ha ha). I like to get those kind sometimes, telling me how much you love me, dear. Yes, we both love each other so much — we are very sure of that, heh, dearest?

Last night I wrote to Edward and Gertrude telling them that you + I were planning to be married April 22nd if you could get your furlough + asked Ed if he'd give me away — also told them to consider that letter an invitation for all of them to come to the wedding. I gave Gertrude your new address too in case she writes to you.

Cele called up two places last night to inquire about a breakfast + reception. One was the Candlelite (that's the place on River St. that's been all renovated recently — Dot Blake had her reception there) + the other place was Roseland. Neither place would give too much information over the phone. The Candlelite said they charge $2.00 per person for a dinner — not including a cocktail + that we'd have to bring our own food for a reception. Imagine that! Roseland charges $1.75 for a dinner without a cocktail but wouldn't set any price for a reception. They said they didn't like to quote prices over the 'phone — that we should go out there + talk it over. They couldn't serve sandwiches already made up — everyone would have to make their own. So you can see neither one of those places sound very good, heh, dear?

Remember Sunday, Walt, when Mrs. Champ said they figured 75¢ per person for a reception + $2.10 per for a dinner? Well figuring 100 people at 75¢ for the reception is $75.00 plus $52.50 for 25 dinners — comes out to $127.50 — I don't see how she figures $150.00 minimum do you, Walt? Then the $15 tip for the waiter would make it $165.00 (at least). If I happen to talk to her again I'll bring this to her attention. Of course I know you can't figure right to the penny but there is a big difference in the price she gave us + the price when you figure so much per person. Well, we'll see, dear.

I bought an orchid flower to go with my suit. It's a pretty one I think — is very frilly.

Darling, you have $210.00 altogether saved. I've drawn out the $100.00 I had saved + have used it for putting deposits on the suit + coat + buying things I need. What I have left will pay for my dress + veil. So, Walt, I won't take out any of the $210.00 until just before the wedding for your expenses. I thought I'd mention all this to you so you'd know what you have on hand, etc. Dear, try to keep as much of the money you have now with you during the next two weeks so you'll have enough to come home next time. I hope you have enough to hold you over.

I didn't receive any mail from you today, dear, but probably will get yesterday's letter tomorrow. I know you don't have a chance to write during the day now.

Well, dearest, be a good boy. You are a good one, Walter dear. I'll be thinking of you. Just think, darling, if your plans work out in 6-1/2 weeks we'll be Mr. + Mrs. Walter J. Klein. I can hardly believe it. I know we'll be very happy.

Love Always,

xxxxxx Rita xxxxxx

"Bunny"+"Spitfire"

(when I'm good)(when I'm bad)

ha ha ha

Monday 3/13/44

Hello Dearest,

Received your nice letter you wrote Friday.

You said you hoped my gown didn't have to be altered much – well, dearest, it didn't too much – they ordered a size 9 + it just had to have the usual alterations – the bottom of the skirt – a little thru the waist etc. It will fit nice.

It was pouring rain this morning so I decided I'd take the day off + go to the doctor for a check-up as I told you last night. I went to Dr. James + explained just how I felt – that "achy" feeling, etc. I told him I was discouraged feeling like this now because I'm planning to be married in about six weeks. He said he'd try to build me up – that I was run-down + that the "achy" feeling I have is in the muscles – it comes when a person is run-down. He gave me a prescription to take – they are pills containing liver + iron + I'm to take six a day. They are quite powerful. They are the same as an injection only of course in pill form. I'm to go back to him this coming Friday + he might start a treatment on me of injections – I'm not sure yet.

Don't worry, dearest, about this, I'll be feeling a lot better soon I'm sure. I think marriage will help me a lot. I'm going into work Wednesday.

Cele + Charlie went to Alice Cierran's in Devon last night as you know + Alice is planning to be married next month but doesn't know just what day – her boyfriend expects to get a furlough the week before Easter. She isn't going to have a big wedding at all tho – it'll be very quiet – she is going to wear a suit + isn't even sure if she'll bother with a wedding breakfast. Cele told Alice + her mother + father about our plans + they think it's foolish to fuss so much – as times aren't normal, etc. Well, that's just the way they feel – they think it's even foolish to wear white. I'm glad you + I don't feel that way, dearest.

Walter dear, I enjoyed the week-end with you a lot. It's too bad I wasn't feeling the way I should but you understand me, heh, darling. Please don't worry about me, dear, now that I've put myself in the doctor's care I'm sure I'll be alright. Your kindness, patience + understanding helps a lot – try not to be discouraged, dearest, I know how you feel, dear. In going into marriage with me you'll want to be sure I'm healthy which is the most important factor in a happy marriage. If I thought I was so physically run-down that it would interfere with our marriage I wouldn't want us to be married but I'm confident, dearest, that I'll be very well soon, so don't worry, darling.

April 22nd would be better than right after Easter but we'll work things out the best we can, darling.

I'll be thinking of you, dear.

Love Always,
xxxxxx Rita xxxxxx

Tuesday, Mar. 14th

Hello Sweetheart,

How are you this beautiful day? I hope everything is well with you + that you are rested after the tiresome trip back to Camp Sunday night.

Last night — rather - late yesterday afternoon I went over to Dot Smith's to say goodbye to her. She left for Alabama this morning. I stayed for supper over there + we had a nice time chatting, etc. Mr. + Mrs. Smith were also there. I left there about 9 o'clock. Dot said she had a nice time here — it was nice seeing her mother, father + friends but still she was anxious to get back to Ernie — She said once you are married + go away, your home never seems the same to you when you come back — naturally, your husband or wife comes first I guess that's true, heh, dear? She said if Ernie is stationed in Alabama in the summertime, she'll come home again then. She feels bad that she won't be at our wedding, darling. It is a shame but that's just one of the things that's due to the abnormal living we're experiencing now — on account of the war.

It'll be so nice when we are all together after this mess, heh, dearest? — You, Dot, Ernie + I — won't it be wonderful?

This afternoon, in order to get some air + sunshine I took the bus downtown + went window-shopping then had my suit fitted. The waist of the skirt had to be taken in, that's all. It'll be ready soon. It's beautiful out today — it seemed so good to be able to walk in the sun instead of being in that old office for 9 hrs. per day.

Dearest, Cele + Charlie want me to take a 2-month leave of absence from work, so I'll get built up — especially since we're getting married. I could go back to work in May. They said if E.W.C. didn't want to let me have a leave of absence, then they could give me a release + I could get a job someplace else. What do you think of the idea, dearest? I imagine you're wondering what I'm going to use for money all that time but the way things stand now I have practically everything I need for the wedding + won't need any more clothes — the only thing I don't like to live on Cele + Charlie without giving them any money. I guess I could make that up to them, tho, when I start working again.

I have to go back to the doctor Friday + I think he'll prescribe a rest first of all + maybe injections as he knows I'm planning to be married soon + that would be a quicker treatment than just taking medicine.

Cele + Charlie both think that we should have just a breakfast + no reception. They said it would be better to have your family + ours – then pick one from each of the Lavery families too – this would make about 40 or 45 people + would come to about $80 or $85 for the breakfast which would be better than $150 or $165.00. What do you think of this, dearest? It seems the best way to me.

I imagine I'll get mail from you tomorrow, dearest, telling me what date you can make it. As soon as we are pretty sure about the date then we can first of all tell the priest, + then reserve that date for the breakfast. Another thing about having just a breakfast. If we could have use of a nickelodeon (I'm sure we could) we could have music during the dinner + dance too if we wanted to amongst ourselves. Well, dear, at the end of this week we'll decide definitely – but I think that's the way it will be.

Please don't worry about me, dearest. By the time we are married (by the middle of April or so) I'll feel better than I did before. I'll have gained weight by that time too. The doctor knows that I want to feel at my best at that time so I have faith in him – he really knows his business.

I think I'll go into work tomorrow noon + tell the office manager that I'd like either a leave of absence or a release – whatever he wants to give me. It's really the best way, dearest.

I'm so thankful I'm going to marry a type of person as you, dearest. I don't think I could ever have met anyone so understanding + kind. Please again, dear, don't worry about me – when you come home next time you'll see a big improvement in me. I love you so much, Walter. I'm going to try my utmost to make you happy always as I've told you so many times before.

Isn't it odd, darling, it seems no matter how our physical condition is – if we are way below par or not, we still have a desire to let our emotions go – we don't really want to but our sexual systems are all keyed up even when we don't feel so well – like last week for instance – I should never have let myself become aroused at all but you know how everything was – we only saw each other alone for about ½ hr. + tried to crowd everything into that time. We were worse off than before we started by the time you left. Well, we realize our mistakes anyway + when we're married everything will take its course – s l o w l y.

Darling, this is a long letter – I hope you don't mind. I'll close now + mail it.

Lots + lots of love + kisses,
xxxxxx "Bunny" xxxxxx
I love you, dearest.

Wed. Mar. 15th 3 p.m.

Dearest,

I'm eating a nice chocolate Nestle bar as I'm writing this. I bought three of them from Agnes last week + kept them in the Frigidaire + now every day about this time I eat one.

After looking in the mail basket twice this morning + twice this afternoon I've come to the conclusion that there's not going to be any mail from you today, dearest. I know you must have written but it's just slow in coming. I hope I get some tomorrow (Thurs.).

I didn't go out to see the office manager today after all. It's raining that's why. I talked with Cele again last night about my asking for a leave of absence + asked her what she thought of the idea of my working just afternoons for a while. She thinks that's a good idea too. I'd at least be able to make a little money for the hours I worked + contribute a little something here in the house. It's bad enough to have Thomas around here without giving anything towards running the house without my doing that too. In that way I could keep out of debt too. I think I'll ask Charlie Thibault (our office manager) if I can do that for a while – I'll probably go out to the office Friday + talk to him. I could sleep in the morning until quite late + get the rest I need – that's what I need more than anything – the doctor says. I feel a whole lot better today than I have during the past two weeks.

I hope I get a letter from you tomorrow, dearest, telling me what date you can get home on furlough. You'd better take the furlough whenever you can get it – if you let it go you might never get one. I hope everything works out for the best, dearest.

It doesn't seem possible, does it, Walter dear, that you + I will be married soon. It will be wonderful sharing each other's companionship – I think it will be a different kind of companionship than we share now – then, just being together – doing everything together – after we adjust ourselves to each other we can plan towards our future – a home + children.

You + I, dearest, are starting off right – there are no misunderstandings between us. We understand each other's ways + actions better than a lot of other couples getting married – I'm sure our love is so strong it'll carry us through any difficulties we might have later in life. You will always be first in my thoughts, dearest – in fact my whole life will be you. We surely will have a fine life together, heh, dear?

Walter, the next time you come home maybe it would be a good idea to bring your bag with the clothes you'll need when you're on furlough – like socks, handkerchiefs, underwear, pajamas etc. – not too many things but enough to hold you over while you're here. If you need any of these things you could buy them here in Bpt. a few days before. Use your own judgment, dearest.

I guess we won't be seeing each other this week-end, dearest, but you'll probably call up Sunday noon, heh, darling? I'll be thinking of you, dearest.

Love Always,

xxxxxx Rita xxxxxx

Friday 3/24/44 – 1:15 p.m.

Dearest Walter,

As I mentioned in one of my other letters I'm going to meet Helene this afternoon at 2:30 – I'm writing this before I go.

In Wednesday's letter (I got it this morning) you said as far as you knew then – that you'll probably be home this week-end. That'll be wonderful, dearest, if you do. I'll be so glad to see you.

Darling, you said we shouldn't make a deposit at Roseland until about a week before the wedding if possible. They wouldn't reserve the date that long, dearest, without a deposit. Cele said when she does give him the money she'll explain that it's going to be a furlough wedding + if something should happen the last minute that they should make some allowance at least. The best thing to do is just hope nothing does prevent your getting your furlough. It's a gamble no matter how anyone looks at it. We'll just hope for the best, Walter dear. Everything seems to be in your favor so far (+ my favor).

Maybe you'd like to have Eddie Hammer for an usher, dear. Vin will be one but we should have two – to lay the rug for my train. I think he'd be willing to oblige, don't you? If he just came to see the wedding he'd probably have to take time off anyway – very few people have Saturday mornings off these days.

Dearest, $7.50 doesn't seem like very much money to hold you over 'til you get home. I could enclose $5.00 or so in this letter but I'm afraid by the time Saturday's mail arrives at Camp, you'll be gone. Well, I hope the $7.50 is enough. Don't go without eating, dear, get yourself a sandwich at least on the way.

I got my permanent last night. They've gone way up in price. The one I got was $8.50 that was about the cheapest. It came out nice, tho. It isn't too short. Now I won't have to do my hair up in bobby pins when you + I are on our honeymoon (ha ha ha). I will eventually tho, but you'll get used to seeing me like that (ha ha).

Cele is taking time off from work this afternoon (at 3 o'clock) + is going to meet Helene + I too. She's also going to look for a dress. Then Helen + I are going to the show about 5:30 or 6.

Dearest, I'll be home Sat. night so call as you usually do when you get into Bpt. I hope you can manage to leave Camp early. You're such a sweetheart, Walter dear, I love you so much.

Lots + lots of love,
Rita Marie
(long ones) X X X X X X X X X X X X X

Tuesday 3/28/44 – 2:30 p.m.

Dearest Walter,

I hope you are managing to "buck the wind" pretty well on this very windy March day. The wind must be even stronger 'way up there on the Cape than it is here.

My brother, Ed, stopped in here last night for supper + spent the evening.

He was in New Haven on business so he stopped off in Bpt. to see us. He wanted to know all about our wedding. He thought it was a good idea to have it (the breakfast and reception) in Roseland. He said he wouldn't worry if he were in our place about bringing liquor into Roseland; that the beer will be enough + if anyone wants to drink liquor they can buy their own at the bar. He said to have some here at the house tho if we could, in case anyone wants to come back in the evening. Ed is going to come up here again some day soon + be fitted for the morning suit he'll wear – in that place on Congress St. that rents them. Then he might come up the day before the wedding if he can.

While Ed was here Thomas came home drunk. He knows all about him not working, etc. + wanted to talk to him sober but anyway he did talk to him but I'm sure it didn't do a bit of good. Ed had to take the 10:30 train back + Thomas staggered to the bus with him + I guess asked him for money because he didn't come back to the house after Ed got the bus.

There's a man who works in the American Chain who's quite interested in buying our house so Cele + Charlie said if we can't get six rooms someplace – have to move into five – they'll have to let dear Thomas shift for himself + find a room someplace but I know that'll never happen. If we have to move into 2 or 3 rooms he'll still be with us.

Cele said it's too bad you didn't go + talk with your minister when you were home + now, seeing that you might not be home 'til you get your furlough, told me to suggest that you write him. If you want I could compose a letter for you + you just copy it over + send it. I've enclosed one that explains the situation pretty well but you can use your own judgment in sending it. You'll notice I wrote the letter as tho you were <u>telling</u> him of your coming marriage – not <u>asking</u> because with arrangements in the stage they are now, dearest, I don't see how you could do otherwise. Cele has read it + she thinks you should send it.

Dearest, I've tried to choose the words carefully. It's probably what you would say if you were talking to him in person. Remember, dear, I'm just suggesting that you copy it over in your own handwriting + send it. You can use your own judgment. Let me know what you decide to do. If he doesn't hear about it from one of your cousins you'll be lucky. It would be better if he heard from you direct.

Charlie brought home one of Dr. Fishbiens' books. It's one I think you read. One part of it talks about Sex Hygiene + he thought you + I should both read it. I read it about a year ago. Violet let me take it. I told him I read it before + was quite sure you did too + he got mad. He said he was going to have a talk with you (on the sexual part of marriage I guess) but said if he did I'd probably be insulted or something. He thinks I have an awful attitude about it – that I don't want to be told anything about it.

Well, dearest, it is quite embarrassing isn't it? I'm taking it for granted that you know a lot – you've read a lot haven't you? There are a few things I'd like to ask you but we're never alone long enough + when we are the only thing we do is smooch. We don't talk sensibly about anything. I wish you could come home in a few weeks but I know it'll be hard – everyone will want to go home Easter.

Well, dearest, this is a long letter isn't it? Tomorrow is the night of the shower on me. Can you picture my surprised face? (ha ha).

Take care of yourself, dearest, I'll be thinking of you.

Love Always,

xxxxxx Rita xxxxxx

Wednesday, 3/29/44

Hello Dearest,

I was glad to hear you made good time getting back to Camp – 1:30 – it gave you a little more sleep than usual.

No darling, I wasn't tired after the week end – I had plenty of time to rest.

Tonight is the shower, dearest. I'll feel awfully strange walking in with Eleanor + seeing all the people. There'll be about 24 or 25 there. Just thinking of all the nice gifts you + I will have, heh, dear? I'll tell you about it when I write tomorrow.

Last night after going to Church Cele + I went into Fr. O'Connell to tell him that Fr. Pat wants to marry us. He was very nice about it – he said that's the way it should be – if there is a relative who is a priest in any famiy – he's the one who should marry the girl. He said he'd be on the altar too. Isn't that nice of him? He said he thinks you're a nice chap – you seem to be clean-cut + kiddingly said with a nice Irish girl like me for a wife (ha ha) we should be happy.

Cele + I also spoke to the organist + told her we'd like Bob Greene to sing. She said she'd be glad to play for him – that he has a good voice. They are going to have one song sung – at the end – just before we walk out. The name of it is "Mother At Thy Feet is Kneeling" + it's a beautiful hymn. We could have either that one or the "Ave Maria" but I like the one to the Blessed Virgin better. The words are in English + are beautiful whereas the Ave Maria is in Latin.

Today I received a card from the photographer that the glossy finish picture is ready – the one I'm going to use for the paper. I don't know when to put it in tho, dearest. I think I should wait for a week or two yet – by that time you should be quite sure of your furlough. Maybe by Easter Sunday it could be put in – that would be 2 wks. Before the 22nd. What do you think, dear?

We're going to inquire soon about flowers. We'll try to keep the price down as much as possible. We might just get ferns for the altar + hope that whoever gets married before us will have some on the altar. That would cut expenses quite a bit.

Dearest, Cele said if you do decide to send that letter to the minister that you could put a line in (after the part where I said that we were planning to be married in my church) saying that my cousin is a priest + wants to perform the ceremony – or words to that effect. If you could only come home once more before the 20th you could make it a point to see the minister. As far as your father is concerned, dearest, I'm sure in the end he'll make the best of it + come to the wedding. You could tell him too that my cousin wants to marry us.

Well, dearest, I hope everything is well with you. Please don't worry about anything – I think everything will work out fine. Just try to get here on the 20th that's all. (ha ha) – because if there isn't any groom, there won't be any bride (ha ha).

I love you so much, dearest. I'm sure we'll be happy.

Love Always

big ones →XXXXXX Rita XXXXXX

Date_____

Reverend Conrad Reisch

76 Harriet St.

Bridgeport, Conn.

Dear Pastor,

I wanted to visit you when I was home last week-end but time didn't permit so I am writing these few lines to tell you that I'm planning to get married in April – about the 22nd, if the application for my furlough goes through.

The girl I am planning to marry is a Catholic. We have been going together for the past three years. She is as strong in her beliefs as I am in mine. As I always thought it is a girl's privilege to be married in her own Church, we are planning to be married in the Catholic Church.

I realize it would be much better if we were both of the same beliefs but I am quite sure we will have a happy marriage because we both understand that each of us will be free to follow our own Faith. I fully intend to practice my own Religion as I have in the past.

I am sorry I haven't had a chance to talk with you on this subject. I would rather have told you personally but I am sure you understand the little time we boys have here in the Army.

I would appreciate hearing your viewpoint on the matter + look forward to your understanding.

Sincerely,

Walter Klein

(Your Address Love, Walt.)

Wednesday 3/30/44 – 4:30 p.m.

Hello Darling,

I just finished putting some pork chops in the oven to bake for supper. Yes, Walt – I've really started to practice cooking. You see I'm trying everything out on the family first (ha ha). I put the pork chops in a pan + sliced a couple of onions + cut up some green peppers + put them on top to give the chops some flavor. The other night I made a very good meat loaf with chopped steak, onions, 1 egg, bread crumbs + pepper. It came out really good considering it was the first time I ever tried anything like that. I surprised myself even. (ha ha). I think now I could get a plain, ordinary meal together like — potatoes, vegetable-meat-baked + dessert. Maybe when you + I come back from our trip after we're married I'll make dinner some night + you can sample my cooking. (ha ha).

Well, dearest, the shower is all over now + everything was grand. I received some lovely presents. Enclosed you'll find a list of what I got + from whom. Wait 'til you see the things. You'll notice they are things to be used in our home — altho I got some personal presents too. Everyone seemed to have a good time too. We had lots of laughs because Eleanor's sister, Virginia, was there + she + Cele were saying funny things to make everyone have a good time. Your sister Martha managed to come too. I was glad. She left the children at Fishers + Adolph picked her up after it was over — Helene + Ellen came too. Emma has her top set of teeth out — that's why she didn't come but she sent a very nice gift. I was so excited when I was opening the gifts. I thanked each one individually as I opened them. I'll be more at ease when my cousins give me theirs. They are giving me a big one April 11th.

Yes, dearest, I can see your father's point of view with another mixed marriage in the family but it was your sister's very bad luck to get a husband like Bridges. He is no example of a Catholic — or of anything. You could hardly even call him a Christian. I wish you could come home once more before your furlough + have a talk with your father — I would like to be with you too. I could explain in a nice way that I realize how he feels but that I'll do everything I can to make our marriage a fine one. He might understand when he knows my cousin is going to marry us.

Yes, I was surprised myself when Fr. Pat offered to marry us. We are doubly related — that's why he wants to. He said he wished us the best life has to offer.

Ellen seems to think a tie clip set would be nice for Al. She says he hasn't one but would use it if he owned one.

Dearest — about the silver set — (comb, brush + mirror) — you said you haven't seen any up in Camp Edwards in the P.X. It's too bad because that's the only thing I'd like. I suppose you think I'm awfully selfish in wanting such an expensive present but as I mentioned over the week-end I would love to have something from you that I could keep for the rest of my life. I could always say that's what you gave me on my wedding day. If you could only see one for about $35.00 or $40, you could get it when you get paid Apr. 1st. You wouldn't be any richer by not spending the money, Kleiny (ha ha).

If your furlough goes thru (+ I sure hope it does) you'll be home, dearest, 3 wks. from today. Yes, 3 wks. from this coming Sat. is the 22nd. I hope nothing prevents you from getting your furlough. Well, dearest, I'll be thinking of you. I love you so much, Walter. You're a good boy, heh, dear? Take care of yourself so you'll be fine + dandy for our wedding.

Lots + lots of love, dearest
"Bunny"
xxxxxxxxxx

Here's a list of the presents I received last night. Everyone is so nice.
Your sister, Helene – Embroidered sheet + pillowcases – (beautiful)
Martha – Water glass set – 6 glasses + pitcher – very odd shaped glasses – very nice
Ellen – Knife set – about 6 different kind of knives – carving, paring, bread knife, etc. (very useful).
Emma sent a luncheon cloth + napkins blue + cream color + also 1 set of pillowcases with "Mr" on one + "Mrs" on the other. (very nice)
Cele + Eleanor – a beautiful blue satin negligee + nightgown to match. (oh boy)
Eleanor + Kay Keating – a rose colored set of scarves for the bureaus – one for the chest of drawers, one for the dresser, etc. very nice.
Mary Buccino – 6 glasses - with "RYE" printed on them (for rye high balls) + 6 little individual glass dishes for nuts, candy, etc. (nice).
Mrs. Smith – A beautiful hand-made set of scarves for bureaus + a buffet set (hand-made too) + also 3 yellow + white crocheted pieces for hot dishes. There is about 6 months work in everything she gave me.
Dot Smith – a lovely lacey slip (tea-rose)
Dot's grandmother – 2 beautiful hand-crocheted doilies – quite large.
Virginia Kelly (Eleanor's sister) – a string of lovely pearls.
Gladys Kelly (Eleanor's sister-in-law) – a white silk slip. – very nice.
Ann Fendorak (works with Cele) – a nice kitchen table cloth.
Ethel Greene (from Lordship) 2 large bath towels – 1 yellow + 1 green.
Sadie – (Charlie's sister) luncheon set – (table cloth + four napkins) for a card table or kitchen – nice
Catherine – Sadie's daughter (who's been away) 2 towels (fancy) + face cloths (rose color – nice)
Sarah – Buddy's mother – 1 bureau scarf-lace - + 1 cocktail towel (embroidered).
Helen – Charlie's sister-in-law – 2 nice yellow bath towels. (nice)
Mary Singer – a bathroom set – yellow mat + toilet cover. (ha ha). Nice
Ann Preston + Eleanor – Joe's girl – a lovely buffet set 3 pieces – frosted glass in different colors + 2 pieces are candle holders (holds 2 candles each) + then the centerpiece – a very large bowl.
    I guess that's all, dearest. Isn't that a nice selection of gifts tho? I'll put most of them in my cedar chest – you'll see them next time you come.

Palm Sunday, April 2nd '44

Hello Dearest,
    We talked for quite a little while over the 'phone, heh? I was so glad when

you called. It always makes me feel closer to you.

I'm glad you managed to get away from the Camp last night into Buzzard's Bay for a while — altho I hope you didn't drink too much beer, not that you would intentionally, but I know how you are when you go out with anyone — you don't like to refuse — you always follow the crowd (ha ha).

As I mentioned on the 'phone, dearest, our house was sold Friday to a Mr. + Mrs. Jensen, the people who run the jewelry shop on Stfd. Ave. They got a good price on it I guess — I mean they were able to get it cheap. They are willing to spend $2,000 or $2,500 just for repairs. So now the Lavery-Monahan clan will have to find another rent (ha ha). We'll have about 3 months yet, tho, to look for something. Cele said she's not going to look for a place 'til after the wedding — about May 1st — we can start looking. We might be lucky enough to find a place because quite a few out-of-towners are going back home.

We had some more bad news too over the week-end. Charlie went over to the post office to get the truth about Thomas' job — whether he still had it or not. Russell Neary, who is Acting Postmaster talked with Charlie + said he (Thomas) is definitely through over there. He sent in his own resignation on March 6th, signed, etc. + it has gone thru Washington too. The reason he put down resignation was that he had other employment. Isn't that terrible? Mr. Neary said they've done everything they could possibly do for him to make him come back. They even offered him a private office so he could study 'til he learned the system but he made no attempt — in fact he has never taken the test once + he told us he took it 3 times but didn't pass each time. Cele + Charlie feel so bad about him giving up a job like that + then to think he would act like that after all they've done for him — after all — they came up to this house on account of him. Charlie said he'll have to get out when we move. I doubt it but we'll see anyway.

Well dearest, I seem to be writing all the bad news heh? Our coming wedding is the only bright spot on the horizon right now. As I mentioned on the 'phone, I bought Al a tie clip set yesterday in Reid + Todd's downtown. There are just two pieces + it cost over $5.00 — I used your money. It's rather plain but it's nice. They call it gold-rolled 14-karat so it should be pretty good.

I inquired in Larry's about flowers — also in Horans in the Arcade + both places said to wait until after Easter to put in the order because the prices wouldn't be so high then + that will be plenty of time. They wouldn't give me any prices yet but we'll put an order in after Easter — I don't think it'll be too expensive.

I'm going to take my picture down to the Herald some day this week + have it put in either next Sunday or the following week. It depends on how their space is taken.

It'll be so nice, dearest, if you come home next week-end for Easter. Aren't we lucky tho, Walter, that we can see each other every other week-end? Some fellows can never get home. Mary Monahan, for instance went all the way to Oklahoma to see her husband (Ralph) + when she got there he couldn't get any time off. She was there for a week + had to travel 16 miles every day to see him just for a short while in the day time. He couldn't leave Camp at all. He's in the Infantry + is a cook. He's never had a furlough since he's been in the Army. He went in September. Of course that isn't too long but he's so far away – it's too bad. They've been married 8 years. Another case is Ruth Landry. She hasn't seen her boyfriend in a year + 7 months. He's been in the Aleutians over a year. If you + I had to go that long without seeing each other we'd die, heh, dearest? (ha ha). No, I guess we'd have to make the best of it like other people do but it sure would be hard.

You said in Thursday's letter that you might drop your brother a card + remind him to get his suit fitted in time. Yes, dear, it would be a good idea – altho he doesn't have to have it fitted for about another week + a half. There's a store on Congress St. where Vin + Ed are going to have theirs fitted. They sent them there $7.00 for a day. It used to be $5.00 but prices have gone up. Sometimes they have the person's size right in stock. Tell him they are called a <u>morning</u> <u>suit</u> – striped trousers, cut-away coat, etc. They are worn at all formal weddings.

About asking Eddie Hammer – Do you know his address? You could drop him a card or short letter + say you'll try to see him if you come home in a week + tell him all about the wedding + ask him if he could oblige you by being an usher. If you don't ask him, Charlie can fill in but, dearest, let me know what you want to do. It would be nice to have your brother + Eddie in the party + I would have Eleanor + Vin from my side – it's up to you tho – don't wait too long if you ask Eddie.

I love you so much, darling – you're a good boy. Take care of yourself now. I'm feeling better now so don't worry. Lots of hugs + kisses.

Love Always,

X X X X X X Rita X X X X X X

(your future little wife)

Monday 4/3/44 – 4:15 p.m.

Hello Walter Dearest,

I just came back from downtown – it's such a nice day out I went down and bought some things Cele wanted – crêpe paper to decorate the house for the wedding + I bought shoes to wear with my going-away outfit. They are snake-skin (yellowish color sandals) + are quite nice I think. When I came back the letter you wrote yesterday (Sun.) was in the mail basket.

It was so sweet of you to write, dearest, after calling up. It was such a nice "mushy" letter too. If you hadn't written 'til today I wouldn't have received any mail 'til Wed. but you're such a good boy, dearest. You know that would be quite a while not to get mail.

Yes, darling, I was wishing yesterday you were home too – I just felt like talking to you + being close to you. I can't believe it yet, dear, that we will be Mr. + Mrs. Walter J. Klein in three more weeks (not quite three weeks). It will be so strange being together for ten days – sleeping, eating, etc. I can hardly believe it. We'll have a wonderful honeymoon tho I think, dearest, if we take everything easy + don't strain + tire ourselves out, but we won't will we, dearest? We'll have a nice time in N.Y. + also when we come home to 1440. I'm going to fix the middle bedroom up for us – that is, use some of the presents I got in it like scarves, bedspread, etc. That's where you + I will sleep as long as we stay in this house – after we move I don't know just how things will be – it depends on how many rooms we get, but time will tell – there's no use worrying about that now. I hope you are planning on using 1440 Stfd Ave as your address for Army records after we're married, dearest. It would be better don't you think – because for the duration – whenever you come home, naturally you'll live with me – (Cele, Charlie + Jeanie too).

Helene called me up last night + asked me to go to the show with her. We went to see "Cover Girl" at the Globe. I know you saw it + liked it, dearest. I liked it a lot. Rita Hayworth sure is bee-you-ti-ful (ha ha) – Gene Kelly was good too in it.

You say I'll look exceptionally nice going down the aisle in white. Well, I hope so, dearest. I hope I don't get awfully nervous – I did when I was Dot Smith's bridesmaid so goodness knows how I'll be at my own wedding. Of course you won't be nervous in the least. (ha ha). Oh well, it's to be expected I guess to a certain extent.

Well, dearest, I'd better mail this letter. I'm thinking of you all the time + praying that nothing will prevent you from getting your furlough.

Love Always,

X X X X X X Bunny X X X X X X

P.S. Don't worry too much about the silver comb-brush + mirror set, if you can't find one for about $35 or $40. They cost about $50 in Bpt. + that's too much to pay. I'll try to think of something I could use that's less expensive. On second thought maybe they have those plastic ones – like a nylon material. Ernie gave Dot one a year ago Christmas in plastic + it's very pretty + not so expensive – they come in different colors – blue would be nice. In Dot's set there are about 8 pieces + I don't think it cost more than $20. Use your own judgment, dearest. The rose colored one you gave me 3 years ago is wearing out. (ha ha).

Lots of love, dearest

R.

3:00 pm. Wednesday 4/5/44

Hello Dearest,

How do you like my fancy writing paper with lines on it – (ha ha)? You don't care what kind of paper I use, dear – as long as I write.

I received the letter you wrote Monday night this morning.

Yes, dearest, Sunday if you come home – let's not waste any time – see Eddie Hammer if you can + also your pastor. If Eddie Hammer can't make the wedding then Charlie can be the other usher – only I don't want him to feel that he's second choice, if you understand what I mean. If Charlie thought you were asking Eddie Hammer + then Eddie couldn't make it + you asked Charlie – I don't think he'd like it, in other words, dearest, ask either one or the other + let it go at that. Don't tell Charlie I said this – when you come home – but I think he's sort of taken it for granted he would usher. We'll see, dear, don't worry.

About you + I finding a new address when the three months are up here – Cele + Charlie are going to get as many rooms as they can. They prefer six but it's hard to find that many rooms I guess. They said if they go into 5 rooms, Thomas will have to shift for himself. Let's just take everything as it comes + not worry now about what we would do.

I wrote to Emma too, dearest – last Friday + invited her + Gus to the breakfast + reception. I told them I was sorry the invitation couldn't include the children because if I were to have all the children come from each family there would be quite a number + most places outside now only accommodate a certain number. I told her to call me + let me know within a week or so if she + Gus could come.

Ann Preston invited me to her house tonight for dinner – so I'm going out there about 5:30.

Quite a few of the girls from the office call me up once in a while + Agnes called today + said Betty Hughes is expecting a baby in August. She's still traveling around with Bill. He's stationed right now in Savannah, Georgia + they live in a little government house with another couple. She says she's going to stay with Bill as long as he's in this country even if she has to have the baby in a government hospital (financed by the gov't). She certainly has a lot of courage. She wrote to Agnes + said Bill was so glad about her having the baby he was "walking on air". Imagine! Betty's sister (Bill Marsh's wife) had a baby a week ago – a little boy.

Dearest, if you do get a pass this week-end (I do hope you do) will you call me as soon as you get into Bpt. because I'll keep wondering + wondering if you're coming + won't know for sure 'til you call.

This time I'd like to go out Sat. night – it'll be the last time we'll be going out for an evening of dancing, a snack, etc. while we're single + it's better to go out than to stay inside in such close contact with each other, but of course, dearest, if you're too tired we don't have to go. We'll see.

I love you so much. When we're on our honeymoon in N.Y. it sure will be wonderful having you all to myself – that is being alone + being able to do everything together – go to some good shows, dance, dine + rest of course too – it seems as tho we are hardly ever alone.

I love you so much, dearest, - with all my heart + will surely do my best to be a good wife to you, "to have + to hold – to love + to cherish – in sickness + in health – for richer – for poorer 'til death do us part" – or words to that effect – we will be saying soon – not just saying them with our lips but we will mean them + will fulfill all those vows for the rest of our lives.

Love Always,
big ones →X X X X X X Rita X X X X X X

Wednesday – 4/12/44 – 4:15 p.m.

Dearest Walter,

I'm writing this during one of my breathing spells of the afternoon (ha ha). I've been so busy all day today straightening out all of the beautiful presents I received last night at the shower. Then I scrubbed the floor of the middle bedroom so now I thought I'd relax awhile + write to you.

The shower my cousins gave me last night turned out fine. It was held in the Heirloom Shop on Fairfield Ave + it's a lovely place. They served a supper first – chicken paddies – salad, rolls, dessert + coffee. After everyone finished eating I opened the gifts + received so many beautiful ones that I can't begin to name them all. You can see them when you come home, dearest. Some of the outstanding ones are: a beautiful chenille bedspread (blue), a large table lamp with a crystal base with a white shade with wine color trimming – a set of dishes (service of 4) glass ones – called hobnail glassware – two boudoir lamps from Eleanor + Cele (white with crystal bases), another set of dishes (service of 4) in different colors. Well, that'll give you a little idea of some of the things I received, dearest. As I said before you can see for yourself when you come. I'm sure you'll get a lot of pleasure out of looking them all over.

The Hotel Taft sent me an answer already to the letter I sent for a room + bath for you + I. They said they are reserving a double room, private bath + radio for $5.50 less 10% service discount. This offer is special to servicemen + their wives. They said if we arrive after 9: P.M. at night that we should send them a money order in advance for one night's payment. I told them in the letter we expected to arrive between 8 + 9 o'clock but I'd better send the money order for $5.00 anyway – just to be sure.

I received your Monday's letter this morning, dearest. Yes, I have all the necessary clothes ready – I didn't bring my gown + veil home yet but I have everything else – suit, coat, blouse, hat, shoes, bag, two new dresses, + yes, darling, for your information all the pretty silk things I'll need too. (ha ha).

Albert is having his suit fitted next week + as I told you yesterday seeing he can't make the rehearsal the night before you can go down to church with him a little early the morning of the wedding + tell him what to do. Don't worry about him being ready. Everything will work out.

We have to go out to Roseland tonight + give them the number that will be at the breakfast + an approximate number that will be at the reception. Here's who's going to the breakfast:

Your Family
Helene
Your father
Ellen + Al

Ruth + Gus
Martha + Adolph
You + I
Mine
Cele; Charlie, Jeanie
Edward
Eleanor + Vin
Thomas (???)
Fr. Pat.
Fr. O'Connell (???)
Loretta, John Neary
Irene (Brooklawn)
Florence (Irene's sister)
Frank, Allice, little
Alice Curnin.
Eddie Hammer (if he ushers)

There are 27 — as you can see — that's what we're telling Roseland tonight anyway + about 60 for the reception.

Fr. O'Connell might have to go to another wedding breakfast on that day but we're going to ask him anyway. I don't even know whether my dear brother, Thomas, will go to the Church or not. (ha ha).

Dearest, as I told you before my cousin Eileen is giving a tea + shower on me this coming week-end. (Sat. from 3 to 6 in the afternoon). So I expect to be home by 6:30 or 7. I'd suggest that you come here as soon as you get in Bpt. + Charlie will be here if I'm not. Maybe you won't get into Bpt. 'til about 8 o'clock anyway but if you come about 7 — come to 1440 + I'll be home very shortly if I'm not here already. I sure do hope you can come this week so you can see Eddie Hammer + the minister. Well, dearest, you said you hadn't written to them at the time you write Monday's letter. I think you should write even if you do see them but I know you too well to think you will (ha ha). "Last minute Kleiny" that's you.

I have to go to the store now so I'll close.

Lots + lots of love, dearest.

xxxxxx Rita xxxxxx

P.S. I have the chart on Sexual Rhythm worked out on paper for my system for the next nine months. I'll show it to you when you come home. It's the way I understand it but I'm not sure, tho. It said in the book that you should figure it out for the following 8 mos. To 1 year. We'll see, dearest, when you come home.

Friday 4/14/44 — 5:45 pm

Hello Walter Dearest,

You might not receive this letter tomorrow if you get your pass but I just felt like writing a few lines anyway.

Mr. + Mrs. Smith are coming over tonight for a short visit. Mrs. Smith said something over the phone about bringing over a wedding gift.

This afternoon I went downtown + inquired about wedding pictures in Janetty's – on Broad St. I think it would be a good place to have them taken. I'll tell you all about it over the week-end, anyway, dearest.

Cele + I have to go to Larry's, the florist, tomorrow night at 7:30 to make arrangements about the flowers. We'll probably have to go when we come home from the shower. Well, dearest, if you come you can wait a little while.

I didn't receive any mail from you today. I hope I do tomorrow.

Just think, darling, next week at this time we'll be excited + counting the hours practically – 'til we march down the aisle. I do hope everything works out so there won't be any delay in getting your furlough.

I called up the Fishers last night + invited them to the church + the reception + called Mr. + Mrs. Eisenman today + invited them. I guess they are all going.

I'll be so glad to see you this week-end, dearest. I hope you won't have any trouble getting your pass like you did last week.

Love Always,

Big ones ➔ X X X X X X Rita X X X X X X

P.S. It doesn't seem possible that a week from tomorrow we'll be Mr. + Mrs., heh, dear? I love you so much, dearest. Take good care of yourself.

PART VII: D-Day and the End of an Era

The Separation Ends, Married Life Begins

Although the war was still going on in the spring of 1944 as D-Day approached, Walter and Rita were married on April 22, 1944. They were married in the Church of the Blessed Sacrament, 275 Union Avenue, Bridgeport. The letters show how reluctant Walter was in telling his father that their wedding would be in a Catholic Church. The wedding was referred to as a furlough marriage, as Walter was able to get a 10-day pass.

They had set an original wedding date on or close to June 5, 1944, but the date was pushed forward. Rita wrote in one letter that her parents were wed on June 5, 1901, hence her emotional tie to that date. Walter and Rita spent their brief furlough honeymoon in New York City. I assume they traveled to New York by train from Bridgeport. Neither Walter nor Rita had a car at the time. Gasoline rationing was also a limiting factor.

Shortly after their wedding, the war took center stage. Rita worried that Walter might be reclassified for active combat. On June 6, 1944, Rita heard about the D-Day invasion on the radio, along with most of the country. Other dramatic war news was aired on the radio each night.

Walter enjoyed an extended six-week delayed routing leave in June and into July of 1944. This was prior to a then-pending reassignment. Starting in July of 1944, he was stationed on the West Coast. Rita moved in July 1944 to be closer to him. Once they were living in California, that brought an end to the wartime letters. In all, the letters spanned a period of about 17 months; starting in January of 1943 and ending in June 1944.

The wedding, April 22, 1944. Walter's brother Albert is best man. Eddie Hammer and Rita's brother Vin are ushers. Rita's sister-in-law Eleanor (Vin's wife) is matron of honor.

Letters: May 7, 1944 – June 14, 1944

Sunday, May 7 '44 1:00 pm

My Dearest,

I hope you arrived back safely at Camp + that you aren't finding it too hard to adjust to the old routine.

I've been wondering, Walter dear, if you'd have a chance to call up today. If you don't call, I'll understand, dearest.

This morning I went to 10 o'clock Mass alone – Cele + Charlie weren't ready for 10 so they went to 11. I made our bed (yours + mine, dear) dusted a little downstairs here, read the papers awhile + now I'm writing to my dearest husband. It seems so strange, Walter dear, to call you my husband. I'm not used to it yet.

I miss you so much, dearest, but still I'm very happy because we had such a wonderful two weeks together. All our wedding plans worked out perfectly + the days we spent together – our honey-moon in N.Y. + here at home were such happy days. Last night I prayed for you, dearest, + thanked God for giving me such a wonderful husband. I'll never forget these past few weeks – they were the happiest of my life. I know we'll have a full + rich life together too – we'll be together spiritually – have a fine companionship + as husband + wife when you come home. We'll always be very close to each other even tho we are separated by distance. As time goes by I hope I can show you how much I love you.

You deserve the best life can offer + I'm going to do my utmost to be a good wife to you, dearest.

I'll be thinking of you 'til I see you again, Walter dear. Please take care of yourself – for me – we belong to each other now, darling.

Don't worry about me, Walter. This coming week I'm going to rest 'til I go back to work next Monday. I won't drink too much tea or coffee (ha ha).

Love Always,
Your little wife
Rita Marie

(six for last night → X X X X X X X X X X X X + six for this morning)

Monday, May 8 '44 3:00 pm

My Dearest (Husband),

I hope everything is well with you this beautiful sun-shiny day.

I was so sorry, dearest, that I wasn't home last night when you called. When you didn't call by 1:30 yesterday afternoon I thought you didn't find time + that you knew I was to meet Helene at 5:30 last night to go to the show. Cele said you called from Bedford – that you were there with some fellows. I'm glad you had some time to yourself.

I imagine you are finding it a little difficult to get used to the old Army routine – that is, after being with your "little wife" for two weeks. (ha ha).

Dearest, I went to the bank today + cashed those two small insurance checks I had ($5.00 each). I also deposited $25.00 that the Fishers + Eisenmans gave us, + had the name of the account changed to Mrs. Rita Klein instead of Lavery. Now we have plenty of money left for the pictures + I'll send you $5.00 or so at the end of this week so you can keep it for train-fare – that is, if you don't get paid for awhile. Let me know, dearest, how you make out.

Ann Preston called me up today and said Willie came home over the week-end. He stayed at his own home tho in Long Island + Ann went down there over the week-end. I think they're going to be married soon. Ann said they haven't made any decision yet but they are weakening + if they do decide to it will be in July because Willie is due a furlough then. I guess it's catching – the desire to get married. Ann says all her girlfriends are getting married or are already married. I told her to think it over thoroughly before she decides – she's so young – altho she's much more matured than I am even now. I told her what a fine fellow you are + how happy we are.

I miss you so much, Walter dearest. A week ago today you + I were here together doing all the household chores + having a lot of fun. Remember, dearest, when you + I went to the Prestons for dinner + ended up cooking it? (ha ha). My darling thought he was going to a swanky house + was almost afraid to breathe (ha ha).

I love you with all my heart, dearest + am thinking of you all the time. You are my life now + it will be such a pleasure for me to do everything possible to make you happy. Every night I pray that God will keep you close to me + watch over you.

Lots + lots of Love, dearest.
Rita, your loving wife.

P.S. Here are 24 kisses (2 dozen) one dozen for last night + one for today
X X X X X X X X X X X X X X X X X X X X X X X X

Tuesday, May 9th 3:45 pm.

Dearest Walter,

It was so strange this morning opening your Sunday's letter addressed to "Mrs. Walter J. Klein" – it was a nice feeling tho, dear + your first letter to your "little Rita" was so nice – that is, your first letter since we've been married.

Yes, Walter dear, I was very lonesome for you Sat. night + Sunday just as you were, but we'll both adjust ourselves the best we can, heh, dear? We both love each other so much, it's hard tho.

I just came back from downtown after taking our proofs back. We'll have some beautiful pictures when they're finished, four of the group, four of you + I together (the smiling one), three of the half-pose of myself – you know, dearest the one sitting down, three of myself (full length – showing the gown, train etc.) + one of Ed + I that makes a total of 15 altogether. The photographer is giving us a large one framed – whatever one we want made up for nothing (no charge) but I'll decide which one when I get the pictures. I think one of you + I together would be nice.

Mr. Jannetty likes the serious one of me (the half pose) – the one you, I + everyone else <u>didn't</u> like. He's going to use it for display – he says it's a very unusual expression. I told him I thought I looked mad in it but he says that's because it isn't re-touched yet. I just laughed + said you thought the smiling one was more natural of me (ha ha). I paid $21.00 more on the pictures – there isn't so much of a balance now, dearest. I have the amount on hand when they're ready. They'll be ready a week from this coming Sat.

When I go into our room at night, dearest, I see all of your things around + it makes me feel closer to you – your hat, brush, shaving utensils, etc. I want to leave them around like that – it makes me feel – not so lonesome.

Sometimes I like to think of different things you + I did together during the past two weeks. We sure had a wonderful time together. I'll be glad when I go back to work next week. It'll keep me very busy.

Are the boys wearing sun-tans yet in Camp? I imagine it's still quite cool up there. Don't catch cold, dearest. Keep well + as happy as you possibly can. I love you so much.

Love Always,
Your Wife Rita
long ones → X X X X X X X X X X X X X
just the kind you like, dearest.

Thursday, May 18th 6:00 pm.

Dearest Walter,

It's so nice to come home from work every night + find your letter waiting for me – I enjoy them so much, darling, I just finished reading Tuesday's letter – I know how hard it must be for you to write sometimes – you're so nice, dearest, to write each day to your little wife.

Gertrude sent me the negatives of some pictures she took at our wedding – outside of the church – I'll have them developed – I think they should be good because they were taken at a very close range.

I was so glad to hear you can probably get a three-day pass about the middle of June – it should be very nice by that time at Lordship.

Dot Liepertz is coming down to the house tonight to show the movies of us, dear, I wish so much you could be here but maybe sometime we could go up to Dot's house + she'll show them to you.

I hope you receive the money I sent you last night ($6.00). Today was pay day in the office but of course I didn't get paid as I didn't work last week. Well,

I have enough 'til next week I guess.

Dearest, I'll be so glad to see you this coming weekend. The past two weeks have been long ones. I want to tell you how much I love you (when you come home) + be nice + close to you, dearest. You're such a good husband to me, dear – so considerate + kind.

This afternoon in the office I was thinking of you – about how you helped me so much when you were home all the little things you did, dearest, here in the house, emptying the ash trays (ha ha), going to the store, drying dishes, vacuuming, helping me make the bed. We had a lot of fun doing it tho, heh dear? When we have our own home (rent) after this awful war is over, I would never expect you to do any of those things, dearest – unless I was sick or something. You were so nice in lots of other ways too, dearest, while you were home – I thought about it for a long while this afternoon + wished I could tell you in person how wonderful I think you are. I hope I can always guide + help you too, dearest, if you have any difficulties or problems.

Dearest, I'll be looking forward to hearing from you Sat. (by phone) when you get into Bpt. I hope nothing prevents you from getting a pass.

Love always,

Rita

long ones →X X X X X X X X X X X X

Friday, May 19th 7:00 p.m.

Dearest,

Just received your Wednesday's letter telling me about the trip that is scheduled for you in the Command Car with Colonel Stadler.

No, dearest, you couldn't very well refuse to drive it home. As you said, it doesn't pay in the Army to say "no" to some things. It'll be awfully tiring for you, tho, dearest, to drive all that distance + especially when you're driving back Sun. night. You say you'll probably have to stay with the car while it's on display for about four hours. Well, dearest, it's too bad to waste four hours like that but we'll make the most of the time we are together – At least we can be with each other Sat. night + the rest of the time left Sun.

The movies of our wedding are very good. Dot Liepertz showed them last night – The colors look so nice – I'll probably tell you about them over the week-end, darling. Dot said you could see them any time you like, so maybe the next time you come home we can go up to her house – you'd get a big kick out of seeing them. (seeing yourself in the movies – ha ha).

Dearest, I'll be so happy to see you Sat. I can hardly wait to see you, dearest. We'll give each other some nice kisses + if you're tired after driving I'll soothe your brow for you (ha ha). No, really, dear, you can have a nice rest – I imagine you'll be rather tired.

Lots and lots of love, dear,

Rita Marie

big ones→X X X X X X X X X X X X X
P.S. I don't know whether the Jensens will let you park the car in the yard.
They are old crabs (ha ha).

Monday, May 22nd

My Dearest,

I hope you arrived back at Camp safe + sound last night. It must have
been awfully hard driving after dark + I imagine my dearest is quite tired today.
I hope you'll have a nice sleep tonight, darling.

I enjoyed the week-end with you so much, dear – just being together Sat.
night + then yesterday going to the luncheon + to church to see the crowning
– the time went by so fast, dearest. Next time you come home let's just stay
together + not even budge from the house, as you said yesterday (ha ha).
Maybe we could go to Lordship tho + get a nice sun bath.

I've been thinking about you all afternoon, dearest + wondering how you
made out with your interview. I've been praying all afternoon that they
wouldn't talk you into having the tissue removed on your arm. I mentioned to
Helene last night after you left that they wanted you to have it done but she
said you definitely shouldn't have them touch you at all. She won't mention it
to your father at all, dear, so don't worry. She said she wouldn't count on those
Army doctors being so skilled.

Dearest, I don't see how cutting the tissue + eliminating the limited
motion of your arm would be such a wonderful asset to you – of course it
could help your motion but it wouldn't make up for all of the effects of the
burn you've been thru in the past + the symptoms you still feel once in a while
– As I mentioned yesterday, it would just give the Army one more man to send
out + then do whatever they felt like once you're "across the pond." As Cele +
Charlie said, they think there is more to the operation than you think – they
said you might suffer more after it – seeing all these years have gone by
without having anything done, it might be more of a shock to your system than
you realize (if you had it done). Besides, dearest, as you + I both know, being
subject to be moved out (if it were done), two years of our lives would be
wasted. The boys now are either sacrificing their lives or wasting years – in my
estimation (yours too I think).

I understand how you feel too, dear, as you said it's easy for us here at
home to tell you what you should do but still you wouldn't want the officers,
or anyone in fact, to think you were "yellow" or trying to get out of something.
Well, Walter dear, you can let me know how you made out + if there are any
new developments. Please let me know, dearest, when you write – don't keep
anything from me. I know you don't want me to worry but I'd really rather
know than to go on thinking everything was fine + dandy + then all of a
sudden be shocked. I'll pray that everything will work out for you, dearest.

Last night Helene + I didn't go to the show after all. We just took a bus
downtown + went window-shopping + then stopped in the "Star" + had a

sandwich + coffee. One of the waiters in there asked Helene if we were sisters. She said "No, sister-in-laws" + he asked her what my name was – he said "Isn't she a pretty little thing, isn't she cute?" (ha ha ha). I think he was a jerk (ha ha).

Irene Noonan gave me a very nice gift today, a scrap book, to keep all the details of our wedding in – there are pages for everything gifts (list of people who gave + what they gave us) – pages for description of flowers, gown, trousseau, honeymoon, pictures etc. It's all white (the binding) + I think I'll put all the cards, etc. I have in it + other data. It'll be nice to keep thru the years.

Dearest, I love you so much. You make me so happy. God has been so good to us both so far – I hope you'll always be close to me. Be a good boy, dearest, 'til I see you again (you always are).

Love Always
Rita Marie
X X X X X X X X X X X X

Tuesday, May 23, '44

Hello Walter, (My Dearest Husband)

I hope you are rested now after the week-end + that everything is fine with you. I've been thinking about you, dearest + wondering how you made out yesterday. Since you didn't call up I'm taking it for granted that every thing is alright, for the time being, anyway.

Bud Monahan is home – he has a ten-day furlough + it came very unexpectedly – he had made application for one a month ago but didn't think he'd get it for quite a while. He was on maneuvers (or bivouac I think) + it came thru Sun. night. He was so glad to get home – he + Arlene, his wife, came over to see Cele + Charlie last night + he said he was so sorry he couldn't be at our wedding. He tried awfully hard to get a 3-day pass but couldn't at the time. He's in the Ordnance + is classified as a carpenter + works from 8 to 5 – then lots of times he has to go on night problems 'til midnight. He says he really has to work hard + considers himself a full-fledged soldier now after what he's been thru in Virginia. He's in Camp Pickett, about 60 miles from Richmond. He was asking for you, dearest + says he hopes you stay in Camp Edwards for a while at least.

Mrs. Smith called me at the office this afternoon + said Dot + Ernie will be home next week, about Wednesday, Ernie's furlough has been pushed up a few weeks. It wasn't supposed to start 'til about June 15th. I don't know whether that's good or bad for him, do you, darling?

It'll be nice if you can get a pass the week-end of June 3rd, then you + I can see them both. I figured that will be your week-end off if everything is still alright by that time (let's hope so, heh dearest?)

I was surprised tonight to find that there was a letter from you, Walter dear. I didn't think I'd get Monday's letter 'til tomorrow – your letters take two days. Thanks so much, dearest, for the $2.00. I'm glad you have enough 'til you get paid. It was nice of your father to give you $5.00. Yes, I can use the $2.00 as you know. It was nice of you to send it. I'll get paid this Thurs. so everything will be alright.

Glad you made the trip back in 5-1/2 hrs. + that you, too, enjoyed the week-end so much, darling. Yes, Walt, Cele + Charlie are good to us. From now on I'm going to try + give Cele more money – to make up a little for the time I didn't work. It's hard with Thomas not working + then having to move + everything. It takes a lot of money to run this house – food, rent, electric light, gas, telephone, + then supporting Thomas too. Cele + Charlie are sorry they didn't buy a house after they were first married – they had the money but were always afraid something would happen. Now they can't buy one + it's hard to find a rent where they could feel that they could stay permanently. Anyone who owns their own home is better off these days. I often wonder if you + I will have our own place when we're as old as they are. (about 15 yrs. from now). I hope we have. It's awful to keep moving from one place to another.

Well, dearest, I've certainly talked a lot, heh? I hope you're not bored stiff (ha ha). I hope I get a letter from you telling me that you made out alright yesterday, dearest.

I think of you constantly, dear + miss you so much. What a wonderful day it will be when this mess is over + you + I can be together for the rest of our lives.

Love Always
(long ones) X X X X X X Rita X X X X X X

Wednesday, May 24th 4:00 pm

Hello my Dearest Soldier Boy,

How are you, Walter dear on this very rainy + dreary day? I hope you are fine + everything is going along smoothly with you.

I called up home this morning and Jeanie said there was a letter from you so I'm hoping that's the one you let me know how you made out Monday afternoon with the doctor – I can hardly wait to get home tonight to find out.

Mr. Trefry has gone to New Britain this afternoon so your little wife is by herself in the office. Irene Noonan is here of course but she is outside in the ladies' room resting more than she's in here (ha ha).

Last night I wrote quite a long letter to Dot Smith answering her last letter. In that letter she told me you had written to Ernie + Dot said you were still "up in the clouds" from the wedding + said she could tell you + I are both very happy. She said you referred to her + I as "sweet little wives". Since you + I got married, dearest, I've been telling Dot in my letters how nice you are, how all our plans worked out perfectly as far as the wedding, etc. is concerned + how happy I am. Even here in the office the girls know how happy you + I are, dear. I guess they can tell from the "light in my eyes" (ha ha). They kid me a lot.

Dearest, I'll finish this when I get home tonight.

6:45 Just finished reading your very nice letter, dear, (written Mon. night). I'm so happy, Walter, that they didn't talk you into having the tissue cut on your arm, that is, for the time being, at least. (down + kissing you I'm so happy) You just missed by the skin of your teeth twice so be careful next time (ha ha). If they'd only leave you alone, heh dearest? I think it was my prayers that saved you this time too, dearest. I'll continue to pray for you, my dearest, I'm sure God will take care of you.

Yes, it will be wonderful, Walter dear, if you can come home June 3rd. I love you so much, dear.

Yes, I have enough money. I'll be getting paid tomorrow anyway.

I just feel like telling you over + over, dearest, how much I love you. You are my life now, Walter + I want to help you in every possible way. You have often helped me, dear, lots + lots of times. Yes, as you said, Walter. We sure do "click" right – we both work together. We must continue to do just that so that we'll have a wonderful life together.

Please take care of yourself, Sweetheart, you are always in my thoughts.

Love Always,

X X X X X X "Bunny" X X X X X X

just like the kind you like, dear (long ones)

P.S. (1) Next time you come home, let's spend the time together – just the two of us, heh darling?

(2) You'd better tear the 2nd page of this letter up very thoroughly. I said a little too much, heh dear? It's true tho – I get mad every time I think of those dumb clucks (ha ha). [Referring to the girls in the office]

Thursday, May 25th

Dearest Walter, (My Very Nice Husband)

Lots + lots of love to you, dear. I'm writing this letter in the office because I'm going to meet Ann Preston after work tonight – eat + go to the show with her. If there is a letter from you, dearest, when I get home tonight, I'll answer it tomorrow – I'll bet there is a nice letter too.

We'll probably see "Pin Up Girl" with Betty Grable or "Four Jills in a Jeep" (both comedies).

Today is pay day here in the office. My withholding tax will be less now that I'm married. They used to deduct $4.80 but now they'll deduct only $2.40. It pays to get married, heh dearest? (ha ha) I don't know exactly what my pay will amount to now because when I was out there was a general increase went through. (5¢ an hr. more – ha ha) + I don't think I'll get it because I was given one early this year + no one else was. (So they said).

Have an enjoyable week end as you possibly can, dearest – I mean if you have any free time go to a good movie or out with some of the boys. I'll be home if you call Sunday, dearest, about 12:30 or so.

I have to get back to work now, Walter dear, - I'll be thinking of you over the week-end (as always).

You're such a good boy, dearest. I love you so much. You're so good to your "little wife" – so kind + understanding. I wish so much that we could be together for always but as it is now, we can at least dream + look forward to the time we will be together – we can save + work together for our future home (and children I hope). I hope + pray we'll be together before too many years go by – after all, we don't want many years of our lives to be wasted. Even two more years will be bad enough, heh dearest? I'm really looking forward to the time when I can be a real wife – and mother too. No marriage is wholly complete without a home + children is it dearest?

So, darling, just think of all the happiness that must be in store for you + I. Take care of yourself, dearest, your wife wants you to have plenty of rest + as much diversion as possible too (you know how much you can take, dear).

Love Always

for Sat. → X X X X X X Rita Marie X X X X X X

for Sun → X X X X X X X X X X X X X

P.S. I just got paid ($39.00 gross pay – after all deductions – net pay - $31.61) My weekly insult (ha ha).

Sunday, May 28th 1:00 p.m.

My Dearest Husband, Walter

I had to laugh when you called today + were eating an ice cream cone at the same time. I even asked you what kind it was, heh, dear? You're such a good boy, dearest, to call your little wife on Sunday. I love to talk with you even if it is only for a few minutes.

It's too bad you have to chase prisoners this week-end. Did the fellow who was supposed to have the job just go a.w.o.l. or did he get a pass? I should think he'd get into a lot of trouble if he did go a.w.o.l.

As I mentioned on the 'phone I stayed home last night + worked a little bit on our scrap book. There's a lot more I can put into it yet tho.

Cele + Charlie put an "ad" in the paper for a rent – It's been in now for the last few days + will probably seen for this week too. So far, we've had two responses to it. One woman called + said she was going to have a rent soon (in the north End – I don't know what street) + wanted a lot of information as to how many of us there are, etc. She said she'd call again. Another woman called last night + said she'd have one soon, the address was 1872 Boston Ave. (almost in Stratford) – five rooms + sun parlor $45.00 third floor. Cele + Charlie drove up there this morning but they wouldn't go in because it looked like an awfully small place – flat roof + the "sun parlor – (so called) was about as big as our front porch. It wasn't worth $45.00 at all. Besides there were a lot of people talking some foreign language outside the house so you can imagine how it would be to live there. They looked up in the Stoney Brook project (housing) but Cele said the houses are like cigar boxes + there are hundreds of children running around wild – colored + every other kind (ha ha). So many people recommend those projects to us, Success Park, Yellow Mill, Stoney Brook, etc. but Cele + Charlie don't want to go into them unless they really have to. Half of them are very poorly constructed have bad foundations etc.

Gosh, I hope we get one soon. If we still don't find one by Aug. 1st, I think we can get an extension but it will be very little time. Whenever Cele + Charlie do look at any rent + the people ask how many are in the family, they say <u>four</u> + that my husband, who's stationed rather close, comes home once in a while making <u>five</u>. They still keep saying Thomas is not going to be with us but I don't believe it. By the way, darling, he's not working again – he never went back to that job he had. His foot is all better now but he doesn't make any attempt to look for anything. He lives like a king (as you would say) – gets lots of rest, plenty to eat + makes life miserable for everyone. Jeanie calls him a parasite. I don't know how he can be so brazen living on people like he does.

I don't have to work Tuesday, Decoration Day. It'll be nice to have a day off. Quite a few factories here are working tho. I guess you boys in the Army won't hardly know if it's a holiday, heh dear? Remember last year it was on Sunday, dearest + you were home? We went to the Stfd. Parade.

I hope you don't mind my asking you this, dearest, but do they have any silver compacts in the P.X. [Post Exchange] any more? If they do, maybe you could get me one when you get paid – (not an expensive one tho) because the one I'm using now is very shabby. I've been using it every day since you gave it to me about three yrs. ago. I'll always keep it of course but I remember your saying you could get a nice silver one in the P.X. without paying the 20% tax. It's very hard to get sterling silver now here in anything. A nice round one, not fancy, + medium size would be attractive I think. I know you have good taste, dearest, in picking anything out. I'm sure I'd like it (if they have any). You could bring it with you next week-end. I guess I'm a big show off. I'd like to show it to everyone + tell them it was from you (ha ha).

Dearest, I love you so much I do hope you can get a pass next week. We can give each other some very nice kisses, heh, dear? I think of you all the time, darling + look forward so much to seeing you. You're a good boy, Walter dear.

Love Always

(long ones) X X X X X X Rita X X X X X X

just the kind you like.

Thursday, June 1st. 6:00 p.m.

Hello Sweetheart Darling,

I hope it isn't as hot on Cape Cod today as it is here. It's very muggy + damp+ no air at all – just the kind of weather my dearest hates. I hope you are quite cool these days, dear.

Tomorrow is the first Friday of the month so I'm going to Confession tonight + to Communion tomorrow at 6:30 in the morning. I'll offer it up for you, Walter dear, so that God will keep you close to me – for a while at least.

Cele's going too.

I had to laugh at your Tuesday's letter, dearest, where you said I use different kinds of approaches – on the page of my letter where I said I had all kinds of excuses to kiss you – you said yes, + all kinds of approaches too (ha ha).

I met Mr. Trefry's daughter today for the first time. She came in the office to borrow her father's car + he introduced me to her. He calls her "Bunny" – I told her I had the same pet name as she has. She's quite a "glamour puss" – ha ha. – is about 18 yrs. old + goes to Junior College. She's her father's pride + joy + after talking with her I came to the conclusion I'm not so spoiled after all. Wow! She's a spoiled girl. (ha ha).

I got paid today but had to send $13.11 away for insurance. Oh dear, there goes my budget again. I mustn't forget to have you make one out for me, dearest.

Ann Preston stayed 'til 11 o'clock last night – I'm not used to that "night life" any more (during the week) + I was falling asleep on her – practically. (ha ha). Oh well, we had a nice time gabbing anyway. I've been giving her a lot of information about details she'll have to take care of for the wedding.

Well, dearest, I hope your trip down to Bpt. isn't too tiresome this week-end + that it isn't too warm. Please take care of yourself, darling, I'll be waiting for you anxiously – in fact with bells on (ha ha). Something tells me I'm going to smother you with kisses, Sat. + Sun. dearest. You'll just love it too, heh, sweetheart?

Love Always
Rita your "Bunny"

Lots + lots of them too besides this dozen. → X X X X X X X X X X X X
I'd rather give them to you in person, dearest.

Friday, June 2, '44

My Dearest Walter,

Just one more day + I'll see my dearest. I'll be so glad to be with you, over the week-end. I hope nothing prevents you from getting your pass, darling.

Buddy left Wed. morning after his furlough. Arlene, his wife, didn't even get up to get his breakfast so he went to Sarah's (his mother's) to have some + say goodbye. He cried his eyes out when he was leaving – He thinks he's going out I guess – soon although he didn't really say so. He's having extensive training so it does look bad for him. I hope not tho.

Cele and I got up at ten minutes to six this morning + went to Communion. I feel as tho I've been awake for about nine hours already + it's only 10:00 A.M. in the morning. (ha ha) I'm writing this during my rest period but guess I won't have time to finish.

3:30 P.M. I guess I'll mail this from the office after all, dearest. We might eat out tonight + I won't have time to finish it then.

The office is like an oven again this afternoon – the temperature in here is

88° now; there isn't a breath of air.

I love you so much, dearest – you're such a good boy. I hope you don't mind the train ride down here tomorrow too much. I guess it'll be awfully hot traveling. Hope you get in about 7:00 pm.

Lots + lots of love 'til tomorrow, dearest (+ always)

big ones → X X X X X X Rita X X X X X X

June 5 '44, Monday

My Dearest,

I hope you managed to get some sleep on the way back to Providence last night, also that you didn't have to wait too long there for the fellows to ride back with them.

I enjoyed the week-end so much, dearest – I hope you did too. I'm so glad we spent yesterday morning + afternoon together instead of visiting here + there like we used to. I hope I make you as happy as you make me when we're together. You always tell me what a good wife I am to you, dearest, but this morning I had the feeling I could have been nicer to you this past week-end – I mean when I kept mentioning that you should change your clothes + telling you that you aren't neat, etc. (as fussy as you were about clothes before you went in the Army). Darling, I hope I didn't hurt you by saying those things – but you understand me, don't you, dearest? I'm an old fuss-budget about neatness + cleanliness – too fussy, I guess. I won't say anything any more, dear, about those things.

After Helene + I left you last night we took a walk up Main St. + stopped in the Pickwick + had a Tom Collins + later some coffee + pie. I was home at 9:30. I'm going to meet Helene Thurs. + we're going to the show.

Dearest, I guess you know without my saying how stunned I was Sat. when you said you were to be moved back to Devens, have about 8 wks. training + are in the p.o.m. [Components Program Objectives Memorandum] category. I didn't want to talk about it too much when you were home – I didn't want to be reminding you of the fact all the time + spoil your week-end – it's bad enough, heh dearest, without talking about it all the time. Besides I would probably cry + I know you wouldn't like that – tears won't help anyway if you do happen to be moved out – but everyone does experience a great deal of heartache when it happens – even tho we know nothing we can do, think or say will help much.

As I mentioned to you yesterday, dearest, the fellows who are sent out are either wasting their lives or those in Combat are losing them + it's all so futile – if anyone gained anything by this war there would be some sense to it but the only ones who are gaining anything by it are the politicians + those few who are running the show. Well, dearest, I know you feel the same way + there's nothing we can do about it. That's how I feel about all of it – I just wanted to tell you, dear.

So, darling, when you are sent to Devens it might be good if you had another physical – there would be different doctors + it might help you. I know you'll use your best strategy if you do have another physical – if you have a chance to explain about some of the symptoms you have occasionally, this time don't say you feel a "little dizziness" or you get "slight headaches" but say you get bad headaches + dizziness that lasts for a period of time.

If anything new develops in the next few weeks, please let me know, darling in your letters. I think it's better than waiting 'til you see me. I hope you can manage to get a "delayed route" between the 17th + 24th of this month – but of course I realize how the Army is – they change things so often + so quick, one never knows.

I love you, dearest + will be thinking of you constantly 'til I see you again. Please take good care of yourself – you are my life, Walter dearest. I'll keep on praying for you so that God will keep you safe.

Love Always,
Rita Marie
X X X X X X X X X X X X

P.S. Today is June 5th, the day you + I were going to be married – at first – remember, dear, we always had this date in mind? It would be my mother + father's anniversary too (about 43 yrs.) I'm glad we were married on April 22nd, aren't you dear? You probably wouldn't have been able to get time off now anyway. Lots of big hugs + kisses, dearest.

Love,
Rita

June 6th, Tuesday

Walter Dearest,

This morning Charlie woke us up (Cele, Jeanie + I) at a quarter to seven + told us the invasion had started sometime last night – he had the radio on + on every station was news of it - in fact all night there were broadcasts about it. I said some prayers + Cele did too when we heard it – not only for the ones we know over there but for all the boys. I think it really started last Friday or Saturday, don't you, dearest when that so called false report came thru. We have two radios going here in the factory today – I haven't listened to anything tho – I know if you were home you wouldn't even have the radio on heh dear? You don't believe anything you hear or read (ha ha). What do the boys up there think of the invasion, dearest – or aren't they interested at all? I imagine they are worried more about where they'll be from now on.

I talked with Dot Smith this noon on the phone + she said she + Ernie went to see Dot Grant + Jeremy last night. Dot is living with her mother – they've already broken up their home – they put their furniture in storage + Jeremy is going next Tuesday. Dot Smith said they treated them very nice + said they were going to N.Y. for a few days this week. Their anniversary will be next Monday (1 year). Jeremy is going in the Navy.

I was talking to Ruth Sorenson ("Swede's" sister) on the bus this morning. I asked her how John liked the Navy + she said, "alright – he doesn't complain at all" he'll be home July 4th after he finishes his "boot training". Ruth refers to Meta as his girlfriend – I knew she liked "Swede" but I didn't think he cared for her. The way Ruth spoke she's (Meta) at Sorenson's house quite a bit lately since she came home from school.

I told Ann I'd go out to her house for a short visit tonight – I don't feel much like going but I promised her last week. She'll probably be asking me a lot of questions about the details of our wedding so she can follow suit. Well, I don't mind giving her any information – as long as it's not personal (ha ha).

Dearest, there are a few questions I'd like to ask you – could you please answer them if you know yourself? When you are sure of getting the "delayed route" could you let me know + do you think you'll have your 8-weeks training at Devens or some other place + if you do have it at Devens, do you think you'll be home at all during those weeks? Please let me know when you find out because if I thought I couldn't see you during those weeks at all I would definitely take one week off if you get the so called "delayed route". Let me know what you think about it, dearest? I don't want to be a pest asking questions you can't even answer yourself but I don't think I'd have too much trouble getting some more time off + I really would like to, dear. After all, you're more important to me than my work here – you're my life, dear Walter. I'd like to know what you think about it. You said when you were home last week-end that you didn't think I should take any more time off – just a day or so but, darling, if you think it over again you might feel differently. Let me know, dearest, heh?

The latest report we just heard here in the office about the invasion is that there is no opposition at all so far from the Germans. That seems strange doesn't it – they've advanced 10 miles so far with no opposition at all. Adolph might have some "slick tricks" up his sleeves (I hope not).

Isn't it awful when you think of the whole mess? I was just thinking this morning – the average span of life is about 65 yrs. This world was created by God – the earth belongs to him – we people are really living here on borrowed time you might say + here is practically the whole world fighting over this wonderful earth, God's world - no wonder He lets the war rage on – there is so much rotten-ness + greed among all the races. Why can't we live peacefully for the short time we're on this earth? It's all so futile, isn't it, dearest?

I'll pray hard for you, dearest, so that you'll be safe + as close as possible – I love you so much dear – I hope my love can help you if you are lonely or depressed.

Lots of nice kisses, dearest.

Love Always,

Rita Marie

big ones → X X X X X X X X X X X X X

Wednesday, June 7th

Hello Walter Dearest,

I called up home a little while ago + Jeanie said there's a letter from you. I'm so glad, dear, because I didn't get any mail Monday or yesterday.

Everyone here (in the office + home) is living in high tension ever since the news of the invasion – especially people who have close relatives over there – everyone goes home from work at night + keeps their ears glued to the radio. Last night Cele + Charlie said St. Charles + St. Ambrose churches were crowded with people making visits + praying for the boys. As you said Sunday, darling, if people prayed years ago there probably wouldn't be a war on now – all of a sudden the papers + radio are making a big issue of how much prayer is necessary. That's all we can do now I guess is hope + pray. A few places here are closed today to observe a day of prayer.

Last night at a quarter to 12 we heard a broadcast right from the battle area by a commentator who was aboard ship between Cherbourg + Le Havre, France. It was awful to hear the planes (ours) + bombs dropping – it was so clear you'd think you were there. When I went to bed I was so depressed I felt sick – I guess I shouldn't listen to those things.

We had a bond rally here this morning – a sailor + marine spoke who had been in several campaigns + who were home on leave recuperating from wounds. The Fifth War Loan has started + they expect us to have $10.00 a week deducted for 10 weeks – I don't see how they'll meet the quota of $18,500.00 just for our plant.

I didn't get home from Ann's house 'til so late last night. You know how it is, darling, when you visit there – you can never leave early. Ann says Willie expects his furlough to start June 26th instead of July 1st + in that case they'll be married Thurs. June 29th because they'll be engaged a year on the 29th. That doesn't give her much time at all (3 wks) to take care of all the details.

Dot wants me to go over to her house tonight – I will for a short visit I guess + bring the pictures over + show them (the big ones). I think I'll give Mrs. Smith + Dot one each because they gave me two of Dot's.

Charlie met your sister-in-law, Ellen, outside of the house last night about 11 o'clock. She had been to the Hippodrome + was going to get a bus home. Charlie asked her to come in because she said she was wondering if we had the pictures yet from Jannetty's. She came in (after a lot of coaxing) + Cele gave her one of the group – she liked them. Now there is just Emma left + she wants one of the two of us. Let's stop up there, dearest, next time you come home + give it to her.

I don't know whether the check has come to your house yet from the government. If it has I imagine Helene will give it to me tomorrow – we're supposed to go to the show. I hope it has come – I'll deposit it with $30.00 of what you gave me last week-end. That'll make $80.00 altogether that we'll have. I have to get a few things I need with it.

Dearest, I've been wondering how everything is with you this week. Please keep me posted won't you, dear, if there are any new developments as to your moving status, etc. I'd rather know those things than have you tell me in front of Cele when you come home.

6:15 pm. Just finished reading your Monday's letter. So glad you enjoyed the week-end so much, dearest — we are always so happy when we're together. Glad you got to bed early Monday night to catch up on your sleep.

You're a good husband to me too, dearest. You're so kind + considerate. I love you more than I can say.

Love Always,
"Bunny"

Here are some nice long kisses for you, dearest — special ones}
X X X X X X X X X X X X

Thursday — June 8th

Walter Dearest,

How's my very nice husband on this beautiful day in June? I hope you are in "tip-top shape" + everything is fine with you.

I was supposed to go to the show with Helene tonight after work but Ellen called up last night + said Helene fell down the steps of the back porch Monday when she was hanging out clothes. She didn't hurt herself badly — just her leg a little but since she fell she's had a headache off + on + is going to the doctor today for a check up just to make sure she's alright. I guess she hit her head slightly as she fell so it's a good idea to see that everything's OK. Ellen said she was going to a Dr. Lesko on Barnum Ave., Stfd — he's supposed to be a specialist of head injuries, etc. I'm quite sure it's nothing serious because she's able to be up + around + feels alright except for the slight headache. I told Ellen to tell Helene to call me + let me know how she was after seeing the doctor.

I went over to Dot's house last night + had a nice visit. Mr. and Mrs. Smith were there + of course, Ernie + Dot. I brought over the large pictures with me + gave them one each. Dot picked one of the group + Mrs. Smith picked one of me alone (full length). They would rather have had one of you + I alone but there are only two of those left + one is for Emma + the other for ourselves. I should have had more of those made up + less of myself alone. Oh well, it's hard to please everyone. I'm not going to worry about it (ha ha).

6:00 p.m. I only worked 'til five tonight, dear. Your Tuesday's letter was so nice, Walter dear — two whole pages on both sides — gosh, dearest. I sure do appreciate getting such nice long letters from you. I know it takes time + effort to write so much — I like them so much, darling. You're such a sweetheart to write each day.

I doubt very much, dear, if you'll get more than 5 days delayed route seeing you had your furlough so recently, however, it'll be wonderful if you get 5 days — it'll really be a week won't it, dear — from about the 17th 'til the 24th or so — am I right, dear? I have a good idea, but I don't know whether it will appeal to you, dearest. I was thinking if you did get five days it would be nice to go to

Boston (you + I) just for one night + stay at a Hotel. We could go in the morning (during the week) + come home the next night. I could make a reservation at the Statler or some other hotel next week if you like the idea. I've never been to Boston + although I know there's nothing out of the ordinary up there, I'd like to go. I've always wanted to. I imagine Klein is saying to himself "where does that little wife of mine think the money is coming from?" (ha ha ha). Well, dearest, I thought of that but I don't think it would cost too much – trainfare (??) I don't know how much that is but you do - + one night at some hotel we don't have to stay in an elaborate hotel + food. Let me know how you feel, dear, that is, if you're quite sure of getting the time, etc.

I don't think the check came for me at your house. I think Ellen would have said something about it on the phone last night if Helene had received it. Maybe I won't get it 'til July 1st + then will get two. It must have gone there tho because I wouldn't have received that dependency notice from New Jersey. Oh well, there's no use worrying (ha ha). What you never have, you never miss (ha ha). It'll come some time or other.

Glad you enjoyed going to B.S. Church Sunday. Next time you come, it would be a good idea to go to St. Paul's + see your minister, dear. Of course I always like to have you go with me but the minister might think you are being swayed or something. When you do go, dearest, you should make sure he sees you – talk with him if it's only for a short while.

Dearest, I'll have to go + mail this now – it's getting late. I love you so much, Walter, you're my wonderful husband, my friend, companion, + partner – you're such a dear.

Love Always

Ritamarie

each one a long one → X X X X X X X X X X X X X

Friday, June 9th

My Dearest,

I hope you have a little free time over the week-end so you can relax + enjoy some good diversion. I hope you have a chance to call me Sun. about 12 or 12:30-noon. I'll be thinking of you – as I always do.

Ed stopped in to see us last night. He was in Devon on business. He stayed for about an hour + a half + had another fellow with him. I gave him the picture of him + I together – he liked all the pictures a lot – I also gave him the cuff links – engraved. He insisted that I take $5.00 for the picture. I wanted to give it to him but he made me take the money, said he realized how expensive pictures are. He said he was very tired + needs a vacation badly. He wants Cele + Charlie to see if they can get a house at Lordship or someplace else for him – also Gert + the girls for two weeks. He only took one week last year + should have had three weeks.

I called Ellen last night + asked her how Helene made out with the doctor. He said there wasn't much – in fact nothing at all to worry about – he said she hit her head right in a spot that caused a very slight concussion but that with a few days rest she'd be perfectly alright. He gave her some pills to ease her headache. Ellen said he examined her thoroughly.

Dearest, I meant to tell you this last week-end. Cele thinks we should have given Fr. Pat a little money for marrying us – the money we did give went to Fr. O'Connell + she said seeing he was the one who really married us we should have given him $5.00 or so. So, dearest, I was thinking – it would be a good idea the next time you come home to go out to Brooklawn to the house + give him $5.00 – he's usually there. It isn't too late now. I'd like you to see their house – you've never been out there, heh dear - + that would be a good excuse, heh dear? (ha ha). It's a beautiful place + I know they'd like to have us go out. I'll save the $5.00 Ed gave me + give it to Fr. Pat, O.K dear?

Dearest, I asked Cele last night if she thought it'd be a good idea if you + I went to Boston for 2 days (+ one night) if you got 5 days delayed route + she said she thought it was a good idea – she said "Why don't you both go – it would be a change?"

Tonight is the usual weekly "thorough cleaning" night of our house I always clean our bedroom, dearest (thoroughly) do the stairs, vacuum + dust downstairs. Cele does her bedroom, scrubs the bathroom + kitchen (sometimes Charlie does the kitchen) so you see we have a regular system worked out (ha ha).

6:15 p.m. All of the above was written in the office, dearest during my rest period + at lunch time.

Just finished reading your Wed. letter. Thanks for answering the questions I asked you, dear – about your delayed route + going to Devens, etc. That will be wonderful, dear, if you can come home during those 8 weeks. I think I should take some time off during the week of the 19th don't you, dearest? I'd like to take the whole week if I could but if not, at least a few days – after all we don't know how much longer we'll be together – that is, that you'll be able to come home week-ends.

Yes, dearest, I'll try to take your advice + not worry – whatever happens will be God's will + everything might happen for the best after all. I'm still praying for you every night, darling, also so that this mess won't be a long-drawn out affair + praying too for the boys who are in the midst of it.

Dearest, I love you so much I'll be thinking of you over the week-end. I wish we could be together for always.

Love Always,

XXXXXX Rita XXXXXX

P.S. I feel like being close to you + just tell you how much I love you + give you some nice long kisses. Next week I hope, heh dear?

R.

P.S. I still think going to Boston for a few days is a good idea, what do you think, darling? You can tell me on the 'phone Sun. The Copley Plaza is a nice hotel I understand, + of course the Statler (the largest). We could make it sort of a second honey-moon (ha ha). You know you'd just love it, dearest – (ha ha)

June 12th, Monday

Dearest Walter,

Hope you arrived back safely in Camp, that you met the boys without any delay + had a good night's sleep.

We had such a wonderful week-end, didn't we, dearest? Just being together was so nice. You're so good to me, dearest + we have such a wonderful companionship together.

Guess what, dear! C. Thibault, our office manager (so called) said it was perfectly alright for me to take the whole week off. Imagine that! He was very nice about it. He said they could bring in Margaret Anton from the outside office to do my work for that week. He said under the circumstances it was natural for me to want to spend the whole week with you. Isn't that wonderful, dear? I'm tickled. I hope you can get the five days now without any trouble.

I'm going to make reservations tonight (by letter) at the Hotel Pennsylvania for the 21st of June. By the way, dear, we'll be spending our two months' anniversary (ha ha) in N.Y. Isn't that nice? Monday + Tuesday of next week we can do all of the necessary visiting + the balance of the week we can spend together – alone – going to the beach, etc.

I'm surprised that they didn't make a big fuss over my asking for time off seeing I had eight weeks a short while ago, but they said it's a very good reason why I want the time off (in case I don't see you for a long time).

I'm using your pen to write this letter, dearest. I filled it in the morning so I'll see how long the ink stays in. I'll bring it into Matthews (where I bought it) Sat. because it's a life-time pen + there shouldn't be any trouble with it.

Dot called me up last night about 9 o'clock to say goodbye. They could have come over to the house yesterday afternoon but they went to the show instead – guess they thought we wanted to be alone – of course we didn't heh, dear? (ha ha).

Last night after I left you, dearest, I felt so lonesome all by myself – I took the bus home – Cele + Charlie were out but Jeanie was home – I pressed a blouse for today, talked with Jeanie a while + went to bed at 10:30.

I had to laugh at you yesterday, dear – on Saturday, rather, when I showed you the new dress I bought + hat – you got such a big kick out of it – the fact that you bought the things for me, heh dear?

Dearest, I was thinking today, the time from April 22nd 'til now has been the happiest days of my life – even tho we haven't been together all during that time – but just knowing you are a part of my life – a part of me, really, + knowing you love me so much has given me an abundance of happiness, darling. I hope I've made you as happy + even tho we're apart now, dearest, we'll be happy, Walter dear, because my happiness comes first in your thoughts + yours comes first with me, darling. We have a lot of happy years ahead of us yet, I'm quite sure.

Maybe you are right, dear, in thinking you might just be moved to another Camp – it would be wonderful if it were only here in the U.S. You say I'm sure it will be further than that. Well, dearest, it isn't that I'm positive that you won't be here — it's just that I haven't as much confidence as you have — I wish I could feel differently, darling. I'll sure try — after all, I shouldn't give up hope — you're still here + anything can happen in your favor too rather than against you.

Keep well, dearest + get plenty of rest this week + next week you + I will have a grand week together. Love Always,

X X X X X X Rita X X X X X X

Tuesday, June 13th

My Dearest Walter,

I hope this letter finds you very well + rested after your week-end at home with your little wife. (ha ha).

We're having some sandblasting done on the outside of E.W.C. (on the building) + we can hardly breathe in the office today from the dust + dirt coming in the windows. The job is being done by the E + F Construction Co. (greasy Italians) ha ha - + after they sandblast the entire building they're going to re-paint parts of it. The dirt in here today is an inch thick all over everything (ha ha). Mr. Trefry has gone out to lunch so I thought I'd start my daily letter to you, dearest. It's not 12 noon yet.

Charlie deposited the check for me, dear, in the bank. We now have $51.00 in the bank, dear + I have $35.00 home that we can take to N.Y. with us.

Last night I washed a few of your clothes, dear, (1 pr.) socks, 2 hankies, 2 shorts, 2 shirts (under-shirts-ha ha) + pajamas. I left them out on the line all night + took them in this morning + they were all dry. When you come home Sat., dearest, you'd better bring a few extra sets of underwear to last you for the week (if you get the time).

Irene Noonan told me about a good place to eat near the Hotel Penn. The name of it is "Shines" + they're Irish people who run it — she said the prices are very reasonable + the food very good. I told her we didn't have too much money to spend + she said she'd tell me some other places to go when we eat, too. Nice of her, heh dear?

I made reservations last night (by letter) at the Hotel Pennsylvania. I should have a reply by Thurs. or Fri. If you find the last minute that you can't get the time off I can call up there directly + cancel them. Ann Preston said it isn't necessary to send a money order for the room at the Penn. She + Ruth stayed there last year + liked it a lot.

Darling, I'll finish this letter tonight when I go home.

6:30 pm. Didn't receive mail from you today dearest, but I know you wrote + I'll receive it tomorrow — hope so anyway.

I'm glad today is over (as far as working is concerned in the office). The week can't go by too fast for me — It'll be so wonderful being with you next week, dearest. I do hope nothing prevents you from getting the time off.

I called up Mrs. Smith just to see how she was, etc. She is quite lonesome but knows she probably won't see Dot for a long while unless Ernie goes over.

She said they left Bpt. at 7:50 yesterday + will get into Ozark early tomorrow morning. Mrs. Smith doesn't feel well at all. She's been doctoring for anemia but the injections the doctor gave her haven't helped much. I told her she worries too much over her housework + works too hard.

Well, dearest, I'm going to eat supper now – I'm starved (ha ha). I'll be thinking of you, dearest, 'til I see you again. (Sat.). I love you so much dear, you're a grand husband to me. Take good care of yourself, sweetie pie (ha ha)

Love Always,
Rita

long ones →X X X X X X X X X X X X X

Wednesday, June 14th

Walter Dearest,

Received your two letters tonight when I came home from work – one written Tues. noon + one Mon. night.

I was very much surprised, dearest, to hear you are getting 15 days delayed route – I thought the most you'd get would be ten. It's wonderful, darling, that you're getting that much time. Yes, dearest, Capt. Becker + the clerks are swell fellows to give you boys all that time. Imagine, dear, the boys who are getting 25 days – why, that's almost a month.

I think I'll still take next week off tho, dearest, rather than from the 26th of June on – I don't think I could get that week off anyway because vacations are starting in the office + the girl who is going to do my work next week will be busy, so dearest, I'll take next week off instead + then Monday, July 3rd – the day before you go back I'll take that day off, O.K. dearest? We'll keep the reservation I made to N.Y. at the Penn. I should be getting a reply from them tomorrow as to the price, etc. of the room.

Yes, dearest, you + I will have a wonderful two weeks together. Let's really relax + enjoy ourselves + not worry about anything.

Irene Noonan gave me the names of quite a few places that we could go to eat in N.Y. – they are supposed to be good – reasonable prices + good food. We could try a few of them, at least, heh dear? Mr. Trefry said we should eat once (at least) in the Penn. Hotel – the Café Rouge I guess it's a room like the Taft Grille room – I told him I could imagine the prices would be very high + he said they were a little, but it was a beautiful place. Oh well, we'll see, dear. I'm glad you are enthused now, dear over our coming little trip. I think it'll be wonderful we'll have it to remember later on just as we will our honeymoon.

Dearest, I'll be waiting for you Sat. between 5 + 6 o'clock. I'll be home all evening – no matter what time you get home so you don't have to call up, darling, unless you want to.

I'm so happy tonight, dearest, because we'll be together for 15 days. Whatever extra clothes you bring, Walter dear, you can leave them here – I mean underwear, socks, etc. You'd better bring a few sets of underwear + prs. of socks at least, dearest, because we don't want to spend our time washing the few that are here (ha ha) for the next two weeks. I'll have lots of time to wash everything when you're gone to Devens. You only have 1 good set of underwear here + 1 old set + 2 prs of socks. You have plenty of hankies + ties. I'll bet you're laughing at my telling you all this, heh dearest. (ha ha).

Love Always

X X X X X X Rita X X X X X X

PART VIII: After the War

Adjusting to a New Life

Following the move to California, Walter and Rita rarely visited back home, though Walter was good about writing and sending photographs to various Klein family in Connecticut.

And despite their few visits to Connecticut, Walter and Rita never returned to live there. In California, Walter worked for the Los Angeles County water department. To my knowledge, Rita worked in some form of secretarial capacity. Around 1955, they moved into a newly constructed home in Granada Hills, California. Their home was in the San Fernando Valley, north of Los Angeles. At that time, the area was rural and agricultural. As the years passed it became suburbia. Walter and Rita had one son, John Klein, born April 5, 1954.

Walter developed a sideline moonlighting business of servicing automatic transmissions. His customers were mostly neighbors and area farmers. The transmission work was performed behind his house in the adjacent alley.

Walter's collection of used transmissions grew; to the point that the small fenced backyard became stacked several feet deep with transmissions. There was no lawn to the rear of the house, just narrow pathways as one walked through a sea of stacked transmissions. Eventually, vines and ivy foliage covered the mass of transmissions.

Aunt Rita passed in 1988 due to breast cancer complications at age 69. Walter passed on or about April 17, 1995 at age 79. Following Rita's death, Uncle Walter lived by himself. On Easter Sunday, April 16, 1995, Walter visited his son John and family. Following Easter, a neighbor notified John that Walter had not picked up the newspapers on the doorstep for several days. My cousin John, Walter's son, responded. John had difficulty getting into the locked house; his key somehow didn't work. After jimmying a window, John gained entrance. Walter's body was found in bed. The death certificate indicated heart disease issues as the cause of death. While Walter was found and pronounced dead on April 20, evidence indicates he had died several days prior. The date of April 17, 1995 represents a best guess.

Walter and Rita smiling in sunny California after the war ended.

PART IX: Story of the Letters

A Wartime Love Story Lives On

The story of how the collection of letters survived for three-quarters of a century is almost as exciting as Rita and Walter's story itself.

When Walter would return to Connecticut on weekend passes, he would bring Rita's letters home in small bundles. These precious packages were given back to Rita and placed in a box for safekeeping. Consequently, virtually all letters both ways ended up being stored in the same small cardboard storage box.

At the close of the war and the return of peace, Walter and Rita decided to remain in their new home in Southern California. The warmer weather and palm trees must have been like heaven due to Walter's scarred tissues and nerve damage. Recall also, Walter was a packrat and saved nearly everything. Personal items boxed up in Connecticut but not essential to daily life were stored as opposed to being transported to California or disposed of. Walter and Rita opted to store the boxed letters along with other items in the home of Walter's sister, my Aunt Martha Mahlo. The house was located in Easton, Connecticut, which is just north of Bridgeport. A likely estimate for when these items were placed in the Easton house would be 1946, as some additional letters dated up to 1946 were included.

Walter also stored things in my parents' home in Stratford. Additionally, he left things in his father's garage at 163 Jackson Avenue, Stratford.

The years passed. Walter never retrieved his stored belongings. My father eventually had to decide what to do with it all. In the later war years, when Walter was stationed on the West Coast, he sent an assortment of items, including military issue clothing and army boots, to our Reed Street home in Stratford. During that time, Walter had been assigned to the Quartermaster Corps and since he had access to military stuff, that was what he commonly shipped home. After our house became infested with moths, my father put an end to that. He mailed Walter some money, declaring that Walter's stuff in our attic on Reed Street was now ours. Our family then opened the many boxes and bags, thus getting at the heart of the moth infestation problem—Army-issue woolen socks in one of the duffel bags. The moth-infested items were burned.

As a teenage kid, it was common for me to wear WWII military clothing from the former Walter parcels. My mother loathed the black scuff marks I left on her kitchen floor from my WWII-era army boots. Rubber was in critical short supply during the war, so army issue boot heels were made of some synthetic that left scuff marks.

Meanwhile, Walter's belongings stored in Easton, at Aunt Martha's house, must not have caused any problems other than to occupy space. The years and decades passed.

Walter and Rita never made any effort to retrieve their things, not even a stash of wedding gifts received in 1944, gifts that my mother, Ellen Klein (1914-2002), later claimed were never opened.

As for the letters, they didn't come into my possession until much later. Following the close of the war, the letters were stored in Aunt Martha's house in Easton, Connecticut where they remained untouched for half a century, not being disturbed until 1997.

Uncle Adolf Mahlo (1900-1973), married to my Aunt Martha, passed at age 73 due to cancer. Aunt Martha survived Adolf by about 25 years. Following Adolf's passing, she lived by herself in the Easton house up until suffering a stroke, circa 1996. Aunt Martha then went to live with her daughter, my cousin Joyce Mahlo Nagel, in Sandy Hook, Connecticut. At some point during the winter of 1996/1997, the Easton house, being vacant for an extended period, experienced a furnace failure. With nobody there to check on things, the house lost its heat. Due to the cold winter temperatures, pipes froze, including the pipes that serviced the baseboard radiators. Water burst forth from frozen pipes and ruined much of the household contents, especially in the then-crammed basement. To compound matters, field mice entered the unoccupied house, which still contained food in the kitchen cupboards. The house and contents became permeated with and smelled of mice urine and droppings. In sum, the Easton house was no longer habitable. To rent or sell the house, the Town of Easton inspectors would have to visit, inspect, and sign off on the property. Obviously, the house was in no condition to pass an inspection. Getting an occupancy permit was not a trivial option.

My cousin Joyce Nagel made all decisions pertaining to the Easton house and its contents, as she had authority to manage her mother's affairs. In the midst of this debacle, Walter and Rita's boxed items remained undisturbed and unclaimed in the Easton house.

On the weekend of my 40th high school reunion, on Sunday, September 14, 1997, I visited Aunt Martha and Cousin Joyce at Joyce's home in Sandy Hook, Connecticut. Aunt Martha, then age 80, was incapacitated due to her previous stroke; she was wheelchair-bound and no longer able to speak. Joyce did most of the talking, while Aunt Martha smiled and nodded her head in agreement with the conversation. After a pleasant visit with Aunt Martha, Joyce and I drove the brief 15-mile trip to inspect the then-unoccupied Easton house. As we inspected the house and its deteriorated condition, I noticed some boxes of Walter's stuff in the basement. While Joyce was contemplating gutting and landfilling the destroyed contents, I asked for the boxes containing Walter's stuff. In all, there were about eight. One box, as it turned out later, contained the collection of Walter and Rita's wartime courtship letters.

I had flown commercially into the Hartford-Bradley airport, so carrying eight boxes of Walter stuff with me on my return flight was not feasible. I stayed in a hotel on Sunday night near the Hartford-Bradley airport. On Monday morning, September 15, 1997, prior to returning my rental car, I drove to a local post office. I posted the Walter boxes as parcel post to myself at my Dewey, Illinois address.

During this visit to Joyce and Aunt Martha in 1997, Joyce shared that she felt overwhelmed. The contents of her parents' house had negative value.

Please recall that both Walter and Rita were deceased at this point. One saving grace was that the Walter boxes, while in the water-soaked basement, had fortunately been placed high on a ledge and were only slightly impacted by the water. Subsequent inspection of the letters showed that only a small portion of Rita's letters were water damaged. Approximately six letters from the era of December 1943 were affected.

Given these grim circumstances and at my request, Joyce gave Walter and Rita's stuff, including the letters, to me. My visit and actions snatched the letters from certain destruction—and in the nick of time. Aunt Martha passed from this life in July 1998, ten months following my 1997 visit. Soon after that visit, Joyce's son Mark Nagel gutted the Easton house. Four 20-cubic-yard containers of debris were removed and landfilled. Mark Nagel remodeled and restored the house. He and his family currently reside there.

At times, the descriptions by both Walter and Rita used terminology that might today be deemed as inappropriate, offensive, or not politically correct. As editor, I preserve the language and descriptions as written. Walter and Rita's letters represent a unique historical look at life in America during WWII. The letters also provide incredibly detailed insights into Klein family history. Certain aspects of the family story involve sensitive topics. Again, as editor, I opted to preserve the letters as written. There is nothing to be gained by altering history. If transgressions were ever made, as judged by today's standards, then in order to learn from these transgressions, the record must be preserved as it was written. I am reminded of a common street saying from when I was a kid. The saying was used as a rebuttal or retaliation to some other kid calling somebody a name. It went simply, "Sticks and stones can break my bones; but names will never hurt me."

No words written 75 years ago in personal letters by people who are now deceased can ever hurt you. In short, if somebody calls you a dirty name or says something unkind, the best advice is to shrug it off and move on. The only person who controls each life, short of being physically assaulted, incarcerated, or denied food and water, is the person—nobody else and certainly not the words shared on these pages, written nearly eight decades ago.

In my experience as a kid growing up in that era, the family history contained mysteries and voids. My father, for example, never once in his life, at least to my knowledge, ever mentioned his mother, my grandmother. There were no photographs. I never even knew her name until many years later. Over the years as I conducted research into the Klein family, my hope was to somehow find a letter, or anything written by or about my grandmother Eva Sablofski Klein. The 1910 U.S. Census indicated that both John and Eva Klein could read and write in English. In contrast, two pieces of evidence surfaced stating that my grandmother was in fact illiterate. First, the 1920 U.S. Census recorded that Eva Klein was illiterate. Next, her hospital file from the Connecticut Valley Hospital for the Insane described Eva as illiterate. The hospital file added that she was "extremely ignorant." For example, she could not name the U.S. President. She could not identify Chicago on a United States map. She was incapable of performing modestly simple additions and subtractions. She was not able to say or remember what she had for breakfast that morning. Obviously, no letter written by Eva Klein will ever surface.

In contrast, the accumulation of Walter and Rita's wartime correspondences represents the mother lode. And for this mother lode to materialize, three factors had to come into play: the letters had to be written and on a faithful and almost daily basis; the letters had to be preserved and thus be accessible to readers today; and lastly the letters had to be worthy of telling their story. The letters contain daily descriptions of the family and life in America during the 17 months spanned by the letters (starting on January 13, 1943 and ending in June 1944). I feel a sense of joy and honor to have helped to preserve these letters, and to be an instrument in sharing them. The story told reveals much about the Klein family. The story told reveals much about America in the era of WWII—a time characterized by a massive national mobilization and personal sacrifices. The letters make clear the intense devotion and love that Walter and Rita shared.

Upon completion of the transcribing, it is our intention to see that the original letters are properly archived, notably by enclosing the letters and related artifacts in an inert (non-oxygen) environment. We will also explore and be receptive to sharing the letters with a reputable museum devoted to preserving WWII history. I continue to be impressed and inspired by the letters.

About the Editor

Richard, by his own admission, is an incurable romantic and altruist. His writings and musings are filled with hope and bright horizons despite having lived through World War II and the Korean War as a child, both of which deeply impacted his worldview. Through his books, he aims to point the way towards a better internal mindset and a better world.

Richard earned his Ph.D. in engineering from Purdue University in 1969 and taught systems theory for three decades at the University of Illinois in Urbana-Champaign before retiring in 1995. He holds a particular interest in bicycle stability and control, and has devoted much of his time and energy to the development of a national program for teaching children with disabilities to master bike riding. Visit iCanBike.org and RainbowTrainers.com for more info.

Richard and his wife of more than 50 years, Marjorie Maxwell Klein, reside in the St. Louis area. They have two children and six grandchildren. Richard writes for them and for generations to come.

Acknowledgements

I wish to acknowledge and thank Jessica Marie Tatko, my grand-daughter-in-law. Jessica diligently typed these letters so that they could be shared. The typing and organizing consumed months of Jessica's time.

Thanks are extended to Ellen M. Meyer for her conscientious formatting and getting the manuscript in publishable form. Many steps were required to organize this historic collection of letters into themes to be able to tell the stories that have remained hidden for seventy-five years.

28737892R00292

Made in the USA
Lexington, KY
20 January 2019